Land Battles of the
Civil War, Eastern Theatre

Land Battles of the Civil War, Eastern Theatre

Bruce H. Stewart, Jr.

McFarland & Company, Inc., Publishers
Jefferson, North Carolina, and London

The present work is a reprint of the illustrated case bound edition of Land Battles of the Civil War, Eastern Theatre, *first published in 2002 by McFarland.*

Library of Congress Cataloguing-in-Publication Data

Stewart, Bruce H., Jr., 1955–
Land battles of the Civil War, eastern theatre / Bruce H. Stewart, Jr.
p. cm.
Includes bibliographical references and index.

ISBN 978-0-7864-6119-6
softcover : 50# alkaline paper ♾

1. United States — History — Civil War, 1861–1865 — Campaigns.
2. East (U.S) — History, Military — 19th century. I. Title.
E470.2 .S845 2011 973.7'3 — dc21 2001007410

British Library cataloguing data are available

Manufactured in the United States of America

Cover photograph: Soldiers of the First Connecticut Heavy Artillery man a battery of 13-inch sea coast mortars, enforcing the siege of Yorktown, Virginia, in April 1862. © 2011 Corbis Images

McFarland & Company, Inc., Publishers
Box 611, Jefferson, North Carolina 28640
www.mcfarlandpub.com

To
my wife, Julia D. Stewart
my father, Dr. Bruce H. Stewart
my grandfather, General John C. Persons

Acknowledgments

Maps on pages 183, 188, and 193 from *Embrace an Angry Wind: The Confederacy's Last Hurrah* by Wiley Sword. Copyright © 1990 by Wiley Sword. Reprinted by permission of HarperCollins Publishers, Inc.

Maps on pages 16 and 69 from *Stonewall Jackson* by James I. Robertson, Jr. (Macmillan, 1997). Reprinted by permission of the Gale Group.

Maps on pages 112 and 113 from *High Tide at Gettysburg* by Glenn Tucker. Maps on pages 117 and 121 from *Chickamauga Bloody Battle in the West*. Both by Glenn Tucker. Reprinted by permission of W. S. Konecky Associates, Inc.

Maps on pages 98 and 103 from *Chancellorsville 1863* by Ernest B. Furgurson, copyright © 1992 by Ernest B. Furgurson. Used by permission of Alfred A. Knopf, a division of Random House, Inc.

Maps on pages 30 and 32 reprinted with the permission of Simon & Schuster from *Shiloh* by Larry Daniels. Copyright © 1997 by Larry Daniels.

Map on page 70 reprinted with the permission of Scribner, a division of Simon & Schuster, from *R. E. Lee*, Volume II, by Douglas Southall Freeman. Copyright 1934 by Charles Scribner's Sons; copyright renewed © 1962 by Inez Goddin Freeman.

Maps on pages 6, 8, and 43 reprinted with the permission of Scribner, a division of Simon & Schuster, from *Lee's Lieutenants*, Volume I, by Douglas Southall Freeman. Copyright 1942 by Charles Scribner's Sons; copyright renewed © 1970 by Inez Goddin Freeman.

Map on page 95 reprinted with the permission of Scribner, a division of Simon & Schuster, from *Lee's Lieutenants*, Volume II, by Douglas Southall Freeman. Copyright 1943 by Charles Scribner's Sons; copyright renewed © 1971 by Inez Goddin Freeman.

Maps on pages 110 and 125 reprinted with the permission of Scribner, a division of Simon & Schuster, from *Lee's Lieutenants*, Volume III, by Douglas Southall Freeman. Copyright 1944 by Charles Scribner's Sons; copyright renewed © 1972 by Inez Goddin Freeman.

Maps on pages 36, 38, 42, 44, 48, and 50 from *To the Gates of Richmond* by Stephen W. Sears. Copyright © 1992 by Stephen W. Sears. Reprinted by permission of Houghton Mifflin Company. All rights reserved.

Maps on pages 21 and 26 from *Stonewall in the Valley* by Robert Tanner, Stackpole Books, 1996. Used with permission of Stackpole Books.

Map on page 12 reprinted by permission of Harold Ober Associates from *The Seven Days* by Clifford Dowdey.

Map on page 134 from *The Shipwreck of Their Hopes* by Peter Cozzens. Copyright 1994 by the board of Trustees of the University of Illinois. Used with the permission of the University of Illinois Press.

Maps on pages 127, 175, 179, 181, and 182 from *Jubal* by Charles Osborne. Copyright © 1992 by the author. Reprinted by permission of Algonquin Books of Chapel Hill, a division of Workman Publishing.

Maps on pages 141, 146, and 147 from *Decision in the West: The Atlanta Campaign of 1864*, by Albert Castel, published by the University Press of Kansas © 1992. www.kansaspress.ku.edu. Used by permission of the publisher.

Map on page 161 reprinted by permission of Louisiana State University Press from *The Battle for Spotsylvania Court House and the Road to Yellow Tavern: May 7–12, 1864*, by Gordon C. Rhea. Copyright © 1997 by Louisiana State University Press.

Maps on pages 153, 155, and 156 reprinted by permission of Louisiana State University Press from *The Battle of the Wilderness: May 5–6, 1864*, by Gordon C. Rhea. Copyright © 1994 by Louisiana State University Press.

Maps on pages 107, 160, and 171 from *Richard S. Ewell: A Soldier's Life* by Donald C. Pfanz. Copyright © 1998 by the University of North Carolina Press. Used by permission of the publisher.

Maps on pages 169 and 176 from *Forrest, First with the Most* by Robert S. Henry. Used by permission of Broadfoot Publishing Company.

Maps on pages 4, 10, 18, 34, 35, 58, 59, 63, 64, 66, 73, 74, 77, 79, 86, 158, 163, and illustration on page 208 from *Battles and Leaders of the Civil War* (originally published 1884–1887, Century Magazine).

Table of Contents

1863

List of Maps

PREFACE

Many excellent books have been written on the Civil War, but this book fills a need that up till now has not been addressed. While almanacs, dictionaries, and encyclopedias abound, this book is the first comprehensive chronologically arranged work devoted solely to the land battles of the Civil War's Eastern Theater.

With this book the reader can obtain information about individual battles without having to trace their course through an entire chapter or book. For readers who find themselves wanting more details, each entry provides references for further reading. Maps are provided as well, to give the reader a sense of the action and the lay of the land.

The book covers land battles that took place east of the Mississippi River, with two exceptions. First, because of their minor impact on the Civil War in general, as well as the scarcity of actual infantry battles in the state, actions in Florida are not included. Second, minor skirmishes have been omitted, along with cavalry actions normally categorized as "raids." Most noteworthy in this regard would be Stuart's famous "Ride Around McClellan." However, actual cavalry battles, such as Yellow Tavern and Brice's Cross Roads, are included.

Although naval battles are not within this book's purview, battles that combined infantry on land with navy on rivers are included. For example, Vicksburg, Island No. 10 and Drewry's Bluff are covered.

Battles that occurred within a larger campaign are discussed within the entries for those campaigns, in the order in which they occurred, rather than as individual entries. Thus for example such battles as Kernstown, McDowell, Front Royal, Winchester, Cross Keys, and Port Republic are treated within the discussion of Stonewall Jackson's Valley Campaign (March 23–June 9, 1862), although each was obviously a separate engagement. The interested reader can locate these battles by name through the book's index.

1861

April 12–14, 1861
Fort Sumter

P.G.T. Beauregard (CSA) — R. Anderson (USA)

The events which occurred during this battle are well documented. With the escalation of political tensions, military action had finally been taken. Any possibility that war might be averted was now eliminated. However, three days in April do not tell the entire story.

Fort Sumter lies on an island in the middle of Charleston Harbor. The enclosure is surrounded by several significant points of land. Fort Moultrie lies to the north, on the tip of Sullivan's Island. To the south, Cumming's Point reaches out into the water from Morris Island. Due west, Fort Johnson rises from James Island. A bit farther to the west lies the city of Charleston. The fort is almost completely surrounded, and is a most difficult place to defend.

On December 26, 1860, Union Major Robert Anderson and his command were transferred from Fort Moultrie to Fort Sumter.[1] It must be remembered that the state of South Carolina had seceded from the United States only six days before, on December 20.

The next several months were spent increasing the Federal garrison. Men, equipment and guns were needed to make the fort ready for combat. Construction went on for heavy artillery pieces, as heavy cannon were mounted along the parapets.

In late spring, the Federal government became alarmed for the safety of the garrison on the island. President Abraham Lincoln met with his cabinet on March 28. He had become convinced that it would be necessary to relieve the island by forcible means.

President Lincoln handed the following directive to the Secretary of the Navy, Gideon Welles: "I desire that an expedition, to move by sea, be got ready to sail as early as the 6th of April next, the whole according to memorandum attached, and that you cooperate with the Secreatary of War for that object."[2]

The memorandum designated the warships *Pocahontas* and *Pawnee* as well as a revenue cutter to be employed in the mission. Three hundred seamen and two hundred other men[3] were to be on board the ships.

In reality, the "relief" expedition was much larger. The warships *Pocahontas, Pawnee, Powhatan* and *Harriet Lane* along with the steamers *Uncle Ben, Yankee* and *Freeborn* formed a convoy with one merchant ship, the *Baltic*. According to the Federals' own statement, the expedition consisted of "eight vessels, carrying twenty-six guns and about fourteen hundred men."[4]

Politics played a very important role in the battle of Fort Sumter. On the Union side, President Lincoln was trying to maneuver the South into actually firing the first shot. Confederate President Jefferson Davis did not want to comply, as he did not want to alienate the South's many sympathetic friends throughout the northern states.

The Confederate forces in the Charleston area were under the command of General Pierre G.T. Beauregard. On April 11, the graycoats made one last attempt to prevent any outbreak of hostilities. Under a flag of truce, Beauregard sent out his aides James Chesnut and Stephen D. Lee.[5]

Upon reaching Fort Sumter, the two Confederates met with Major Anderson. The major looked at Chesnut and said, "I will await the first shot.[6] If you do not batter us to pieces we will be starved out in a matter of days."[7]

Anderson's reply placed President Davis in a quandary. He did not want to fire upon the fort and initiate hostilities with the United States government. On the other hand, it was vital that the garrison not be reinforced.[8]

Jefferson Davis conferred with Confederate Secretary of War Leroy P. Walker. The two men sent this telegraph to General Beauregard: "We do not desire needlessly to bombard Fort Sumter. If Major Anderson will state the time ... at which he will evacuate, and agree that in the meantime he will not use his guns against us unless ours should be employed against Fort Sumter, we will abstain from opening fire. You are thus to avoid the effusion of blood. If this or its equivalent be refused, reduce the fort as your judgment decides to be the most practicable."[9]

Major Anderson had a terrible dilemma as well. He realized that food was running low, and the relief convoy was already overdue. He was an officer in the United States Army. However, unlike the government in Washington, D.C., Robert Anderson did not wish to actually provoke hostilities.

At 2:30 A.M., April 12,[10] he sat down to compose his reply. "I will, if provided with the proper and necessary means of transportation evacuate Fort Sumter by noon of the 15th instant, and I will not in the meantime open my fire upon your forces unless compelled to do so by some hostile act against this fort or the flag of my Government by the forces under your command." He paused. At this point his mind must have been racing, and the major wrote on: "should I not receive prior to that time controlling instructions from my Government or additional supplies."[11]

It was this last condition which sealed the fate of Fort Sumter. Major Anderson handed the communication to Colonel Chesnut. The Confederate, who had hoped for a solution to the tension which had engulfed the nation, knew the terms were unacceptable. The flotilla was bound to arrive any moment.

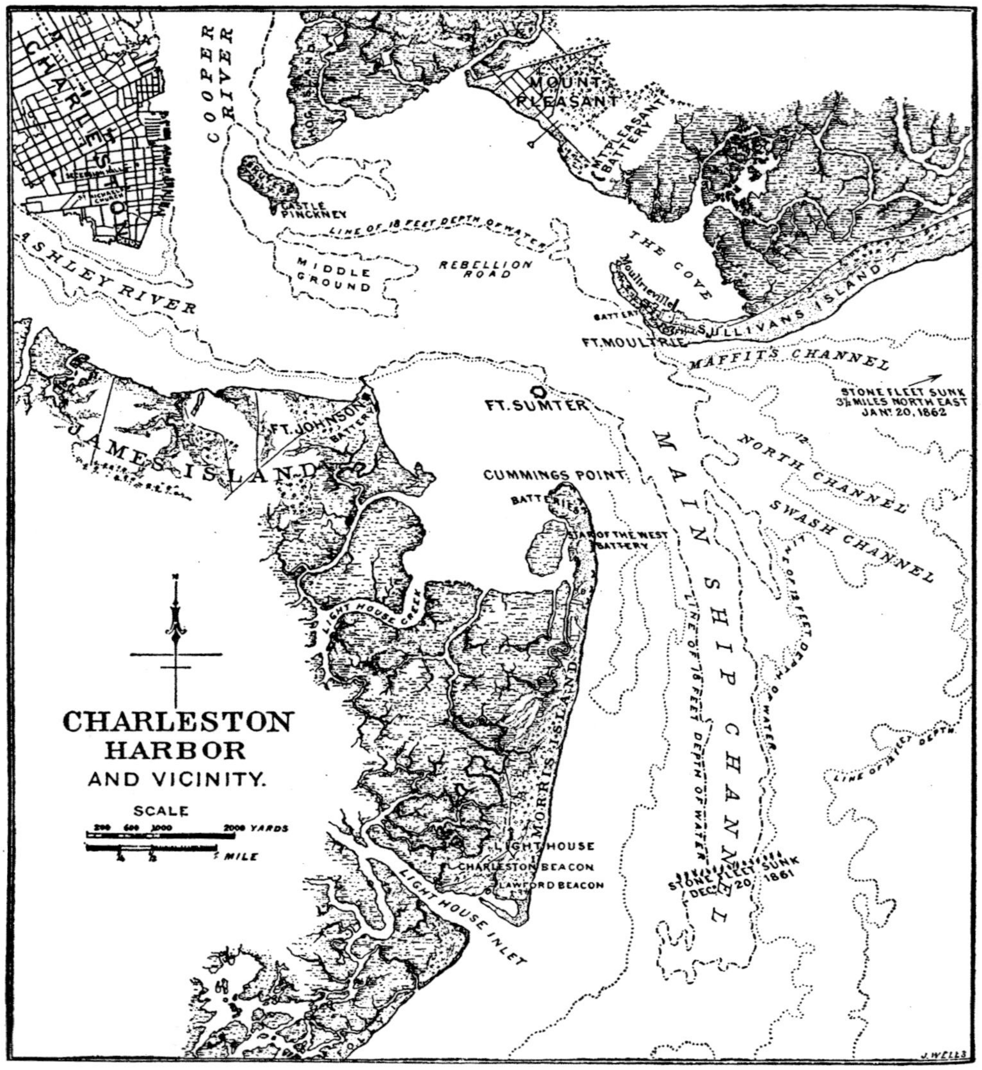

Charleston Harbor and vicinity. Map by Jacob Wells.

The Civil War was about to begin!

At 4:30 A.M., the artillery at Fort Johnson opened.[12] In the darkness, neither side had much success, but as the morning light illuminated the fort, the Confederates were able to inflict more damage. Several fires broke out inside the fort, and soon the gunpowder magazine was in grave danger of exploding.[12a] The Union fire was sporadic, and no shells were sent into Charleston.

During the afternoon the Union ships arrived, but the Confederate artillery prevented the naval vessels from reaching their destination.[12b]

At 12:48 P.M. on April 13,[13] the Union flagstaff was shot in two. Seeing the flag fall down, the rebels were provided with a most curious opportunity.

Former Senator Louis Wigfall observed the collapse of the flag. He believed that he could stop the cannonade. Wigfall commandeered two negroes as oarsmen, and the three men set out in a rowboat for Fort Sumter. Shells continued to explode over their heads, but the rowboat finally reached the fort.[14]

Though Wigfall had no authority to meet with the enemy, Major Anderson believed he was a Confederate emissary with full powers to negotiate peace terms. Discussions took place, and soon thereafter General Beauregard watched the United States flag come down. The white flag of surrender rose in its place.[15] At 2:30 P.M. on April 13, Robert Anderson surrendered Fort Sumter.[16]

The Federals had received 34 hours of continual bombardment.[17] Approximately 4,000[18] artillery shells had fallen on the garrison.

There were no casualties on either side. However, on Sunday, April 14, the Union troops fired a 100-gun salute to their flag. The 50th gun exploded, killing one private and wounding five other men.[19]

Obviously, the events surrounding the attack on Fort Sumter leave several questions open to debate. Who fired the first shot? This seems to be the lone historical fact which is not subject to interpretation.

Other, more complex questions remain. Did Abraham Lincoln provoke the start of the Civil War by sending armed warships to relieve Fort Sumter? Should the Confederates have waited, hoping to starve the Federal garrison into submission? Could the Confederates have afforded to wait, with relief expected at any moment? Did Robert Anderson need to attach unacceptable conditions in his reply to General Beauregard? Could Anderson have waited, in the hope that the ships would arrive? Should Anderson have surrendered Fort Sumter at all?

These questions are left for the reader to answer. However, after the shots were fired on April 12, there would be no turning back. The Civil War had begun.

June 10, 1861
Big Bethel

J.B. Magruder (CSA) — B.F. Butler (USA)

In comparison with later battles, the action at Big Bethel would seem like nothing more than a skirmish.

The action was brief, and casualties on both sides were few,[1] but in June of 1861 it seemed to be a contest of great importance.

The Confederates were led by John B. Magruder, Colonel of the Virginia Volunteers. On May 21 he had been placed in command of the troops on the lower Peninsula, a narrow strip of land separating the York River, on the north, and the James River, to the south. He found the equipment poor, his infantry force small, and he had no cavalry at all. Nevertheless, he persevered, and his efforts to obtain more men for his small command were rewarded.[2]

Shortly after Magruder arrived in the area, a regiment of 1,100 men from North Carolina was sent to his aid, under the command of Colonel Daniel Harvey Hill.[3] Both Magruder and Hill were to become generals for the Confederacy later in the war.

The North Carolinians were so well trained that on June 6, Magruder sent the regiment along with four artillery pieces and a few other troops to an advanced position at Big Bethel Church, which lay on a branch of the Bark River, 13 miles from Yorktown, and only eight miles from Hampton. The Union forces were currently deployed at Hampton and Newport News,[4] and commanded by General Benjamin F. Butler.

On June 10, 1861, the Federals moved forward, their inexperienced troops taking casualties by firing into one another as Colonel Hill ordered his Confederates out to meet the assault. This was one of the few battles of the war in which the Confederates were actually better equipped than their opponents. Several Parrott type cannon had been purchased by Virginia in 1860 and sent to Colonel Magruder.[4a] The Yankees recoiled, and D.H. Hill led his men after the foe as far as his judgment would allow. The rebels were finally recalled to their camp for the night, and the battle of Big Bethel was over.[5]

Reports of this victory were received in Richmond with joy and celebration, and it was magnified by the local papers far beyond its small size. The *Richmond Dispatch* asked, "Was not the hand of God manifest in such a triumph over such odds?"[6] Clearly, the victory at Big Bethel had been blown up out of all proportion.

The Confederates lost only one man killed and seven wounded, of approximately 1,400 engaged in the action, while the Union lost 18 killed, 53 wounded and five missing, for a total of 76 out of 2,500 participants.[7]

The effects of the battle of Big Bethel were profound. John B. Magruder and Daniel H. Hill were each promoted to the rank of brigadier general.[8] Spirits were lifted throughout the South. A large part of the civilian population, allowing patriotic fervor to take the place of careful analysis, felt that the entire conflict would be finished quickly. Most experienced military men, however, realized that the government of the United States was not an opponent to be taken lightly. Many of the Confederate officers had served in the U.S. Army prior to the outbreak of hostilities. They knew only too well the capability of the war machine in Washington. Magruder, like Robert E. Lee, foresaw a long, protracted war.[9] Unfortunately, they would be right.

July 11, 1861
Rich Mountain

R.S. Garnett (CSA) — G.B. McClellan (USA)

Rich Mountain lies in what is now West Virginia. At the outbreak of the Civil War, it was still part of Virginia.[1] Economically, the region was closely tied to the Ohio River.[1a] Unlike the eastern part of the state, there was strong Union sentiment in the area.

On June 11 the western counties broke away from the remainder of secessionist Virginia in an attempt to join the Union. To support the pro–Union counties, General George B. McClellan accompanied 20,000 troops into western Virginia.[2]

In order to block the Federals, the Virginia state government sent General Robert S. Garnett with 4,500 men to the small town of Beverly, located 50 miles west of the Shenandoah Valley.[3] Although the Confederates tried to gain additional recruits from the surrounding area, they were unsuccessful among the loyal Unionists.[4]

When General McClellan arrived on July 9, he found the Confederates deployed on Rich Mountain and Laurel Mountain, which protected Beverly on the west and north, respectively.[5] Despite the fortifications of the enemy, McClellan decided to attack.

On July 11, he sent a Union brigade under the command of General William S. Rosecrans to assault the heights of Rich Mountain. In a pouring rain[6] the Ohioan led his men up the steep sides of the mountain. General Garnett, believing that the precipice was too steep to

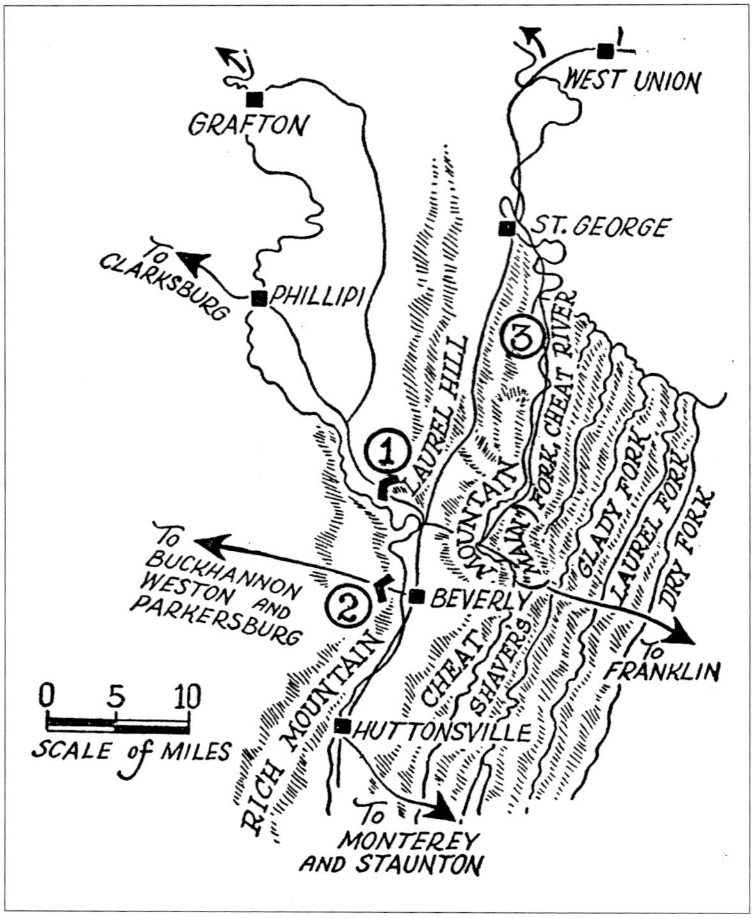

The region of Gen. R. S. Garnett's operations in Western Virginia, in a general sketch by John T. Draper. Positions are as follows: (1) rough approximation of Garnett's line on Laurel Hill, of which no detailed map is known; (2) Pegram's line on Rich Mountain, (3) Carrick's Ford on Shaver's or "Main Fork" of Cheat River. This ford is about four miles south of the town of Parsons and east of U.S. Route 219. Approached from the opposite direction, Carrick's Ford is about 17 miles northeast of the present city of Elkins. Contemporary maps of the region are scarce and unreliable.

attack successfully, left only 1,300 Confederates under John Pegram to defend Rich Mountain.[7]

Rosecrans was able to overrun the rebels with relative ease.[8] The Federals lost only 12 killed and 49 wounded. The rebels had left 20 wounded soldiers on the field, and suffered the loss of 63 men captured, but reliable estimates of Confederate killed in this engagement are not available.[8a] The loss of Rich Mountain was very significant because it jeopardized the Confederates remaining on Laurel Mountain. The Yankees under General Rosecrans now stood upon the Confederate line of retreat from Laurel Mountain to Beverly.[9]

General Garnett attempted to escape. On July 12 he marched to Kaler's Ford, on the Cheat River, and the rebels made camp in a pouring rain.[10] The next morning the Confederates continued to move onward, until they reached Carrick's Ford, some 3½ miles from Kaler's. The current of the Cheat River was very swift, and many of the wagons were unable to make the crossing.[11]

The 23rd Virginia regiment was deployed as a rearguard against the pursuing Federals. The Virginians were able to delay the enemy long enough to allow the wagons to gain some distance from the bluecoats.[12]

General Garnett began to direct the placement of his troops, as he realized that the Yankees would arrive shortly. The Confederates needed only a few minutes before Union troops came into view. Approaching cautiously, the Federals came within 50 yards[13] of the Confederate position. A Union sharpshooter took aim and fired, striking his target in the back. General Garnett fell from his horse, mortally wounded. On July 13, Robert S. Garnett would become the first general officer in the Civil War to be killed in action.[14]

Casualties at Carrick's Ford were heavily in favor of the Union. The Northerners lost no more than 50 men in the brief engagement. While Garnett's command had roughly 20 men killed and 50 captured, Pegram surrendered 553 soldiers to the Federal authorities.[15]

Operations in the western part of Virginia had not gone well for the Confederacy. New leadership was needed. In a somewhat advisory role, Robert E. Lee would soon be sent from Richmond to lead the Southern forces in the area. In stark contrast to his future results, Lee's performance here would be a weak one.

Most of the battles in this section of the country were small, isolated affairs, with little impact on the war in general. However, on the Union side, George B. McClellan had met with great success. His victories here would propel him to the overall command of the Army of the Potomac. In the summer of 1862, Lee and McClellan would meet at the outskirts of Richmond. The outcome would be quite different.

July 21, 1861

First Manassas (Bull Run)

P.G.T. Beauregard	I. McDowell
J. E. Johnston	(USA)
(CSA)	

First Manassas has great significance in the history of the Civil War as it was the first engagement fought on a large scale. There had been other, smaller affairs, but casualties were few and the action was brief. At the onset of hostilities, there were many on both sides who sincerely believed that this War Between the States would be over very quickly. The carnage at First Manassas changed their minds.

The Confederates were positioned just north of Manassas Junction, Virginia. The troops were deployed along the little stream known as Bull Run. However, the organizational structure was not complete. The task of appointing brigadier generals fell to President Jefferson Davis. Among the new general officers were two who were already stationed at Manassas, Richard S. Ewell and David R. Jones. Three other appointees were to figure prominently in the annals of the Civil War: Barnard E. Bee, Edmund Kirby Smith and Thomas J. "Stonewall" Jackson.

Confederate General Pierre G.T. Beauregard now faced the somewhat daunting task of organizing the nineteen regiments[1] under his command. There were approximately 22,000 Confederates at Manassas. In addition, Joseph E. Johnston had 11,000 graycoats stationed at Winchester in the Shenandoah Valley and Theophilus H. Holmes had a small force of 3,000 men at Fredericksburg.[2]

Opposing these widely scattered Confederates were about 35,000 Federals in front of Washington, commanded by Irvin McDowell, and 15,000 troops at Winchester, led by Robert Patterson.[3]

By July 17 it became apparent that General McDowell was moving his force toward Manassas Junction. Beauregard urged Johnston to come to his support.[4] In his desire to receive reinforcements, General Beauregard had overlooked the fact that if their forces were combined, General Johnston, by virtue of his seniority in rank, would be in command.[5]

On the 18th of July the Confederates were strung out along Bull Run. To prevent the bluecoats finding an easy point to cross the water, General Beauregard made sure that all of the fords were protected. On the Confederate right, Richard "Dick" Ewell was at Union Mills. To his left was D.R. Jones at McLean's Ford. James Longstreet was at Blackburn's Ford and Milledge Bonham covered Mitchell's Ford. Finally, Philip St. George Cocke guarded the fords between Mitchell's and the Stone Bridge, which was shortly to become so famous.[6]

Blackburn's Ford lies about half a mile from both McLean's and Mitchell's Fords.[7] It was here, against Longstreet's men, that the first action occurred. McDowell sent a division forward to test the strength of the Southern forces. Soon bullets began to fly back and forth. The glory of war faded away as men began to fall. James Longstreet was absolutely unflappable in the heat of battle,[8] and he steadied his men. The first attack was repulsed, but the Northerners regrouped. The Northerners moved forward again, but the Confederates held firm a second time.[9] However, the Federals were still at Blackburn's Ford in force. The enemy might test Longstreet's men once more. Beauregard had ordered the brigade under Jubal Early to move to Longstreet's assistance.[10] Early's infantry fired into the Union ranks, and at this point the Confederate artillery opened fire on the Yankees. The Federals withdrew their troops, and the small affair at Blackburn's Ford was over.

Although the casualties on both sides during July 18 had been very few, the action in front of Longstreet's men had a more important result. The armies now had an idea of each other's strength. The larger battle on July 21 would be fought with each side trying to attack the other's left flank.[11]

The next few days were spent shifting troops into position, and making general preparations for an assault. Joseph E. Johnston had been transferred to Manassas from Winchester, and by July 20 his men began to arrive. Theophilus Holmes brought his small force from Fredericksburg. By the next day the opposing forces would be almost equal.[12]

Irvin McDowell had been searching for an unguarded crossing of Bull Run. He finally found one. Sudley Ford, which lay north of Beauregard's left flank, had no Confederates behind it. His plan was to feint against the enemy right, then send approximately 13,000 men in a night march to Sudley Ford. Sweeping down on the Confederate left, McDowell's men would drive the rebels from the field.[13]

Pierre G.T. Beauregard, for his part, massed most of his troops on the Confederate right. His left, which was about to receive McDowell's attack, had the smallest concentration of defenders. As morning broke on July 21, the action was about to begin.

Shortly after 5:00 A.M.[14] a messenger delivered a report from General Bonham. Stationed at Mitchell's Ford, he had noticed Federals in force on his left. Gunfire was now audible in the direction of the Stone Bridge,[15] which was the main crossing of Bull Run.

Orders went out to different Confederate commanders, with various instructions. Most important were those on the left. General Cocke, to the right of the bridge, and Colonel Nathan G. "Shanks" Evans, just to the left of it, were told to hold their positions to the last extremity.[16] Colonel Evans was to play a vital role in the drama which unfolded.

In addition, General Beauregard began deploying the troops he had held in reserve. Around 7:00 A.M.[17] Gen-

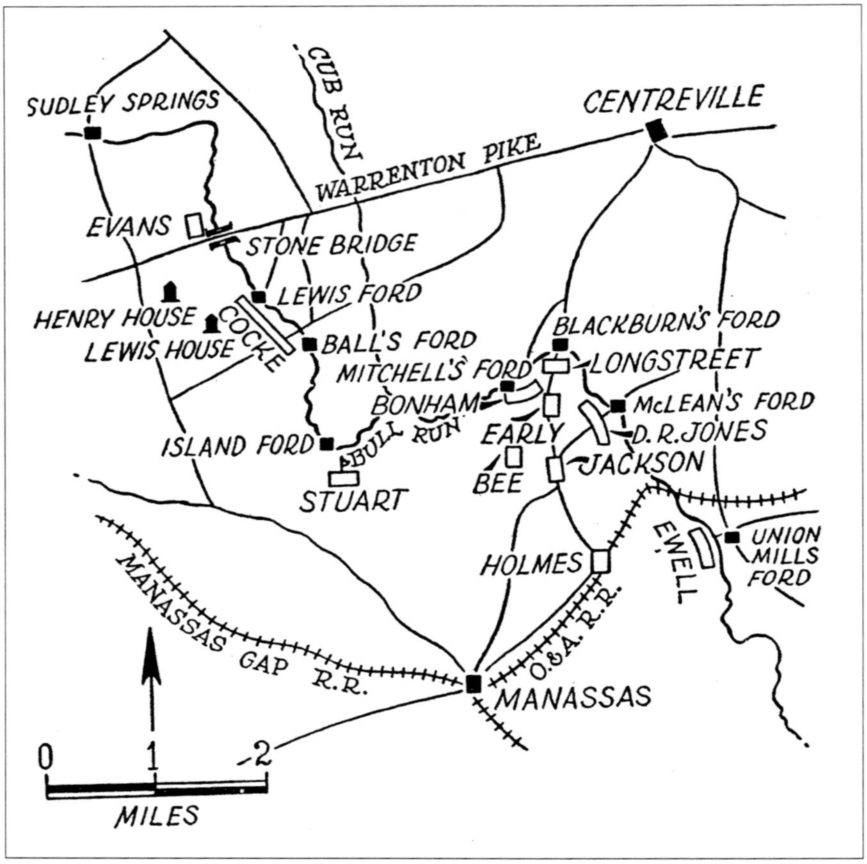

First Manassas (Bull Run): position of Confederate forces, July 21, 1861, sunrise. Map by John T. Draper after R. M. Johnson.

eral Barnard Bee and Colonel Francis Bartow were ordered to hurry to reinforce the left. Combined, their commands came to 2,800 men.[18] General Thomas J. Jackson was to move with his brigade and nine artillery pieces to fill the space on Bonham's left and Cocke's right.[19] By the end of the day he would be forever known as "Stonewall."

About 9:00 A.M. Beauregard received a message from E. Porter Alexander. Alexander would go on to fame in the artillery service, but today the young captain was working as a signal officer. He notified the general that the enemy had crossed Bull Run two miles above the Stone Bridge, with both infantry and artillery.[20]

Troops must be sent to the threatened sector with all possible speed! Bee was directed to continue his march past the bridge and move toward Sudley Ford. Jackson, as well as Colonel Wade Hampton with his 600 South Carolinians, would strengthen the left as well.

By 11:00 in the morning the sounds of battle on the left were growing. General Johnston, though technically in command of the Southern forces, had respectfully allowed General Beauregard to conduct the battle. Johnston, however, became more and more apprehensive as the noise increased. After a new blast of artillery from the left, he turned to Beauregard and said, "The battle is there, I am going!"[21]

The battle had already started. McDowell had moved his troops to the Sudley Ford. Opposing the bluecoats was a small band of Confederates. Shanks Evans had his men stationed just to the north of the Stone Bridge. He noticed that the enemy was moving along Bull Run. Without waiting for orders, Evans took 1,100 muskets to block the Union advance.[22]

General Bee arrived, and with the commands of Bartow and Hampton, threw his men against the foe. Despite combining all of their forces these Confederates were still heavily outnumbered.[23] They fought valiantly, but were at length compelled to retire to the hill behind them. The rebels sought to regroup around the house of the widow Henry.

Jackson had been moving to his left to take up a position between Bonham and Cocke, but he heard the sound of the battle on the left, and marched to Henry Hill.[24] Jackson's men got into position shortly before Johnston and Beauregard arrived.

The tenacity of the graycoats under Evans, Bee, Bartow and Hampton, along with Jackson's timely arrival, had saved the Southerners from destruction. However, if McDowell could bring up General Patterson's men quickly enough from the northwest, the Confederates would be doomed.[25] The battle was clearly a race against time.

Colonel Evans had been fighting for five hours, and the issue was still in doubt. Would the Federals be able to get around the Confederate left and outflank Johnston's army? At 2:00 P.M. Beauregard ordered a charge to clear the bluecoats off Henry Hill. The right of his line charged forward, and momentarily cleared the plateau.[26] But the enemy reappeared and took possession of the hill again.

General Bee rode across the field to his West Point comrade Thomas J. Jackson. Saluting, he said, "General they are driving us!" Looking to the northwest, Jackson sternly replied, "Sir, we will give them the bayonet."[26a] Bee rode back to his lines, where officers were trying to reform the broken fragments of the brigades which had fought so hard that day. Pointing with his sword, his voiced boomed above the roar of the battlefield. "Look, men, there is Jackson standing like a stone wall! Let us determine to die here, and we will conquer! Follow me!"[26b] Barnard Bee would not survive the day, but he gave the world the most famous sobriquet in American military history.

General Beauregard knew that the hill must be retaken. He ordered another charge from his center and right. Could his men take the hill before Union reinforcements arrived? This time, the Confederates cleared the hill, but the cost was heavy. General Bee and Colonel Bartow went down. The Federals were slow to regroup, and the rebels took the hill for good.[27]

Finally Confederate reinforcements arrived, and the left was extended. Two South Carolina regiments had been sent from General Bonham, the 28th Virginia arrived from General Cocke, and three more regiments had detrained at Manassas Junction. Under the command of E. Kirby Smith, they had been rushed to the action. Still, the battle hung in the balance. The Union troops were trying to extend their own right, and get around Beauregard's left flank.[28]

Looking through his binoculars to the southwest, General Beauregard saw a column of troops marching in his direction. But who were they? The flag lay against its mast, with no breeze to show its colors. It could well be General Patterson, with fresh divisions to seal the Southerners' fate.[29]

The column came into full view. Suddenly, a gust of wind burst across the battlefield. General Beauregard put his binoculars to his eyes and watched the flag unfurl. The troops belonged to Jubal Early![30]

The Confederates cheered the timely arrival of General Early's men, who quickly fell into position on the left of the line. To the great joy of the grayclad infantry, the enemy in front was no longer extending those blue lines around Beauregard's left flank. The rebels could sense victory in the air. The entire line surged forward, and the Federal front collapsed under the charge. As the Southerners rushed forward, the collapse turned into a rout.[31]

The last step for the Confederates was the pursuit of a beaten foe. It was 4:40 P.M.[32] In a flurry of orders from Johnston and Beauregard, the pursuit stalled. A false rumor kept Ewell and Holmes at Union Mills, and Bonham's troops did not receive orders in a timely manner. His men had made a very difficult march before they became entangled with Longstreet's division along the Manassas-Centreville highway. The cavalry under General J.E.B. Stuart was impeded by many prisoners, and deprived of virtually all of its striking power.[33] The next day saw a heavy rain cover the area.[34] The dirt roads turned to mud and any chance of a pursuit on July 22 was lost.

When the fighting was over, the Confederates had possession of the battlefield. They had seen 387 men killed, 1,582 wounded and 13 captured or missing, for a total of 1,982. McDowell's Union army had lost 460 soldiers killed, 1,124 wounded, and 1,312 captured or missing, for a total of 2,896.[35]

Clearly, the Confederacy had won the day. President Jefferson Davis was elated with the victory.[36] General Beauregard, however, was not. The Creole from Louisiana felt that much more should have been accomplished.[37] While the Southerners had taken more prisoners, won possession of the field, and acquired more military equipment, he realized that there was a big difference between victory and complete victory.

September 10, 1861

Carnifix Ferry

H.A. Wise	W.S. Rosecrans
J.B. Floyd	(USA)
(CSA)	

The Confederate troops in this part of western Virginia were severely hampered by the inability of the Southern commanders to work together. General Henry A. Wise and General John B. Floyd held separate commands, and each seemed determined to try to win the war alone.

The action at Carnifix Ferry, West Virginia, took place due east of Charleston, near the present-day town of Summerville, located in the central section of the state. In 1861, West Virginia had not yet become a state.[1] The western counties of Virginia were tied economically to the Ohio River, and as a result, there was a great deal of Union sentiment in this area.[2]

Both sides of the conflict maintained scattered forces throughout the state. General Floyd's command was the first of the Confederate troops in the area to move forward.[3] Floyd marched his 2,600 troops[3a] northwest up the Kanawha Valley, crossing the Gauley River at Carnifix Ferry.[4]

The graycoats were threatened by a large Union force under General William S. Rosecrans. General Wise warned Floyd against being trapped against the river, but Floyd allowed his high self-esteem to block sound military logic. When Floyd's Confederates became endangered, Wise refused to send him reinforcements.[5]

The Gauley River flows in a southerly direction, then changes direction, running due west.[6] The Confederates faced northwest, with each flank against the water, and

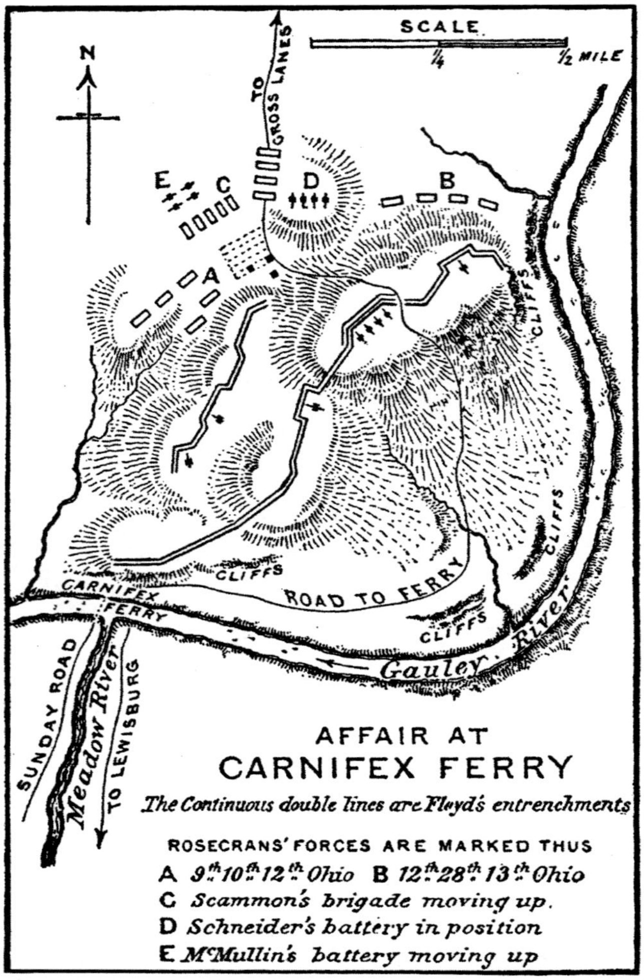

Affair at Carnifix Ferry. The continuous double lines are Floyd's entrenchments. This map uses the slightly less common spelling, "Carnifex." Map by Jacob Wells.

the bend in the river behind them.[7] On September 10, General Rosecrans attacked with three Ohio brigades, easily forcing the Confederate pickets back and capturing a few supplies in the process.[8]

During the night the Confederates slipped away, and the ferry was destroyed, eliminating any possible pursuit.

Casualties seemed to favor the graycoats in a battle which was small by later standards. The Confederates reported only 20 total casualties, whereas the Union forces had lost 17 men killed and 141 wounded in the fighting that day,[9] but the action at Carnifix Ferry had much deeper ramifications. Amazingly General Wise, and not Floyd, was blamed for the fiasco on September 10.[10] However, the Confederate government realized that leadership in the western part of the state was lacking. The Richmond authorities decided to entrust the rescue of the region to a general who at this point in the Civil War had not yet commanded Southern troops in the field. His name was Robert E. Lee.

September 11–13, 1861
Cheat Mountain

R.E. Lee (CSA)	J.J. Reynolds (USA)

Cheat Mountain was Robert E. Lee's first endeavor in western Virginia. Union victories at Philippi and Rich Mountain earlier in the summer had secured the sector for the Federals. The two victories by the enemy had brought General Lee to the area in order to see if the western counties could be recovered for the Confederacy.

Cheat Mountain was strategically important, as it controlled several mountain passes, along with the Staunton-Parkersburg Turnpike. The Union force of about 2,000 men was under the command of General Joseph J. Reynolds. It had been split in two, with Colonel Nathan Kimball and the 14th Indiana regiment atop the Cheat Summit, while Reynolds and five other regiments guarded the turnpike at Elkwater.[1]

From the Southern perspective, the key position was the high ground around Huttonsville, which dominated the road in the rear of Cheat Mountain. It might be possible to get around the enemy before the Yankees realized that they were in danger.

General Lee assumed command of about 15,000 Confederates,[2] and divided the rebels into five columns. This did not sit well with General William Loring, who had been sent to western Virginia by Lee less than two weeks before.[3] Now it seemed to him that Lee had come to supervise the operations.

Several factors entered into Lee's assessment of the situation. The ground was very difficult, there were no roads to speak of, and the face of Cheat Mountain was covered in a dense blanket of mountain laurel, which would certainly retard any attack Lee might decide to make. The exact strength of the enemy was not known, and the Confederates had a large part of their troops out sick, but the possibility of surprise still existed.[4]

On September 8, General Lee issued his orders for attack. He tactfully wrote the orders in the name of General Loring, to smooth any ruffled feathers.

Colonel Albert Rust had found a hidden route to Kimball's right. This was two miles west of the mountain's crest, and led to Colonel Kimball's supply lines.[5] General Samuel Anderson's brigade would cut the wagon trail behind Cheat Summit. Rust would lead one attack force of about 2,000 men. General Henry Jackson would lead a march on the Staunton-Parkersburg turnpike, as soon as Rust opened the way. Two other brigades, under General Daniel Donelson and Colonel Jesse Burks, would be ready to advance on Elkwater along either side of the Tygart River. One more brigade would be held in reserve, commanded by William Gilham.[6] The guns of Rust's command would signal the attack.

With the three remaining Confederate brigades, Lee would go after Reynolds. Two brigades were assigned to General Loring. General Lee was to be undermined by Loring's lack of enterprise, poor weather, and inexperienced soldiers recruited from a civilian population.[7]

On September 10, in steady rain,[8] the graycoats advanced. At 9:00 A.M., Anderson's brigade moved out. The graycoats marched all day, but the going was very slow.

One day later Reynolds met Loring's brigades at Conrad's Mill, then withdrew to Elkwater. The gunfire from this minor skirmish eliminated any chance of surprise.[9]

September 12 brought some success to Lee's operation, as General Anderson cut the wagon road behind Kimball. However, Colonel Rust was deceived into believing he was marching into a trap. Despite having 2,000 men to Kimball's 300, the Southerner thought he was outnumbered.[10] The activity from Rust was nowhere to be heard. Robert E. Lee was growing impatient. The only solution left was to open the battle with the troops west of the mountain. Rust and Jackson would simply be unavailable.[11]

By the 13th, the attack which had seemed so promising had quickly turned into disappointment. Lee soon realized that the prospects for success were slim. The terrain was rugged, the enemy was on the alert, and supplies were low. There was no choice but to abandon the effort.

The episode at Cheat Mountain must be counted as a dismal failure in the career of Robert E. Lee. Still, it would have been extremely difficult to succeed. Weather was poor, sickness was rampant, and subordinates such as Loring and Rust had not served him well.[12]

For his part, Lee's performance was also wanting. He did not push Loring forward aggressively enough. Born and bred with extreme tact, Lee's lack of firmness with his subordinates would remain with him throughout the war. Second, he should never have allowed Rust to have led the advance. Rust did not have an experienced soldier at his side to make a proper reconnaissance of the Federal position, and he was easily deceived by Union prisoners as to the actual strength of his opponent. In addition, Lee's intricate plans for the coordination of so many different attacking columns were too complex for the unseasoned Confederates of 1861.[13]

On the positive side, the mistakes made in the rugged mountains by Robert E. Lee were rarely made again. He learned from this wretched experience, and his understanding of the common soldier laid the groundwork for the superb morale which would exist in the Army of Northern Virginia.[14]

October 21, 1861
BALL'S BLUFF (LEESBURG)

J.E. Johnston (CSA)	G.B. McClellan (USA)

During October 1861, both armies were quietly facing each other in eastern Virginia. There had not been much activity for either side since the Confederates won the battle of First Manassas on July 21. The Southerners were still encamped around Manassas Junction, which lay due west of Washington, D.C. General Joseph E. Johnston of Virginia was in command. General George B. McClellan had his Federal troops positioned from Maryland down into Virginia, between the rebels and the capital. It was of the utmost importance to Abraham Lincoln and his cabinet to keep Washington safe from invasion.

McClellan assumed that the Confederates were deployed around Leesburg. Gradually, he began moving divisions of his army to the northwest, with the purpose of crossing the Potomac River from Maryland into Virginia. This would place the Union forces between Washington and Leesburg. One of these divisions was led by General Charles P. Stone, and contained a brigade under Colonel Edward Baker, a political appointee who was a personal friend of President Lincoln.[1]

As McClellan moved his men across the Potomac, the General wanted to know whether the Confederates had changed their position. He directed General Stone to observe the situation, and also suggested that a "slight demonstration"[2] might force the enemy to withdraw.

General Stone assigned this task to Colonel Baker, giving him the option of either pulling his troops back to the Maryland side, or reinforcing his own brigade for just such a demonstration. Baker, eager for the opportunity to punish the Confederates, plunged forward without making a thorough reconnaissance of the area.[3]

Baker had crossed the Potomac to attack the Confederates he thought were near Leesburg. He found no rebels in his immediate vicinity and decided to await

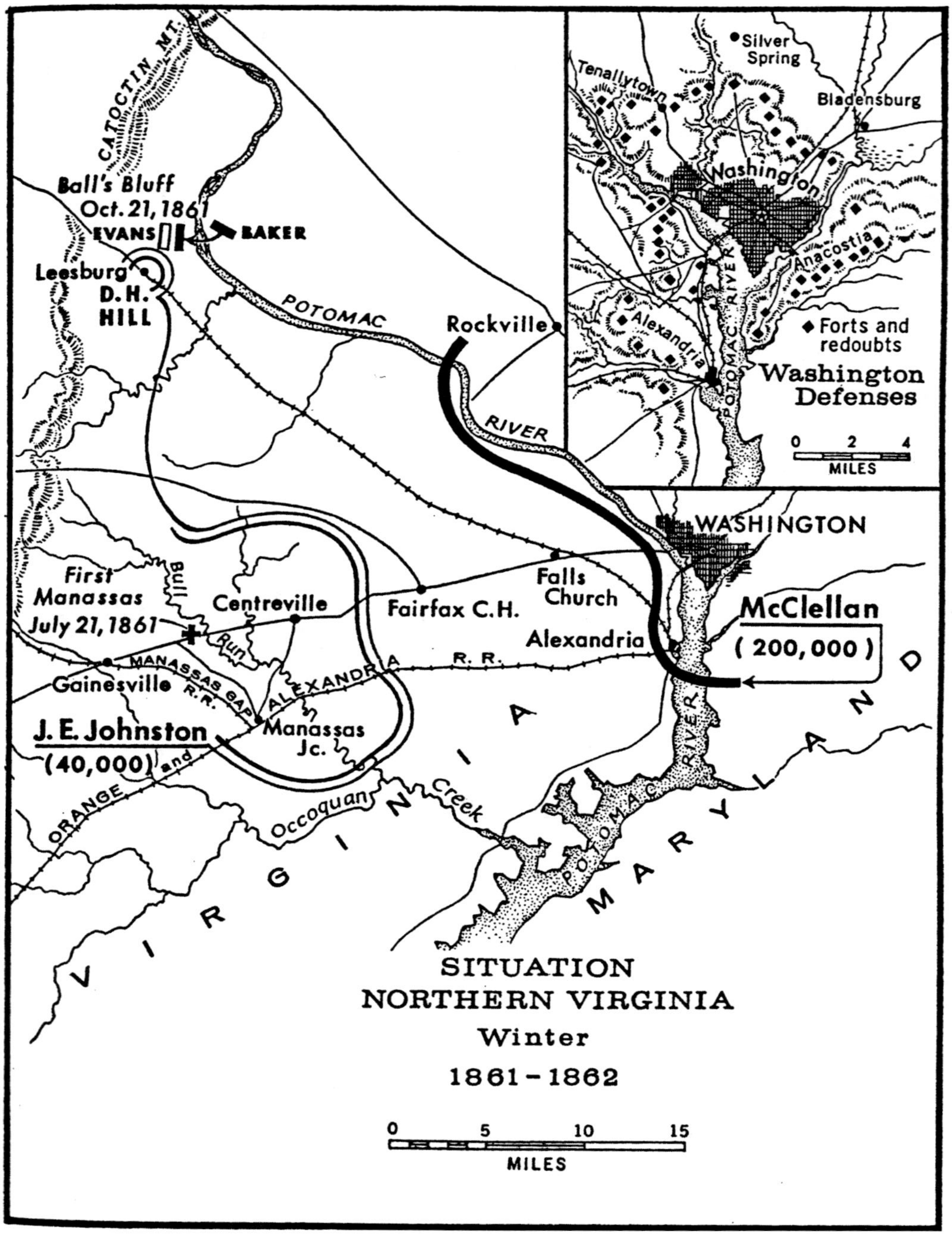

Situation in Northern Virginia, winter 1861-1862.

developments. The Colonel assumed a very weak defensive position, with his back to the water.

Nathan G. "Shanks" Evans was a South Carolinian with a very strong combat record. He perceived the weakness in the Federal deployment and attacked ferociously. He brought up three regiments and a cavalry unit and enveloped both of Baker's flanks, forcing him to retreat to the river. With his back to the Potomac and Evans in his front, Baker's troops were quickly destroyed. His brigade lost 49 men killed, 158 wounded and 714 missing, for a total of 921.[4] Edward Baker was killed in the action.[5] The Southerners had 33 soldiers killed, 115 wounded and one missing, for a total of 149.[6]

The results of this small action had great repercussions. George B. McClellan decided to await better weather, and abandoned any idea of attacking the Confederates in 1861. He also gave up any idea of a frontal attack against Johnston's men. In a letter to President Lincoln, General McClellan wrote that he was considering "another plan of campaign that I do not think at all anticipated by the enemy."[7]

This was the beginning of the Peninsula Campaign, which would begin in late March, 1862.[8] In this campaign, General McClellan would lead an immense force by water down to the neck of land in Virginia known as the Peninsula. It separated the York River on the north, and the James River on the south. The Federal plan was to march inland and capture Richmond, which lies on the James. Instead, he would see his dreams shattered at the hands of Robert E. Lee.

1862

January 1–February 23, 1862
THE ROMNEY CAMPAIGN

T.J. Jackson (CSA)	F.W. Lander (USA)

The village of Romney, Virginia, is located along the South Branch of the Potomac River, and as it was the county seat of Hampshire County, it was the principal community in the South Branch valley.[1] It was not populous, containing some 500 inhabitants in 1862,[2] but it had great military importance.

Romney was surrounded by hills and mountains. The farmland in the area was very fertile, while the lush pastures were ideal for cattle. Whoever controlled the town would be able to control the whole valley.[3]

Significant Union plunder of the area had already taken place. In a small 17-mile area, 41 homes had been burned.[4] The same fate could await Winchester, not far to the southeast. For the moment, though, the Confederate army was stationed there, led by General Thomas J. "Stonewall" Jackson.

Although the Federal armies were very large when combined, they had weakened their defenses by placing small outposts almost everywhere. This seemed like an ideal opportunity to defeat the fragmented Federal forces one at a time. Jackson's plan was to march north to the town of Bath and overcome the garrison there. Once Bath had been taken, the rebels would continue north across the Potomac River and capture the neighboring town of Hancock, Maryland. This would give the Confederates a secure base from which to operate. From this point, Jackson could turn his attention southwest in the direction of Romney.[5]

January 1 was much warmer than usual. Graycoats shed their overcoats as the temperature rose on a mild winter day. As they left Winchester in the direction of Bath, the Confederates had no idea of the freezing weather which was about to come their way.[6]

The Southerners had four brigades which constituted Jackson's command. Three of these were led by General William W. Loring, while the other was a small group of militia under General Gilbert S. Meem.

Jackson was not very familiar with any of these troops, and the march did not get started in good order.[7]

The afternoon brought a bitter wind, and the temperature began falling fast. The troops without heavy coats began to suffer. It was impossible to light campfires in the swirling conditions. January 2 saw no improvement. The temperature never exceeded 27 degrees[8] and the biting winds made it feel much colder to Jackson's grayclad troops. Conditions were difficult as a heavy blanket of snow impeded the Confederates' progress, and turned the roads to ice.[9]

The Confederates were heading toward Unger's Store, a small village on the way to Bath. By the time the men reached their destination, they had been a day and a half without food or warm clothing, and had marched a meager 15 miles in two days[10] through the frigid cold. Jackson's men were suffering severely, and the campaign which was to end in Romney had only just begun.

Late in the evening of January 2,[11] the troops were relieved to see the supply wagons pull into camp. Food had finally arrived. In addition, some of the militia joined Jackson's main body, bringing the small force under Stonewall to some 8,500 men.[12]

On January 3 the weather got even colder.[13] Not all of the men had received their rations yet, but the village of Bath was only a few short miles ahead. There was considerable disagreement between Jackson and his subordinates. Jackson wanted to push ahead, the troops wanted to eat. Jackson compromised, with the men eating what they could carry as they headed north, continuing on their journey.

Stonewall Jackson devised a two-pronged plan of attack. The militia would march to the left of the rest of the army, approaching Bath from the west, while the remainder of the Confederates, led by General Loring, would attack from the south.[14]

By midafternoon the rebels had covered 11 miles, although the conditions were severe. Unexpectedly, Loring's men ran into Union pickets three miles before reaching Bath. The Union men opened fire upon discovering the approach of Jackson's column. Secrecy was now lost.[15]

The Union forces around Bath numbered only 1,400 men[16] and Jackson believed the town could be taken before dark. However, Loring had ordered his troops to make camp for the night, so the assault would have to wait another day.[17]

On Saturday, January 4, the ground was covered with snow. The militia had good intentions, but the men lacked experience. They came upon a few Federals and each side fired one volley, then fled in opposite directions. It looked as if Jackson's attack would have to come solely from Loring's men, still slowly advancing from the south.[18]

As Loring moved forward, it became apparent that the militia had failed to close off the Union escape route from Bath. The Confederates overwhelmed the thin resistance, but were unable to do more than capture a handful of prisoners as the little town fell into Southern hands.[19]

Poor roads, freezing weather, inexperienced commanders and a lack of close cooperation with subordinates on Jackson's part[20] had gotten the first stage of the campaign off to a most inauspicious beginning.

On January 5 General Jackson turned his attention

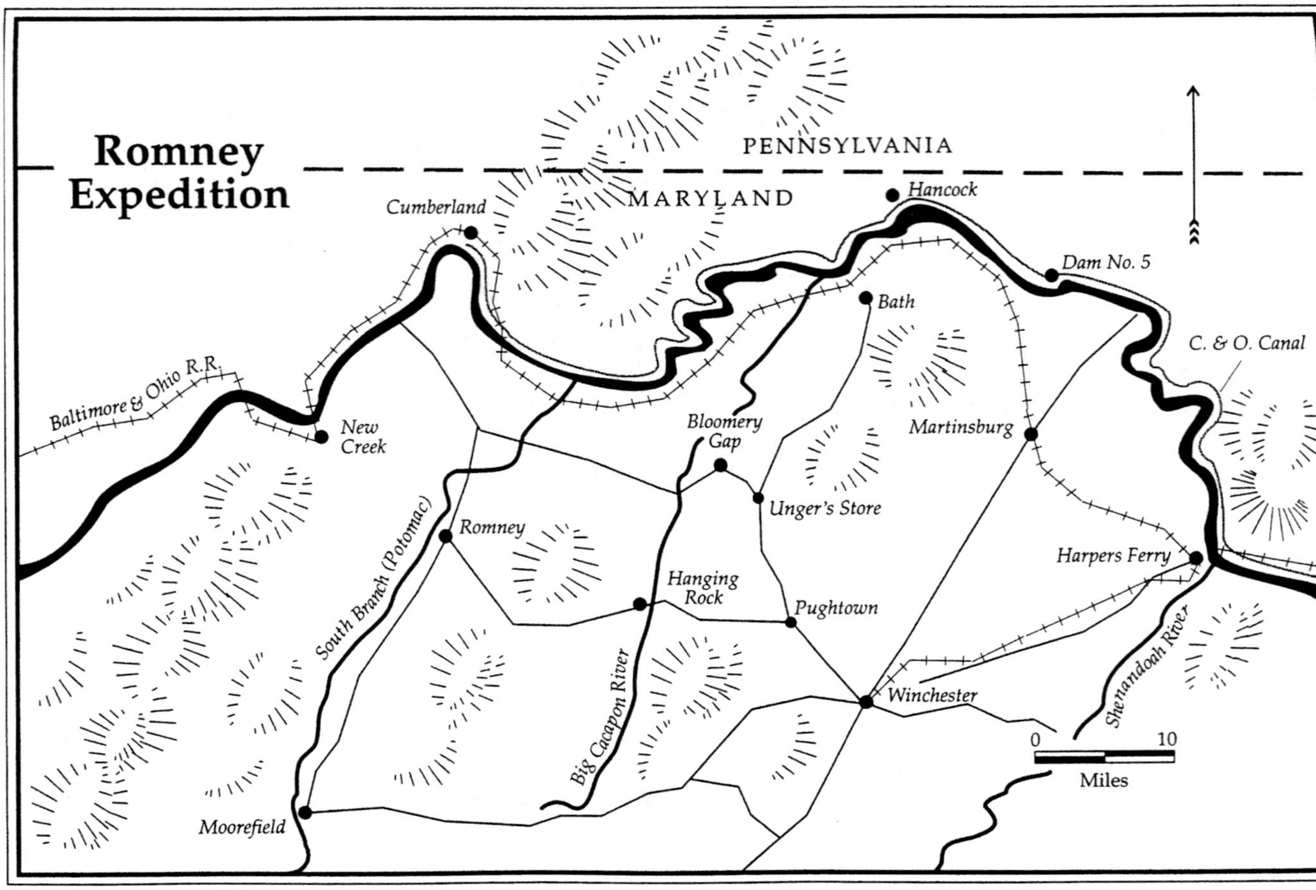

Romney Expedition. Map by George Skoch.

to Hancock, just across the Potomac River. He asked for the surrender of the garrison in order to spare any needless bloodshed, but the Federal commander, Frederick W. Lander, refused the overture.[21]

The Confederates unleashed an artillery bombardment, and the Union cannon responded, although no casualties were inflicted by either side. The next day brought reinforcements to the bluecoats, and a thick blanket of snow made operations increasingly difficult.[22] Hancock could still be taken, but at a much higher cost to the Confederates than Jackson was willing to pay. After all, Romney was the main objective, not Hancock.

January 7 saw the Confederate army on its way back to Unger's Store. Strong men succumbed to the wind and cold. Straggling was severe, as the Southerners searched for any food, warmth or shelter they could find. The weather was just as hard on animals and equipment. On at least two occasions, General Jackson had to dismount to help prevent a wagon from slipping across the frozen hills.[23]

Upon reaching Unger's Store, Jackson was greeted by worrisome news. Approximately 2,000 Federals had captured 700 Confederate militia at Hanging Rock.[24] That was the only garrison of Confederates on the Winchester-Romney road. Despite the sudden advantage, the bluecoats abandoned the position at Hanging Rock, and for some unexplained reason returned to Romney.[25]

The next several days were spent in the misery of camp life around Unger's Store. Men were constantly exposed to the elements, food was scarce, and predictably, sickness increased. Preparations were made for a final drive toward Romney. One brigade of militia would guard Jackson's left; another would protect the right. Jackson ordered the Confederate cavalry, led by Turner Ashby, to determine the strength of the opponent still garrisoned at Romney.[26]

Stonewall Jackson was astounded when he heard the news from his chief of cavalry. The Federals had evacuated Romney! Union estimates of Confederate numerical strength were exaggerated throughout the war, and this was no exception. Upon learning that Jackson was in the area, the Northerners decided to fall back against an enemy they believed had numerical superiority.[27] This may have had some influence on their behavior at Hanging Rock. Little did they know how small Jackson's tired little column actually was.

On January 13 the Confederates broke camp and headed for Romney. The weather had improved somewhat, and the dirt roads had thawed into a heavy mud. By the next day, Stonewall led his troops into the little town. The glory of an epic battle to crown his campaign was missing. General Loring arrived with his troops two days later.[28]

Up to this point, the struggles of Jackson's men had been rewarded. Approximately $60,000 worth of supplies had fallen into Confederate hands. This had been accomplished at a cost of only four dead and 28 wounded, although the sick list was very heavy.[29]

After the occupation of Romney, Stonewall Jackson made a serious mistake in diplomacy. He believed that Loring's troops were unaccustomed to hard marches, and had become demoralized. Therefore, he left Loring's men in Romney to guard the town and the surrounding valley. The Stonewall Brigade, which was Jackson's former command, was to make the long march back to Winchester. Although Jackson's men were forced to make a longer march, Loring had been left in Romney, a location detested by all of the Confederates, regardless of rank.[30] The town was filthy, and the Union army was only 20 miles away.[31]

The perceived favoritism toward the Stonewall Brigade engendered feelings of resentment in Loring's graycoats.[32]

Had Jackson been more open as to why he believed it was vital to guard Romney, Loring's troops may well have reacted in a more receptive manner. As it was, they believed that their exposed position in a town without comfort was ordered simply to protect the Stonewall Brigade.

On January 23 Jackson's troops began the march back to Winchester. Loring's soldiers were glad to see them go, but the ordeal in Romney was not yet over.

Overlooked amid the sudden animosity among the Confederates were the accomplishments on the Southern side. The Yankees had been driven out of the area, Winchester was protected for the present time, Romney belonged to Jackson, and any Federal offensive had been prevented.[33]

However, the situation at Romney would deteriorate in a hurry. Although there was no present danger, General Loring believed his command to be in great peril. The streets were still open sewers, and the courthouse was full of rotten meat, left there to decay by the Yankees as they evacuated.[34]

In addition, morale was poor among officers and men.[35] The hard marches, freezing cold, increased sickness and the orders to remain in Romney had combined to leave the Confederates despondent and rebellious. Officers began writing old friends in the Confederate Congress, protesting Jackson's severe and inhuman treatment of their men. Next came a petition signed by 11 officers, which was addressed to General Loring, repeating the complaints.[36] While criticism of Jackson was widespread, it was instigated by two colonels, Samuel V. Fulkerson and William B. Taliaferro. Taliaferro even managed to gain an audience with Vice President Alexander Stephens, followed by a conference with President Davis himself.

The flurry of reports to Richmond caused grave concern in the capital. Although there was no basis in fact in any of them, the politicians rashly jumped to the conclusion that Loring was needlessly exposed. On January 31, Jackson received a telegram from Secretary of War Judah P. Benjamin, which read as follows: "Our news indicates that a movement is being made to cut off General Loring's command. Order him back to Winchester immediately."[37]

This telegram signaled a critical turning point in Jackson's military career. As a soldier, Jackson immediately obeyed the order, but he realized that all of the hard work and accomplishments of the Confederate troops were about to be reversed in a matter of minutes by the civil authorities in Richmond. The undermining of his authority was more than he could take. Within the hour he had sent a reply to Secretary Benjamin and resigned from the army.[38]

Fortunately for the future of the Confederacy, Stonewall Jackson was not without friends as well. One of these was Governor John Letcher of Virginia. Jackson knew that it would take time for his letter to reach Secretary Benjamin, so he sat down and penned a long letter to Governor Letcher. Another good friend was Congressman Alexander Boteler. These two men intervened on Jackson's behalf, and President Davis refused to accept the resignation. It was clear that Benjamin had blundered. A crisis was averted. With constant efforts and appeals to Confederate patriotism, Letcher and Boteler were able to persuade the general to withdraw his resignation.[39]

Stonewall Jackson was back in command, and he set about restoring the morale of his battle units. Loring was sent to southwestern Virginia, but the Virginia regiments remained with Jackson. A personal triumph had been won, but the gains of January would soon evaporate.[40]

As soon as General Loring had been recalled to Winchester, Union troops moved back into Romney. The entire area was soon in Federal hands. Repairs were made to the Baltimore & Ohio Railroad and by February 23 the Yankees had connections all the way to Hancock.[41]

Simply put, the gains of early 1862 were made due to tremendous efforts by both Jackson and the common soldier in the face of tremendous adversity. Those gains were quickly lost by the machinations of Jefferson Davis and Judah Benjamin.[42] Unfortunately for the Confederacy, interference from Richmond would continue throughout the war.

January 19, 1862
Mill Springs (Logan's Crossroads)

G.B. Crittenden
F.K. Zollicoffer
(CSA)

G.H. Thomas
(USA)

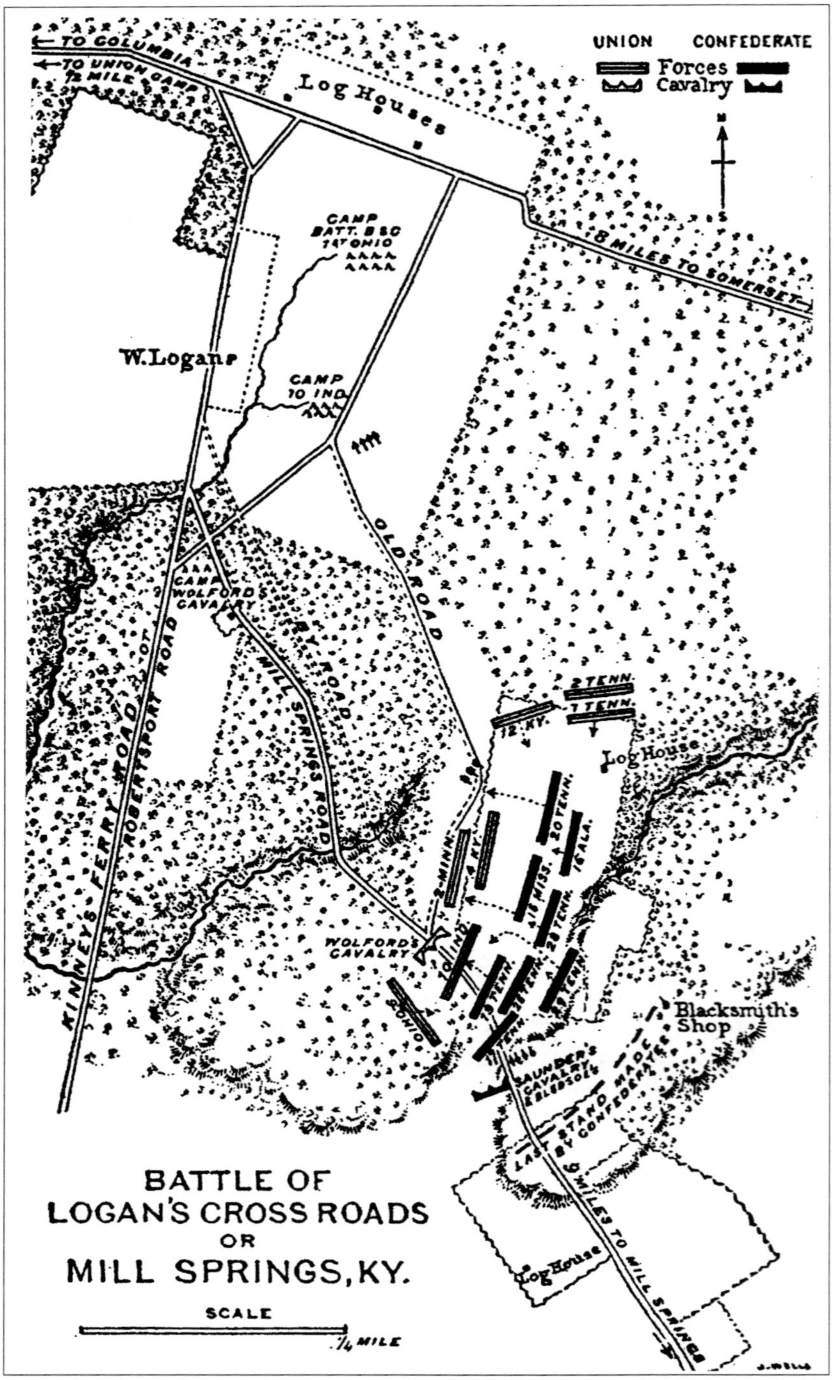

Battle of Logan's Crossroads or Mill Springs, Kentucky. Map by Jacob Wells.

In the early stages of the Civil War, conflict raged over the occupation of the state of Kentucky. From a strategic point of view, the state was important to both sides. For the South, it held the possibility of new recruits to the Confederate forces. In addition, the threat of invasion across the Ohio River would detain Federal soldiers in the midwest, instead of allowing them to be sent to Virginia.

The Yankees needed entry into Tennessee. Control of Kentucky allowed President Lincoln to send Northern troops south into the Volunteer State. Kentucky never actually seceded, and the state sent troops to the Union and the Confederacy as the war progressed.

In the middle of January the United States government had posted three brigades in the vicinity of Logan's Crossroads, Kentucky. An insignificant little spot, the crossroads is about ten miles west of Somerset[1] in the eastern portion of the state. On January 17,[1a] General George H. Thomas arrived to take command. A Virginian by birth, Thomas fought on the side of the Union. These three brigades numbered approximately 4,000 men,[1b] although there were reinforcements close at hand.

To the south lay the Confederates, about ten miles away as well, but on the north side of the Cumberland River.[2] Across the water from the graycoats was the town of Mill Springs. Led by General George B. Crittenden, the rebels also numbered 4,000 soldiers.[3]

General Crittenden faced a serious dilemma. The Cumberland was behind him, and the Southerners did not have the means to ford the river. The only course of action left was to strike Thomas before reinforcements could be of any assistance.[4]

The attack was led by Felix K. Zollicoffer, followed by William H. Carroll. The Confederates faced west as they moved forward. After a march of nine miles on the morning of January 19 they encountered the Federal pickets, and a stubborn fight ensued. The main body of the Federal troops was alerted, and the bluecoats ran to their posts.[5]

Colonel Speed S. Fry formed his Kentuckians (Union) in a position near the woods with his right resting on the Mill Springs Road. In front of his men was an open field, and he awaited the impending attack. A ravine ran across the field parallel to the Union position.[6]

The Confederates took shelter in the ravine, then delivered a furious volley of musketry, covering the field with smoke. A Southern horseman approached and fired at Colonel Fry as the graycoats moved forward. Several Yankees fired their guns, and the shots were fatal. It was General Zollicoffer.

The loss of their commander threw the rebels into disarray, and two of Zollicoffer's regiments fell back. Crittenden brought Carroll's troops up in support of the attack. Though Carroll's men fought with great courage, the Northerners had the better position on the field of battle.[7]

Union forces had been able to reach around the flanks of the enemy. The 12th Kentucky (Union) pressed the Confederates on the Federal left, while the 9th Ohio held the right. While the most of the Federals faced east, the Ohioans turned their line northeast, and charged furiously, driving the rebels back at the point of the bayonet. The vigor of the charge broke the Confederate line, and the Southern left flank collapsed. As the left flank gave way, the entire Confederate position crumbled.[8]

The Federals had planned to pursue Crittenden's men the next morning, but the Confederates had escaped across the river in small boats. The graycoats then destroyed the boats, and no pursuit was possible.

Casualties favored the soldiers in the north. When the day was done, General Thomas had lost 40 men killed, 207 wounded and 15 captured or missing, for a total of 262. General Crittenden's ill-fated attack had cost 125 lives, 309 men were wounded, and 99 captured or missing for a total of 533.[9]

Moreover, the Federal troops captured many supplies, as well as food and medicine which were badly needed by the Southern troops. As the graycoats fell back from the action at Mill Springs, desertion increased, and the command under Crittenden lost the ability to function as an effective fighting force.[10]

February 6, 1862
Fort Henry

L. Tilghman (CSA)	U.S. Grant (USA)

Fort Henry was situated on the east bank of the Tennessee River, very close to the Kentucky border. The location of the post contained several inherent drawbacks, which made it very difficult to defend. Built on very low ground, parts of the fort were subject to flooding.[1] Moreover, there was high ground outside the walls which was ideal for enemy artillery.[2]

The Confederate garrison stationed at Fort Henry was not a large one. General Lloyd Tilghman realized that his poorly equipped[3] force of 2,600 men[4] was insufficient for an adequate defense. He appealed to both military and civil authorities to improve conditions at the fort, but to no avail.[5] On February 6, as the Union force of approximately 16,000 approached, he sent most of the garrison to Fort Donelson,[6] 12 miles to the east on the Cumberland River.

General Tilghman knew that his small band of rebels was no match for the much larger contingent of bluecoats. The Southern soldiers were hopelessly outnumbered on land, and the enemy had brought in the firepower of seven gunboats on the Tennessee River. Altogether, General Grant aimed 54 pieces of artillery at Fort Henry. Tilghman had but 12 pointed at the river.[7] He hoped to save as many men as possible, and delay the Federal advance with the remainder of the Confederates. Returning to the fort, he fought side by side with a skeleton force[8] in a short but gallant defense.

Against such odds, the fort could not last long. The gunboats advanced around 11:45 A.M., and by 2:00 P.M. the fighting was over.[9] General Tilghman had surrendered Fort Henry.[10] The Confederate garrison never really had a chance, but the fall of the fort was hastened by the rising waters of the Tennessee River,[11] flooding parts of the stronghold.

Casualties in the brief engagement were very light. The Confederates reported five men killed, 11 wounded and about 94 captured, while the Federals lost 11 killed, 31 wounded and five missing.[12]

Although the action would seem minor when compared with larger battles later in the war, the loss of Fort Henry was very significant. Only ten days later Fort Donelson would fall. Together, these two defeats opened up the state of Tennessee to Union occupation. The Volunteer State would never again be completely free of the Union Army.

February 13–16, 1862
Fort Donelson

J. B. Floyd (CSA) — U. S. Grant (USA)

Fort Donelson lay on the west bank of the Cumberland River. Like many forts of its time, it was not much more than earthen entrenchments,[1] formed in a semicircle high above the river. Twelve miles to the northwest, on the east bank of the Tennessee River, lay Fort Henry. The Confederates believed that with these two strongholds situated on the two major rivers of the state, they could control west Tennessee. These long, winding waterways meander through the state, and near the Kentucky border, northwest of Nashville, they flow very close together. The proximity of the forts to each other gave the government in Richmond great confidence, the thinking being that troops could be easily moved from one location to the other should the need arise.

The flaw in this line of thought was that part of Fort Henry was subject to flooding in high water, while Fort Donelson was poorly supplied, in both men and equipment.[2] Should these forts fall, the entire state of Tennessee would be wide open to the bluecoats.

However, the situation changed on February 6, 1862, when General Ulysses S. Grant captured Fort Henry. Confederate resistance there was weak, and the loss of Fort Henry greatly alarmed John B. Floyd and Gideon J. Pillow, the Confederate commanders at Fort Donelson.

General Grant planned to capture the fortifications using his infantry to block the escape of the Confederate garrison while Union gunboats on the Cumberland River shelled the rebels into surrender.[3] On Thursday, February 13, the Federal navy moved up the Cumberland.[4] While the bluecoats had complete control of the water, the fort was on much higher ground, and cannon inside Fort Donelson did considerable damage to the Union fleet.[5] The naval commander realized that the fire was too strong, and abandoned his mission.

General Floyd, despite this success, believed that Fort Donelson was untenable.[6] By Friday evening he decided to try and break out of the trap. Early the next morning, February 15,[7] the Confederates charged out into the bitter cold,[8] catching the enemy by surprise. General Pillow, on the left flank, attacked the Federal division of General John McClernand.

This attack opened an escape route to Nashville, but inexplicably, General Pillow ordered a withdrawal. He had been overcome by his fear of an impending attack on the thinly held Confederate right flank.[9] Regrouping, General Grant had his men counterattack, and the Confederates' window of opportunity was soon closed.

Floyd and Pillow decided to surrender, but neither man was willing to perform the distasteful task. They assigned the duty to General Simon B. Buckner, and the next day escaped in boats with roughly 2,500 men. The Confederate cavalry, under General Nathan B. Forrest, was able to fight their way to safety.[10]

The loss of Fort Donelson was a tremendous blow to the Confederacy. General Buckner surrendered 11,600 men on February 16, 1862.[11] Additional battle casualties on the Confederate side were not reported. Federal casualties, army and navy combined, were only 510 killed, 2,152 wounded, and 224 captured or missing, for a total of 2,886.[12] Up to this point in the war, it was the worst defeat for the Confederacy. The road to Nashville was open to the Union Army, and it appeared that Kentucky was irretrievably lost. Slowly but surely the Federal forces were beginning to command more and more of Tennessee. The small Southern armies still scattered throughout the state would be unable to hold off the forces of Ulysses S. Grant and Don Carlos Buell, currently headquartered at Louisville. As the citizens of Tennessee began to comprehend their predicament, they finally realized that a terrible conflict was just beginning.

March 23–June 9, 1862
The Valley Campaign

T. J. Jackson (CSA) — N. P. Banks, J. C. Frémont, J. Shields (USA)

The Valley Campaign of 1862 which was conducted by Stonewall Jackson must really be viewed as a series of events. It took place in the Shenandoah Valley of Virginia, and over the course of the next several months, the rebels marched up and down the valley. They were constantly pursued by three separate Union forces. Nathaniel P. Banks, John C. Frémont and James Shields attempted to defeat Jackson's elusive little band. Their efforts would be in vain.

It was vital to the Southern cause that the Shenandoah Valley be defended. It contained some of the most fertile farmland in Virginia, and the food supply was critical to the soldiers in the field. As the Civil War progressed, the ability to feed his troops would become increasingly important for General Lee.[1]

As the month of March opened in the Shenandoah, Jackson was technically under the command of General

Joseph E. Johnston. Johnston's Confederates were stationed in central Virginia around Manassas Junction, and he wanted Jackson to guard the left flank of the Southern army and secure the passes in the Blue Ridge Mountains from enemy attack.[2] Johnston did not regard Jackson's command as an offensive weapon.

The overriding concern in Richmond was that Jackson must prevent the Federals in the valley from combining forces with the Yankees in front of Johnston. Somehow, Stonewall Jackson must make sure that Banks, Frémont and Shields remain west of the Blue Ridge Mountains. This was the campaign that would launch Jackson's career.

General Jackson's ragged band of Confederates marched south from Winchester along the Valley Pike, through Strasburg until they reached Mount Jackson on the 20th of March. This section of Virginia was extremely rugged. To the west ran the long ridge which made up the Allegheny Mountains. To the east were the Blue Ridge Mountains. In between these two formidable outcroppings of rock ran a series of ridges called Massanutten Mountain, or simply the Massanutten.[3] For 50 miles[4] just east of the Valley Pike the Massanutten accompanied Stonewall's troops.

Speed and mobility were to be the watchwords of the Confederates in the valley. On March 21 Jackson received a dispatch from General Johnston. His superior feared that Jackson's men were not pressing the enemy closely enough to contain them. Accordingly, Stonewall was ordered to march north to Winchester.[5]

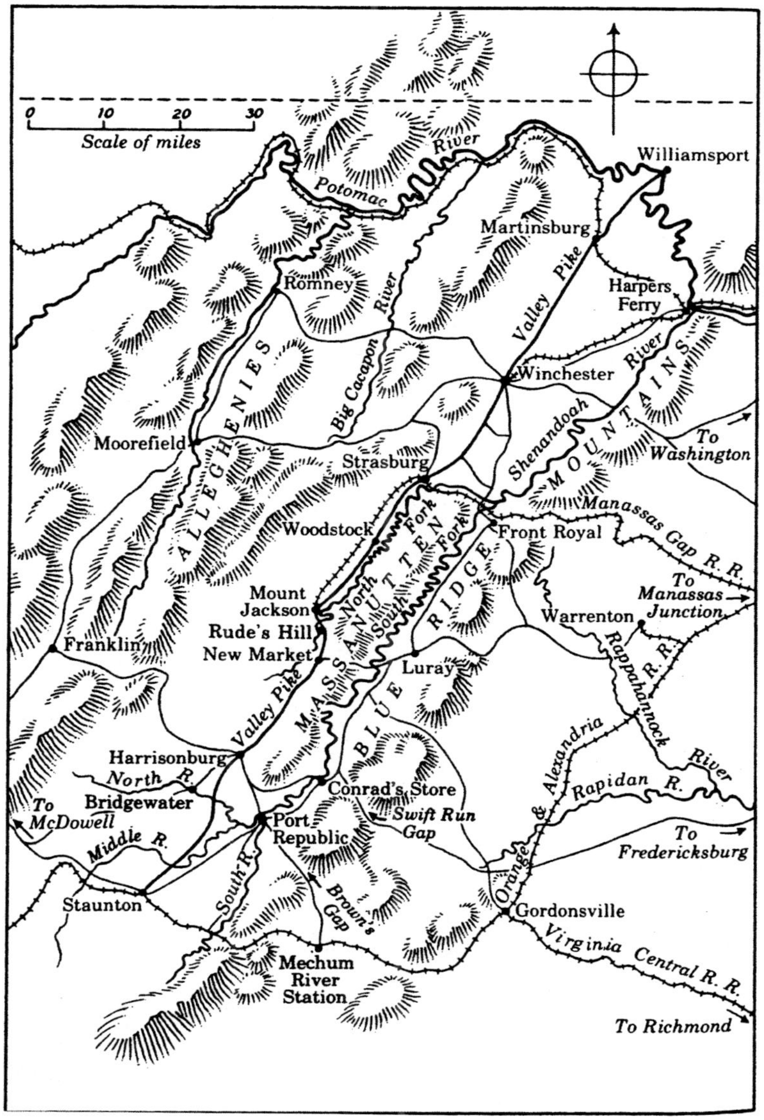

The Valley

Mount Jackson was 40 miles[6] from Winchester, but Jackson's rebels moved out. It was a very difficult march, but they reached Strasburg by the evening of the 22nd.[7] Harsh conditions had reduced the troops to less than 3,500 men.[8] The Confederate cavalry under Colonel Turner Ashby had begun skirmishing with Union troops under General Nathaniel P. Banks. Ashby's horsemen had camped for the night at a little village just south of Winchester called Kernstown.

For his part, General Banks just could not believe that there would be a battle any time soon, and certainly not here. After all, Joe Johnston had begun pulling back from Manassas[8a] and no troops were on their way to reinforce Stonewall Jackson in the valley, therefore, a battle was not likely. In Winchester he conferred with General James Shields, who was convalescing from a recent wound to his left arm, and Shields came to the same conclusion.[9]

Accordingly, General Banks pulled his forces out of Winchester, leaving Shields in charge of the Union forces around the town. As he was wounded, Shields directed Colonel Nathan Kimball to take command of the area. Any real fighting was sure to wait until his injury had healed.

Turner Ashby was an excellent horseman, and was well liked by his men, but he was not an accomplished cavalry scout. As a result, he gave General Jackson some information which stated that Winchester was held by only four Union regiments.[10] This false piece of information would govern Jackson's thinking for the coming battle.

As March 23 dawned, the weather was clear[11] and Stonewall was confident. He knew that the march from Mount Jackson to Strasburg had been hard on his men, but a mere four regiments of the enemy should not prove too difficult to overcome.[12] The rebels would have to make another forced march, this one 14 miles.[13] At 2:00 P.M.[14] Jackson's three infantry brigades arrived on the south side of Kernstown.

The most predominant feature of the terrain in front of Jackson was the rise of ground called Pritchard's Hill. It appeared to anchor the Union right flank, and Colonel Kimball had posted an artillery battery on the crest. These guns were already shelling Ashby's men as Jackson rode up to get a clear view of the situation.

General Jackson quickly formulated a plan of attack. By gaining control of Sandy Ridge, which was a mile and a half west of the turnpike, the Confederates could outflank the enemy and cut off the line of retreat to Winchester.[15]

Jackson would send his three infantry brigades to accomplish this task. Commanded by General Richard B. Garnett, Colonel Jesse Burks and Colonel Samuel Fulkerson, the graycoats advanced. The brigade under Burks made up the Confederate center, just west of the Valley Turnpike. Fulkerson, followed by Garnett, moved forward through the woods on the left. Ashby's horsemen made up the Confederate right, and were stationed east of the turnpike.[16]

Opposing Jackson's troops, Nathan Kimball also had three brigades: his own, Colonel Jeremiah Sullivan's and Colonel E. B. Tyler's. Combined with the artillery and cavalry still on hand, the Union force was considerably larger than a mere four regiments. Sullivan was on the Union left, facing Ashby; however, he would later shift to the right. Tyler was on the right, and Kimball's own brigade was in the center, although it was farther to the rear.[17]

On the Confederate left, the rebels soon met heavy resistance. The enemy was there in force. Garnett had been ordered to support Fulkerson as they both moved through the woods, but Jackson had never informed Garnett what Fulkerson's orders were. This created a great deal of doubt in the mind of Richard B. Garnett. Before he could communicate with Jackson, Garnett ordered his troops to fall back. As he did so, Colonel Fulkerson's right became exposed. He, too, had to give ground to avoid being overwhelmed by the onrushing bluecoats.[18] Jackson's flank attack was falling apart.

The 14th Indiana regiment had succeeded in moving around the Confederate left flank.[18a] The rebels held fast, but the opposition was too strong. The Northerners had simply turned the tide of the battle. As the day wore on, the 13th Indiana made the final breakthrough, just after 6:30 P.M.[18b]

Jackson thought that there were reserves in the area, but General Garnett had ordered the two regiments in question to remain where they were and cover the retreat of the infantry and artillery.[18c] There would be no reinforcements for the Confederate left. General Jackson decided to break off the action and regroup at a more advantageous location.

The problem lay not with the Confederate troops themselves, but with faulty information and poor reconnaissance. Jackson's enemy was not four regiments, as Ashby had suggested, but James Shields' division of 9,000 men. These troops had moved from Winchester back to Kernstown. Had Stonewall Jackson made a proper and thorough examination of the area before ordering the attack, these Yankees would surely have been discovered.[19]

The casualties at Kernstown were not particularly heavy; later battles in the Civil War would see far more blood. The Confederates lost 80 men killed, 355 wounded and 263 captured or missing, for a total of 718. The Union forces had 118 soldiers killed, 450 wounded, and 22 captured or missing, for a total of 590.[20]

It would appear that the Southerners were the losers in this confrontation. They had lost more men, and Nathan Kimball's troops had driven Stonewall Jackson's graycoats from the field. However, the battle of Kernstown had far greater ramifications. Due to Jackson's activity, the Union troops under Nathaniel Banks stayed in the Shenandoah Valley. Banks feared this recent aggression, and felt that it was safer to remain where he was. The government in Washington, D.C., was also alarmed. General Irvin McDowell, commanding the Federal forces surrounding the capital, was ordered to safeguard Washington.

There would be no union between Banks and McDowell. General McDowell would also not be able to combine forces with General George B. McClellan for a planned invasion of Richmond during the spring of 1862. The immediate threat in the eyes of the Federal government was now Jackson.[21]

While the actual battle had been lost, the net results of the battle of Kernstown made it one of Jackson's better strategic victories.[22] The benefits to the Confederacy were enormous. The Yankees would now continue their attempts to put Stonewall Jackson out of business.

On Monday, March 24, the Confederates worked their way slowly southward along the Valley Turnpike. The destination was Rude's Hill. The march was not as difficult as the approach to Kernstown. It was at this point that Jackson decided that a change in command was necessary. Still furious at Garnett for retreating at Kernstown, Jackson replaced him with General Sidney Winder. Winder was a strict, competent officer, but was not popular with the men in the ranks.[23]

The next two weeks were spent at Rude's Hill. The men and horses needed rest from the arduous marching leading up to Kernstown. In April Jackson received some news from General Johnston, and it would affect operations in the valley.

Johnston's army was moving south, and only the division of General Richard S. Ewell would remain behind. The good news was that Johnston authorized Jackson to utilize Ewell's troops in case of necessity. Should the Confederates in the valley march further south, General Ewell would unite with Jackson, giving the Valley Army valuable reinforcements.[24]

On April 19 the graycoats headed farther south. The new destination was a good one. Jackson would camp at Conrad's Store, at the southern end of the Massanutten. If Banks moved past Jackson to attack Harrisonburg, the Union rear would be exposed. If Banks stayed where he was, in the north, or lower valley, he would be immobilized. The new location afforded the Confederates an ideal spot to observe the enemy,[25] and General Ewell would soon join forces with Jackson.

For his part, General Nathaniel P. Banks was thoroughly confused. Not only was he unable to see Stonewall Jackson, he was unsure as to the precise location of the Confederate force. During a 12-day period beginning on the 19th, General Banks reported Jackson out of the valley, moving toward Gordonsville, at Stanardsville and at Richmond.[26]

By late April, Jackson's Valley Army was much stronger than it had been earlier in the year. The rebels under Jackson amounted to about 6,000 men. Richard Ewell brought approximately 8,000 troops with him. These men were better equipped than Jackson's graycoats, and were camped just over the Blue Ridge. Also, the Confederates had a small force of about 3,000 muskets under General Edward Johnson, guarding the important city of Staunton.[27]

Although none of the Confederates in the Shenandoah Valley were aware of it at this point, there was another development taking place behind the scenes in Richmond. Joseph Johnston was more concerned with the Union Army of the Potomac under George McClellan than he was with the Confederates under Jackson's command. McClellan was in the process of invading Richmond from the east, and the Confederate capital must be defended. As a result, the day-to-day operations in the Shenandoah were turned over to the advisor to President Davis, a man whose aggressive mind thought just like Jackson. Jackson would now begin to work closely with Robert E. Lee.[28]

By the 26th of April, a golden opportunity presented itself. General Banks had finally moved his 19,000-man army from Winchester down to Harrisonburg.[29] Jackson ordered Ewell to move his command to Swift Run Gap. The scattered Federals under Nathaniel Banks were a very inviting target, but the Confederates had to move fast. Edward Johnson and his 3,000 men were not large enough to hold off an invasion of Staunton. To make matters worse, General John C. Frémont led an additional Union force of 20,000 men stationed 75 miles west of Staunton in the Allegheny Mountains.[30]

General Frémont had divided his troops, sending General Robert Milroy toward Staunton with 6,000 Union soldiers.[31] Stonewall Jackson needed a plan, as the Federals seemed to be closing in.

Success would depend on quick strikes and secret marches. General Ewell was to cross the Blue Ridge Mountains and replace Jackson at Conrad's Store. Jackson would take his command and reinforce Edward Johnson, attacking General Milroy's 6,000 men before the remainder of Frémont's troops could come to their assistance. After Milroy had been defeated, Jackson would take his graycoats back to General Ewell, combine forces, and pursue Banks.[32]

By April 29, Richard Ewell's infantry had come in sight of Stonewall Jackson's campfires. Early the next morning, Jackson moved out, and for several days heavy rains would slow the pace of the Valley Army. However, on May 3, the weather improved, and the soft roads began to dry.[33]

Two days later, Jackson had his veterans in Staunton, and again received good news. Federal scouts had placed him all over Virginia, from the Shenandoah Valley all the way to Richmond. The movements of the Valley Army were still a mystery to the enemy.

On the morning of May 7, General Jackson's Southerners marched west from Staunton. If he could combine his troops with Edward Johnson, the Confederates could place almost 10,000 men against 6,000 bluecoats.[34]

On May 8, the united Confederates looked down upon the site of the second battle of the Valley Campaign. The grayclad footsoldiers were in front of McDowell, Virginia. Enemy camps were visible a mile away. The rebels knew that the action was about to begin.

After looking at the topography, Jackson decided to try and move around the Federals in a flanking movement, scheduled for the next day. Leaving General Johnson at the front, Jackson rode back to his headquarters. Milroy, however, did not cooperate. He received a report that the Confederates were about to attack, so the Federal decided to assault immediately. The report was false, but at 4:30 P.M.[35] on May 8, Milroy attacked Johnson.

The Confederate position was along the top of Sitlington's Hill, facing west. General Johnson had four regiments in place. From left to right, the 52nd Virginia, 58th Virginia, 12th Georgia, and 44th Virginia awaited the Union assault. Milroy would not wait to be outflanked. The heaviest attack came against the Confederate right.[36]

Edward Johnson sent the 25th Virginia to the right as the graycoats reached the hill. Jackson had kept the 31st Virginia as a reserve. It became apparent that the rebels were suffering from Jackson's poor deployment of his own three brigades. These men should have been closer to the battlefield. By 6:00 P.M. General Taliaferro's brigade had reached Johnson, and the Virginians were ordered to support the right and center. By sundown the action had spread all along the Confederate front. Suddenly, General Johnson was hit by a Union bullet, knocking him out of action with a painful ankle injury.[37] William Taliaferro was now the highest ranking Confederate on Sitlington's Hill.

Fortunately for the graycoats, the troops were handled with great skill. New regiments were shifted promptly against each Union thrust, until darkness finally covered the field, and the gunfire began to fade away.[38] Taliaferro's good work had saved the day for the South.[39]

The results at McDowell were mixed. The bluecoats had attacked, and had lost 34 men killed, 220 wounded and 5 missing, for a total of 259 casualties. On the other side, there were 116 Confederates killed, 300 wounded, and 4 missing for a total of 420 men.[40] Despite losing more men, the Southerners had repulsed every Union attack, and at the end of the action were in possession of the field. However, as victories go, this was not one of General Jackson's finest.

Stonewall Jackson had no time to relish the defensive work in front of McDowell. He had to turn his attention to Nathaniel P. Banks. It was time to rejoin General Ewell.

While Jackson had been dealing with Milroy, General Ewell had been growing impatient at his lack of activity. On May 13, as Jackson's men were marching back to Staunton, Ewell received a bit of good news. The orders from Stonewall read as follows: "If Banks goes down the valley I wish you to follow him; so that he may feel that if he leaves the Valley, that not only will we occupy it, but that he will also be liable to be attacked as soon as he shall have sufficiently weakened his forces on this side of the Shenandoah."[41] It looked as if there would finally be some action.

For purposes of clarification, it must be remembered that due to the course of the Shenandoah River, "down the valley" means northward, while "up the valley" refers to movement toward the south.

Two days later, Jackson faced a crisis. The bluecoats under McClellan were moving even closer toward Richmond. On May 15 the Confederacy had turned back Union gunboats at the battle of Drewry's Bluff, only seven miles from Richmond on the James River. General Johnston wanted to have General Ewell's troops join him in eastern Virginia. Even with Edward Johnson's men, Jackson knew his Valley Army would not be strong enough to defeat Banks without Richard Ewell's three brigades.

General Banks had begun moving north, or down the valley, in the direction of Strasburg. He had sent General Shields' division to go to Fredericksburg. These developments in the valley were very ominous, and they must be stopped. It was imperative that Banks remain in the valley, and Shields must not be allowed to reinforce the Federal troops opposing General Johnston. Frémont was now of secondary importance. No action against his army could influence Banks or Shields.

Fortunately for Stonewall Jackson, General Lee gave him great discretion in the pursuit of Banks. Lee realized that a strike against Banks could pin the Union general in the valley, while holding Shields away from Fredericksburg. A May 16 letter from Lee to Jackson stated, "Whatever may be Banks's intention it is very desirable to prevent him from going either to Fredericksburg or to the Peninsula.... A successful blow struck at him would delay, if it does not prevent, him from going to either place."[42]

The problem for Jackson was that Lee and Johnston were both his superiors, and their orders conflicted with each other. Which orders should he obey?

Jackson looked at the problem this way. On May 18, he evaluated the situation. The May 13 directive from Johnston which ordered Ewell to leave the valley seemed outdated by Lee's May 16 orders which underscored the importance of a "successful blow."[43] He decided to go after Banks.

Early in the morning on May 19[44] Stonewall Jackson headed north in pursuit of the Federals. Up the Valley Pike the soldiers trudged, until they reached New Market. Once again, the Confederates would use the Massanutten to their advantage. At New Market, the Southerners turned east, slipping through the narrow pass to Luray, where they would meet up with the troops under General Ewell and continue north.

While the Confederates were consolidating, the Union troops were widely scattered. General Banks had 1,000 men at Front Royal, 4,476 footsoldiers and 1,600 cavalry at Strasburg; approximately 1,450 Federals were at Winchester guarding supplies, and 800 more bluecoats were stationed along a 12-mile stretch of the Manassas Gap Railroad from Strasburg to Front Royal.[45] Hidden behind the Massanutten, the Confederates moved closer and closer to their prey.

By the evening of May 22, the rebels were only ten miles from Front Royal.[46] Located at the northern end of the Massanutten, Front Royal had strategic importance due to its proximity to the Manassas Gap Railroad and the South Fork of the Shenandoah River.

Although there were Union troops in Front Royal,

Jackson realized that the town was indefensible. He knew that the town could not be held. High peaks on the west, southwest and east presented an invading force with ideal topography. General Banks did not seem to understand this, and continued to hold his men in widely scattered locations. The problem for the Confederates was not whether or not Front Royal could be captured, but just how quickly it could be taken. Stonewall Jackson wished to trap the Federals in Front Royal and then move toward Banks's rear before the bluecoats in Strasburg could react to the attack.[47]

Jackson's orders for May 23 were very simple. The cavalry were to cross the South Fork and prevent the garrison in the town from escaping to Strasburg. The infantry, with General Ewell's troops in the lead, would march up the oddly named Gooney Manor Road, attacking the Federals from the south.[48]

Everything went according to plan, to the delight of the citizens of Front Royal.[49] At about 2:00 P.M.[50] the Federal pickets were driven back. Southern troops from Maryland and Louisiana poured into Front Royal from the east, but the Federals had fallen back and made a stand north of the town, just east of the Winchester Turnpike.[51] Federal artillery opened up upon the Confederates.

Ashby had taken his cavalry ahead to Buckton to cut off the Federal retreat, but Colonel Thomas Flournoy was at hand, and Jackson ordered him forward. Stonewall could sense the retreating enemy within his grasp, and did not want to let go.

The Confederates had driven the Federals all the way across the Shenandoah River, almost to Cedarville, where a small group of Union men tried to reform once more.[52] Again Flournoy charged the foe, scattering the bluecoats into a nearby orchard, and the rout was complete.[53]

It had turned out that the Federals numbered a mere 1,063 men, while Jackson had been able to throw his combined force of 16,000 against the lightly held town.[54] The Federals had lost 904 men, while the Confederates had suffered less than 50 casualties in the action at Front Royal.[55]

The victory at Front Royal was more than just a severe blow to the bluecoats. The Confederates were on the Federal flank, the road was open to Winchester, and the Valley Army had cut off the avenue of retreat for General Banks.[56]

However, the battle at Front Royal had a more far-reaching effect. On May 24, President Abraham Lincoln ordered General Irvin McDowell to forego his planned move against Richmond, scheduled for the 26th of May. McDowell would be retained in front of Washington to protect the capital. At that moment, although there were three battles left to fight, Stonewall Jackson's men had won the Valley Campaign.[57]

The next target would be General Banks. Jackson analyzed his possibilities within the operational framework of a triangle. The road from Strasburg to Front Royal was the base, with Winchester at the apex. Depending on where Banks moved, the Union troops could be defeated anywhere inside this triangle.[58]

At 10:00 A.M. on May 24[59] Nathaniel P. Banks ordered the Federals to retreat down the valley to Winchester. The Confederates were in hot pursuit. General Ewell's troops came from Ninevah, approaching Winchester from the southeast, while Jackson moved north from Middletown, attacking from the southwest.

The Federals had placed 1,000 troops opposite General Ewell, but the main force was on the hills southwest of town. Jackson's approach to Winchester was guarded by two lines of hills, the second about 400 yards behind the first. On the second group there were about 4,000 bluecoats and a dozen cannon.[60]

General Winder was in command of the Stonewall Brigade, and Jackson wanted the graycoats to take possession of the high ground west of the Valley Turnpike. He sent forward the brigade under Colonel John Campbell for support. Around 6:00 A.M., May 25, Jackson ordered three artillery batteries to the crest of the first ridge.[61] They opened fire on the Federals and an artillery duel ensued. This lasted for about an hour, as both sides suffered severe damage to their big guns.

With the Confederate left under pressure from the superior Union artillery, Stonewall Jackson directed General Richard Taylor to move at once against the Federal cannon. Pointing to the enemy position, Jackson's orders to Taylor were unmistakable: "You must carry it."[62]

Taylor's Louisiana brigade worked their way along Abraham's Creek around the Union right. Artillery shells burst among them, but they relentlessly continued. At the base of the hill which contained the Federal guns, Taylor joined Fulkerson's Virginians. Virginia followed Louisiana in the march up the hill. Half way up, the Union cavalry contested the advance, but the Confederates scattered the horsemen with a concentrated volley.[63]

As the Louisianans surged forward, the Union line crumbled under the weight of the onrushing graycoats. The entire Confederate line rushed forward, inspired by Taylor's gallant charge. The brigades of Isaac Trimble from the east, Sidney Winder and John Patton[64] from the south, and Taylor and Fulkerson from the west poured through the Federal defenses.[65]

The day had been won, but the Confederates were not yet finished. They pushed north, through Martinsburg and almost to Williamsport on the Potomac River. By May 29 Jackson's men had made a demonstration at Harpers Ferry.

However, the Union army had not been idle. General

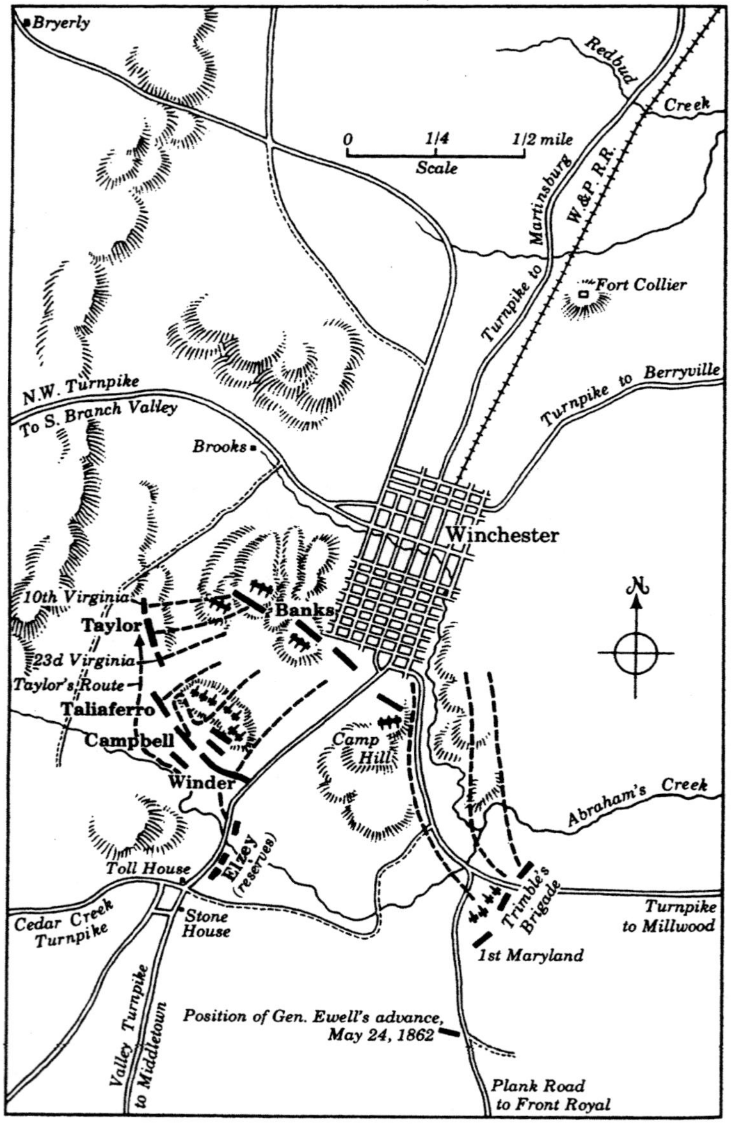

Battle of Winchester, May 25, 1862.

Frémont had moved his troops north as well, and was now closing in from the west. Banks still hovered along the waters of the Potomac River to the north. General McDowell had returned General Shields to the Shenandoah Valley. He led two brigades forward, advancing from the east. The end of May found a noose of 50,000 Federal soldiers closing around Stonewall Jackson's neck.[66] The speed and endurance of Jackson's "foot cavalry" were about to be sorely tested.

Jackson realized that the Valley Army was in a terrible predicament. On May 31, the Southern troops began to evacuate Winchester.[67] Fortunately for the grayclad veterans of the Shenandoah Valley, the Union generals were snatching defeat from the jaws of victory. General Frémont and General Shields had moved extremely slowly to close the trap around Jackson's men. Each man was convinced that Jackson's Confederates outnumbered his own force,[68] overlooking the reality that concerted action between them, combined with Banks's troops, could overwhelm Jackson's small command.

While the Federals seemed frozen in their tracks, Jackson led his men south down the Valley Turnpike. None of Jackson's foot cavalry had eaten for two days, but they had marched 35 miles, and men were dropping from exhaustion.[69]

On June 1 the Confederates reached Strasburg in one of the more remarkable marches of the Civil War. As the troops realized that they were safe, morale improved among the ranks. However, the next day the march resumed, as rain pelted the graycoats, trudging south upon the Valley Turnpike.[70]

While the infantry marched on, Ashby's cavalry continued to harass Frémont, slowing the Federal pursuit.[71] Jackson crossed the North Fork of the Shenandoah on June 3, and the fast rising river washed away Union attempts to bridge it. Stonewall's men now had a full day's lead over Frémont.[72]

James Shields was mired in the mud caused by the heavy rains. His bluecoats were strung out for 20 miles in the Luray Valley, incapable of a vigorous pursuit.[73] The Confederates struggled as well, but they were marching on the hardened Valley Turnpike, which was somewhat firmer than the dirt roads on which the Yankees traveled.

By June 6, the Confederates marched into Port Republic. They had marched over 100 miles without a day's rest. Fully 20 percent of the Valley Army was missing. Sickness and straggling had taken their toll, but the majority of this total were men who had simply given out.[74]

General Ewell's command arrived at Cross Keys, roughly halfway between Harrisonburg and Port Republic. The Confederates would finally receive a chance to rest for a few days.

All seemed peaceful on the battlefront, until Jackson received a stunning report on the evening of the 6th of June. About two miles south of Harrisonburg, Turner Ashby had fought a rearguard action against the Federal horsemen. His horse had been shot from under him, and Ashby had led his men back on foot. Earlier that evening, the popular cavalry leader had been killed instantly by a bullet passing through his right forearm and left breast.[75]

The village of Port Republic lay in the angle formed by the confluence of the North Fork and the South Fork of the Shenandoah River. A commanding line of bluffs rose up just west of the town, on the south side of the North Fork. Artillery placed here would have an unobstructed view of the entire village. Equally important were the river crossings. A long wooden bridge crossed the North Fork at the northern end of the main street. There were no bridges across the South Fork, but there were several fords.[76]

General Frémont was closer to Port Republic than was General Shields. General Jackson hoped that Frémont might attack Ewell at Cross Keys before Shields could arrive. June 7 passed quietly, but on the next day events began to unfold.

At about 9:00 A.M.,[77] a Confederate cavalryman rode up to Jackson, reporting that Federals had forded the South Fork and were already in Port Republic! As the bluecoats galloped down the main street of Port Republic, Stonewall Jackson heard gunshots from the north end of town. Leaving his headquarters at the home of Dr. Kemper, Jackson walked over to investigate, and saw the enemy cavalry racing toward him. He quickly mounted his horse and narrowly escaped, but several members of his staff were taken prisoner.[78]

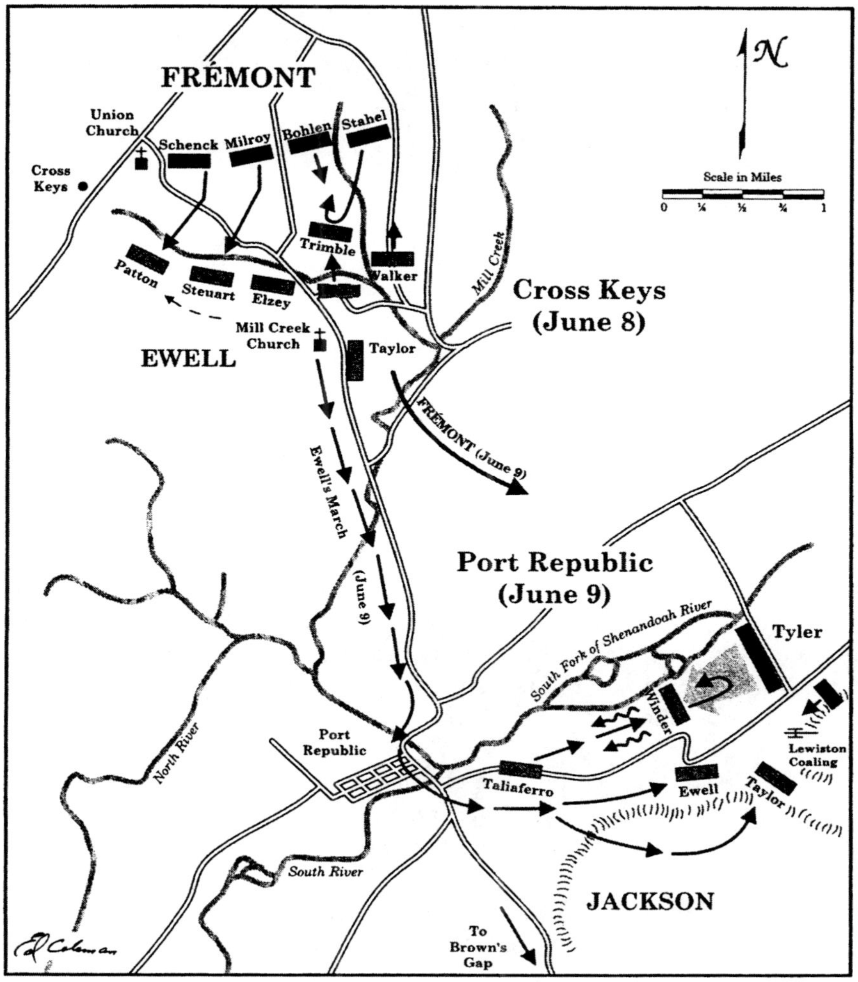

Cross Keys and Port Republic. Map by Ed P. Coleman.

It looked as if the Confederate ammunition train would be captured. There were only 12 pickets from the 2nd Virginia regiment, led by Captain Samuel Moore, standing between the Southerners and disaster. When the main street of Port Republic reaches the Kemper property, it turns to the right (west) at a ninety degree angle. The Northerners rode after the wagon train, when at a distance of 100 yards, Captain Moore and his rebels opened fire from behind a white picket fence.[79]

Though small, the attack was a complete surprise. Suddenly the Confederates burst forth from behind the picket fence, firing as they ran, forcing the startled cavalry back into the town. Meanwhile, the Charlottesville Artillery had been resting in a field near Moore's heroic stand. Three artillery pieces opened fire on the main streets while Captain Moore's men fired furiously at the Yankees. Together, this action had stopped the enemy from advancing.[80]

As soon as the gunfire ceased in Port Republic, Stonewall Jackson heard cannon open fire to the northwest. Instantly, he knew what had occurred. Ewell was locked in combat with Frémont at Cross Keys.

At 10:00 A.M.[81] on June 8, Frémont had moved forward. Richard Ewell had chosen a sound defensive position. He had placed George H. "Maryland" Steuart's brigade on the left, Arnold Elzey's troops in the center, and Isaac Trimble's men on the right. Each flank was protected by an expanse of woods.[82]

By 10:30 A.M. artillery pounded away at each side, and it became clear that Frémont intended to attack the Confederate right, where Trimble was stationed. The former railroad executive was now 60 years old. Feisty by nature, he was a commander who loved to fight. He told his troops to hold their fire until the enemy was within 50 yards.[83]

The Northerners calmly advanced, and at Trimble's signal his graycoats unleashed a furious volley into Frémont's ranks. The blue lines halted, then received another shower of lead from the rebels, whereupon the Yankees fled for cover in the nearby timber. Trimble, however, was not satisfied. Spotting a Union artillery battery half a mile away, he ordered a counterattack. The sight of the onrushing Confederates was too much for the Federals; they broke and ran. Trimble's men did not stop until they had moved forward a full mile from their original position.[84]

The soldiers continued to fight during the day, but by the end of June 8, the Confederates were in control of the ground from which Frémont had begun his advance. Clearly, Ewell had carried the day. With a loss of only 288 men, the Southerners had lost less than half the total of the enemy.[85]

Stonewall Jackson spent most of the day at Port Republic. He inspected his troops and supervised the placement of the artillery. He expected General Shields to attack the next day. As darkness fell upon the little village, the wagon trains were ordered forward so that the men could get something to eat. He knew his men would need strength for the following morning.[86]

From the very beginning, Jackson had planned to divide the enemy, and defeat each isolated fragment of the Union force in the valley.[87] Thus far the strategy was working.

After 10:00 P.M.,[88] Jackson met with General Ewell and Colonel Thomas Munford of the cavalry. The strategy for the next day was outlined to both men. Ewell was to take food and ammunition from his wagon train that night, then send the wagons through Port Republic to Brown's Gap. Munford was ordered to ensure that the road to Brown's Gap remained open. At daylight, Ewell would take most of his troops and join Jackson, leaving only Trimble's men to contain Frémont. Taliaferro was to secure Port Republic with his brigade. Jackson would take the four remaining brigades and attack Shields.[89]

At 7:00 A.M. on June 9, Jackson rode out to the battlefield. The Confederates were slowly executing his plan of attack. The Southerners faced to the northeast. On the left was the South Fork of the Shenandoah. The center was open ground, covered in wheat. To the right was a spur of the Blue Ridge Mountains, rising some 50 feet above river bottom land. The crest of the height was a "coaling" or flat expanse used in the production of charcoal. The Federals had already placed artillery on the hill and were shelling the rebels, still a mile away.[90]

Stonewall Jackson had not done a good job of reconnaissance. He did not have enough men at his disposal to face two Union brigades and 16 guns. General Erastus Tyler commanded the bluecoats on the field. His right was anchored on the South Fork, and his center was on the Port Republic Road, but the Union left, with six guns on the coaling, was clearly the Federal strongpoint.[91]

Against this position Jackson committed his regiments in piecemeal fashion. He did not launch a well-coordinated assault against the enemy. The superior strength of the Union artillery tore huge gaps in the advancing lines, and Jackson soon realized that the battle was going against him.

Stonewall looked to the rear for reinforcements. First he ordered Taliaferro's brigade to the front, then searched for Richard Taylor's Louisiana troops. As he saw Taylor approaching, Jackson turned to his aide, Jedediah Hotchkiss. He pointed to the coaling and screamed above the artillery: "Take General Taylor around and take that battery!"[92]

General Tyler was preparing to counterattack. If the Ohioan was successful before Taylor could reach the battery, Jackson's lines would disintegrate. The only help could come from Ewell. His men were en route from Cross Keys, but were arriving in disjointed sections.[93] The battle was still hanging in the balance.

As Jackson was still trying to send more graycoats to the front, the battery on the coaling suddenly ceased fire. In furious hand-to-hand fighting, Taylor's men had captured the six guns which had wreaked such havoc among Jackson's troops. Three times the artillery pieces were won and lost, until the Louisianans finally emerged victorious.[94]

This put a stop to Tyler's planned counterattack in the center. General Winder had put together all available men and led the first concerted effort on the Confederate side. At 11:00 A.M. the Union lines broke, and General Tyler ordered a retreat.[95]

Isaac Trimble had crossed the river to join the battle, and he burned the bridge behind him, leaving Frémont stranded on the other side of the water, watching as Shields retreated.

Casualties on the Confederate side amounted to about 800 men, while Tyler had lost 1,018 soldiers.[96] The Federals had no more than 3,000 troops against Jackson's 8,000 rebels, and it had taken Stonewall over four hours to dislodge a much smaller foe.[97] The casualties on the Confederate side were higher than they should have been. The battle of Port Republic had not been well managed by Jackson, despite the fact that he had won the contest in the end.

The Valley Campaign of 1862 must not be judged purely on what occurred in the Shenandoah Valley. With a Confederate force which never exceeded 17,000 men, Stonewall Jackson was able to defeat three separate commands which totaled more than three times his number. The Valley Army had inflicted almost 5,000 casualties, captured 9,000 small arms and many tons of valuable supplies, all at a cost of approximately 3,100 Southern troops. The enemy had been routed from the Shenandoah Valley.[98]

However, that was not the extent of the Valley Campaign. Some 40,000 Union soldiers had been held at Fredericksburg in order to protect the capital. This had a detrimental effect on the Union invasion of Richmond.

Finally, the victories in the Shenandoah raised morale throughout the South. Both the military and civilian population were hungry for good news after Confederate losses over the winter.

For Stonewall Jackson, there would be no rest. His tattered graycoats would soon be on the way to eastern Virginia. Joseph Johnston had been wounded at the battle of Seven Pines, and Jackson was about to begin a remarkable journey under a new commander. His name was Robert E. Lee. Together, they would seem invincible.

April 6–7, 1862
Shiloh (Pittsburg Landing)

A. S. Johnston
P. G. T. Beauregard
(CSA)

U. S. Grant
(USA)

The Tennessee River winds through the Volunteer State, flowing in a westerly direction from Chattanooga. As the water meanders through northern Alabama and Mississippi, it changes course to run back into Tennessee. On the west bank of the river, the village of Pittsburg Landing appears, followed shortly thereafter by Crump's Landing. A short distance inland lies the small community of Shiloh. It was here in Tennessee that one of the greatest dramas of the Civil War was about to unfold.

The battle came about as a result of the Federal desire to strike deep into the Confederacy. Shiloh itself had little importance; the real target was the Memphis and Charleston Railroad.[1] If Union General Ulysses S. Grant could interrupt traffic on this line, it would be a serious blow to the Southerners.

The Confederates under General Albert Sidney Johnston had encamped around Corinth, Mississippi, in the northern part of the state. General Johnston had four army corps under his command, led by Leonidas Polk, Joseph Hardee, Braxton Bragg and John C. Breckinridge. Combined, the Confederates comprised a force of some 40,000 men,[2] although estimates of troop strength vary for both sides.

As the month of April dawned, General Johnston moved northward. General Hardee was to lead the way, followed by General Polk. They would head toward the small hamlet of Michie, Tennessee. Further east, Breckinridge would follow Bragg's men from Corinth to Monterey, a distance of only 12 miles.[3] Unfortunately, the march from Corinth proved to be a slow and deliberate one for the graycoats. The rebels were delayed in their departure, and different commands became intermingled, further hindering their progress.[4]

By April 5, Johnston's men approached the battlefield, but unity was lacking among the southern generals. P. G. T. Beauregard, who was second in command, preferred to retreat to Corinth without a battle. Braxton Bragg concurred. However, Johnston and Hardee believed that it was possible to gain a great victory, and were in favor of an attack.[5] As the senior commander, Johnston gave the orders for the following day.

Against this army of Confederates, the Federals actually brought two armies to the field. The largest, commanded by General Grant, was made up of six divisions. Generals John A. McClernand, W. H. L. Wallace and Lew Wallace led the first three, while the Yankees under Stephen A. Hurlbut, William T. Sherman and Benjamin M. Prentiss were to play an equally important role in the days to come. General Grant had approximately 37,000 men[6] at his disposal.

In addition to this force, the Federals had some 25,000 men[7] under General Don Carlos Buell. However, these troops were stationed in Nashville, and were unable to arrive at Shiloh until April 7, the second day of the struggle. Buell's men were divided into four divisions, commanded by Alexander McCook, William Nelson, Thomas Crittenden and Thomas Wood. These men would play an absolutely critical role in the final outcome of the battle of Shiloh.

While the railroad continued to be the central target for the Federal troops, it was of paramount importance for General Johnston to prevent the Union forces from combining their strength.[7a] Grant must be defeated before Buell could arrive from Nashville.

Both sides would come to realize that the battlefield was a small area, approximately nine square miles in size.[8] The Tennessee River formed the eastern boundary, with Lick Creek to the south and Owl Creek to the north. Shiloh Church was the most significant feature to the west, and it was after this small building that the battle was to draw its name.

As the Union forces moved inland from Pittsburg Landing, they found that the two creeks converged. The opening between the small tributaries narrowed to a gap of only three miles.[9] General Johnston's Confederates would not have much room to maneuver.

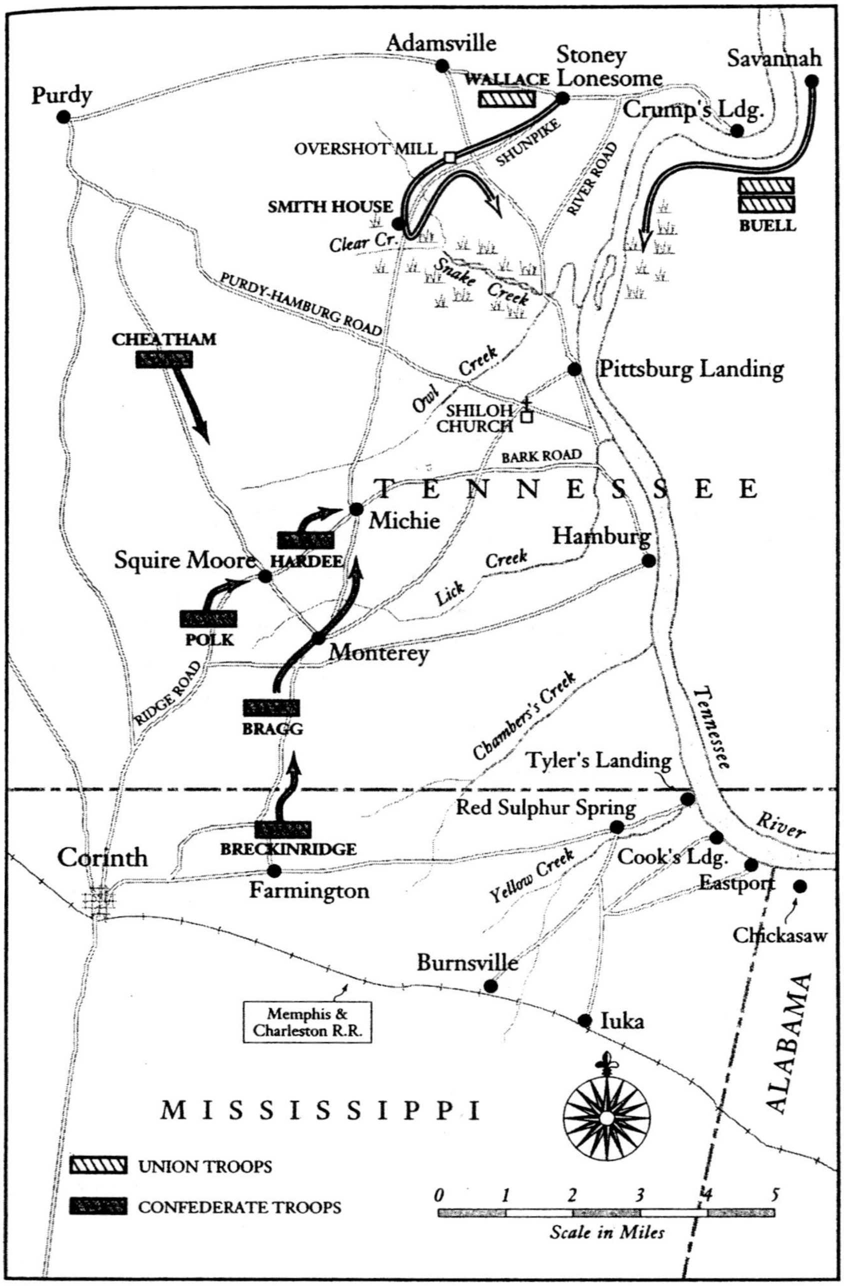

The Shiloh Campaign

men under General Breckinridge were held back as a mobile reserve in case of necessity.[11]

Against the gray attackers General Grant had scattered his forces. To the west of the church were Sherman's bluecoats, while Prentiss stationed his division to the east. These troops would bear the brunt of the initial onslaught.[12]

McClernand's men were behind, and between the first two divisions. General Hurlbut and General W. H. L. Wallace were located behind McClernand, closer to the Tennessee River. Lew Wallace would not take part in the early action, as his division was farther north at Crump's Landing.[13] As the battle progressed, these positions would change considerably.

Shortly after 5:00 A.M. on April 6,[14] the grayclad veterans of Joseph Hardee emerged from the dim light. They had come upon the right flank of the Union troops under Benjamin Prentiss. S. A. M. Wood, R. G. Shaver and Aaron Hardcastle[15] hit the Yankees hard, and the battle was under way. At the edge of Fraley Field, Major James Powell would be the recipient of the Confederate attack.

David Moore and Everett Peabody were ordered to Powell's assistance, but the bluecoats were roughly handled. Wood and Shaver pushed forward along the Pittsburg-Corinth Road. The Confederates moved to the northeast, and the Yankees fell back before them.[16]

The Federals were able to briefly halt the onrushing rebels, but the stand was short indeed. By 8:30 A.M.[17] the Union camps had been captured, and the Northerners were forced to scatter. Powell was killed,[18] and the Federals broke in disarray. The impact of Hardee's thrust sent the battle moving northward.[19] General Sherman was about to receive some very unwelcome visitors.

Much of Tennessee was rural during this period, and the area around Pittsburg Landing was no exception. There were wooded sections, but three dozen farms covered the land.[10] Military action would take place in separate theaters, all of which lay between Lick Creek and Owl Creek.

On the morning of April 6, Sidney Johnston moved his troops forward, marching north toward Shiloh Church. General Polk held the left, with Hardee in the center, and Braxton Bragg's men on the right. The

Just east of the Pittsburg-Corinth Road lay the little church at Shiloh. This area was also the headquarters of General William Tecumseh Sherman. His Yankees faced south, on either side of the road. The left side of his alignment looked out over Rea Field.[20]

Shortly after 7:00 A.M.[21] Pat Cleburne's brigade of Confederates hit Sherman's left, attacking the 53rd Ohio regiment.[22] The rebels received a thick volley of musketry, stopping the momentum of the charge. Casualties were heavy, especially for the 6th Mississippi.[23]

However, the inexperienced bluecoats had not been prepared for the sudden assault. Hastily, the Yankees ordered a retreat, and the Ohioans fell back. Sherman's left had given way, hoping to consolidate their forces a bit further to the rear.

Fighting raged along the line, and by 8:00 A.M.[24] the Union right was engaged. Cleburne had divided his forces, sending four regiments to his left.[25] The graycoats struck Ralph Buckland's brigade. Buckland's 2,200 men not only outnumbered the 1,500 Southerners in their front, but the Union men outflanked the enemy as well, extending well past Cleburne's left.[26]

Raked by Union artillery, the Confederates suffered heavy casualties here also. Still, General Sherman had been forced back under the pressure of the assault. By 10:00 A.M. it seemed as if Sidney Johnston would accomplish his mission and carry the day for the South.[27] Sherman's entire division was in retreat.[28]

When the firing started on April 6, General John McClernand sent a courier to Sherman requesting information. It became obvious that there was a gap between Sherman's 5th Division and the 6th Division of General Prentiss.[29] Unfortunately for the bluecoats, McClernand's troops were not concentrated. His camps extended back for quite a distance, giving his reinforcements great depth. However, the formation was not very wide, and it might prove difficult to fill the break between the Union divisions, who were trying their best to reform their shattered lines.[30]

As McClernand moved forward around 8:00 A.M., his Northerners ran right into the battered remnants of Sherman's division. Organization was not good. Battle units from Sherman, McClernand and W. H. L. Wallace became mixed up with one another. The action was centered around the intersection of two main highways: the Purdy-Hamburg Road ran east and west; the Pittsburgh-Corinth Road ran north and south. Facing south, the bluecoats determined to hold their ground.[31]

The Tennesseans under General Alexander P. Stewart attacked the center of the Union position, moving north along the Pittsburg-Corinth Road. Stewart's brigade suffered heavy losses, but with the assistance of Wood's and Shaver's Confederates on the right, the graycoats continued to roll back the foe before them.[32]

The Southerners had captured 18 artillery pieces, and nine Union officers lay wounded. By 11:20 A.M., the rebels held complete possession of the Pittsburg-Corinth Road.[33]

General Johnston appeared to be in control. Each Union division in action thus far was in serious trouble. However, Sidney Johnston had placed too much emphasis on his left flank. This allowed the Federal center and left to steady their forces and prepare for an attack.[34]

Once again the Federals fell back to a new position. By late morning they had moved northeast, hard pressed by Confederates from all four southern corps.[35] The next struggle seemed to be for the area around Jones Field.

At 11:30 A.M.[36] the Yankees organized their first counteroffensive of the day. Sherman and McClernand sent their troops forward, and the surprise attack caught the rebels off guard. McClernand followed this thrust with a bayonet charge. The Confederates had brought up reinforcements, and Jones Field was hotly contested. Finally, the Federals withdrew, but again had inflicted heavy casualties in the Southern ranks. Confederate manpower was falling, and future attempts on the center and right might well be in danger of succeeding.[37]

The Union left did not have the troops that the right received, but Johnston had not attacked as heavily in this sector as he might have. Colonel David Stuart held the far left of the Union line. In contrast to the mass of graycoats Sherman had faced, Stuart saw only a part of Braxton Bragg's command.

About 10:00 A.M.,[38] the Yankees realized that their small command was outnumbered, and Stuart pulled his men back to reform. James Chalmers threatened the Federal left, while John Jackson's rebels attacked the right.[39]

Stuart's men attempted to maneuver into a better position, but became hopelessly entangled. Confusion reigned, and the brigade began to disintegrate. Attempting to rally his men, Colonel Stuart was hit in the shoulder by a bullet.[40] Organization on the Union left was lost.

Opportunity stared the Southerners in the face. If the rebels could reach the Tennessee River, the Union escape would be cut off. Despite the confusion along the enemy front, the Confederates were unable to take advantage of the situation. Ammunition was low, and the soldiers began to pillage the Union camps, slowing the advance.[41] The door was open to Pittsburg Landing. The Confederates would fail to march through it.

Like the Union right and left, the center of the battlefield contained a mixture of commands. Prentiss had seen his division severely beaten, and he had pulled back to safer ground. Stephen Hurlbut led the Union 4th Division forward, and W. H. L. Wallace brought up his troops to assist as well. This formation in the center of the battlefield would turn out to save the day for the Union. The combat was so ferocious that the Confederates called this spot the "Hornet's Nest."

By 11:00 A.M. the Confederates had turned both flanks of General Grant's army.[42] Only the center remained. The bluecoats formed along a sunken road. Facing southwest, Hurlbut placed his 4,000 men on

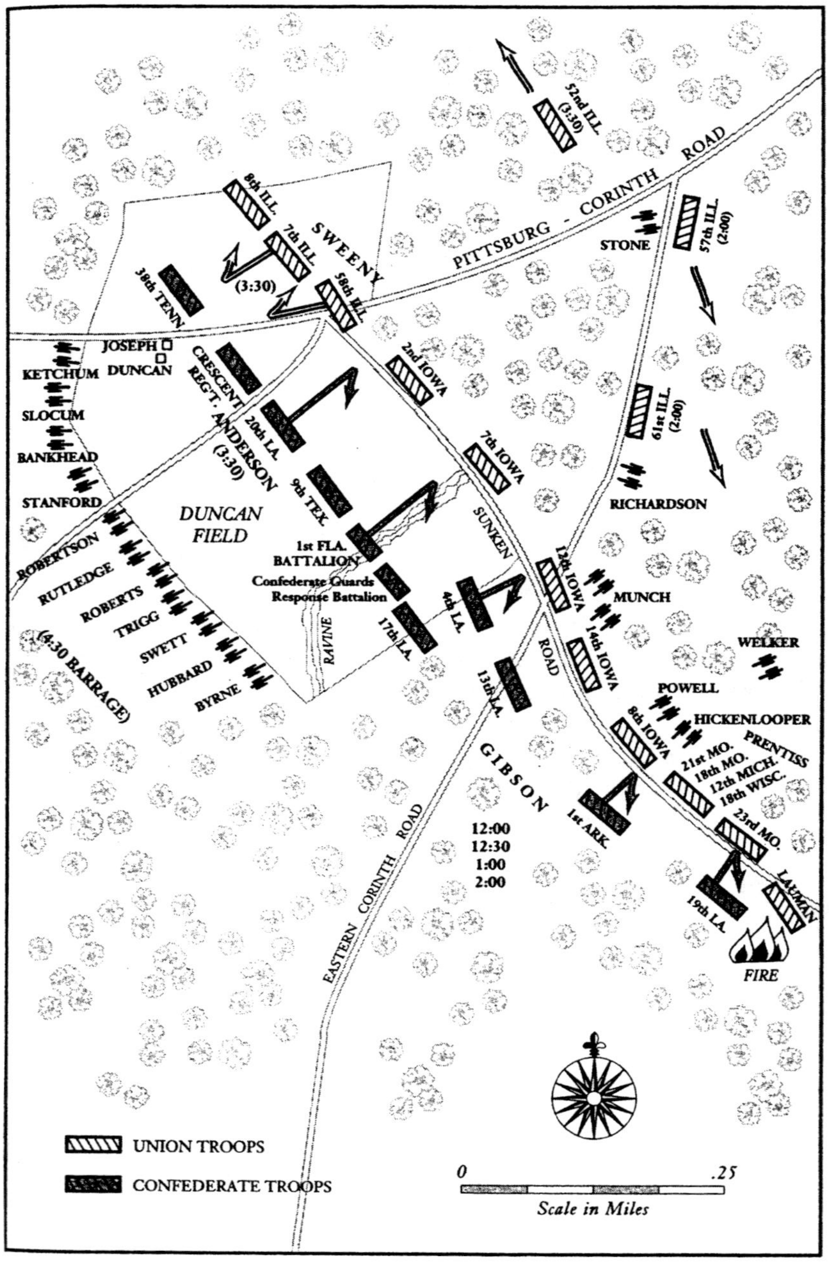

Shiloh: "The Hornet's Nest," 2:00–4:30 P.M., April 6, 1862.

the left, Prentiss was in the center, with some 1,200 soldiers, while W. H. L. Wallace held the right with 5,000 troops.[43]

Braxton Bragg led approximately 10,000 Confederates in a frontal assault on the Hornet's Nest.[44] Throughout the afternoon the rebels assaulted the Union position. General Bragg should have maneuvered around the flanks of the enemy, but instead he decided to utilize continual frontal assaults. The constant pressure forced the Federals back, eventually succeeding, but the price was dear in Confederate blood. Bragg's performance cannot be regarded in a positive light, as the sacrifice of so many Southern lives was a loss the Confederacy could ill afford.[45]

The Federals had started off facing southwest, but Bragg's pressure had changed conditions considerably. By 4:45 P.M. the Northerners were surrounded, and now faced east and south.[46] A long day of constant combat had combined different Confederate commands as well. There was no escape left for the majority of the Yankees, although the 7th Illinois and 3rd Iowa regiments were able to make their way to safety.[47]

It was almost 6:00 P.M. when Prentiss surrendered.[48] While estimates vary, Prentiss reported that 2,200 Union soldiers were captured.[49] The heroic stand by these Federals prevented the annihilation of the rest of Grant's army. The action at the Hornet's Nest was undoubtedly the key to the battle of Shiloh.[50]

In the early afternoon, the Confederacy would suffer a serious blow. Directing troops in front of Breckinridge's lines, General Johnston was suddenly struck by four different bullets. The most serious severed an artery behind his right knee. Johnston remained on the battlefield, but by 2:30 P.M., he was dead.[51] General Beauregard would assume command.

There is no question that the death of Sidney Johnston damaged the organization of the Confederates. However, there were others factors at work which would allow the Union forces to triumph on April 7. Johnston had committed too many troops on his left. The Federals had been beaten, but the Confederate casualties were very heavy. The opportunity to destroy Stuart's Yankees on the Union left had been lost. Finally, General Lew Wallace had begun to arrive from Crump's Landing.[52] Enemy reinforcements were now at hand. Could General Buell be far behind?

As the sun dropped on the field of battle, General Beauregard made a momentous decision. The Federals were in considerable disorder, and great progress had been made. It appeared as though the victory was in hand. Beauregard decided to call off the Confederate attack. Any further action could certainly wait until tomorrow.[53]

This decision was particularly important, because

it set the stage for the reversal which occurred on the following day.[54] April 7 would belong to the Union.

Throughout the night Federal reinforcements continued to arrive at Pittsburg Landing. These were General Buell's men, and they would have a telling effect on the action to come.

Casualties had been heavy for the South. Fresh Union troops under Lew Wallace had reached the field, and Don Carlos Buell began to send his men forward. The depleted ranks of the Confederacy would be outnumbered.

The initial action on April 7 took place in Jones Field. Wallace's division faced south, on the far right of the line in blue. To his left were the men under Sherman and McClernand, facing southwest. Generally speaking, Grant's men would form the Union right, while Buell's troops made up the left. This formation held true throughout the day.[54a]

Opposing the Northerners was Braxton Bragg's Corps, on the left and right, combined with the remnants of Pat Cleburne's command in the center. The Confederates faced northeast, but Cleburne's left flank was unsupported, or "in the air."[55]

General Bragg ordered Cleburne to attack,[56] but the small force was hurled back with ease. General McClernand's men swept forward, recapturing the camps which had been lost in the prior day's action.

The Tennesseans under Benjamin Cheatham blocked the Union advance, even making some initial progress against Sherman's Federals. However, with Wallace on the left, Sherman in his front and McClernand to the right, Cheatham's rebels had little chance of success. The entire Confederate front was being pushed back. By 1:30 P.M. the graycoats had retreated across Review Field, and the fight centered around Water Oaks Pond.[57]

Confederate resistance was stubborn, and General Sherman was becoming impatient. Fortunately, the Ohioan looked to his left and saw Buell's troops moving forward. Two Union brigades under General Lovell Rousseau and Colonel Edward Kirk struck the Southerners in the right flank, forcing them back.[58] By 2:30 P.M., the Purdy-Hamburg Road was back in Union hands.[59]

Braxton Bragg pulled the Confederates back to Shiloh Church, and the graycoats reformed. It was clear to all that General Buell had arrived. Threatened by superior numbers, Bragg's lines were in serious danger.[60]

The graycoats retreated once more. They established a position along Shiloh Branch, a small creek south of the church. The troops were pieced together from different commands, but most of the men belonged to General Breckinridge. At 4:00 P.M.[61] the 38th Tennessee regiment startled the Federals with an aggressive charge. The Yankees simply regrouped, and pressed their numerical advantage. One hour later[62] the Confederates had completely withdrawn.

The battered Union troops did not offer much in the way of a pursuit as the Confederates struggled southward again. The battle was over.

Casualties at Shiloh were staggering. The Union forces had seen 1,754 men killed, 8,408 wounded and 2,885 missing, for a total of 13,047. The Confederate side had lost 1,728 soldiers killed, 8,012 wounded and 959 missing, for a total of 10,694.[63]

From a military standpoint, what were the results of so much bloodshed? Shiloh was a battle the Confederacy simply had to win. A victory would have restored the balance of power west of Virginia, the frontier to Kentucky would be open once again, and the Mississippi Valley would be saved.[64] All of the fruits of success from the first day had been dashed at the hands of General Don Carlos Buell. His timely reinforcements had saved Grant from disaster, and won a crucial victory for the North.

However, there was another, perhaps more immediate result of the combat in Tenneessee. In two days, one battle had produced more casualties than in all American wars combined up to that point.[65] The horrors of the Civil War were now too readily apparent to the civilian populations on both sides of the conflict.

April 7, 1862
Island No. 10

J. P. McCown	J. Pope
W. W. Mackall	A. H. Foote
(CSA)	(USA)

With the fall of Vicksburg in the summer of 1863, control of the Mississippi River was securely in Union hands. However, in the early stages of the conflict, the Federal grasp was not so firm. About 60 miles[1] below Columbus, Kentucky, the course of the river makes a sharp bend, and the Confederates had built fortifications there on the bluffs overlooking the water. They believed that the artillery posted on these heights could command the enemy traffic on the Mississippi.

The river actually changes direction, flowing north for a short distance. In the middle of this curve was a little spot of land called Island No. 10.

Ten miles downstream at New Madrid,[2] Confederate guns protected the western approaches to the peninsula known as New Madrid Bend. Together, the rebel force comprised some 7,000 men.[3]

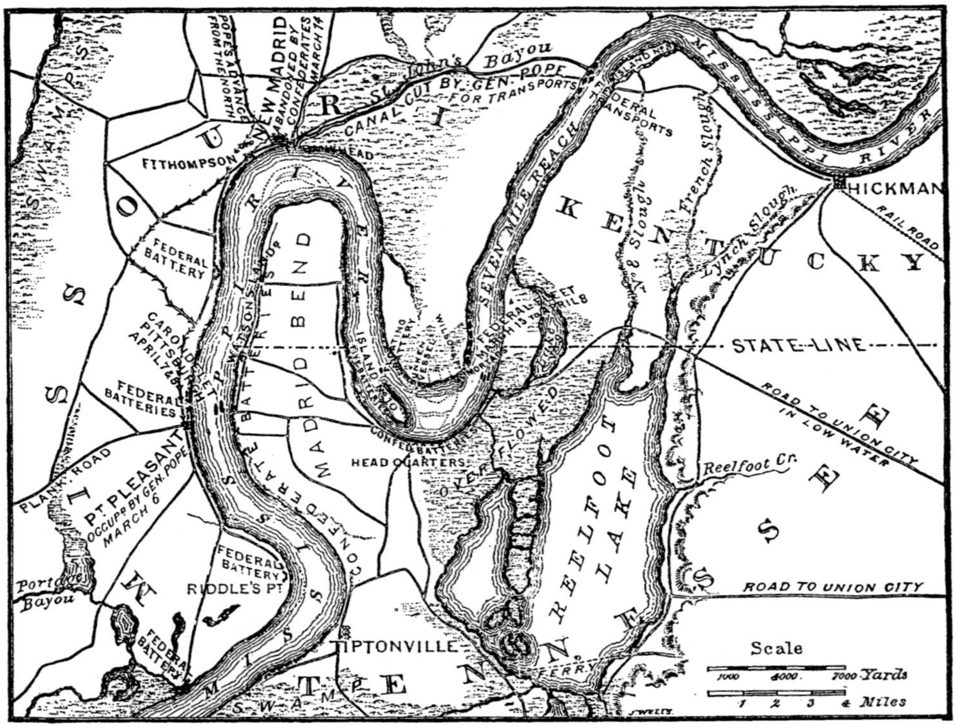

Military and naval operations about Island Number 10. Map by Jacob Wells, based on the two maps by Captain A. B. Gray, C.S.A., made in March 1862, and on official reports.

The Union assault force would be a combined effort, which would include both naval and land forces. General John Pope would lead the infantry of the Army of the Mississippi, some 20,000 soldiers,[4] while Flag Officer Andrew H. Foote commanded a flotilla of 6 gunboats and 11 mortar boats.[5]

The stage was set for the capture of Island No. 10 on March 13, when General Pope forced the evacuation of New Madrid. Pope approached the town from the north, and General John P. McCown pulled his graycoats back across the river to the peninsula. The Union occupation of New Madrid isolated Island No. 10. The Federals controlled the Mississippi River above and below the Confederates.[6]

General William W. Mackall replaced McCown,[7] only to find he had inherited a most precarious situation. On April 4, the gunboat *Carondelet* ran past the Confederate artillery. Three days later, the *Pittsburg* safely passed the Southern gauntlet, while General Pope landed four troop-laden steamers on the eastern shore of the Mississippi.[8]

Trapped between Federal forces, Mackall surrendered some 3,500 men on April 8.[9] The capitulation of New Madrid and Island No. 10 opened the Mississippi River to the Union as far south as Fort Pillow, Tennessee. Slowly but surely the United States government was beginning to take control of the river, but it would be over a year before the fall of Vicksburg finally sliced the Confederacy in two.

April 10–11, 1862
Fort Pulaski

C. H. Olmstead (CSA) — D. Hunter (USA)

Fort Pulaski is situated on Cockspur Island, at the mouth of the Savannah River. The island itself is formed of rather marshy soil, and broad channels of water course around it. The best approach to Cockspur from firm ground is from the southeast, over two miles away.[1] Many Confederates believed that the location of the fort provided a great deal of protection from enemy attack. As a result, it was not strongly fortified.[2]

Union General Thomas W. Sherman had a different opinion. He felt that these obstacles could be overcome. In November 1861,[3] he directed the Expeditionary Corps to investigate the feasibility of capturing Fort Pulaski. It was determined that Tybee Island, southeast of Cockspur Island, was the most suitable starting point for such an attack. Here, too, the ground was soft, but the industrious Yankees went to work, reinforcing the entire area. Eventually, several artillery batteries began to take shape.

However, Tybee Island was not the only place where bluecoats were hard at work. Two other batteries were constructed, each about four miles from the fort. The first was situated on Jones Island, northwest of Fort Pulaski. Located at Venus Point, it consisted of six guns. The other battery was on Bird Island, which lies in the middle of the Savannah River, just south of Jones Island. The Federals placed six guns here as well.[4]

The slow, arduous process of reinforcing the muddy terrain seemed to have no end. Sandbags and wooden planks were laid down, and the heavy artillery pieces put in place. By April 9, 1862,[5] the Federals were ready. Fort Pulaski would be trapped in the crossfire from the Union guns.

About 8:00 A.M. the next morning,[6] the bombard-

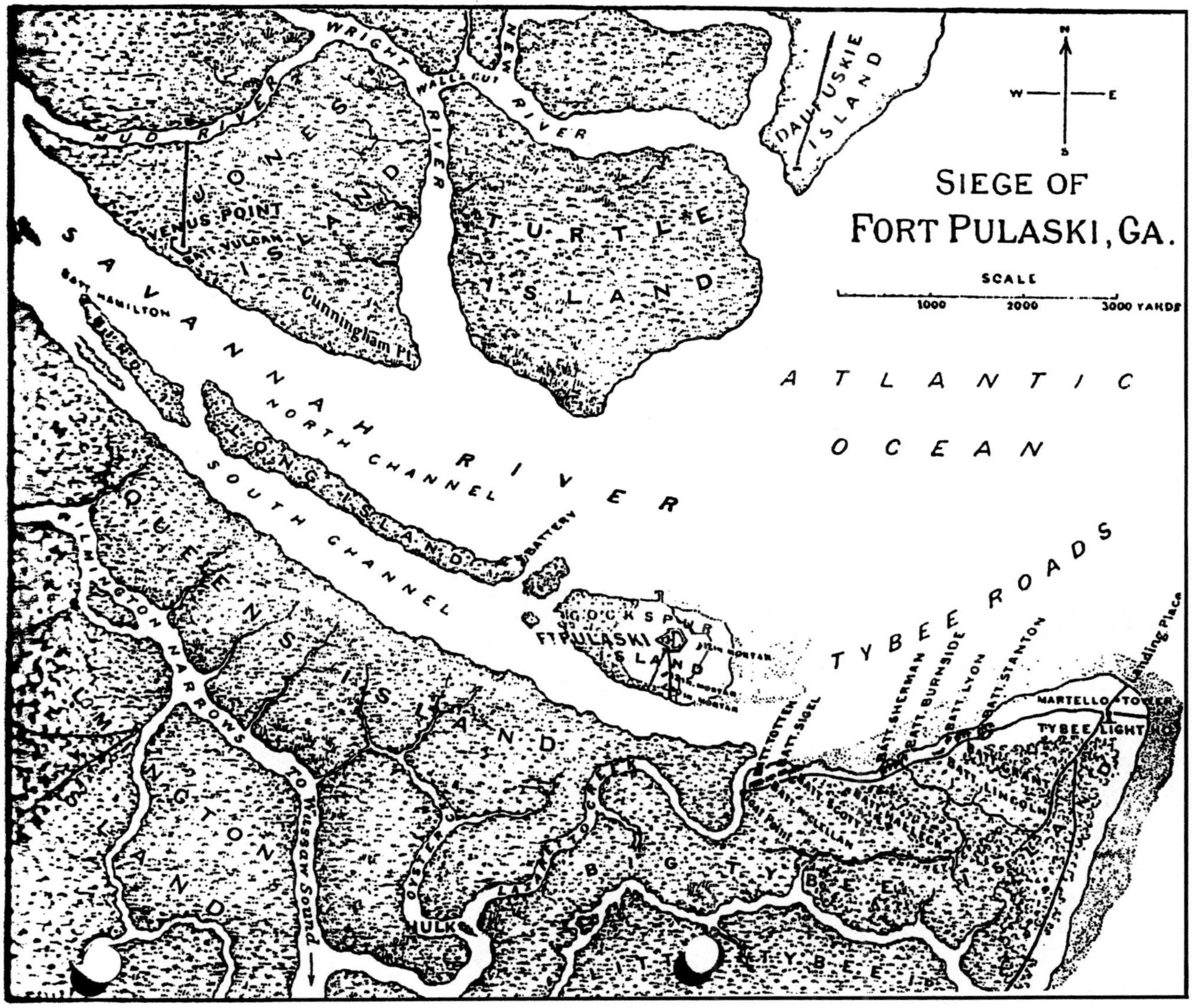

Siege and capture of Fort Pulaski. Map by Jacob Wells.

ment began. By the end of the first day the artillery shells had done considerable damage to the fort. Gradually, some of the Confederate guns within the fort fell silent under the steady pounding from the surrounding islands.[7]

Shortly after sunrise on April 11, the Yankees resumed their fire. Repeated explosions against the walls of the fort ripped gaping holes in the sides of the enclosure. It was obvious to the defenders that the situation was hopeless. At 2:00 P.M. a white flag appeared above Fort Pulaski.[8]

As this battle had been a long-range artillery duel, casualties were very slight on both sides.[9] However, the capture of Fort Pulaski was not without important consequences. The Savannah River was now closed to blockade runners. The Federal navy which had been occupied in Savannah could now be transferred to other Confederate ports,[10] such as Charleston, Wilmington or Mobile. Inch by inch, the Union was closing its grip on the southern seas.

April 5–May 3, 1862
Yorktown

J. B. Magruder (CSA)	G. B. McClellan (USA)

Although Yorktown was most certainly a battle, it was part of the much larger Peninsula Campaign. Union General George B. McClellan had decided to bring an

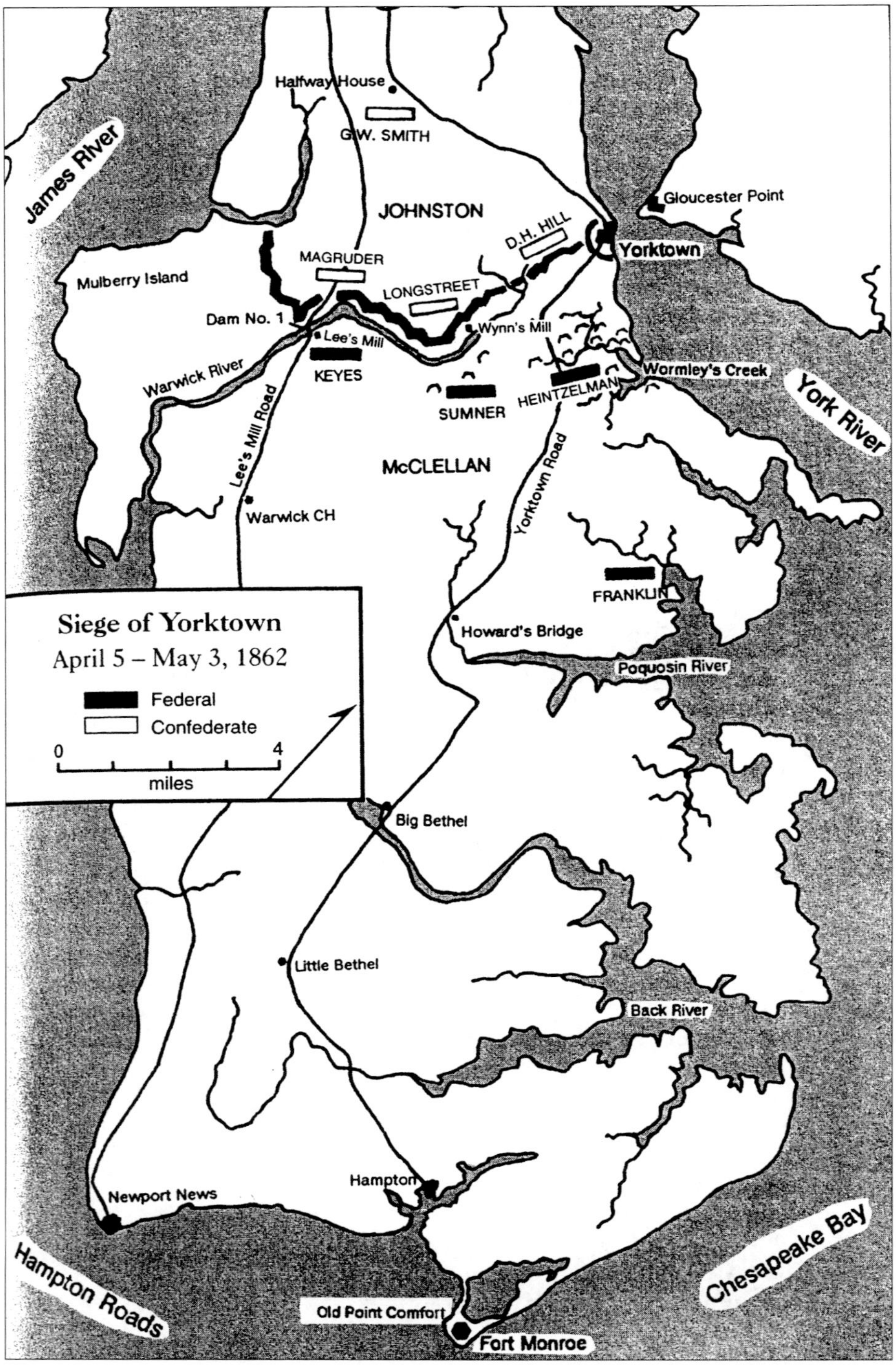

Siege of Yorktown, April 5–May 3, 1862.

amphibious force up the Peninsula, a narrow strip of land in Virginia which separated the York River, to the north, and the James River, to the south. He believed that his Army of the Potomac could defeat any opposition they encountered, move northwest, and capture Richmond, which lay on the banks of the James. In so doing, General McClellan foresaw a quick end to the conflict, and a glorious chapter in his own military career.

General McClellan was inherently a very cautious man. Before the bluecoats moved forward, he wanted to be sure that his men were adequately supplied. During March and into April, ships sailed constantly through Chesapeake Bay, landing at Fort Monroe on the tip of the Peninsula. The Union army transported 121,500 men and 14,592 animals to Fort Monroe in less than three weeks.[1]

General John B. Magruder was quite the opposite in personality. Nicknamed "Prince John" in the Confederate army for his theatrical style,[2] he realized that the Confederates would be hopelessly outnumbered. Against the Union horde, the graycoats could muster only 13,600 troops.[3]

Nevertheless, Magruder was determined to use deception and daring to delay the cautious Yankee advance into Virginia as long as possible. The weather would help the Confederates as well. Saturday, April 5, saw a morning rain which stopped the Yankees in their tracks.[4]

As the Federal columns finally moved inland, Magruder took his small band of rebels and marched them back and forth. This gave the enemy the impression that the Confederates had large numbers of defenders, and were being reinforced.[5] Equally important were the fortifications stretching across the Peninsula. George McClellan wanted to find exactly what he expected, without any surprises. Now he had to deal with something very different.[6] The Union commander was faced with a dilemma. Should he attack, or await Union reinforcements? The military situation worsened when a telegram arrived from Washington. General McDowell's I Corps had been removed from the Army of the Potomac in order to protect the capital. There was simply no doubt about it. In McClellan's own mind, Magruder's band of rebels must certainly outnumber his force of Yankees. Prince John's bluff had worked.[7]

Over the next few days, Confederate reinforcements actually did arrive. General Joseph E. Johnston brought additional troops to the Peninsula and assumed command. By April 10 the Southern ranks had swelled to 34,400.[8]

Confederate guns at Gloucester Point across from Yorktown prevented the Union naval forces from sailing past Yorktown, while the ironclad *Merrimack* protected the James River. General McClellan would have to capture Richmond by land.[8a]

Gradually, the Union forces moved forward. Samuel Heintzelman advanced on the right with the III Corps, in the center was Edwin Sumner's II Corps, and on the left marched the IV Corps of Erasmus Keyes. William Franklin's division of the I Corps was held in reserve. Arrayed against this force of bluecoats was the small force of rebels, holding the Yorktown line with grim determination. On the Confederate left was the division of Daniel Harvey Hill, his left anchored on the town itself. In the center were the men under James Longstreet, while the right was held by the troops of Magruder's command. Gustavus W. Smith held his troops in reserve to move wherever needed.[9]

The morning of April 14 saw General Johnston back in Richmond for a meeting with President Davis. Also present were Secretary of War George W. Randolph and General Robert E. Lee, who at this point in his career was still a military advisor to President Davis. Johnston was accompanied by generals James Longstreet and Gustavus W. Smith. Johnston sought to shift Magruder's line at Yorktown back to Richmond. Smith and Longstreet supported Johnston's plan to withdraw, while Lee and Randolph felt that the Peninsula must be held. If the current position was abandoned, the city of Norfolk would have to be sacrificed, which would be a great blow to the Southern cause. Davis listened, then sided with Lee and Randolph. The Peninsula was to be defended.[9a]

Two days later McClellan decided to bombard the Confederates with his siege guns, and soon realized that the Union army had superior artillery. The Union commander from Pennsylvania probed for a weak spot in the Southern defenses, sending General Baldy Smith with his division against the Confederate right. The Northerners attacked at a place on the Warwick River called Dam No. 1 but were thoroughly repulsed, losing 165 men.[10]

The next several days were spent fortifying the Federal lines. Due to wet weather and the inflated estimates of Confederate strength, McClellan felt that a siege of Yorktown was the best way to reduce the city. The Yankees brought in no fewer than 70 heavy field pieces. President Lincoln had created an army capable of delivering 7,000 pounds of shell into the enemy lines. This advantage in firepower was not unnoticed by General Johnston.[11]

It soon became apparent to Johnston that his cautious adversary was saving up ammunition to deliver a stunning blow. On April 29 Richmond was notified as follows: "The fight for Yorktown, as I said in Richmond, must be one of artillery, in which we cannot win. The result is certain; the time only doubtful.... I shall therefore move as soon as can be done conveniently...."[12] As soon as the line from Yorktown to the Warwick River was abandoned, Norfolk would be left undefended.

With continued reinforcements the Confederate force on the Peninsula had grown to 56,600 men.[13] It would not be possible to evacuate Yorktown unnoticed. However, during the night of May 3[14] the rebels opened up a random bombardment, spewing shells everywhere. The bluecoats were forced to duck for cover, as artillery shells burst all around them. Finally, the guns ceased, and an eerie silence covered the field. At first light, General Heintzelman rose above the field in an observation balloon. The Confederates had simply disappeared.[15]

Casualties for both sides combined had been under five hundred.[16] Johnston would be blamed for not only leaving the Peninsula prematurely, but leaving too much equipment behind as well. He would fall back and attempt to vindicate himself at Williamsburg.

May 5, 1862
WILLIAMSBURG

J. E. Johnston (CSA)	G. B. McClellan (USA)

On May 3 General Johnston had pulled the Confederate forces out of their defenses at Yorktown. His intent was to seek a more favorable defensive position, much closer to Richmond. Johnston's men marched inland on two roads. One led from Yorktown in a northwesterly direction straight up the Peninsula, the narrow neck of land in Virginia which separated the York River, to the north, and the James River, to the south. The other road paralleled the Yorktown road about one mile from the James. The roads came together approximately two miles southeast of Williamsburg, the old colonial capital.[1]

The graycoats were separated into four infantry commands, under James Longstreet, Daniel Harvey Hill, Gustavus W. Smith and David R. Jones, who had assumed the leadership of the ailing John B. Magruder's troops. Jeb

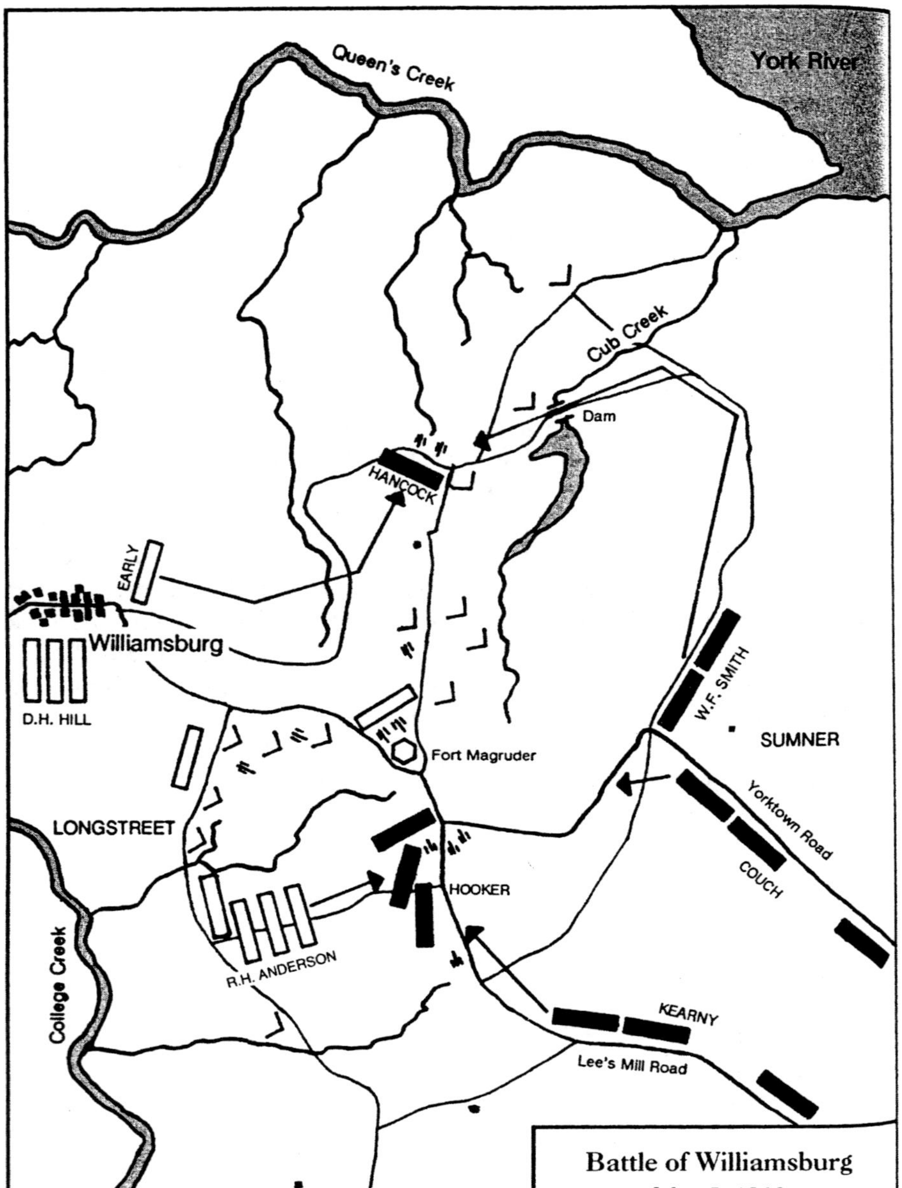

Battle of Williamsburg, May 5, 1862.

Stuart's cavalry formed the rear guard, ever watchful for pursuing Yankees.[2]

By the afternoon of May 4 all four commands were at or beyond Williamsburg.[3] Although Johnston would have preferred to make it all the way to Richmond, steady rains had turned the roads into mud. The Confederates would have to fight where they were.

At this point the Peninsula is only seven miles wide. Queen's Creek on Johnston's left and College Creek on his right narrowed the area the rebels had to defend even further.[4] In order to hamper the advancing bluecoats, trees were felled as obstructions.

George B. McClellan was having great difficulty moving the troops of the Army of the Potomac through the mire. The Union pursuit had been delegated to General Edwin V. Sumner, a 65-year-old army veteran who had risen far beyond his capacity. His limitations would hinder the Union assault at Williamsburg, as he would never quite understand the battle that was developing around him.[5]

On Sumner's left was the division of General Joseph E. Hooker of the III Corps, marching on the Lee's Mill Road. Known as "Fighting Joe" in the Union ranks, he was full of confidence in his own ability. Still a few miles behind Hooker was General Philip Kearny, a highly respected officer who was to die four months later at the battle of Chantilly.[6] On Sumner's right was Baldy Smith's division of the IV Corps. Other divisions of the IV Corps were trying to assist General Smith, but they too had been unable to reach the field of battle.[7] None of General Sumner's troops in the II Corps had arrived at this point, but the general was accompanied by two other corps commanders: Samuel Heintzelman of the III Corps and Erasmus Keyes of the IV Corps.

Poor weather had reduced the Federal pursuit to three corps commanders in charge of two divisions. Smith was so much further inland than Hooker that the two Union divisions would be fighting on different fields. The bluecoats hoped that their remaining divisions would be able to conquer the quagmire in Virginia and take part in the action to come.

Unlike General Sumner, James Longstreet would perform quite well at Williamsburg. By the 5th of May he had deftly shifted the men under his command, and was able to place 10,350 Confederates in front of the 9,000 Federals under Hooker.[8] The rebels were able to move through a sheltered ravine to Hooker's left, and the Yankees were in danger of being outflanked.[9]

West of the Lee's Mill Road, General Hooker saw his line of battle bend backward. Four New York regiments suffered most severely[10] as the Confederates pushed the foe back to the road, overrunning the Union position. As they reached the road, the grayclad Mississippians carried off four guns, but were unable to drag the remaining six artillery pieces through the mud. They turned the cannon around and fired at the Northerners.

After a retreat of half a mile, the Yankees reformed and waited for Longstreet's assault. As the Southerners came within range of the second Federal artillery position, the cannons opened fire. The graycoats ducked for cover among the trees as General Hooker shouted encouragement to his troops.[11]

At that moment the battle was saved for the Union by the timely arrival of Phil Kearny's division. With the reinforcements, the III Corps was able to drive the Confederates back off the Lee's Mill Road.[12] Hooker's left flank was saved.

On the Union right, a very different battle was taking place. Baldy Smith had sent General Winfield S. Hancock on a lengthy two-mile march in an attempt to attack the Confederate left.[13] At 3:00 P.M.,[14] Hancock had 3,400 men on the enemy flank.[15] He intended to accomplish in this sector what Longstreet had almost done against Hooker.

D. H. Hill's men stood squarely in Hancock's path. Hill advanced the brigade of Jubal Early, a feisty, aggressive soldier who thrived on combat. Early proposed to move to the Confederate left and hit Hancock's men in the right flank. Hill liked the plan and gave his approval. The only problem for the graycoats was that the exact position of Baldy Smith's troops was not yet known. Nevertheless, Jubal Early ventured forth.[16]

Unfortunately for the Confederates, the enemy artillery was not where Early thought it was. As the 24th Virginia emerged from the safety of the woods on the Confederate left, they were not on Hancock's flank, but squarely in front of the Union men.[17] Early led two Virginia regiments on the left, while D. H. Hill's North Carolinians were on the right.[18] In the thick, swampy underbrush, Hill's men became separated from Early's Virginians. Without waiting for the rest of the brigade, Early shouted "Follow me!" and led the Virginians straight toward the guns.[19]

Brave and gallant though this attack may have been, it was doomed from the start. Hancock had 3,400 men and eight artillery pieces. Early had under 1,200 men and no artillery support at all. Hancock counterattacked and the result was predictable. While the Union side lost 100 men, General Early's brigade suffered 508 casualties.[20] The Union right was faring much better than the left.

General McClellan, with his penchant for overestimating the Southern forces, would claim another "brilliant victory" by his outmanned army.[21] Reality, however, might tell a different story. On the Confederate side, Joe Johnston had lost a total of 1,682 men, including cavalry skirmishing on May 4. Federal losses came to 2,283.[22] While Jubal Early had not acquitted himself well, on the whole the management of the battle was much worse on the Union side. General Baldy Smith summed up the action for the Army of the Potomac when he said that it was a "beastly exhibition of stupidity and ignorance."[23]

The performance by Edwin Sumner would hardly enhance his reputation. At every point during the action the Federals had more men and more guns. The bluecoats should have won the day. Not only had he not understood the enemy's troops, he had failed to understand his own.

May 7, 1862
Eltham's Landing

J. B. Hood (CSA)	W. B. Franklin (USA)

On May 5, the Confederates completed the withdrawal from Williamsburg. The graycoats were moving in the direction of Richmond. General Joseph E. Johnston, commanding the southern troops, felt that the Peninsula was untenable, and desired to seek the safety of the capital.

The Federal forces were led by one of the Union army's finest officers, General William B. Franklin. He had graduated first in the class of 1843 at the U.S. Military Academy, and was a close personal friend of General George B. McClellan, commander of the Army of the Potomac.[1]

General Franklin had decided to take his division up the York River on an amphibious expedition which would land on the Eltham plantation. The York River is formed by the confluence of the Pamunkey River and the Mattapony River. In between these two rivers lies a narrow strip of land which contains West Point, Virginia, the terminus of the Richmond and York River Railroad. Opposite West Point, on the south bank of the York River, was Eltham's Landing.

Unfortunately for the bluecoats, General Franklin did not arrive until May 7. Had he disembarked two days earlier, he might have been able to cut off the Confederate retreat from Williamsburg. As it was, the Confederates were already at Barhamsville, five miles down the road.[2]

Franklin decided to get his troops into position and await reinforcements. Three other Union divisions were still at Yorktown. They would be able to join him soon, and then the Federals could attack.

On the Confederate side, Joe Johnston wanted no part of a full-scale assault. It was his idea to determine the strength of the enemy lines, then gradually retreat toward Richmond.[3] Johnston's instructions to General John B. Hood were "to feel the enemy gently and fall back."[4]

John B. Hood and his Texas brigade did not know how to "feel the enemy gently." Aggressive by nature, Hood led his troops forward, searching for the bluecoats. In order to avoid casualties from friendly fire, the Confederates were ordered not to load their muskets. Suddenly, the Texans came upon Union pickets, patrolling the area in front of Franklin's main force. Fifteen feet in front of General Hood, an enemy corporal raised his rifle, and a shot rang out. The corporal dropped dead. Private John Deal of the 4th Texas regiment had disobeyed orders and loaded his gun. As a result, Hood's life was saved.[5]

Hood's brigade pushed forward through the woods until they came upon Franklin's troops in brigade strength. Gunfire broke out along the line. There were several charges and countercharges, but the Yankees believed that their flanks were being turned. Several Union regiments broke for the rear, hoping to reform back at Eltham's Landing. The bluecoats were reinforced at the landing, and their lines held at that point.[6]

General Hood could not detect any other opportunity to gain an advantage, so he decided to obey Johnston's original orders, and broke off the fighting.[7]

The action at Eltham's Landing was not much more than a skirmish, particularly when compared to some of the larger battles later in the war. Hood had suffered 48 casualties, while Franklin had lost 186 men in two hours of combat.[8]

The results here did not change the strategy for either side. General Johnston resumed his retrograde movement toward Richmond, General McClellan continued in cautious pursuit. This would all culminate in less than one month at the battle of Seven Pines.

May 15, 1862
Drewry's Bluff (First)

E. Ferrand (CSA)	J. Rodgers (USA)

In the spring of 1862, the Union Army of the Potomac landed on a narrow strip of Virginia soil called the Peninsula. It lies between the York River, to the north, and the James River, to the south. Under the leadership of General George B. McClellan, 121,500 Yankees[1] moved inland. McClellan's intent was to combine infantry power on land with gunboats on the rivers. He believed that the inevitable result would be the fall of Richmond.

Victories at Yorktown and Williamsburg[1a] by the Federals cleared the entrance to both rivers for the warships of the U.S. Navy. On the night of May 3, 1862, the Confederates evacuated Yorktown.[2] Two days later, Williamsburg fell under Union control.

The capital of the Confederacy lay upon the banks of the James River. At the beginning of the Civil War, Richmond was a bustling city of approximately 40,000 inhabitants.[3] Despite its importance as the largest city in Virginia, there were few fortifications around it, and now there was an urgent need to build defensive works in case of a Union attack.

Drewry's Bluff was ideally suited for Richmond's protection. It is located only seven miles south of the city, where the James River becomes fairly narrow. The south, or right bank of the James is a sheer cliff rising about one hundred feet above the water. Perched upon this bank was a small enclosure, a redoubt in military terminology, officially known as Fort Darling. However, as the owner of the property was Augustus Drewry, it had become known as Drewry's Bluff.[4]

Robert E. Lee's eldest son, General George Washington Custis Lee, supervised the placement of heavy artillery pieces at the fort. At the same time, engineers sank ships in the middle of the river as obstructions.[5] As most of the rebels stationed here were navy men, Commander Ebenezer Ferrand was placed in charge. It was hoped that this blockade would prevent Union ships of war from sailing into the Richmond harbor.

Around 6:30 A.M.[6] on the 15th of May, 1862, the Federal warships sailed into view, with John Rodgers in command. The ironclads *Monitor, Galena* and *Naugatuck*, along with the wooden gunboats *Aroostook* and *Port Royal* were determined to concentrate their firepower on Drewry's Bluff, and then pound Richmond into submission. The results of Custis Lee's efforts were about to be tested.

At 7:45 A.M.[7] the *Galena* sailed to within 600 yards of the bluff,[8] its big guns aimed directly at the rebels.

Fortunately for the Confederates, the obstacles in the water were impassable to the large naval vessels. Unable to maneuver in the narrow sections of the James,[8a] the ships would have to fight it out from below the cliffs. The Southern guns roared from the bluff, hitting the ironclad with the first two shots of the battle. The resounding cannon echoed for almost four hours, trading shots along the water, with the Union fleet getting the worst of it. The *Galena* was hit 40 times, and was severely damaged. The *Naugatuck* was put out of action about halfway through the fight when her 100-pounder Parrott gun exploded. The *Monitor* suffered no damage, but her guns would not elevate high enough to reach the Confederates on Drewry's Bluff. When the grayclad cannoneers discovered that they were in no danger, they did not fire on her again. The wooden ships were forced to keep their distance from the artillery on the bluff, and were never a factor in the battle.[9]

Union Commander Rodgers had no choice but to turn his squadron away. All of the hard work of Custis Lee and his small band of engineers had paid off. For the moment, the streets of the capital would be safe from Union gunboats. Although the naval portion of General McClellan's plan to capture Richmond was a failure, the Federal infantry was not yet finished. Within one month, the bluecoats would be staring at the spires of Richmond's churches. Nonetheless, just two weeks after that, McClellan's plans would be in ruins, shattered by Robert E. Lee.

May 27, 1862
HANOVER COURT HOUSE

L. O'B. Branch (CSA)	F. J. Porter (USA)

During the Spring of 1862, the Union Army of the Potomac had undertaken a campaign to force the surrender of Richmond, Virginia. General George B. McClellan had moved his bluecoats along the Peninsula, a narrow strip of land between the York River, to the north, and the James River, to the south.

As the Federals marched further west, they found that the land narrowed as smaller rivers meandered their way across the Virginia landscape. To the south, the Chickahominy River flowed into the James. On the Union right, the Pamunkey River wandered into the York.

The Army of the Potomac contained just over 98,000 men, divided into five corps.[1] When General McClellan reached the vicinity of Richmond, he placed the III and IV Corps south of the Chickahominy. The Union II, V and VI Corps were north of the river, facing southwest. They seemed so close to the Confederate capital, yet were still blocked by the water.[2]

Confederates were gathering at Hanover Court House, 14 miles north of Richmond, and just south of the Pamunkey. If the right flank of the Army of the Potomac were to be secure, McClellan realized that this threat would have to be eliminated.[3] The assignment would go to his favorite lieutenant, General Fitz-John Porter.[4]

General Lawrence O'Bryan Branch commanded a force of some 4,000 Confederates.[5] The graycoats were guarding the Virginia Central Railroad, which was the main artery from Richmond to the fertile Shenandoah Valley.[6]

Branch had his troops posted on the railroad near Peake's Crossing, some four miles southwest of Hanover Court House.[7] The rebels would be outnumbered by approximately three to one.[8]

Rain had turned the dirt roads into a quagmire. On May 27, the Yankees labored through the heavy mud,[9] and at noon[10] reached a Confederate outpost at a crossroads just south of Hanover Court House. The Confederates faced east, while the Federals, with more troops, faced both south and west.[11]

The 25th New York regiment led the way forward for General Porter, and the New Yorkers sustained heavy casualties while the remainder of his force made their way through the mud.[12] There was a sharp fight around the house of Dr. Kinney, a local resident. The contest lasted about an hour, and the Confederates retreated north in the direction of Hanover Court House. Porter ordered a pursuit, leaving the 25th New York behind to guard the crossroads.[13]

At this point, both commanders made errors in judgment. Porter believed that the main body of the enemy lay to the north, and turned the Yankees away from Branch, who was still at Peake's Crossing. Branch did not realize the numerical advantage his adversary possessed, and unwisely gave battle when it would have been wiser not to fight at all.[14]

Under the false impression that the enemy force was a small one, Branch attacked the crossroads. The bluecoats were in trouble, and couriers dashed off in order to recall General Porter. The Confederates surged out from the protection of the woods and into a wheat field, and the Yankees opened fire, dropping the rebels in rows. The Southerners were forced to fall back before the power of the Union guns.[15]

The action soon became a struggle for control of a hedgerow between two fields. Branch's North Carolinians and bluecoats from Maine fired at point-blank range. Suddenly, Porter's troops returned, pouring into the rebels.

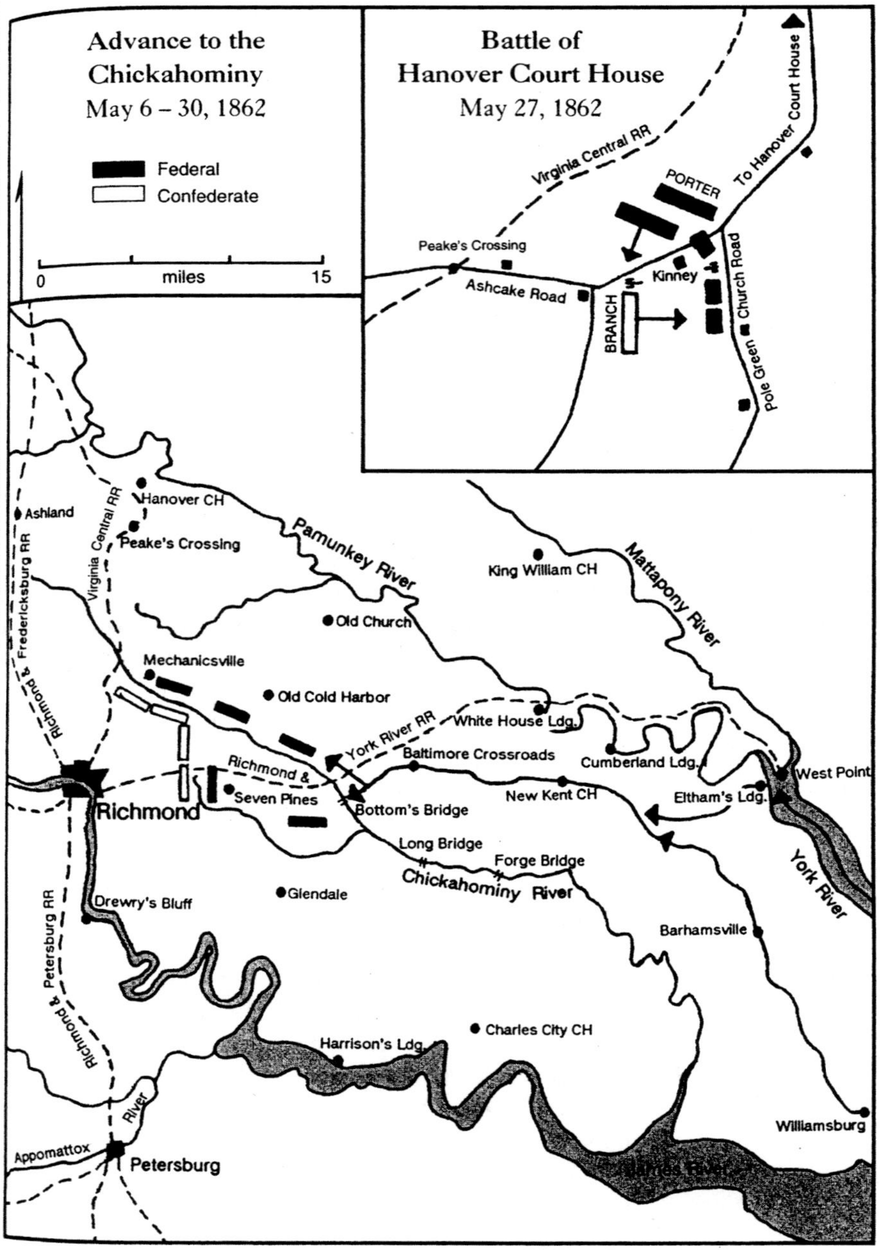

Advance to the Chickahominy, May 6–30, 1862.

The effect was overwhelming, and the Confederates were driven from the field.[16]

Casualties at Hanover Court House went in favor of the Union. While each side lost approximately 285 men killed and wounded,[17] the Confederates had seen 731 of their men captured, whereas Porter had lost only 70 soldiers to the enemy.[18]

On the surface, it would appear that the battle had been a resounding victory for the Union. In reality, Porter's activity against a small band of Confederates had cost the Federals a full week's delay in their attempt to capture the capital of the Confederacy.[19] In the weeks ahead, the Union forces would pay dearly for their failures.

May 31–June 1, 1862
SEVEN PINES (FAIR OAKS)

J. E. Johnston (CSA) — G. B. McClellan (USA)

During the spring of 1862 the Federal Army of the Potomac had launched a grand offensive with the purpose of capturing Richmond. General George B. McClellan had led his bluecoats to victories at Yorktown and Williamsburg.

Joseph E. Johnston had ordered his Confederates to fall back before the Union army, seeking the protection of Richmond's defenses. The numerical strength of the enemy seemed overwhelming.

In front of the Confederates, General McClellan had a force of some 98,000 men.[1] Against the tide of blue, the Confederates could muster approximately 60,000 troops.[2] To the north, at Fredericksburg, the Federals had the I Corps, currently under the leadership of General Irvin McDowell. Assigned to protect the nation's capital, Fredericksburg contained 30,000 Yankees.[3] It was extremely important to the South that these two Union armies remain apart.[4] The combination of McClellan and McDowell would pose an insurmountable obstacle.

With their backs to Richmond, the Confederates decided to attack McClellan before he could affect a junction with McDowell.

The Federal commander had allowed the Chickahominy River, which flowed generally southeast, to divide the Army of the Potomac. The Union II, V, and VI Corps were north of the river. They were commanded by Edwin Sumner, Fitz John Porter and William Franklin, respectively. McClellan had also placed two corps south of the

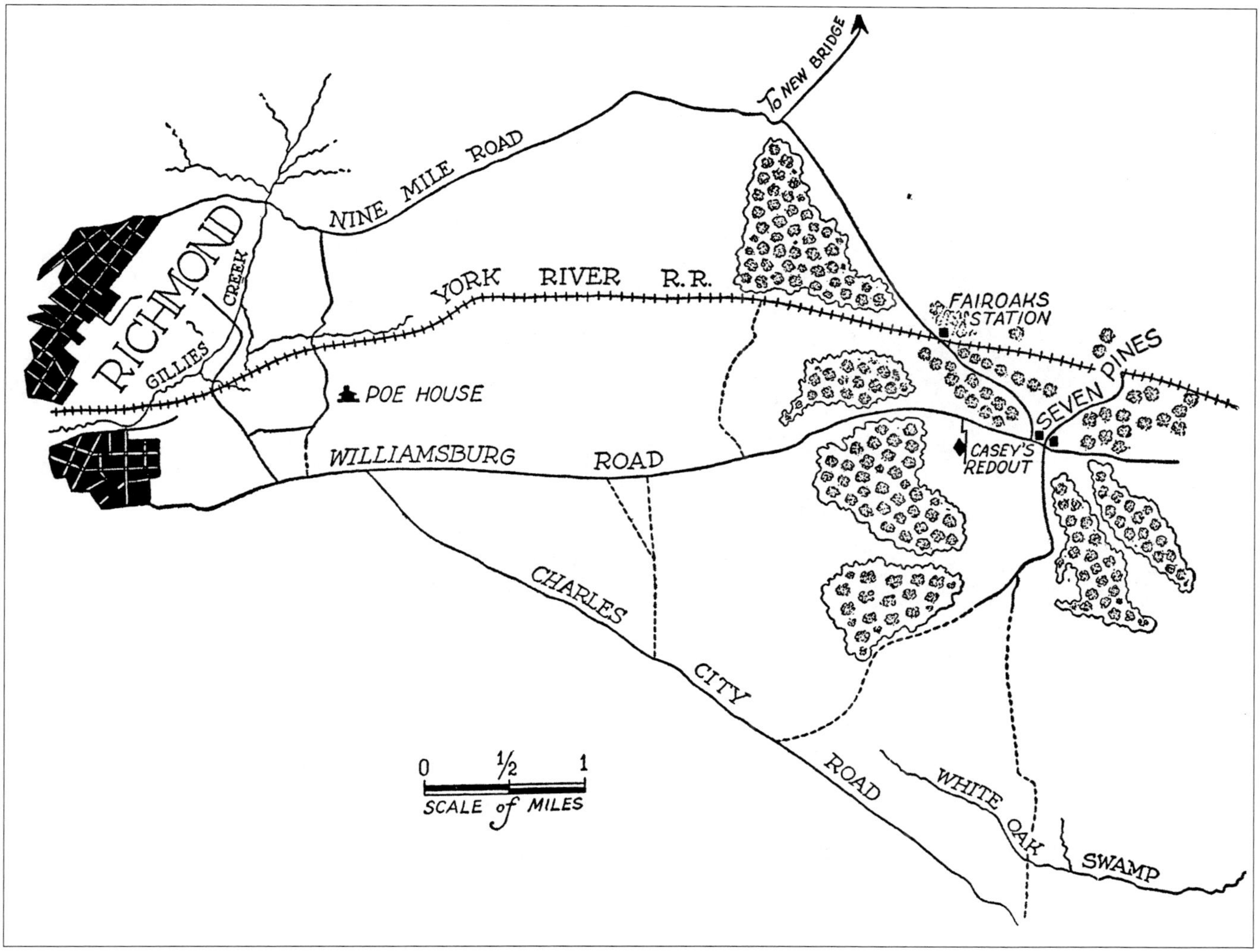

Lines of advance eastward from Richmond to Seven Pines as used for the attempted concentration of May 31, 1862. Map by John T. Draper.

Chickahominy. The III and IV Corps, under Samuel Heintzelman and Erasmus Keyes, were the bluecoats which General Johnston wished to attack.

The Confederate plan was straightforward and very direct. They would attack the enemy in front, while simultaneously striking both flanks of the Union columns.[5] Most of the action would take place between the James River, to the south, and the Chickahominy River, to the north.

General Keyes and the men of the IV Corps would receive the initial attack. The Union III Corps was farther east. Johnston intended to defeat Keyes before Heintzelman could offer any assistance.[6] The Confederates would attack on May 31, at a place called Seven Pines.

There were three main highways which led to the Union position. The first, closest to the Chickahominy River, was the Nine Mile Road. Leaving Richmond, it ran east, then turned southeast to Fair Oaks Station, a stop on the York River Railroad, only six miles from the capital of the Confederacy.[7]

Next was the Williamsburg Road, just over two miles[8] to the south. From Richmond, it ran due east for seven miles until it reached Seven Pines.[9]

The third road was the Charles City Road. Just over two miles east of Richmond, it branched off of the Williamsburg Road, running southeast. As the distance increased between these two roads, the White Oak Swamp arose in between them. This could make communication between the two roads difficult.

Despite the potential hazards, Joe Johnston was confident that the battle plan was sound. The advantage in numbers held by the Union Army of the Potomac had been eliminated by the Chickahominy River. Johnston's plan called for over 51,000 Confederates to take part in the attack, while the Union III and IV Corps combined totaled just over 34,000.[10]

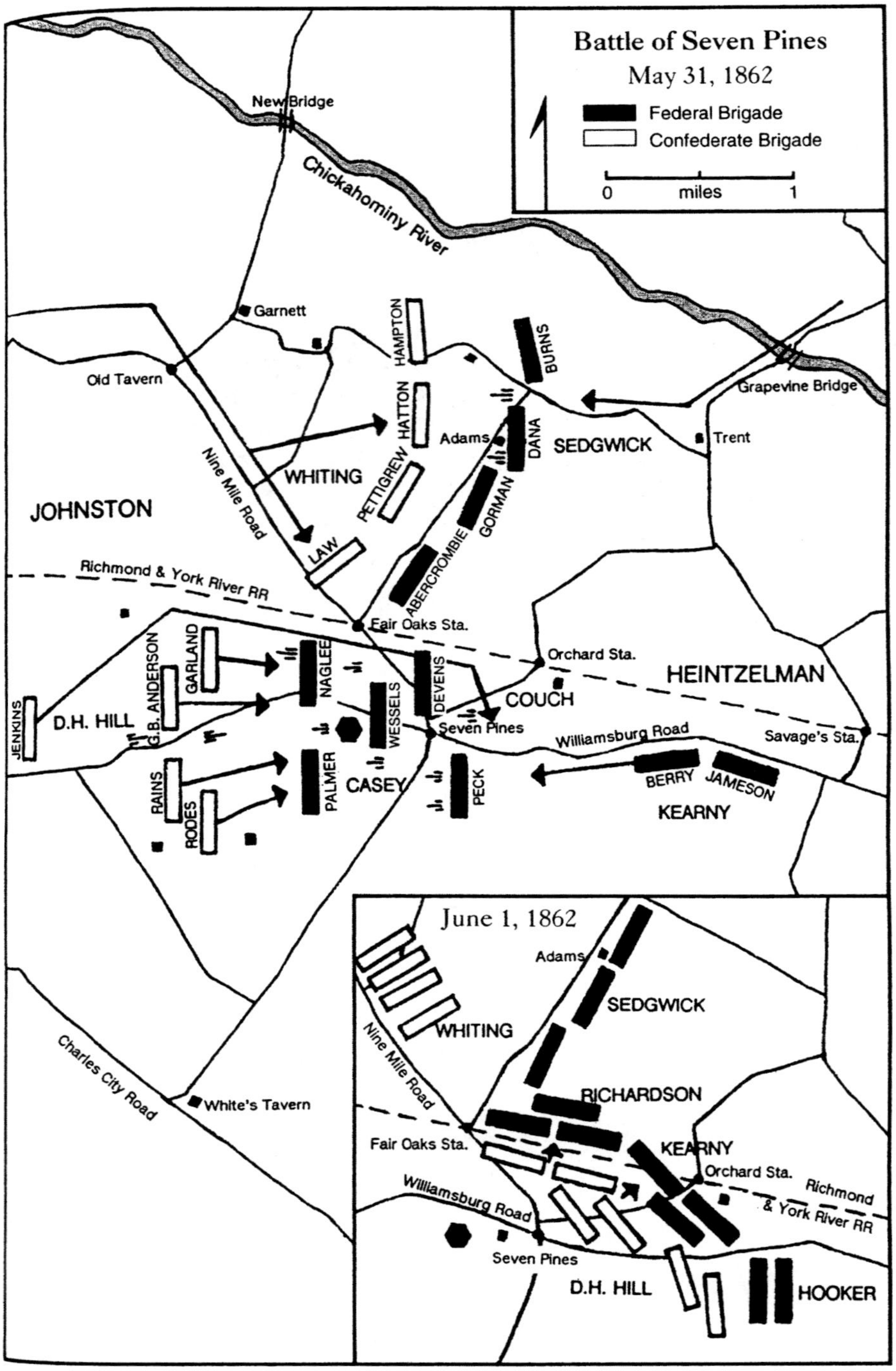

Battle of Seven Pines, May 31, 1862.

The rebels would be divided into two "wings" for the coming assault. Operations on the smaller left wing were under the direction of General Gustavus W. Smith. General Longstreet commanded the powerful right wing, which contained most of the Confederate firepower.

The Confederate plan of attack called for James Longstreet to march along the Nine Mile Road, D. H. Hill to take his men down the Williamsburg Road, and Benjamin Huger's troops to take the Charles City Road. John Magruder's command would be used as a mobile reserve, and would follow Longstreet on the Nine Mile Road.[11] The Confederates were to arrive simultaneously at Seven Pines, and the Union IV Corps would be overwhelmed.

Unfortunately for the Confederates, Johnston's plan was not executed as he had intended. General Longstreet, instead of marching down the Nine Mile Road as ordered, took the Williamsburg Road. This created a large delay in the Confederate advance.[12] The Charles City Road branched from the Williamsburg Road. Unless General Huger had already passed, not only had Longstreet's mistake blocked Hill's division, but Huger was blocked as well.[13]

General Johnston was further hindered by poor staff work. He was some two miles from the spot of the proposed attack, but knew very little of the positions of either his own commanders or their troops.[14] Uncertain of Longstreet's whereabouts, Johnston did know that the Nine Mile Road was empty. Although actually part of General Smith's left wing, the division under General W. H. C. Whiting was close at hand. They could move down the Nine Mile Road and assail the Federals in the right flank.

General Johnston gave the orders, and Whiting's men were soon in motion. On May 31, these troops were about to begin the battle of Seven Pines.

On the Confederate left, Whiting had four brigades at hand. A fifth, under John B. Hood, was positioned on Whiting's right to connect with Longstreet's left. Attacking north of the Nine Mile Road, his graycoats hit the Federals under John Sedgwick. "Uncle John," as he was known to his men, had brought his troops across the

Chickahominy River, and stood squarely in the path of Whiting's advance.[15]

The Southerners gallantly advanced, but were easily repulsed. The assault was not well coordinated, and different commands were sent forward in piecemeal fashion. As a result, the Confederate thrust in this sector was not as powerful as it might have been.[16] Casualties were heavy, and little progress resulted from the attacks on the left.[17]

While Whiting was occupied at Fair Oaks on the Southern left, Longstreet and Hill had struck the bluecoats at Seven Pines on the Confederate right.

At approximately 1:00 P.M. on May 31, D. H. Hill gave the order to attack. On Hill's right, Robert Rodes would lead the attack. However, as Rodes advanced, his Alabama troops became bogged down in the marshy ground between the Williamsburg and Charles City roads.[18]

This delay gave the bluecoats under Silas Casey an initial advantage, but the Southerners quickly overcame their difficulties, and the Federal earthworks were outflanked. The Confederates pushed the enemy backwards, capturing eight artillery pieces in the process.[19]

Some 150 yards[20] behind Casey's original position, the Yankees reformed. Taking cover in the woods, they were determined to stop General Rodes. For a moment the Confederate left was in danger. The graycoats were saved by the King William Artillery, commanded by Captain Thomas H. Carter. The sudden barrage drove the Federals back again, and the Confederate left was secure.[21]

With his left flank out of danger, Rodes sent forward his center and right. In the belief that additional Confederates would protect his right flank, he allowed these men to become exposed in the open ground before the woods. Unfortunately, there was no support on his right flank.[22]

The Federal troops concealed in the woods were not about to let this oversight go unpunished. They opened fire and the graycoats dropped in rows. The Union soldiers were finally forced from the woods, but at a heavy cost in Confederate blood.[23]

On the north side of the Williamsburg Road, the rebels fared no better. Muddy water three feet deep[24] slowed the advance. Commands became entangled, lines overlapped, and as officers fell the organization began to deteriorate.[25]

Despite poor management on the Confederate side, the enemy was gradually pushed back. General R. H. Anderson came forward, dividing his brigade of Confederates. He took command of one column, assigning the other to Micah Jenkins of the Palmetto Sharpshooters. The South Carolinians charged furiously, overrunning the Federal camps and storming two artillery positions.[26] Darkness brought an end to the combat on May 31.

Although the Federals had received the worst of the action on the final day of May, the Yankees had managed to inflict one very important casualty on the Southern side. Joseph Johnston had been observing Whiting's affair at Fair Oaks from a knoll 200 yards north[27] of the train station when he was wounded in the right shoulder.[28] The wound, though not mortal, was a severe one. His services would be lost to the Confederacy for six months.[29]

The conduct of the battle for June 1 would fall to General Gustavus W. Smith. The responsibilities of high command seemed to be too much for Smith's nervous system. Nevertheless, Smith suddenly found himself in command of the Army of Northern Virginia.

Due to hesitation and conflicting orders from General Smith, there was very little action on June 1. There seemed to be an opportunity for Longstreet on the Confederate right, but the attack was feeble in nature and easily repulsed by the Union forces.[30] It was soon apparent to all that the Confederate commander would have to be replaced.

The action at Seven Pines was not James Longstreet's finest hour. With 13 brigades at his disposal, only six were used in the actual assault — two from D. H. Hill and four of Longstreet's own command.[31] Furthermore, due to Longstreet's abandonment of the Nine Mile Road, the attack point was not made at Fair Oaks, where the Federals were most vulnerable, but at Seven Pines, a much stronger defensive position.[32]

The result of the mismanagement on the Confederate right was that despite having more men at the battlefield, the Confederates consistently had fewer troops at the actual point of attack.[33]

The battle had basically been a draw. The Union troops had won at Fair Oaks, and called the battle by that name, while the Confederates had been victorious at Seven Pines, and chose to refer to the action as the battle of Seven Pines. However, the Confederates had failed miserably in both their execution and management of the battle.[33a]

Casualties had been severe for both sides. The Confederates had lost 980 men killed, 4,749 wounded and 405 missing, for a total of 6,134. The Federals had seen 790 of their soldiers killed, 3,594 wounded, and 647 missing, for a total of 5,031.[34]

The Confederate president had been observing the action, as the battle had occurred so close to the Confederate capital. When Jefferson Davis turned his horse back toward Richmond, he realized that he must make a very difficult decision. It would be the most famous decision of his life.

General Johnston was seriously wounded. General Smith was personally courageous, but unfit for high command. The Army of Northern Virginia must have a new commander. At his side was a general who was currently his military advisor in Richmond. As of June 1, 1862, the Army of Northern Virginia would be led by Robert E. Lee.

June 6, 1862

MEMPHIS

J. E. Montgomery
M. J. Thompson
(CSA)

C. H. Davis
(USA)

Confederate policy during the Civil War regarding the city of Memphis is very difficult to understand. It was a large city, located on a major river, and could provide a sound base for offensive operations in Missouri, Kentucky or Tennessee. On the other hand, there were many difficulties which a defense of the city would present. The Confederate States had no navy to speak of. In February, Forts Henry and Donelson had fallen, giving control of northwest Tennessee to the Federals. Two months later the area would be further solidified for the Union with their triumph at Island No. 10. April also saw the graycoats defeated at the battle of Shiloh, due east of Memphis.[1]

In short, the city was surrounded by Union victories. Union dominance of the Mississippi River was increasing. It was simply not possible for the South to maintain possession of the city. Nevertheless, the Confederate government in Richmond would continue to attach a much greater importance to Memphis than was warranted.

Although the Confederates did not undertake a vigorous campaign to occupy the city, they did not altogether abandon the area. A token force of infantry under General M. Jeff Thompson along with a squadron of rams on the Mississippi River would contest any Union advance. The rams were commanded by Captain James E. Montgomery.

This small group of graycoats was not sufficient to prevent a large contingent of Federal soldiers from taking possession of Memphis, yet the resources in manpower were not combined with any other Confederate troops to strengthen an existing command.

This is a good illustration of the policy of diffusion used so often by President Jefferson Davis. He attempted to defend every inch of the Confederacy at the same time, which compromised the defense of each area. Naturally, this policy came under the attack of many Confederate military leaders.[2]

The Union squadron approached Memphis from the north, under the command of Captain Charles H. Davis. At 4:20 A.M. on June 6, the vessels left Island No. 45, about two miles north of Memphis.[3] At 5:40 A.M., the navies clashed in a most unequal contest which would determine the fate of the city.[4]

The two sides bombarded each other in a long-range artillery duel, but the damage was negligible. The Union rams began to turn the tide in favor of the North. The Confederate rams *Sumter* and *General Bragg* were soon disabled and run aground. Two more Southern vessels, the *General Beauregard* and the *General Price* collided. Finally, the *General Thompson* was set on fire by cannon shots from the Union ironclad *Benton*. It burned down to the waterline, then exploded.[5] Only one of the Confederate rams escaped unharmed.

Thick black smoke covered the water, making visibility extremely difficult. Battle reports on the Confederate side were incomplete; however, estimates place their fatalities at close to 100, with perhaps another 100 men captured by the Union navy. The Federal troops suffered minor casualties, and only one man was killed as a result of the action on the water.[6]

Memphis was forced to capitulate. The mayor officially surrendered the city to Captain Davis between 10:00 A.M. and 11:00 A.M., and Union troops occupied the streets before noon.[7]

Possession of the city of Memphis was vital to future operations for the United States government. West Tennessee was now firmly under Union control, and the bluecoats would use the city as a supply base for the campaign on Vicksburg. Although there would continue to be fighting throughout Tennessee, this part of the state would never be recovered.

June 16, 1862

SECESSIONVILLE

N. G. Evans
(CSA)

H. W. Benham
(USA)

While the Civil War raged in Virginia, both sides had forces in the Carolinas as well. If the United States could establish a strong presence in the region, Confederate troops might be prevented from serving in Virginia or Tennessee. From the Southern perspective, it was vital to keep the ports of Charleston and Wilmington open for commerce.

In order to protect the area, the Confederates had constructed a fort near the village of Secessionville, South Carolina, located in the southeast corner of the state. The small inlet next to the fort was armed with a floating battery of artillery. Under the overall command of Nathan G. "Shanks" Evans, the resident commander of the fort was Colonel Thomas G. Lamar.[1]

The Federal troops were stationed just south of Charleston, South Carolina, under General Henry Benham. The bluecoats had taken a position just west of James Island, in wet, swampy ground. Two divisions, led by Horatio G. Wright and Isaac I. Stevens, were assigned the task of removing the troublesome graycoats.[2]

Wright's men were encamped with their backs to the Stono River. Stevens placed his troops a bit farther south. East of Stevens' division and northeast of Wright's Federals lay the Confederate works at Secessionville.[3]

In early June General Benham had been able to silence the floating battery, but Union artillery had not inflicted substantial damage to the Confederate guns inside the fort.[4]

On June 16, Benham ordered 3,500 men from Stevens' division to accompany 3,100 of Wright's men. Between 2:00 A.M. and 3:30 A.M.,[5] the Yankees moved forward into the darkness.

By 3:30 A.M. Stevens' Federals had captured the Confederate pickets who stood guard outside the fort. These Union troops would lead the assault. Wright's division, led personally by General Benham, would follow.[6]

At 4:00 A.M. Colonel Lamar's artillery ripped huge gaps in the swarming lines of blue. The first attack was repulsed within 15 minutes. Shortly thereafter, General Evans arrived with additional Confederate reinforcements. Nevertheless, Benham ordered first a second and then a third attempt to take the fort. Some of the Yankees were able to reach the parapets of the fort, but both attacks were turned away by the Confederate garrison. By 10:00 A.M., General Benham ordered a retreat.[7]

Casualties ran in favor of the Confederacy. The graycoats lost 204 men, while the Union suffered 683 total losses. There were no great repercussions in the Civil War as a result of this minor engagement at Secessionville, but there were significant changes of a more personal nature. Evans praised the work of the Confederate troops, and the fort was renamed Fort Lamar.[8]

Henry W. Benham received sharp criticism by the United States government for his overzealous attack. The Lincoln administration claimed that he had brought on the action in violation of instructions not to instigate a battle. Accordingly, on August 7, 1862, Benham was quietly mustered out of service to the United States.[9]

June 25–July 1, 1862
THE SEVEN DAYS

R. E. Lee (CSA)	G. B. McClellan (USA)

Although he was to gain greater fame in future battles, Robert E. Lee first won the hearts of the southern people during the battles of the Seven Days. At the beginning of the war, General Lee was not well known throughout the South. Working diligently as an assistant to Jefferson Davis, his time was spent in the government offices in Richmond. Dutifully performing all the tasks that were asked of him, he longed for a field command.

At the close of May 1862, General Joseph E. Johnston was wounded at the battle of Seven Pines, and President Davis chose General Lee to command the Confederate forces as of June 1, 1862.

General George B. McClellan had cautiously moved the Union Army of the Potomac, comprising over 105,000 men, to the outskirts of Richmond, his troops only five miles from the capital of the Confederacy.[1] While others feared that the city might have to be evacuated, Lee was adamant that the capital must be defended.[2]

Against a numerically superior foe, the Confederates could count on approximately 85,000 men. These troops of the Army of Northern Virginia were commanded, north of the Chickahominy River, by Thomas J. "Stonewall" Jackson, who was positioned on the Confederate left, with 18,500 men. To his right was his brother-in-law, D. H. Hill, and 9,000 men. In the center, A. P. Hill led 14,000 troops, and on the far right, James Longstreet's division, also 9,000 strong.

South of the Chickahominy, General Lee had John B. Magruder, with 12,000 men, along with Benjamin Huger's 9,000 man division. Stationed on the James River were H. A. Wise's 1,500 men and T. H. H. Holmes's division of 6,500.[3]

In addition, the Southerners had cavalry under J. E. B. Stuart, of approximately 3,000 horsemen, and a reserve artillery section under the command of W. N. Pendleton, which numbered another 3,000 men.[4]

Any attempt to coordinate the movements of so many different commands would have been difficult under the best of circumstances, but during the early stages of the Civil War it was to prove an impossible task. A

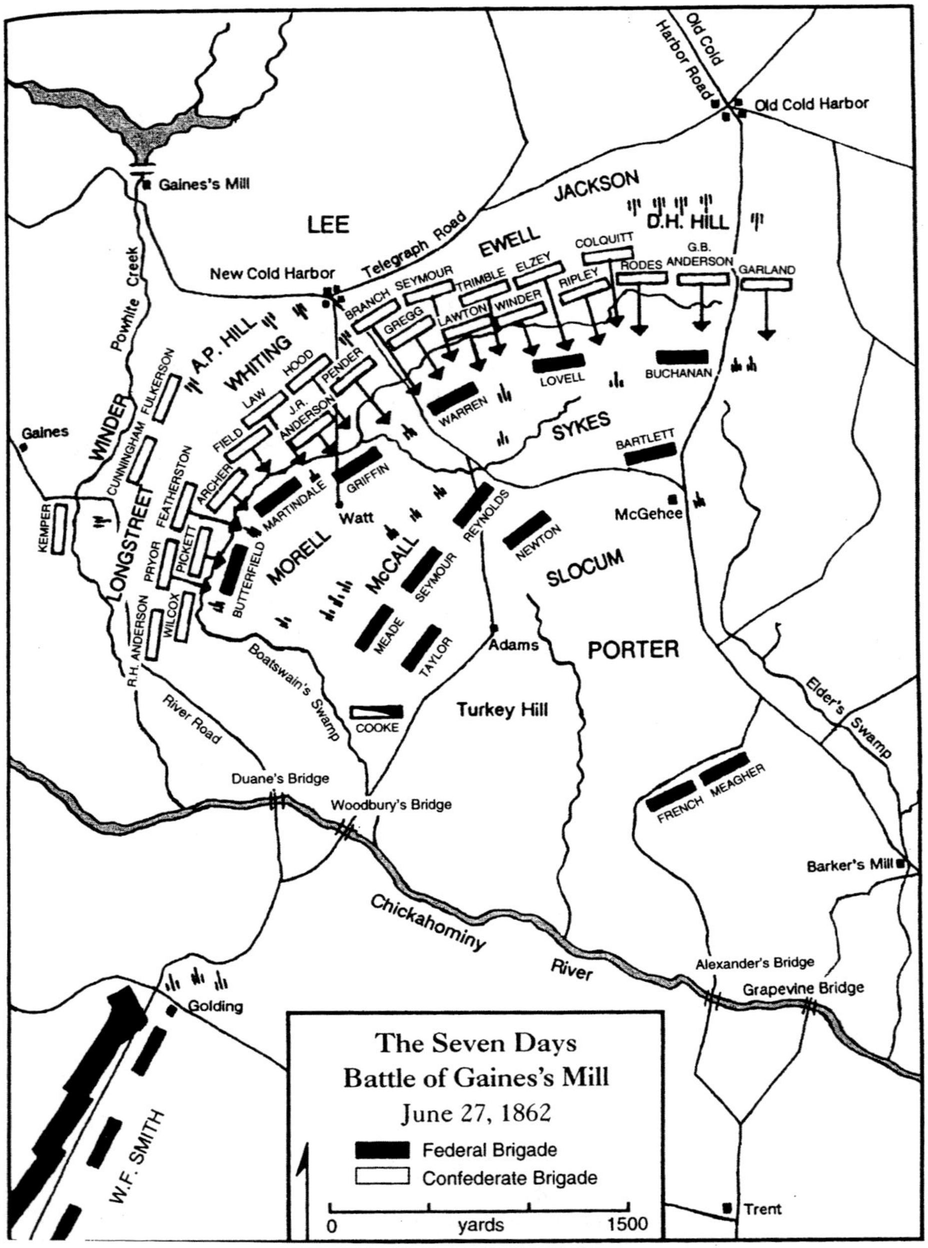

The Seven Days — Battle of Gaines's Mill, June 27, 1862.

battle plan which was too complicated, poor maps,[5] and a general staff which was not large enough to help coordinate so many different forces would contribute to the lack of the complete victory that Lee envisioned.[6]

As the Federals had advanced to the very gates of Richmond, General Lee's overall objective was a simple one: he must drive the Union forces back and eliminate the threat to the Confederate capital. His basic battle plan was to turn the enemy's right flank, and compel him to retreat away from Richmond.

At a council of war on June 23, Lee met with generals Jackson, Longstreet, A. P. Hill and D. H. Hill and outlined his plan of attack.

Because General McClellan had placed his men astride the Chickahominy, the river divided the Union forces. The Federal right wing, which lay north of the river, was the one which General Lee wished to attack.[7] In order to achieve greater striking power, Lee's plan called for some 56,000 of his troops to fall upon McClellan's right. The date for the attack was set for June 26, with the rebel forces converging on a little village called Mechanicsville.

Before this action could get under way, a smaller engagement commenced, just south of the river, on June 25. General McClellan wanted to move forward, along the Williamsburg Road, and occupy the ground in front of the Federal left, opposite Benjamin Huger's Confederates. Orders went out to the aggressive Yankee, General Joseph Hooker, to move his division forward, which started the battle of Oak Grove. In terms of casualties, Oak Grove was just a prelude of what was to come: the Confederates suffered 66 killed, 362 wounded, and 13 missing, for a total of 441. Union casualties were slightly larger: 68 killed, 503 wounded, and 55 missing, for a total of 626.[8]

Although the action on June 25 was not large in terms of casualties, it was significant in the context of the Seven Days, because it was the only battle in which the Union forces fought on the offensive. In each succeeding engagement, it was the Confederates who were to be the attackers.

The following day the battle of Mechanicsville was to illustrate just how difficult it was to connect large bodies of troops together, none of which could see each other. The biggest problem lay on the Confederate left. In Lee's plans for the 26th, Jackson was to turn the Federal right flank and link up with A. P. Hill's left, while Longstreet and D. H. Hill moved northeast up the Mechanicsville

Turnpike, then turned east, attacking General McClellan's favorite lieutenant, General Fitz-John Porter of the Union V Corps.

Of all the Confederate generals, Jackson's line of march was the longest. Due to a late start, he was nowhere to be seen, and A. P. Hill's division was dangerously exposed. Lee had intended for General Hill to hold Porter in place while Jackson rolled up his right flank; however, Jackson had not yet arrived, and Hill's troops rushed in too soon. As a consequence, of Lee's planned attack force of 56,000 men north of the Chickahominy, he was able to get only 11,000 into action, losing nearly 1,500.[9] The Federals, who were able to get 14,000 men into battle, lost 361.[10] The Confederates had paid dearly for their failure to cooperate with one another.

Mechanicsville was Robert E. Lee's first battle in charge of the forces of the Army of Northern Virginia, and his inexperience was revealed. However, there was poor communication among all of the generals involved on the side in gray.[11] While there was particular disappointment in the performance of Stonewall Jackson[12] (the Union victory here would later be attributed by some to Jackson's failure to arrive[13]), General Lee had been able to seize the initiative and achieve his overall objective to drive the bluecoats away from Richmond. Just five hours after the battle had ended, General McClellan decided to begin his retreat.

June 27 found the Union V Corps anchored on a plateau, still facing west, waiting for the oncoming Confederates. To the west and north of the plateau ran a sluggish little stream called Boatswain's Swamp,[14] which slowly made its way into the Chickahominy River. Stationed just behind Boatswain's Swamp, the bluecoats were in a very strong defensive position. The Federal troops were located on the property of a Dr. Gaines, the largest landowner in the area, and as such, the battle became known as Gaines's Mill.[15]

Including infantry, artillery and cavalry, General Fitz-John Porter had assembled 27,160 men in this area.[16] The Confederates advanced in a southeasterly direction, D. H. Hill's division on the left, Jackson to his right. A. P. Hill was to advance down the Telegraph Road, and Longstreet would take the River Road, all converging around Dr. Gaines's property. General Lee hoped that his force of 54,300 men would drive Porter farther away from Richmond.

The Confederate plan of attack at Gaines's Mill was much the same as it had been at Mechanicsville. Stonewall Jackson was to turn Porter's right flank. D. H. Hill was to support Jackson's turning movement, while A. P. Hill and Longstreet were to assail the Union front.[17]

Once again, perfect coordination failed the Confederates. D. H. Hill had managed to get his troops down the road to attack the Yankees, but he was far ahead of Jackson's column. As Hill's men advanced, they came under severe artillery fire from the Union batteries. Not expecting such a rough introduction, General Hill felt it best to wait for Jackson.

On the other side of the Confederate formation, Ambrose Powell Hill began deploying his own men around 1:00 P.M., facing the center of the V Corps, with Longstreet's division to his right, and slightly behind him.[18] At 2:30 P.M., General Hill signaled for the advance.[19]

While the duel was approximately equal in numbers of infantry, the Union artillery had a huge advantage, and it began to tell. Hill's attackers were decimated in a series of attacks, and the rebels were unable to penetrate the position behind Boatswain's Swamp. The casualties mounted for the second day in a row in his division, and the question still remained on the Southern side: where was Jackson?[20]

As Powell Hill was seeing his men get cut down in front of Union artillery, Stonewall Jackson was getting off to yet another poor march. Through a misunderstanding with his guide, Jackson marched in one direction and then retraced his steps. It was not until 3:30 P.M. that his lead division, under General Richard S. Ewell, finally reached the field.[21] Making matters worse, the grayclad troops were sent in piecemeal, thereby losing maximum effectiveness.[22]

Over on the Confederate right, generals Longstreet and A. P. Hill attempted a diversion, to take some pressure away from Jackson's men on the left. Before long, the superiority of the Union artillery posted on the plateau told Longstreet a greater effort was needed to drive Porter's men from their position.[23]

As the light began to slip away, Jackson also knew that the battle must hang in the balance no longer. A concentrated effort could dislodge the stubborn Yankees. While it was common in Civil War battles for men on each side to claim that they had faced "overwhelming odds" when estimating the enemies' forces, the opposing troops at this point in the action were approximately equal.[24] It was almost 7:00 P.M., and Lee was going to throw everything he had at General Porter, in one last attempt to push the Union army away from Richmond.[25]

On the Confederate left, D. H. Hill's men charged valiantly, but became disorganized upon reaching the soggy ground of Boatswain's Swamp, and were unable to maintain their alignment. In the center, Jackson's brigades swelled forward, but they too were broken up by the smoke and dust which lay thick over the battlefield, making it very difficult for regiments and brigades to stay together. To make matters worse, one of Jackson's largest brigades, under General Alexander Lawton of Georgia, had never been in battle before, and did not have the

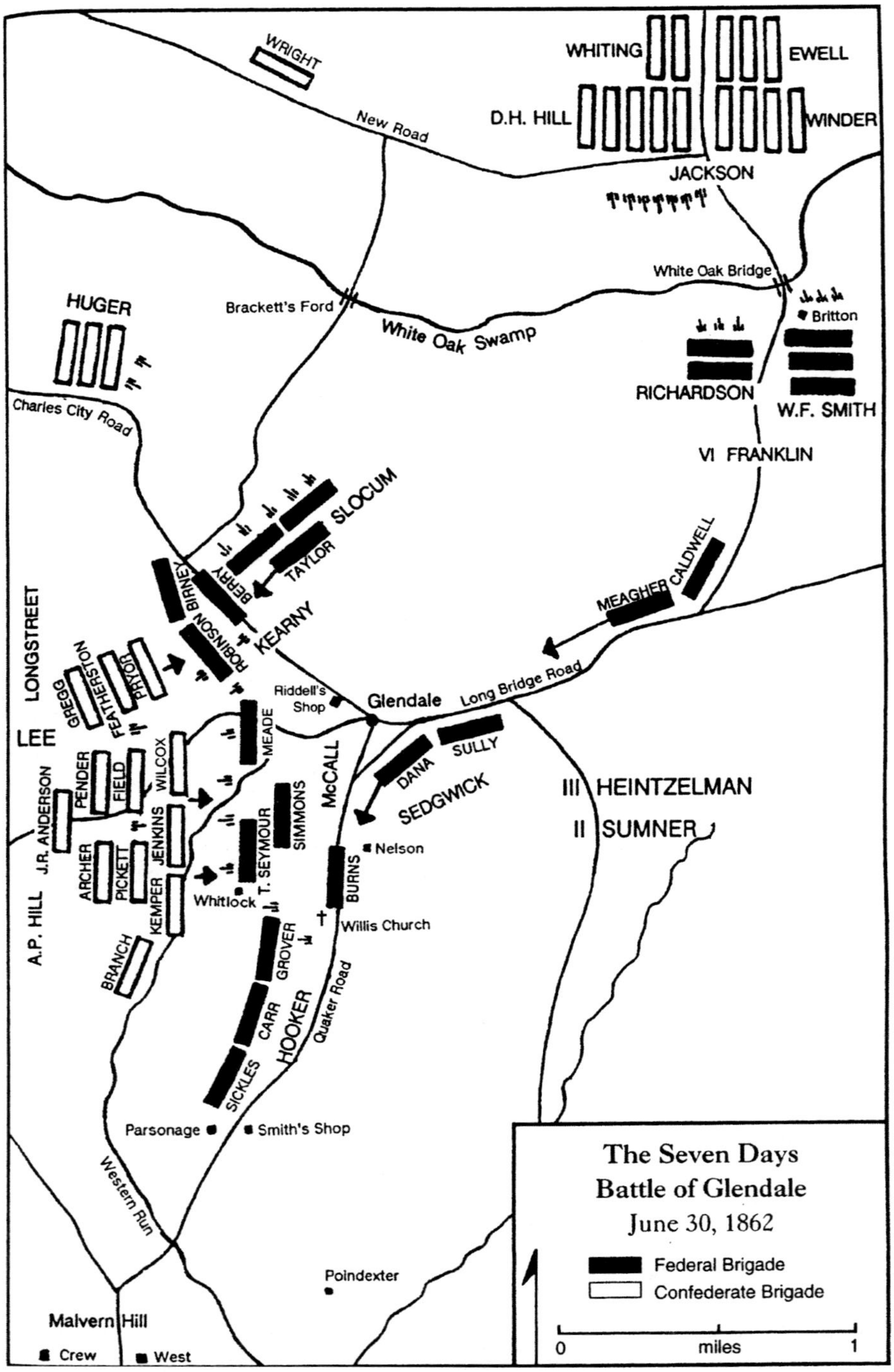

The Seven Days — Battle of Glendale, June 30, 1862.

military discipline of other units. On the right, Longstreet was having problems of his own. As his front was closest to the Chickahominy River, he had to overcome long-range artillery fire from Union forces posted south of the Chickahominy, as well as attack Porter's V Corps, on the north side.[26] As his men stormed up the plateau, they were met with a shower of bullets. It was unsafe to retreat, but even more dangerous to stay where they were, so they charged forward, taking heavy casualties as they went.[27]

The defenders had the advantage of position on all fronts, so there was no room for the Confederates to maneuver. To overcome this, General Longstreet had his men advance without firing a shot, preparing to use the bayonet to sweep the Federals from their front. Longstreet knew that Porter's men would not be able to reload their guns fast enough to stop the swarming rebels. Although the Confederate losses mounted, there were simply too many men for the bluecoats to resist. All along the line General Lee's men broke through the Union ranks, shattering their defenses.[28]

At this point, the Federals had no choice but to retreat. As the Confederates poured after the bluecoats, they set their sights on the artillery pieces forming the first line of defense on the plateau. The Union soldiers resisted stubbornly, but lost ten guns to the onrushing rebels. Before the night was over, nine more guns would be captured.[29]

As darkness enveloped the field, the Confederates could hear the unexpected sound of cheering from the retreating columns of blue. Reinforcements had finally arrived, but unfortunately for General Porter, they were too late to do any good. The brigades of Thomas F. Meagher and William H. French, belonging to General Sumner's II Corps, had crossed the river, but they could only cover the retreat of Porter's men. The firing slowly died away, and the Union forces slipped away into the night.[30]

Gaines's Mill was the largest and costliest battle of the Seven Days. As in all Civil War battles, estimates of casualties vary, particularly on the Southern side. The Confederates had lost 1,483 killed, 6,402 wounded, and 108 missing, for a total of 7,993. Fitz-John Porter lost fewer men: 894 killed, 3,114 wounded, and 2,829 captured, for a total of 6,837[31]; however, he had been driven from the field.

From the Union perspective, General McClellan had been very fortunate not to have lost the entire V Corps. E. Porter Alexander, an artillerist under Longstreet, put it this way: "Had Jackson attacked when he first arrived, or during A. P. Hill's attack, we would have had an easy victory — comparatively, & would have captured most of Porter's command."[32]

There was little action on June 28, as the Federals continued their retreat, moving farther away from their original objective, Richmond, and continuing in a southeasterly direction. There was sporadic fighting as General Porter's troops marched back to the south side of the Chickahominy, and casualties were slight,[33] but it was also a day of planning, especially for General Lee. It seemed as if he had General McClellan in full retreat, but he was not positive what the Union general would do.

General McClellan had three options: he could remain close to the Chickahominy River and try to maintain his railroad connections northward to a place called White House, which lay on the Pamunkey River. This would still afford him the opportunity to place Richmond under siege. Second, he could fall back down the Peninsula which divided the York River, on the north, and the James River to the south. In essence, he would be withdrawing over the land he had fought so hard to take earlier in the spring. The third possibility would be to retreat southward, giving up his defenses along the Chickahominy entirely, and attempting to find a position close to the James River, where he could be protected by the powerful guns of the Federal navy.[34]

Lee reasoned that General McClellan had not rushed toward Richmond during the battle of Mechanicsville or Gaines's Mill, so it was unlikely that he would try it now. It was more probable that the Yankees were heading toward the James. To be sure, he ordered General Ewell's infantry division and General Stuart's cavalry to take possession of the railroad, and to observe possible crossings of the Chickahominy.[35]

Upon reaching White House, J. E. B. Stuart and his horsemen found great stores of supplies on fire, the Yankees hoping to destroy anything which the Confederates might use. Stuart's men were able to salvage some of the provisions, as well as fodder for their horses, but were amazed at the vast quantities of delicacies available to the Union army. Food of any kind was always in short supply for General Lee's men, and the chief of cavalry had discovered pickled oysters, canned ham, and iced lemonade among the wreckage, a veritable feast for Stuart's hungry troopers.[36]

With the information that White House had been abandoned, General Lee realized that McClellan had indeed changed his base of operations. The Union commander was moving southeast in the direction of a small village called Savage's Station.

General Lee wanted not only to liberate Richmond from a painful siege, he wanted to cut off the retreat of the Army of the Potomac and destroy it, thereby winning a complete victory.[37]

In order to accomplish this objective, a vigorous pursuit was needed. There were four roads stretching in a southeasterly direction which General Lee could use to get behind McClellan's men. The direct pursuit was assigned to General John B. Magruder, affectionately nicknamed "Prince John" in the Confederate army due to his stylish dress and theatrical manners. He was to move due east, along the Williamsburg Road, forcing the Yankees to delay their retreat as they paused to fight. General Benjamin Huger, on Magruder's right, was to take the Charles City Road, so as to intercept the Union forces at Glendale. Generals Longstreet and A. P. Hill would march along the Darbytown Road, which would also lead to Glendale, while the southernmost of the roads would be taken by General Theophilus Holmes. This was the River Road, and it led to a point of high ground known as Malvern Hill.[38]

In addition to these troops, Lee had Stonewall Jackson, who still had D. H. Hill attached to his command. They had the shortest distance to march, and were to move due south. They would effect a crossing of the Chickahominy River at Grapevine Bridge, which had been destroyed by the Federal army, and take a position on Magruder's left. Thus, Lee's plans for battle at Savage's Station had Jackson on the left, Magruder in the center, and Huger on the right.[39]

However, once again Lee's best intentions failed to materialize. Benjamin Huger, observing the quiet around 2:00 P.M. on General Magruder's front, sent a message saying that he would continue with his two brigades down the Charles City Road, assuming that Magruder would not require his assistance. Jackson, for his part, had a courier tell Magruder that he would be unable to cooperate, as he had "important duty to perform."[40] Instead of the three-pronged attack which General Lee had planned, John B. Magruder was now facing the Yankees with his men alone.

This left Confederate troops under "Prince John" amounting to only about 14,000 men, facing General Sumner and approximately 26,600 troops.

Not liking those chances, Magruder went forward very cautiously. He could not understand what had happened to Jackson. Stonewall Jackson had once again been unable to move his men forward with the speed which had made him famous during the Valley Campaign, conducted earlier in the spring of 1862. He had simply failed to rebuild the Grapevine Bridge at his crossing point over the Chickahominy River, detaining his entire command.[41]

Huger also failed to grasp Lee's intention to have him cooperate closely with Magruder. As he continued farther down the Charles City Road, he widened the gap between his left and Magruder's right. He seemed to be more apprehensive of an imaginary attack against his rear than in participating in the overall plan.[42]

Magruder was very fortunate that Edwin Sumner had managed the battle so poorly on the Union side. General Sumner had 26 regiments of the II Corps available to him, but managed to put only ten into action.

For his part, "Prince John" was just as cautious, engaging only a small part of the Confederate force. However, in looking at the larger picture, he had accomplished General Lee's overall goal of forcing the Federals to turn and fight, thereby delaying the retreat of the Army of the Potomac.[43] If he could bring General McClellan to battle, there was a chance to capture the entire Union Army.

When nightfall ended the battle of Savage's Station on June 29 at 9:00 P.M., the lack of aggression on both sides was apparent, as each army was in the same position they were at 5:00 that afternoon. Casualties were greater on the Union side, with a total loss of 919 men, as opposed to 444 for the Confederates.[44]

Once again, Stonewall Jackson had failed to do his part. His lack of cooperation and poor staff work from General Lee's assistants had left Magruder at a terrible disadvantage, dooming the Confederate pursuit to failure.[45] Another chance had slipped through his grasp, but there was nothing left for General Lee to do but make his plans for the next day. Despairing about the past would do him no good.

Robert E. Lee had one overriding characteristic: audacity. Although the disappointing results were not entirely Magruder's fault, Lee had unjustly blamed him nonetheless. Dissatisfied with the caution shown at Savage's Station the day before, Lee ordered Magruder to act in support of Longstreet and A. P. Hill, giving the pursuit for June 30 to Stonewall Jackson.[46] General Lee was hopeful that the aggression Jackson had shown in his Valley Campaign would resurface on the way to Glendale. Jackson was to march to White Oak Swamp Bridge, cross there, and attack the Yankees in the rear.[47]

All of the roads along which both armies marched led toward Glendale. It was a small community, originally known as Frayser's Farm. It was of great strategic importance, as the Federal armies had to funnel through the village.[48] If McClellan's men were to escape to the James River, they would have to defend Glendale, and the Union general knew it.[49]

General Lee thought he could bring the Federals to battle at Glendale, and in so doing might capture all of the Union army. This required a two-part approach. He would order the larger part of the Army of Northern Virginia, six divisions of 44,800 men, to attack Glendale from the west, cutting the Army of the Potomac in two. At the same time, Lee would use the four divisions under Stonewall Jackson, 25,300 troops, and move south, attacking McClellan's rearguard. These Union men had been stationed just south of a winding little stream called White Oak Swamp. Their purpose was to prevent any Confederate pursuit, and allow the remainder of the Army of the Potomac to reach the safety of the new base of operations on the James River.[50]

According to Lee's plan for June 30, General Benjamin Huger's division, 12,000 strong, would begin the battle. They had the shortest distance to march, only three miles along the Charles City Road, and had not suffered many casualties thus far in the fighting.[51]

The divisions under James Longstreet and A. P. Hill had crossed the Chickahominy River the day before, and were still seven miles from Glendale, marching east on the Darbytown and Long Bridge roads. Together, this force amounted to 19,200 men, and was under the command of General Longstreet. General Lee had placed Magruder, with his three divisions, which came to 13,600 men,[52] under Longstreet as a reserve in case they were needed.

The opportunity for the Confederates was huge. Two-thirds of the Army of the Potomac still remained in and around Glendale.[53] According to Porter Alexander, there were only a very few times during the war when "we were within reach of military successes so great that we might have hoped to end the war with our independence. ... This chance of June 30th '62 impresses me as the best of all."[54]

By this point in the fighting General McClellan had lost the will to command. His dreams of capturing Richmond had quickly vanished. While his subordinates were trying to save the Union army, he had retreated to the safety of the gunboats on the James River. Aboard the *Galena* he had lost the determination to fight, and the capacity to act. His demoralization was complete.[55]

Located just south of White Oak Swamp, in a very strong defensive position, was the Union rearguard, led by General William Franklin. Facing Stonewall Jackson, Franklin could count approximately 25,200 men under his command, along with six batteries of artillery.[56]

In order to attack General Franklin, Stonewall Jackson needed to cross the thick, muddy White Oak Swamp. This would not be easy, as the horses were sinking up to their stomachs in the awful mire. Jackson summoned Colonel Thomas Munford of the 2nd Virginia Cavalry, to see if he could find a passage across the swamp. Munford rode downstream a quarter mile and discovered a crossing which was uncontested by Federal infantry. A second crossing, not quite as far downstream, was discovered by the cavalry troopers of General Wade Hampton.[57]

Munford and Hampton reported their findings to Stonewall Jackson. Jackson seemed stalemated by the Yankees across the swamp, and issued no orders at all. The full extent of the physical and mental exhaustion which had plagued him throughout the Seven Days was apparent during dinner, as the general finally collapsed in a deep sleep, his dinner still between his teeth.[58]

Although he was hopeful of making great progress the next day, the Confederate troops around Glendale needed him to act immediately.[59] Jackson's inertia proved to be critical during the fighting on June 30. Even if he could do nothing at all against Franklin's men, the most cursory demonstration downstream would have prevented any troops from being sent back to Glendale as reinforcements. As it was, General Franklin was able to release four brigades, amounting to 11,700 men,[60] which were to prove critical in the action opposite General Longstreet.

The remainder of the Federal force was stationed west of Glendale, in an irregular line north to south. The absence of any direction from General McClellan left the Yankees somewhat disorganized, and there were many gaps in the Federal defenses which faced west and northwest, against Longstreet, A. P. Hill, Magruder and Huger.[61]

In the action just west of Glendale, the troops of Longstreet's division moved forward alone. General Huger was obstructed on the Charles City Road, and had effectively removed himself from this part of the battle. Led by Cadmus Wilcox, Micah Jenkins and James Kemper, General Longstreet's three brigades of 4,700 men[62] formed the initial line of assault, running north and south. Longstreet's remaining brigades and the men of Magruder's and A. P. Hill's divisions were close at hand. Opposing the Confederates were parts of the Union II, III, V and VI Corps.[63]

The initial assault hit the Union center. These were the troops of George McCall's division. The Confederates concentrated their striking power in a narrow area, and McCall's command was decimated.[64] The Federals were able to bring up fresh troops to fill the breaks in their lines, but the fighting was so fierce at some points that the stubborn Yankees and onrushing rebels were locked in hand-to-hand combat. With the daylight starting to wane, the battle of Glendale would turn on the strength of reinforcements.[65] The Confederates under General Wilcox were brought forward. In a short time, their efforts decided the contest in the South's favor.[66] The Federals fell back, believing that more Confederate reinforcements were close at hand,[67] and darkness ended the bloodshed.[68]

Casualties at Glendale, also called the battle of Frayser's Farm, were heavy, but close to equal on both sides. The Confederates lost 638 dead, 2,814 wounded and 221 missing, for a total of 3,673. Union losses were 297 dead, 1,696 wounded, and 1,804 missing, for a total of 3,797.[69]

Who had really won or lost at Glendale? From the Confederate perspective, when the day was done, the field was theirs. The Union forces were once again in retreat, heading for Malvern Hill. They had sustained fewer total casualties, and the enemy was moving farther and farther away from Richmond. Yet, it was not the complete victory that Lee had envisioned. His intent throughout the Seven Days was not only to win a battle, but to capture the Union Army in the process. In addition, the overall plan had not been executed. The troops belonging to Longstreet and A. P. Hill had fought valiantly, yet 50,000 men under Jackson, Huger, Magruder and Holmes had remained completely idle.[70] When asked if he thought the enemy might slip through his grasp once again, General Lee's temper uncharacteristically surfaced, as he angrily said, "Yes, he will get away because I cannot have my orders carried out."[71] There was no doubt that he was not pleased with the performances of Jackson and Huger, and a tremendous chance for the Confederates had been missed.

From the Union point of view, the Army of the Potomac had not been cut in two as Lee had desired. The retreat had not been cut off, and even though the Union side had suffered more total casualties, the men in blue had just thwarted Robert E. Lee's best laid plans. Simple survival was a victory of sorts. The campaign would have to move to another field of combat.

As the Federals moved ever closer to the James River, it became clear that the end of the terrible bloodshed might be close at hand. With the Confederates in front and the river at their back, the next battle could determine the outcome of the Seven Days.[72]

Malvern Hill seemed to be a good place to fight, if you were fighting for the Union. Instead of the fragmented dispositions used thus far in the campaign, the Union troops were all located in one place.[73] The terrain was very favorable for defense. In addition, General McClellan had returned from the gunboats, which raised morale as he was very popular with the men in the ranks.

It was not really a hill, but an open plateau which ran just over a mile, north to south, and was approximately three quarters of a mile wide. Situated just under a mile north of the James, Malvern Hill was about 130 feet higher than the river. Turkey Island Creek had two branches, Turkey Run and Western Run, which framed the sides of the plateau. Strangely, Western Run was on the east side of the plateau. While there was some open ground on the surrounding farms, the ground close to

Western Run was densely wooded, with soft, marshy soil. It would be very difficult for onrushing Confederates to charge up Malvern Hill.[74]

General McClellan's main concern was the Union right. He was attempting to move his men down to the James River, to a spot called Harrison's Landing. As he was very worried that General Lee might move around the Federal right flank, cutting off the retreat, most of the Federals were placed on this side.[75]

It was up to General Lee to determine just how to attack these Federals. Although the Federal Army had been continually pushed back farther from Richmond, each day had brought the Confederate leader some measure of disappointment. Lee had not achieved his initial goal, that of the destruction of the Army of the Potomac. His frustration had reached a climax at Glendale, as Lee knew how large an opportunity had been lost.

This frustration colored his judgment, and plunged the Confederacy into a battle that should never have been fought.[76] The overwhelming desire to strike a crippling blow against the Army of the Potomac allowed Lee's natural aggression to dominate his analysis. As a result, he was consumed by only one thought at Malvern Hill: attack!

Robert E. Lee fully appreciated the effects of the fighting at Glendale on the troops under Longstreet and A. P. Hill. Physically, they were exhausted. Any fighting on Day 7 would have to be done by the men under Jackson, Magruder and Huger. Their divisions were fresh, not having taken part in the fighting on June 30.[77]

It was vital to Confederate plans that John B. Magruder cooperate with Stonewall Jackson and Benjamin Huger for a final thrust against the Yankees. Once again, the Confederacy was victimized by poor maps. General Magruder took the wrong road, making a mistake similar to the one Jackson had made at Gaines's Mill. By the time he had corrected the problem, Prince John was over three hours behind schedule.[78]

Jackson, for his part, took up his familiar position on the Confederate left, and D. H. Hill stationed his men on Jackson's right, making up the Confederate center. Lee's plans had called for Magruder to fall in on Hill's right, but as he was not yet on the field, that position went to two of Huger's divisions, commanded by Lewis Armistead and Rans Wright. General Huger, and two of his other divisions, were nowhere to be found.[79] Magruder would have to fall in on the far right when he arrived.

General Lee occupied a central location behind the Confederate lines for his field headquarters, and from this post, he reconnoitered the Confederate left himself. Lee ordered Longstreet to perform the reconnaissance on the right, while keeping his own troops in a reserve role. On the far right, Longstreet discovered a position which he thought could contain as many as 60 artillery pieces. Lee had found a similar position on the Confederate left, under Jackson's command. Both positions were on high ground, the elevation approximately the same height as Malvern Hill, and when massed together, the Confederates would have the Army of the Potomac caught in a crossfire.[80]

After comparing their findings, Lee and Longstreet decided to establish two "grand batteries" which would pour such a destructive fire upon the Federals on Malvern Hill that an infantry assault would be assured of success.[81]

Colonel Robert H. Chilton, Lee's chief of staff, wrote the order for the upcoming attack. Colonel Chilton, as he was to demonstrate throughout the course of the Civil War, was not adept at writing precise orders which were easily understood. Like many of his directives, this order was very vague, creating much confusion. The July 1 battle order read: "Batteries have been established to act upon the enemy's line. If it is broken as is probable, Armistead, who can witness effect of the fire, has been ordered to charge with a yell. Do the same. R. H. Chilton, A.A.G."[82]

This left Lewis Armistead, who was commanding his first battle, to judge the effect of the artillery bombardment and to decide whether to attack or not. The only signal would be the "rebel yell," which might prove to be confusing to the Confederates as well as the Yankees amid the many sounds of a battlefield. Finally, Colonel Chilton failed to indicate the time the orders were sent, which only added to the confusion of the officer receiving them.[83]

While it is unlikely that Robert E. Lee ever saw such a poorly drafted order, it is an indication of the loose supervision he used with his subordinates.[84] However, it was his style to let his generals manage the battles and his staff write the orders. Tight, rigid control was not in his nature.

The devastating crossfire from Confederate artillery was a good plan in theory, but the reality was something very different. On the left, Jackson simply did not have enough guns. Instead of the mass of field pieces Lee and Longstreet had envisioned, Stonewall could manage to bring up only 16 guns. The Union troops facing him had 37, and against such odds the Confederate artillery could inflict little damage. The situation on the Confederate right was just as bleak. Huger had six batteries, only two got into action, and of Magruder's 16 batteries, just two were brought forward. A. P. Hill sent one battery to the right, but the artillery pieces were brought in separately, and in any case this was far from the 60 guns Longstreet had originally envisioned.[85]

The Confederate artillery bombardment was a dismal failure. Units of infantry moved forward at different points along the line, but instead of charging forward in a steady line, there were five separate advances.[86] The Federal sharpshooters had an easy time, and General Lee's men never had a chance against the massed Union guns in such a strong defensive position at Malvern Hill. Charge after charge resulted in rebels falling by the score, and the Confederacy had nothing to show for their fruitless assaults.

Perhaps the most remarkable fact of the battle of Malvern Hill was that it lasted as long as it did. Union artillerist Henry Hunt stated, "the battle was desperately contested, and frequently trembled in the balance."[87] While better management by both Magruder and Huger might have resulted in a Confederate victory,[88] Malvern Hill was unquestionably one of Robert E. Lee's worst conducted battles.[89] The position of the Federals was extremely strong, and should probably never been assailed. Ultimately, the destructive firepower of superior Union artillery was brought to bear. As night fell over both sides and the cannon grew quiet, the Confederates were left to count the losses of a costly repulse.

Casualties for the Army of Northern Virginia at Malvern Hill were severe — 869 killed, 4,241 wounded and 540 missing for a total of 5,650. The Army of the Potomac lost 314 killed, 1,875 wounded and 818 missing — a total of 3,007.[90]

Malvern Hill was, in the narrow sense, a staggering defeat for General Lee. However, viewed in the larger perspective, he had accomplished his mission. Despite the victory which the Union had won on July 1, General McClellan issued the orders to retreat. His dream of taking Richmond had been dashed, and he was now moving backward.

For the entire campaign, the Confederate losses came to 3,286 dead, 15,909 wounded and 946 missing, or a total of 20,141. On the Union side, there were 1,734 killed, 8,062 wounded and 6,053 missing, for a total of 15,849.[91]

Throughout the Seven Days, the Confederates had been plagued by poor communications and vague orders from General Lee. This was his first battle in charge of the Army of Northern Virginia, and it was not the fighting machine it would become later in the war. Each day one general after another failed to perform up to Lee's expectations. When one considers that the Seven Days were fought in the early stages of the Civil War, the intricate, complex plans of attack demanded too much. Their maps had been poor and they were operating in unfamiliar country. The obstacles to Confederate success were many, and heavy casualties were the result of desperate assaults, but when the fighting was finished the Federals were heading for the safety of Harrison's Landing, and Richmond was saved.

To the reader, the only question which may remain lies in the physical condition of Stonewall Jackson. He had won great fame during his Valley Campaign of 1862, and would be immortalized for his performance at Chancellorsville in May 1863. Why had such an accomplished general, at that time the most famous general in the Confederacy, performed so poorly?

The answer appears to be in the degree of clinical exhaustion, which is today termed battle fatigue, from which General Jackson was suffering. He had been riding, marching or fighting almost continuously since March, 1862. By early June, the effects began to show. On his route to link up with the Army of Northern Virginia, he had had little or no sleep for an extended period of time. Most sources[92] attribute his poor showing at the Seven Days to his tremendous physical exhaustion at that time.

August 9, 1862
Cedar Mountain

T. J. Jackson (CSA)	J. Pope (USA)

Seventeen freight trains creaked over the dilapidated tracks of the Virginia Central Railroad. The cargo this July was 11,000 Confederates[1] under the command of Thomas J. "Stonewall" Jackson. They were headed west from Richmond to Fredericks Hall, located in the Piedmont region of central Virginia.[2] Opposing this ragged band of rebels was Union General John Pope, with approximately 17,900 men.[3] They appeared ready to strike the Virginia Central at any moment. Pope had two army corps at his disposal, the II Corps under General Nathaniel P. Banks, and the III Corps under General Irvin McDowell. The Federals had placed 11,000 additional troops at Fredericksburg with about 500 cavalry.[4] It was imperative that Jackson prevent these two forces from uniting.

Jackson moved part of his army to the vicinity of Gordonsville on July 19. It was the most important town in the area, and he realized it must be secured.[5] While the next week was spent resting the men and horses of the Confederacy, good news was received on July 27 in a letter from Robert E. Lee. Reinforcements were on the way, possibly as many as 18,000 men.[6] They would be led by Ambrose Powell Hill. A. P. Hill was an excellent fighter in combat, and his fine troops would be an asset to any command. By the first week in August he had arrived at Stonewall's headquarters.

On August 5, John Pope had devised his plan of attack. The Federals were stationed at Culpeper, which was due north of Gordonsville. Pope would move south to the Rapidan River, and then make a demonstration with the Union right toward Charlottesville. This feint was designed to give Stonewall Jackson three options: he could fall back from Gordonsville to protect Charlottesville, he could send part of his army back to Charlottesville, thereby weakening the force in front of Pope, or he could move northward and fight on terrain unfavorable to the Confederacy.[7]

However, Stonewall Jackson was not a general who would simply do as his enemy wished. On August 7, he led his grayclad veterans northward, but to fight when and where he chose. The Confederates had only three divisions, led by Richard S. Ewell, A. P. Hill and Sidney Winder. These were the best troops in the South,[8] and Jackson had great confidence in them.

The flaw in the Union plan lay in the deployment of their troops. Their left was encamped around Fredericksburg; the right was at Sperryville, 55 miles to the west.[9] When General Banks was ordered to move out from Culpeper, he would be isolated. Jackson intended to concentrate on Banks, defeating him before reinforcements could arrive.

The Confederates marched northward eight miles, stopping for the night around the county seat of Orange. Jackson issued the marching orders for August 8. Ewell was to take the lead, followed by Hill and Winder. At this point, a curious turn of events occurred. Jackson changed his mind, sending an aide off with verbal orders for Richard Ewell. General Ewell was to split apart from the rest of the Southerners, and after crossing the Rapidan, would reunite with the other divisions at a place called Barnett's Ford.[10]

As the morning dawned on August 9, Culpeper was still eight miles away. The lead brigade of Ewell's division, commanded by the irascible Jubal A. Early, approached a fork in the road. The left went northwest to Madison, and the right veered in a northeasterly direction to Culpeper. In the middle of the "Y" was a clump of woods. "Old Jube," as he was affectionately called, could see Yankee cavalry on a ridge up ahead. General Early called up a battery of artillery, which scattered the horsemen, but received cannon fire in return from behind the ridge.[11] General Banks and his Union infantry were not far behind.

The topography influenced Jackson's plans. The dominant feature of the area was Cedar Mountain. Cedar Creek flowed around the base of the mountain, giving rise to the name, although many of the locals referred to it as Slaughter Mountain.[12] The undulating ridges covered the Confederate right and the Union left. General Ewell was to send his two remaining brigades, led by Isaac Trimble and Henry Forno, over the mountain and turn the Federal left. Early would take his brigade and continue up the Culpeper Road. Winder had orders to support Early, but in addition, he was to extend the left of the rebel troops to be able to get around the right flank of the bluecoats.[13] While this would leave the front slightly concave, the artillery on each flank could aim their field pieces in a converging fire on the Yankees.

Stonewall Jackson decided to occupy Banks with Jubal Early in the center. Trimble and Forno would strike the Federal left, while Winder attacked the Union right at the same time.[14] However, Jackson did not make an adequate reconnaissance, and was not fully aware of the position of his foe.[15] This oversight would almost cost him the battle.

Jackson's troop dispositions were predicated on all of the bluecoats being on the east side of the Culpeper Road. They were not. As the cannon roared that August afternoon, Jubal Early began to receive fire from an unexpected direction: his left. To make matters worse for him, as Trimble and Forno crept around the Federal left, a gap developed between Early's right and their left. Old Jube was clearly in trouble. Fortunately for the Confederacy, Stonewall Jackson saw it. He sent orders to Powell Hill to come to Early's aid with the utmost speed.[16]

The Federals were swarming around Early's men. On the Confederate left, the valiant Sidney Winder had been mortally wounded. Leadership would fall to the senior brigadier, William Taliaferro. This was a most difficult time to change command.

Jubal Early had stubbornly managed to keep his lines from breaking, but at 5:45 P.M. Banks sent three more regiments and part of a fourth to assail the Jackson's left. Although Banks could have sent in more men than he did, the Federals found a seam among the exhausted rebels and burst through it, using the weight of numbers to drive the graycoats back. The Yankees managed to get behind Taliaferro, forcing him to pull his Confederates back. As he did so, Early's left became exposed to the swarm of Union men.[17]

It seemed as though Stonewall would be outflanked. He searched the battlefield for help. Through the roar and dust rode a red-shirted horseman at the head of fresh troops. It was A. P. Hill. His men rushed to the rescue of the Confederate left, as "Little Powell" directed horses and artillery into position.

With the reinforcements now at hand, the Confederate left and center began to stabilize, but the enemy had one more charge left in them. The 1st Pennsylvania Cavalry sent 164 troopers storming southward, determined to break through Early's lines. They rode straight into the Southern artillery, which unleashed a furious barrage of canister. The Pennsylvanians turned around in a hasty retreat; 93 saddles were empty.[18] This typified the Union failure of the day.

A. P. Hill had turned the tide in the favor of the Confederacy. With the left and center secure, General Ewell ordered Trimble and Forno to attack the Federal left. The Federals were in trouble, and their lines were caving in on all sides. However, a simple victory would not suffice for Stonewall Jackson. Now was the time to vigorously pursue the enemy. With good fortune, Hill's men could drive the bluecoats all the way back to Culpeper. Darkness, dust, heat and fatigue were just too much for the men in gray.[19] Jackson was forced to let his exhausted men camp for the night.

Although Cedar Mountain was a clear victory for the Confederates, there was a price to pay. The rebels had lost 223 men killed, 1,060 wounded and 31 missing, for a total of 1,314. On the Federal side, there were 314 dead, 1,445 wounded, and 622 captured, for a total of 2,381.[20] In addition, the Confederates had possession of the battlefield.

This was a battle the Confederacy should have lost. Jackson had not made a proper reconnaissance of the area. He had allowed his left to be unprotected or "in the air."[21] Finally, in uncharacteristic fashion, he had failed to exercise control over his troops.[22] Banks, while not using his men as judiciously as possible, had still managed to turn Jackson's left flank. He had enough troops to repel a Confederate assault, but not enough for a successful attack. A greater concentration of Union force in this area could have routed the Confederates.

Despite the somewhat lackluster performance of Stonewall Jackson, A. P. Hill had been very solid, and Jubal Early had been excellent, holding his men firm under tremendous pressure. Were it not for the heroics of these two men, the outcome of Cedar Mountain would have been very different indeed.

August 14–October 8, 1862
The Kentucky Campaign

E. K. Smith	D. C. Buell
B. Bragg	(USA)
(CSA)	

Like Maryland and Missouri, Kentucky was called a "border state." Although it never actually seceded from the United States, there were many Kentuckians fighting on each side. Politically, it was evenly divided. Governor Magoffin supported the Confederacy, while the state legislature was equally split.[1]

President Abraham Lincoln placed a very high value on Kentucky. He felt that it was vital to the preservation of the Union.[2] The loss of the state would place the Confederates on the Ohio River, and invasion of Illinois, Indiana, or Ohio would be a simple matter. On the other hand, firm Union control of the Bluegrass State would offer President Lincoln's men entry into Tennessee.

During the spring of 1862, the Confederacy had suffered a number of military reversals.[3] The graycoats desired to regain their lost territory

The Confederates had divided their forces into two wings, under the overall command of General Braxton Bragg. Edmund Kirby Smith took the right, or east wing north from Knoxville, Tennessee, on a march in the direction of Richmond, Kentucky. From central Tennessee, Bragg headed north toward Louisville.[4]

Far to the west of Bragg's troops, Union General Don Carlos Buell's Army of the Ohio marched north from Nashville. The Kentucky campaign would become a race between the opposing forces.

By the end of August, Smith's 10,000[4a] Confederates had crossed the state line and advanced close to Richmond. Smith sent a division forward under Patrick Cleburne. On August 29, Cleburne's troops ascended Big Hill, over 60 miles[5] north of the Tennessee line. The rebels then headed north on the road to Richmond.[6]

Confederate cavalry under Colonel John Scott found the enemy located at Kingston, five miles south of Richmond.[7] General Smith decided to attack immediately.[8]

Cleburne's division would lead the assault for the rebels. At 5:00 P.M.[9] artillery was heard, but the precise location of the Federals was still unknown. The Confederates halted, and began to form their lines of battle. It was after dark when the final arrangements were completed.[10]

Union cavalry charged the rebels, but the footsoldiers quickly dispersed the foe. Sharpshooters from the 48th Tennessee regiment were pushed forward, and the grayclad infantry returned with 30 prisoners and several horses.[11]

At daylight on August 30th[12] Pat Cleburne led his troops forward to locate the Federals. The Union soldiers were camped about half a mile north of Kingston.[13] Facing south along the Richmond Road, the Northerners awaited the attack.[14]

The Confederates deployed behind a low hill which ran parallel to the Federals, some five hundred yards to the south.[15] For over two hours the artillery exchanged salvos, as the Union infantry attempted to move around the Confederate right flank.[16]

Kirby Smith arrived upon the field, bringing with him additional reinforcements. In a mirror image of their opponent, the Confederates decided to assault the Union right, and began massing troops in that sector of the field. Union General Mahlon D. Manson seemed to

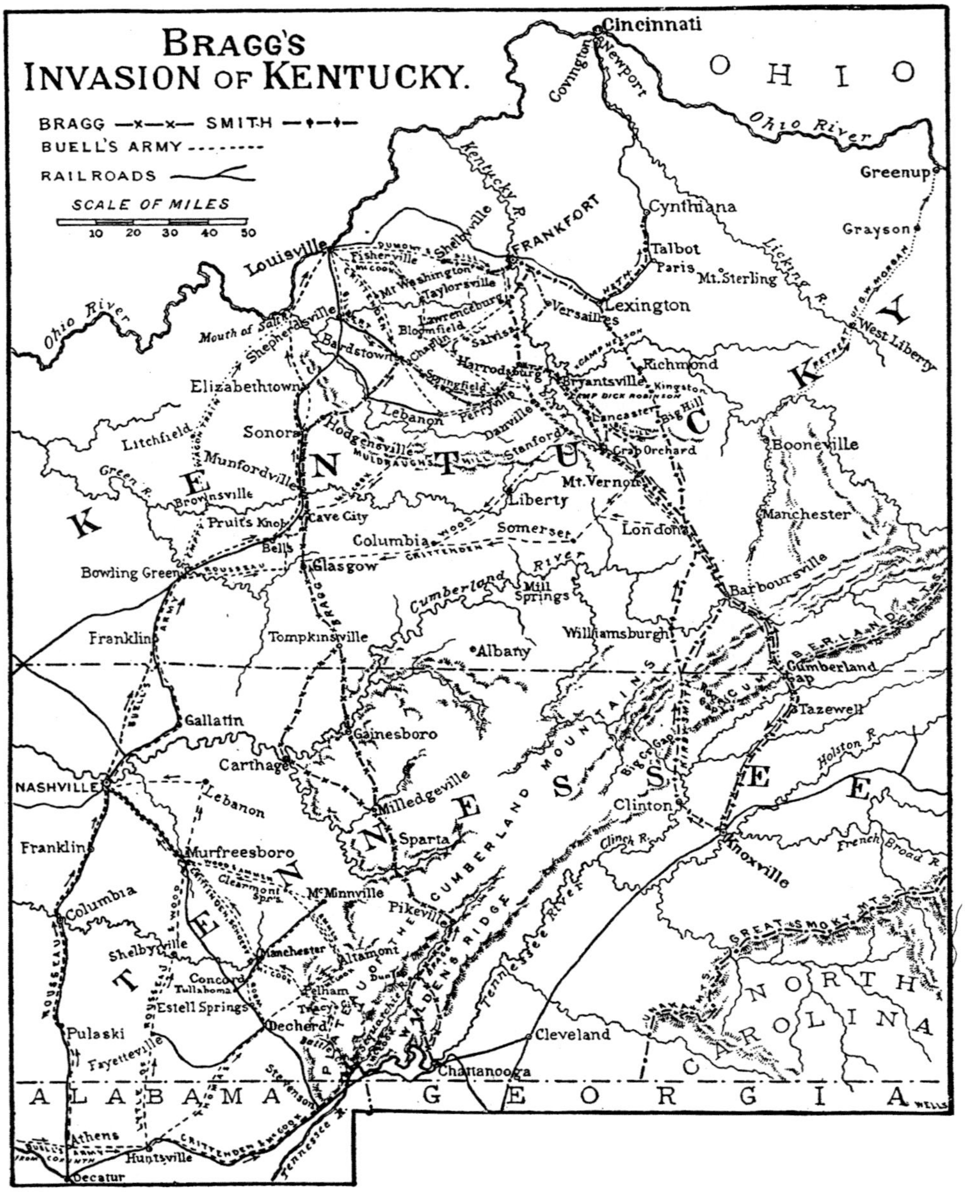

Bragg's Invasion of Kentucky. Map by Jacob Wells.

ignore the Confederate movement, still intent on the other flank.[17]

General Cleburne realized that the heavy concentration by the enemy against the Confederate right flank would weaken the enemy center. He devised a simple plan to defeat the opponent. When the rebels opened fire on the right, other troops would attack in the center at the same time.[18] As he was arranging the Confederate artillery and checking on the alignment of his brigades, a Union bullet ripped through Pat Cleburne's cheek. Although the wound was not a fatal one, the inability to speak left him temporarily disabled. Colonel Preston Smith would assume command of the Southern forces.[19]

The Confederates moved forward on both sides of the road to Richmond. Pressing the enemy steadily, the graycoats swarmed through the town. The Federals withdrew, leaving Richmond in Southern control. The rebels pursued the foe three miles farther, but the chase yielded no meaningful results.[20]

Despite his wounding, Pat Cleburne had won the day for the Confederacy. Kirby Smith reported 78 men killed, 372 wounded and 1 missing, for a total loss of 451 soldiers. The Federals lost 206 killed, 844 wounded, and 4,303 captured, for a total loss of 5,353 men.[21] Union General William Nelson, the district commander, was wounded, and General Manson was captured. In addition, the Confederates took nine artillery pieces, 10,000 stands of small arms, and a large quantity of supplies.[22]

Shortly after the battle of Richmond, the Confederates under General Harry Heth arrived to join Kirby Smith. The troops pushed northward, to the vicinity of Lexington. This forced the evacuation of Cumberland Gap, which had been in Federal hands.[23]

While Kirby Smith was moving through Kentucky, Braxton Bragg had not been idle. He had organized his 30,000 troops[23a] in Chattanooga into two wings. The right wing would be under Leonidas Polk, while the left would be commanded by Joseph Hardee. The Federals headed north from Nashville. Don Carlos Buell was determined to catch Braxton Bragg. Although the adversaries were starting from different points, both men were headed in the direction of Louisville. Which side would get there first?[24]

On September 14 the bluecoats arrived in Bowling Green, Kentucky. General Buell then changed direction, moving 50,000 men[24a] in a northeasterly direction toward the small town of Munfordville, about 45 miles north[25] of the Tennessee line. Confederate cavalry under Joseph Wheeler blocked the road, and reported the presence of the enemy to General Bragg. James Chalmers led his rebels forward on the morning of the 14th, but was easily repulsed by the Union forces already stationed in Munfordville. At a cost of only 37 men, the Northerners had inflicted 337 casualties on the Confederates.[26]

The Southerners surrounded the enemy, and at 9:30 A.M., General Chalmers demanded that the garrison surrender.[27] Union Colonel John T. Wilder refused, and the small Kentucky outpost remained under siege.[28]

The Confederates attempted to strengthen their position. General Bragg moved General Polk's men around the Federals, placing his troops behind the foe. General Hardee's corps remained in front of the town.

By September 16, all of the dispositions were ready. At 6:00 p.m Bragg again asked for the capitulation of the Union forces. This time Wilder hesitated, and asked for more time. Under a flag of truce, the Union colonel met with the Confederates. After he had seen the Southern infantry and artillery, Wilder realized that he was in a hopeless predicament.[29]

On September 17 the siege of Munfordville was lifted. The Federals reported 15 men killed, 57 wounded, and 4,076 prisoners, for a total loss of 4,148.[30]

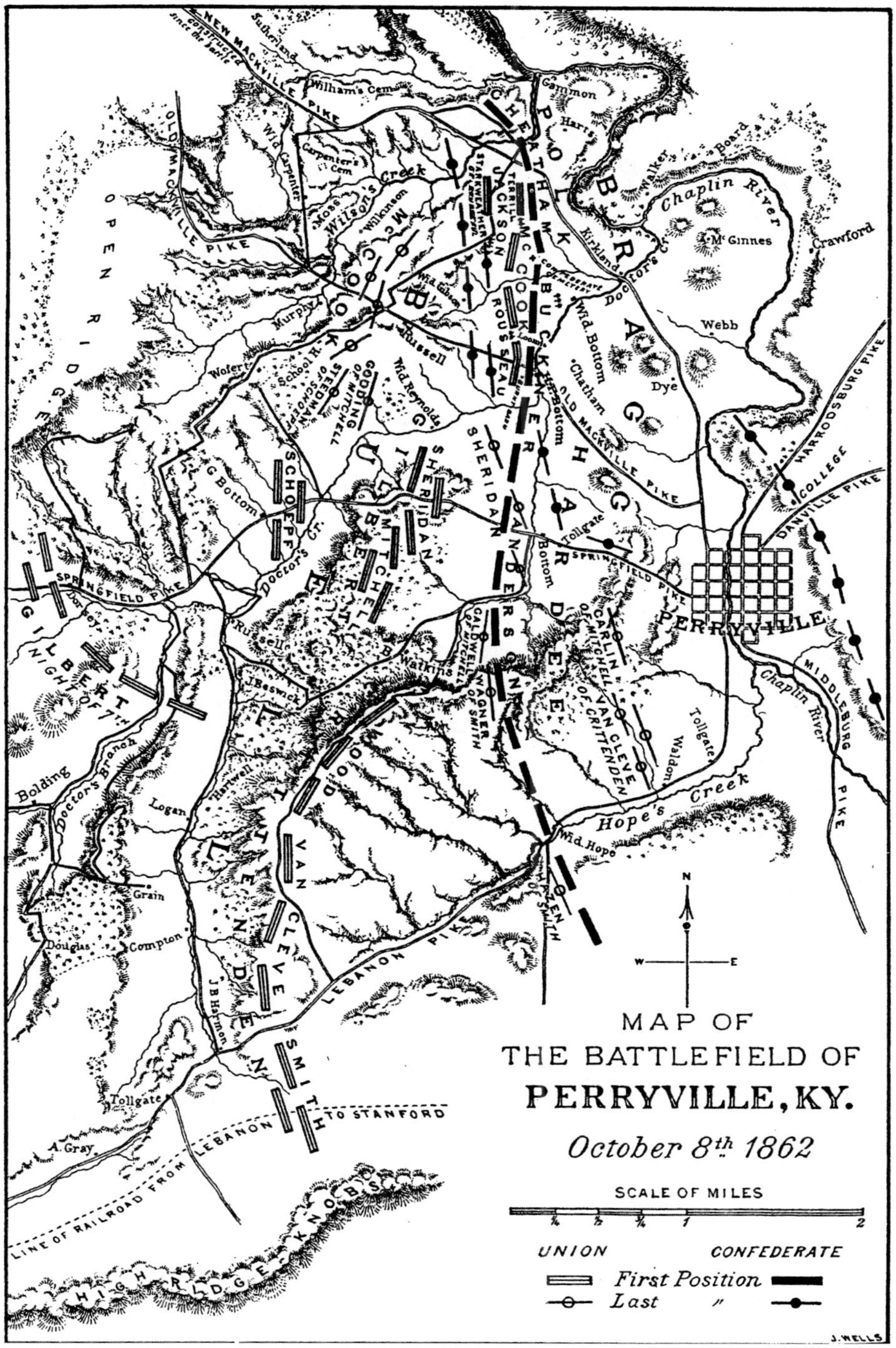

The battlefield of Perryville, Kentucky, October 8, 1862. Map by Jacob Wells.

While the month of September had been a success for the rebels, there was still work to be done. The troops in Munfordville had been captured, but General Buell was still at large. It would be wiser to consolidate the forces of Bragg and Kirby Smith before undertaking a major offensive. In addition, the delay over a small village had prevented the rebels from reaching their true goal, which had been the capture of Louisville.

Buell marched his men northward toward Louisville, with no opposition, while Bragg led his graycoats to the small village of Bardstown, just south of the enemy. The Federals would be able to rest and reorganize their forces, and Buell might be able to gain reinforcements from troops currently stationed in Cincinnati. Bragg wished to unite the separate Confederate commands. The next battle would take place in a small town called Perryville.

October 1 saw General Buell leave the confines of Louisville, and the chase resumed. Could he intercept Bragg before the Confederate commander united with Kirby Smith?

The Union infantry was organized into three army corps, each containing three divisions. On the Federal left was the I Corps, under Alexander McCook. These men were ordered to proceed through Taylorsville. In the center, Thomas Crittenden led the II Corps through Mount Washington. The III Corps was under the command of Charles Gilbert, and they would take the road through Shepherdsville and make up the Federal right wing.[31]

Braxton Bragg spent the first week of October moving east, attempting to join forces with General Smith. The Federals must not be allowed to attack each Confederate army separately. Accordingly, General Bragg headed in the direction of Perryville.

By October 7, the Federals approached the town. McCook still held the left, but Gilbert's troops had shifted to the center, and Crittenden took position on the right.[32]

Perryville is located approximately 70 miles[33] southeast of Louisville. The graycoats took up a position slightly west of town, facing west. Joseph Hardee's troops were on the left and Leonidas Polk's men held the right.

The battle plan was to turn the left flank of the Army of the Ohio.[33a] At about 1:00 P.M. on October 8, the Confederates attacked.[34] B. F. Cheatham's division struck the Union left, supported by Simon Buckner's troops. On the left, Bushrod Johnson's men led the advance. Pat Cleburne had recovered from his wounds at Richmond, and moved forward on Johnson's right.[35]

The Federals took shelter behind strong fortifications along a ridge. Buell's troops poured a destructive fire into the advancing Southerners.[36] However, the Southerners held their ground, and slowly the Northern lines were pushed backwards.

As soon as the Yankees fired their muskets the rebels were upon them. The blue line broke in disarray and although the rebels attempted to pursue, darkness covered the field.[37] It had been a bloody struggle, but the gray lines had surged forward almost a mile.[38]

Casualties had been severe for such a small contest. The Southerners lost 510 men killed, 2,635 wounded, and 251 missing, for a total of 3,396. The Army of the Ohio had seen 845 troops killed, 2,851 wounded, and 515 captured, for a total loss of 4,211.[39]

The battle of Perryville was not a particularly well-managed affair by either side. The Confederates were able to get only 16,000 troops into the struggle, while the Federals left Crittenden's command almost completely unengaged.[40]

This action closed the inconclusive campaign for control of Kentucky. Despite Confederate victories in the field, the state remained neutral. The additional recruits to the armies of the Confederacy simply did not materialize. The Civil War would shift southward again, and by the end of the month both armies were back in Tennessee.[41]

August 28, 1862
GROVETON

T. J. Jackson (CSA)	J. Pope (USA)

In late August the Federal troops were centered around Manassas Junction. The large Union supply depot was filled with military supplies and foodstuffs of all kinds. Such a large quantity of stores were a very attractive prize for hungry Confederates.

Commanded by General John Pope, the Yankees were not far from Washington, D.C. Posing additional difficulties for the Confederates was the proximity of another Union army. Reinforcements for General Pope were close at hand. General George B. McClellan's Army of the Potomac could merge with Pope's troops within five days.[1]

Robert E. Lee did not want to assault the enemy in the open, but it seemed possible to maneuver the foe into a corner. The key to Confederate operations was the control of the Orange and Alexandria Railroad. This line linked Pope to Washington, and the Federals depended upon it for their supplies.[2]

In order for General McClellan to reinforce Pope, McClellan would have to come from Fredericksburg, located to the south. While this would increase the strength of the enemy from 50,000 to 130,000 men,[3] it also forced General Pope to maintain contact with Fredericksburg. The Union left flank would be pinned down, thus opening a possibility of attack against the Union right.

John Pope had two choices. He might remain where he was, hopeful of receiving reinforcements, or he could retreat toward the safety of Washington. In either case, General Lee recognized a momentary window of opportunity.

On Sunday, August 24, General Lee met with Stonewall Jackson, James Longstreet and J. E. B. Stuart, his chief of cavalry. Lee outlined a bold plan. The Confederates would detach General Jackson to cut off the

Union supplies. The target was not Manassas Junction, but the Orange and Alexandria Railroad itself. The gamble was enormous. If Pope learned of Jackson's departure, he might first defeat Jackson, and then concentrate on Lee's remaining forces, defeating the graycoats in separate pieces. Speed and secrecy were of the essence.[4]

Early in the morning of August 25, Jackson's troops moved out.[5] Stonewall would take three divisions of approximately 23,500 men.[6] Richard S. Ewell would be in the lead, followed by Ambrose Powell Hill's division. In the rear would be Jackson's old division, now under the command of William Taliaferro.

By 9:00 A.M., Union scouts had notified General Pope of the Confederate movements. However, General Pope drew an incorrect conclusion. He believed that the Southerners were marching toward the Shenandoah Valley, and thus were not a threat to his right flank.[7]

General Ewell's division camped for the night at Salem. The Confederates had covered 26 miles. The grayclad veterans knew that tomorrow would bring another grueling march. No rations were available, so most of the men simply lay down to sleep right where they were.[8]

The next morning the men noticed that the march had changed direction. General Ewell now led his troops east, in the direction of the Bull Run Mountain range. In the center was Thoroughfare Gap. If Pope had any Yankees stationed along this narrow pass, the action would get hot in a hurry. Gunfire from any combat here would bring the rest of the Union army quickly to the rescue.

Fortunately for Jackson, the pass was undefended. The Confederates could relax a bit. At Gainesville the road forked. The left went to Manassas, the right went to Bristoe Station. Stonewall decided to head for Bristoe. From the current position, the road to the Orange and Alexandria Railroad was two miles shorter from Bristoe Station.[9] As the railroad had been the objective all along, the rebels headed to the right.

The Confederate cavalry rode next to each flank of the foot soldiers as the long columns began the four-mile[10] journey. There was not much daylight left as the grayclad troops heard the sound of a train whistle heading northward. The Northerners spotted their enemy, and sporadic gunfire broke out from Bristoe Station. The rebels tried to derail the train, but it managed to make it through the village, heading for Manassas Junction. Soon, all of the Union troops there would learn of Jackson's advance.

Confident that another freight train would soon be on the way, the Confederates prepared to stop it. Their suspicions proved correct. This time they opened a derailing switch, and when the train came through it plunged down an embankment. Before the Confederates could plunder the freight cars, a third train whistled, and twenty empty boxcars shattered into splinters against the wreckage, blocking the railroad from any further use.[11] However, the serious work was yet to come.

Stonewall Jackson had marched an astonishing 56 miles[12] in two days. His mobile strike force was right where General Lee wanted them to be: behind Pope's army and between Pope and Washington.[13]

Despite the good fortune, Jackson realized that there was a more valuable prize to be had at Manassas Junction, only seven miles away. The Federals had organized a huge supply base there, stocked with numerous items which were scarce in the Confederacy. Darkness had fallen, but no time must be lost. Could the graycoats reach Manassas before Pope could either receive reinforcements or destroy those supplies?

But who could Stonewall send on such an expedition? Every man was exhausted. General Isaac Trimble volunteered to lead the attack. Jackson ordered him to take some 600 men of the 21st North Carolina and the 21st Georgia, and at 9:00 P.M. Trimble's men moved out. As an afterthought, Jackson felt cavalry support would lend strength to the operation, so General Stuart was ordered forward as well.[14]

Around midnight[15] there began a rare occurrence in the Civil War: a night attack. General Trimble sent forward a small party which opened fire upon the enemy. When the Federal cannon returned the fire, the Confederates were able to determine the position of the bluecoats. The Union pickets fired a few shots, then fled to the rear of their lines. Trimble yelled "Charge!" and the rebels stormed down on Manassas Junction. In just a few minutes the Confederates were in control, having captured 300 prisoners, eight cannon, 175 horses and the full stock of the depot. This had been accomplished at the cost of only 12 Confederate casualties.[16]

On August 27 Jackson ordered the rest of his men northward. This time Taliaferro and A. P. Hill led the way, and Ewell's division remained at Bristoe Station. General Ewell was to delay any Federal pursuit, then burn the bridges behind him as he joined the Confederates at Manassas Junction.[17]

At 7:00 A.M. the Confederates had barely reached the junction when Jackson peered through his binoculars. The glint of bayonets in the distance had aroused his concern. The Federal War Department had sent four New Jersey regiments under General George W. Taylor to secure the vital Bull Run Bridge. Other reinforcements would be arriving soon at Manassas Junction.[18]

The Bull Run railroad bridge was north of Manassas Junction, but Taylor detrained his troops due to a collision on the tracks, and the Northerners moved south. General Taylor believed that his enemy was a small force, so his troops marched all the way to Manassas Junction, even though they had no artillery. At about 10:00 A.M., the bluecoats formed their battle lines, and advanced straight toward A. P. Hill, positioned on the Federal left.[19]

Jackson's artillery opened fire, and the unequal contest was over by 11:00 A.M., though no real effort was made to annihilate the New Jersey brigade. Hill's division took about 300 prisoners. However, the Federal killed and wounded did not exceed 135.[20] General Taylor fell, mortally wounded.

Back at Manassas Junction, famished Confederate soldiers feasted on delicacies provided by the United States government. Even the simplest military fare was always in short supply for the grayclad troops, and they were not used to seeing such abundance.

General Ewell's men arrived at Manassas during the afternoon, hoping to partake of the spoils. Unfortunately, there was not much left. To make matters worse, Federal reinforcements were moving swiftly toward the rebels, and Jackson realized that the supplies still left must be destroyed, before they fell into Union hands.

The Confederates marched north around midnight,[21] with the explosions of Pope's supply depot at their backs. The rebels would try to rendezvous at Groveton.

On Thursday, August 28, General Pope arrived at yet another wrong conclusion. He believed that Jackson was at Manassas Junction, and would do battle there. The bluecoats headed in that direction.

Around noon, a messenger arrived at Jackson's camp with a captured order.[22] A large body of Union troops was marching north from Manassas Junction in the direction of Centreville. Stonewall Jackson wasted no time with deliberations. Turning to General Taliaferro he said, "Move your division and attack the enemy." The orders to General Ewell were simply "Support the attack."[23] Both divisions were off as the graycoats were now getting ready for battle.

Later that afternoon[24] an exhausted courier rode up to Jackson with a message from General Lee. The other half of the Confederate army was moving through the west face of Thoroughfare Gap. The rebel forces would be united once again by the next morning.

As the sun began to sink from view, a column of Union troops appeared. General Rufus King's division of 10,000 men were marching along the Warrenton Turnpike toward the little stream known as Bull Run. The Confederates had Taliaferro on the right, Ewell in the center, and Hill on the left. The rebels surged forward, hitting the Yankees in the left flank.[25]

Gunfire erupted along the lines, as volleys were delivered at close range. Two of the most famous units in the entire Civil War went head to head, the Union Iron Brigade, and the Confederate Stonewall Brigade. Neither gave an inch. Smoke and confusion covered the battlefield.

Only darkness brought an end to the battle. Losses were heavy on both sides in the brief contest. On the Union side, the bluecoats had lost approximately 1,100 men of the 2,800 engaged, while the Confederates had suffered some 1,200 casualties among 4,500 participants.[26]

Confederate losses were particularly concentrated, with the Stonewall Brigade losing roughly 40 percent of its strength. General Taliaferro was hit three times, and was out of action for some time to come. Even more serious was the wound to General Ewell. He was hit in the left knee and tibia. The leg would have to be amputated, and Ewell was lost to the army for months.[27]

The stalemate at Groveton produced no tangible results for either side, and was really poorly conceived from the Southern point of view. The Confederates had tried to blast away at the enemy in headlong assaults, when a flank attack might have proved more profitable. Jackson had lost two of his best division commanders, to no apparent gain. The army would now have to be reorganized.

General Pope was now aware of the location of General Jackson, and began his preparations accordingly. The drama would continue to unfold only one day later at the battle of Second Manassas.

August 29–30, 1862

Second Manassas (Bull Run)

R. E. Lee (CSA)	J. Pope (USA)

The summer of 1862 had been kind to the Confederate Army of Northern Virginia. Robert E. Lee had survived a critical test in June, as the Union forces under George B. McClellan reached the outskirts of Richmond. General Lee pushed the Yankees back in a series of battles known as the Seven Days.[1]

Abraham Lincoln yielded to pressure on both the military and political fronts, and General McClellan was relieved from command. Three separate forces[2] were combined into one army, led by the bombastic Union general, John Pope. The Confederates would have a new opponent.

The campaign began in earnest on August 15. The day found 54,500 Confederates[3] under General Lee in Gordonsville, Virginia. The town was a stop on the Orange and Alexandria Railroad, just south of the Rapidan River.

In this part of Virginia, the Rapidan flows east as it makes its way to join the Rappahannock River, which flows in a southeasterly direction. The Union army of some 70,000[4] was camped in between the two rivers, a mere 20 miles away.[5] It would be very difficult for such a large body of men to escape if they were suddenly attacked. General Pope had already made a grave mistake, and Robert E. Lee was determined to make him pay for it. The main route of escape for Pope's troops was the bridge at Rappahannock Station.[6] Could the Confederate cavalry destroy it in time to isolate Pope? General J. E. B. "Jeb" Stuart and his horsemen would have to try. Confederate success would depend on speed and secrecy.

Almost immediately, General Lee's plans began to unravel. Fitzhugh Lee, the nephew of the commanding general, announced that his horses would need rest before they undertook such a difficult expedition. The commissary wagons of James Longstreet's command had not arrived with food for his men. The trap would have to wait.[7] Lee postponed the advance until August 19. Later, he changed his plans again. The attack would take place on the 20th.[8] The delay had allowed the Yankees to escape. As the Confederates crossed the Rapidan on August 20, they discovered that the bulk of the Union army had already moved to the north side of the Rappahannock. The fords were heavily guarded.[9] General Lee would have to find another way to attack the enemy.

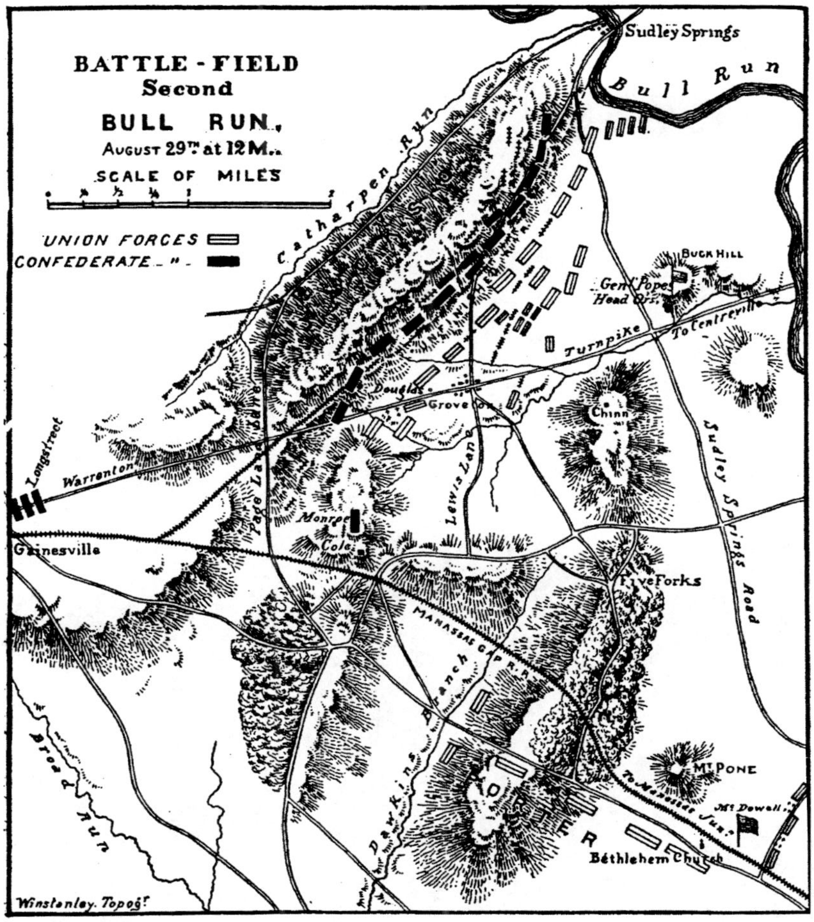

Second Manassas (Bull Run): General Pope's view of the situation at noon, Friday, August 29, with Longstreet placed at Gainesville; but according to Longstreet and others, Longstreet was at that hour on Jackson's right and capable of resisting an attack on the part of Porter. For a discussion of Longstreet's location, refer to *Battles & Leaders Vol. II*, pages 510 and 525. Map by Jacob Wells.

On August 22 the Confederates received some important news. A daring cavalry raid at Catlett's Station had produced the captured battle plans of the Federal army. General Pope intended to merge his army with General McClellan's troops. McClellan and his soldiers would take boats to Aquia Creek, move inland to Fredericksburg, then march west to join Pope. The two Union armies would be able to unite within five days. The junction of their forces would create an opponent with 130,000 men.[10] General Lee would have to attack Pope before McClellan arrived.

Robert E. Lee came up with a bold plan, full of risks. He realized that in order to win the race against time, audacity was required. The Army of Northern Virginia had established headquarters in Jeffersonton, a quiet village between the Rappahannock and the Rapidan. The past several days had been spent in an attempt to probe the enemy lines and move north. All of that would have to change. General Lee was about to embark on a quick offensive strike behind enemy lines.

The Confederates would split the army in two. Stonewall Jackson would march north with his three divisions, led by William B. Taliaferro, Richard S. Ewell and A. P. Hill. They would first head north, then turn east. Their purpose would be to get behind Pope, severing his communications with Washington, D.C. Jackson's force would total approximately 23,000 men.[11]

General Lee would retain Longstreet's troops, or about 32,000 muskets.[12] Longstreet would attempt to occupy Pope's attention, allowing Jackson more freedom of movement. The two Confederate forces would then reunite as soon as possible. The danger in this plan was that Jackson would be between Pope and McClellan. Stonewall would have to strike quickly and then disappear before his small force was obliterated.

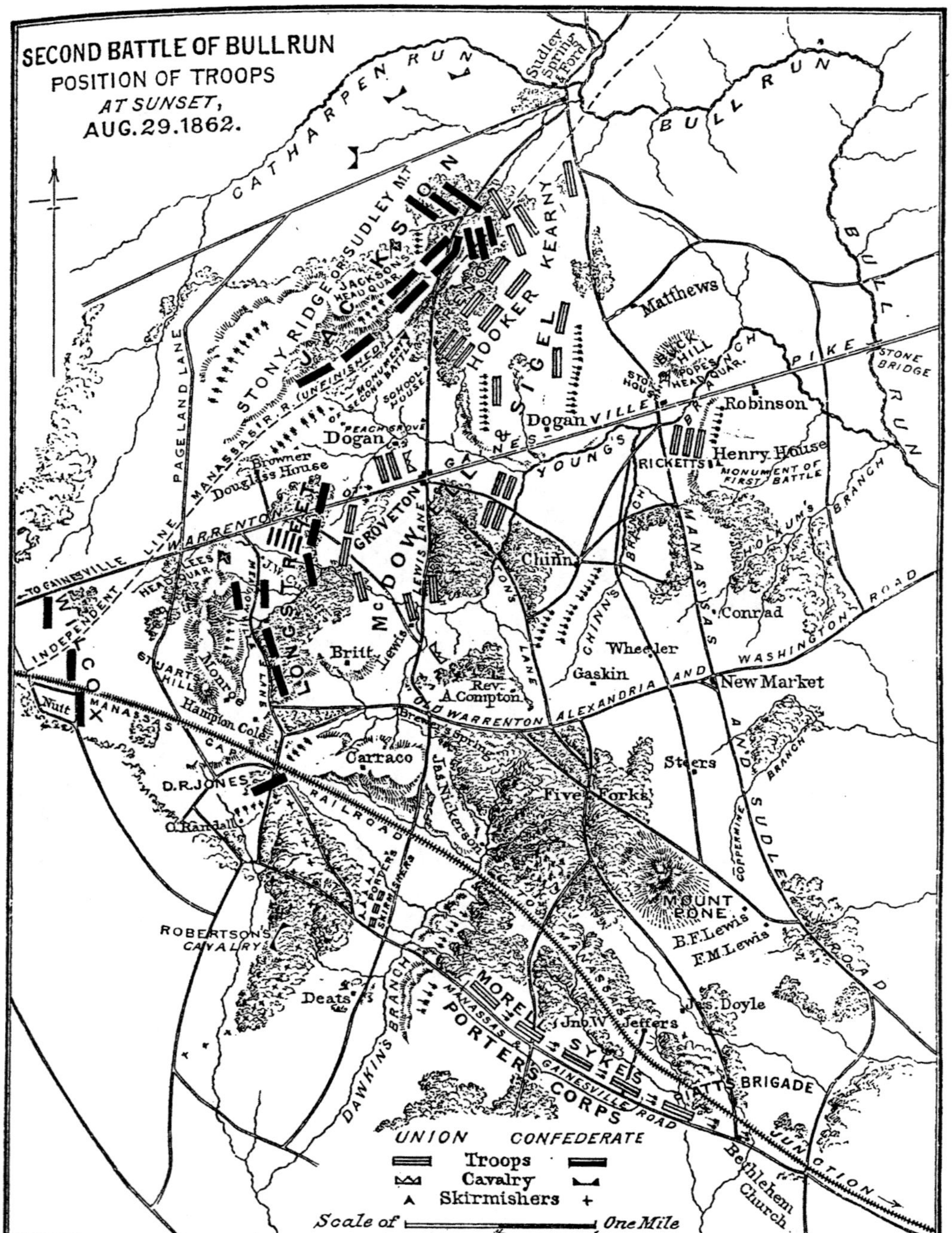

Second Manassas (Bull Run): relative positions at sunset, Friday, August 29. At noon of that day Porter's corps was in much the same position as at sunset. According to General Pope, at noon Porter, with very little resistance to overcome, might have occupied the hill of the Monroe and Hampton Cole houses, a position of great importance. But, according to other authorities, Longstreet was in position between Jackson and Porter by noon. At that hour the right of the Union army was arrayed in a continuous line in front of Jackson from a point on the turnpike three-quarters of a mile west of Groveton to the point where the Sudley Springs road crosses the unfinished railroad which was Jackson's stronghold. The map above illustrates the situation at the time of the greatest success on the Union right, when Jackson's left had been turned upon itself by Kearny's, Reno's, and Hooker's divisions. For a further discussion of Longstreet's position, see *Battles & Leaders Vol. II*, page 527. Map by Jacob Wells.

On the morning of August 25,[13] Jackson began his journey. On the 26th he passed through Thoroughfare Gap, and joined the Confederate cavalry under General Stuart. The Northerners extended their right flank in search of the foe, but without success. Nightfall found most of Jackson's command at Bristoe Station.[14]

Events were unfolding exactly according to General Lee's plans. Stonewall Jackson had made a night attack against Manassas Junction, only seven miles from Bristoe. The graycoats had captured a great deal of military supplies. News of Jackson pillaging his supply depot forced Pope to turn backward, and away from General McClellan.[15]

Now was the time for Longstreet to move. He too would advance through Thoroughfare Gap, and on August 28, the Confederates began to make their way through the passage in the Bull Run Mountains.[16]

Although the rebels had made great progress behind the enemy, Stonewall Jackson was not comfortable in a stationary position. He quickly moved his troops from Manassas Junction, and on August 28 Jackson's men won a decisive victory at the battle of Groveton.

According to the latest intelligence reports, John Pope was nine miles[17] away from Lee, camped around the town of Warrenton. Could General Lee bring Jackson and Longstreet together before a major battle took place?

On August 29 the Confederate forces came together. Stonewall's troops held the left wing of the Confederate position, and Longstreet would deploy his men farther south as soon as they reached the battlefield. Jackson took a position facing east and southeast along an unfinished railroad cut. Jackson's own division, led by William Starke,[17a] was on the right. Ewell's division, temporarily under the command of A. R. Lawton,[18] held the center, and A. P. Hill had been given the left.[19]

General Longstreet arrived later in the morning and placed his left flank on the Centerville Turnpike, close to Jackson's right. Facing east, this was the division under John B. Hood. Nathan G. "Shanks" Evans and his men were in immediate support. Three brigades led by Cadmus Wilcox were behind Hood's left, while James Kemper and three more brigades were behind Hood's right. D. R. Jones' division lined up on Hood's right, with his command extending southward to the Manassas Gap Railroad. The strongest point of the line was the center, just west of Groveton.[20]

Opposing the graycoats, General Pope had five[21] Union corps. On August 29, Pope made another mistake. Instead of uniting his forces in a concerted thrust against one wing of the Confederate army, he attacked in a disjointed, piecemeal fashion.[22] Parts of different commands would take center stage as the day wore on.

The initial activity took place on Stonewall Jackson's front. As the battle opened, two divisions of Heintzelman's corps held the Union right. Philip Kearny's men deployed on the Union right, while Joseph Hooker led his troops to a central position behind Sigel's corps. The Union left was held by John Reynold's division, which belonged to McDowell's corps. Finally, most of Jesse Reno's corps was also pushed forward.[23]

The beginning of the day saw sporadic bursts of gunfire, but without serious consequences. Around 10:00 A.M. the Union artillery opened up on Jackson's right, and the Confederates responded.[24] Under the cover of the artillery barrage, the Federal soldiers began shifting their position to Jackson's left.[25]

The bluecoats had discovered a gap in the lines of A. P. Hill's division. Maxcy Gregg's South Carolinians on the far left, and Edward Thomas's Georgia brigade had failed to close up their defenses, leaving an opening of some 175 yards on the northernmost end of the line.[26]

General Pope pounded away at Jackson's left flank, but without success. Four separate assaults had left Union bodies piled in heaps along the unfinished railroad cut. Nevertheless, there was no indication that the day was over.[27]

By early afternoon, Longstreet's troops were in position, and the Army of Northern Virginia looked like a giant trap ready to snap its jaws shut on any unsuspecting Yankees who might wander into the middle. Much to Lee's dismay, John Pope would not take the bait.

General Lee wanted Longstreet to attack the Union left flank, but Longstreet was reluctant to move. He feared for the safety of his right flank if the Confederates advanced too far. Fitz-John Porter's corps was in front of the rebels, and a battle on two fronts would not take place until the graycoats had more information on the precise location of the enemy.[28]

While the Confederate right wing hesitated, Jackson's left was growing even more precarious. Hill's troops had repulsed each Federal assault, but ammunition was running low and the men were exhausted.

The Southerners had fallen back some 300 to 400 yards, and Gregg's position on the far left had become isolated from the rest of Jackson's command.[29]

Wave after wave of blue continued to charge forward, breaking, then charging again. The fighting was desperate, as sheets of flame erupted within ten paces of the opponent.[30] The slaughter was horrific on both sides. Suddenly, the South mounted a counterattack, led by General Jubal Early's fresh troops. Six regiments of 2,500 men ripped into the battered ranks of the enemy, and drove them back to the railroad cut.[31] Darkness ended a long day of fighting on the Confederate left.[32]

As the sun set over the battlefield, each army needed to rest. Facing west, troops under Jesse Reno and Samuel Heintzelman held the Union right flank. Behind these two corps were the men under Franz Sigel's command. Generally speaking, all of these soldiers blocked Stonewall Jackson's advance. In the Union center, along the Centerville Turnpike, was Irvin McDowell's command, while Fitz-John Porter's corps still held the ground near the Manassas Gap Railroad, on Longstreet's right flank.[33]

On the first day General Pope had concentrated his attacks in Jackson's sector, albeit in a very disjointed fashion. August 30 saw an escalation of the contest, as the battle moved along the entire front.

The Confederates had performed admirably, but General Lee had not desired to bring on a general engagement. He had intended to maneuver Pope into a full retreat, hoping to recover more of Virginia soil for the Confederacy.[34] Perhaps a new day would see the Yankees leave the state.

Around 8:00 A.M. the Union artillery batteries opened a slow fire, but to little effect.[35] For about an hour the guns roared, until they soon fell silent.

General Stuart reported that the Federals were massing their troops in three lines on Jackson's front.[36] Perhaps Pope was planning an assault. The Confederates

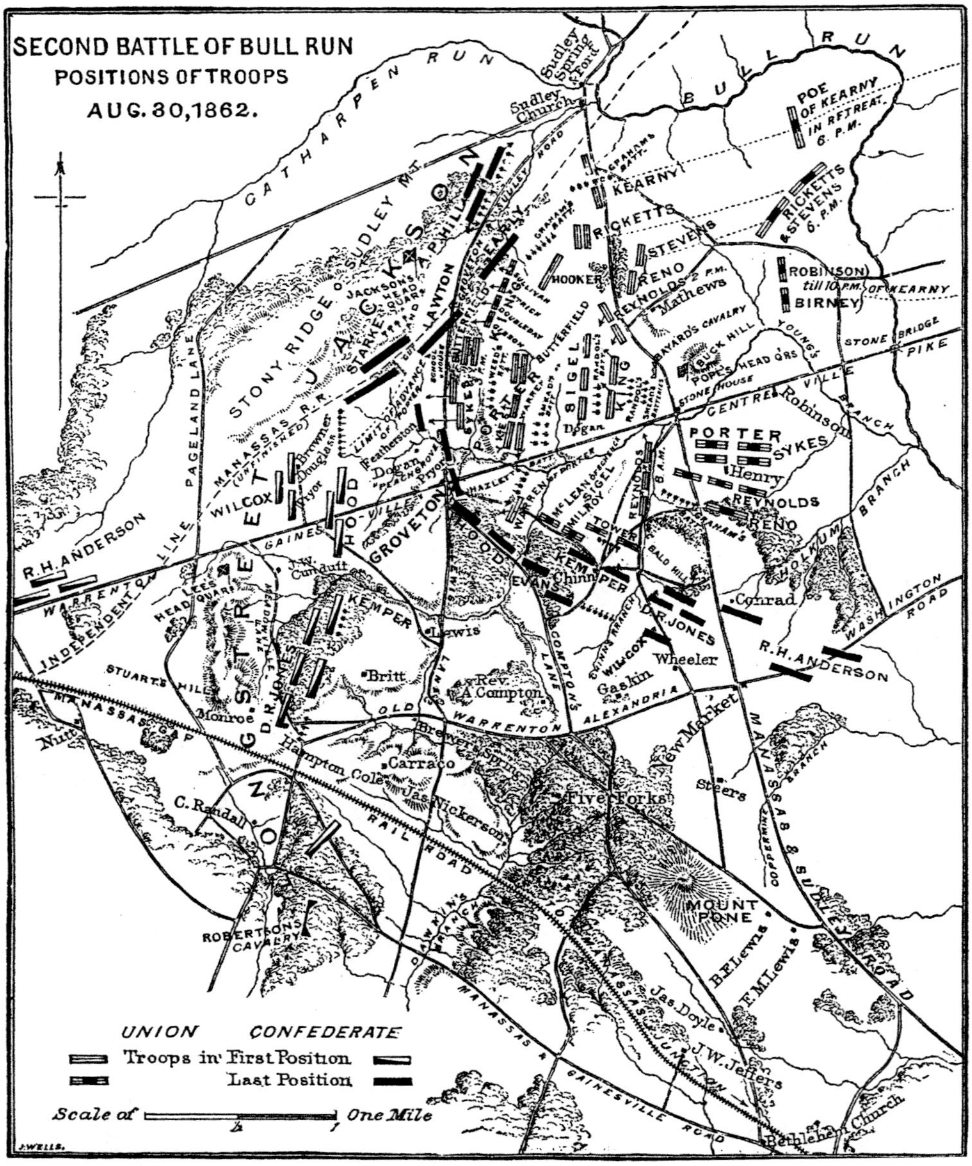

Second Manassas (Bull Run): first and last positions in the fighting of August 30. During the assault by Porter's corps and King's division, Jackson's forces were behind the unfinished railway. When that assault failed, the Unionists north of the turnpike were attacked by the brigades of Featherston and Pryor (of Wilcox), which were acting with some of Jackson's troops and with one brigade of Hood. Wilcox, with his own proper brigade, passed far to the right and fought his way to an advanced position, after Evans and D. R. Jones had compelled Sigel and McDowell to loosen their hold on and west of Bald Hill. (*Note:* Tower, Milroy and McLean, on the map, should be placed more to the east on and near Bald Hill.) At dark the Confederates were somewhat in advance of the positions indicated on the map. Map by Jacob Wells.

waited, expecting a vigorous attack at any moment. Nothing happened. Noon came and went, and the Yankees finally began to move around 2:00 P.M.[37]

At this point, Pope believed that Jackson would do just what the Federals expected him to do. Once again, the Union high command had made a critical mistake. Jackson had fallen back to strengthen his lines. Therefore, Jackson should be retreating. Without making a thorough reconnaissance to determine the Confederate position, Pope ordered his forces forward "in pursuit of the enemy and press him vigorously during the whole day."[38]

Fitz-John Porter would sweep around Jackson's right, and cut off his escape. By the end of the day Lee's army would most certainly be destroyed. Unfortunately for the bluecoats, Jackson was not in the process of retreating, and James Longstreet stood squarely in the path of any advance by General Porter.[39]

Shortly before 3:00 P.M.,[40] a lone Union cannon fired a shot to signal the start of a general advance. From Starke's position, Jackson beheld a tremendous display of some 12,000 Federals.[41] Onward they came, and the Confederates opened fire with muskets and artillery. Row after row of Yankees fell, but the bluecoats were undaunted.

Ammunition was running low and the weight of the attack had pushed the Southerners back. Starke's troops were bent back, Lawton held the center, and Hill was frantically trying to tighten his lines. For almost two hours, the Federals had been pounding the Confederate left wing. Jackson would need assistance in order to survive.[42]

General Pope had committed all of his reserves in a last-ditch effort to turn Jackson's left wing. Portions of all five Union corps had assailed the stubborn graycoats. As General Porter attacked Jackson's right, Porter's left flank became exposed to Longstreet's corps to the south.[43]

James Longstreet was quick to seize his opportunity. He ordered his artillery to open fire, and the Yankees began to fall. The Northerners saw that their left lay bare. Southern cannon boomed, and the Federals broke off their assault as panic came over the troops.[44]

Porter's attack began to falter as the men dashed for safety. Longstreet knew he had his adversary on the run. The Confederate infantry swept forward. Almost 25,000 men[45] surged ahead, crushing the Federal left flank.[46]

As the Federal left collapsed, Jackson attacked, striking the other end of Pope's formation. The Federals had been bent into a horseshoe, and the rout was on.[47] The Army of the Potomac had been shattered, but was saved as rain and darkness covered the field.

August 30, 1862, had been a banner day for the South, as the Army of Northern Virginia had triumphed once again. However, a problem persisted which would dog General Lee for the remainder of the war. The graycoats had just enough men to drive the foe from the field, but not enough troops to gain the decisive victory which Lee had envisioned.[48] Casualties at the battle of Second Manassas were heavily in favor of the Confederacy. General Lee had lost 1,553 men killed, 7,812 wounded, and 109 soldiers captured or missing, for a total of 9,474. General Pope had seen 1,747 men killed, 8,452 wounded, and 4,263 captured or missing, for a total of 14,462.[49]

In addition, the Confederates had taken possession of the field and driven the Yankees back toward Washington, D.C. Due to the defeat at this battle, John Pope was relieved of command, and the Army of the Potomac would once again be led by General McClellan.

The Federals would have to reorganize, and fast. On the Confederate side, morale was soaring after a stunning victory. The rebels would win again on September 1 at Chantilly, then both sides marched onward, locking horns in the bloodiest battle of the entire war: Sharpsburg.

September 1, 1862

Chantilly (Ox Hill)

R. E. Lee (CSA)	J. Pope (USA)

The Confederates were flush with victory after their performance at Second Manassas. On August 29 and 30 Robert E. Lee had dealt the Union Army of the Potomac a stunning blow. If he could only destroy General Pope's army before they retreated to the safety of Washington's defenses, perhaps the war could be brought to a close.

The Union forces were located around Centreville. General Lee believed that the most effective pursuit of his foe was with the "foot cavalry" under Stonewall Jackson. Jackson would take his men north from Groveton to the Little River Turnpike, crossing Bull Run at Sudley Ford. Upon reaching the road, the Confederates would turn sharply to the southeast. By marching in the direction of Fairfax Courthouse the graycoats would be able to cut off the Federal line of retreat. The troops under General James Longstreet would remain on the battlefield of Second Manassas, bury the dead, and then follow Jackson.[1]

It had rained heavily on August 31, and the dirt roads had turned to mud.[2] Nevertheless, Jackson's force plodded on. After crossing Bull Run, the men found the turnpike. As A. P. Hill's lead division reached Pleasant Valley, they bedded down for the night.[3]

Rain continued into the night. The Southerners were exhausted from recent fighting and marching, no food was available and water was scarce.[4] Due to the condition of the roads, marching was slow.

By the next morning, military discipline had given way to hunger. Soldiers stole what they could from nearby farms. The rain stopped around 8:00 A.M. on September 1, but famine and fatigue persisted.[5] Union cavalry had discovered Jackson's columns, and while the horsemen did little damage, the element of surprise had disappeared.

General Longstreet was ten miles behind Jackson. General Lee had directed that Jackson not bring on a battle until the Confederates were reunited, so Stonewall called a halt to rest his weary men. By noon, Longstreet had closed to within two or three miles, so the foot cavalry took up the march once again.[6]

After another three miles the Confederates reached the mansion of Chantilly. General J. E. B. Stuart of the Confederate cavalry met Jackson at the intersection of the turnpike and Ox Road. Stuart had scouted on ahead and reported Federals immediately in front.[7]

From Jackson's point of view, much had been gained thus far, and with little loss. General Pope had already been maneuvered from his position at Centreville. He would certainly have to fall back. It would be wise to wait until Longstreet arrived.[8]

The Federals did not intend to let Jackson have his own way. Around 4:00 P.M.,[9] generals Isaac Stevens and Philip Kearny brought their divisions forward. The Confederates were aligned on the south side of the road, facing almost south. A. P. Hill was on the right, Richard Ewell held the center, and Jackson's old division was on the left. It was now led by General William E. Starke, who had assumed command after William Taliaferro had been wounded at Groveton on August 28.[10]

A thunderstorm broke over the field, the rains lashing out against the soldiers.[11] Ammunition was wet for both sides, and the contest might be decided by the bayonet. The fighting was heaviest in A. P. Hill's sector. Brigades were thrown forward, with neither side gaining much of an advantage. Both sides refused to give ground.

Two unexpected developments decided the action in Jackson's favor. General Stevens was killed early in the action, leading a New York regiment in a charge. In the confusion of the battle, Phil Kearny rode into the Confederate lines, and was killed instantly.[12] The deaths of their two field commanders caused the Federals to end the action and withdraw from the battlefield.[13]

In comparison with larger battles, the losses were few. The Confederates lost just over 500 men, while the Union forces suffered close to 1,000 casualties.[14] In addition, the bluecoats lost two valued generals. While it cannot be said that either side gained much from the action at Chantilly itself, on September 2 the Federals were headed back to Washington, most of Virginia was safe from the enemy for the moment, and the second great campaign of Manassas had been mercifully brought to a close.[15]

September 13–15, 1862
Harpers Ferry

T. J. Jackson (CSA)	D. S. Miles J. White (USA)

At the outset of hostilities, the Southern states did not have a great stockpile of military supplies with which they could arm their troops. Harpers Ferry, Virginia, was of vital importance due to the large quantities of munitions held there. Located at the confluence of the Shenandoah and the Potomac rivers, the town changed hands many times during the course of the war. The most significant action took place in the middle of September 1862. The conquest of Harpers Ferry was to play a large role in the battle of Sharpsburg.

General Robert E. Lee had decided to march his Confederates northward into Maryland. Two important factors played a major part in his decision. Both armies had fought valiantly in the struggle, and as a result much of the farmland in Virginia had been exhausted. The food supply for the Army of Northern Virginia was of vital importance to General Lee.[1] In addition, the Civil War had taken the lives of many Southern soldiers, men who would be difficult to replace. General Lee believed that new men could be recruited in the state of Maryland.[2]

On September 4,[3] General Lee's Army of Northern Virginia crossed the Potomac River. Initial recruits in Maryland were certainly fewer than the Confederates had anticipated. While the troops were politely received, the large numbers of reinforcements General Lee had hoped to gain simply were not forthcoming.[4]

Lee knew that in order to secure the state of Maryland for Confederate military operations, Harpers Ferry must be controlled. On September 8, he outlined his plan of attack to Stonewall Jackson.[5] General Jackson would be entrusted with leading the expedition to capture the town. Lee divided the remainder of his army. Further north, some men would be in the vicinity of South Mountain, while others went to Hagerstown.[6]

Harpers Ferry must be taken quickly. The Confederates were located at Frederick, Maryland, and the Union Army of the Potomac under General George B. McClellan was only 35 miles away.[7] Lee wanted to be able to consolidate his troops in case of an enemy attack.

Three separate columns would move independently to reduce Harpers Ferry. They would approach the town from the west, north and east. When the graycoats had surrounded the ferry, Jackson would have control over operations.[8]

Stonewall Jackson would take his three divisions to Bolivar Heights, attacking from the west. General Lafayette McLaws was ordered to lead his division to Maryland Heights, approaching from the north. General John G. Walker's small division must cross the Potomac River, and take possession of Loudon Heights, blocking the Federal escape across the Shenandoah River.[9]

By September 9, the Union Army of the Potomac was only 25 miles from Frederick, Maryland.[10] The Yankees were getting closer.

The timetable was a tight one for General Jackson. Lee had allowed only three days for the reduction of the ferry. Jackson was then directed to rejoin the Army of Northern Virginia at Boonsboro.[11]

At this point, fate intervened on the side of the Union. Robert E. Lee had written detailed instructions, known as Special Orders No. 191, which explained the movements and destinations of each Confederate general officer. A copy of the orders went to each division commander. As a matter of courtesy, Jackson sent a copy of the orders to his brother-in-law, D. H. Hill. This resulted in Hill possessing two copies of the orders — one from General Lee and one from General Jackson.[12]

Inadvertently, the copy from Jackson was lost. It resurfaced, wrapped carelessly around three cigars. Staring intently at the precise movements of every Confederate command was Union General George B. McClellan![13]

On September 11, Jackson headed west on his march to Bolivar Heights. He crossed the Potomac at Williamsport, Maryland, and turned south for Martinsburg,

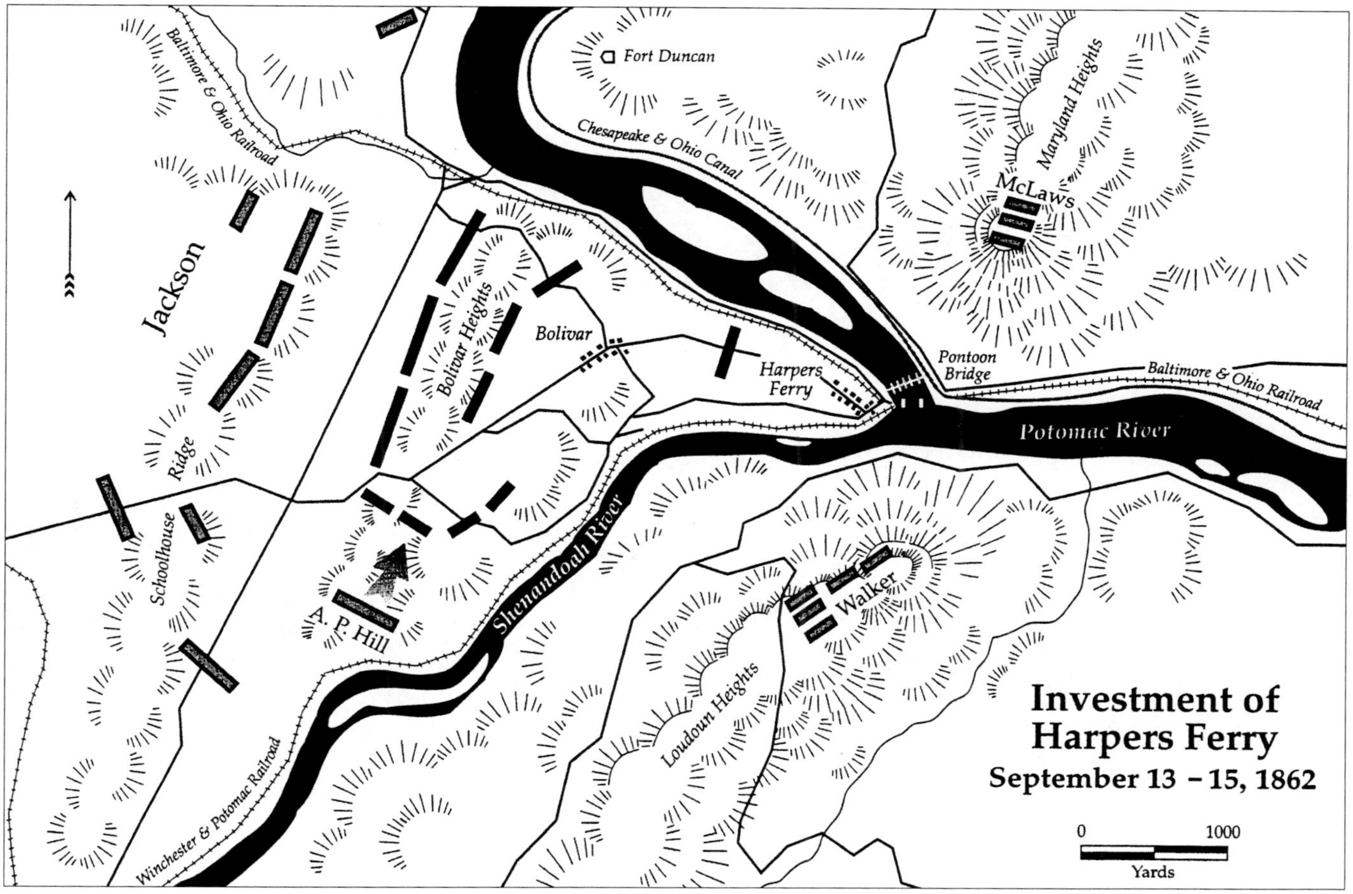

Investment of Harpers Ferry, September 13–15, 1862. Map by George Skoch.

Virginia. At each point of the journey, eager townspeople wanted to have a glimpse of the famous Stonewall Jackson. By the 12th the grayclad troops were entering Martinsburg.[13a]

Back in Virginia, the crowds of admirers slowed the progress of the Confederates. Jackson was now a day late in Lee's timetable.[14]

The rebels were up before dawn the next morning, and on September 13, the Confederates came in sight of Bolivar Heights, the great eminence which covered the approach to the ferry from the west. Jackson looked for a position from which he could observe Maryland Heights and Loudon Heights.[15]

Lafayette McLaws had been assigned a difficult task. His distance had been the shortest—only 20 miles.[16] However, the march to Maryland Heights was very arduous, and the outcroppings of rock would be very difficult to capture if the Yankees already held the heights.[17] The route was rugged indeed, and McLaws decided to divide his force of some 8,000 men.[18]

On September 12, he sent two of his best brigades, Joseph Kershaw's South Carolinians and William Barksdale's Mississippians, up the difficult climb to seal off the north, while his remaining troops blocked the escape routes to the east.

Kershaw and Barksdale reached the summit by 6:00 P.M. on the 12th.[19] Was the enemy in their front? Cautiously, the Southerners advanced. The rocky terrain slowed their progress, but the fortifications of some 2,000 Federal soldiers caused the Confederates to halt for the night.[20]

At 6:30 A.M. on the 13th, the mountaintop erupted in gunfire. Three Union regiments defended the summit, but only two, the 39th New York and the 32nd Ohio, had any combat experience. The Northerners had placed the 126th New York in the center of their line. The action was fierce, but when their Union colonel was wounded, the New Yorkers broke and fell back to a new position. At 10:30 A.M. the Confederates began to advance, trying to establish a new position. At 3:30 P.M. the contest began anew, but this action was shortlived. By sundown McLaws had possession of Maryland Heights.[21]

For his part, Walker's journey was uneventful. By 2:00 P.M. on September 13, his 2,400 men held Loudon Heights.[22] Stonewall Jackson had surrounded Harper's Ferry, but could he force the enemy to capitulate?

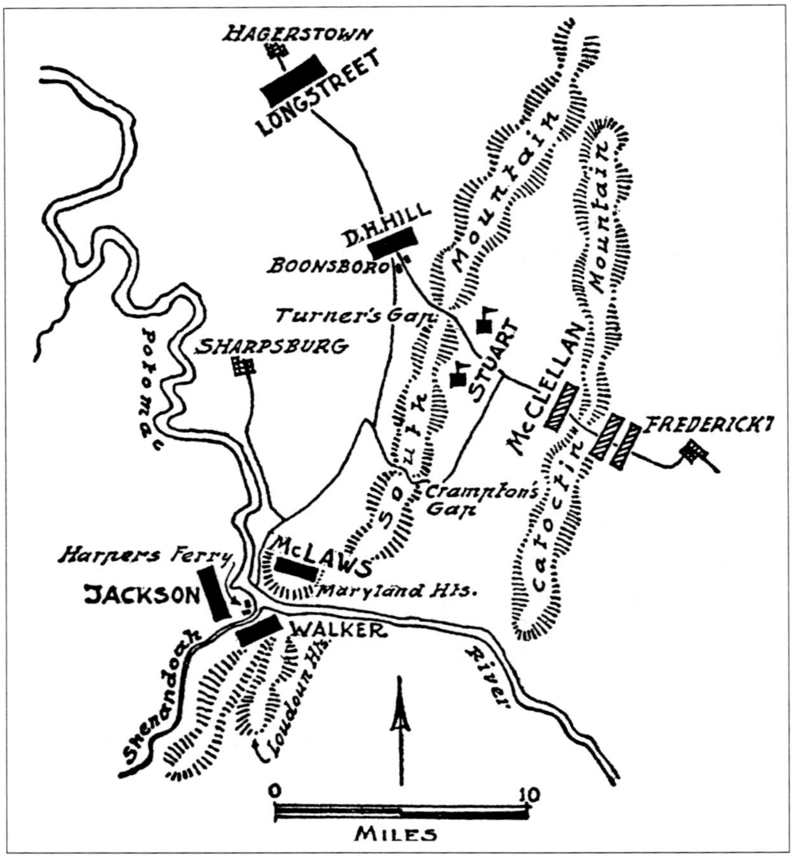

Disposition of the Army of Northern Virginia on the evening of September 13, 1862. Map by John T. Draper.

On September 14, the Southerners opened fire with artillery upon the town. The Federal garrison was helpless to return the fire, as the surrounding elevation gave the Confederates a commanding position. The Union commander, Dixon S. Miles, was mortally wounded, and on the morning of September 15, a white flag rose inside the ferry.[23]

General Julius White had assumed command of the Federal troops, and around 8:00 A.M.[24] he met with Confederate general A. P. Hill, who escorted him to Jackson. The terms for surrender were to be unconditional, and White had no choice but to accept.[25]

The casualties at Harpers Ferry were overwhelming in favor of the Confederacy. The rebels lost 39 men killed and 247 wounded, for a total of 286.[26] The Federals had 44 men killed, 173 wounded and 12,520 captured, for a total of 12,737.[27] In addition, the Confederates took possession of 73 cannon, 12,000 firearms, 200 wagons and 1,200 mules, all of which were in short supply in the Army of Northern Virginia.[28]

While the victory at Harpers Ferry had been impressive, Jackson's absence at South Mountain had cost the graycoats dearly on September 14. D. H. Hill did not have enough men to hold the mountain passes, and George McClellan was in possession of the Confederate battle plans. Hill was defeated at South Mountain, and General Lee fell back to Antietam Creek to unify his forces. On September 17, Jackson would be back with General Lee, hotly engaged at the battle of Sharpsburg.

September 14, 1862
SOUTH MOUNTAIN

R. E. Lee (CSA)	G. B. McClellan (USA)

In early September, the Confederate Army of Northern Virginia was full of confidence. They had good reason to be optimistic. The last week had seen Southern victories at Groveton, Second Manassas and Chantilly.

While the military situation was quite good, General Robert E. Lee had several problems which simply would not go away. War had ravaged Virginia, as both armies had marched back and forth across the state. The Confederates needed additional troops, and a bold stroke by the men in gray might persuade the United States government to seek a peaceful solution to the conflict.

General Lee looked north, to Maryland. Maryland was known as a "border state." She sent her sons to fight on both sides of the Civil War, and the Confederate authorities believed that thousands of new recruits were waiting to join Robert E. Lee. With the prospect of additional manpower from such a tempting target, General Lee decided to take the war outside Virginia soil.

On September 4, 1862, the Army of Northern Virginia began to cross the Potomac River. By the 6th, Lee had set up new headquarters in Frederick, Maryland. Public reception of the tattered graycoats was mixed. The citizens were polite, but somewhat indifferent. New recruits were scarce, and did not approach the numbers the Confederacy had hoped to receive.[1]

Lee had also expected that the Union troops stationed at Harpers Ferry would be transferred to the vicinity of Washington, D.C., as the Army of Northern Virginia crossed into Maryland. This had not occurred. Harpers Ferry was still occupied by the enemy, and it seemed that a thrust deeper into the state was in order. Frederick was no longer a desirable base of operations.[2]

On September 9, General Lee decided to separate his forces. General James Longstreet would march his troops in the direction of Hagerstown, Maryland, in the western part of the state. Another column was to move against Harpers Ferry, Virginia. These men would be led by General Thomas J. "Stonewall" Jackson.

A rear guard was left at South Mountain, under the command of Daniel H. "Harvey" Hill. General Hill's force was not large enough for the task he was to perform. This would turn out to be very important in the days ahead.

The plan of attack for Harpers Ferry would capitalize on the rugged country around it. Located at the confluence of the Potomac and Shenandoah Rivers, the town was surrounded by high bluffs which looked down into the Union garrison below.

General Jackson was to take three divisions and occupy Bolivar Heights, thus investing Harpers Ferry from the rear. Maryland Heights would be taken by one other division, while still another Confederate force would scale Loudon Heights. Completely surrounded, the bluecoats stationed in Harpers Ferry would be forced to surrender.[3]

While Jackson was pleased with the possibility of an offensive thrust, General Longstreet was nervous about the separation of the Confederate forces.[4] Jackson would be at Harpers Ferry, Longstreet at Hagerstown, and Hill at South Mountain. It seemed ominous indeed.

Despite Longstreet's reservations, the rebels were to move out on September 10. The schedule provided for Jackson to reach his destination on the 12th, while John G. Walker and his division were to seize Loudon Heights on the same day. Lafayette McLaws was given the responsibility for Maryland Heights.[5]

On September 12, Jackson's troops entered Martinsburg, Virginia. The next morning, his men saw the rising ground of Bolivar Heights. Plans were going on schedule.

While Jackson and Longstreet were fulfilling their missions with relative ease during the middle of September, the scene of action shifted to General D. H. Hill. The overall plan did not anticipate any activity in front of General Hill. Union general George B. McClellan was east of South Mountain, and moving very slowly. Confederate cavalry watched his every move. General Lee seemed confident that Jackson would capture Harpers Ferry and then rejoin Hill before McClellan initiated any attack.[6]

Harvey Hill was almost unconcerned about an attack from the east. He turned his attention to the south, in the direction of Harpers Ferry. General Hill set up headquarters three miles west of Turner's Gap, the main pass through South Mountain, and began to deploy his troops.[7]

His force was not a large one, and Hill compounded the problem by his failure to study the terrain around him. He was depending on the Confederate cavalry, under General J. E. B. "Jeb" Stuart, to protect Turner's Gap. For his part, Stuart thought that defense of Turner's Gap was more a precaution than a necessity. He believed that Harpers Ferry had already capitulated, which it had not, and Jackson's infantry would soon be at the side of Harvey Hill.[8] Stuart withdrew from his position east of South Mountain back toward the mountain itself, and notified Hill of this change. Hill ordered the brigade under Colonel A. H. Colquitt forward to support the cavalry at Turner's Gap.[9]

On the evening of September 13, General Hill received an alarming message from Colquitt. The Colonel had seen Union campfires in great numbers, far more than the Confederates had suspected. Could this be the beginning of a major Union offensive?[10]

Daniel Harvey Hill suspected the worst. Harpers Ferry had not yet been taken. If General McClellan quickly overwhelmed Hill, General McLaws might be defeated on Maryland Heights. Harpers Ferry might yet be relieved, and then the Yankees could attack Jackson and Longstreet separately, beating each one in detail. The situation appeared truly desperate.[11] It would get worse.

At this point, chance intervened on the side of the Union. Suddenly, the events at South Mountain on September 14 and Antietam Creek three days later were dramatically changed.

Just after noon on September 13,[12] Private B. W. Mitchell of the 27th Indiana Infantry picked up a crude package on the ground at Frederick, Maryland, formerly occupied by D. H. Hill's men. It was nothing more than three cigars, wrapped in paper, carelessly left behind. The paper, however, was a copy of Special Orders No. 191, Army of Northern Virginia. It was addressed to D. H. Hill. This was taken to division headquarters, where it was authenticated. It was the entire battle plan for the Army of Northern Virginia, and it was resting in the hands of George B. McClellan.[13]

McClellan was a very deliberate, slow-moving general. Suddenly the Union Army of the Potomac was moving with good speed, and they were headed straight for D. H. Hill.

Hill's force numbered some 3,000 in five brigades.[14] His orders were to prevent the escape of any Yankees from Harpers Ferry, and also to guard the pass at Turner's Gap which led to the town of Boonsborough. It did not seem possible to carry out both orders, but he would try.

The Federals were in fact attacking in great force. The Union I and IX Corps, led by General Ambrose E. Burnside, comprised the Federal right wing. The center, under General Edwin V. Sumner, was composed of the II and XII Corps, while the enemy left, led by General William B. Franklin, was comprised of the VI Corps and one division of the IV Corps.[15]

At 3:30 P.M.[16] the troops under Longstreet began to arrive. It was welcome relief to Daniel Harvey Hill. General Hill deployed his troops facing east along the crest of the mountain against his most formidable opponent. To the left of Turner's Gap went Robert Rodes' division, with A. H. Colquitt's astride the main road through the pass. On the right, or south side of the gap were the brigades of G. B. Anderson and Roswell Ripley, with Samuel Garland's men on the far right of the formation.[16a]

The impact of the Federal thrust was taken by Garland's brigade. In his attempt to rally his troops Samuel Garland was killed. Leaderless, his North Carolinians began to waver, then broke for the rear under the Union onslaught. Longstreet's men provided support, and the line held for the moment. It soon became evident that the main attack would be against the Confederate left, where General Rodes was putting up a stubborn defense.[16b] His men were pushed back, but with Colquitt's assistance the Yankees were unable to break through to the main road.[16c]

After darkness covered the battlefield the thin line of graycoats had no choice but to fall back to a safer position.[17] Estimates of casualties vary widely, as the Confederate losses were not separately tabulated. The Union forces had 325 men killed, 1,403 wounded and 85 missing, for a total of 1,813. Confederate losses are estimated at 1,800 soldiers killed or wounded, with the greater part of Garland's command captured, representing total casualties of about 2,700.[18]

South Mountain was a battle which Robert E. Lee never intended to fight. Taken by surprise, the Southerners took senseless casualties, then had to retreat westward in the direction of Sharpsburg. The graycoats could ill afford such losses only three days before the bloodiest single day in the entire Civil War.

September 14, 1862
Crampton's Gap

W. A. Parham (CSA) — W. B. Franklin (USA)

In the fall of 1862, the Confederate Army of Northern Virginia moved across the Potomac River into Maryland. By the second week of September, the different commands had become widely scattered: Robert E. Lee had decided to send James Longstreet to Hagerstown, Maryland; Thomas J. "Stonewall" Jackson led an expedition against Harpers Ferry, Virginia; and a small force under Daniel H. Hill was ordered to secure the passes around South Mountain.

South Mountain is a range of hills in western Maryland which runs roughly north to south. General Hill took a position about three miles west of Turner's Gap, one of the principal passes in the mountain.[1] Five miles further south,[1a] Colonel William A. Parham defended Crampton's Gap. This opening in the mountain had great strategic importance, as it was less than ten miles northeast of Harpers Ferry.[2]

If the Union forces broke through the Confederate lines, the bluecoats could attack the rebels who were investing Harpers Ferry. Part of Stonewall Jackson's force, these 8,000 troops[3] were led by General Lafayette McLaws, and it would prove disastrous to the Southern cause if he were to be defeated.

Nevertheless, Colonel Parham had only two regiments of cavalry and three of infantry at his disposal.[4] It was very important to reinforce the position.

On September 14, the Federals attacked. Union General William B. Franklin sent his troops forward as Parham's small force stubbornly resisted. Henry Slocum initiated the assault, but was unable to break the stout defenses. After several attempts, the troops under William F. "Baldy" Smith were added to Slocum's left.

William Parham had been able to make some limited progress during the day. The graycoats now occupied the eastern part of the mountain. However, the farther Parham moved forward, the more vulnerable the flanks became. If the Federals were victorious at Crampton's Gap, the Union forces would be between Lee and Jackson. The Confederates would then be defeated individually.

Southern reinforcements were soon sent to Crampton's Gap. Four regiments under Howell Cobb and additional troops under Paul Semmes[5] tried in vain to stem the tide of the Union assault.

Late in the afternoon, the sound of battle drifted to General McLaws, and he became very concerned about the safety of his men. His Confederates had approached Harpers Ferry from the east in order to occupy Maryland Heights. Still, the rebels were vulnerable to an attack from the rear. Could Colonel Parham hold his position? McLaws decided to make a personal reconnaissance of the situation.[6]

The long day of combat finally became too much for the beleaguered Confederates. The center of Parham's command collapsed under the weight of the Union pressure. The Confederates began to crumble under the onslaught.[7] The Federals moved forward, taking possession of the pass.[8]

The Confederates retreated in great disorder down the western side of South Mountain. Despite the apparent chaos, Lafayette McLaws refused to panic. He formed a new line of defense about 1½ miles[9] below Crampton's Gap, and the troops rallied around the new position. The rebels at Harpers Ferry were saved.

General McLaws had been very calm under tremendous pressure. Still, he was not without friends in the Union army, and the Federals had not capitalized on their opportunity. Once the pass in the mountain had been secured, the Yankees decided to camp for the night, and darkness played a large role in averting a much larger disaster.[10]

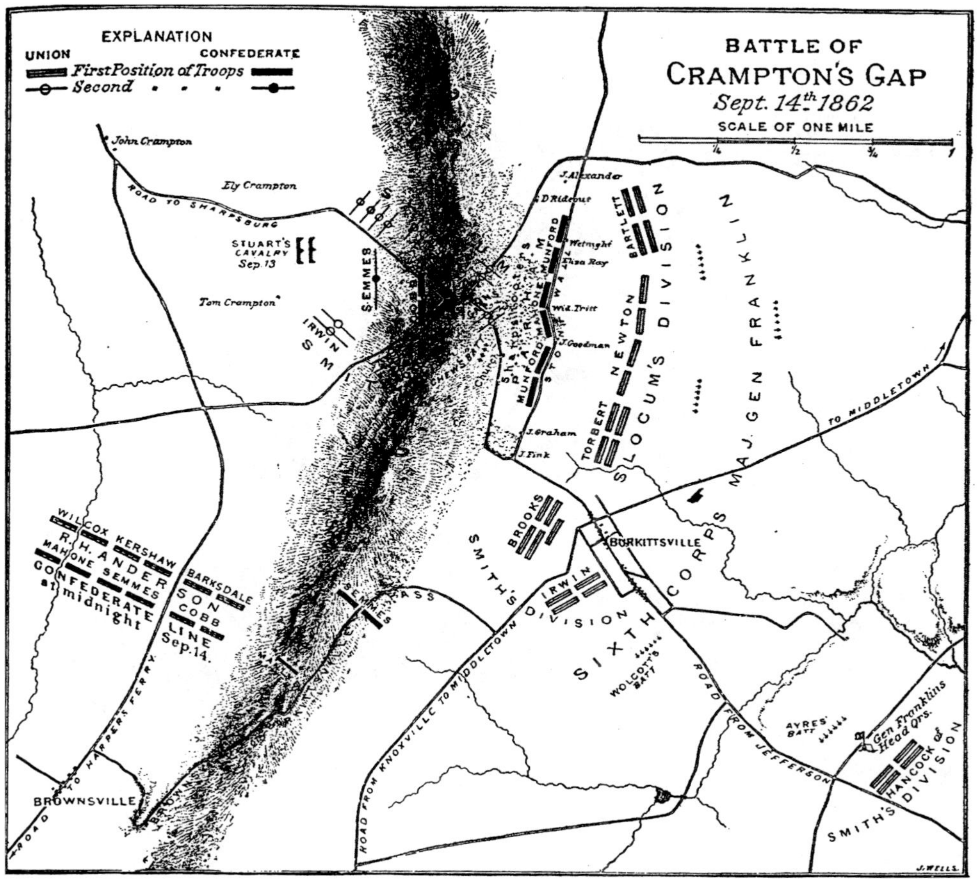

Battle of Crampton's Gap, September 14, 1862. Map by Jacob Wells.

Casualties at Crampton's Gap were in favor of the Union. At a cost of only 533 men, General Franklin had inflicted approximately 1,000 casualties on his opponent.[11] On the surface, it seemed as if the Federals had carried the day.

Unfortunately for the Union, the action here had much greater ramifications. Franklin's hesitation at Crampton's Gap had ensured the success of Stonewall Jackson's attack on Harpers Ferry. On September 15, Jackson's troops received the surrender of 12,520 Federal soldiers.[12]

Stonewall Jackson was able to reunite his command with the Confederates under Longstreet and D. H. Hill. While Jackson would not arrive in time to prevent the Confederate defeat at South Mountain, his troops would play a critical role on September 17 at the bloody battle of Sharpsburg.

September 17, 1862
SHARPSBURG (ANTIETAM)

R. E. Lee (CSA)	G. B. McClellan (USA)

The Union Army of the Potomac had the enemy on the run. On September 14 the Union forces overwhelmed the Confederates at South Mountain, a range of hills in western Maryland. The opportunity arose to capture the entire Southern army. The result would be the bloodiest single day of the war.[1]

Robert E. Lee needed to consolidate his forces. Different commands of the Army of Northern Virginia had become separated. James Longstreet was in Hagerstown, D. H. Hill had been defeated at South Mountain, and Thomas J. "Stonewall" Jackson had just captured Harpers Ferry. In order to withstand a Union attack, the graycoats must reunite.

Longstreet and D. H. Hill retreated to the west. The rebels crossed Antietam Creek and took a position just east of the little town of Sharpsburg.[2] Jackson left one division under A. P. Hill at Harpers Ferry, and on September 16 Stonewall rejoined the army.[3] When General Lee assembled all of his men together, he would have some 40,000 troops at his disposal. George B. McClellan led 87,000 Federals in pursuit.[4]

When dawn broke on the 17th of September, the rebels faced tremendous odds. Sharpsburg was actually three battles rolled into one. Each sector would see furious action.

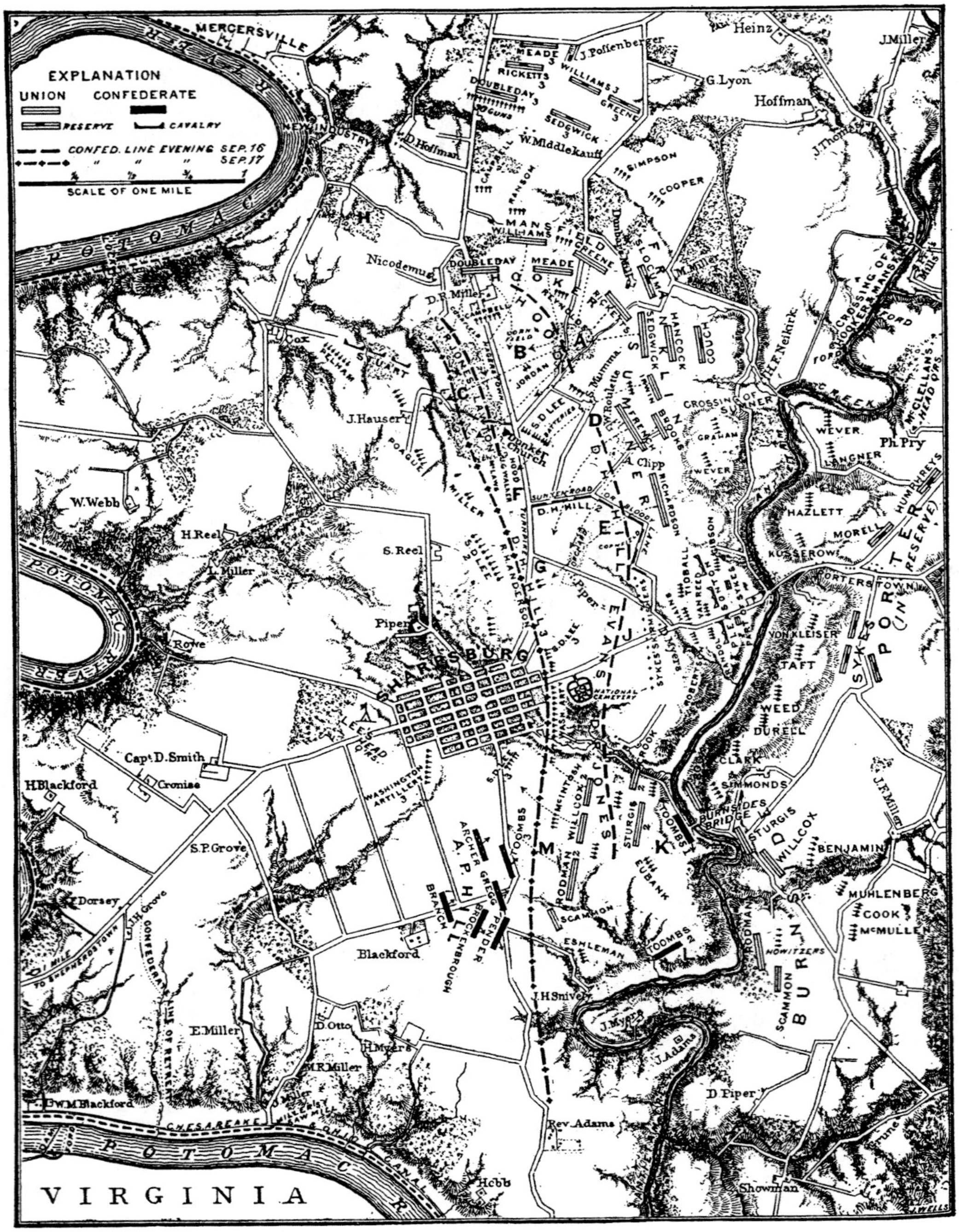

The field of Antietam. Map by Jacob Wells.

Stonewall Jackson placed his troops on the Confederate left, facing north. Jubal Early's men occupied the far left of Jackson's line. The dominant feature in the area was the Dunker Church. West of the Church was a clump of trees, known as the West Wood. The Hagerstown Turnpike separated the opposing sides, and continued all the way into town. A few farms dotted the countryside, but while the Confederates had some protection, much of the Union advance this day would come over open fields of grain.[5]

The center of General Lee's defense was held by D. H. Hill. The men were across the Hagerstown Turnpike, and had taken a position along a small dirt road, facing northeast. The road zigzagged back and forth. An insignificant country road would go down in history as "Bloody Lane."[6]

On the right, James Longstreet's troops were the closest to Antietam Creek. Their front was generally southeast. The ground was open on both sides of the water.[7] Later in the day, a stone bridge would witness a struggle which hung in the balance until A. P. Hill turned the tide in favor of the South.

The battle of Sharpsburg began shortly after 6:00 A.M.[8] On the far right of the Union line, General Joseph E. Hooker led an assault on Jackson. The bluecoats immediately pierced the center of the Confederate position, and were moving south down the Hagerstown Road.[9] A gap had opened between Jackson's troops and the left flank of D. H. Hill.

Stonewall had to move fast. Orders went out immediately to General John B. Hood, a furious combat fighter. Hood's men were eating breakfast in the West Wood. At 7:20 A.M.[9a] the rebels jumped to action. Only 2,300 strong,[10] they seemed to be but a tiny fragment compared to the blue horde swarming through the Confederate lines.

There was only one thing left for Hood to do. He must counterattack, and now! He led his troops forward, slamming into Hooker's Yankees. Hood's veterans forced the enemy back some 400 yards.[11]

However, the carnage was absolutely frightful for both sides. The armies had charged into close contact with one another, and the artillery blasted into tightly packed soldiers, dropping them in rows. The fury of Hood's charge had stunned the Northerners.[12]

Still, Lee was desperate. Not all of the Confederates had arrived at Sharpsburg. The men from Harpers Ferry were still on the way. The Confederate left would need help, and soon. Where would Lee find the troops?

In the early going, the Confederate right had not been pressed. Lee shifted three brigades from the right to help the beleaguered Jackson.[13]

The reinforcements were badly needed. At 7:30 A.M.[14] the Federals attacked again. Around the Dunker Church, Union General Joseph Mansfield's corps lunged into the battle. The Confederate left was in grave danger once again. Fortunately for the rebels, General Mansfield had been killed as he led the Union charge, removing the leadership from the enemy. Still, the fighting continued for another 90 minutes.[15]

The Union attacked for the third time on the Confederate left around 9:00 A.M.[16] Desperate to overwhelm Stonewall Jackson, Edwin Sumner hurried one division forward.[17] Had he waited for the rest of his command to form, the damage might have been far more severe.

General Jackson responded promptly. Lafayette McLaws brought his division forward, and the graycoats were soon locked in a deadly struggle. The arrival of General McLaws finally halted the enemy advance around the Dunker Church.[18] Sumner's lone division was caught in a crossfire, and driven back with heavy loss.[19] The action settled into a stalemate, neither side willing to give an inch. The fighting drifted to the south.

Daniel Harvey Hill held a critical sector of the field. The Union attack in this area was started by two of Sumner's divisions, which had failed to participate in the attack against Jackson. The bluecoats had veered to their left, striking D. H. Hill's troops in the left flank.[20]

As the combat died down on the Confederate left, Robert E. Lee furiously shifted his troops to the area in greatest need. Richard. H. Anderson now ordered his men to the support of D. H. Hill. Anderson's division numbered fewer than 4,000 men,[21] but the Southerners would need every one.

General Hill deployed his men along a sunken road which came to a point, facing the enemy. One mile northeast of Sharpsburg,[22] the Confederates constructed fortifications for protection, and awaited the Union charge. At 10:30 A.M.,[23] the Federals dressed their ranks and charged. The sunken road would soon become known by its more grisly name, "Bloody Lane."

Before noon,[24] the Union troops under General William Franklin moved forward to assist Sumner's Yankees. It seemed impossible that D. H. Hill could hold his position. But he would.

Casualties were staggering. Union General Israel Richardson sent his division forward, led by the intrepid Irish Brigade. Unfortunately he was mortally wounded, dealing a crippling blow to the Federals.[25]

Three separate assaults had been made against Hill's thin line. Confederate Colonel John B. Gordon had taken five bullets, and had to be dragged from the field. With Gordon wounded, orders to shift were mistaken for orders to fall back. The Confederates abandoned Bloody Lane. General Lee waited for the massive, final thrust which would shatter the Confederate center. It never came.[26]

Around 1:00 P.M.,[27] the Confederate right came under intense pressure. A stone bridge crossed Antietam Creek. General Ambrose E. Burnside had led his Union forces toward the bridge earlier in the day, but each attempt had been repulsed by the Confederates.

A concerted effort finally took the bridge for the Union, as the rebels slowly fell back under the weight of the assault. To Longstreet's right, a Federal division under Isaac Rodman forded the shallow waters of Antietam Creek. On the left, D. H. Hill had withdrawn his forces, and Longstreet had no support.[28]

Once again, General Lee found a disaster in the making. Robert Toombs found himself in command of a few thin Georgia regiments, staring at four entire Union divisions.[29] Lee had been forced to take troops from Longstreet to save Jackson. Would Burnside exploit his advantage?

Amazingly, Ambrose E. Burnside waited. Two hours went by. At 3:00 P.M.,[30] the slow tide of blue crept gently up the hill. However, the delay had saved the Army of Northern Virginia from certain destruction. At 1:00 P.M., Lee did not have a single regiment to send to the Confederate right.[31]

Seventeen miles away[32] at Harpers Ferry, A. P. Hill had leaped into action. As Stonewall Jackson was attempting to fend off "Fighting Joe" Hooker, Hill's 3,000 men headed north.[33] Clad in a bright red battle shirt, Hill knew that the fate of Lee's army might depend on his ability to march, and march quickly. Furiously he urged his men onward.

As Longstreet contested every inch of ground, Burnside slowly pressed the graycoats back. The delay had given General Hill the time he needed to arrive. By 4:00 P.M.,[34] the men had formed their lines of battle. Suddenly, A. P. Hill slammed into the exposed left flank of the Union Army of the Potomac. The entire left wing reeled under the unexpected assault. Burnside's troops fell back to Antietam Creek, and the Confederate right was saved.[35]

The counterattack by A. P. Hill ended the fighting at the battle of Sharpsburg. When darkness brought a close to the day, the Confederates tensely held their position. General Lee invited the enemy to attack on the 18 of September, but the Federals did not advance. During the night of the 18th, General Lee led his battered troops back into Virginia.[36]

The casualties for both sides were absolutely horrendous. General McClellan saw 2,108 Union soldiers killed, 9,549 wounded, and 753 captured or missing, for a total of 12,410. The Confederates had lost 1,512 men killed, 7,816 wounded, and 1,844 captured or missing, for a total of 11,172.[37]

Both sides were filled with valor and courage. However, the Union leadership had failed the men. The Union attacks were not sent in together, and the troops attacked in piecemeal fashion.[38] This robbed the Federals of the strength which would have resulted from a unified, concerted thrust. Even worse, General McClellan let 25,000 men [39] sit by without taking part in the action. The Confederates performed admirably, but they were heavily outnumbered. Competent Union leadership should have won this battle.

For all of the slaughter and carnage which characterized the battle, Sharpsburg was a draw. Neither side gained much of an advantage during the actual fighting. Each attack had been met, and stalemate reigned all along the line. The ramifications, however, were substantial. The net results were a loss for the Confederacy. The battle put an end to Robert E. Lee's invasion of Maryland. The new recruits that Lee had hoped to enlist in the Army of Northern Virginia had not materialized.[40]

General Lee had to reorganize his shattered forces, and it would take some time to make up the losses from this campaign. Fortunately, the enemy was in no hurry. Sharpsburg had been devastating to both sides. In the end, one fact seemed inescapable: war would return to Virginia.

September 19, 1862
Iuka

S. Price (CSA) — W. S. Rosecrans (USA)

Iuka, Mississippi, is a very small town near the border of Tennessee. It lies some 20 miles east of Corinth on the Memphis & Charleston Railroad.[1] In the fall of 1862, there were several Union forces located in the area. Ulysses S. Grant was in overall command of troops under generals E. O. C. Ord, and William S. Rosecrans.

General Don Carlos Buell was leading a Union campaign in middle Tennessee. The Confederates believed that the Yankees in Mississippi might be sent north to reinforce General Buell. It was vital to prevent such a junction.

Sterling Price led a small band of some 14,000 rebels.[1a] Alone, he was no match for the Federal armies, but he had received permission to call for the assistance of the graycoats at Vicksburg, under General Earl Van Dorn.[2] Together, they might be able to prevent the Union forces from leaving the state.

On September 14, General Price and his Army of the West marched into Iuka.[3] While the Confederates were concerned about Union soldiers being sent to Tennessee, the Northern generals worried that the rebels would march into the Volunteer State as well.[4]

General Grant wanted to keep Price pinned down in Mississippi. The Federal plan was to launch a coordinated attack with different forces. Currently seven miles northwest of Iuka, General Ord would leave Burnsville with 8,000 men.[5] General Rosecrans was at Jacinto, some 14 miles west of Iuka. With 9,000 troops at his disposal, Rosecrans would attack the town from the south.[6] Ord was to assemble his force on September 18, with the attack scheduled for the next day. Rosecrans would cut off the Confederate escape route to the south.[7]

Sterling Price faced a difficult decision. General Bragg in Tennessee wanted him to march toward Nashville, but the union with General Van Dorn had not yet occurred. He was relieved from his dilemma when President Jefferson Davis directed Van Dorn to take command of the Army of the West, and join the two Confederate armies.[8]

On September 19 General Price received the news that the Confederate pickets had been forced to retreat on the Jacinto Road. General Rosecrans had announced his presence. The bluecoats were within a mile and a half of the center of town.[9]

The Federal intent had been for Ord to attack the Confederates. However, during the 19th he sat by while Rosecrans did all the fighting. General Ord later claimed that he heard no gunfire. This seems to have been a rare instance of acoustic shadow, an occurrence during the Civil War in which sound was muffled.[10] At any rate, he remained northwest of Iuka, wondering where General Rosecrans could possibly be.

The action on the Jacinto Road was heating up. General Price threw in more and more Confederates against the advancing Yankees, and the foe was driven back some 600 yards.[11] The graycoats surged forward, capturing nine artillery pieces.[12]

The Northerners regrouped and found reinforcements, but darkness covered the field. Success had been won, but at a dreadful cost. General Price had lost his favorite lieutenant, General Henry Little.[13] Struck in the forehead by a bullet as he led his men to the attack, he died instantly.

There was great apprehension among some of the Confederate leaders. They had suffered tremendous losses in the day's combat, and were fearful that the enemy would shortly overwhelm their position. General Price could not persuade his subordinates that their concerns were groundless, and without the confidence of his generals, he gave the order to move out of Iuka. The rebels fell into line and marched southward that night.

General Price had thrown 3,179 soldiers into the battle of Iuka. The Southerners lost 86 men killed, 408 wounded, and had to leave about 200 rebels behind who were too sick to be moved,[14] for a total loss of approximately 700 men. Union losses were slightly higher, with 141 men killed, 613 wounded, and 36 Northerners captured or missing, for a total of 790 Federals.

The casualties were light, when compared with larger battles later in the war. Both armies would have to rest and regroup, for in two weeks the action would shift to the northwest, where the soldiers locked horns again in the battle of Corinth. As it turned out, neither side made it to Tennessee.

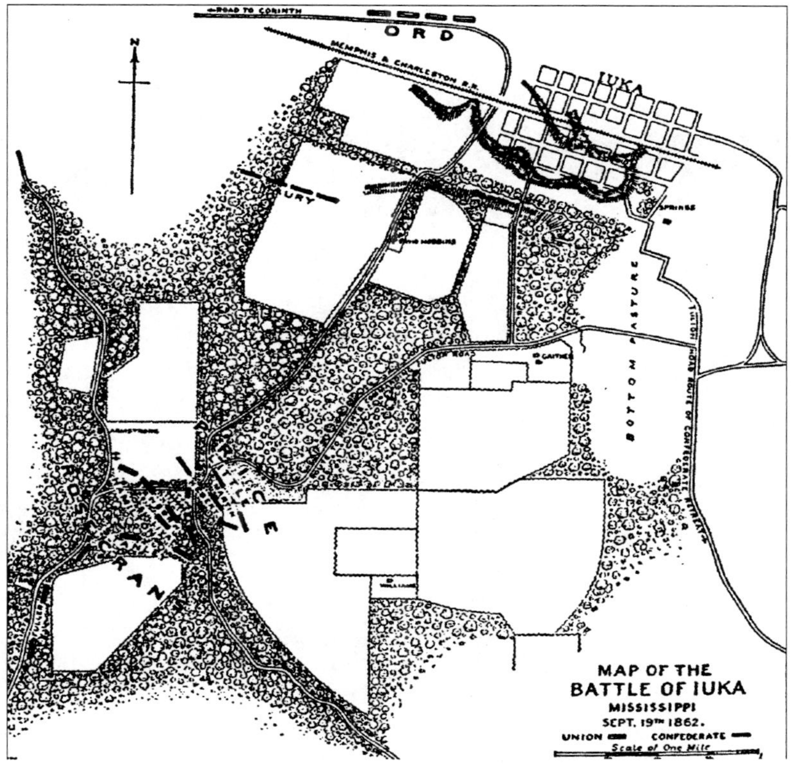

Battle of Iuka, Mississippi, September 19, 1862. Map by Fred E. Sitts.

September 19–20, 1862
SHEPHERDSTOWN (BOTELER'S FORD)

A. P. Hill (CSA) — F. J. Porter (USA)

Robert E. Lee and the Army of Northern Virginia were in full retreat. The graycoats had been repulsed at the battle of Sharpsburg, along Antietam Creek. It was time to leave the state of Maryland, and march back to the safety of Virginia. On September 18–19 the rebels crossed the Potomac River at Shepherdstown, Virginia, a small town only nine miles northwest of Harpers Ferry.[1] Speed was of the essence, as the Yankees were close behind.

Lee had given precise orders to General William Pendleton, the Confederate chief of artillery. With two brigades and 45 cannon, Pendleton was to hold the crossing at Boteler's Ford, near Shepherdstown.[2] The position was to be held all day on the 19th, and through the night if necessary. It was vital that the army cross the river in safety. General Fitz-John Porter and the Union V Corps were determined to capture the Confederates.

General Lee had his most trusted lieutenants close at hand, including Thomas J. "Stonewall" Jackson. In the early morning[3] of September 20, a frantic Pendleton rushed into Jackson's camp with a most alarming report. The Federals had crossed the river, defeated the infantry, and captured all of the Confederate guns![4]

Jackson could hardly believe such a wild rumor. Nevertheless, there was no time to consider such a catastrophe. The fate of the Army of Northern Virginia was at stake.

Immediately Jackson sent instructions to General A. P. Hill, a tenacious fighter in battle.[5] Hill led his men back toward the waters of the Potomac. Half a mile[6] from Boteler's Ford, he halted his men in a cornfield opposite Porter's bluecoats.[7]

On the Maryland side of the Potomac stood 70 artillery pieces of the Union V Corps. The heavy guns were massed on the hills. They were a formidable sight indeed.[8] The task at hand for A. P. Hill was to dislodge the Federal troops already on the Virginia shore. They must be forced back into Maryland.

The Confederates formed two lines of battle. The brigades of Dorsey Pender, E. L. Thomas and Maxcy Gregg made up the first line, supported by the troops under James Archer, James Lane and J. M. Brockenbrough.[9]

As the graycoats stepped forward, they were greeted by a thunderous volley of Union artillery. General Hill described it as "the most tremendous fire of artillery I ever saw."[10] On Hill's right and center, Gregg and Thomas hurled back the enemy with destructive force. However, on the left the bluecoats had massed their troops against Pender. Porter had extended the Union lines, attempting to outflank the North Carolinians.[11]

William Dorsey Pender had no intention of allowing a Confederate defeat. He wheeled one regiment to meet the threat. He then notified James Archer of the danger. Archer quickly shifted his men to prolong the Southern flank. Together, the two brigades advanced on the double. After they had gained the crest of the hill in their front, the enemy began to fall back. The rebels then poured a heavy volley into the backs of the Yankees, who were in full flight toward the Potomac River.[12]

The Federals splashed frantically for the Union shore. The Confederates aimed their muskets at the struggling foe, reloading as fast as they could. The shores of Virginia were safe again in the hands of the Southerners.

Upon closer reflection, General Pendleton had exaggerated the scope of the disaster. Instead of losing over 40 guns, it was revealed that only four had been taken. Nonetheless, Hill's timely counterattack saved the Army of Northern Virginia.[13]

Casualties had been slight, as the action at Boteler's Ford had been a sharp but brief encounter. The Confederates had lost 261 men; the Federals had 71 men killed, 161 wounded, and 131 missing, for a total of 363 soldiers.[14]

Although the action would certainly not qualify as one of the major battles of the Civil War, it was not without its importance. General Lee's troops had finally gained the time and freedom they needed to rest and recuperate from an arduous campaign in Maryland. The coming months would see the graycoats back in Virginia, where they would fight a tremendous battle on the streets of Fredericksburg.

October 3–4, 1862

Corinth

E. Van Dorn (CSA) — W. S. Rosecrans (USA)

Corinth, Mississippi, is a railroad junction in the northern part of the sate, just below the border with Tennessee. The town had strategic importance during the Civil War,[1] as it lay upon the intersection of the Mobile & Ohio Railroad and the Memphis & Charleston Railroad.

On October 3 the Confederates were camped some ten miles to the northwest[1a] in Chewalla, Tennessee. Led by General Earl Van Dorn, they numbered 22,000 men.[2] The rebels were aligned in three divisions, with Mansfield Lovell on the Confederate right, Dabney Maury in the center, and Louis Hebert on the left. Van Dorn would attack from the northwest,[3] and attempt to carry the town by surprise.[4]

The Federals at Corinth were under the command of General William S. Rosecrans, a Cincinnati native with four divisions at his disposal. At 9:00 A.M.[5] the bluecoats had Charles Hamilton's division on the right, with Thomas Davies to his left. Next in line were the troops under Thomas McKean, while David Stanley's men made up the far left of the Union alignment.[6] General Rosecrans held a slight numerical advantage, with about 23,000 muskets[7] covering the approaches from the north, northwest and west.[8]

The defenses at Corinth were protected by an outer line of earthen entrenchments, with an inner defense some 400 yards[9] closer to the town. In between lay a wide swath of felled timber.

The Confederates concealed themselves in the woods, then charged the works, storming over the thinly held outer defenses. By 1:30 P.M.,[10] the bluecoats had been forced back to the second line. This allowed the Union troops to form a more compact battle front.

Heat, fatigue, and a shortage of water[11] worked against the Confederates. A one-hour halt in the advance was called, and the time allowed the Federals to regroup and further strengthen their position. The assault continued, beginning with Lovell's troops, and then extending all along the front.

Around 3:00 P.M.[12] Rosecrans ordered General Stanley to move his men forward, providing reinforcements for McKean's and Davies' weary veterans. It had been an exhausting day for both sides, but up until this point Stanley's men had been held in reserve, and were relatively fresh.

The Confederates were not able to advance any further, and darkness put an end to the fighting on October 3. Although the Southerners were within 600 yards[13] of Corinth the performance of General Lovell's troops had not delivered the desired result.[14]

The Confederates planned to renew the contest at dawn on October 4. General Hebert would strike the Union right flank, while Maury would press forward in the center. Lovell would swing to the far right, attacking the enemy from the southwest in an attempt to outflank the Union left.[15]

Despite precise plans for the attack, the Confederates were not well coordinated on the second day. Hebert reported ill, and his division was commanded by General Martin E. Green. The change in command caused some delay, and Maury's troops led the advance. Green followed in close support, but Lovell did not attack at all.[16] General Maury was able to reach Corinth itself,[17] but the charge was thrown back by a stout defense. Without the cooperation of Lovell's division, Maury and Green had little chance of success.

By noon[18] the Confederates had withdrawn along the road which led back to Chewalla. The Federals, exhausted after two days of difficult fighting, did not pursue. Over the next two days, Van Dorn's command retreated to Ripley.

Casualties at the battle of Corinth favored the Federals. General Rosecrans lost 355 men killed, 1,841 wounded, and 324 captured or missing, for a total of 2,520. The Southerners lost 505 soldiers killed, 2,150 wounded, and 2,183 captured or missing, for a total of 4,838.[19]

The Maryland Campaign.
Map by Jacob Wells.

Not only had General Rosecrans won the battle for the Union, but General Hebert and General Lovell were relieved of command only a few weeks later. For the moment, Corinth was firmly in control of the Northern forces.

October 16, 1862–July 4, 1863
The Vicksburg Campaign

J. E. Johnston	U. S. Grant
J. C. Pemberton	(USA)
(CSA)	

The campaign of Vicksburg was characterized by continual failures. Time and time again, the Union forces began a march toward the hill city, only to be stymied by treacherous terrain and Confederate soldiers.

Despite a series of setbacks, lack of cooperation by the Southern generals and the tenacity of General Ulysses S. Grant would eventually carry the day for the Union.

One of the larger problems for the Northerners to overcome was the sheer size of the Confederacy. The land mass from the Atlantic Ocean to the state of Texas represented an immense geographic area. The conquest of the rebellious states appeared to be a tremendous undertaking.

Railroad transportation in the south was very poor.[1] This was due in part to the many rivers which meandered their way across the Confederate states. Easy transportation by water had retarded the development of an efficient rail system.

The largest, and most important of these waterways was the Mississippi River. On the Mississippi side, about midway up the state, lay the formidable citadel, Vicksburg. The winding course of the water, with many bayous, lakes and tributaries on both sides, made Vicksburg seemingly impregnable.

However, the difficulties in the capture of the city made it all the more attractive. General Grant realized that Union possession of Vicksburg would give the Federals control of the Mississippi. This, in turn, would slice the Confederacy in two, making it extremely difficult for the graycoats to receive food, supplies, medicine and troops from the states west of the river.

The Union strategy was essentially twofold. Grant would move south through Mississippi; at the same time, General Nathaniel P. Banks would move north from New Orleans. The two armies would squeeze the fortress in a pincer movement, forcing Vicksburg to surrender.[2] However, it would take time for Banks to move through Mississippi, and cooperation with Banks would delay Grant's plans considerably. Ultimately, Grant's Army of the Tennessee would have to capture Vicksburg alone.[2a]

The Vicksburg campaign got under way in earnest on October 16, 1862. The Federal armies were reorganized, and General Ulysses S. Grant took command of the Department of the Tennessee. This department would include north Mississippi, Cairo, Illinois, and the areas of Tennessee and Kentucky which lay between the Mississippi and Tennessee rivers.[3]

His opponent would be John C. Pemberton, a Pennsylvanian by birth who was fighting for the Confederacy. As head of the newly constituted Department of Mississippi and East Louisiana, Pemberton would be responsible for the security of Vicksburg.[4]

Working in cooperation with General Pemberton would be General Joseph E. Johnston. President Davis had given him the title of commander of the Department of the West. While Johnston's area of responsibility reached all the way to Chattanooga, he was given authority for the defense of Vicksburg as well.[5] The arrangement by Jefferson Davis would not turn out well for the Confederates.

Ulysses S. Grant knew the value of his own supply lines. The fall of 1862 was consumed organizing the Union forces for a drive deep into the heart of the Confederacy. Supply depots were established in Columbus, Kentucky, and Memphis, Tennessee. As the troops marched south into Mississippi, the Army of the Tennessee would operate along the lines of the Mississippi Central Railroad.[6]

Unfortunately for the bluecoats, the Confederates understood just how much the Federal troops depended on these supply lines. As December dawned in Mississippi, the Southerners were preparing to strike Grant's most important supply base, located at Holly Springs.[7]

Holly Springs, Mississippi, lies in the north central part of the state. While Grant was busy constructing a huge supply depot, a new idea occurred to him. The graycoats were situated almost due south at Grenada. He would occupy the Confederates stationed there, and send General William T. Sherman south from Memphis. Sherman would move past the enemy, and head straight for Vicksburg.[8]

On December 20, General Sherman left the city of Memphis. On the same day, Grant's new strategy began to fall apart. He was unaware of the Confederate plans. Three days before, on December 17, the Confederate cavalry under General Earl Van Dorn had left Grenada. With 3,500 men,[9] he headed northeast, in the direction of Ripley, Mississippi, and on the 19th, turned west, in the direction of Holly Springs.[10]

During the night of the 20th, Van Dorn divided his troops. At daybreak[11] the Confederates struck the depot, attacking from the east, northeast and north. The Federals tried to save the supply base, but the element of surprise had worked against them. After sweeping away a feeble defense, Van Dorn's troopers set fire to the depot.[12]

To make matters worse, telegraph lines and railroad tracks were destroyed. Over one million dollars[13] worth of damage was done to the Union war effort. The cavalry raid had a tremendous impact on the Union plans to attack Vicksburg. On December 21, General Grant began to pull back his Federal troops.[14] Because the Federals had intended to supply their army from this base, Van Dorn's raid was devastating to the Union cause.[14a] It looked as if the campaign would have to start over.

General Grant was not a man to be idle for long. He was determined to force the rebels to retreat. The Confederates were still located around Grenada, on the Yalobusha River. Grant was confident that Sherman could reach the enemy. By Christmas, 1862, General Sherman and his troops were on a naval convoy, heading south along the Mississippi River.

On December 26, Sherman would receive a painful experience in the swampy Mississippi bayous. The bluecoats landed at Johnson's Plantation, opposite the mouth of Steele's Bayou. North of Vicksburg, they were still four miles from the Confederate positions outside the city.[15]

The Mississippi River on the right and Thompson's Lake on the left created a narrow passageway for the Yankees. The Confederate front was only three miles wide.[16] The rebels were strongly posted, facing west and northwest atop the bluffs on Walnut Hills, also known as Chickasaw Bluffs.[17] To make matters more difficult for the

Federals, General Pemberton had reinforced the Southerners with Confederates from Grenada.[18]

Sherman attempted to bombard the enemy with Union gunboats on the Mississippi, but little damage was done. The Confederates had felled trees in the flooded bayous, slowing the Federal advance. Sherman continued to search for the best route to attack.

On Sunday morning,[19] December 28, Union General Frederick Steele led his men forward. Moving east, he encountered resistance from grayclad troops behind a levee. The Southerners had strengthened their position by digging entrenchments. Steele's advance came to an abrupt halt.[20]

The soft, wet ground prevented the Federals from bringing up artillery support, and the infantry's advance was slowed to a crawl by the difficult terrain. The Confederates had posted their field pieces on high ground, giving the graycoats a clear field of fire into Steele's invaders. As a result, the Union soldiers were at a considerable disadvantage.[21]

December 29 opened with a long-range artillery bombardment by the Northerners, as Sherman hoped to soften up his foe prior to a general assault. George Morgan and Frederick Steele's men would lead the attack. Again the terrain worked in favor of the Confederacy. The Yankees received a shower of fire from both muskets and artillery.[22]

The Federals advanced to within 150 yards[23] of the Confederate positions, but were driven back with heavy losses. Five separate assaults were made on the center of the enemy, but to no avail. Each time the Union forces were handily repulsed.[24] General Sherman lost 2,000 men in one day, while the Confederates suffered only 187 casualties.[25]

Once again, the Union war effort had reached an impasse, with every attempt foiled. A series of construction projects were about to begin. General Grant's ultimate goal was to isolate Vicksburg, forcing a surrender without a direct frontal assault.

Several canals were dug across narrow points of land, in an attempt to close the Union ring around the city. Each[25a] met with failure, frustrating both officers and men. It was not until April 1863 that the final Union drive on Vicksburg began to materialize.[26]

After months of frustration, Ulysses S. Grant solved the problem of supplies. The bluecoats simply operated on the Louisiana side of the Mississippi River, and established headquarters at Milliken's Bend, just upriver from Vicksburg. By mid–April the Northerners had sent XIII Corps south, led by General John A. McClernand. The Yankees would march through Louisiana until they reached Hard Times Landing. This would set the stage for Grant's next target: an attack on Grand Gulf, Mississippi. Once established back in Mississippi, the Yankees could then proceed with the campaign on Vicksburg.

The Union XIII Corps would make up the right wing of the Federal army. General James B. McPherson would lead the XVII Corps in the center, while Sherman's XV Corps would follow, comprising the left wing.[27] The marching order was to remain until the troops reached Hard Times.

On April 26, General McClernand began to send his troops down the Mississippi River. The Yankees left Hard Times for the short journey to Bruinsburg, Mississippi.

Observing all of this activity on the water was Confederate General John S. Bowen. Charged with the defense of Grand Gulf, Bowen recognized that the Union troops in the area meant trouble for the Confederacy. The presence of eight gunboats[28] under the command of Admiral David Porter only underscored the problem.

The Confederate defenses at Grand Gulf were not nearly as formidable as those at Vicksburg. Above the town, Fort Cobun was protected by a parapet nearly 40 feet thick. Three quarters of a mile downriver lay Fort Wade. A double line of rifle pits connected the two positions.[29] The Union navy would attempt to capture the town with a concentrated bombardment.

At 7:00 A.M.[30] on the morning of April 29, the gunboats left Hard Times, and moved past Grand Gulf. The vessels opened fire on Fort Cobun at 7:50 A.M.[31] Porter's fleet continued downriver, shelling Fort Wade as soon as it came in range.

The gunboats moved past Fort Wade and turned around, heading upriver. The Union navy repeated the process. The Confederates vigorously returned the fire, but little damage was done to the fleet by the artillery on the shore.[32]

Due to the long range nature of this particular conflict, casualties at Grand Gulf were slight. The Federals had 18 men killed and 57 wounded, for a total of 75 casualties, while the Confederates lost only 3 men killed and 19 wounded, for a total of 22. Despite a continual bombardment, Admiral Porter had failed to knock out the batteries on the shore.[33]

While General Grant had a clear understanding of his own intentions, General Pemberton was completely in the dark. The Confederates had some 50,000 men, but they were widely scattered along a 200-mile front, from Fort Pemberton in the north all the way down to Port Hudson, Louisiana. The Confederates simply did not know where Grant would strike next.[34]

Undaunted by the failure of the navy to eliminate the defensive works at Grand Gulf, Grant simply turned his attention further south, to the small town of Bruinsburg, Mississippi. By noon on the 30th of April,[35] most of the

XIII Corps had been transported down the Mississippi and was already on the east bank of the river.[36]

At 4:00 P.M.,[37] the bluecoats marched north for Port Gibson. If the Federals could take Port Gibson, then Grand Gulf would be untenable. The ring around Vicksburg was getting tighter.

Dawn on May 1 revealed the approach to Port Gibson. The task at hand seemed almost impossible. The hilly terrain was marked by levees and ridges, running in all directions. Each one seemed to be separated from the next by a ravine covered with trees, vines, and impenetrable canebrakes.[38] Port Gibson was only eight miles[39] from Vicksburg, but the journey would be difficult.

McClernand's men were moving inland, in an easterly direction. When they had reached the Rodney Road, the bluecoats discovered that they were blocked by Confederates under General Martin E. Green. To the north, in the direction of Port Gibson, lay the Bruinsburg Road. Perhaps this might afford a better avenue of travel. However, this direction was shut off as well — General Edward Tracy had deployed his Alabama troops across the Union line of march.[40]

General Bowen's command included the defense of Port Gibson. For the moment, he had done a very thorough job. There must be a better way to attack the Confederate position, the Northerners thought.

The Federal artillery opened fire on the graycoats to the north in an attempt to develop the strength of the Southern position. As the 49th Indiana regiment advanced, the Confederates pulled back.[41] McClernand did not believe that the enemy had sufficient manpower to stop a concerted assault.

By 8:15 A.M.,[42] the Yankees were ready to attack. The Federals surged forward, and the Alabama lines collapsed. The lines had gained some 400 yards, but were stopped by the rugged terrain and Tracy's second line of resistance.[43]

Although Tracy's defense had held for the moment, the Confederate position was in trouble. The situation deteriorated when General Tracy, attempting to encourage his men, was shot by a Union sniper. He died almost instantly.[44]

The Federals extended their flanks in both directions. Tracy's men were in serious trouble. Increasing pressure on all fronts, the bluecoats gradually moved forward throughout the afternoon.

The Union XIII Corps was doing well as they moved toward the Bruinsburg Road. The conflict was more difficult down by the Rodney Road. McClernand decided to mass his troops and strike the center of the Confederate position in a frontal assault.[45]

There were simply too many Union soldiers for the Confederates to resist. The graycoats fell back, trying to delay the advance. As the wave of blue swept over the field, the Southerners retreated to the east and the north.

Bowen's men had given a good account of themselves at Port Gibson, but in the end were not able to resist the numerical superiority of the foe. McClernand had 17,696 men, against approximately 6,800 for the Confederacy.[46]

The Union had lost 131 men killed, 719 wounded, and 25 missing for a total of 875, while the Confederates had 60 soldiers killed, 340 wounded, and 387 missing, for a total of 787.[47] However, with the Union victory at Port Gibson, Grand Gulf was outflanked. It would be extremely difficult to defend.[48]

On May 2 the rebels evacuated Grand Gulf. The Union forces were moving closer to the city of Vicksburg itself. During the month of May, General Grant would engage the enemy four times in a series of battles which would determine the fate of Vicksburg.

By the 11th of May, General Pemberton had established his headquarters in Vicksburg. He had approximately 23,000 men under his immediate command. However, two days later the graycoats would have a second force in Mississippi. Headquartered at Jackson, General Johnston arrived on May 13 with some 24,000 troops.[49] The failure of these two forces to work in concert would have a telling effect on the campaign in Mississippi.

The Union Army of the Tennessee, it will be remembered, was located to the south of Vicksburg. From Port Gibson, they had moved north to Grand Gulf, which the Confederates had evacuated. General Grant now moved in a northeasterly direction, to the small town of Raymond.

On May 11 the bluecoats advanced along a broad front. Sherman's XV Corps held the center. The XIII Corps under McClernand was on the Union left, closer to the Big Black River. General McPherson and the XVII Corps anchored the right, closer to Jackson.[50]

By the 12th McPherson's troops were approaching Raymond, defended by General John Gregg's Confederates. Gregg was soon to make a costly error in judgment.

Both General Gregg and General Pemberton believed that the advance on the Union right was only a diversion; the real attack would come elsewhere. As a result, Gregg seriously underestimated the strength of the Yankees in front of him.[51]

At 9:00 A.M.,[52] General Gregg deployed his troops. Generally, the Southern lines faced southwest. General Hiram Granbury led the 7th Texas regiment to the right of the formation. The 3rd Tennessee held the center, with the 50th Tennessee on the left. In close support of the Confederate left was a combination of the 10th and 30th Tennessee regiments.[52a] Gregg had held two commands[53] in reserve.

At about 10:00 A.M.,[54] the two sides collided. McPherson had sent forward skirmishers from General John A. Logan's division. The Yankees ran into the rebels and bullets began to fly.

Logan immediately placed one brigade on the left of a dirt road, commanded by Elias S. Dennis, while John E. Smith's brigade took their positions to the right of the road. The action began about two miles southwest of Raymond.[55]

At noon,[56] Gregg began to deploy his men for a counterattack. The advance would begin on the right, with Granbury's Texans, and would continue down the line. When General Gregg gave the signal, the Texans moved forward. The enemy broke in confusion, some running forward, some retreating.[57]

Fighting was difficult and sporadic. Due to the limited contact with the enemy up to this point, John Gregg still believed that he faced only one brigade, not parts of three separate brigades. Only two Union regiments had been sent into action, but in reality, there were 13 Federal regiments at Logan's disposal.[58]

As the afternoon wore on, more and more Union troops were sent forward. It became obvious to the Confederates that the enemy was there in force. The counterattack was brought to a sudden stop, and the graycoats fell back to Raymond. Pursuit by the Union forces was minimal.

Casualty reports for the action around Raymond vary widely, even by Civil War standards. Gregg's reports were incomplete at best, but the Confederates had 73 men killed, 252 wounded, and 190 missing, for a total of 515. The Federals lost 68 men killed, 341 wounded and 37 missing, for a total of 446.[59]

With the victory at Raymond on May 12, General Grant decided on a new plan, one which would ultimately result in the capture of Vicksburg. There were rumors that Joe Johnston was moving toward Jackson, leading another Confederate force. Grant would consolidate the Union forces under McClernand, Sherman, and McPherson. Then the Yankees would strike the enemy at Jackson, moving in the opposite direction from the graycoats at Vicksburg. Once Johnston had been defeated, the Federals would then turn their attention to the goal of the entire campaign: Vicksburg.[60]

As the Northerners moved toward Jackson, the situation for the Confederates began to deteriorate. Pemberton wanted help from Johnston, but did not wish to venture too far away from Vicksburg, leaving the city undefended. Johnston wanted Pemberton to attack Grant, but was not inclined to offer any assistance. The Union army was trapped in between two Confederate forces, but General Grant would succeed by defeating each adversary separately.[61]

On May 14, General Sherman's XV Corps was approaching Jackson. The Confederates had taken a position behind Lynch Creek, astride the Raymond-Jackson road. Facing southwest, the rebels waited for the Federals.[62]

Just after 11:00 A.M.,[63] the blue columns came into view. The Southern cannon roared. The advance was momentarily checked, but little damage was done. The Union artillery was vastly superior, and Sherman's guns soon replied. The rebels were forced to fall back under the pressure of the Federal cannonade. The XV Corps crossed Lynch Creek, and the Yankees were quickly advancing upon the town.[64]

To the north, the Confederates were struggling as well. McPherson's XVII Corps was marching due east toward Jackson on the Clinton-Jackson road. General Gregg sent Colonel Robert Farquharson with one brigade to the Confederate right, in an attempt to strike the Union left flank. Along the road, three regiments blocked the Union advance.[65] The 46th Georgia was on the right, with the 14th Mississippi in the center and the 24th South Carolina on the left.[66]

At 11:00 A.M.,[67] McPherson ordered his troops forward. A blast from artillery forced the XVII Corps to pause, but the Federal troops were far more numerous. The Yankees regrouped and charged again, forcing Gregg's men to fall back.

Confederate resistance at Jackson was very slight. Joe Johnston had ordered the men to fall back, literally abandoning the town to the Federals. Johnston retreated to the northeast, in the direction of Calhoun. By 4:00 P.M., Jackson was firmly in Union hands.[68]

Johnston had arrived in Jackson just in time to retreat. Pemberton expected to assail Grant from one side, while Johnston attacked from the other. Grant, for his part, thought that Johnston's Confederates would move forward. Instead, Johnston pulled his forces back, while Pemberton remained inactive as well.[69]

The Union forces lost 42 men killed, 251 wounded and 7 missing in this brief affair. Most of the Confederate commanders did not file battle reports, but one brigade opposite McPherson's XVII Corps had 17 men killed, 64 wounded and 118 missing, for a total of 199 casualties. Of course, this does not begin to approximate the total loss for the Confederacy. The city had been captured, 17 cannon taken by the Federals, and according to one estimate, some 800 Confederates seized.[70]

Ulysses S. Grant had everything going his way. Joe Johnston was in full retreat, and John Pemberton was consumed with indecision. Finally, on May 13, part of the garrison at Vicksburg tentatively stretched forward, crossing the Big Black River. The Confederate division was led by General John S. Bowen.[71]

The bluecoats now headed west, toward Vicksburg. General McClernand divided his forces, sending two divisions on the Raymond Road, and farther north, two more divisions on the Jackson Road. Still farther north were men of McPherson's XVII Corps. With cooperation, XVII Corps might be able to strike the grayclad foe in the left flank, forcing Pemberton to abandon his advance.[72]

The Confederates had three divisions at their disposal. On the right, General W. W. Loring guarded the Union approaches along the Raymond Road. Bowen's troops held the center of the Southern defenses, while General Carter Stevenson's division occupied the Jackson Road. Pemberton's position was a strong one, as the troops faced east, along a heavily wooded ridge.[73] The northern end of the Confederate position was a 140-foot-high cliff, named Champion Hill, after a local landowner.[74] The 23,000 graycoats were slightly outnumbered, as the Federals brought about 30,000 soldiers toward the enemy.[75]

The first action on May 16 took place on the Raymond Road in General Loring's sector. The far right of the Confederate position was held by Lloyd Tilghman's brigade. To his left were the rebels under Winfield S. Featherston. Both of these brigades were south of the Raymond Road. North of the road were Abraham Buford's men. The far left was anchored by Martin Green's brigade, which was actually part of General Bowen's command.[76]

Two Union divisions under A. J. Smith and Frank Blair made contact with the rebels, but did not attack aggressively. An artillery duel commenced, and superior Federal artillery carried the day. By 11:00 A.M. the bluecoats occupied General Loring's original line. A. J. Smith would try to consolidate all of the Federals before launching an all-out attack.[77] The action would shift to the north.

On the Jackson Road, the Federals were massing their forces for a two-pronged assault. While McClernand sent his two remaining divisions forward from the east, McPherson would attack from the north.

At 10:30 A.M., McPherson gave the order, and two divisions surged forward.[78] While Alvin Hovey's division struck the center of the Confederate position around Champion Hill, John Logan moved his blueclad troops forward on Hovey's right. Carter Stevenson's rebels were in danger of being outflanked.[79]

If Logan got behind Stevenson, the Confederates would be cut off from Vicksburg. As a result, the Southerners kept shifting their men to the left. By 11:30 A.M.[80] the Federal advance was approaching the stiffest line of Confederate resistance. The battle might soon be decided.

Slowly the Yankees inched forward. They paused, only 75 yards from the graycoats, fixed bayonets and charged. The rebels would have time to fire only once. The plan worked. Stevenson's Confederates fought stubbornly, but by 1:30 P.M. the Union pressure had become too great.[81] A powerful thrust by Hovey in the center and Logan to his right gained possession of the Jackson Road.[82]

General Pemberton had waited all day to see where the enemy would attack. When it became apparent that the main assault had struck the Confederate left, General Bowen was ordered to support Stevenson's battered command. At 2:30 P.M.,[83] Bowen's two brigades launched a vicious counterattack against Hovey's Federals. The Confederates were led by three of their finest commanders: Bowen, Martin Green, and Colonel Francis M. Cockrell.[84]

The 5,000 Arkansans and Missourians were the best combat troops in either army,[85] and they were in no mood to be stopped by a few Yankees. Sixty minutes later, Champion Hill was back in Southern hands.[86]

To Bowen's left, Confederates attempted to move forward, but General Grant continued to bring up reinforcements. Bowen had advanced so far forward that he was without support on either flank. There was no choice for his graycoats but retreat. At 4:00 P.M.,[87] the men fell back. Champion Hill changed hands once again.[88]

The Confederates had been hurled back on both the Raymond and Jackson roads. Pemberton pulled his forces back in the direction of Vicksburg.

Casualty reports are incomplete on the Confederate side, but estimates give their losses as 381 men killed, 1,018 wounded and 2,441 missing, for a total of 3,840. The Federals had only 396 men killed, 1,838 wounded and 187 wounded, for a total of 2,421.[89]

John Pemberton had failed at Champion Hill. Perhaps the Yankees could be halted along the Big Black River. The very next day would provide the answer.

On May 17 the Confederates were facing east, defending the bridge over the Big Black River. It represented the gateway back to Vicksburg. General Bowen was in command. The lines were anchored on the left by the meandering course of the Big Black. The right rested on Gin Lake. Martin Green held the left, Cockrell's troops were on the right, and General John C. Vaughn's brigade in the center. As the Federals moved west, General McClernand's XIII Corps prepared to assault the Confederate fortifications.[90]

There was little activity on either flank of the Confederate army. Around noon,[91] Cockrell heard sharp gunfire to the north. The Federals had massed their forces for a tremendous assault against Vaughn's Tennesseans. The surging blue soldiers were too numerous to resist. With a gaping hole in the Confederate center, Cockrell and Green were forced to withdraw,[92] although they had suffered very few casualties.

The force of the Union thrust was so successful that the action at the Big Black was very brief. Most of the Confederate losses on May 17 were prisoners. Approximately 1,800 Southerners fell into Union hands. Federal losses in the fight for the bridge over the Big Black River were less than 300 men.[93]

Pemberton's command withdrew into the defenses around Vicksburg. The Union plan was succeeding, but for General Grant, the hardest part lay ahead.

On May 18, the Union Army of the Tennessee placed Vicksburg under siege. The bluecoats surrounded the city in an attempt to force General Pemberton to surrender.

The siege got under way with two fruitless assaults by the Federals. On May 19 and May 22, the Union troops attempted to storm the city, but were repulsed both times with heavy losses.[94] Vicksburg remained under siege until July 4, 1863, when General Pemberton finally surrendered the entire garrison of 29,491 men.[95]

Obviously, the capture of Vicksburg had enormous ramifications. The Mississippi River was now open to Union naval operations, Confederate supplies and reinforcements would have a difficult time freely crossing such a broad river, and Union troops could move along the water without opposition. These military objectives would greatly assist President Lincoln in his war effort. However, perhaps the greatest damage was psychological. A symbol of invincibility had been torn away.

The capitulation of a fortress the Confederacy had deemed impregnable marked the end of a chapter of some of the worst generalship the Confederacy would produce. The campaign is certainly a credit to the tenacity of Ulysses S. Grant. However, the loss of the city is more of a reflection of the failure of General Johnston and General Pemberton to work together. Grant had placed the Union forces in between two enemy forces, which early in the struggle outnumbered the Federals. Had the Confederates attacked simultaneously, the results in Mississippi might have been quite different.

December 13, 1862
FREDERICKSBURG

R. E. Lee (CSA) — A. E. Burnside (USA)

Fredericksburg is located on the west side of the Rappahannock River in central Virginia. The Confederates, some 78,000 strong under General Robert E. Lee,[1] occupied a strong defensive position west of the town. On the east side of the river was the Union Army of the Potomac, a force of 125,000 troops[2] commanded by General Ambrose E. Burnside.

Although the position held by the Army of Northern Virginia was impregnable, neither Lee nor "Stonewall" Jackson wanted to fight at Fredericksburg. Both men conceded that the position was sound from a defensive standpoint, but they realized that due to the imposing terrain on the east side of the river, the Confederates would be unable to follow a victory with an aggressive pursuit.[3] On the other hand, James Longstreet, a defensive general by nature, thought that the ground was ideal. He hoped that the Yankees would attack.

Despite his misgivings, General Lee was unwilling to retreat farther and expose more of Virginia to the enemy, so he decided to give battle right where he was.[4]

Fredericksburg was really a story of two battles. The action opened on the Confederate right, where Thomas J. "Stonewall" Jackson held his sector against the Federals under William B. Franklin.[5]

December 12 produced fluctuating temperatures, creating heavy fog at the break of day.[6] The topography gave Jackson a huge advantage. Between the Rappahannock River and Jackson's front line of defense there was a wide, open plain. Running through the plain were the tracks of the Richmond, Fredericksburg and Potomac Railroad. Should the enemy be able to pass the R. F. & P., there was a slope 100 to 200 yards wide before Prospect Hill, where Stonewall had deployed his men.[7]

The rebels displayed a front 3,300 yards in length.[8] Jackson concealed the troops under A. P. Hill in the woods on Prospect Hill. From left to right, the brigades of Dorsey Pender, James Archer, and James Lane held the front line.[9]

There was a second line farther back, with Maxcy Gregg's brigade behind Archer and Lane. The divisions under John B. Hood, Jubal Early, D. H. Hill and William Taliaferro were held as reinforcements. The cavalry, led by J. E. B. "Jeb" Stuart, secured Jackson's right flank. Overall, the Confederates had 35,000 men in the area.[10]

In theory, this looked like a strong position. Unfortunately, it had one vital flaw. In the center of the line, between Archer and Lane, there remained a gap some 600 yards wide.[11] It is generally accepted that Stonewall Jackson knew about A. P. Hill's troop dispositions.[12] Perhaps the rebels were unconcerned as they felt that that the enemy would not be able to pierce the Confederate defenses without encountering a murderous crossfire from the Southern artillery.[13] At any rate, the gap in General Hill's lines was largely ignored.

On December 13, around 10:00 A.M., the fog lifted, revealing three rows of blue soldiers with glistening bayonets as far as the eye could see.[13a]

In command of the sea of bluecoats was General Franklin. His imposing force numbered 60,000 strong.[14] Cautious by nature, Franklin would employ only two divisions in the attack. About 1,200[15] yards away, the Yankees moved forward. The assault was under way!

The wide rows of enemy soldiers provided a tempting

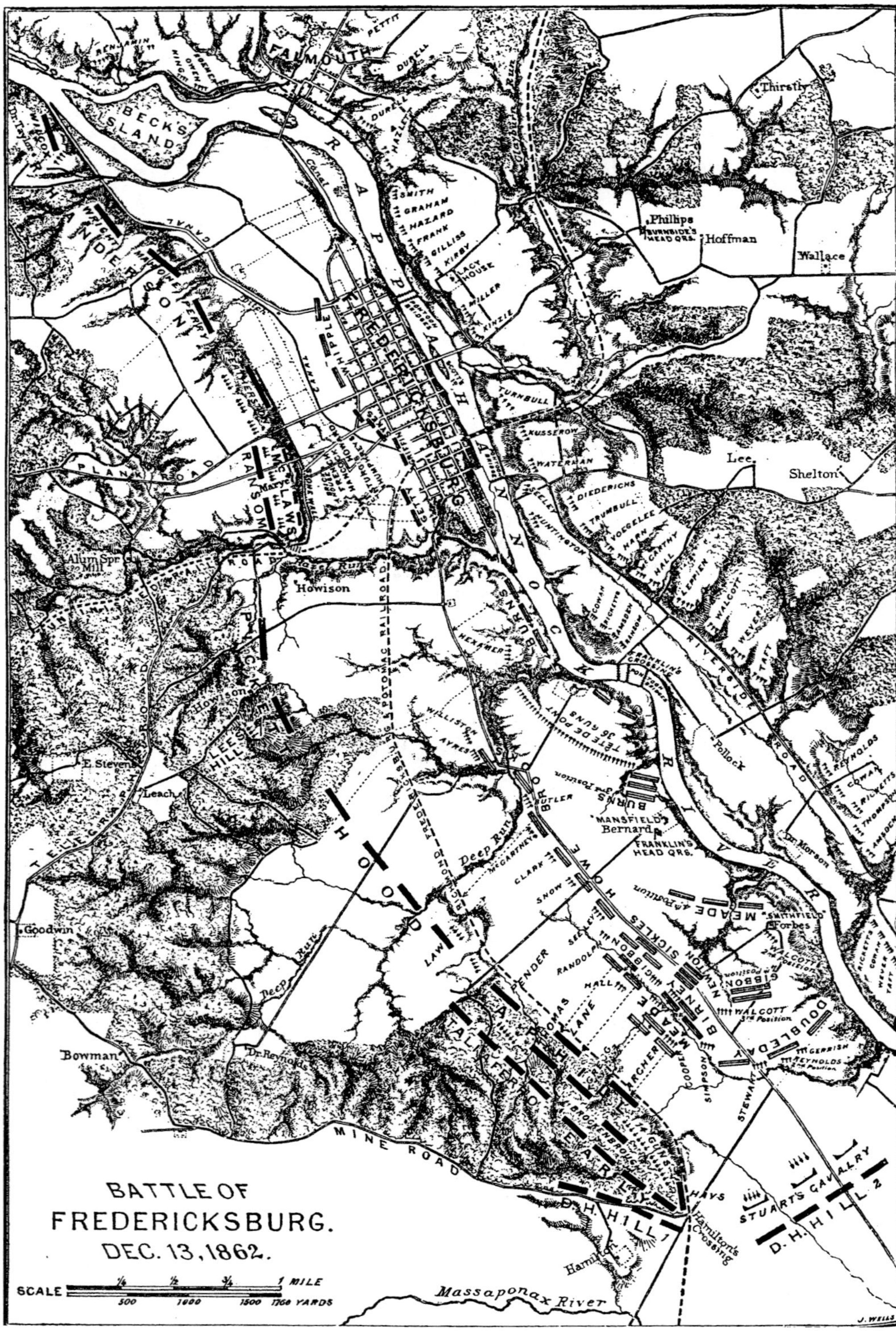

Battle of Fredericksburg, December 13, 1862. Map by Jacob Wells.

target for the Confederate artillery. In addition to the regular artillery, Stonewall Jackson decided to employ Major John Pelham, an artillerist serving in the cavalry. He let loose a barrage from the Confederate right, disrupting the Federal advance. Moving his two field pieces forward, Pelham was causing great damage, when suddenly a Union shell knocked out one of his guns.[16]

John Pelham was widely recognized as the most skilled artillerist in the Confederacy.[17] He moved his one remaining gun, a 12-pounder Napoleon cannon, back and forth so swiftly that the Federals believed the graycoats were firing several guns at the same time.[18] With their long lines raked by the fire from the Confederate right, the Union advance stalled.[19]

Three times General Stuart ordered Pelham to withdraw. The young Alabamian was undeterred, continuing to fire his lone cannon in the face of all odds. Finally, his ammunition gave out and he was forced to fall back.[20]

Federal artillery bombarded the woods where Hill's men were stationed, but there was no reply. Assuming that the Confederate artillery had been knocked out, the Federals moved forward. Slowly, the artillery fell silent, and the advance resumed.[21]

In the lead were the 5,000 Pennsylvanians under General George G. Meade. John Gibbon's division was on

Meade's right, and slightly behind him. Around noon the bluecoats were only 800 yards from Jackson's rebels.[22]

Just before 1:00 P.M., the Federals moved through the swampy bottomland and into the gap between Archer and Lane. Jackson's impenetrable defense had been pierced![23]

Maxcy Gregg's troops were unprepared for the onslaught they received. The Northerners fired a point blank volley into the graycoats. In attempting to rally his men, Gregg fell mortally wounded.[24]

Meade's breakthrough had lasted an hour and fifteen minutes.[25] Gibbon's men were battling Lane's North Carolinians when Stonewall Jackson hurled his reinforcements into the action. Jubal Early's division, plus the brigades of Dorsey Pender, Frank Paxton and Edward Thomas, hit the enemy with all of their fury.[26] Archer's brigade regrouped and descended upon Meade's exposed left flank. The Pennsylvanians were hammered from two directions.[27]

No army could withstand such pressure. The bluecoats withdrew from the woods back onto the open plain. Once the Federals reached the open ground, it became a race for the safety of the Union lines. Confederate infantry and artillery inflicted many casualties as their foe retreated.[28] Stonewall Jackson had dealt the Federals a crushing defeat on the Confederate right.

However, the battle of Fredericksburg is best known for the defensive stand of General James Longstreet. General Burnside ordered charge after charge of Union troops to their death in front of a strongly posted contingent of graycoats. This action took place in the town itself.

The ground rises on the western edge of town to an eminence known as Marye's Heights. In front of the heights lay a sunken road, protected by a stone wall four feet high. Artillery posted on Marye's Heights and the surrounding hills commanded the streets below. It would be too much for General Lee to ask that the enemy would actually attack this position. But charge they did.

General Longstreet had placed his infantry under Lafayette McLaws behind the stone wall. The brigades of T. R. R. Cobb and Joseph Kershaw, numbering some 2,500 men, awaited the oncoming bluecoats.[29] Behind these troops was the Washington Artillery, with the North Carolinians under Robert Ransom for support.

The Federals had decided to attack the strongest part of the Confederate position. General Burnside threw his men into the face of the Southern artillery. The infantry was hardly engaged as the cannon roared, cutting huge gaps in the Union lines.[30]

Again the Federals charged, only to be thrown back over their dead and wounded. A third charge resulted in more Union dead on a battlefield now thickly strewn with Burnside's casualties. General Lee became uneasy at the persistence of the enemy.

After the third charge, Lee commented to Longstreet, "General, they are massing very heavily and will break your line, I am afraid." Confident in his reply, Longstreet asserted, "General, if you put every man now on the other side of the Potomac on that field to approach me over the same line, and give me plenty of ammunition, I will kill them all before they reach my line."[31]

General Longstreet was not far from the truth. As the Federals continued their fruitless charges at Marye's Heights, the graycoats kept up the massacre. General Cobb was mortally wounded in the battle, but the casualty list was frightful, particularly on the Union side. Most of General Lee's losses occurred in Jackson's sector, as his troops did not have the protection of a stone wall.

The Confederates lost 608 men killed, 4,116 wounded, and 653 captured or missing for a total of 5,377 at the battle of Fredericksburg. Union losses were 1,284 killed, 9,600 wounded and 1,769 captured or missing, for a total of 12,653.[32]

The battle of Fredericksburg produced a shocking defeat for the United States government. President Lincoln responded by removing Ambrose Burnside from his post on January 25. Although he would continue his career in the army, it had become quite clear that he was unfit for higher command.

December 31, 1862

Parker's Cross Roads (Red Mound)

N. B. Forrest (CSA)	C. L. Dunham J. W. Fuller (USA)

Throughout the Civil War the Union infantry and cavalry had struggled with their inability to capture the notorious Southern horseman, General Nathan Bedford Forrest. Aggravation mounted as he continually frustrated Federal efforts to bring his mounted attack force under control.

Although he possessed no formal military training, Forrest was an outstanding cavalry officer.[1] He conducted his operations mainly in Tennessee, Alabama and Mississippi. Famous for his mobility and elusiveness, he would continue to plague the Union high command for the duration of the conflict.

As Christmas dawned in 1862, General Forrest found himself in a most precarious situation. He was stationed at Union City, Tennessee,[2] in the northwest corner of

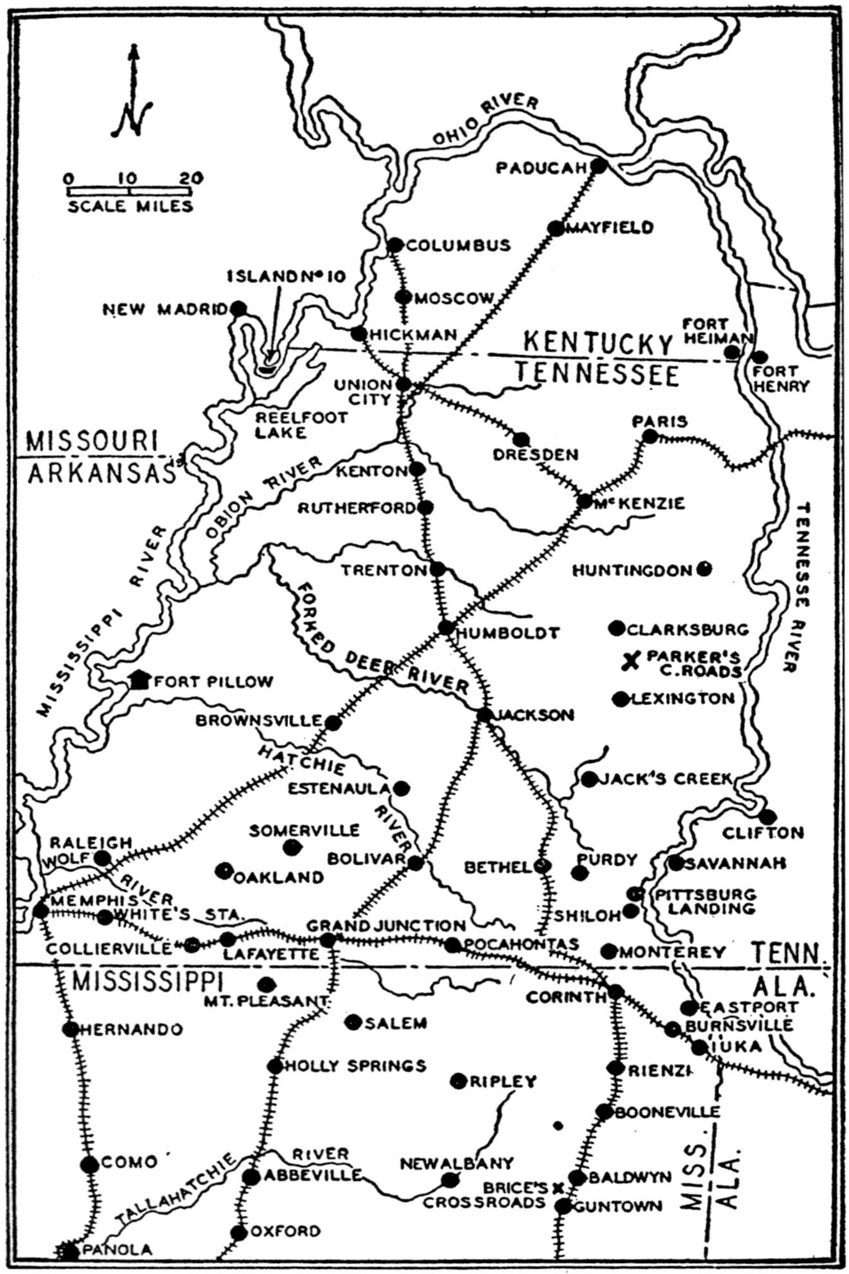

West Tennessee and Kentucky and Northern Mississippi

the state. His force of some 2,000 men[3] seemed to be surrounded.

Due north, at Columbus, Kentucky was a garrison of some 7,000 enemy troops.[4] To the south, at Jackson, Tennessee, General Jeremiah C. Sullivan had two brigades, each one as large as Forrest's own command. Additional Union forces were stationed at Fort Henry, Tennessee and Corinth, Mississippi. A third brigade in Jackson, though not under General Sullivan's command, made the Confederate plight a dire one indeed.

Forrest intended to break out of this trap by riding southeast, and crossing the Tennessee River at Clifton. This would give the graycoats some measure of security. However, there would certainly be fierce opposition on the journey.

On December 31, 1862, the Confederates came in contact with one of General Sullivan's brigades, under the leadership of Colonel Cyrus L. Dunham. The opposing forces collided at the small village of Parker's Store.

At the same time, Forrest sent a small detachment to Clarksburg. These troopers were to watch the Union forces at nearby Huntingdon, and report any movements. This small scouting party failed to report the presence of Sullivan's other brigade,[5] led by Colonel John W. Fuller. This oversight almost cost the Confederates the battle.

The fighting started out as a long-range artillery duel. It began on the west side of the Huntingdon-Lexington Road, and the slow-moving action moved in an easterly direction. By 12:00 P.M., however, Forrest intensified the pressure. Cannon were aimed at the Federal flanks, and A. A. Russell was ordered to take his men around Dunham's right, while J. W. Starnes would maneuver around the other flank.[6]

The Confederates soon captured three artillery pieces, the Union wagon train, and about 300 men. Upon the appearance of several white flags, Forrest demanded that the enemy surrender.[7] Dunham refused, but it still looked as if the graycoats had the situation well in hand.

Despite the best preparations, the day was not yet over for the Southerners. Within thirty minutes[8] Fuller's brigade struck the Confederates in the rear, taking Forrest completely by surprise. He had expected that his scouts would keep him aware of the position of the Union troops.

Russell and Starnes heard the gunfire behind the Confederate position. At this point, their men were behind Dunham. Thinking quickly, they charged Colonel Dunham's bluecoats, preventing his troopers from concentrating on Forrest.

Forrest and the remainder of the Confederates were caught between two lines of Union cavalry, but most of the men were able to escape as Dunham was held at bay.

Some 300 dismounted cavalrymen were lost to capture after the Northerners stampeded their horses.[9]

No official casualty report exists for the Confederate side at Parker's Cross Roads; however, Forrest estimated his losses as 60 men killed and wounded. The Federals had 27 soldiers killed and 140 wounded. Each side had approximately 300 men captured.[10]

The Federals did not offer any pursuit, and the Confederates were able to ride 12 miles south to Lexington that night, crossing the Tennessee River at Clifton one day later.[11] For the time being, General Forrest had his troopers safe across the water.

The conflict at Parker's Cross Roads was not a major battle in the Civil War, but it was not without significance. When it was over, the Confederates had added new recruits to their ranks, captured equipment and supplies, and defeated another attempt to imprison their commanding general. To the United States government, the mystique of Nathan Bedford Forrest was greater than ever.

December 31, 1862–January 2, 1863
STONES RIVER (MURFREESBORO)

B. Bragg (CSA)	W. S. Rosecrans (USA)

Murfreesboro, Tennessee, was a small community during the Civil War. As late as 1864 there were only 4,000 inhabitants.[1] It lay just east of the Nashville & Chattanooga Railroad, some 30 miles[2] southeast of Nashville. Stones River flows through this part of Tennessee, with the East Fork passing to the north and east. The West Fork runs just west of Murfreesboro, and it was in this area that the battle would take place.

On November 26, 1862, the Confederate forces moved into the town.[3] General Braxton Bragg had no desire other than to occupy middle Tennessee. The Union Army of the Cumberland under General William S. Rosecrans was stationed in Nashville. The fortifications there seemed too strong to attack, and it appeared wiser for General Bragg to stay where he was and await developments.[4]

Militarily, this was not a strong position for the Confederates. It was very easy to move around the Southerners. General Bragg was not familiar with the country in this area,[5] and a better position should have been selected.

For his part, General Rosecrans was in no hurry to assault his adversary. However, on December 26,[6] the bluecoats moved forward. He divided his 47,000 men[7] among three generals: the right wing was led by Alexander M. McCook, the center was under George H. Thomas, and the left was commanded by Thomas L. Crittenden.

The Confederates were deployed about a mile and a half[7a] northwest of Murfreesboro, the Southern lines were bisected by the Nashville Turnpike and the West Fork of Stones River. General Bragg had 38,000 graycoats under his command.[8]

The Federals took three days to reach the battlefield. On December 29, General Rosecrans arrived in the vicinity of Murfreesboro, but the entire army would require still another day to get into position.[9]

The Union battle plan was relatively simple. The bluecoats faced east and slightly southeast. General Crittenden on the left would align his men on both sides of the West Fork of Stones River. If he could capture the high ground on the east side of the water, the Union artillery could command the field, and turn the right flank of the enemy. General Thomas would hold the center, and advance as far as the river, while General McCook was ordered to turn his right to the southeast, and receive any Confederate attack. If Bragg did not attack, McCook would occupy the enemy forces in his front.[10]

The Confederates had concocted a mirror image of the Union plan. Facing west, General Joseph Hardee's corps was on the left, and his object was to attack the enemy's right, in this case McCook's men. Hardee was to continue to turn to his right. In the center was the corps under General Leonidas Polk. He would move forward, and turn to his right as well. The rebels had some additional troops on the other side of Stones River as reserves, commanded by General John C. Breckinridge. The Confederate intent was to push the Army of the Cumberland back into Stones River.[11]

Unaware of each other's intentions, both sides wanted to attack the enemy's right flank.[12] The coming battle would turn on execution.

On the morning of December 31, a gray fog covered the battlefield.[13] At 6:22 A.M.,[14] the rebels moved through the mist. John P. McCown's 4,400 men[15] led the assault, followed by Pat Cleburne's 5,000[16] Confederates, only 500 yards behind.[17]

The bluecoats were calmly eating their breakfast when McCown delivered a vicious blow to the unsuspecting Yankees on McCook's far right. These were the brigades under August Willich and Edmund Kirk. Kirk was wounded, and his troops disintegrated.[18] Willich's men fared no better. With the remnants of Kirk's shattered brigade streaming at them, Willich was soon overpowered as well. General Willich was captured.[19]

A few regiments attempted a feeble defense, but the

field soon belonged to McCown.[20] Union General Richard W. Johnson had suffered the destruction of his entire division.

As the Confederates overran the Union position, McCown's assault began to come apart. Instead of turning to his right, the men drifted too far to the west. Cleburne's division was no longer a second wave of shock troops; they now occupied the front line, with McCown on Cleburne's left.[21]

The next group of bluecoats was the division of General Jefferson C. Davis. The Indiana native shifted his lines, and deployed his men facing south on either side of Gresham Lane. General Cleburne sent the Tennesseans under Bushrod Johnson to attack Davis's new position.[22]

Although there were woods to the east of the lane, Davis's men had a clear field of fire directly in front of them. Union artillery opened up, and the Tennessee Volunteers were hit hard, but they persisted, and the Southern field guns answered. Regrouping, Johnson's men surged forward.[23]

The Northerners were forced to withdraw their artillery from the field, and Johnson's troops overran the enemy. West of Gresham Lane, the 22nd Indiana Regiment collapsed, followed by the 77th Pennsylvania. On the other side of the road, the graycoats were having a more difficult time. Johnson's Tennessee regiments had become tangled up with one another, and the assault in this area lacked cohesion.[24] Johnson's advance stalled.

At 7:30 A.M.,[25] the rebels met a second line of defense: the Union brigade led by Colonel Philemon Baldwin. The Confederates belonged to McCown's brigade, under the command of General St. John Liddell. While Liddell's men advanced in the lead, fragments of Bushrod Johnson's Tennesseans were advancing along the west side of Gresham Lane, and additional Confederates loomed just behind Liddell on his left. Baldwin's men fell back without a fight.[26]

The Southerners under McCown and Cleburne had been successful. General Hardee's troops had performed valiantly against the divisions of Johnson and Davis. However, the attack would now shift to General Polk's graycoats, and the next opponents they encountered would be tough ones.

The action continued to move in a northerly direction. At approximately 8:00 A.M.[27] the battle reached the Union forces under General Philip H. "Little Phil" Sheridan.

Sheridan's division now made up the remaining portion of the Union right. He was determined to give a good account of himself, and his troops did not let him down.

The Federal troops fought stubbornly for over two hours, until they finally ran low on ammunition.[28] Casualties were high among the Northerners, but Polk's troops suffered even more severely.[29] Finally, the feisty New Yorker was forced to give ground, but not before dealing the enemy a serious blow.

With Sheridan finally defeated by Polk, Hardee could now reform his exhausted men and resume his quest for the Nashville Turnpike. If Hardee could capture the pike, the Federal escape route would be cut off.

As the contest shifted to the center of the field, Braxton Bragg's focus became a small wooded spot of land, known to later generations as the Round Forest. Cedar and oak trees dominated the area. Union Colonel William B. Hazen commanded the ground. Hazen would fight well on December 31, but Bragg's preoccupation with this small group of trees would cost him the battle.[30]

Just after noon[31] the Confederate assault finally died back. The graycoats approached the Nashville Turnpike, but they did not have enough men to capture the road.[32]

Although it is true that the Confederacy could certainly have used more men, it accentuates a striking difference in the performance of the two commanding generals. William S. Rosecrans was constantly in motion, reviewing troop dispositions and bringing forward reinforcements. On the other hand, Braxton Bragg was almost detached from the battle. He allowed Polk's men to be sent forward in a piecemeal, uncoordinated fashion, weakening that assault considerably. While Rosecrans was utilizing every available man, Bragg allowed four brigades under General Breckinridge to remain on the east side of the river.[33] A magnificent opportunity for a Confederate victory was squandered due to poor leadership.

Throughout the afternoon the carnage went on, with the Yankees repelling charge after charge. Belatedly, General Bragg was able to move Breckinridge's troops forward, but they were far too late to do any good.[34] The attempt to carry the Round Forest had failed, and darkness covered the field.

January 1, 1863, was a day of rest. Both sides remained inactive, and licked their wounds from a bloody battle. However, neither army left the field, and the conflict would resume the next day.

By January 2, the Federals were strongly entrenched. East of Stones River, Union troops held the high ground. Bragg decided that since Breckinridge possessed the freshest troops, his division would make the assault.[35] Naturally, Breckinridge was against the order. The terrain was very unfavorable to the Confederates. On the other hand, the Union position was a strong one, and the rebels would have to advance over open ground with little protection.[36]

General Breckinridge advanced at 4:00 P.M.[37] The attack had some limited success at first, but soon the Federal artillery began to assert its power. Captain John Mendenhall, Crittenden's chief of artillery, had collected 45 guns[38] to thwart the Southern assault. Massed together, the artillery would have a tremendous effect when trained on the onrushing graycoats.

Mendenhall had selected an ideal position: on the west side of the river, the guns were higher than Breckenridge could place his infantry. As the graycoats moved forward, they were greeted by the explosions of the Union field pieces. As the cannon roared, the Confederate advance was immediately checked. In addition, Union reinforcements poured across the river and over the field to chase the rebels back. General Bragg's plan of attack for January 2 had been soundly defeated.[39]

Casualties at the battle of Stones River were very heavy for both sides. The Confederates lost 1,294 men killed, 7,945 wounded and 1,027 captured or missing, for a total of 10,266. This does not include a few additional casualties in John Pegram's cavalry brigade. The Federals had 1,730 soldiers killed, 7,802 wounded and 3,717 captured or missing, for a total of 13,249.[40]

Who really won the battle of Stones River? When the day was over, the Federals had lost more men, but the bluecoats were in possession of the battlefield. Although the Union Army of the Cumberland did not pursue their foe, Braxton Bragg retreated some 36 miles.[41]

Over and above the immediate results, the battle had great repercussions which would last for the duration of the Civil War. The action at Stones River brought about the Confederate loss of middle Tennessee. This opened the gates to Chattanooga and Atlanta for the Union, as the Federal government solidified its control of the Volunteer State for good.[42]

1863

March 17, 1863
KELLY'S FORD

F. Lee (CSA) — W. W. Averell (USA)

The winter of 1863 was marked by inactivity along the southern front. The graycoats under Robert E. Lee were camped along the Rappahannock River in eastern Virginia, awaiting a move by the Union commander, General Joseph E. Hooker.

The only move of note was a thrust by William Averell in the direction of Culpeper, which lay upon the Orange and Alexandria Railroad. On March 16, Averell assembled 3,000 horsemen[1] and headed west. The Yankees were riding for Kelly's Ford.

The object of the New Yorker's attention was General Fitzhugh Lee, a Confederate cavalry officer who was the nephew of the commanding general. Fitz Lee led a brigade of troopers currently stationed at Culpeper.[2]

Other events at Culpeper brought General J. E. B. "Jeb" Stuart and Major John Pelham to the town. Stuart was the chief of cavalry for the Army of Northern Virginia, and Pelham was a brilliant young artillerist in the cavalry. A court-martial was in session, and Stuart had been called as a witness. The trial was over by Saturday the 16th, and as the two Southerners had no military responsibilities, they decided to remain one more day and turn their attention to the ladies of the town.[3] Their decision would turn out to be a fateful one for the Confederacy.

Fitz Lee realized that if the Yankees were to move south of the Rappahannock River, they would probably cross the river at Kelly's Ford. He stationed 60 men along the Orange and Alexandria Railroad, guarding against a surprise attack.[4]

However, on March 17, Lee received the news that the bluecoats had indeed crossed the river, and had captured 25 Confederates in the process. It was vital to defeat the foe before Averell could reach the railroad tracks.[5]

The Confederate cavalry under Lee numbered no more than 800 men.[5a] The odds were long, but this was the type of desperate action which got John Pelham excited. Jeb Stuart could smell a battle in the air, and he wanted to be on hand when the fighting started. At this point there was nothing Major Pelham could do. The artillery attached to Fitz Lee's command had not yet arrived on the scene, but perhaps the major could perform some other service for the graycoats.[6]

The Union forces were not moving up the road from

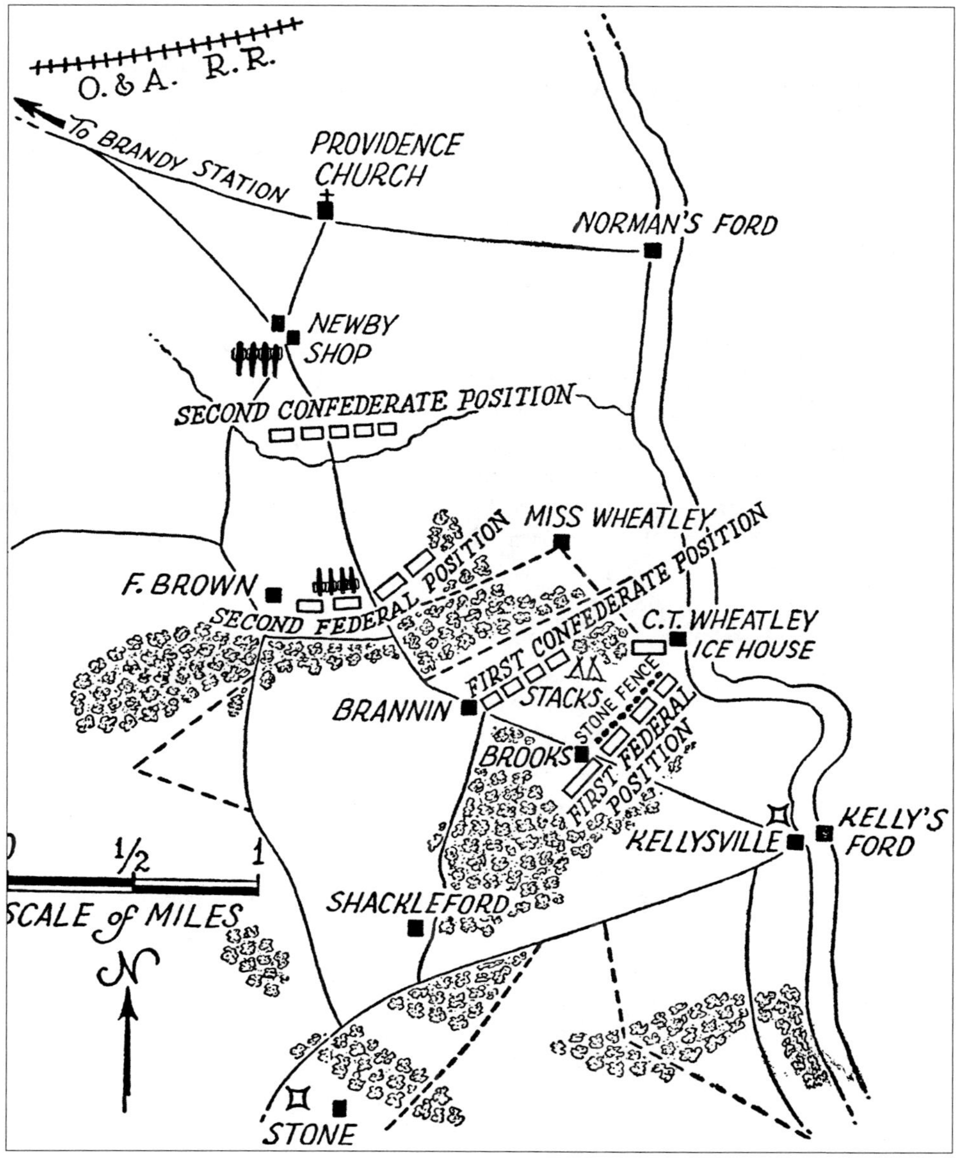

Scene of the action at Kelly's Ford, March 17, 1863. Map by John T. Draper after H. B. McClellan.

Kelly's Ford. They were over the river, but what were they doing? Fitzhugh Lee was not about to wait and see. If Averell was not going to advance, then the Confederates would go after him. Lee's cavalry mounted their horses, and rode off in the direction of Kelly's Ford, with Stuart and Pelham at their side.

As the graycoats approached from the west, they came upon the enemy. The Federals' left flank was anchored by dense woods. In front of the woods on the Federal right was a stone fence, defended by Union sharpshooters.[7]

General Lee decided to attack at once. Stuart agreed, and remained at the front to observe the sharpshooters, while Major Pelham went to the rear in an attempt to bring up the missing artillery. When Pelham returned, he found the action developing very quickly.[8]

The 3rd Virginia Regiment was charging the stone fence. They intended to scatter the bluecoats, with sabers drawn and pistols ready. The Virginians were searching for a gate or gap in the fence where they would be able to break through the Union line. The southern horsemen were heading for the farm buildings on their left,[9] belonging to the estate of C. T. Wheatley.

Here was an opportunity for battle which John Pelham simply could not pass up. It was in his blood. He leaped to his horse and encouraged the rebels. "Forward!" he shouted, and raced toward the action. Fortunately, Lee's troopers had found an opening at a gate, and were pouring through it. The young major halted and stood high in his stirrups, waving his friends forward.[10]

Suddenly a terrific crash was heard overhead, as a Union artillery shell burst above Pelham. His horse reared back, and the major toppled from his steed. The smile remained on the face of the young man from Alabama, but a small shell fragment had entered the back of his head, just at the hairline.[11]

He was taken to the rear, and presumed to be already dead. At the Shackleford home in Culpeper, his limp body was taken down from his horse. To everyone's amazement, his heart was still beating. However, a steel tip of a Union shell had penetrated about two inches into his skull, causing a fatal wound.[12] He died at approximately 1:00 P.M.,[13] March 17. He was only 24 years old.[14]

The Confederate charge had lost its force, and the action degenerated into demonstrations by both sides. Nightfall brought about the withdrawal of the Northern cavalry. Casualties were 133 on the Southern side, while Averell had lost approximately 78.[15] However, the graycoats had lost Major Pelham, a crippling blow to the cavalry. He had organized General Stuart's horse artillery, a very mobile strike force which could be easily shifted from one point to another.

His rise had been rapid within the artillery arm of the service, and his eye was uncanny in his understanding of the terrain in front of him. The death of Pelham extinguished the star of an officer most certainly destined for greatness.

April 27–May 6, 1863
CHANCELLORSVILLE

R. E. Lee (CSA)	J. E. Hooker (USA)

The stage was set for the battle of Chancellorsville on January 25, 1863. Abraham Lincoln had lost confidence in General Ambrose E. Burnside, and replaced him with Joseph E. Hooker. Nicknamed "Fighting Joe" in the Union Army of the Potomac, he boasted loudly of victories soon to be his. President Lincoln had chosen Hooker for his aggressive nature. The Federal government had grown weary of a succession of commanders who had been unable to suppress the rebels. In Lincoln's view the past was colored with caution and incompetence, but now he finally had his man.

Hooker's first task was to improve the sagging morale of the Union army. He started by reorganizing the units under his command. The Army of the Potomac would be comprised of seven corps, and it was important to place strong leadership at the top of each one. The end result was an improvement over the prior winter, but complete success would not be attained.

Command of the I Corps was given to General John F. Reynolds, a capable officer who was highly respected within the ranks of the Army of the Potomac. The II Corps would be led by General Darius N. Couch. Hooker had great confidence not only in Couch, but in his subordinates as well. General Daniel Sickles was in charge of the III Corps. This was a controversial appointment because Sickles was a politician, not a military man, and some Union officers felt that he was not qualified for such responsibility. The V Corps went to General George G. Meade. In contrast to Sickles, Meade's appointment was well-deserved. The commander of the VI Corps was General John Sedgwick. As popular with the common soldier as Hooker himself, Sedgwick had won the nickname "Uncle John." His troops adored him, and would follow him anywhere. The XI Corps was led by General Oliver O. Howard. His bravery was unquestioned — he had lost an arm in the battle of Seven Pines — but the native of Maine had replaced the beloved Franz Sigel at the head of a corps which still retained its German flavor. Finally, the XII Corps went to General Henry W. Slocum.[1] With only two divisions, it was small in size, and this lack of manpower was to be very important in the coming months.

Another change which General Hooker brought to his troops was the institution of insignias and badges for each division. In this way, the men were no longer in an impersonal army, but each battle unit could be readily identified by the designs on their cap or sleeve. This appears to be trivial, but it instilled a sense of pride in the common soldier.[2]

In short, the Army of the Potomac was a much better fighting force in the spring of 1863 than it was only a few short months before. "Fighting Joe" Hooker had no doubt that this was an army to be reckoned with.

Not all of the important activity occurred on the Union side. In February,[3] two divisions[4] of Lee's Army of Northern Virginia under General James Longstreet were sent to North Carolina to gather food. Lee miscalculated both the strength of the enemy and his own need for Longstreet's troops.[5] The failure to recall these divisions was one of Lee's few mistakes,[6] and it would result in a lost opportunity for the graycoats.

Although there were many activities which formed a backdrop to the battle of Chancellorsville, they should be looked upon only as a prelude of what was to come. The events belonging to the battle itself began on April 27, 1863.

Chancellorsville was really just a few outbuildings, centered around the Chancellor farmhouse,[6a] located in a place called the Wilderness. The Wilderness is an area of Virginia woodland of about 70 square miles along the Rappahannock River. In colonial times the Wilderness had witnessed the development of the iron industry, and most of the trees had been cut down. The second growth timber had emerged as a dense tangle of dwarf pine, cedar and hickory, along with a scrub oak known locally as blackjack.[7] Soldiers on both sides who fought in the area would long remember the thickness of the underbrush. It had a tremendous impact on both movement and vision.

At the end of April, Robert E. Lee commanded an army of 60,892 men, just south of the Rappahannock River. Joseph E. Hooker had 133,868 Union troops at his disposal,[8] but they were located on the north side of the water. Very soon these large forces would come together.

Although General Lee's attack at Chancellorsville is well documented, it was actually General Hooker who started the battle on the offensive. He had a very sound plan, and during the last few days of April, it was the Federal forces who were in control of events. But would "Fighting Joe" see his plan through to completion?

The Union plan of attack sent Howard's XI Corps, Slocum's XII Corps and Meade's V Corps, in that order, along the Rappahannock to the Federal right. These troops would cross the Rappahannock at Kelly's Ford. Moving south, they were then to cross a second river, the Rapidan, which flows into the Rappahannock. Approaching from the west, the intent was to get behind Lee's army, striking the graycoats in the left flank.[9]

General Couch would divide the men of his II Corps. One division was ordered to Banks' Ford, another to U.S. Ford, and a third marched in the direction of Fredericksburg. It was important to General Hooker that General Lee focus his attention on Couch in his front; he would thus fail to see the approaching Yankees on his left.[10]

The Federal left wing would be made up of Reynolds' I Corps and Segwick's VI Corps. They would be placed opposite Fredericksburg. Daniel Sickles' III Corps, located between the left and right wings, must be prepared to move either way.[11]

General Hooker had designed a wonderful plan for his infantry, but it was at this juncture that he committed a critical blunder with his cavalry.[12] He detached the Federal horsemen under George Stoneman to raid the Confederate supply lines.[13] The eyes and ears of the Army of the Potomac were gone.

However, the advantage was still with the Northerners. Hooker's brilliant flanking maneuver had taken Lee completely by surprise. By April 29, the right wing of the assault force was across both the Rappahannock and the Rapidan.[14] It was not until this point that the Confederate cavalry, led by General J. E. B. Stuart, informed General Lee of the enemy's movements. On the Union left, Sedgwick's VI Corps was across the Rappahannock just below Fredericksburg.[15] If the rebels retreated, he was to pursue, but Sedgwick's basic purpose was to prevent any Confederates in the area from reinforcing Lee. Further downstream, Reynolds brought the I Corps across with little difficulty. The Confederates were still unclear as to Hooker's intentions.[16]

Partially negating this advantage was the inability of the Federal command to pinpoint the location of the Confederate defenders, particularly the elusive Stonewall Jackson. As a result, Hooker overestimated the number of men facing Sedgwick, and underestimated the strength of Lee's left flank.[17]

April 30 saw the movement of Union divisions as they crept toward Chancellorsville. Without much opposition, the bluecoats had steadily moved into the tiny settlement. It looked as though the movement of the Federal right wing had been a rousing success. General Hooker was unaware that April 30 would be the high point of his military career.[18] The left wing spent an idle day, watching the Confederates in their front, wondering when the impending battle would begin.

By May 1, all uncertainty had disappeared in the

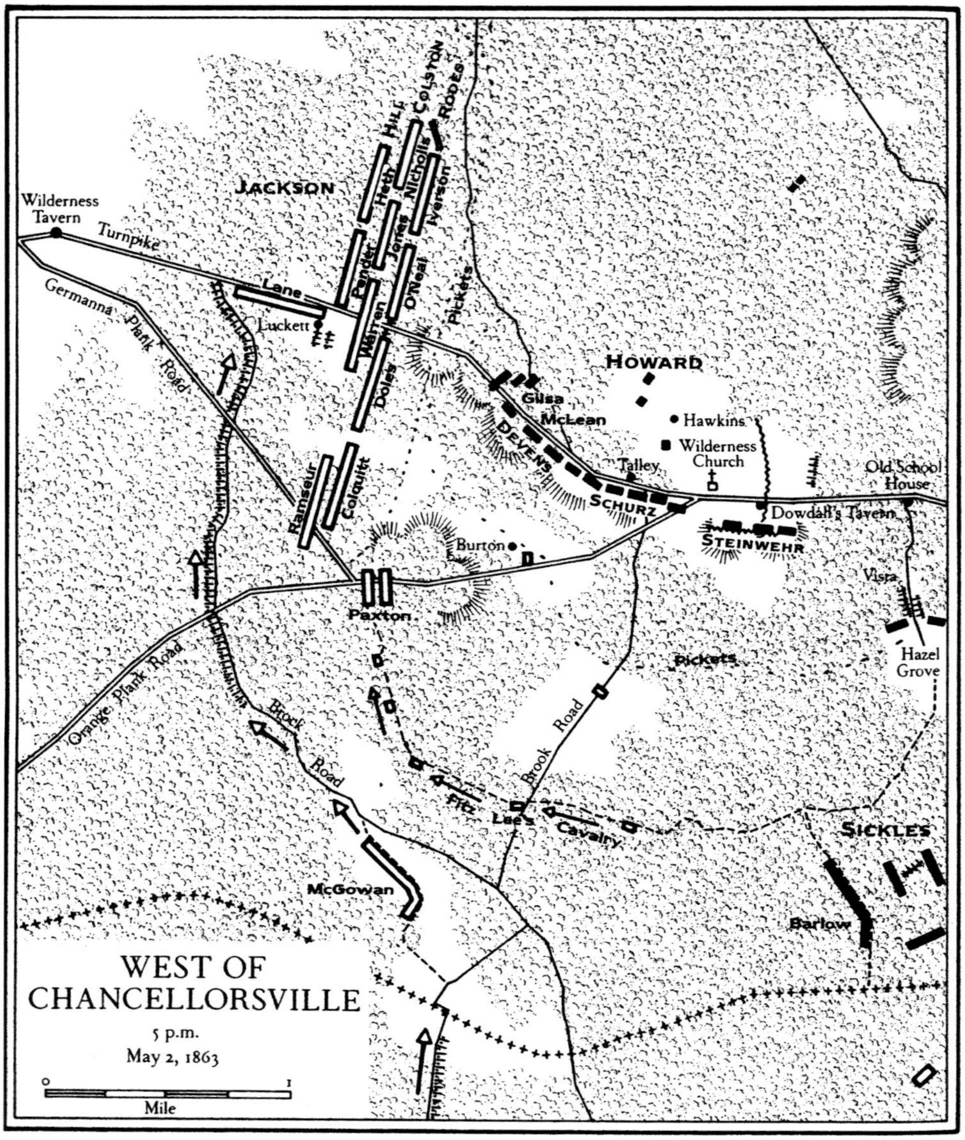

West of Chancellorsville: poised to strike. Jackson spreads his infantry through the undergrowth for a mile on each side of the turnpike, positioned to overlap and roll up Howard's unsuspecting corps. Three of Jackson's brigades and most of his artillery are still strung out in the Wilderness. Map by William J. Clipson.

mind of Robert E. Lee. He knew where the enemy was, and decided to take bold steps to stop the invaders. Knowing that he was heavily outnumbered, he determined to divide his army in the face of the enemy. It was the most famous maneuver of his life.

Special Orders No. 121 governed the transfer of Confederate troops from the Fredericksburg area to Chancellorsville. General Lafayette McLaws would leave one brigade behind. This would be Barksdale's Mississippians. He would move with the remainder of his force in a westerly direction toward Chancellorsville and reinforce General Richard H. Anderson. This movement would place Anderson on the Confederate left, with McLaws in the center. The second point dealt with Stonewall Jackson. Jackson would leave one division, under General Jubal A. Early, in Fredericksburg. At daylight on May 1 Jackson was to take the remainder of his corps west, also reinforcing Anderson.[19]

This left General Early with slightly over one division, against the two corps under Sedgwick and Reynolds. Jubal Early had just over 10,000 men; he would be facing over 45,000.[20]

The first brilliant strategical move had been made by Hooker, in moving his troops to strike the enemy's left flank. At this point Lee would neutralize Hooker's gem with one of his own. General Lee shifted his army, concentrating the rebels at Zoan Church.[21] He now stood directly in the path of the Union right wing. This caused Hooker to worry that Lee would defeat one wing of his army, then turn the Confederates loose on the remaining wing, beating half of Hooker's army at a time.[22]

In making this move to counter his adversary, Robert E. Lee exhibited the remarkable sense of perception that followed him throughout the entire Civil War. He was the only Confederate general who realized that Sedgwick's assault at Fredericksburg was a distraction, and that the real attack would come against the Confederate left.[23]

For his part, General Hooker had an entire half of his army across two rivers. With 70,000 men and 184 cannon[24] on Lee's flank, the plan simply must work. He ordered an advance eastward. Meade's V, Slocum's XII, and Howard's XI Corps marched toward Chancellorsville. Hooker was exhibiting a trait which would cost him dearly: his mental vision was limited to his exact physical vision.[25] He assumed that nothing could disrupt his plans. Robert E. Lee was about to teach him a very painful lesson.

Everything seemed to be going according to the Union attack plan. There was little or no resistance as the blueclad corps marched past Chancellorsville toward the Confederate left flank. Suddenly, out of nowhere, the enemy appeared. On the Orange Turnpike, General George Sykes of the V Corps collided with Lafayette McLaws' graycoats. South of the turnpike, on the Orange Plank Road, General Slocum's XII Corps met Stonewall Jackson's men.

This aggressive action by General Jackson took Hooker by surprise. He had not expected to be attacked on May 1.[26] The Union commander was unnerved, and he faced a dilemma. He had wanted to fight a battle, but not here and not now.[27] Lee had forced Joe Hooker to make a decision. It would be the most important decision of his life.[28]

General Hooker must now choose between attacking in full force and retreating. A weakness appeared in Hooker's outwardly boastful, arrogant nature. He lacked firm moral stamina. In addition, he may have suffered a nervous collapse due to the excitement and fatigue of the four preceding days. On May 1, he ordered the army to retreat to Chancellorsville.[29]

Now was the time for Robert E. Lee to take center stage. Lee was an aggressive, offensive general by nature, but his outstanding characteristic was his audacity.[30] He was determined to strike the Northerners, pushing the foe back across the Rappahannock. There were three directions in which Lee could attack. On the Confederate right, General Early was doing his best at Fredericksburg. He held the town, but was heavily outnumbered. Making matters worse, the high ground on the opposite bank of the river was ideal for Union artillery.

In the center, Hooker had a strong position, and could be reinforced with relative ease by both wings of the Army of the Potomac. Offensive operations against the Union center did not seem too promising. There must be another way to attack this invader.

When evaluating an attack of the Federal right, the difference between the Southerners' use of cavalry and the Union failure in this regard cannot be emphasized too heavily. Lee knew approximately where Hooker's right flank was; the problem was how to get there.[31]

General Lee decided to take a bold step to move around the Federal right flank. In his plans, he would violate every maxim of military convention. The Army of Northern Virginia had been divided once already around Fredericksburg, but the Confederates would split their forces yet again. Lee would retain the divisions of Richard Anderson and Lafayette McLaws, some 14,000 men, and occupy the Confederate center. Stonewall Jackson would take 28,000 troops[32] on a circuitous march. Heading first to the west, he would then turn south, west and north. This would place Jackson's assault force facing east, outside the right flank of the XI Corps,[33] under General Oliver O. Howard.

Although Jackson intended to begin his march very early in the morning of May 2, he got a late start. General Robert Rodes' division was to lead the attack, and by the time his men broke camp it was close to 7:00 A.M.[34] The divisions of General Raleigh E. Colston and A. P. Hill would follow Rodes. The Southerners headed west toward an old foundry called Catherine Furnace. Here they would turn south on the route to outflank the bluecoats. Amazingly enough, Jackson's men at Catherine Furnace were actually observed by Union troops. General Sickles' III Corps was stationed at Hazel Grove, and saw the graycoats as they moved past.[35]

Jackson realized that the Confederates had been spotted. As they passed Catherine Furnace, Union artillery began to bombard the column. He ordered Rodes to detach a regiment to guard against any surprise attack from Hazel Grove. Jackson's infantry was ordered to move at double time past the danger, and the wagons were sent on a safer, more southerly route until the threat was over.[36]

Hearing the sounds of gunfire erupt on his left, General Lee sent two brigades from General Anderson's division to Jackson's aid. General Carnot Posey and General A. R. "Rans" Wright rushed their brigades forward, striking Sickles' troops in the flank.[37]

At this point, Dan Sickles made a decision which would be very significant later in the day. Due to the stiff resistance from Posey and Wright, General Sickles borrowed Francis Barlow's brigade from Howard's XI Corps. In addition, General A. S. Williams' division was moved out of its position on the right of Hazel Grove to meet the Confederate threat. This left a large, undefended gap between Sickles's III Corps and the XI Corps under Howard.[38]

Despite the fact that the rebels had been seen, no one in the Army of the Potomac seemed alarmed. It looked from a distance as if Jackson was retreating.

While the tail of Jackson's column fought off trouble from the bluecoats, Robert Rodes moved his troops south down the Furnace Road, then turned west again. Out of view of the enemy, Rodes moved his grayclad Southerners north to the Brock Road. The rebels crossed the Orange Plank Road and continued until they reached the Orange Turnpike. Here they turned east, feeling for the vulnerable right flank of the XI Corps. Close to 3:00 P.M.,[39] Jackson jotted a quick note to Lee. The Confederate left was about to strike.

The situation on the Confederate right was not as promising. General Barksdale's brigade of Mississippians still held possession of Fredericksburg. Hooker had ordered Reynolds' I Corps to withdraw from his position, but Sedgwick still had his entire VI Corps in place. At 11:00 A.M. General Early was observing the movements of the I Corps, trying to determine what the enemy was doing, when a messenger arrived from Lee's headquarters.[40]

It was Colonel Robert H. Chilton, Lee's chief of staff. Chilton delivered a verbal message to Early to move his force toward Chancellorsville. Jubal Early was incredulous. He knew he could not leave Fredericksburg without being seen, and as soon as the Yankees knew that it had been evacuated they would take possession of both the town and the surrounding area. Chilton was insistent that General Lee did indeed mean for Early to withdraw, and General Early began pulling his troops back toward Chancellorsville.[41]

Colonel Chilton had been mistaken. A note from Lee arrived well after the graycoats had left Fredericksburg, stating that Early was to withdraw only if he could do so safely. General Early now had a decision to make. Should he go west and join General Lee, or try to retrace his steps back to Fredericksburg?[42]

Early assumed that the Northerners had observed his withdrawal, so he continued west. One mile later, he was informed that the brigade left to guard the town was in jeopardy. General Barksdale had returned to Fredericksburg to help the beleaguered Louisianans, commanded by General Harry Hays.[43]

Jubal Early was absolutely furious. He had landed in a terrible predicament, his tiny little force had been split apart, and it seemed as if the Confederates would be captured or destroyed, all because Colonel Chilton had misconstrued General Lee's intentions. General Early turned his command around, and headed back to Fredericksburg to unite his army. Fortunately for the bewildered graycoats, the situation was not as desperate as it had seemed. The Federals had failed to take advantage of their opportunity, and that very evening the rebels were back in the emplacements they had left earlier in the day.[44]

Evening was fast approaching on Stonewall Jackson's eager assault force. The troops were aligned in three lines roughly parallel with each other, all facing east along the Orange Turnpike. Robert Rodes had his division in front. From the Confederate left to right, were the brigades of Alfred Iverson, Edward O'Neal, George Doles and Alfred Colquitt. Stephen D. Ramseur had dropped off of Rodes' right flank to prevent any surprise attack. His brigade took a supportive position just behind Colquitt's men on the Confederate right. About 150 yards[45] behind them were the Southerners under Raleigh Colston. The brigades of Francis Nicholls,[46] J. R. Jones and E. T. H. Warren made up this second line. A. P. Hill's command brought up the rear. Harry Heth and Dorsey Pender placed their brigades to the left of the Turnpike, but James Lane's brigade had not quite reached the field yet, and was still marching along the Turnpike. Sam McGowan's men were still farther back, moving forward on the Brock Road.[47]

Right in front of the Confederates was the exposed right flank of General Howard's XI Corps. Both Howard, and the Union brigadier on Howard's far right, Charles Devens, were unaware that an enemy force was about to attack at any moment. Their lack of concern and attention to detail would cost the Federals dearly in the moments to come.

Fighting Joe Hooker was very concerned about the dispositions of the XI Corps. With generals Barlow and Williams supporting the III Corps, Howard had fewer than 11,000 men remaining on the Union right flank.[47a] There were gaps in between the divisions of the XI Corps.[47b] Finally, almost half of Howard's men were in action for the first time.[47c] Hooker had tried to move Reynolds' I Corps to support it, and it was that movement which Jubal Early had already observed at Fredericksburg. However, it was not likely that Reynolds would arrive in time.[48]

The Union XI Corps was clearly the weakest link of Hooker's point. Not only was it the smallest, but it was also the poorest in quality. Hooker did not have much confidence in Howard's ability and he had placed him on the far right to keep the XI Corps out of the line of fire.[49]

It seemed as if Howard was depending on the dense Wilderness as his first line of defense. Only two regiments[50] faced west, as well as the reserve artillery, posted about a mile or so to the rear. Everyone else faced south.[51]

The sun had started to slip away on May 2. It was 5:15 P.M.[52] The Confederates were lined up just as Jackson wanted them. The unsuspecting quarry lay right in front of the Southerners, cooking their supper and talking casually. With most of his assault force at hand, Stonewall Jackson sat on his horse next to Robert Rodes. "Are you ready, General Rodes?" he asked, in a calm voice. "Yes, sir." "You can go forward, then."[53] He had unleashed the greatest assault in Confederate military history.

General Rodes' division moved through the Wilderness. There was half a mile[54] to go before they reached the Yankees' first line. In only 15 minutes,[55] the Confederates had delivered their first volley into the Union ranks. Two German regiments[56] were so surprised that they turned and ran without firing a shot.[57] Some Federals tried to fire into the onrushing horde of graycoats, but resistance was weak, and the collapse quickly became a stampede.

The Confederates seemed to be charging from everywhere, pouring over the Union lines. Panic ensued, and as each regiment fled, they created utter chaos in the Federals behind them. Among the hail of bullets flying all around him, General Howard tried to stop the flood of bluecoats running for safety,[58] but it was to no avail. While his personal courage was unquestioned, his lack of preparation had cost the Yankees dearly.

While it would appear at first glance that the Confederate assault had been executed to perfection, errors had indeed occurred. General Rodes had led his men forward with resounding success, but Jackson's attack was actually less powerful than it might have been.

General Alfred Colquitt, positioned on the right flank of Rodes' division, was cautioned not to stop for any reason, and to charge forward into the enemy lines. Nevertheless, he became worried about Federal forces to his right. General Stuart's cavalry had been stationed there, precisely to prevent any halt whatsoever in the advance. When Colquitt suddenly halted his brigade, he blocked the path of General Ramseur's brigade as well. This eliminated 13 regiments and about 5,000 men from Jackson's force.[59]

Despite the inactivity in Colquitt's brigade, the Southerners pressed on. Robert Rodes exhorted his men onward. Riding high above the swarming graycoats, he shouted encouragement to his troops: "Forward, men, over friend or foe!"[60]

The biggest problem for the Confederates was the lack of sunlight. As May 2 slipped away, visibility became difficult. Howard's XI Corps had been routed, and the bluecoats were on the run. Would Jackson have enough light left to finish them off?

General Rodes and General Colston had seen their men overtake the enemy, but the Confederates had become disorganized by the pursuit. At about 7:15 P.M.,[61] Rodes was ordered to halt his men and reorganize the Southern forces. Colston's second line had become entangled with Rodes' troops, and the rebels would have to sort out the problems. By 8:00 P.M., the thick branches of the forest in the Wilderness cast a shadow of darkness over the action.

However, Stonewall Jackson was not to be deterred by fading light or the few regiments of enemy infantry which had attempted a weak defense. The Yankees must be pursued, and with all possible speed. The first two assault divisions were exhausted, and all battle formation had been lost. Now it was A. P. Hill's turn. Pushing his brigade forward, the North Carolinians of General James Lane advanced. The 28th and 18th North Carolina regiments deployed to the left of the Plank Road, with the 37th and the 7th North Carolina to its right.

General Jackson instructed A. P. Hill to press on, as the enemy had been routed. Jackson then moved forward on the Orange Plank Road, past Lane's men. He wanted to make a personal reconnaissance of the Union position. Continued pursuit was the only thing on his mind. None of the officers in Lane's brigade were notified that first Jackson, and then Hill had ventured forward beyond the Confederate lines.[62]

At this point, Stonewall Jackson was not expecting any danger. However, he was closer to the enemy than he realized. Off to his right, a single shot rang out. Then suddenly, as if in response, the 37th and 7th North Carolina opened fire. Both Jackson and Hill were trapped! Men and horses went down instantly. The gunfire intensified, and unknowingly, the 18th North Carolina had opened fire on General Jackson and his aides. The sound of so many horses in front of General Lane's troops sounded like Union cavalry. Lieutenant Joseph G. Morrison leaped from his horse, shouting "You are firing into your own men!"[63]

In the dark, the Confederates thought that this was a trick, and redoubled their fire. A. P. Hill had also shouted for them to stop. Finally, the gunfire died down among the Southern soldiers, but not before Stonewall Jackson had been hit three times.

At first, his wounds were not deemed serious, but closer inspection would reveal otherwise. He had been shot once in the right hand and once in the left forearm, but the most serious problem was the bullet which shattered the bone in his upper left arm.[64] The small party in the woods needed to get the general medical attention as quickly as possible.

General Jackson said that he was able to walk with some assistance, but he moved with great difficulty. Soon a litter was brought, and he was carried at a faster pace. A burst of fire opened from the Union lines, and one litter bearer was wounded. The rebels placed the litter on the ground, and waited until the air grew silent. On they went, through the thick woods, as this seemed safer than the middle of the road. Here one of the litter bearers tripped over a root or vine, and Stonewall Jackson tumbled out of the stretcher. Landing awkwardly, right on his injured arm, he groaned in agony.[65]

Finally, he reached friendly lines, and Dr. Hunter McGuire arrived with an ambulance. Jackson was gently loaded into the vehicle and transported to Guiney's Station, located 18 miles south[66] of Chancellorsville.

He fought a hard battle against his injuries. His left arm was amputated, but pneumonia had developed, and on Sunday, May 10, 1863, Stonewall Jackson uttered his last words: "Let us cross over the river and rest under the shade of the trees."[67]

Jackson had been wounded, but the fighting on May 2 was by no means over. A. P. Hill had also been hit, though not severely. He was wounded by a shell fragment across the back of the legs.[68] He was, however, no longer capable of commanding his troops.

General Hill decided that he was obliged to turn over the command of the Second Corps to Robert Rodes, who was present and could press forward. At the same time, he knew that he should send for J. E. B. Stuart, who was the only major general still left in the corps.[69]

Robert Rodes could have taken command, as he was present and Stuart was not. However, he was a very dedicated officer, and patriotic to the Southern cause, and immediately stepped aside, realizing that the leader of the cavalry was both well known and well liked throughout the army. For the remainder of the battle of Chancellorsville, General Stuart would be in command.

With a change in command, a tremendous battle, and the darkness in the Wilderness, the Confederates were in disarray. General Stuart was on his way to assume command of Jackson's troops, but the next action would occur on Lee's right, over in Fredericksburg.

On May 3, John Sedgwick still had the Union VI Corps facing the Confederates under Jubal Early. However, the situation had changed in a matter of hours. Had "Uncle John" vigorously pressed the attack the night before as Hooker desired, he would have found Fredericksburg lightly defended, as Early had taken most of his men back toward Lee. By this point, General Early had returned, having overcome the difficulties with Colonel Chilton. Once again, the feisty Virginian had blocked the path of General Sedgwick.

It was here that Fighting Joe Hooker made another momentous decision in the battle of Chancellorsville. It concerned the fate of the Federal III Corps. General Sickles had his men positioned around Hazel Grove, an ideal spot for artillery. Despite the Union advantage in this arm of the service, General Hooker failed to capitalize on this golden opportunity. Hazel Grove, in the words of E. Porter Alexander, the Confederate artillerist, was "an open, grassy ridge, some 400 yards long, extending N.E. and S.W...."[70]

Before sunlight on May 3, Hooker summoned Sickles to his headquarters at the Chancellor house and ordered him to fall back to a position around Fairview.[71] The Hazel Grove location would have been excellent for the bluecoats. In turn, Alexander would make sure that it was just as valuable for the Southerners. Confederate artillery placed there would not only jeopardize the Union artillery at Fairview, it would place the entire Federal position in great danger.[72]

Overnight, the Northerners had contracted their lines. Facing the enemy were the III and XI Corps. Couch's II Corps was behind them. The troops of the V and I Corps were held in a strategic reserve. The XI Corps had been moved to the rear, although nothing was expected of Howard's men.[73]

General Stuart had arrived on the field and assumed command of the graycoats. They faced east, with A. P. Hill's division now in the forefront. It had been placed under General Harry Heth. General Colston still made up the second line, while Rodes' tired rebels comprised the third line of attackers.[74] However, this time all of the Confederates were present in the assault force, although General Stuart had no reserves left to use. In addition, there were the divisions of Anderson and McLaws under Robert E. Lee. They would most certainly be put into action today. Finally, the Confederate artillery held Hazel Grove. Porter Alexander would press his advantage to the utmost.

In the early morning hours, the rebels moved forward. The slaughter was horrible, as the battlefield erupted with the roar of muskets and cannon from both sides. The Confederates were hindered by the slowness of Colston in bringing his troops forward promptly.[75] The Yankees had the advantage in that they were fighting from behind earthworks, and inflicted heavy losses on the charging rebels. Hooker's strategy of defensive warfare seemed to be working.[76] However, "Fighting Joe" Hooker was still waiting for VI Corps under Sedgwick to reinforce his embattled bluecoats. Sedgwick was not moving with alacrity. He seemed almost stationary.

General Stuart brought up his third line, still attacking from the west. General Lee sent in Anderson and McLaws from the south. The Confederates charged forward, the Yankees began to waver, and then began to run low on ammunition. Their fire started to wane, and gradually, Hooker's troops fell back. The firm grip of Fighting Joe on the battle of Chancellorsville had been broken, but the cost was high in Confederate blood. Ramseur's brigade had lost over half its strength.[77] Other brigades lost heavily as well.

The Union artillery had pulled back as the Southern shells exploded around the Fairview position. The Confederate artillery had been better handled, from a more advantageous position. That advantage was beginning to tell. The action at Hazel Grove would prove to be one of the best examples of offensive artillery in the entire war.[77a] Porter Alexander had learned that the Chancellor house was Hooker's headquarters. General Hooker stood next to a column on the porch as the battle raged around him. Suddenly a shell exploded, splitting the column in two. Word soon spread among the Union troops that Fighting Joe Hooker was dead.[78]

He was not. But from the Union perspective, the situation was even worse. He was injured so severely that he could not effectively command the men in the field, yet he failed to promptly turn over the army as he should have. General Hooker had suffered what would be diagnosed today as a concussion.[79] Effectively, the head of the Army of the Potomac had been removed from the battle-

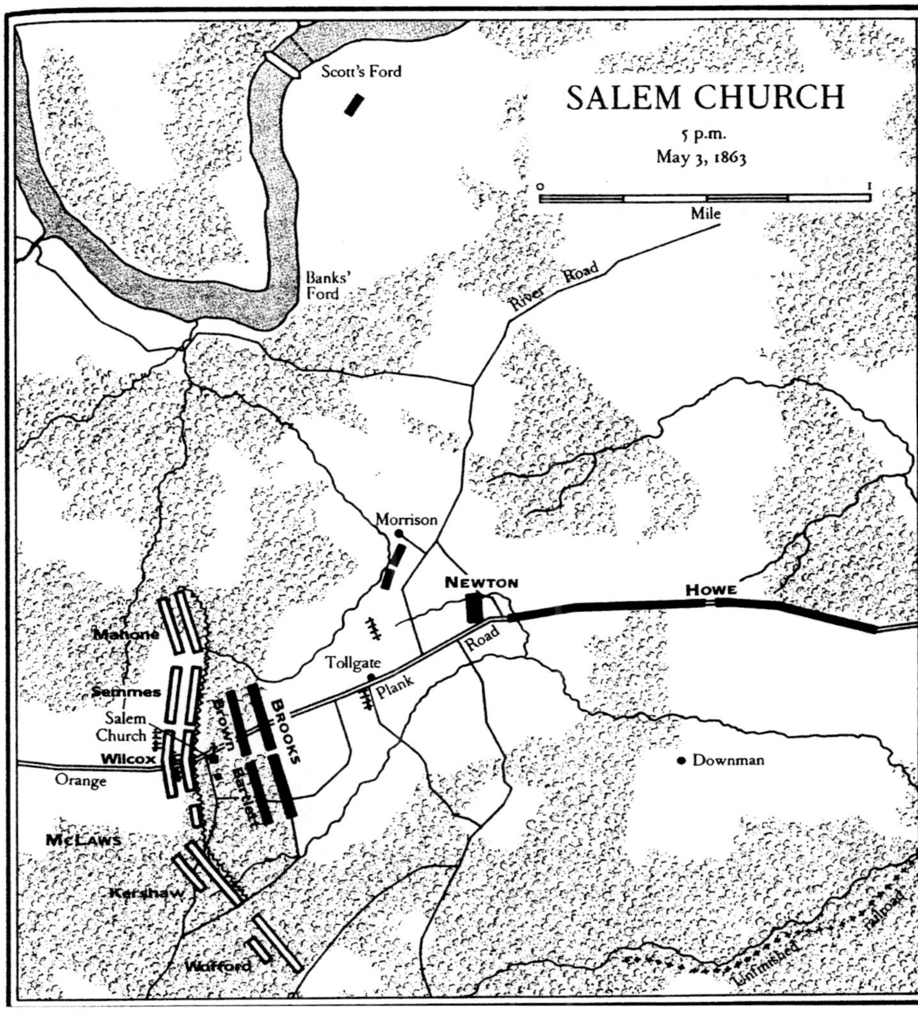

Salem Church, May 3, 1863, 5 P.M. Fire in the pulpit. After delaying Sedgwick again at the tollgate, Wilcox is reinforced by McLaws. Wilcox's Alabamans and Semmes' Georgians play the major role in throwing back Brooks's advance at Salem Church. Map by William J. Clipson.

field. Orders would now come from General Couch, who was second to Hooker in rank.[80] The Federals would have to fall back again.

By about 10:30 A.M., the last of the bluecoats had withdrawn past Chancellorsville. General Lee mounted Traveller, his favorite horse, and rode from Hazel Grove to Fairview. Confederate artillerists had moved forward and were throwing shells at the retreating Yankees.[81] Traveller brought the general into Chancellorsville, and as he came into view of the tattered graycoats, a cheer rose among them for their beloved chieftain.

Lee, Jackson and the troops they led had executed a miraculous maneuver on the Confederate left. But May 3 was not over. On the Confederate right, General Early was in trouble again. At Fredericksburg, the Confederates were stretched in a thin line from the Orange Plank Road near Marye's Heights all the way down to Hamilton's Crossing.[82]

General Sedgwick had finally moved forward, and was attempting to join the rest of the Army of the Potomac near Chancellorsville. The small band of rebels under Jubal Early blocked his path. The ground around Marye's Heights would be hotly contested.

In this sector the Confederates had approximately 1,200 men and only eight artillery pieces. Most of the strength of Early's command was farther south, where the graycoats were more vulnerable. The Union VI Corps had over 27,000 troops and 66 guns with which to storm the position at Marye's Heights.[83] Clearly, General Early was in trouble.

The Confederates had received the transfer of one brigade under General Cadmus Wilcox, but were still heavily outnumbered. Attacking around 10:30 A.M., the bluecoats moved forward along a broad front.[84] As the assault force approached, the grayclad Southerners opened fire, cutting large holes in the Union ranks. The advancing columns staggered, and fell back under the shower of lead.[85] However, there were simply too many Yankees. The Federal divisions stormed the heights, the rebels were pushed back, and Marye's Heights fell into Union hands.

To the right of Marye's Heights three divisions under General Albion P. Howe punched through the Confederate lines, splitting Early's defenses in two. Had Sedgwick concentrated his efforts on Jubal Early, the entire force around Fredericksburg might have been captured. As it was, the cost had been heavy; the assaulting bluecoats had lost nearly 1,100 men to 475 for the Confederacy.[85a] But Hooker had ordered Uncle John to move toward Chancellorsville, so the Yankees headed west.[86]

Although the Northerners had been successful on that morning, they were not free just yet. Cadmus Wilcox had no intention of giving up without a fight. His men slowed the Union advance, but he was soon outflanked, and had to fall back.[87]

Back in the Confederate center, a messenger from

Fredericksburg arrived with somber news for General Lee. The position had been lost, and the Yankees were moving against the rear of Lee's divided force![88] Once again, Lee would divide his army in the face of the enemy. Hooker must be held in check, so General Lee retained Anderson, and sent McLaws to aid General Early.[89]

General Cadmus Wilcox would perform his greatest service on the fields of Chancellorsville. Although heavily outnumbered, he continued to delay Sedgwick in his attempt to rejoin Hooker. His Confederates on the Orange Plank Road would fight, then fall back to a new position, slowly giving ground, before repeating the process again.

Late in the afternoon of May 3, General Wilcox had taken up a position around Salem Church. Five brigades would attempt to hold off the Yankees once again. William "Billy" Mahone was posted on the Confederate left. To Mahone's right were Paul Semmes' troops. Wilcox held his brigade astride the road, with Joseph Kershaw's South Carolinians and William Wofford's Georgians next in line.

Salem Church stood on the south side of the Orange Plank Road, five miles west of Fredericksburg and six miles east of Chancellorsville.[90] Three Union divisions under William Brooks, Albion Howe and John Newton were determined to clear the way for Hooker's troops.

The Yankees under General Brooks moved along the Plank Road until they came in contact with the graycoats in the Confederate center. Wilcox's men held their fire until the enemy was only 80 yards away[91] and then let loose a terrible volley. Holes opened in the Federal ranks, but the Northerners kept coming. They drove the 10th Alabama back, but the 8th and 9th Alabama counterattacked, pouring a furious fire into Brooks' division, and the Yankees were compelled to retreat.[92]

Next to Wilcox, the Georgians under Paul Semmes were fighting off a New Jersey brigade. The Yankees had charged forward, but were thrown back repeatedly. After several assaults had failed, the attackers had begun to fall back. The Southerners noticed the charge of Wilcox's men to their right and lunged after the bluecoats. The Union VI Corps had met yet another repulse.[93]

Once again, despite having fewer men available on the entire battlefield, the Confederates brought more men to the point of impact.[94] The VI Corps suffered 1,523 total casualties at the battle of Salem Church on May 3, while Wilcox and Semmes lost only 674 men, less than half as many.[95]

From the Union perspective, Stonewall Jackson had shattered the XI Corps at Chancellorsville, Jubal Early had tenaciously held Fredericksburg, and Cadmus Wilcox had attacked William Brooks with great ferocity at Salem Church. Where did Lee get all of this firepower? Had Longstreet arrived on the scene with even more men? Where would the rebels strike next? The Federal high command was getting very nervous as the day drew to a close.[96]

Of course, had Joe Hooker utilized his cavalry properly, he would have known that General Longstreet was nowhere near Chancellorsville. But while the Union cavalry was off raiding supply lines and doing minimal damage to the Southern war effort, Robert E. Lee was busy planning how to push the Federals back across the Rappahannock River.

General Lee had heard the sound of battle at Salem Church. Aggressive by nature, he considered this to be an opportunity to attack the bluecoats again, not to retreat. General Early forwarded a plan to retake Marye's Heights, which was Sedgwick's link to Fredericksburg. The Confederates would return to Marye's Heights, and strike the VI Corps from the east, while McLaws attacked from the west. Lee approved the plan, and urged McLaws to press Sedgwick vigorously, so that he could not turn unmolested against Early.[97]

On May 4, Jubal Early sent the brigade of Georgians under John B. Gordon forward to retake Marye's Heights. Gordon's men charged forward and drove the enemy from the hill. The Union VI Corps was now in a bit of a bind. This charge secured the ground for the Confederacy, but it also cut off the escape routes through the town. Around 8:00 A.M., Early listened for McLaws opening fire. All he heard was silence.[98]

Lafayette McLaws was a solid, dependable soldier, but he was not a risk taker. He had asked Lee for reinforcements, and the division of Richard Anderson was sent on its way. McLaws was going to wait until the reinforcements arrived.[99]

Again, Lee had gambled by dividing his forces. With only three divisions under Heth, Colston and Rodes he would try to contain Hooker, while destroying Sedgwick at the same time.

It was almost 6:00 P.M. when three cannon shots signaled the attack.[100] The bluecoats scrambled for the rear as Early's men rushed forward. The Confederates pushed the foe back to the Orange Plank Road, and the Southern brigades of John B. Gordon, Harry T. Hays and Robert F. Hoke went up against the division of General Howe. This fight near Bank's Ford against Howe cost Early 1,200 casualties against only 900 for the bluecoats. However, Sedgwick had ordered a withdrawal across Bank's Ford for that very night.[101]

When General Lee awoke on May 5, he intended to attack VI Corps once again. Instead, he found that the enemy had crossed the Rappahannock River. The threat to the Confederate flank had evaporated. For his part, General Hooker had already made up his mind to move the remainder of the Army of the Potomac back to the north side of the river, and by May 6, he was gone.

In retrospect, the quick exit was most fortunate for the Army of Northern Virginia. General Lee, always the aggressor, had planned a frontal assault against a strongly fortified Union position, but it would have been very costly in Confederate lives. The Union evacuation made sure that the attack never took place.[102]

Estimates of casualties vary, particularly on the Southern side, as some battle reports were incomplete. The Federals had 1,606 men killed, 9,762 wounded and reported 5,919 captured or missing, for a total of 17,287.[103] The Army of Northern Virginia lost 1,649 men killed, 9,106 wounded and 1,708 captured or missing, for a total of 12,463.[104]

The action at Chancellorsville went much further than the casualty lists. Other battles were more famous, but no other battle had a more far-reaching influence on the outcome of the Civil War. The loss of Stonewall Jackson cannot be underestimated. The entire Army of Northern Virginia was reorganized as a result of his death. It set off a chain of promotions in which officers were thrust into positions for which they were not ideally suited.

Future battles, Gettysburg in particular, were profoundly affected by these changes. Robert E. Lee felt that the Confederacy would have been victorious at Gettysburg had Jackson been present.[105] With his loss at Chancellorsville, Lee had lost his most valuable offensive weapon. Douglas Southall Freeman, Lee's biographer, states flatly that the loss of Jackson was "the turning point in the history of the Army of Northern Virginia."[106] It was a loss that the South could never overcome.

The flanking maneuver at Chancellorsville would go down as Lee and Jackson's supreme moment. A numerically superior foe had been sent back across the Rappahannock River. However, the Confederates had dealt the Army of the Potomac a staggering blow, but not a finishing one. In that sense, great though the victory was, it did not accomplish its mission.[107] Robert E. Lee always pursued the complete victory, not the partial victory. That was something Jefferson Davis would never understand.

June 9, 1863
Brandy Station

J. E. B. Stuart (CSA) — A. Pleasonton (USA)

Brandy Station was a stop along the Orange and Alexandria Railroad, located in central Virginia about four miles southwest of the Rappahannock River. In and of itself, it was a small little railroad station. However, it would prove to be the site of the largest cavalry engagement of the entire war.

General Joseph E. Hooker commanded the Union Army of the Potomac. It was rumored at the time that the Confederates were planning a major offensive. As it turned out, this would be the campaign which ended at Gettysburg. Hooker wished to know the exact position of General Lee's Army of Northern Virginia.

On June 8 the Union cavalry left Falmouth, moving along the Rappahannock in the direction of Culpeper, where most of Lee's troops were stationed.[1] The horsemen were supported by two brigades of infantry and some light artillery. All together, the troops under General Alfred Pleasonton comprised a force of 11,000 men.[2]

On the opposite bank of the river were the cavalry of General J. E. B. Stuart. The Confederates were spread out, patrolling the fords, ready to contest any Yankee advance.[3] The Union attack plan called for an advance on the following day.

On June 9, General Pleasonton's force moved out in two columns. Screened by a morning mist,[4] the bluecoats plunged into the waters of the Rappahannock. At 4:00 a.m.[5] General John Buford's Union division crossed at Beverly Ford. Surprising the Confederates under W. E. "Grumble" Jones, the Northerners quickly captured 150 prisoners.[6] However, Jones' troopers regrouped, and contested any further advance as they fell back towards Brandy Station.[7]

Four miles downstream at Kelly's Ford, David Gregg's Yankees pushed past Beverly Robertson's graycoats to connect with Buford's troopers.

General Stuart was busy concentrating his scattered brigades. Wade Hampton was ordered to reinforce Jones, but the rebels were unable to halt Buford's attack. The Northerner eventually worked his way around the Confederate right flank, at which point the 12th Virginia Cavalry counterattacked.[8]

The Southern horsemen pushed Buford's cavalry back, and appeared to have the upper hand. Then Gregg's troops arrived on the scene, and another counterattack ensued. Here Hampton's Confederates were thrown into the fray. Attacks and counterattacks continued through the day, until General Pleasonton observed the dust clouds of approaching Confederate infantry. At this point, he called off the fight.[9]

The casualties are not comparable to a major infantry battle. The Confederates lost 523 men; Pleasonton's Union force suffered 936 casualties.[10]

The significance of the battle of Brandy Station lies not in the sheer number of men who died on June 9, but in the repercussions of the action that fateful day. There were two very important consequences, and they would turn out to be enormous. Both would have a profound impact on the battle of Gettysburg, which would be waged in early July.

Prior to the engagement at Brandy Station, the Army of the Potomac was unaware of the precise location of General Lee's Army of Northern Virginia. This action disclosed very important information to General Hooker and the Union Army of the Potomac. The Yankees now knew exactly where the Confederates were, and more importantly, that the rebels were moving north. Up to this point General Hooker had been very content to be encamped at Falmouth, but this cavalry battle set the Northerners in motion, and greatly reduced any element of surprise General Lee had in an invasion of Pennsylvania.[11]

Second, the embarrassment of a surprise attack and near defeat humiliated General Stuart. Although he was a very talented scout, he had a terrible weakness, a love of praise,[12] and on the march to Gettysburg, he would allow himself to become separated from General Lee while pursuing a Union wagon train. The cumbersome prize would not be as valuable as the loss of the eyes and ears of the Army of Northern Virginia. There have been many Confederates, including General Lee himself, who have suffered blame for the defeat at Gettysburg, but in Robert E. Lee's own opinion, nothing could make up for the absence of his cavalry.[13]

The casualty reports at Brandy Station would indicate a Confederate victory, but the reality was that the Union gained far more than they lost, quite possibly saving the day at Gettysburg.

June 14–15, 1863
WINCHESTER (SECOND)

R. S. Ewell (CSA)	R. H. Milroy (USA)

The second battle of Winchester occurred during the Confederate campaign to invade Pennsylvania. On June 3, 1863, the Army of Northern Virginia left Fredericksburg and headed west. General Robert E. Lee intended to take a circuitous path, unobserved by the Federal troops which were currently in eastern Virginia. The Southerners would march through the Shenandoah Valley, then turn north, in the direction of Gettysburg.

In the lead was the Confederate Second Corps, under the command of Richard S. Ewell. On June 13, his graycoats reached Berryville, Virginia, a small hamlet only 12 miles east of Winchester.[1]

The Union forces had possession of Winchester, but the Federals had only 6,900 men in the town, with an additional force of 1,800 in Berryville.[2] Both Union forces would need to be defeated before the Confederates could proceed safely into Pennsylvania.

The Confederates had three divisions in General Ewell's Second Corps. Two divisions, led by Jubal Early and Edward Johnson, would attack Winchester. Ewell's third division, under the command of Robert Rodes, would march to Berryville to defeat the Federals there. In addition, a 1,500-man brigade of cavalry under Albert Jenkins reported to General Ewell. The horsemen would accompany General Rodes.[3]

Federal troops at Winchester were under the leadership of Union General Robert H. Milroy. If Milroy could mount a sustained defense of the post, the bluecoats would be able to disrupt General Lee's northern invasion. Confederate success depended on good coordination and quick execution.[4]

Capture of the town might not be easy. The Federals had constructed several forts north of Winchester, and the key to the Union defenses was Fort Milroy,[4a] the largest of the enclosures. Two thousand feet to the west, Flint Ridge rose above the fort. If the ridge could be taken, Fort Milroy would become untenable.[5]

However, an open earthwork known as West Fort occupied the ridge. The Confederates would have to approach West Fort from Little North Mountain, a rise of ground which ran roughly parallel to the Union fortifications.

General Ewell decided to hit Winchester from three sides. Approaching from the east, Edward "Old Allegheny" Johnson would attack along the Berryville Road. On the south, John B. Gordon would take his own brigade, along with some Maryland troops, and move north. On Little North Mountain, Jubal Early's troops would attack West Fort, and then Fort Milroy.[6] The rebel assault on the town would begin the next day.

With his troops in position, Richard Ewell was ready to attack. At 6:00 P.M. on June 14, Jubal Early's artillery unleashed a furious barrage on West Fort. The small enclosure was not strongly defended, and after a 45 minute bombardment the Southern infantry charged forward. Harry Hays' Louisiana brigade swept over 200 yards of open ground, leaping past the walls of the earthworks. The bluecoats attempted a feeble defense, but the fort was soon in Confederate hands.[7]

General Early informed Ewell that he would attack again during the morning of the 15th. Ewell realized that with West Fort in Southern control, the Federal garrison at Winchester was in trouble. The only logical course of action was to retreat.[8]

In order to evacuate the city, the Yankees must use

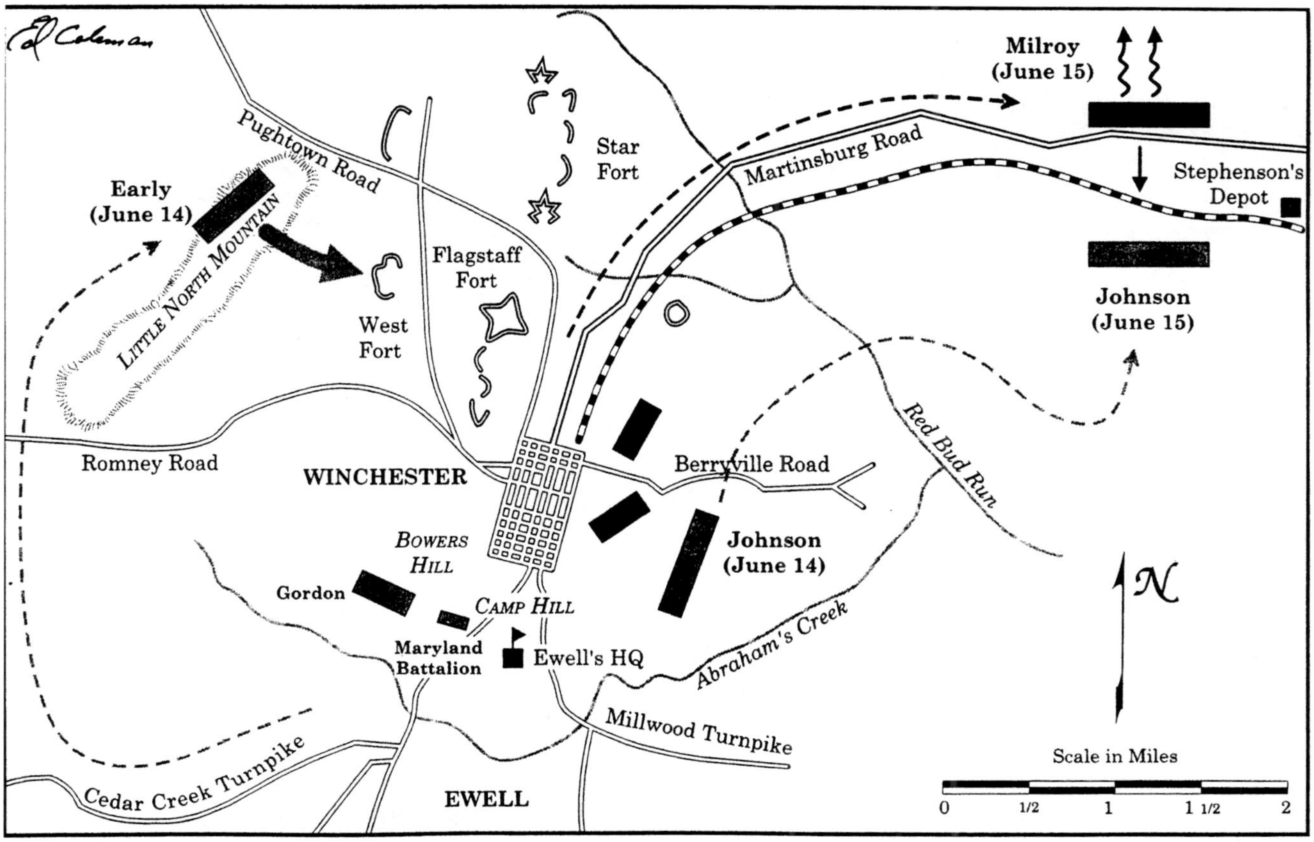

Second Winchester. Map by Ed P. Coleman.

the Martinsburg Road. This route would take Milroy's command in a northeasterly direction. Accordingly, Ewell ordered Edward Johnson to take a position some 2½ miles from Winchester, blocking the Federal escape.[9] If Milroy decided to remain in Winchester, "Old Allegheny" would be in position to support Jubal Early's attack the next morning.[10]

June 15 found the Federals attempting to escape the net General Ewell had thrown around them. Johnson's men had taken a position along a railroad cut near Stephenson's Depot. The graycoats faced north, just south of the Martinsburg Road.[11]

Milroy attacked, trying desperately to cut his way to freedom. When Johnson blocked the frontal assaults of the Union soldiers, the Federals tried to envelop the Confederate flanks. However, Johnson shifted reinforcements to the endangered points, and the Federal attacks were repulsed.[12]

Demoralized, some 2,500 Union soldiers surrendered.[13] Additional troops were captured as daylight broke over the battlefield.[14]

From his headquarters on the south side of Winchester, Richard Ewell could hear the gunfire at Stephenson's Depot, but the general was still unsure of exactly who was involved. Could Milroy still be in Winchester?

At first light, General Early entered Winchester from the west. He was soon joined by General Gordon, leading his men into the town from the south. The enemy had abandoned the town.

The Federal garrison at Berryville had shared the fate of their compatriots at Winchester. The bluecoats had learned of General Rodes' impending attack, and had fled to Winchester, only to evacuate the town.[15]

The results of the battle of Winchester were heavily in favor of the Confederacy. Union forces had seen 95 men killed and 348 soldiers wounded. The Confederates had taken over 4,000 prisoners, 23 artillery pieces, 300 horses, and an extensive supply of equipment. In addition, the Federal troops in the area had been driven out of Virginia and into Maryland. General Ewell had accomplished all of this at a cost of only 47 men killed, 219 wounded, and 3 missing.[16]

While the Confederate victory had been decisive, and many prisoners had been taken, Robert H. Milroy was not among them. Milroy had been able to elude Johnson's troops, fleeing in the direction of Harpers Ferry.[17]

Few Confederate victories had been so one-sided. However, the success at Winchester would prove to be short-lived. The graycoats would continue northward in the invasion of Pennsylvania, only to meet defeat on the fields of Gettysburg.

June 17, 1863
Aldie

T. Munford (CSA) — A. Pleasonton (USA)

In the weeks leading up to the battle of Gettysburg, information on the movements of the enemy was particularly important for both sides in the conflict. Lack of information was a major problem for the Union Army of the Potomac. The Federals were commanded by General Joseph E. Hooker, and General Hooker did not have a clear idea of the Confederate intentions.

At the beginning of June, the Army of the Potomac was encamped around Falmouth, Virginia, located on the north bank of the Rappahannock River. Across the water to the south, General Lee's graycoats had pitched their tents near Fredericksburg.[1] However, the Confederate route to Pennsylvania would be a circuitous one, meandering through the Shenandoah Valley, and the Confederates vanished from the immediate sight of the Federal scouts. It was vital to General Hooker that he knew the whereabouts of his adversary.

On June 17, the Federal cavalry under General Alfred Pleasonton was directed to ascertain the location of the Confederates. The horsemen rode northwest from Manassas Junction to Aldie,[2] a small town on the way to the Blue Ridge mountains.

Suddenly, gunfire broke out east of the town. Judson Kilpatrick, a brigadier in David Gregg's division, had come upon part of Thomas Munford's Confederates, commanded by Thomas Rosser. The 5th Virginia Regiment charged the enemy, driving Kilpatrick to the west and through Aldie itself.[3]

Confederate sharpshooters were deployed under Captain Boston in a strong position north of Snicker's Gap Road,[4] and Rosser notified Colonel Munford of the situation. Munford arrived with three regiments, and a brisk series of charges and countercharges got under way. The action was furious, but the battle shifted to the west,[5] along the Snicker's Gap Road.

Boston's men were ordered to remain where they were,[6] although the actual combat was moving away from them. This left his men somewhat isolated from any Confederate assistance, should the need arise. Presently, Gregg's troopers surrounded the sharpshooters, and Boston was compelled to surrender.[7]

As the daylight waned, Munford halted the enemy progress. However, the fighting on June 17 had not come without a price, as the Southerners had lost 119 men at the battle of Aldie. General Gregg reported total casualties of 385 soldiers.[8]

July 1–3, 1863
Gettysburg

R. E. Lee (CSA) — G. G. Meade (USA)

In order to fully appreciate the events at Gettysburg in the first week of July, it is necessary to examine the events leading up to the battle. At the beginning of June, the Union Army of the Potomac was headquartered at Falmouth, Virginia, just north of the Rappahannock River. The troops were not led by General Meade, but by the boastful New Englander,[1] General Joseph E. "Fighting Joe" Hooker.

Robert E. Lee's Army of Northern Virginia was camped across the river to the south, at Fredericksburg. The decision had been made to invade Pennsylvania, and the Confederates would soon be on the move. To avoid detection by the enemy, General Lee would march to the west, through the Shenandoah Valley.

On June 3, the graycoats broke camp and began their journey. General Lee had three corps of infantry under his command. James Longstreet led the First Corps, and Richard S. Ewell directed the Second Corps. The recently created Third Corps was under A. P. Hill. The Confederate cavalry was led by the flamboyant J. E. B. "Jeb" Stuart. All told, the Confederates had some 70,000 men.[2]

General Lee issued instructions for each of his lieutenants. These orders would govern the Confederate movements during the first stage of the march. Richard Ewell's Second Corps would take the lead. His troops would cross the Blue Ridge Mountains at Chester Gap, and this would bring the men into the Shenandoah Valley. General Ewell would then turn north toward Winchester, Virginia. At this point, the Second Corps would change direction and march northeast. Crossing the Potomac River at Williamsport, the rebels would continue until they reached Hagerstown, Maryland.[3]

James Longstreet would take the First Corps along

the Blue Ridge Mountains, but in contrast to Ewell, Longstreet's forces would stay on the east side of the mountains. In so doing, the First Corps would guard the Shenandoah Valley from any unsuspected Union attacks.[4]

A. P. Hill would follow General Ewell's route. At the beginning of the march, Hill's Third Corps would be in the rear. However, his troops were ordered to continue past Longstreet's Corps. This would ensure that Ewell and Hill would be able to cross the Potomac unmolested. Finally, Longstreet would cross the Blue Ridge at Snicker's Gap, and then turn north, also crossing the river at Williamsport.[5]

Although it may not have seemed significant at the time, perhaps the most important set of orders General Lee gave out in early June were his instructions to the Confederate cavalry. The performance of General Stuart was absolutely critical in the outcome of the battle of Gettysburg.

The purpose of the Southern mounted forces was to keep the enemy as far to the east as possible, and to continue to gather information for General Lee.[6]

More specifically, Jeb Stuart was to make sure that he protected the right flank of General Ewell. As the rebels marched north, Stuart was to ride north along with the infantry.[7] In this manner, the Confederate cavalry would always be between Lee's three corps of infantry and the Union Army of the Potomac.

Perhaps Robert E. Lee was not emphatic enough with his chief of cavalry. Perhaps the commanding general gave his subordinate too much latitude. As the campaign wore on, General Stuart would become separated from the Army of Northern Virginia. The absence of cavalry would be the most important factor in the outcome of the conflict ahead.[8]

The Federal troops presented an approximate mirror of the Southern movements. On June 13, General Ewell was in the Shenandoah Valley. He would win a decisive battle over the next two days at the Second Battle of Winchester. General Hooker spent the next two weeks moving his forces northward. The bluecoats took a more direct route, stopping at Frederick, Maryland.[9]

It cannot be emphasized too strongly how important the position of Jeb Stuart was at this time. He was actually east of the Union army.

General Stuart had pursued an enemy wagon train around the entire Army of the Potomac. The eventual capture of 125 wagons was a fine prize, but the cost to the Confederacy was the eyes and ears of General Lee.[10]

It was not until June 28 that General Lee finally learned that the Yankees were north of the Potomac River. Furthermore, President Abraham Lincoln had appointed a new commander to lead the Northern forces. His name was George G. Meade.[11]

By the end of June, both sides were converging on the most famous battlefield the Civil War would produce. However, as the action was about to begin, neither side was a compact fighting force.

The Confederate First Corps was camped around Chambersburg, almost due west of Gettysburg. A. P. Hill's troops were located in Fayetteville, some ten miles east of Longstreet's position. The Second Corps was widely scattered. Some of General Ewell's men were in Carlisle, while another division was almost in York. Generally speaking, the First and Third Corps were west of Gettysburg, the Second Corps was northeast of the town.[12]

General Meade was gradually bringing the Union army into the area. The Federal troops were approaching from the south and southeast.[13]

The Army of the Potomac was divided into seven corps. The I Corps was under John F. Reynolds, a talented officer who would not survive the battle. The II Corps was also in capable hands, as it was led by Winfield S. Hancock. The III Corps was commanded by Daniel Sickles, a controversial appointee, as he was not a military man, but a lawyer from New York. George Sykes was in charge of the V Corps, with John Sedgwick directing the VI Corps. Known as "Uncle John" to his men, Sedgwick was one of the most popular men in the Union army. The XI Corps was under O. O. Howard. These men were still under a cloud of suspicion as the troops had been shattered by Stonewall Jackson at Chancellorsville only two months earlier. Finally, the XII Corps was led by Henry Slocum.

Union infantry continued to march through Pennsylvania during late June, but the Northern cavalry were the first Yankees to actually occupy the town of Gettysburg. On July 1, the mounted troopers under General John Buford would open the action.

In comparison with the major cities of the time, Gettysburg was only a small town. Some 2,500 inhabitants[14] made their homes here, and it had no military significance. However, ten roads came together at Gettysburg. For this reason, it assumed an importance much greater than its small size.

On July 1, the Confederates of A. P. Hill's Corps gingerly moved forward. As Harry Heth's division of Confederates pressed forward too, the rebels encountered John Buford's cavalry. The battle of Gettysburg was about to erupt!

General Lee had not wanted the battle to begin this early.[15] At the time of Heth's attack, General Longstreet's troops were still on the way to Gettysburg, and General Ewell's Corps had not arrived either. Due to the absence of the Confederate cavalry, Lee was unclear as to the strength or exact position of his foe. The graycoats must make the best of a difficult situation.

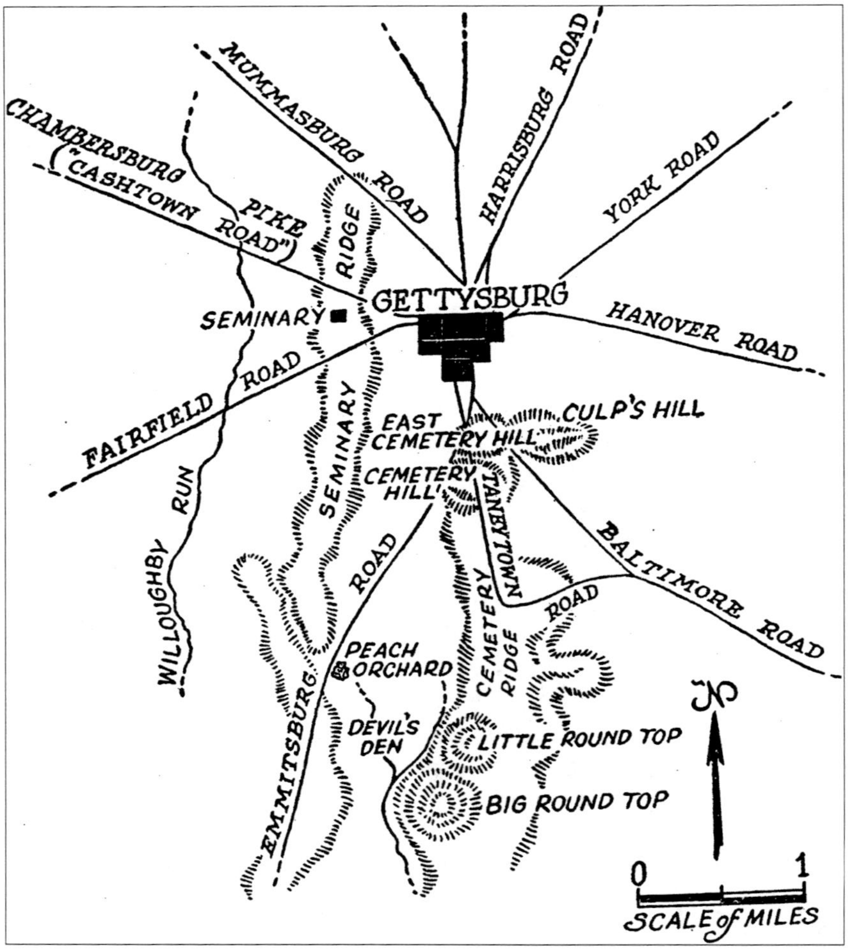

Gettysburg and vicinity. Map by John T. Draper.

Archer and Davis had come upon the famed Iron Brigade, a tenacious outfit of midwesterners.[19]

Unfortunately for the Confederates, the Federal line extended beyond Archer's right flank. In a few minutes the rebels were overwhelmed, and General Archer was captured. On the left, Davis was unable to control his troops, and two of his regiments ventured too far ahead of the rest of Davis's command. They too were taken prisoner by the Iron Brigade.[20]

While it seemed as if the bluecoats were in control, fate would intervene on the side of the Confederacy. As he was leading his men forward, General John F. Reynolds was suddenly cut down by a Confederate sharpshooter. Command of the I Corps would fall to General John Newton.[20a]

After the defeat of Archer and Davis, the rebels fell back and regrouped. Heth had a decision to make. Should he retreat, or form his troops and renew the attack?

North of the Chambersburg Turnpike lay an unfinished railroad, and General Heth decided to reform his command in a wooded ravine to the right of it. He knew that reinforcements were close at hand. General Dorsey Pender's division would provide ample support.[21] Perhaps a counterattack could push the Yankees back and gain control of the area for the South.

Around 2:30 P.M., the Federal troops in front of Heth began shifting to the north.[22] General Ewell and the Second Corps had arrived!

Robert Rodes brought his division forward on the Carlisle Road to a position almost perpendicular to Heth's men. Rodes' artillery began to bombard the Yankees from the side, causing great concern among the Union I Corps. With five brigades under his command, General Rodes anchored his left flank, and attacked with the right side of his formation.[23]

The graycoats were the aggressors, but trouble was brewing. Although Rodes was unaware of the situation, his own division, with help from Harry Heth's men, were the only Confederates facing the entire I Corps of the Union army. Making matters worse, the XI Corps under General Howard was moving up fast on Rodes' left.[24] General Ewell was bringing grayclad reinforcements, but would they arrive in time?

The left side of Rodes' attack received a destructive fire from the Union troops. The right moved forward, but

The battle of Gettysburg would see the Confederates formed in the shape of a fishhook. General Ewell would make up the left of General Lee's line, and his men would face south. On Ewell's right was A. P. Hill. The Third Corps faced east and southeast. Hill's troops constituted the Confederate center. Longstreet would face east, and complete the deployment. His soldiers comprised the right flank of Lee's army.

General Heth had sent his men toward the town at about 5:00 A.M.,[16] marching in a southeasterly direction along the Chambersburg Turnpike.[17] Joseph Davis commanded the graycoats on the left side of the road, while James Archer's brigade was on the right. About three miles west of Gettysburg, Heth's troops sighted enemy cavalry. As the Southerners advanced, the Union cavalry withdrew.[18]

The Confederates continued, until they reached Willoughby Run, a small stream in the area which ran north and south. As the men began to cross the stream, they were greeted by a burst of gunfire. Infantry from the Union I Corps had arrived to support Buford's cavalry.

received no cooperation from Heth. General Lee did not want to exhaust Heth's men so soon, as Longstreet's men were still en route to Gettysburg.[25] Prospects looked grim for the Confederacy. Just as the Federals appeared victorious, fresh Confederates appeared on Rodes' left flank. General John B. Gordon led his men into the contest. General Lee realized that the time had come to release Heth's men, and a gray wave poured forward.[26]

The Federal troops fell back under the Confederate onslaught, taking heavy casualties as they tried to reform in Gettysburg. The weight of the assault was too much to withstand. The Union forces were attacked from both their front and flank, with some 5,000 prisoners[27] falling into Confederate hands. The XI Corps alone left 7,500 men dead or wounded.[28] Confederate losses had been substantial,[29] but I and XI Corps had been shattered. Losses had been heavy for both sides, but the first day of Gettysburg was far from over.

As the Federals retreated, the action shifted south of the town itself. A range of hills would form part of the next Union line of defense. About one mile south of Gettysburg was Cemetery Hill, rising 80 feet into the air.[30] Closer to town was a smaller eminence, East Cemetery Hill. Approximately half a mile to the northeast was Culp's Hill. Slightly larger, Culp's Hill was 100 feet high.[31] These hills would form the Union right flank. The center of General Meade's line was a long ridge which ran north and south. It was known as Cemetery Ridge.

The Union left would be anchored by two large hills on the southern end of Cemetery Ridge. The smaller of the two was named Little Round Top. Further south was a larger hill, known as Round Top. The Union position was strong from a defensive standpoint, but if either end of the formation were to fall into Southern hands, General Meade would be forced to evacuate Gettysburg. As a result, control of the hills would be of vital importance to both sides. A. P. Hill had been on center stage as the battle opened. The action would now turn to the area around Culp's Hill. At this point, Richard S. Ewell became the pivotal figure in the drama.

As General Ewell surveyed the situation in his front, he could see that Federal troops occupied Culp's Hill and Cemetery Hill. He did not know how many of the bluecoats were present, or what reinforcements the enemy might have close at hand. It was not yet 4:00 P.M.[32]

A swift, vigorous attack might well take the hills for the Confederacy. However, there were not specific orders from General Lee to advance. Richard Ewell would have to act on his own initiative. In one of the more crucial moments of the entire war, Ewell lost his aggression. He decided to move forward, and then halt until he received definite instructions.[33]

There can be no doubt that the correct course of action was a vigorous assault. There is also no doubt that Ewell's lack of enterprise cost the Confederacy dearly on the 1st of July. However, part of the blame for the failure to occupy these hills must rest with Robert E. Lee.

General Lee told Ewell to take the hills in his front "if practicable." Richard Ewell was not Stonewall Jackson — he needed specific direction from his commanding general. Instead, he received vague instructions, filled with many possibilities.[34] The Confederate inertia allowed the Federal troops to bring up reinforcements, and a golden opportunity was lost.

July 2 dawned with the Union forces still deployed from Culp's Hill and Cemetery Hill on their right, along Cemetery Ridge to the base of Little Round Top. The remnants of Howard's XI Corps and Newton's[35] I Corps held the Federal right, with Slocum's XII Corps in a reserve position south of Howard and Newton. Winfield S. Hancock posted the bluecoats of the II Corps on Cemetery Ridge. To his left, General Sickles placed the III Corps out in front of the ridge. This created a gap of about one mile between his men and Hancock's forces. The V Corps under George Sykes was behind the III Corps, located near the base of Little Round Top. The VI Corps, led by John Sedgwick, was en route to the field, but when the day started, Sedgwick had not yet arrived.[36]

Neither of the Round Tops was occupied by General Meade's men.[37] This fact would turn out to be extremely important. On the Confederate side, General Longstreet had arrived. He took his place to the right of A. P. Hill's troops. On Longstreet's left was the division under Lafayette McLaws; on his right were the grayclad veterans of John B. Hood's division.[38] A. P. Hill remained in the Confederate center, although his role in the battle of Gettysburg would not be as prominent as it was on the first day. Richard Ewell held the left, his troops still facing south in front of Culp's Hill and Cemetery Hill.[39]

George Meade was convinced that the Confederates would renew their offensive in the morning. He believed that Culp's Hill was the weakest point of the Union line. Therefore, the rebels would attack the Federal right.[40]

The Union commander was only partially correct. General Lee recognized that possession of Culp's Hill would bring tremendous advantages to the graycoats. However, the Round Tops were undefended, and Southern artillery posted on the heights would force the Yankees to abandon Cemetery Ridge. Lee decided that he would attack on both flanks.[41]

On the Confederate right, Longstreet was ordered to launch an invasion, while Ewell would organize a "demonstration" on the left. If the opportunity presented itself, General Ewell was given the authority to develop his attack, and capture the hills in his front.[42]

Unfortunately for the Confederacy, James Longstreet

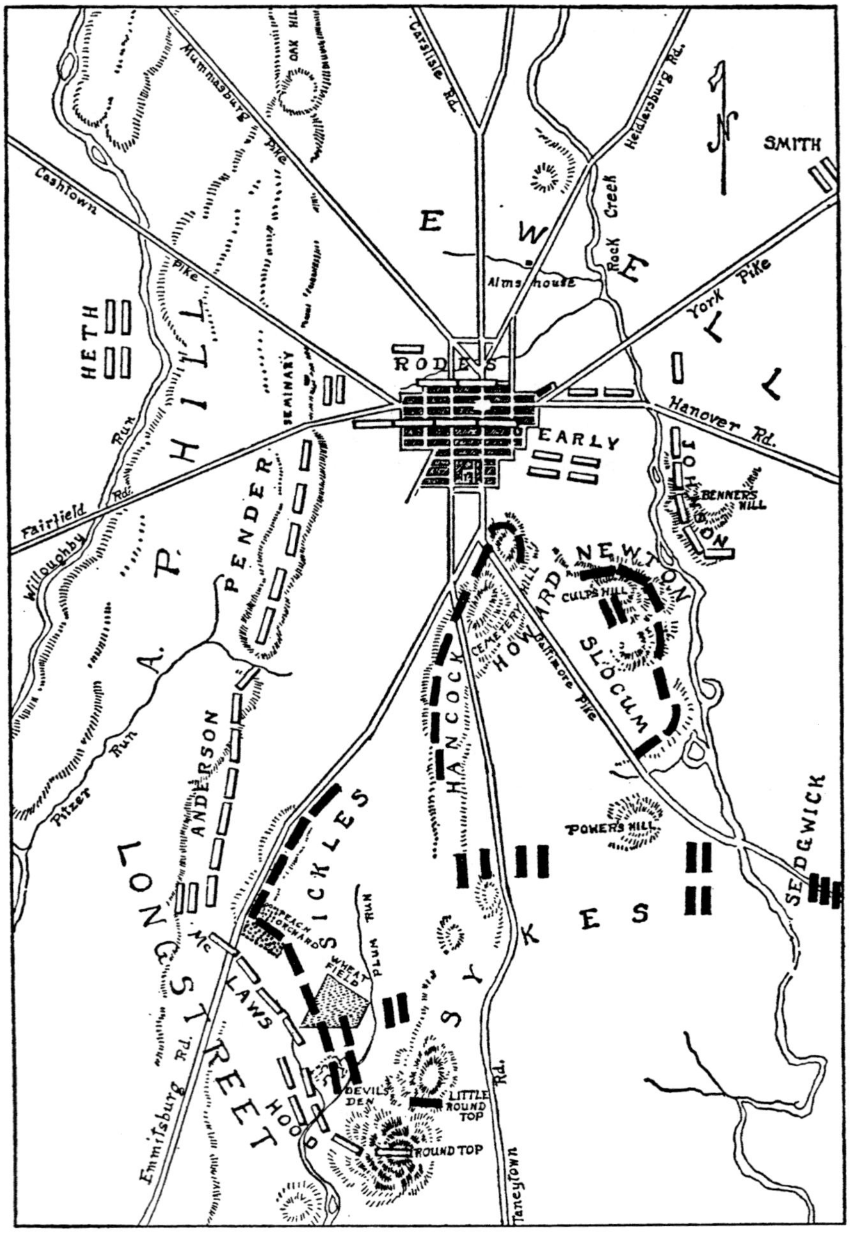

Attack on Federal left, July 2, 1863, 4:00 P.M. Map by Dorothy Thomas Tucker.

had other ideas. He wanted to move around the Union left flank, placing the graycoats between Gettysburg and Washington, D.C. With the threat to the nation's capital, the enemy was sure to retreat.[43]

General Lee, in contrast, wanted to actually attack the Union left flank. John B. Hood's division would take the lead, followed by the troops under Lafayette McLaws. Richard Anderson's command would support the attack, forming on the left of McLaws. The Confederates would move across the Emmitsburg Road, with Hood on the right and McLaws on the left.[44]

The Confederates were to cross small patches of ground which have since become famous. Just east of the Emmitsburg Road was the Peach Orchard. The trees stood in front of the Union III Corps, under General Sickles. Behind the orchard was an open plot of ground, known today as the Wheat Field. A bit further east, and in front of Little Round Top, was Devil's Den, which formed the left of III Corps.[45]

Lee had intended for the assault to begin early in the day. Longstreet, however, was very slow. A deliberate general under the best of circumstances, his disagreement with General Lee had put the Georgian in a particularly foul mood. The graycoats did not move forward until 4:00 P.M.[46] Longstreet's delay on July 2 robbed the Confederates of any advantage a prompt attack might have brought.[47]

Making matters worse, the assault was poorly coordinated.[48] General Hood had wanted to attack the Yankees in the flank, and take possession of the Round Tops. Longstreet merely repeated Lee's orders, which were to move across the Emmitsburg Road. Lee was not present, and could not know that his orders had become outdated. Current conditions favored Hood's plan. Still, the Confederates were unable to move in concert, and the initial thrust was repulsed by the Union III Corps.[49]

However, the Confederate attack was simply too powerful for Sickles' isolated command. Hood swept forward, and his thrust finally captured Devil's Den. McLaws, in the center, followed suit. His division shattered the III Corps, as the graycoats plunged through the Peach Orchard and the Wheat Field. Anderson hit Sickles' right flank, and the III Corps was quickly decimated.[50]

The situation on the Union front was a dire one. General Hancock desperately attempted to shift troops from the II Corps on Cemetery Ridge. General Sykes and the V Corps was behind Sickles. Would the reinforcements arrive in time to save Sickles' broken command?

Up until this point, July 2 had been very costly for both sides. In his defense of the salient in front of the Union lines, Daniel Sickles had shattered his right leg. Sickles would lose not only his leg, but some of his reputation as well.[51] On the Confederate side, John B. Hood

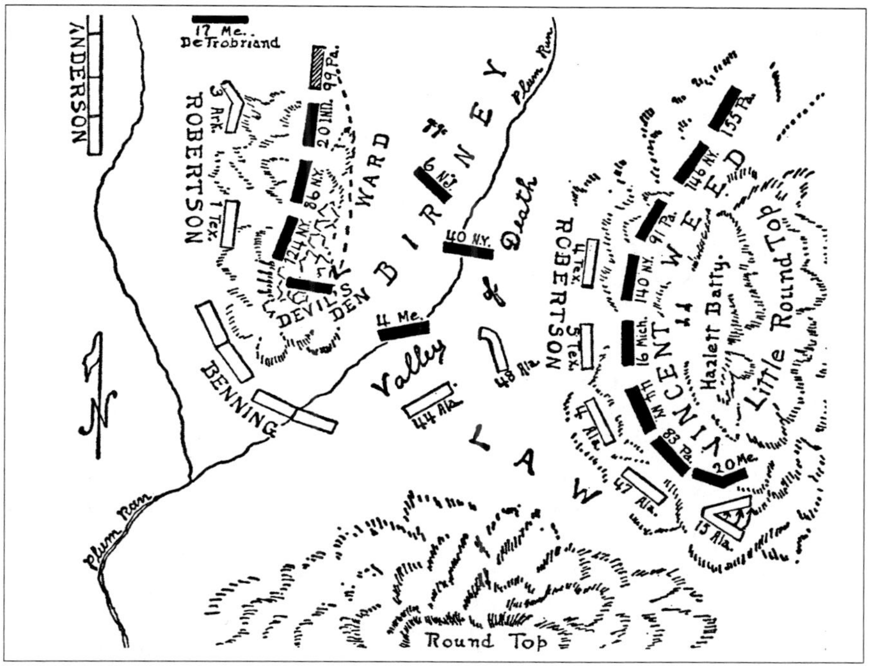

Defense of Little Round Top and Devil's Den, July 2, 1863. Map by Dorothy Thomas Tucker.

had been wounded in the left arm only 20 minutes after his assault began. Command of the division fell upon Evander Law, a capable brigadier, but he did not have Hood's battle experience.[52] In McLaws' sector, the lead brigade under William Barksdale began to disintegrate when Barksdale was mortally wounded. This reduced the striking power of the troops on Hood's left.

Hood's attack had reached Little Round Top, and it was on top of this large hill that some of the most vicious fighting of the battle took place. If the Confederates could hold it, Hancock's corps would be destroyed by Southern artillery. If the Yankees could defend it, it might well mean the repulse of the entire Confederate army, and General Lee would be defeated. Who would prevail?

Most accounts of the battle of Gettysburg center upon the well-known generals. However, the critical prize of the battle was contested by two colonels. William Oates of the 15th Alabama regiment and Joshua Chamberlain of the 20th Maine were about to engage one another in a struggle of wills and fate. Possession of Little Round Top would belong to the victor.

As General Law ascended Little Round Top, the most critical position went to Colonel Oates. The 15th Alabama regiment held the far right of the Confederate line. The 47th Alabama was next in line, with the 4th Alabama in the center.[53]

On the left side of the formation were two regiments of Texans, the 5th Texas, and the 4th Texas, commanded by Jerome B. Robertson.[54]

Union Colonel Strong Vincent held the left of the Federal position, and their right was led by General Stephen Weed. Colonel Chamberlain and the 20th Maine were on the far left, right in front of Colonel Oates and his Alabamians.[55]

The fight for the summit of Little Round Top was a desperate one, and the Confederates almost turned the flank of the Union army. However, fate would intervene on the side of the bluecoats.

The rebels had one brigade in reserve, under Henry L. "Rock" Benning. His troops were between Robertson and Law. As he moved forward, Benning decided to support Robertson instead of Law. As a result, the Confederate attack against the Union left did not have the striking power necessary to turn the flank and capture the summit of Little Round Top. Colonel Chamberlain "refused" or bent back his lines, so as to give added protection to the Union left. In furious hand to hand combat the Yankees' lines held firm. Chamberlain would receive the Congressional Medal of Honor for his valor.[56]

As darkness fell over the mountain, Union reinforcements continued to arrive, and General Meade's left flank was at last secured.[57]

Most of the action on July 2 occurred on the Confederate right, or Longstreet's sector. However, the center and left were not altogether idle.

Part of the problem lay with General Lee's overall plan of attack. The battle units were ordered to attack *en échelon*, which meant that each command depended on the Confederates next to it for support, in a series of individual attacks.

In the center, A. P. Hill had three divisions at his disposal. R. H. Anderson held the right, with Dorsey Pender on the left. Harry Heth's troops were in reserve.[58] As the graycoats moved forward, some progress was made against the base of Cemetery Ridge. Meade had weakened the center of his lines in order to save his left flank.

Anderson's forces met Hancock's bluecoats. Cadmus Wilcox held the far right of the assault force. David Lang[59] to his left was supported by A. R. "Rans" Wright in the center. The three brigades advanced until 7:00 P.M., each one gaining some measure of success. Unfortunately, the brigade led by General Carnot Posey was next in line. By the time Posey attacked, Wright had been defeated.[60]

General Posey's assault was stopped by five companies of the 12th New Jersey regiment, and the Confederate attack in the center ground to a halt. His failure to advance caused both Pender and Heth to remain inactive, and the Southern troops in A. P. Hill's sector of the field would accomplish very little on the 2nd day of July.[61]

Richard Ewell was well aware of his missed opportunity to seize Culp's Hill on July 1. He still held the Confederate left. He ordered Edward Johnson's division forward. The hill was held by only one brigade of Yankees, but the New Yorkers were well entrenched. They had erected strong barricades, and would be very difficult to dislodge.[62]

General Johnson made four separate assaults, and each one was repulsed. Finally, the attack began to lose steam, and Jubal Early took two brigades up a ravine which separated Culp's Hill and Cemetery Hill. The Confederates were able to capture several artillery batteries in vicious hand-to-hand fighting.[63]

General Early received a severe counterattack from a combination of Hancock's men as well as remnants from the Iron Brigade.[64] There would be no further progress by General Ewell that day.

Although the sun was sinking on July 2, the Confederates had done well thus far. The Union I, III, and XI Corps had been destroyed. While General Meade had not been driven from the field, the graycoats had dominated the first two days of action.

From the Union perspective, they had not been driven from the field, and they knew it. General Hancock still held a strong position on Cemetery Ridge. The II, V, VI and XII Corps were not about to give up easily. The battle of Gettysburg was far from over.

On July 3 General Lee knew that he had attacked both flanks of the enemy, without success. The battle would turn on Lee's final decision. The precise location of the Confederate assault would turn out to be extremely important.

Lee believed that an attack on the Union left offered the best chance of success. However, due to Longstreet's continued reluctance in this approach, Lee changed his mind. Instead of striking the left and left center of the Union lines, the rebels would charge the center of the Federal position.[65] This would prove to be a fatal mistake.

General Longstreet's corps would lead the attack, and for this reason he was given the honor of its coordination. Artillery under E. Porter Alexander would open a bombardment upon the Federals, providing some protection for the advance.

Approximately 15,000 men[66] would constitute the assault force. These were solid, veteran troops, but they were too few in number, and were making a frontal assault against an enemy in strong fortifications on Cemetery Ridge. It had little hope of breaking the Union lines.

Perhaps Longstreet realized as much, as he opened up an exchange of notes with Alexander, almost giving the artillerist the responsibility for the beginning of the advance.[67]

July 3, 1863, has become better known as "Pickett's charge" in honor of General George E. Pickett, who led the Southern advance. In reality, nine brigades stormed Cemetery Ridge, only three of which belonged to General Pickett.[68]

From left to right, Pickett's brigades were led by Richard B. Garnett, Lewis Armistead, and James Kemper. General Johnston Pettigrew would lead four divisions on Pickett's left. The remnants of Archer's[69] brigade would form on Garnett's left, followed by Pettigrew's own brigade.[70] Joseph Davis placed his men next in line, followed by the command of Robert Mayo.[71]

Behind Pettigrew were two more brigades under General Isaac Trimble. James Lane and William Lowrance would advance in the center of the attack, adding strength to Pettigrew's assault.

While the Union forces on Cemetery Ridge were strongly posted and heavily entrenched, the graycoats advanced over open ground with little or no protection. At 1:00 P.M.[72] Confederate artillery opened fire, but with little effect. In contrast, heavy Federal guns blasted huge gaps in the Confederate lines.

Still, the graycoats moved onward, constantly reforming their lines as men dropped by the scores. The Confederates had some success, many of the rebels reaching different parts of Cemetery Ridge, only to be killed as they reached the end of their journey.

Again, the Confederates attacked *en échelon*, and again the coordination broke down. Pickett's charge became a series of isolated, unsupported attacks, lacking unity and strength. The Confederates would surely have had greater success with massed artillery on the Union flanks. Instead, 56 guns under Ewell and A. P. Hill remained silent while a frontal assault disintegrated on the slopes of Cemetery Ridge.[73]

The carnage was horrific, and casualties were heavy. General Hancock was wounded, and General Armistead was mortally wounded. In the end, it was an assault doomed to failure. As Robert E. Lee surveyed the field, he watched the destruction of his ill-fated charge. As the survivors sought the safety of Confederate lines, he could only say "It was all my fault."[74]

While General Lee had performed very poorly here, the loss at Gettysburg was most certainly not all his fault. There were numerous causes of the failure in Pennsylvania. Historian Clifford Dowdey put some perspective on the action with the following summation: "the third day occurred because of Ewell's failure on the first and Longstreet's failure on the second, within the pattern made necessary by Stuart's failure to provide reconnaissance."[74a]

Jeb Stuart, Richard Ewell and James Longstreet had

all made horrendous mistakes. A. P. Hill had been almost invisible after opening the battle. At a lower level, Harry Heth and Robert Rodes had also turned in very poor accounts of themselves.

In spite of failings on the Confederate side, credit must be given to the Union leadership, particularly that of Meade and Hancock. Hancock was simply superb, holding the Union center and left while the Confederacy was winning the early part of the action.

The Gettysburg Campaign. Map by Jacob Wells.

George Meade had turned away the Confederate thrust into the North. The bluecoats had lost more men, but Gettysburg remained in Union hands. The Federals had lost 3,072 men killed, 14,497 wounded, and 5,434 missing, for a total loss of 23,003 soldiers. The Confederates had 2,592 men killed, 12,709 wounded, and 5,150 missing, for a total of 20,451.[75]

Gettysburg remains the most well documented of all Civil War battles. What were the results of this month-long campaign? The Federals had lost more men, but these troops could be replaced more readily than the Southern casualties. The Union forces had prevented a victory on Northern soil. That fact alone made Gettysburg significant. However, George G. Meade knew that he had not won in resounding fashion, and Robert E. Lee understood that despite the carnage on the last day, the Army of Northern Virginia had not been destroyed.[76]

The Shenandoah Valley was clear of Federal troops, the Yankees would have to regroup in order to move South again, and for the time being, Virginia would no longer be the battleground for this bloody conflict. The campaign had not accomplished all that Lee had desired, but it was not without positive results.[77]

In looking back on Civil War battles, many questions always arise. At Gettysburg, speculation will continue on the course the battle might have taken had Stonewall Jackson been present. His death at Chancellorsville was keenly felt throughout the Army of Northern Virginia. Richard Ewell was a capable subordinate, but his failure to capture Culp's Hill on the first day of the battle showed his lack of initiative.

Perhaps no one missed Jackson as much as Robert E. Lee. The Confederate invasion of Pennsylvania had been turned away in July, but Lee believed that Gettysburg was lost at Chancellorsville.[78]

July 14, 1863
FALLING WATERS

R. E. Lee (CSA)	G. G. Meade (USA)

On July 4, the Confederate army began its retreat from the fields of Gettysburg. Thoroughly repulsed, the Army of Northern Virginia had been turned away by the Union Army of the Potomac, commanded by General George G. Meade. Casualties for both sides had been heavy, but General Lee was worried that the bluecoats might pursue his tattered Confederates on the road back to Virginia.

A. P. Hill's Third Corps would take the lead, followed by James Longstreet and the First Corps. Richard Ewell and the Second Corps brought up the rear. Heavy rain began to fall shortly after noon,[1] and progress was slow for the Confederates.

Lee's troops headed down the Fairfield Road, in the direction of the Potomac River. Hearts were heavy as the troops were saddened with failure. The long line of rebels stretched out 17 miles in length,[2] and headed for Williamsport, Maryland.[3]

On July 6 the Confederate cavalry under General John Imboden held off about 7,000 enemy horsemen.[4] The situation was do or die for the graycoats, and every man realized that failure here meant the capture of General Lee's entire army. Southern reinforcements arrived from General J. E. B. "Jeb" Stuart's cavalry command and order was restored.[5] It had been a very close call.

The infantry reached Williamsport during the morning of July 7. The rebels guarded the crossings of the Potomac River between Williamsport and Falling Waters, just a few miles downstream. At this point, the Confederates rested. There was not much activity for several days, and gradually morale improved. If the Federals attacked, the Army of Northern Virginia would be ready.[6]

On July 12 the Union infantry appeared. However, instead of a full-scale assault, the Federals simply entrenched. It seemed as if Meade's Army of the Potomac was expecting the Southerners to attack them.[7]

The Confederates used this time to build pontoons to cross the river. The rains had been furious, swelling the waters of the Potomac. Fortunately the rebels had a man whose talents were equal to the task. Stonewall Jackson's former quartermaster, Major John Harmon, supervised the construction.

By the 13th the Potomac had fallen somewhat. It was possible to cross at Williamsport, and a pontoon bridge was ready at Falling Waters. Most of the Confederates crossed into Virginia in the night and during the next morning. By 11:00 A.M., all of the Army of Northern Virginia was safely across, except for two divisions at Falling Waters under General Harry Heth.[8]

On July 14, Meade ordered a reconnaissance in force. At 7:00 A.M.[9] the Northerners moved out. They found Williamsport deserted, but ran into Heth's troops at Falling Waters.

General Heth was responsible for watching not only the Confederate army as the men moved back into Virginia, but the Yankees as well to make sure that enemy aggression was held in check. Two Union cavalry divisions surprised Heth's men before the rebels could cross the Potomac. The rivers were high, but Heth was able to discharge his duty with the loss of only two cannon and some 500 stragglers who were unable to keep up with the remainder of Lee's troops.[10]

Although General Johnston Pettigrew was mortally wounded in the initial attack, Heth's loss was small. Lee's defeated Army of the Potomac was back in Virginia, and the United States government felt that the Confederates had been allowed to escape.

September 19–20, 1863
CHICKAMAUGA

B. Bragg (CSA)	W. S. Rosecrans (USA)

The summer of 1863 had not been kind to the Confederacy. A decisive victory in May at Chancellorsville had given way to defeat at Gettysburg on July 3. The very next day, the garrison at Vicksburg surrendered after a lengthy siege, giving the Union control of the Mississippi River. The troops in gray needed to beat the Federals in the field to lift morale throughout the South.

General Braxton Bragg commanded the Confederate Army of Tennessee. Unlike their counterparts in Virginia, the Army of Tennessee had not met with much success. Very gradually, the Union forces had taken control of the Volunteer State.

In early September the Union soldiers were headquartered in Chattanooga, Tennessee, under the command of General William S. Rosecrans. The Cincinnati native had divided his men into three forces, led by George H. Thomas, Alexander McCook and Thomas Crittenden.

The topography around Chattanooga is very mountainous. The hills stretch down into Georgia, and they provide great opportunity for an army to either hide or attack. The first meaningful action in September occurred at a little place in North Georgia called Dug Gap.

On the eastern side of Missionary Ridge, another mountain range known as Pigeon Mountain extends farther south into Georgia. In the center of Pigeon Mountain a narrow opening allows passage through the hilly terrain. This is Dug Gap.

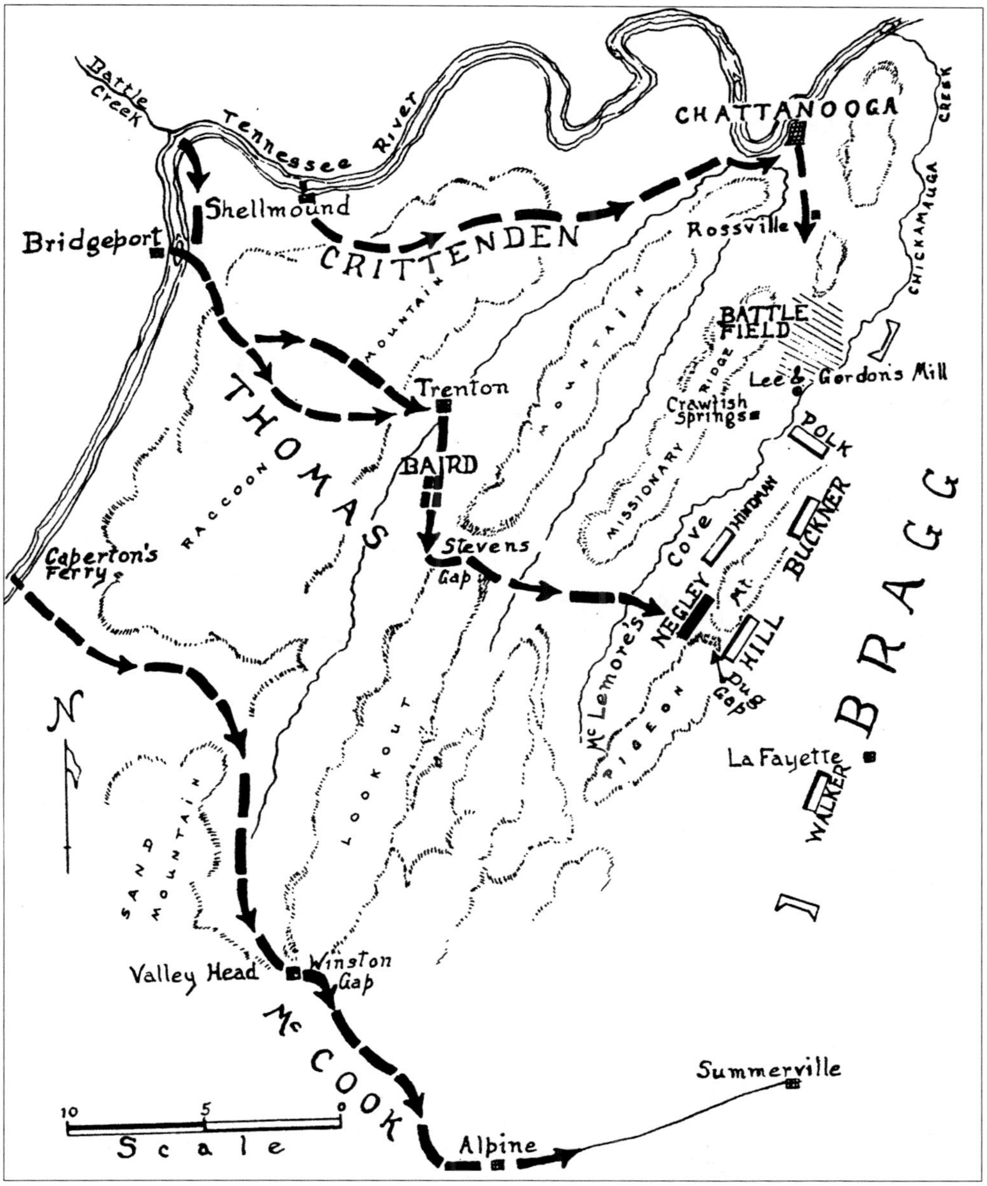

Rosecrans' hazardous dispersal of his corps crossing Lookout Mountain. Negley's exposed position is shown in McLemore's Cove. Map by Dorothy Thomas Tucker.

On the western side of the mountain were the bluecoats under General Thomas. By September 10 they were stationed in a small, secluded tract of land by the name of McLemore's Cove.

The rebels of General Patrick R. Cleburne's division held the gap, as well as the eastern side of Pigeon Mountain. Some 15 miles[1] farther north, Confederate General Thomas C. Hindman was ordered to move his troops forward the next morning. This would signal the start of the attack.

William Rosecrans had already made a serious mistake. The Union forces were widely scattered. Crittenden was to the north, Thomas was around McLemore's Cove, and McCook too far to the south. None of the Federals could come to the assistance of the other. This was a golden opportunity for the Confederates.

At 8:00 A.M. on the 11th, Cleburne had his graycoats in position. Only a small ridge separated the opposing forces. The Irishman waited for the sound of Hindman's attack, but silence covered Pigeon Mountain. By 11:00 A.M., General Hindman had still not brought his men forward. When combined, the Confederates outnumbered their foe by almost four to one.[2] By the time that the Confederates finally attacked, the Federals had slipped away to the west.

While Hindman had needlessly feared that Crittenden and McCook were about to attack his lines, part of the blame for the failure must rest with Braxton Bragg as well.[3] As the commanding general he should have made sure that the Union mistakes were exploited. Confederate leadership had been severely lacking on September 11 but the next day would bring still another chance.

Although the Confederates had let Thomas escape, Bragg was now aware of the position of the enemy. General Crittenden and his men were all alone, isolated from any assistance. On September 12 it would be a simple matter to defeat these Yankees. The task for tomorrow would fall on Confederate General Leonidas Polk.

Thomas Crittenden had placed his troops along the La Fayette Road, just north of Lee & Gordon's Mill. The Federals were some 12 miles from General Thomas.[4]

At 3:00 A.M.,[5] Bragg gave Polk his orders. Three times he repeated his order to attack.[6] For additional support, Bragg decided to use Hindman's Division, a corps under General Simon B. Buckner, plus the Confederate Reserve Corps, commanded by General William H. T. Walker. The assault was to take place almost due south of Lee & Gordon's Mill, at Pea Vine Church.

Leonidas Polk had grossly overestimated the enemy force confronting his men. He believed that a second Union corps was behind Crittenden,[7] ready to act as reinforcements. Failing to aggressively assail the enemy, Polk was no better than Hindman. The Confederates lost a second chance at Pea Vine Church.

The Southerners had thrown away two opportunities that rarely come along in the course of an entire war. However, the enemy was still dangerously divided on September 13. General Rosecrans had not yet united his three corps. A ten-mile gap remained between Crittenden, at Lee & Gordon's Mill, and the left flank of General Thomas. Some 30 miles of difficult terrain separated Thomas and the left flank of General McCook.[8]

The graycoats held one more advantage. In a rare occurrence during the Civil War, at this point the Confederates actually outnumbered the Federals. Bragg had approximately 68,000 men at his disposal, while Rosecrans could count only 63,816.[9] Both sides would attempt to bring up reinforcements.

Over the next week the soldiers of each army would move in a northerly direction. This part of Georgia was very rugged, with spurs from Missionary Ridge breaking the contour of the land. Several farms dotted the landscape, with Chickamauga Creek running north and south as it meandered through the wooded countryside. Small back roads crisscrossed the area, but the main artery was the La Fayette Road, which ran north and south. Visibility in the forest extended only a few feet, as officers struggled to maintain control over their commands.

As the combat unfolded, the fighting on the first day would move generally east to west and north to south, although each farm seemed to be the sight of a daylong contest. Battle units on both sides would become intermingled and confused.

By September 19, the opposing armies were finally ready to fight for control of this forest. The battle of Chickamauga was about to get under way. The Confederates faced west, and General Bragg had divided his army into two wings. The right wing was under Polk. His right flank was protected by the cavalry of General Nathan B. Forrest. The left wing was under the command of General James Longstreet, who had just recently arrived from Virginia with reinforcements.[10] General Longstreet would not only assume command of the left wing, he would win a decisive victory for the South. There was also cavalry on the left flank, led by General Joseph Wheeler.

General Rosecrans had worked hard to consolidate his troops. Thomas led six divisions on the Union left, while McCook's two divisions made up the Federal right. Crittenden had taken on a reserve role, as General Rosecrans wished to be able to deploy these men wherever they might be needed.[11]

Most of the infantry were on the east side of the La Fayette Road, as the action at the beginning of the battle centered along Chickamauga Creek. The initial confrontation would take place at a seemingly insignificant little spot known as Jay's Mill.

Colonel Dan McCook came from a well-known military family in the United States Army. His brother, General Alexander McCook, occupied the Union right. On September 19, Dan McCook would begin the battle of Chickamauga.

Colonel McCook had been sent to Reed's Bridge to reinforce other Union troops in the area. About one mile west and south[12] of Reed's Bridge, McCook found what he believed to be a single, isolated Confederate brigade. These were the graycoats under General Evander McNair.[13]

Dutifully, the Federal brigadier reported his findings to General Thomas. There were other Federal units close at hand, and it seemed as if this lone enemy brigade could be easily captured.[14]

Thomas sent two divisions to Jay's Mill. John M. Brannan's men took the lead, with Absalom Baird's bluecoats in close support. The order to Brannan now placed the Yankees on the offensive for the first time. Up until this point, Bragg's Confederates had been the aggressors. Instead of Bragg outflanking the Union left, Thomas now extended past Bragg's right.[15]

Colonel John T. Croxton led Brannan's Second Brigade forward and drove the enemy from the field. However, Confederate cavalry were waiting. Croxton advanced to a distance of perhaps 150 yards, and with approximately 1,000 soldiers against 250 horsemen,[16] pressed his advantage. Slowly but surely, George H. Thomas was being drawn into a battle.

Brannan hoped to capitalize upon the disparity in numbers. He sent Colonel Ferdinand Van Derveer to turn the Confederate right. Unfamiliar with the country, the colonel marched very slowly. While Croxton was still engaged with General Forrest's cavalry, the bluecoats lost a chance to envelop the Confederate right.[17]

Although Van Derveer had lost a chance for the Union, Forrest understood the severity of his plight and decided to strike back. He sent Colonel George Dibrell along the Reed's Bridge Road, with the intent of moving around Croxton's left flank. Around 9:00 A.M. Dibrell moved out, but instead of completing a simple maneuver against Croxton, he marched directly into the slow-moving Van Derveer.[18]

With Confederates on Croxton's flank and Van Derveer engaged, General Brannan ordered his third brigade to move forward. The Yankees were under the command of Colonel John Connell, but they had not yet reached the action.

George Thomas had no intention of losing an entire division without a fight. He ordered Absalom Baird to bring his division up and support Brannan at Jay's Mill.[19]

The reinforcements were timely, but the Union coordination was not good. The broken country, dense underbrush, and confusion of the battle made cooperation difficult. The graycoats managed to escape with minimal damage, and by 11:00 A.M. the heat of the battle subsided as both sides chose to reorganize their lines.[20]

The battle of Chickamauga began to drift in the direction of the La Fayette Road. West of Jay's Mill, Confederate General St. John Liddell ordered two brigades, under Daniel C. Govan and Edward C. Walthall, to attack the Federal right. They would meet General Baird's three Union brigades north of the Brotherton Road.[21]

Baird had placed Colonel Benjamin F. Scribner's brigade in front of the graycoats. Attacking due north, Walthall's Mississippians hit the Union left, while Govan charged the right. Scribner's Federals never had a chance, losing nearly half of the brigade.[22] John Starkweather commanded Baird's Second Brigade. His men were behind, and slightly to the right of Scribner's troops. The Confederate onslaught overwhelmed Starkweather as well, and the bluecoats disintegrated.[23]

Walthall's assault continued, rolling up John King's Third Brigade. Many Federals had simply deserted their posts, as they fled under the weight of the attack. The Northern troops finally reformed among Croxton and Van Derveer's men. A fresh Union division under General Richard W. Johnson had made its way to the sound of the action. Combined, this was a powerful force, and the Federals counterattacked. The Yankees drove Govan back, and General Liddell was forced to withdraw his exhausted rebels.[24] Both sides began to bring up reinforcements.

The tension of the battle had brought out General Rosecrans' worst traits. An impulsive, emotional man by nature, he was gradually becoming unglued. His grasp of the situation would continue to deteriorate as the action intensified.[25]

By 2:00 P.M., the conflict had moved farther west, to the intersection of the Alexander's Bridge Road and the Brotherton Road. The Confederate division under General Benjamin F. Cheatham held the crossing, while the Union divisions of John M. Palmer and Richard W. Johnson approached.

With ammunition running low,[26] Cheatham sent his troops forward, but the Confederate attacks were made in uncoordinated, piecemeal fashion. By 2:30 P.M., the Yankees had pushed the graycoats back across the Brotherton Road.[27]

General A. P. Stewart moved his Confederates to Cheatham's left. He had stabilized the situation for the Southerners, and forced the battle closer to the La Fayette Road.[28]

Cheatham's left was secure, but his right was not. General George Maney received a furious charge from the bluecoats under August Willich and Joseph Dodge. These two brigades pressed in on Maney's flanks, and forced him to pull back.[29]

As the Federals gained control of the action, Maney's troops gave way, and the Yankees poured through the woods. On Maney's left, General Otho F. Strahl ordered his rebels to fall back. The air grew quiet over the farm of the Brock family, as the Union forces did not offer pursuit. For the moment, it was clear that the Northerners had gained control of the area.

The Confederates had been pushed back, but the grayclad men of Polk's right wing continued to fight. General Polk sent Liddell's two brigades forward. Had Walthall and Govan entered the fray earlier in the day, much more could have been accomplished. By the time the Southerners crossed the field, it was after 3:00 P.M.[30] General Liddell had intended to form his troops on Maney's right, but the Tennesseans had already broken apart under the Federal onslaught. Unable to attack in unison with Maney and Strahl, the Confederates were easily repulsed.

The drama shifted to the Brotherton property, where the Brotherton Road meets the La Fayette Road. A small, one-room log cabin was the only building on the farm, but every inch of ground was fiercely contested. Like many other areas in the battle of Chickamauga, the densely wooded country obscured a soldier's vision to only a few feet around him.

The Brotherton property was approximately the

center of the Union line. If the rebels could break through here, General Bragg would have a decided advantage.

The Yankees formed in lines perpendicular to each other. Some troops faced south, while others faced east. They allowed the enemy to approach to within 50 yards, then let loose a terrific volley. This stopped the Southerners and their lines recoiled under the impact of the blast. The Northerners had the advantage of numbers, and surging forward they pressed the graycoats back. However, shortly before 4:00 P.M.,[31] an Alabama brigade counterattacked.

These were battle-hardened veterans under Colonel James Sheffield. Their opponents, though numerous, were inexperienced. Initially, Sheffield had great success, but his troops outdistanced the other Confederates, and soon were fighting alone. The enemy finally reformed, and delivered a counterattack of their own. Eventually, Sheffield was pushed back to the safety of his compatriots.[32]

Although the Federal center had held, the Union right flank was in trouble.[33] Confederate General Bushrod Johnson had seen the weakness on the Union right, the sector held by Colonel Edward King. Johnson's boys stormed past the Federals, and the bluecoats were forced to retreat to avoid capture.[34]

The Federals were running low on ammunition, and only the left of the formation was east of the La Fayette Road.[35] How much longer could the men hold their ground?

On the left side of the Federal alignment, William Grose held his men fast. They faced a somewhat southerly direction against William Bate's troops. Grose was posted on a gentle rise of ground, and had placed artillery on the crest of the knoll. The Confederates attacked from each side, and the Yankees were caught in a crossfire.[36] By 4:15 P.M.,[37] Grose was forced to retire. The Union left retreated across the Brotherton Field, as the flank collapsed in disarray.[38]

Federal reinforcements arrived, stalling Bate's assault. As in many battles, the graycoats did not have enough men to follow up their success. General Bate tried to reform his lines, but a second assault just north of the Brotherton property was easily repulsed.[38a]

No further progress was made by either side in this area of the battlefield. Each army had fought stubbornly. The quiet gave the men some relief, and as the sun set upon the Brotherton Farm, both sides buried their dead.

Further south lay the Viniard Field, and the combat continued to move in this direction. At 1:30 P.M.,[39] Union General Jefferson C. Davis crossed the La Fayette Road with two of his own brigades and three others which belonged to General Crittenden. Although Davis was able to make some progress, the graycoats held their ground. Three Confederate brigades under John Gregg, Jerome Robertson and Robert Trigg faced east, and refused to allow the Federals to advance. As Robertson attacked in the center, his men relieved the pressure on General Gregg.

Fortunately for the Confederates, confusion intervened among the bluecoats. The visibility was very poor, and two Federal brigades became entangled. Colonel Sidney M. Barnes, on the Union right, had led his men across the path of General William Carlin, in the center. At this point, Trigg and Robertson attacked. Striking Barnes in the right flank, Colonel Trigg caught the Northerners by surprise.[40]

As the Federals fell back, the troops reformed along the La Fayette Road. They refused to be pushed back any farther, and General Davis was able to bring up reinforcements. The Confederates moved forward through the fields of the Viniard Farm, when the Southerners were suddenly stopped in their tracks.[41]

On the Union left was the 35th Illinois Regiment. The rebels swarmed around their left flank, heading straight toward the Brock House at the north end of this section of the battlefield.[42]

Colonel John T. Wilder had brought his men up to hold the Union left. They were armed with new Spencer repeating rifles, which could deliver a shower of bullets in a very short time. The Confederate threat to the Union left was over as soon as it began.[43]

Both sides reformed their lines, as the contour of the ground made intricate maneuvers very difficult. By 5:00 P.M., there was nothing left to do but charge the enemy.[44]

Colonel Luther Bradley's Federals attacked from the southwest corner of the field. The graycoats added the Georgians under Henry "Rock" Benning who took their positions on Robertson's right.

As the daylight faded, Colonel Bradley gallantly led his brigade across the La Fayette Road. The silhouettes made fine targets for the Southern marksmen and his attack was easily repulsed. Casualties were heavy for the men in blue, though they were able to withdraw in good order. Darkness seemed welcome by both sides, and gunfire died away at Viniard Field.[45]

There were very few attacks at night during the Civil War. Visibility in open ground made operations difficult at best, and as commands became intermingled, more often than not each side would end up firing upon its own men.

The dense woods of Chickamauga compounded the problem. Nevertheless, there was one more act to play out on September 19, and Pat Cleburne's Confederates were about to attempt just such a risky maneuver. General Leonidas Polk, commanding the right wing, made the decision to order the Irishman forward.

Around 6:00 P.M.,[46] General Cleburne arranged his

division astride the Brotherton Road, just east of the Winfrey Field. S. A. M. Wood's brigade held the left, south of the road. On his right were the troops under Lucious Polk, the nephew of Leonidas Polk. On Wood's left were Confederate horsemen.

Opposing the graycoats on the other side of the clearing were the Federal troops under Philemon Baldwin, August Willich, and Joseph Dodge. These three brigades had support to their left by Scribner and Starkweather.

General Wood's troops moved forward across Winfrey Field, and initiated the attack. The soldiers could not see the Federals, and fired at the flashes of the enemy muskets. Imaginations ran wild for both sides, as the tension mounted.

Wood's troops had struck the bluecoats under General Baldwin, who fired one volley, then fell back. Baldwin was killed in the early action, and the Union organization began to disintegrate. Wood's brigade was able to pierce the enemy lines, as Baldwin and Willich retreated.

Lucious Polk was to enjoy even greater success. Scribner and Starkweather struggled to organize their lines, but to no avail. With minimal casualties, Polk took 50 prisoners and recaptured three cannon which had been lost earlier in the day.[47]

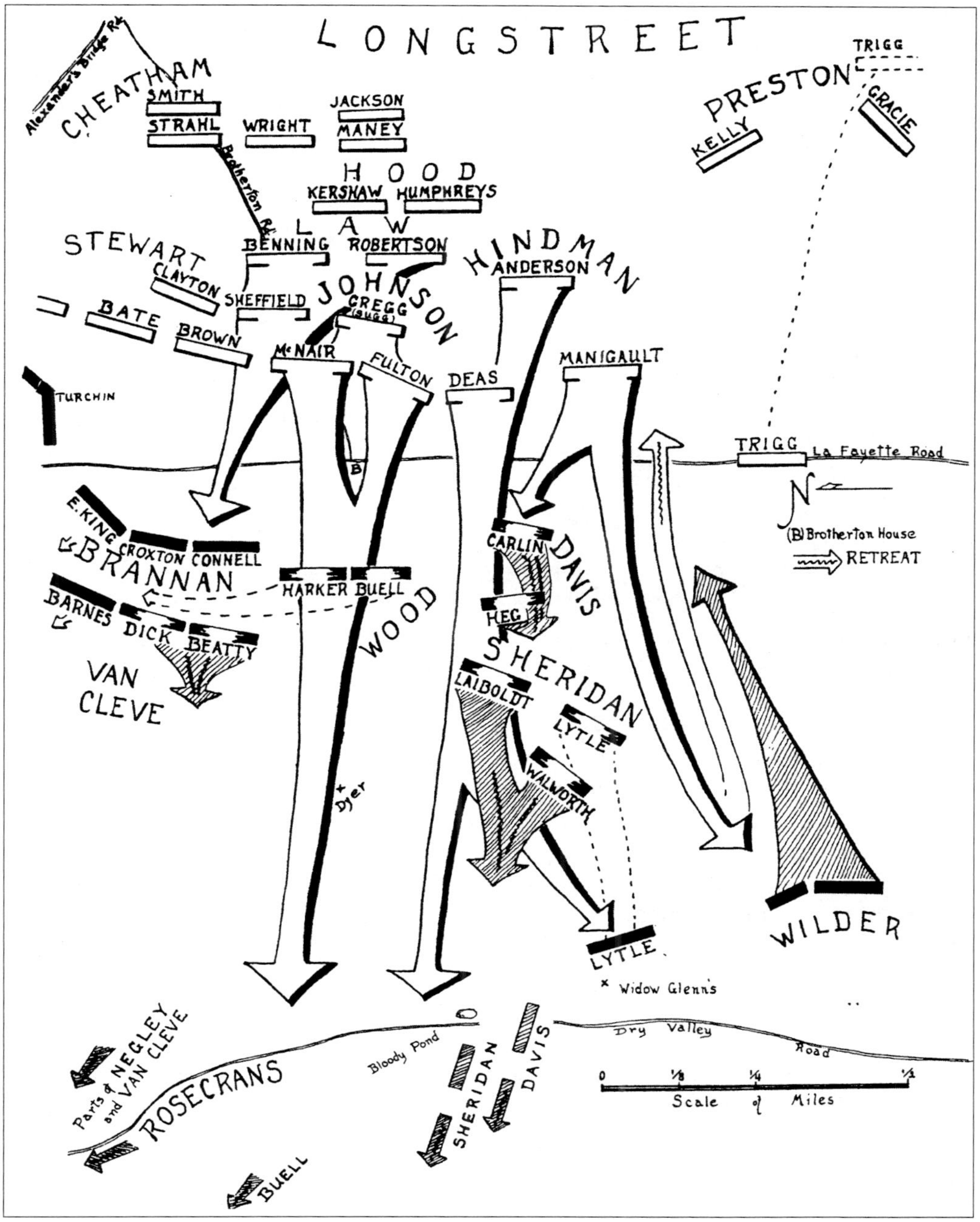

Longstreet's massed attack on the Federal right. Bushrod Johnson's division moves through the gap left by Wood and cleaves through the Federal right center. Hindman's division routs divisions of Davis and Sheridan and Rosecrans' right wing is driven from the field. Map by Dorothy Thomas Tucker.

While the Confederates had achieved some success, the darkness prevented any disciplined pursuit. Leonidas Polk's night attack had ended in confusion.

After the first day of combat, the Federals had been pushed back to the vicinity of the LaFayette Road, but generals Bragg and Polk had not acquitted themselves well. The Confederate attacks had been made in a piecemeal, isolated fashion. Had the assaults been simultaneous, their effect would have been more powerful.

On the 19th of September, the action had been concentrated on the right wing of Bragg's Army of Tennessee, which was managed by General Polk. Tomorrow, the contest would shift to the left wing, which was under the control of General James Longstreet. The results would be quite different.

General Rosecrans spent the night attempting to consolidate his forces. The alignment for both sides on September 20 would be very significant. George Thomas still held the Union left. He commanded six divisions facing east, in the following order from north to south: Baird, Richard Johnson, Palmer, Reynolds, Brannan and Negley.[48]

Next to Thomas were McCook's two divisions, under Union generals Davis and Sheridan. It must be remembered that General Crittenden still held his troops in reserve.[49]

Unlike Leonidas Polk on the previous day, James Longstreet had massed his graycoats on the left wing in a very powerful assault formation. From his left to right (south to north) Longstreet had placed four divisions, under A. P. Stewart, Bushrod Johnson, Hindman, and William Preston.[50] General John B. Hood's division was just behind Johnson. The Confederates had amassed eight brigades, five lines deep, over some 70 acres of land east of the Brotherton farm.[51]

At 11:00 A.M.,[52] the order was given which changed the course of the battle of Chickamauga. Through a terrible misunderstanding on the Union side, Longstreet's troops were about to burst through the Federal lines.

The Federals were very nervous, perhaps justifiably so, as they had been pushed from Jay's Mill to the La Fayette Road only the day before. Although the Confederates were massed around Brannan's position, General Rosecrans seemed to be preoccupied on the far left of Thomas' line. This was about to cause tremendous confusion.

Rosecrans believed that General Brannan had moved from the center to reinforce Thomas on the Union left. Brannan had in fact not moved at all. Therefore, Rosecrans now thought that a gap existed to the right of Reynolds.

As a result, Rosecrans sent an order to General Thomas J. Wood, moving Wood closer to Reynolds. This accomplished nothing, as Brannan had not moved. There was no gap next to Reynolds. However, this did leave a large, yawning space in front of the Confederate formation.

James Longstreet was not about to let such a mistake go unpunished. At 11:10 A.M.[53] he sent General Bushrod Johnson forward, and the graycoats poured through the opening in the Union lines.

Wave after wave of Confederates overran the Union right. The troops under General McCook were quickly shattered. Longstreet's charge surged forward, then turned north, toward Dyer Field. The left wing of the Southern army had done a magnificent job, and the bluecoats were in full retreat.

The right wing had not produced such spectacular results. The Federal troops were stationed just east of Kelly Field, and the Confederates were able to extend their right flank to get around the enemy left. Generals Marcellus A. Stovall and Daniel W. Adams moved their brigades forward, and both brigades turned so that by 11:00 A.M.[54] they faced south, with Adams on the right.[55] The Confederates forced the Union left to pull back their lines, but Adams and Stovall were not supported by additional troops, and the Federal lines finally held.

With Confederates on the flank and in the center of the enemy, the right wing had a great opportunity. Once again, General Polk let a golden chance for the Confederacy escape his grasp. The failure to crush General Thomas would be critical in the days ahead.[56]

Despite the failure by Polk on the Confederate right, the Union troops were still in dire straits. General Thomas had been forced to contract his lines. McCook had been routed by Longstreet, and the Federals attempted to consolidate the remnants of McCook's broken command with Thomas's men to the west.

General Thomas had retreated in a westerly direction to a gentle rise known as Snodgrass Hill. While he had his headquarters in the fields of the Snodgrass family, the troops in blue were deployed along three hills which extended southwest of Snodgrass Hill.[57] Together, these hills made up part of what was called Horseshoe Ridge, though it was not shaped like a horseshoe.

General Brannan's men occupied the Union right. It was a sound defensive position, as the bluecoats could fire their guns down the slope upon the advancing enemy. To the Confederates, the task at hand seemed a simple one: the Federals held the heights; they must be removed.

General Joseph Kershaw's South Carolinians looked up at Brannan's troops and at 1:00 P.M.[58] began to advance on the Confederate left. The assaults were not well organized, and the graycoats were easily repulsed. On Kershaw's right, General Benjamin Humphreys attacked along the southern end of Snodgrass Field. Thomas had managed to piece together enough troops to hold off this attack as well.

The day wore on for General Thomas, but the Federals held on. Casualties were heavy on both sides as repeated assaults at the Union lines took their toll in bloody repulses. Still, at the end of the day George H. Thomas still stood atop Snodgrass Hill.

General Thomas refused to give ground. He had stopped the Confederate assaults almost single-handedly, as he had received almost no help. Rosecrans, McCook and Crittenden had left the battlefield in disgrace, riding back to Chattanooga.

As the daylight faded,[59] Thomas began to withdraw the troops still left at Kelly Field, then finally pulled back his men from Horseshoe Ridge. The Union forces retreated safely into Chattanooga. He had saved the Union Army from destruction, and it was on this day that he earned his nickname The "Rock of Chickamauga."

The casualties for the battle of Chickamauga were severe for both sides, although estimates vary considerably. The Federals, fighting much of the time from behind fortifications, lost fewer men. Still, the Union Army of the Cumberland had 1,656 men killed, 9,749 wounded, and 4,774 captured or missing, for a total of 16,179.[60] The Confederates had lost 2,389 men killed, 13,412 wounded, and 2,003 captured or missing, for a total of 17,804.[61]

It would appear that the Confederates did indeed win a big victory on September 20. However, despite General Longstreet's heroics, the victory at Chickamauga was not as beneficial as it might seem. The Confederacy lost a tremendous number of soldiers, without destroying or capturing George Thomas and his command.

Despite the objections of Longstreet, Forrest, Polk and Bushrod Johnson, General Bragg allowed the enemy to retreat into Chattanooga without a vigorous pursuit.[62] When the final results of Chickamauga were viewed in retrospect, many on the Southern side came to view the battle as a victory that the South could not afford.[63]

While this is true in some respects, it should be viewed less as an analysis of the performance of James Longstreet, and more as an indictment of Braxton Bragg.

October 5–10, 1863
Blue Springs

J. S. Williams (CSA)	A. E. Burnside (USA)

The conflicts at Blue Springs, Tennessee, were actually part of a larger campaign by the Confederacy. The rebels desired to dislodge Union General Ambrose E. Burnside from his position in Knoxville. Blue Springs was actually three battles. The first occurred on October 5, with another on the 7th, and the final engagement on the 10th. The expedition was a combination of cavalry, infantry and artillery. These battles in East Tennessee were the last attempts by the Confederacy to remove Burnside from Knoxville, before the graycoats placed that city under siege in November.[1]

The Confederate infantry was under the overall command of General Robert Ransom. On October 1 the rebels arrived in Jonesborough, Tennessee, located in the far eastern corner of the state. Cavalry General John S. Williams was ordered to take 1,700 men and move southwest to the East Tennessee and Virginia Railroad. The Southern troopers were to stop near Bull's Gap, in the vicinity of Greenville, Tennessee. Ransom would then head north and seize Cumberland Gap.[2]

However, Williams and his command slightly overstepped their authority. The graycoats rode about eight miles west of Greenville,[3] and at this point, ran into trouble. On October 3, the Confederates clashed with Union horsemen under Samuel Carter. General Carter was unsure of the Confederate intentions, and fell back. Williams deployed his men west of Blue Springs, and light skirmishing occurred for the next two days.[4]

Carter knew that there was Union infantry at Bull's Gap, so on October 5, he ordered a daring evening attack against the Confederates. After two hours, his Federals withdrew to the west.

General Williams did not wish the enemy to know exactly how many soldiers he had at his disposal. As a result, some deception was called for. Extra campfires were lighted, and buglers sounded roll call for troops which did not exist.[5] Hopefully, this would delay or prevent any further Union aggression.

However, on October 7, Carter was back. He tested the front of his foe, and after more minor skirmishing, withdrew his blue-clad troopers once again.[6]

The Federal troops had twice probed the Confederate lines, but had really just felt the strength of the enemy. At 10:00 A.M. on October 10, the Federals returned, and this time they came with a strong force.[7]

General Burnside had brought a Union cavalry brigade along with an entire division of infantry. The mounted troopers led the advance, and Williams and his Confederates fell back to deploy their troops.[8]

The Southerners retreated east of Blue Springs. The infantry took up a position in front of a ridge, while four cannon and four rapid-fire guns were placed in the rear.[9]

The Federals advanced, gradually extending their lines as more Union reinforcements arrived. Burnside's intent was to move around the flanks of the Confederate infantry. As the more numerous Yankees lengthened each side of the formation, the graycoats were forced to stretch their lines to counter the threat.[10]

At 5:00 P.M. on October 10, Burnside's troops charged forward. The wooded terrain was rough and uneven. The Confederate flanks bent back, almost broken by the weight of the charge. The Federals reached a point 250 yards[11] from the enemy rear, but were suddenly greeted by a blast of artillery. Canister ripped through their ranks, forcing them to fall back. The Yankees immediately sought the protection of the trees. General Williams urged the rebel infantry to action, and bullets rained on Burnside's command.[12]

As darkness finally covered the field, the Federals retreated, while the Confederates went back to their defensive positions.[13]

Perplexing news followed the Confederates. An order from District Commander General Samuel Jones ordered Williams to retreat from Blue Springs. The graycoats would now attempt to unify their somewhat scattered forces. Ransom's expedition to Cumberland Gap had been canceled, and the entire battle at Blue Springs had been unnecessary.[14]

In comparison with other battles of the Civil War, the needless affair at Blue Springs produced very few casualties. Burnside's Northerners recorded 100 men killed and wounded, while the Confederates had lost 261 soldiers.[15] The Confederates fell back into Virginia, while Burnside would soon experience an arduous November in the siege of Knoxville.

October 14, 1863
Bristoe Station

A. P. Hill (CSA) — G. G. Meade (USA)

In the aftermath of Gettysburg, the Union Army of the Potomac had moved south into Virginia. Led by General George G. Meade, they numbered just over 80,000 men.[1] By early October, the Federals had reached Warrenton Junction, a stop on the Orange and Alexandria Railroad.

Stationed at Culpeper, the Army of Northern Virginia blocked the Union advance. Robert E. Lee commanded three corps, but the First Corps, under James Longstreet, had been dispatched to Tennessee. These men had been victorious less than one month ago at the battle of Chickamauga. The Second Corps, under Richard S. Ewell, along with the newly created Third Corps under A. P. Hill, gave Lee slightly less than 50,000 troops.[2] General J. E. B. "Jeb" Stuart led the Confederate cavalry.

Despite a numerical disadvantage, General Lee was in no mood to retreat. He wished to attack whenever possible. If Meade could be driven back along the railroad to the Potomac River, the Confederacy might be able to spend the winter of 1863 in peace once again.[3]

The Union Army was spread out on a ridge north of Culpeper. Lee wanted to move around the right flank of the enemy, force Meade to retreat, and strike the bluecoats when an opportunity presented itself. In order to catch the Yankees by surprise, Ewell and Hill would need to take circuitous routes, both ending up in the town of Warrenton. On October 12, the two Confederate corps left Culpeper, with the cavalry under Jeb Stuart hiding their movements from Federal eyes.[4]

On the afternoon of October 13, General Ewell's men reached Warrenton. A. P. Hill, with the longer march, arrived as darkness fell.[5] It was too late to mount an attack. Offensive operations would have to wait until tomorrow.

During the night, Lee received information from General Stuart that the Army of the Potomac was moving in a northeasterly direction along the Orange and Alexandria Railroad. It looked as though Meade was moving toward the fortifications around Washington.[5a] The enemy had a head start, but with a fast march Lee might yet be able to intercept the Yankees at Bristoe Station.

Dick Ewell was very familiar with this section of Virginia, having grown up here. Upon reaching the little town of Greenwich, he gave the direct road to Bristoe Station to General Hill. General Ewell decided to use back roads, and he kept the march of the Second Corps about a mile to Hill's right. Lee rode with Ewell, and was not in visual contact with the Third Corps.[6] Suddenly, Lee heard a burst of gunfire from his left, and knew instantly that a battle had begun. Lee and Ewell did not arrive until the action was over. As they would soon discover, it was as poorly managed an affair as the Civil War would produce.[7]

As A. P. Hill approached Bristoe Station, he noticed a large group of bluecoats on the near side, and many more on the far side of Broad Run. It was a small stream which ran north and south until it reached the Orange and Alexandria Railroad, where it turned due east. Hill was marching from the west, placing the north-south section of the stream directly in his front.[7a] As he came close to Broad Run, he saw large quantities of discarded camp equipment from the Army of the Potomac. Campfires were still burning and it appeared as if they had left in a hurry.[8] He had his quarry on the run, now he must finish them off.

Sensing the possibility of a great victory within his grasp,[8a] Hill deployed the division of Harry Heth facing the stream, intending to cross the little watercourse and attack the enemy in his front. Only two brigades were in position, John Cooke's on the right and William Kirkland's on the left, when they received orders to attack immediately.[9] Just as Cooke began to advance, his brigade received heavy gunfire from their right, from behind a railroad cut. Hidden from view was the Union II Corps, under General Gouverneur K. Warren. They lunged forward as the Confederates marched into their trap.[10] Intent on capturing the troops in front of him, A. P. Hill had not made a thorough reconnaissance of the surrounding area.[11]

The battle of Bristoe Station was over in 40 minutes.[12] Neither Lee nor the Second Corps could be of any assistance. Had Hill delayed his impetuous attack even half an hour, the Union troops could well have been isolated and cut off.[13]

Two brigades had borne the brunt of the slaughter. Both Cooke's and Kirkland's commands had been decimated.[14] The casualties in Heth's Division were 1,361,[15] while Warren lost 548.[15a]

Robert E. Lee was not a general who sharply criticized his subordinates. Nevertheless, he knew when and where mistakes had been made. For his part, A. P. Hill had the courage and fortitude to place all of the blame upon himself. The next morning, as the two men walked over the battlefield, Lee put an end to the matter with the sternest rebuke possible: "Well, well, General, bury these poor men and let us say no more about it."[16]

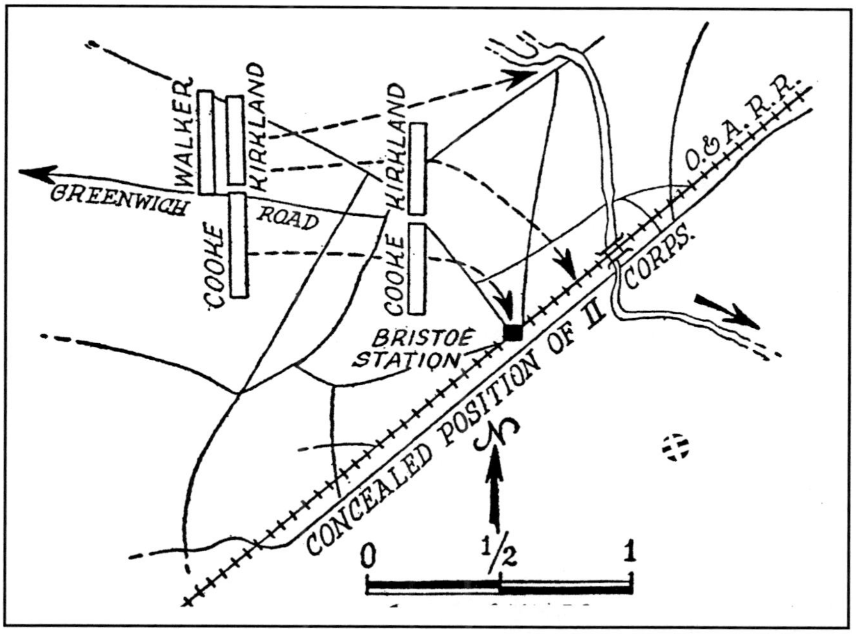

The attack of Cooke and Kirkland at Bristoe Station, October 14, 1863.

November 4–December 14, 1863
THE KNOXVILLE CAMPAIGN

J. Longstreet (CSA) — A. E. Burnside (USA)

Confederate General James Longstreet had been a most outspoken critic of Braxton Bragg, who was his immediate superior in the fall of 1863. Longstreet, along with many other general officers, believed that Bragg should have pursued the Federals more vigorously following the victory at Chickamauga.

General Bragg decided to remove his harshest critic, and on November 4 General Longstreet was sent north with two divisions[1] against the Federals in Knoxville under General Ambrose E. Burnside. The addition of 5,000 cavalrymen[2] under General Joseph Wheeler brought Longstreet's entire force to approximately 17,000 troops.[3]

The march was extremely slow. Trains were in short supply and some of the soldiers had to move on foot. It was not until November 14 that the Confederates reached the southern approaches to Knoxville.[4]

It must be pointed out that the transfer of Longstreet to Knoxville had several very important repercussions. General Bragg ordered this move primarily to remove General Longstreet, not to actually accomplish anything from a military standpoint.[5] Second, and most important, the transfer of infantry, artillery and cavalry would severely weaken Bragg's forces still in Chattanooga. Longstreet's men would be badly needed at the battles for Chattanooga, less than one month away.

There was a striking contrast in the overall esprit de corps which existed in the western armies and the morale in the Confederate troops fighting in Virginia. The contentious, fault-finding atmosphere and complete lack of camaraderie which existed among officers and enlisted men under Braxton Bragg was quite different from the attitude which prevailed under Robert E. Lee.

On November 14th, General Burnside sent Federal troops to the southwest in an attempt to rescue Union forces around Loudon, Tennessee. If the bluecoats could retreat to the safety of the Knoxville defenses they would be able to avoid capture.[6]

The next day, Longstreet's Confederates set out in hot pursuit. Only one mile[7] separated the opposing forces, and the race was on to Campbell's Station, a stop only ten miles to the northeast[8] on the Kingston Road.

Heavy rains had turned the dirt roads into quagmires,[9] slowing the pace of both armies. On the 16th the Federals arrived at Campbell's Station only minutes ahead

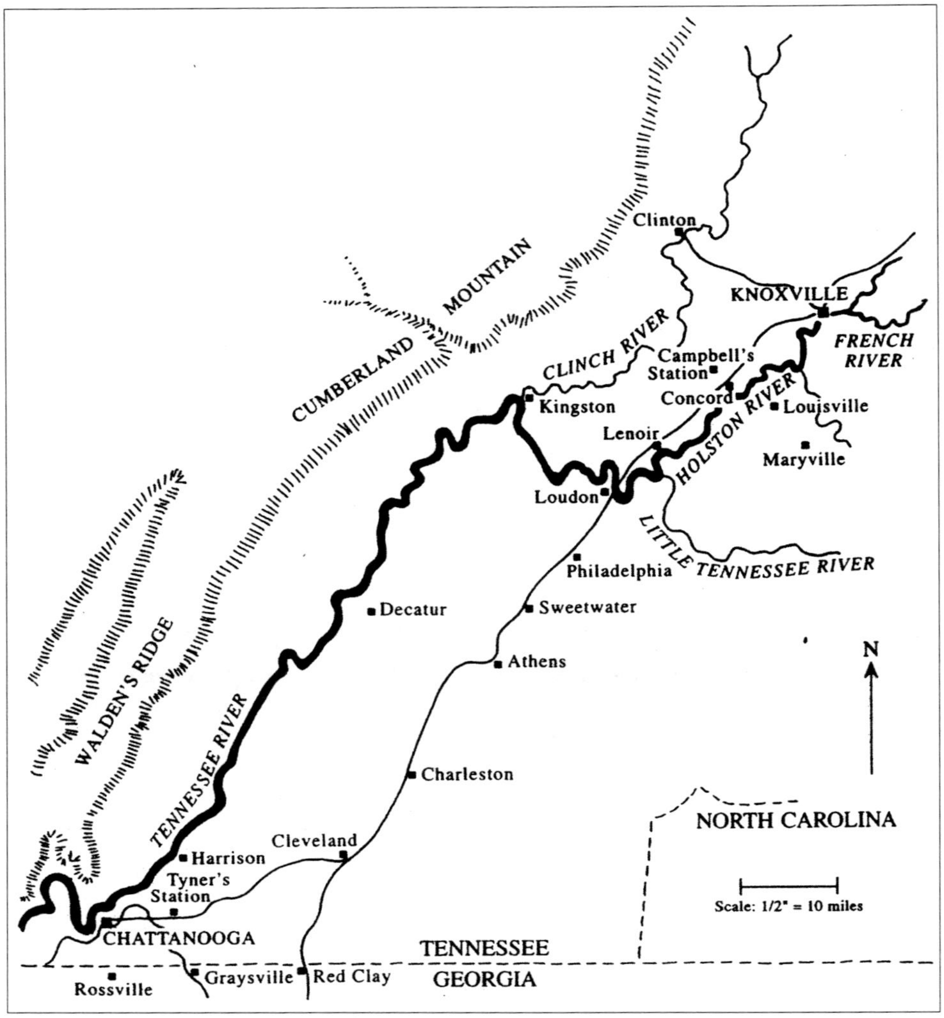

Chattanooga–East Tennessee Operations, October–November 1863.

of the rebels, and began to deploy their troops.[10] General Edward Ferrero would hold the Union right, while Colonel John Hartranft placed his troops on the left.

General Longstreet assailed the Federal right, as Lafayette McLaws vainly attempted to break the enemy lines. This attack was followed by another against the Union left. Micah Jenkins tried to move beyond the Federal left flank, but ended up in front of Hartranft and his men. The attacks on the Federal position were easily repulsed.[11]

Casualties were slight at Campbell's Station. The Federals lost 318 men, while the Confederates reported only 174 casualties. However, the Yankees had escaped to the safety of the defenses around Knoxville.[12]

Although Longstreet had proclaimed his desire for the offensive operations which had been missing under General Bragg, Confederate activity around Knoxville was anything but aggressive. Instead of a direct attack, the Confederates lay siege to the city.[13]

There was some minor skirmishing as the days wore on, but the next real combat took place on November 29, just west of the city, at a place known as Fort Sanders. Knoxville lies on the northern bank of the Holston River, and Fort Sanders seemed to be somewhat isolated. The Confederates believed that it might be possible to gain access to Knoxville by an attack in this area.

Around 6:00 A.M.,[14] the Confederates bombarded the fort with artillery. The graycoats then rushed the walls. The ditches around the fort were steep and difficult to climb. The rebels did not have any scaling ladders, and were subjected to a terrible fire from the garrison inside. Some of the Southerners were able to reach the parapet, but they were all either killed or captured.[15]

Shortly thereafter, the order to suspend the attack was given. There was some delay in this order reaching one brigade, and one more futile attack was given, but it too, was easily repulsed.

On the 29th of November General Longstreet received confirmation of the Confederate defeat in the battles for Chattanooga. There might soon be Yankees ready to attack him from behind. Longstreet had no choice but to withdraw from Knoxville. The rebels waited a few days, hoping to still put some pressure on General Burnside. However, by December 4, the siege was lifted.

From Knoxville, the Confederates headed northeast, in the direction of Rogersville. The march took five days, and the graycoats were finally able to rest for a few days to gather food and supplies. On December 13, Longstreet led his men back to Bean's Station, located on the banks of the Holston River. The Confederates attempted to surround the enemy, but their organization was poor, and some 4,000 Federals were able to fall back, momentarily out of danger. A stubborn duel lasted all day on the 14th, as the Federals were determined to avoid capture. When darkness covered the field, Bean's Station had ended the Campaign of Knoxville. Casualties were not more than 200 men on either side.[16]

The Confederate operations around Knoxville had been a dismal failure. The Union forces lost 92 men killed, 394 wounded, and 207 captured or wounded, for a total of 693. The Confederate casualties were 182 soldiers killed, 768 wounded, and 192 captured or missing, for a total of 1,142.[17] The winter of 1863 would curtail active operations, but the spring would see General Longstreet back in Virginia, under the command of Robert E. Lee.

November 7, 1863

RAPPAHANNOCK STATION

R. E. Lee (CSA)	G. G. Meade (USA)

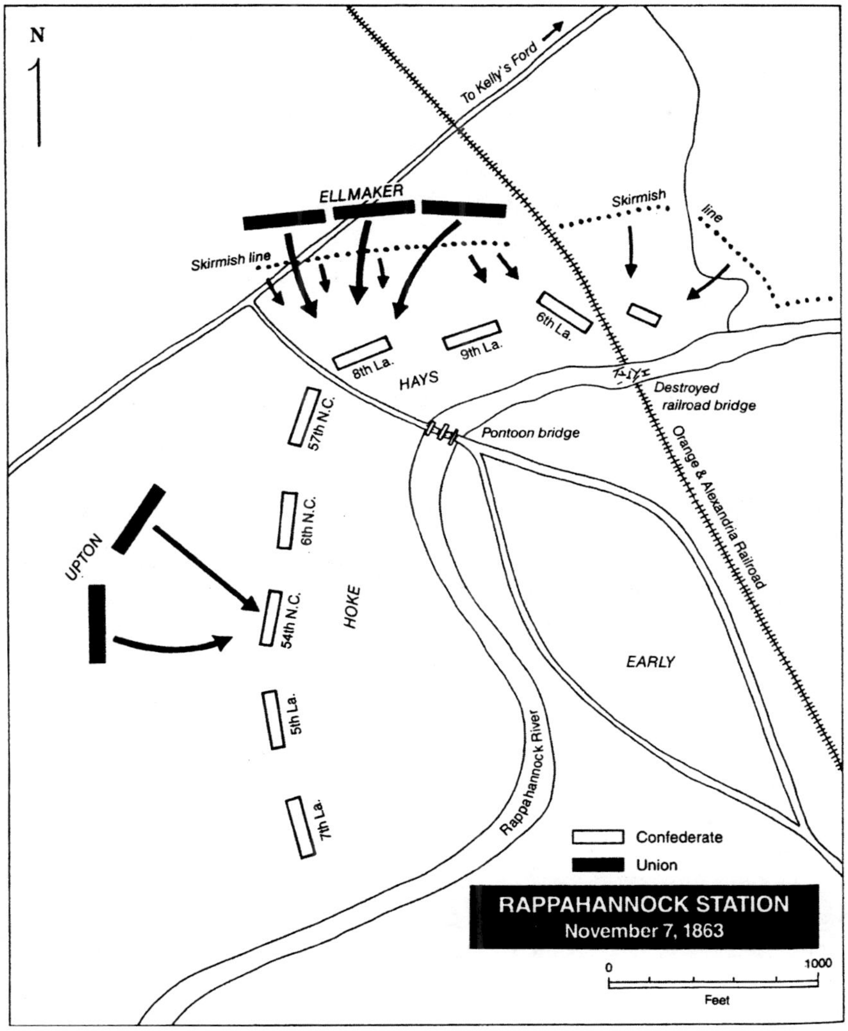

Rappahannock Station, November 7, 1863.

The engagement at Rappahannock Station, Virginia was shaped by Union General George G. Meade's desire to recapture lost territory between the Rappahannock and Rapidan Rivers.[1] The Confede-rates had fallen back to this area following the defeat at Bristoe Station on October 14. General Robert E. Lee had taken up a position along the line of the Rappahannock River and planned to fortify the major river crossings. The Confederates would hold the ground at Rappahannock Bridge and attack the bluecoats at Kelly's Ford, four miles downstream.[2]

The north side of the river was dominated by high ground. It was vital to the Confederates to hold the bridgehead at Kelly's Ford to prevent a surprise attack. As long as the graycoats held the bridge, it would be difficult for the enemy to cross the water.[3] Protection of the bridgehead and the immediate area would fall to General Jubal A. Early, a division commander under Richard S. Ewell.

On the south, or Confederate side of the river, Lee's troops stretched out along the water, with Ewell's command to the east, A. P. Hill's men to the west, and Robert E. Rodes in the area around Kelly's Ford. The Confederates had spanned the water with a long pontoon bridge. This would facilitate movement of the rebels from one side of the river to the other.

On November 7, General Meade divided his forces. The Federal left was commanded by William H. French. General French and his troops crossed at Kelly's Ford, while the Union right, under John Sedgwick, advanced on Rappahannock Bridge.[4] The Yankees began to advance toward Kelly's Ford, and soon had pushed their way across to the Southern side. Upstream, toward Rappahannock Bridge, a strong force of bluecoats were moving against the Confederates on the north side of the river.[5]

Jubal Early could see the flashes of musketry across the water, but was unable to determine the extent of the action. As darkness began to creep across the battlefield, both Early and Lee perceived a slackening of the enemy's fire. The two Confederate generals believed that the fighting had stopped for the time being, as night attacks in the Civil War were very uncommon.[6]

Unfortunately for the Confederates, General French would have a surprise in store. The Yankees had crossed the Rappahannock River at Kelly's Ford and captured the majority of two Confederate brigades.[7]

The affair was truly a disaster for the Confederacy.

Early had lost 1,674 men, and Rodes suffered an additional 349 casualties.[8] Union losses on November 7 were only 370 soldiers.[9]

However, the credit belongs to the Northern generals. John Sedgwick had taken the right flank of Meade's army and occupied the front line of rifle pits without firing a shot. William French had simply overpowered light resistance in his assault at Kelly's Ford.[10]

The result of the fine Union effort was that General Lee found his position untenable. The Union troops were already on the south side of the Rappahannock, and Lee fell back to a new line. Recrossing the Rapidan River, the Confederates knew they would have to regroup.

November 23–25, 1863
CHATTANOOGA

B. Bragg (CSA) U. S. Grant (USA)

The battle of Chattanooga must actually be viewed as three separate and distinct battles: Orchard Knob on November 23, followed by the action on Lookout Mountain on November 24, and culminating in the battle along Missionary Ridge on November 25. When put together, they resulted in the Union capture of Chattanooga, and the Confederate retreat from a seemingly impregnable position.

Occupation of Chattanooga was extremely important for both sides. It was the key to controlling east Tennessee. With several railway connections and water transportation on the Tennessee River, the city was a very attractive base of operations.

With the Confederate victory two months earlier at Chickamauga,[1] the stage was set for the coming engagements. Retreating Federals had streamed into the city. Most Confederate general officers felt that a vigorous pursuit was in order.[2] However, Braxton Bragg did not agree. He believed that a siege of Chattanooga would force the Union forces to capitulate.[3] General Bragg's opinion was supported by President Jefferson Davis,[4] and, obviously, their view prevailed. The siege would prove to be a mistake with grave consequences.

Braxton Bragg and Jefferson Davis were soon to make a second mistake, almost as severe as the long, fruitless siege of Chattanooga. General James Longstreet had been a most outspoken critic of Bragg after Chickamauga. Favoring an aggressive pursuit of the foe, he was adamantly against the siege. General Bragg wanted to rid himself of dissenting opinions, so on November 4, two divisions under Longstreet were sent north with the purpose of invading Knoxville.[4a] The absence of these Confederates would be critical in the days to come.

Much had happened to the Union forces since their defeat at Chickamauga. General Ulysses S. Grant had been transferred to Tennessee to take command of the troops in Chattanooga. He believed changes were in order. While the Army of the Tennessee remained under Grant's favorite lieutenant, General William T. Sherman, the Army of the Cumberland had a new commander, in the person of General George H. Thomas. Finally, the Federal troops had broken the siege and starvation had been averted.

The Confederates were in a much better position. There are several mountains in the Chattanooga area which run roughly northeast to southwest. General Bragg and his graycoats controlled all of them. Most of the Southern troops were located on Missionary Ridge and Lookout Mountain. When the Federals looked up at the enemy, they saw Confederates strongly posted among ominous rock formations. Chattanooga seemed to be a battle the rebels could not lose. But they would.

In comparison with the huge mountain ranges in this part of Tennessee, Orchard Knob is little more than a foothill.[5] It lies between Missionary Ridge, to the east, and the Union encampment in Chattanooga. Some of the advance elements of the Confederate Army of Tennessee had occupied this area.[6] General Grant wished to ascertain the strength of the enemy on Orchard Knob, so he sent forward two divisions of the IV Corps under Generals Wood and Sheridan with orders to make a reconnaissance in force. Grant instructed two divisions of the XIV Corps under Generals Baird and Johnson to act in support.[7] These troops would be able to provide the Union commander with the information he desired.

The immediate question for the Federals was this: how could they get close enough to Orchard Knob to observe the enemy without actually starting a battle? Some deception seemed to be in order. With bands playing and flags flying, the Union troops lined up as if they were on parade, ready for inspection by Generals Grant and Thomas. Suddenly, at 1:30 P.M. on November 23, the Yankees moved forward at double-quick time.[8]

The Southerners were quite perplexed, not quite sure of what was happening. Wood's men had covered 800 yards before the Confederates at Orchard Knob opened fire. By the time they were able to reload their rifles, the swarming Yankees had reached the first line of defenders.[9] Despite this initial success, there was a steep price to pay. The grayclad men on top of Missionary Ridge poured a destructive torrent of lead into the onrushing bluecoats.[10] Casualties varied among Union regiments, but they were heavy. The 41st Ohio lost nearly one fourth of its soldiers; the 93rd Ohio suffered a similar fate. But the Federals pressed on, and perseverance yielded results. Just before 3:00 P.M., Wood signaled to Thomas: "I have carried the first line of the enemy's entrenchments."[11] But how should the victors proceed?

After consultation with Grant, it was decided that the men had fought too hard to give up now. General Thomas signaled to Wood to entrench where they were and hold their ground.[12] George Thomas had good reason to be pleased. His troops in the Army of the Cumberland had acquitted themselves quite well. The first day had gone to the Yankees. The next move belonged to Bragg.

It became apparent to General Bragg that the Confederate right must be reinforced. He transferred General Pat Cleburne to the far right, then assigned the overall command of that sector to his most reliable subordinate, William Hardee. In addition, Bragg shifted some troops from the Confederate left, on Lookout Mountain, over to General Hardee. The center of Missionary Ridge was entrusted to General John Breckinridge. However, the Confederate left had been depleted. Lookout Mountain, under General Carter Stevenson, had only a skeleton force of two divisions.[13] Obviously, it would have been better had Longstreet not been sent to Knoxville.

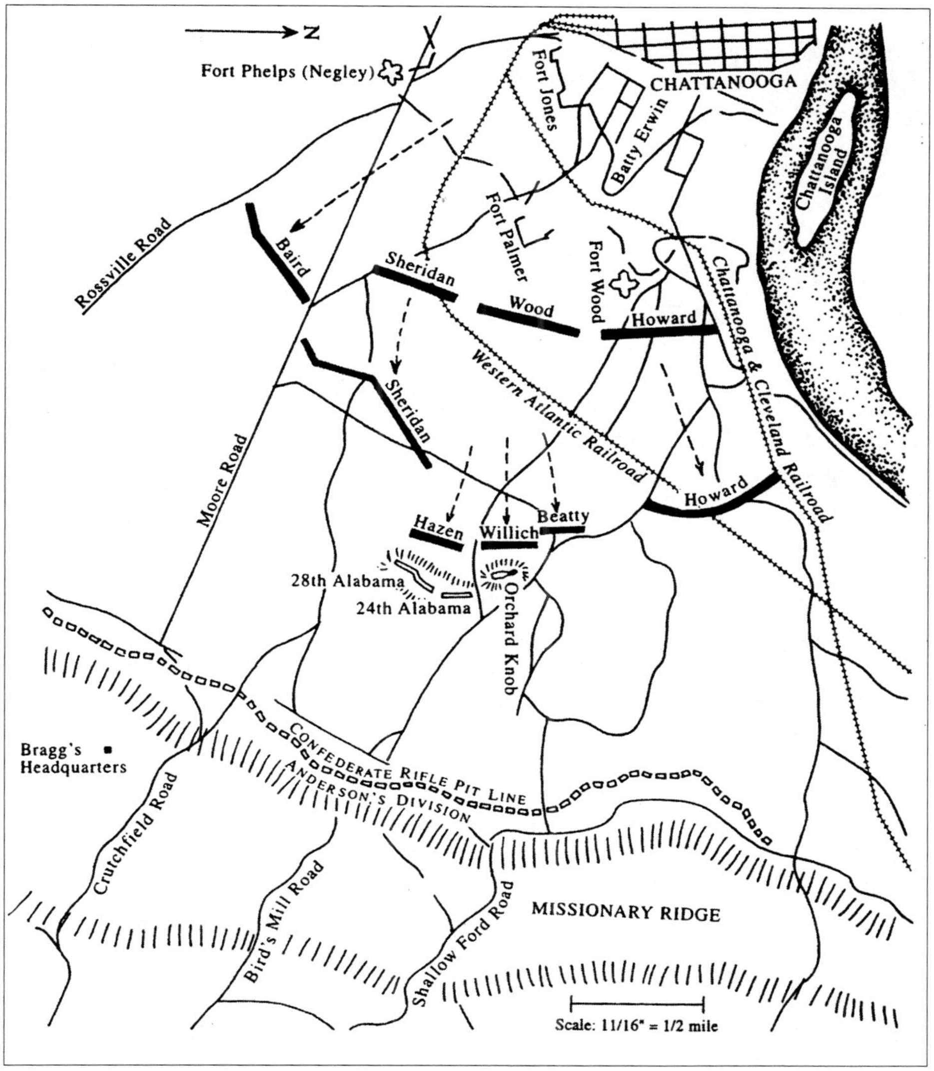

Assault on Orchard Knob, November 23, 1863.

General Bragg now turned his attention to the center of Missionary Ridge. Here he made yet another mistake. Unable to decide whether to defend the crest or the base of the mountain, he settled on a compromise. The troops under Breckinridge would be divided, half on top of Missionary Ridge, the remainder in the rifle pits down below. In splitting his forces in this manner, Bragg weakened each one.[14]

The absence of Longstreet's divisions, combined with curious troop dispositions, had weakened both the left and the center of the Confederate lines. Despite great advantages in both position and terrain, the rebels were throwing them away.

Grant had stationed General Joseph "Fighting Joe" Hooker in Lookout Valley. Lookout Mountain loomed large above him,[14a] but he had three divisions under his command, and knew the mountain was thinly held. Grant felt that a demonstration on the Union right would aid an attack by Sherman against Missionary Ridge, but General Thomas had higher goals. He felt that Lookout Mountain could actually be captured. After much persuasion, Grant finally relented.[15] Hooker would launch his attack on November 24.

Grant, however, still felt that General Sherman was the key to Union success. He would move against the Confederate right on Missionary Ridge. With Sherman on his left, Thomas in the center, and Hooker on his right, Ulysses S. Grant was confident of success.

As dawn broke on November 24, a dense fog settled in over Lookout Valley.[16] Neither side was able to see the other. Hooker's men cautiously advanced, as sharp rocks, heavy boulders and a dense forest impeded their progress.[17] Slowly, the bluecoats moved forward along the narrow footpaths. Finally, about 10:30 A.M., the Yankees came in contact with the first line of grayclad pickets at the base of the mountain. The muskets began to pop, and the fire grew stronger.[18] The fight for Lookout Mountain was about to begin.

The Confederate picket lines had the same problem which plagued General Stevenson's entire command. There were simply not enough men to contest the Union advance — at least six feet separated each of the Mississippians[19] — and Hooker's troops soon overpowered the rebels. Hopelessly outnumbered, some of the Confederates were able to scramble back up the mountain; many more surrendered.[20]

The bluecoats continued upward. At about 11:30 A.M., their climb came to a halt about 300 yards from the summit of Lookout Mountain. The Yankees had come up against another line of defense. Every rock and tree seemed to have a musket behind it, spitting fire into the Union ranks. Hooker's boys began to fall, and the New Yorkers leaped for cover behind anything they could find. Further progress would have to wait.[21]

Fortunately for General Hooker, it would not wait long. Enjoying a four to one numerical advantage, the blue tide seemed to sweep forward, almost without orders, carrying the second line of defense away.[22] The Federals moved across Lookout Creek and paused at the Cravens House, midway up the mountain. The action was no longer visible to the Union troops in Chattanooga. Both sides had simply vanished into the mist.[23]

By 2:00 P.M., the fog had grown even thicker. While the heavy vapor shielded the Yankees from Confederate cannon, it also allowed the Mississippians to fall back and reform their lines. In addition, the poor visibility retarded the Federal advance.[24]

The fighting had reached a stalemate. For the rest of the afternoon and into the evening each side fired at the other, unable to actually see the enemy. Both sides were running out of ammunition,[25] but Hooker's forces were clearly in command. With the Yankees only partially up the mountain, General Stevenson decided to evacuate the summit.[26] As night fell upon the soldiers, the Confederates slipped away under the cover of a total eclipse.[27] Lookout Mountain was lost, almost sacrificed, in what would become known as the "Battle Above the Clouds."

November 25 broke even colder than the day before,[28] but Grant and Thomas eagerly awaited the sounds of Sherman's attack on the Confederate right.[29] William T. Sherman led 16,600 men against the north end of Missionary Ridge. Pat Cleburne blocked his path, stationed at a place called Tunnel Hill. His 4,000 rebels [30] would do their duty, but the situation looked grim for the graycoats.

In the fight for Tunnel Hill, Sherman showed how ignorant he was of the terrain. He had positioned his troops too far to the north. The ground dropped off into a broken ravine, which separated the Yankees from the Texans on the crest of the hill. The Federals would now have to cross very difficult ground and then work their way up the north side of Tunnel Hill. Despite a numerical advantage, the attack was both late in starting[31] and poorly coordinated.[32] A simultaneous assault with all of the Union troops would have been devastating. Instead, Sherman's columns failed to act in concert and the result was a costly repulse.

The first attempt to take Tunnel Hill came from the north. The bluecoats under John Corse advanced on Cleburne's troops and the Southern cannon opened with a fury. Yankees dropped in their tracks as they tried to work their way through the ravine and up the hill. Finally, Sherman had seen enough. By noon the attack was over.[33] He would have to regroup and try again.

The next group of Yankees attacked from the northwest. John Loomis led his brigade out of the woods into plain view of the cannon perched on Tunnel Hill. As they advanced, Loomis opened a gap of about 400 yards between his left and Corse's right.[34] Once the Federals had passed out of the shelter of the woods, they became easy targets for the Confederates. Cleburne's men opened gaping holes in the ranks of yet another Union brigade.[35]

So far, Sherman had managed to place his troops on the wrong hill, start his attack hours behind schedule, fail to coordinate the movements of different brigades, and use only two of the nine brigades under his command. In addition, Corse and Loomis, in their disjointed attacks, had both suffered a bloody repulse. This was not exactly what General Grant had in mind for Missionary Ridge.

As the Federal troops tried to reform and regroup for the fighting which lay ahead, Pat Cleburne remained one step ahead of them. One of the best generals in Bragg's Army of Tennessee,[36] the Irishman continued to anticipate the Yankees' next move.[37] By shifting men from point to point, he was able to place a strong defensive force right at the point of attack.

The Confederates continued to pour lead into the groups of bluecoats pinned beneath Tunnel Hill. By 4:00 P.M., a Federal collapse appeared imminent.[38] With their ammunition low and casualties mounting, the Northerners were running out of options. In the hopes of reversing the tide of the battle, the soldiers were ordered to make a desperate charge for the summit of Tunnel Hill.[39] If the troops were used in concert, Sherman still had a large numerical advantage over Cleburne.

General Sherman had finally sent fresh troops to join

the assault. The exhausted Confederates at the top of Tunnel Hill could not hold out much longer. General Cleburne looked as if his defenses might crack. Fortunately for the Confederates, General Hardee had realized the plight of his lieutenant, and reinforcements were sent to the Confederate right. Hardee knew that Cleburne would use them wisely. Pat Cleburne continued to get his men to the proper place at the proper time, while the Yankees below him were still held back by their lack of cohesion.[40]

Nevertheless, the Yankees just seemed to creep closer and closer to the Confederate breastworks. A desperate measure was in order. General Alfred Cumming suggested to Cleburne that his Georgians charge down the mountain, sweeping the bluecoats away at the point of the bayonet. Cleburne knew that to sit and wait for the Federals was foolish; the sheer weight of numbers would eventually decide the battle in Sherman's favor. He approved the plan. Over the precipice they bounded, through their own breastworks and down the slope.

The bluecoats crumpled under the swarm of gray. Entire regiments seemed to melt away. The result of Cumming's aggression was that the Union infantry in his front ceased to exist as an effective fighting force.[41] The moment belonged to the Southerners.

However, neither Cumming nor Cleburne was satisfied with momentary advantage.[42] After a 15-minute pause, the rebels regrouped for one last charge. Around 5:00 P.M., they started forward. They met little resistance, as the Federals had withdrawn to safety. The fight for Tunnel Hill was over.[43] Pat Cleburne had held his ground.

General Cleburne had done his best, and had performed splendidly. Still, this was a fight that General Sherman should have won. He had enough men, but the generalship was poor. The Union army assaulted Tunnel Hill in fragmented, piecemeal frontal attacks. Sherman should have used all his troops at the same time in a well-coordinated action, and found a way to outflank the Confederates.[44]

The action at Tunnel Hill was over, but the fight for Missionary Ridge was not. Once again, Joe Hooker and his men would be busy. Fresh from the victory on Lookout Mountain the day before, he was ordered down the mountain to assail the left flank of Missionary Ridge. General Thomas was adamant that both flanks of Missionary Ridge must be attacked before he could send his Army of the Cumberland at the center.[45]

At 10:00 A.M. November 25, Thomas ordered Hooker to "move forward firmly and steadily upon the enemy's works in front of Missionary Ridge.[46] Hooker tried to comply, but unfortunately his troops had found a formidable barrier in Chattanooga Creek: the Confederates had burned the main bridge. The Federals would have to build a new one, but this would take time. The Union column ground to a halt.[47]

From the field headquarters on Orchard Knob, General Grant was becoming anxious. On his left, Sherman's assault on Missionary Ridge had been a dismal failure. On his right, Hooker's troops had stalled in front of Chattanooga Creek. Despite Union victories on the first two days of the fighting, the Confederates still held the high ground in their front. The flanks of the enemy had hardly been softened.

Although the Confederate position seemed a strong one, a closer examination of Bragg's defenses revealed the weakness of the center. Both Bragg and Breckinridge, while they recognized that Grant would assail their flanks, believed that he would attack *only* the flanks. The attacks by Hooker at Lookout Mountain and Sherman at Tunnel Hill seemed to confirm this assumption.[48] As a result, they had neglected the center.

Neither general ordered that the top of the ridge should be fortified until the last possible moment. They both believed that the rifle pits along the base of Missionary Ridge would be sufficient. In addition, fall-back positions should have been laid out in case of a defeat, and Breckinridge had made no provision to withdraw the men stationed in the rifle pits.[49]

Obviously, none of the brigadier generals on Missionary Ridge cared for the dispositions. The troops in the center did not have enough axes, shovels, and picks to create adequate breastworks in such a short time.[50] The location of the entrenchments was also faulty. Placed too far behind the crest of ridge, the Confederates could not command the slope in front of them.[51] On the other hand, the problem for the artillery was just the opposite: the guns were too close to the edge of the cliff. As a result, the cannon could not be depressed adequately upon the invading enemy. To make matters worse, they were too widely dispersed, thus negating the potential for massed artillery.[52]

Finally, Bragg and Breckinridge had left no reserves in the center to be used wherever they might be needed.[53] All in all, a very strong position had been transformed into a very vulnerable one.

At 10:30 A.M.,[54] George Thomas ordered his skirmishers forward. The intent was to move out of the wooded area around Orchard Knob and, if possible, capture the rifle pits at the base of the ridge. The sheer number of Union troops created quite a spectacle. The Confederates on top of Missionary Ridge could see every movement, and the view was breathtaking. Unfortunately for the graycoats, good vision led to fear and exaggeration of the situation down below.[55]

As the Army of the Cumberland moved forward, the rebels opened fire. The muskets cracked in rapid

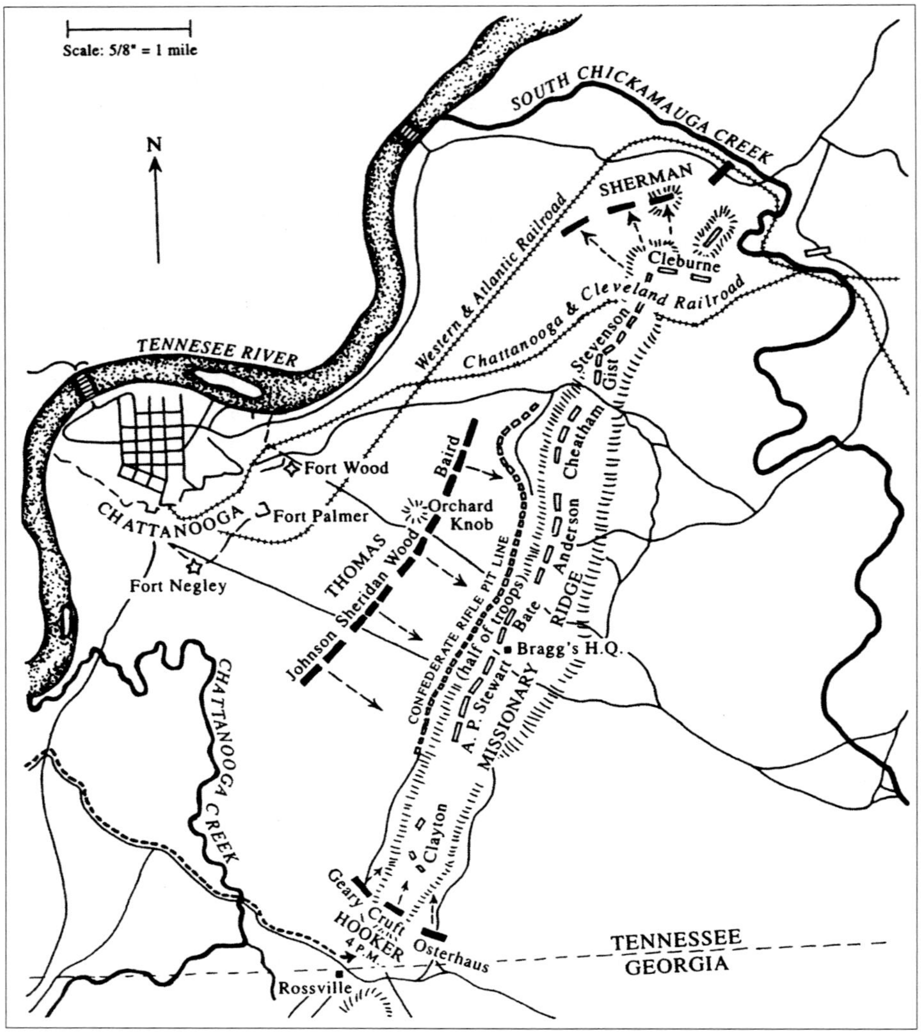

Situation at 4:00 P.M., November 25, 1863, Thomas's assault.

succession, the cannon boomed, and the shells burst all around the advancing bluecoats. However, the artillery range was very poor, and while the noise was deafening, the damage was slight.[56]

The Yankees moved as quickly as possible toward the base of Missionary Ridge. At this point in the assault, Bragg's feeble preparations were revealed. Some of the Confederates held their ground while others tried to scramble back up the mountain, their backs to the onrushing enemy. There was no coordination among Southern infantry units whatsoever.[57]

The rifle pits were easily captured, but the victory proved dangerous indeed. The Federals overpowered the defenders so quickly that they became a tangled mass of blue. Confederates on the crest of Missionary Ridge fired quickly from left and right. The Yankees were caught in a crossfire, and their only thought was to escape.[58] By 4:10 P.M., the organization in front of Missionary Ridge had broken down. Each unit was now fighting on its own.[59]

Back on Orchard Knob, General Grant could hardly believe his eyes. Without any orders,[60] the men had started to make their way up the ridge. Only the first line of rifle pits was to have been captured, and Grant never intended to have his men continue on up the slope. With the men of General Thomas Wood in the lead, halfway up the mountain, other Federal units followed suit. There was no organization whatsoever, but the Union soldiers pressed on, determined to reach the summit.[61]

Wood's plight appeared more dangerous than it was. There were still many Confederates scrambling back up the side of Missionary Ridge. These men obscured the vision of their compatriots on the crest. Unable to get a clear shot at the advancing Federals, many graycoats had to hold their fire. In addition, smoke from the battle settled above the bluecoats, making them almost invisible. Finally, the Southerners' aim was very poor. The Confederates were reluctant to hit their own men, as well as to expose their heads above the trenches on top of the ridge. Combined with the smoke, this sent many bullets harmlessly over the heads of the Yankees.[62] Watching the assault from the top of the mountain, General Patton Anderson gave this assessment of the situation: "Owing to the conformation of the ridge, from which several spurs projected along my front, affording cover to the attacking forces, and protecting them from any but a direct fire and in some places even from that—he was enabled to advance to within a short distance of the crest with comparative impunity."[63] The Floridian's view of the action was all too accurate.

General Wood was concerned that the Confederates in his front would mount a counterattack similar to the one Cleburne had used against Sherman. His troops had expended so much energy in scaling Missionary Ridge that a sudden charge could have been devastating.[64] Fortunately for the Army of the Cumberland, Braxton Bragg had neither the enterprise nor the skill of Pat Cleburne.

The Federals continued their ascent until they

reached a point just below the embankment. Still obscured by the irregular terrain, the Yankees were only a few feet from the Confederates. Here the graycoats paused, and tried to regain their strength. Suddenly, the bluecoats stormed the parapet, and they were upon the rebels before a shot could be fired.[65] Panic ensued among the Mississippians. Many surrendered on the spot, while others turned and fled. Bragg and Breckinridge had left the center so poorly defended that the few who remained were bayoneted where they stood.[66]

Everything that would hinder retreat was thrown away. Officers could do nothing to stop the panic in the ranks. Entire brigades seemed to melt away under the onslaught.[67] Once the Federals had gained the summit, it was simply a matter of numbers. There were not enough gray-clad rebels to withstand the Union divisions scaling the mountain. The Confederacy needed those men under Longstreet on Missionary Ridge, just as they had needed them on Lookout Mountain.

The rout of the troops from Mississippi had placed all of Missionary Ridge in jeopardy. Located in the center of the line, their retreat imperiled the commands on either side. One by one, they began to collapse. Some divisions fell back better than others, but the Confederate position on Missionary Ridge was lost.

The Confederates continued to pull back in an easterly direction toward Ringgold Gap. Cleburne's troops guarded the retreat. By 9:00 P.M., almost all of his command had withdrawn across Chickamauga Creek.[68] Despite being heavily outnumbered, his men had stood firm against Sherman's attacks. The rest of the graycoats had not done so well.

Although some of the defenders of Missionary Ridge had no patience for those who broke and ran, others were more tolerant. Nearly all felt betrayed by their superiors.[69] It was generally felt that Bragg and Breckinridge were to blame for the fiasco on November 25.

Estimates of casualties vary for the three days of fighting for Chattanooga. The Federals lost 684 men killed, 4,329 wounded and only 322 captured, for a total of 5,335. The Confederates suffered 361 killed, 2,180 wounded and a staggering 4,146 captured (although General Grant stated that 6,142 men were captured) for a total of 6,687.[70]

There was no doubt that both the performance and the judgment of Braxton Bragg were not up to those of his subordinates. Bragg and Breckinridge had placed individual divisions in a very difficult position. The defense of Missionary Ridge was severely compromised by the decision to divide Breckinridge's troops between the base and the crest of the ridge. The placement of the entrenchments, as well as the dispositions of both infantry and artillery, were simply deplorable. The lack of preparation, when the Confederacy had occupied the surroundings of Chattanooga for months, was inexcusable.

Bragg's decision to place personal considerations over military logic cost him dearly. In sending James Longstreet to Knoxville with two divisions, the defense of Lookout Mountain and Missionary Ridge was weakened. Those troops could have strengthened the Confederate lines at either mountain. The graycoats had an excellent defensive position along both ranges, and neither should have been lost. Poor leadership cost them both.

November 27, 1863
Ringgold Gap

P. R. Cleburne (CSA) — J. E. Hooker (USA)

The Confederate Army of Tennessee was in full retreat. On November 25, the graycoats had suffered perhaps the most humiliating defeat of the entire Civil War.[1] Despite the possession of a seemingly impregnable position on Missionary Ridge, Federal soldiers had scaled the heights and overwhelmed the Southerners. Braxton Bragg, in command of the rebels, gave orders to fall back to the southeast, in the direction of Dalton, Georgia.

During the early morning of November 27, most of the battered Confederates were still trying to escape the enemy. However, one final attempt would be made to halt the Union pursuit. It would occur at Ringgold Gap.

The defense was entrusted to Patrick R. Cleburne, the finest general in the Army of Tennessee.[2] Two days earlier the Irishman had been ordered to save the north end of Missionary Ridge from destruction at the hands of General William T. Sherman. Heavily outnumbered, the graycoats held their ground. He was now called upon to save the Confederate army a second time. Once more, Cleburne's men would stand tall.

Just east of the small village of Ringgold, Ringgold Gap was a rather narrow passage, only about half a mile in length.[3] About 20 miles southeast of Chattanooga,[3a] the gap was dominated by large rock formations. Ridges appeared in the darkness, running in a generally north-south direction. The troops faced west, preparing for the Union attack. On the Confederate right was White Oak Mountain. Taylor's Ridge protected the left flank. Between the outcroppings of rock, a branch of East Chickamauga Creek meandered its way along the tracks of the Western & Atlantic Railroad.[4]

Pat Cleburne's division counted only 4,157 muskets.[5]

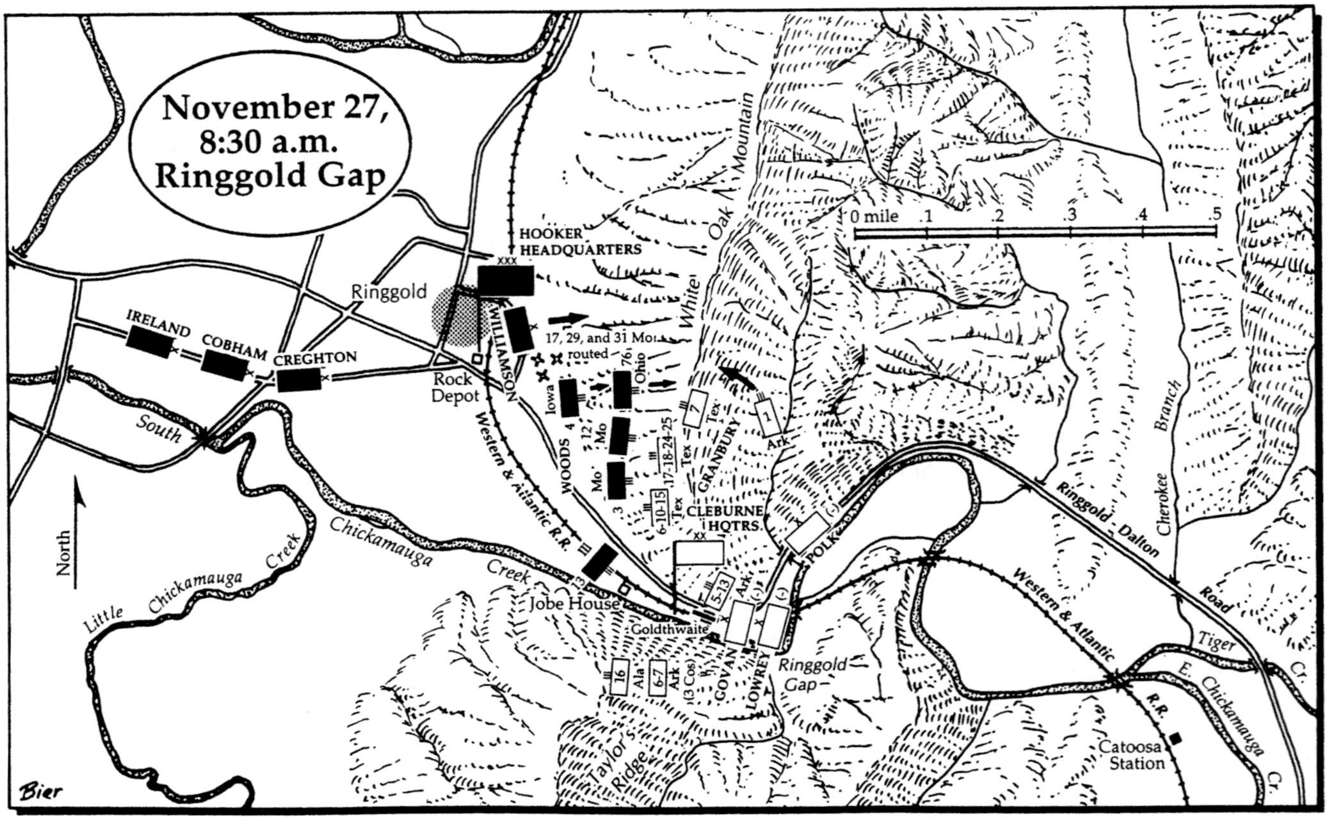

November 27, 8:30 A.M., Ringgold Gap. Map by Jim Bier.

At dawn his troops would receive an attack from General Joseph E. "Fighting Joe" Hooker. The Federals had 8,868 men, eager to destroy another Confederate division.[6]

Great care was exercised in the deployment of the Confederate soldiers. The Texans of Hiram Granbury's brigade held White Oak Mountain. Cleburne then divided the soldiers of Mark Lowrey's brigade. The 16th Alabama Regiment guarded Taylor's Ridge, with some assistance from three companies of Arkansas troops. These rebels were instructed to keep out of sight until the Federals approached. The remainder of Lowrey's command, along with Daniel Govan's Arkansans, occupied the center of Ringgold Gap.[7]

Four short lines of defense were formed. In addition, Lucious Polk's brigade was placed at the eastern mouth of the gap, and stood ready to provide reinforcements to Granbury's troops in case of an emergency.[8]

General Cleburne well understood that he would be outnumbered. He used some deception to turn the odds in his favor. Two hundred troopers[9] of the 9th Kentucky Cavalry were sent out to warn the Confederates of any Union advance. The Kentuckians would fire their guns one time, then turn and gallop away, giving General Hooker the impression that Ringgold Gap was held by only a small force of cavalry.[10]

Shortly after 8:00 A.M.,[11] Pat Cleburne observed the Yankees approaching. The Confederates were concealed behind trees and rocks, and Cleburne's artillery was covered with branches. Hooker marched straight ahead. He was headed for a trap.

The enemy came into view, and the Texans opened fire. Hooker's Missourians recoiled, but soon regrouped, led by Colonel James A. Williamson. As the Federals began to scale the height of White Oak Mountain, Confederate major, W. A. Taylor, extended Granbury's right flank. Suddenly, Taylor counterattacked. The unsuspecting bluecoats broke in disorder. The Northerners fled back across the open fields, seeking the protection of the town of Ringgold.[12]

While the Missourians attacked the mountain, the 13th Illinois Regiment continued heading straight to the gap. The Federals were marching toward an innocent looking clump of trees. When the Yankees were only 50 yards away, the trees exploded with Confederate artillery. Grapeshot and canister tore through the ranks of the Midwesterners.[13]

At the same time, the Arkansans in the gap opened fire. The 13th Illinois was pinned down by the fury of Confederate muskets and artillery.[14]

While the Federals in the center were being cut

to pieces, Granbury had stopped the advance of the Missouri troops on the Union left. There must be a way for Hooker to relieve the Yankees on White Oak Mountain.

The 76th Ohio Regiment was ordered forward. They made their way around Taylor's right flank, and General Cleburne quickly shifted more men to meet the threat. Lucious Polk and Mark Lowrey moved their brigades to the Confederate right.[15]

The Southerners arrived just in time. Several Iowa regiments advanced to assist the Ohioans, and a desperate, short-range struggle ensued. As the morning wore on, General Hooker continued to send fresh troops against the Confederate right, in an attempt to outflank his Irish adversary.[16]

Polk and Lowrey were equal to the task. Hidden behind sharp outcroppings of jagged rock, the Southerners poured a destructive fire into the ranks of the oncoming Yankees. The last Union effort against the Confederate right ended in a thorough repulse.[17]

Shortly before 10:00 A.M., the Federals made their first assault on the Confederate left.[18] Colonel George Cobham's three Pennsylvania regiments rushed forward. The bluecoats made it past the 13th Illinois to an embankment near the railroad, but Confederate artillery and Daniel Govan's infantry brought the Yankees to a sudden halt.[19]

Again, Hooker sent reinforcements forward. At 10:40, Colonel David Ireland's New York brigade went to Cobham's aid. As the New Yorkers marched to the sound of the gunfire, the shattered remnants of the 13th Illinois fell back.[20]

Ireland's brigade was momentarily stopped under a furious counterattack by part of the 16th Alabama. However, the Northerners reformed, and sent a shower of bullets into the 16th, driving the rebels back. The situation on the Confederate left had reached a stalemate. Additional Federal troops were forming in Ringgold, and Hooker's artillery was moving into position for a long-range bombardment. Pat Cleburne realized that conditions were shifting in favor of the enemy.[21]

General Cleburne had given "Fighting Joe" credit for a sense of aggression which the Union general no longer possessed.[22] Hooker had no intention of ordering more men into combat.

At noon,[23] Cleburne received a dispatch from Confederate General Joseph Hardee. The Army of Tennessee was safe. The graycoats could now withdraw from Ringgold Gap. Shortly after 2:00 P.M.,[24] the rebels began to pull back and join the rest of the army. The field belonged to the Union, but the Army of Tennessee had been saved.

At a cost of only 20 men killed, 190 wounded, and 11 missing, the Confederates had inflicted 507 total casualties on Joe Hooker's troops.[25]

The battle of Ringgold Gap was not one of the larger struggles of the Civil War, but it served as yet another illustration of Pat Cleburne's skill as a general. For over four hours[26] he had held back a more numerous foe, allowing the remainder of the Army of Tennessee to save their men, animals, supplies and equipment.

1864

April 12, 1864

Fort Pillow

N. B. Forrest (CSA) — L. F. Booth (USA)

Nathan Bedford Forrest was perhaps the greatest cavalry commander the Civil War produced.[1] He fought in the Western Theatre of Operations, his campaigns mostly in Tennessee, Alabama and Mississippi. Although his victories were numerous, Fort Pillow survives to this day as his darkest and most controversial hour.

Fort Pillow was originally constructed by the Confederates in 1861, and lies on the Mississippi River about 40 miles north of Memphis.[2] As the original work was much too large for any group to defend, the Confederates built a smaller fort within the outer walls.[2a] In the early summer of 1862, Fort Pillow came under possession of the Union forces as the rebels retreated following the siege of Corinth. The Yankees then built a third, smaller enclosure, lower than the original construction.[3]

There were not many troops stationed at the fort, and in order to reinforce the post, four companies of heavy artillery, a section of light artillery, and some colored troops were sent from Memphis. Commanded by Major Lionel F. Booth, the garrison now contained 557 officers and men, of whom 295 were white and 262 colored.[4]

At about 5:30 A.M. on April 12, a force of 1,500 graycoats attacked the fort, and were quickly inside the original, outer walls. From the heights of the walls which had been built in 1861, they fired down into the inner defenses of the Federals. About 9:00 A.M., Major Booth was killed, and his adjutant fell shortly thereafter.[5]

At 3:30 P.M. Forrest's men sent in a flag of truce to Major Booth, not realizing that he had been dead for over six hours.[6] The Yankees needed to play for time, and carried on a conversation in the name of the major, as the troop-laden steamers *Liberty* and *Olive Branch* neared the fort. Believing that the Union troops were awaiting reinforcements, Forrest ordered 200 men down to the steamboat landing and another 200 down to the Coal Creek Ravine, in order to prevent a landing of the steamboats at either point.[7]

This movement caused great controversy, as it was later claimed in the North that Forrest had used the flag of truce to move troops into position to storm the fort. In actuality, the Confederate commander had moved 400 men out of any possible attack force.[8]

As the Federals continued to stall for time, Forrest delivered an ultimatum, still intended for Major Booth "Will he fight or surrender?" The answer came back "I will not surrender." At this point, General Forrest ordered his men to charge.[9] The Confederates swarmed over the parapet, firing a volley at point blank range into the bluecoats. The Yankees attempted to fire at the attackers, but the disparity in numbers was too great. Before the defenders could reload their weapons, the second wave of rebels jumped over the inner walls of Fort Pillow.[10]

The remainder of the Union troops, both white and colored, broke and ran, seeking to escape through the little enclosure of the fort to the brow of the bluff above the river. They leaped over, only to meet a cruel fate.[11] Upon reaching the banks of the Mississippi, the Federals were caught between the two Confederate forces Forrest had detached to prevent the steamboats from landing. Taking a volley from one group of rebels, then the other, the slaughter of these Union men was horrendous.[12]

There is little doubt that some of the Federal troops were killed after they had individually tried to surrender. However, this raises another point of controversy. Fort Pillow itself was never surrendered. Some of the men who surrendered, escaped and rejoined the fight, killing Confederate soldiers.[13] This only served to inflame the passions of the rebels below the bluffs.

Finally, as the Union flag fell inside the fort, General Forrest ordered a cease-fire. The remainder of April 12 was devoted to gathering up the wounded and burying the dead. Shortly after dark, Forrest left Fort Pillow, on his way to Jackson, Tennessee. It was alleged by Federal soldiers that the killing continued into the night. If this did occur, it may have been the work of stragglers or prowlers. It was not done by any organized Confederate forces.[14]

While it is very difficult to arrive at an accurate total of Union casualties, due to men drowning in the Mississippi River, it appears that of the 557 men stationed at the fort, there were at least 336 survivors.[15] Approximately sixty percent of the garrison was either killed or wounded.[16] The Confederates lost 14 men killed and 86 wounded.[17]

The U.S. Congress Committee on the Conduct of the War examined the events. There were various accounts of what had really happened on April 12, 1864. Many of the allegations were correct; many others simply had no basis in fact. Nevertheless, the name of Nathan Bedford Forrest will be forever associated with the fall of Fort Pillow.

May 1–September 2, 1864

The Atlanta Campaign

J. E. Johnston, J. B. Hood (CSA) — W. T. Sherman (USA)

During the summer of 1863, the Union forces looked unstoppable. On July 3, George G. Meade had turned back Lee's thrust into Pennsylvania with a victory at Gettysburg, albeit at a cost of higher casualties than the Confederates. The very next day, the Confederacy was sliced in two, as U. S. Grant's forces received the surrender of Vicksburg, giving the Federal forces control over the Mississippi River. In November, Chattanooga was liberated from a siege, and placed firmly in Union hands.

However, by the middle of 1864 the Federal juggernaut had ground to a halt. The war raged on. Although Robert E. Lee's Army of Northern Virginia had been turned back from Pennsylvania, it was still a very powerful force. General Grant had been transferred to Virginia, with the hope of ending the war once and for all. Instead, Lee had blocked his every move as Grant tried in vain to capture Richmond.

Worse yet, the political situation was darkening for Abraham Lincoln and the Republican Party. There was growing sentiment across the North for putting a stop to the war, as Grant's continued assaults created staggering casualties, too large for the politicians to conceal. This had given rise to the political fortunes of Democrat George B. McClellan, the former Union general, who was running in the election of 1864 on a promise of peace.

With the situation in Virginia a virtual stalemate, President Lincoln needed a victory in the field to ensure the reelection of the Republican Party, and he needed it soon. His attention turned to Georgia.

Atlanta was not only the rail center of the South, with its sprawling network of tentacles capable of sending troops, supplies and equipment to all parts of the Confederacy, it was also the key to the food supply of the Army of Northern Virginia. The capture of Atlanta would most certainly lift the spirits of the Northern people, and send President Lincoln back to Washington to continue his quest to win the war.

The fall of Atlanta was not caused by one single battle. Rather, it was a series of events. Taken together, they tell the story of a Confederate retreat from the border of Tennessee to the outskirts of Atlanta. Eventually, General Sherman would simply march around the city, forcing the southern forces to evacuate. Once Atlanta was occupied, it was an easy journey to the sea.

As the campaign began, the Union forces were headquartered at Chattanooga, Tennessee. Commanded by General William T. Sherman, the 98,000 Federals[1] were divided into three armies: the Army of the Cumberland, under General George H. Thomas, the Army of the Tennessee, led by General James B. McPherson, and the smaller Army of the Ohio, under General John M. Schofield.[2]

General Thomas was in charge of a force so large, that it alone was larger than the entire body of Confederate troops arrayed against Sherman's men. The Army of the Ohio, on the other hand, was actually made up of little more than the XXIII corps itself.[3]

The Confederates were stationed just south of the Tennessee border, in the small town of Dalton, Georgia, about 25 miles south of Chattanooga. Led by the popular General Joseph E. Johnston, the Southern forces were composed of two corps: one under the leadership of John B. Hood, the other under William J. Hardee. A third infantry corps, commanded by Leonidas Polk, was en route from Mississippi, while the cavalry was under the direction of Joseph Wheeler.[4] The total number of Confederates (including Polk's corps) in Dalton was slightly over 60,000 men.[5]

The topography in the Dalton area was dominated by ridges which ran roughly northeast to southwest, and made it very difficult for an army to maneuver.[6] As Sherman moved his giant-sized army southward, it could not go undetected. Joe Johnston was aware of the Union movement, but he was uncertain of the target.[7] At this point the Federals were west and north of Dalton, and marching south. Sherman could simply march around the Southerners on the road to Atlanta. The Confederates must continue to block the enemy's advance.

It appeared as if the bluecoats were headed either to Resaca or Calhoun, six miles further south. After minor skirmishing in the Dalton area, orders were issued to generals Hardee, Hood and Wheeler. The infantry would march south to Resaca, one division was sent to Calhoun, and the cavalry would guard the crossings of the Oostenaula River.[8] On May 13, the Union army entered Dalton. There was little evidence remaining of the fighting which had taken place one day earlier. The graycoats had disappeared.[9]

Approximately 90 miles[10] from Atlanta by rail, Resaca lies just north of the Oostenaula, one of three rivers the Yankees would have to cross before they reached Atlanta. Next would come the Etowah, followed by the Chattahoochee. If used properly by the Confederates, the water could become an imposing obstacle to an army as large as Sherman's.

General Sherman made several mistaken assumptions as the Union army marched south. First, he decided that Johnston would retreat south of the Oostenaula River. Second, he believed that most of the Confederates were still en route to Resaca, and therefore the Federals would be able to get behind the rebels, intercepting the Southerners before they reached Resaca. Finally, Sherman did not realize how difficult the terrain was, and this slowed the progress of the Union troops considerably.[11]

In reality, Joe Johnston intended to make a stand at Resaca. He had no desire to be attacked while he was in

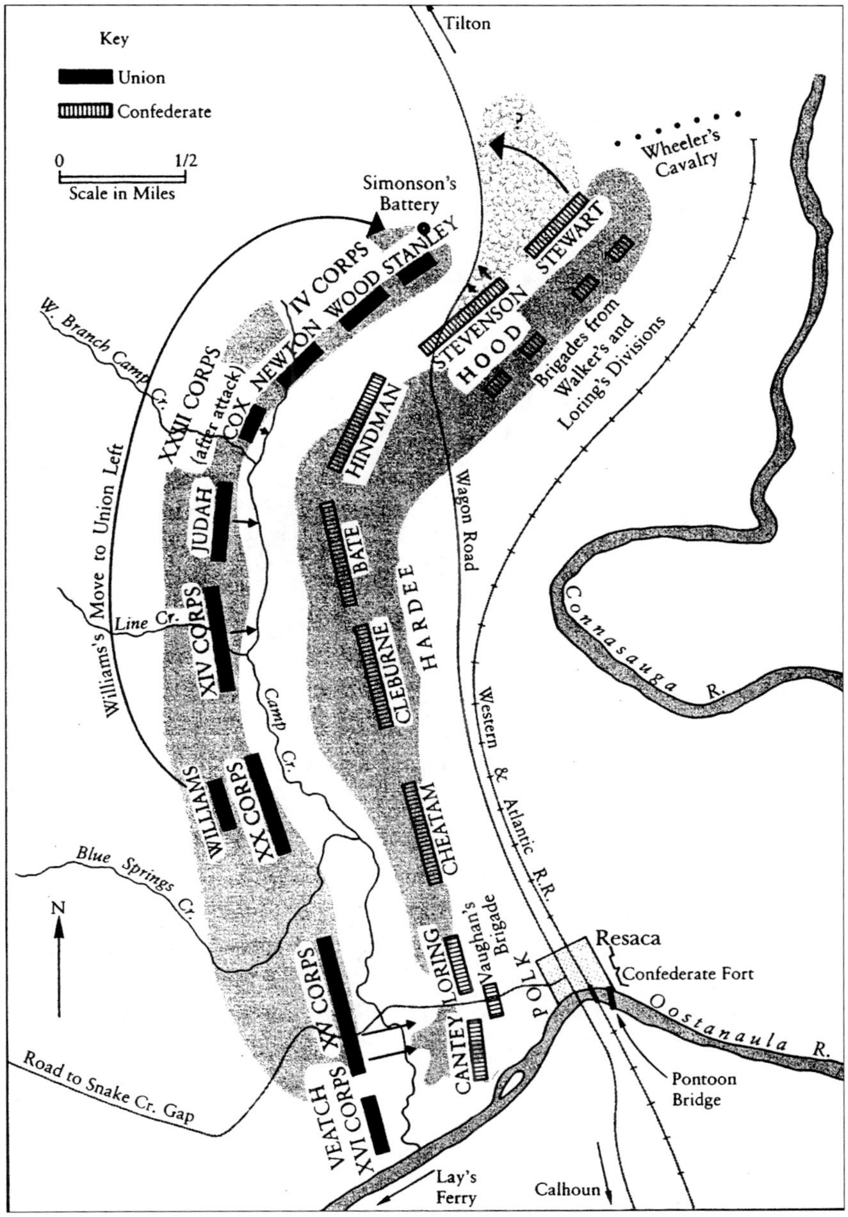

Battle of Resaca, May 14. Map by Laura Kriegstrom Poracsky.

the process of crossing a river. Perhaps more important was the position of each army. While the Union armies were widely separated from one another, the Confederate commands were very close together. Almost all of the grayclad veterans were in Resaca already, or would be by nightfall.[12]

General Johnston placed his men facing west. The Confederate left was anchored on the Oostenaula. These were General Polk's troops. General Hardee was in the center, with General Hood on the right. Arrayed against this formation were two corps of General McPherson's Union Army of the Tennessee. The XVI corps had its right flank secured by the river, with the XV corps to their immediate left. Next came the XX and XIV corps, both of General Thomas's Army of the Cumberland. To their left were the XXXIII and the IV corps.[13] Both sides were ready for tomorrow.

In the Union assault on May 14, Sherman's intent was to attack the Confederate right flank. However, the terrain played a disruptive role in impeding Schofield's advance. Regiments, brigades and divisions became entangled as they attempted to penetrate broken ground overgrown with dense underbrush.[14] As a result, the bluecoats failed to attack in unison. The Federals were repulsed by the right center of the Southern line. By 3:00 P.M., the fighting had ended in total failure.[15]

Having failed in a frontal attack, General Sherman brought out his artillery. The Union army enjoyed a decided advantage over the Confederacy in this area, and it was time to use it. This was the strategy which should have been used to begin with.[16] The heavy guns of Sherman's army had greater range than the Southern field pieces, and the Federals could bombard the enemy with relative impunity.

Had Schofield attacked again after the Yankees pounded the rebel lines with artillery, chances of success would have been much greater than before. However, Sherman did not order him forward a second time that day.[17]

Sherman had other priorities. He wanted to extend the Union left, in order to place more troops in front of General Hood's corps of Confederates. In addition, he hoped to force General Johnston to remain in Resaca so that other Union troops could safely bridge the Oostenaula River at a place called Lay's Ferry. If successful, these Federals would be able to vigorously pursue the rebels further south whenever Johnston decided to evacuate.[18]

Although the Union forces were much larger than their Confederate counterparts, they were by no means out of danger. The IV corps, which was the left flank of Sherman's position, was exposed to a counterattack, and Joe Johnston recognized the opportunity.[19] Fortunately for the graycoats, the attack would be led by one of their finest combat generals: John B. Hood.[20]

Around 5:00 P.M.,[21] Hood's men advanced. The

Federals had attempted to control as much of the ground to their left as possible, which had created a very long, but very thin line. Even so, the Confederate right still overlapped the Union left. The Southerners crashed forward, screaming the terrifying "rebel yell." The Union formations broke under the onslaught and soon the IV corps was fleeing in disarray.[22]

The Southern brigades swarmed down the side of a heavily wooded hill, toward an open field. As they emerged from the protection of the timber, Federal cannon opened upon them, tearing huge holes in the ranks. The onrushing tide of gray came to an abrupt halt. The Federal artillery had saved the day for the Northerners. As darkness fell, the action died down on this sector of the battlefield.[23]

On the other end of the line, General McPherson was moving his XV corps into action. He had learned that the Confederates were shifting men from this part of the field to the north. McPherson heard the sound of firing in that direction, as Hood attacked the IV Corps. The Ohioan wished to prevent any more grayclad men moving from Polk to Hood, and sent the XV Corps across Camp Creek to hold the rebels right where they were.[24] As they moved up the hill in front of Polk's corps, the bluecoats were greeted with a shower of lead from the muskets above them. But Polk's men would not be able to reinforce Hood.[25]

Joe Johnston now faced a dilemma. If McPherson's force pierced the Southern defenses in Resaca, the Union army would cut off Johnston's line of retreat to Atlanta. The Confederates would be trapped. At approximately 7:30 P.M.,[26] General Polk ordered his Tennesseans forward. They would make three separate assaults that evening. The graycoats realized that the situation was desperate, and the action was fierce. Supported by artillery behind them, the ground seemed covered in flames. However, the Northern troops still controlled the hill. After the third attack was repulsed, Polk called off the attack and withdrew his troops to the safety of the Confederate lines.[27]

For William T. Sherman, the day had not gone as planned. He had captured a hill in front of Polk's corps, but had been repulsed in front of Hood's men, the Union troops had not attacked Resaca from the north, and the bridgebuilding efforts across the Oostenaula at Lay's Ferry were still unfinished.[28]

The Union plan of operations for May 15 was the same as that of the day before.[29] While the morning was uneventful, the Federals finally did establish a bridgehead at Lay's Ferry, five miles to the southwest.[30] Slowly but surely, the long arms of General Sherman's army were reaching around the Southern defenders on the way to Atlanta.

Around 1:00 P.M.,[31] the Yankees began their assault. Once again, they were going to try to break through General Hood's corps on the Confederate right. General Howard's IV Corps was in the lead, with the XIV Corps under General Palmer on their right. The main strike force, however, was the XX Corps, led by General Hooker.[32]

As Howard's troops moved forward, they met, in the words of Union General William B. Hazen, "a concentrated fire of great violence."[33] Hazen lost 120 men in 30 seconds. Similar results occurred in other brigades. The bluecoats quickly returned to their starting point.[34]

While General Howard was receiving a warm welcome, the XX Corps was moving into position on Howard's left. Hooker's objective was a hill which anchored the center of the Confederate line. Sherman wanted to seize this hill. If it could be taken, Johnston's entire right wing would have to withdraw into Resaca.

The Union troops attacked from the west, and again the heavy undergrowth disrupted the assault. Battle units became separated, and the piecemeal, disjointed attacks failed to create the mass of blueclad soldiers Sherman wanted. Each time the Yankees moved into range of the Confederate muskets, the advance was repulsed. The operations of Hooker's XX Corps ended in failure.[35]

Although the assault from the north did not succeed, all was not lost for the Federals. They had erected a second bridge across the Oostenaula River at Lay's Ferry. General Johnston, realizing the danger to his line of retreat, met with Hood, Hardee, and several other generals. In order to safeguard the Confederate communications and supply lines, it was decided to move the army south of the river that very night.[36]

By 3:30 A.M. on May 16, the Confederates were across the water.[37] The fight for Resaca was over, and the Yankees marched into the town. Still, Johnston had given the enemy the worst of the fighting. Southern casualties amounted to approximately 3,000 men; Sherman's army lost about 4,000.[38]

The Southern commander believed that a slow movement south was the only course open to him. He would try to best the Yankees wherever opportunity arose. Commenting on Sherman's great numerical superiority, General Johnston explained his thoughts in the following manner: he was "determined to fall back slowly until circumstances should put the chances of battle in our favor, keeping so near the U.S. [Sherman's] army as to prevent its sending reinforcements to Grant, and hoping by taking advantage of positions to reduce the odds against us by partial engagements."[39] This, then, would be the Confederate strategy as long as Joe Johnston was in command.

At 1:00 A.M. on May 17, the grayclad men headed to Adairsville, seven miles farther south.[40] According to

Johnston's maps, this was a strong defensive position. He could attack the enemy again from there.[41]

By the time the Union forces reach Adairsville it was almost dark, and too late to begin an attack. Furthermore, the men were widely scattered once again. General Thomas had most of the Army of the Cumberland at hand, but Hooker's XX Corps was still far to the rear. Schofield, with the XXIII Corps was behind Hooker, while McPherson's Army of the Tennessee had veered off on a different road, and was eight miles to the west of Adairsville. Obviously, the prudent course of action would be to wait until tomorrow.[42]

The battle would have to wait. General Johnston, upon reaching the town, discovered that his maps were more advantageous than reality. There was no position here from which he could give battle. The Confederates could retreat, but to where? After conferring with his generals, Johnston decided to divide his army. Hood and Polk would take their men 11 miles southeast, to the village of Cassville. Hardee and most of the cavalry would march to Kingston, seven miles due west of Cassville.[43]

May 18 found the Confederates in good spirits. About one mile northwest of Cassville, Joe Johnston had concentrated over 70,000 men.[44] Sherman had played right into the hands of the Southern commander. The Federal troops were strung out over a wide area, McPherson on the Union right, Thomas in the center, and Schofield on the left. It was the Army of the Ohio which was most vulnerable.[45] It would remain so for the duration of the Atlanta campaign.

The men of the XXIII Corps made up the smallest of the Union armies. They were isolated, and heavily outnumbered. Despite the attractive prize in his front, Johnston remained noncommittal. That evening Hood, Hardee and Polk urged an attack on the unsuspecting Northerners, but no orders were forthcoming.[46] This lack of aggression is the glaring difference between the cautious Joseph E. Johnston and the audacious Robert E. Lee.

As the next day dawned, General Sherman still felt that the rebels were in the process of retreating. The Ohioan was thinking in terms of pursuit, not an actual battle.[47] However, upon reaching Cassville the bluecoats found Confederates in their front, waiting for the Yankees to attack. Hood was on the Confederate right, Polk in the center, and Hardee on the left. As the day passed, more and more of the Union army arrived on the scene. The Federal artillery began to pound away at Polk and Hood. The few Southern guns which attempted to reply were ineffective, causing minimal damage. Sherman's artillery continued to burst among the graycoats until darkness brought an end to May 19, and the action faded away.

During an evening conference with Johnston, Hood and Polk informed their chief that their positions could not be held. Johnston was reluctant to withdraw, having selected the current position himself. Hood proposed that any action for May 20 be in the form of an offensive thrust. After much deliberation, General Johnston ordered a retreat south of the Etowah River, scheduled to begin immediately.[48] Johnston had let a golden opportunity to strike the XXIII Corps slip away.

It was at this juncture that the administration in Richmond made a serious mistake, which would have a great impact on the entire Atlanta campaign. General Nathan Bedford Forrest was in position to strike the Union supply lines with his cavalry. General Sherman had no fear so constant as that of the incessant meddling of Forrest's horsemen at his back.[49] Prior to reaching Atlanta, the Yankees were very dependent on a long, tenuous supply line which reached back into Tennessee. Johnston, Polk and Hardee urged President Davis to allow Forrest to attack Sherman's lifelines, but to no avail.[50] Prominent Georgians, such as Governor Brown, and General Howell Cobb, sought in vain to persuade the President.[51] Even Robert E. Lee was unable to show the government the merits of this approach.[52]

Due to a perceived Union threat from Memphis, General Forrest was never used against the rear of General Sherman's army. One can only speculate as to what might have been. However, Forrest's combat record, combined with the consternation of Sherman, Grant, and the United States government, suggests that the damage may well have been considerable.

During the night, the Confederates slipped away to the south, through Cartersville and across the Etowah. While Johnston's strategy of a slow retreat was justified on the whole, the Federal armies now stood less than 50 miles from Atlanta.[53]

The graycoats marched on to Allatoona, a small village on the Western and Atlantic Railroad. It too, was a strong defensive position. Flanked by high hills, the town offered Johnston a good chance to rest his men. It was here that Johnston received a telegram from President Davis indicating his severe disappointment in the fact that the Confederates had yet to fight a major battle.[54] The President's patience was wearing thin.

This period around Allatoona marked a relative pause in the campaign that had begun at Dalton. Sunday, May 22 saw religious services in each army. The quiet time was appreciated by the soldiers, but the vacation from the duties of war was about to end.

Monday found the Northern army in motion once again. Keeping McPherson on the Union right, Thomas in the center, and Schofield on the left, Sherman headed for Dallas, Georgia. The bluecoats continued to slowly outflank the Confederates with their numerical superiority. Dallas was 14 miles south of the Etowah River, and only 16 miles west of Marietta,[55] which was Sherman's ultimate objective.

General Johnston surmised that Sherman was trying to move around the Confederate left flank. He sent Hardee's and Polk's corps to Dallas, to stem the most recent threat. The grayclad troops had no river to cross, no wagon train to slow them down, and did not need to worry that they would suddenly be attacked. For the next few days each side was getting into position for the action to come.

On May 25 Hardee was on the Atlanta-Marietta Road, due east of Dallas. Polk was to his right, while Hood had moved his corps to the vicinity of New Hope Church, northeast of Dallas. Marching straight toward Hood's position was the Union XX Corps, under General Hooker.[56]

Sherman was convinced that the Confederates were not in the immediate vicinity, and the XX Corps marched forward. Hood was only able to put 4,000 men in front of Hooker's 16,000, but the graycoats were well concealed, and bullets rained down upon the Yankees.[57] At 7:30,[58] rain and darkness brought an end to the action at New Hope Church. The Confederates of General A. P. Stewart's division cheered loudly as they watched the enemy retreat. Both Johnston and Hood praised the 42-year-old Tennessean for his men's stout defense.[59]

Hooker lost approximately 665 men killed, wounded and missing during the fighting at New Hope Church. Stewart reported a loss of "between 300 and 400."Fully aware of the Union's numerical superiority, Sherman had no praise for Hooker.[60]

The next day was spent shifting troops for another attack. Sherman had not lost sight of his ultimate objective: Atlanta. He would continue to use the Federal strength in numbers to try and march around the enemy. If he was persistent, perhaps Johnston would make a mistake.

On May 27, General Oliver Otis Howard moved the IV Corps against the Confederate right. Howard had part of the XIV and XXIII corps at his disposal as well. He sent Thomas Wood's division forward. Little Pumpkin Vine Creek was to their left, and the underbrush was heavy, but the bluecoats kept moving. Suddenly, they came upon some rebels straight ahead. They were only dismounted cavalry, and Howard had them outnumbered.

The graycoats fell back to a ridge overlooking the ravine which held the IV Corps. If Howard could capture this ridge, Sherman's troops would be able to strike the rear of the Confederate army, and Johnston would be compelled to retreat once again.[61]

However, this would not be easy. The Southern infantry came into view. It was the division of General Patrick R. Cleburne, the stubborn Irishman who had foiled Sherman six months earlier at Missionary Ridge.

The Texans opened fire on the advancing Federals, dropping many in their tracks. The Yankees ducked for cover, and began shooting back in a desperate attempt to take that ridge. For a moment it seemed as if the numbers of the Union side would simply overwhelm Cleburne's men. Fortunately for the rebels, reinforcements were brought up on both sides of the Texans. The Arkansans pushed back the attackers, who were beginning to run low on ammunition.[62]

At 6:00 P.M.,[63] with the IV Corps in confusion, General Howard received a note which stated that General Sherman had canceled the attack. The Northerners were to shift to the defense and await further developments. The two sides continued to fire away at each other until darkness brought an end to the battle of Pickett's Mill.

Before Sherman could undertake offensive operations, he must bring his forces together. McPherson was still too far to the right. Thomas was still in the center with the Army of the Cumberland, but the Army of the Tennessee was ordered to move closer to Thomas's right. For his part, Schofield's Army of the Ohio was still isolated, and he was to march his troops closer to Thomas's left. Once this had been accomplished, the bluecoats would have a compact fighting force, from the Union right to left, of McPherson-Thomas-Schofield.[63a]

Johnston, too, wished to probe the enemy, hoping to discover an opening which the Confederates might exploit. Thus far, the Southerners had been retreating, only stopping long enough at Resaca to bloody the nose of the adversary. In other fighting the graycoats had held their ground, or won minor victories. All that would change on May 28, as the Union army took advantage of Southern mistakes.

General Johnston received erroneous reports that the Federals around Dallas were moving north. Hardee was ordered to have a division determine the strength of the enemy. This assignment fell to the troops of General William Bate, a 37-year-old Tennessean. They occupied the Confederate left, just east of Dallas. Opposing Bate's division was McPherson's Army of the Tennessee.[64]

Bate mistakenly believed that the bluecoats in his front were not there in force, and ordered his men forward. After making some initial progress, the gray-clad boys from Alabama and Mississippi got no further. Union reinforcements came up quickly. Bate tried to cancel the order to attack, but in the confusion of the battlefield, some units received the message, and others did not. Inspired by the earlier charge, the Confederates attempted a futile assault. The heavy underbrush and lack of coordination hampered their efforts.

The rebels had come up against the XV and XVI corps. Around 6:00 P.M.,[65] the Southern charges faded away. The action at Dallas on May 28 was a reversal of Pickett's Mill. Johnston's army had now tasted a real defeat.

Losses at Dallas are difficult to judge. Estimates vary widely, because, in part, some units did not complete battle reports. The Southerners lost between 1,000 and 1,500 men killed, wounded and missing. On the Union side, General Logan lost 379 men in his XV Corps, while other commanders reported very few casualties.[66]

Not only was the battle of Dallas a poorly managed fiasco from the Confederate viewpoint, it was also an unnecessary battle to begin with. If Bate had realized from the outset the strength of his opponent, there never would have been any attack.[67]

The next few weeks were spent gradually shifting troops from one point to another. The results through the month of May had been mixed. The Confederates had succeeded in blocking the Union offensive thrusts. However, the bluecoats were 80 miles closer to Atlanta than they were when the campaign began. Johnston had abandoned several strong defensive positions in a steady retreat. While the Southerners had lost fewer men,[68] the Union losses would soon be made good with the addition of fresh reinforcements. Johnston's casualties could not be replaced.[69]

On June 10, Sherman began moving south again. Thomas held the Army of the Cumberland in the center, but McPherson had been moved to the Union left, while Schofield now held the right. Sherman did not expect any resistance until his troops reached Kennesaw Mountain, due north of Marietta.[70]

Late in the morning,[71] the IV and XIV corps of the Army of the Cumberland came upon rebel skirmishers about a mile from Pine Mountain. This eminence lies between two roads which lead to Marietta. Johnston had posted Bate's division there, hoping that Thomas would be foolish enough to attack the strong Confederate position; however, Sherman's burly lieutenant had no intention of making such a mistake.[72]

From his headquarters at Big Shanty, General Sherman was able to scan the rugged terrain to the south. Big Shanty lay atop the steep grade of the railroad tracks. It is the site of present day Kennesaw, and commanded a panoramic view of Brush Mountain to the southeast, and both Pine and Lost Mountains to the southwest. The general from Ohio stood just over 28 miles from the center of Atlanta.[73]

The next few days were uneventful. On June 14, Sherman looked through his binoculars and noticed a group of Confederates peering at the Yankees from Pine Mountain. Ever mindful of the state of Union morale, he directed the artillery to bombard the graycoats. The Southerners Sherman had found were Johnston, Hardee and Polk. The day's action was singularly unimportant, with the exception that during it, a Union shell exploded, killing General Polk.[74] He would be succeeded by A. P. Stewart.

After some minor skirmishing, the Confederates withdrew again, and by June 22, Johnston had taken up a position on Kennesaw Mountain. The giant outcropping of rock was a formidable opponent for the Northern troops. The Federal artillery could lob shells onto the precipice, but the infantry was unable to scale the heights.[75]

Sherman was still intent on finding a way to get to Marietta. On the Federal left, Joseph Hooker had the XX Corps facing east along the Powder Springs Road. To his right was the XXIII Corps under General Schofield. Still unaware that there were any rebels in the area, the 123rd New York and the 14th Kentucky (Union) moved forward. Lying in wait for the bluecoats was John B. Hood, with his men, about a mile east of the Kolb farm. To Hood's right were Hardee's troops. The Confederates were concealed in the forest, and soon the Yankees came upon their skirmishers.[76]

Hood sent his infantry forward around 5:00 P.M.[77] Hooker's Kentuckians repulsed two charges by the Southerners, then fell back as the New Yorkers on their left gave way. While the 14th Kentucky had performed admirably, the 123rd New York had not fared as well. Hood's men drove them back, but soon came under a crossfire of Union artillery, quickly breaking up the advance. Once again the Federal artillery had carried the day. The battle of Kolb's Farm had cost General Hood 1,500 casualties, while the loss on the Union side did not exceed 250.[78]

Days passed with minor skirmishing until the 27th of June. General Sherman had gotten very impatient in his inability to crack through to Atlanta.[79] Throughout the campaign, he had tried to maneuver around the flank of the enemy, but at the battle of Kennesaw Mountain, he made a tactical mistake, and attempted a frontal assault.

The Union XIV, IV, and XV corps formed an arc opposite Hardee's corps. To Hardee's right were Polk's troops, temporarily commanded by General William Loring. His right extended all the way to Kennesaw Mountain. Little Kennesaw Mountain and Pigeon Hill rose up in Loring's front.[80]

Logan's XV Corps on the Union left made some progress around Pigeon Hill, but then came up against strong Confederate fortifications. General Loring's men poured a concentrated fire down on the bluecoats from the heights, and the advance stalled quickly. Further south, Palmer's XIV Corps attacked Hardee's best

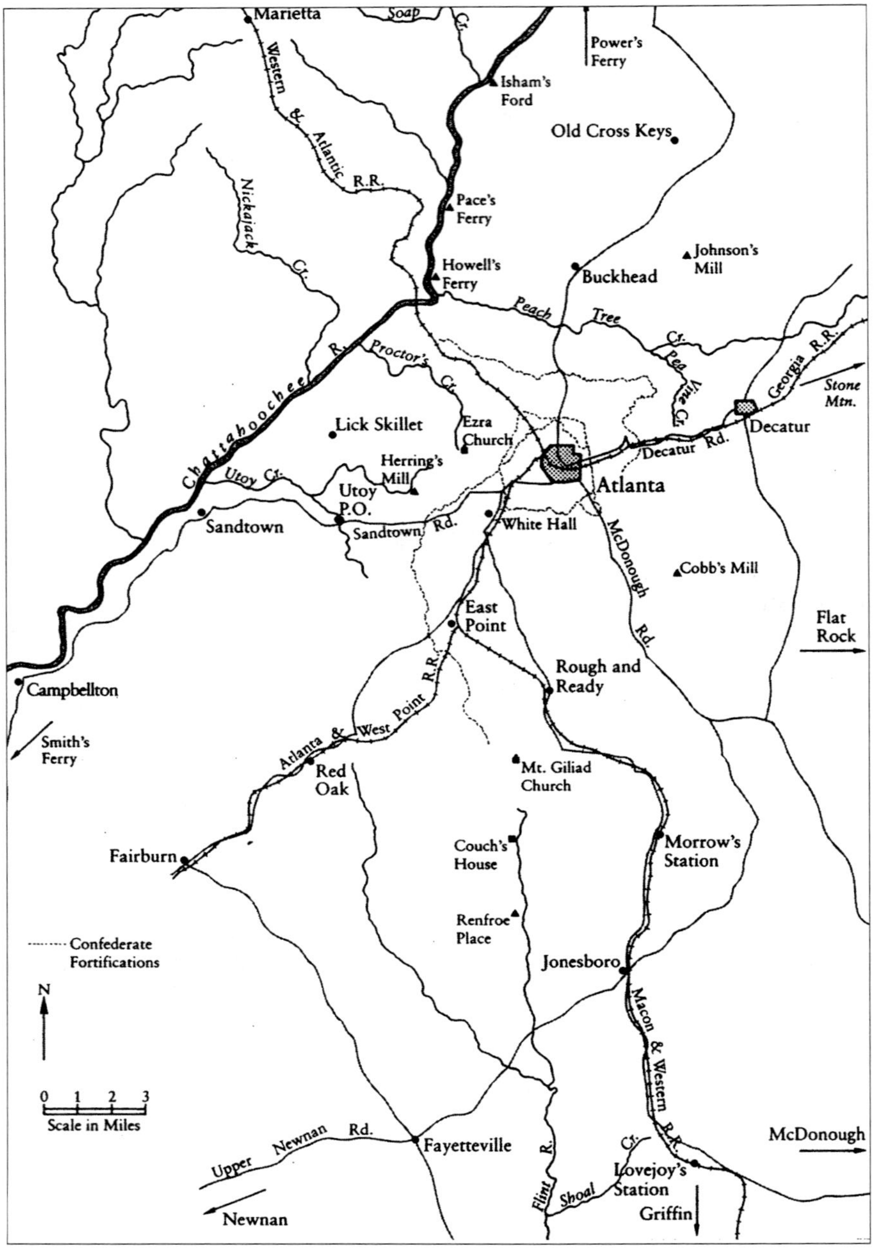

Atlanta area. Map by Laura Kriegstrom Poracsky.

divisions, held under Cleburne and Cheatham. These men were not likely to give way under any assault, but here they were behind strong fortifications, with heavy artillery massed at the Yankees. Palmer did not have a chance.[81]

At 10:45 A.M., Thomas and McPherson telegraphed Sherman that the assault on Kennesaw Mountain has been a failure.[82] The Confederate position was simply too strong to carry by a frontal attack. Casualties for the Federal side on June 27 were approximately 3,000 men, while Johnston lost only 700.[82a]

While the news from his larger forces was not good, Sherman received a more encouraging report from Schofield. The message stated that it was possible to turn Johnston's left flank, but it would require more men than Schofield had at his disposal.[83]

After considering the matter, General Sherman decided that it was wiser to move around Kennesaw Mountain than go over it. There were many of his soldiers who wished that the commander had come to that conclusion 14 hours earlier.[84] The Union army must now shift to the right.

Joe Johnston had won a victory at Kennesaw Mountain, but the situation had not really changed. The bluecoats were now only one day's march from the city of Atlanta, and the Union forces still had the Confederates heavily outnumbered. Sherman had not yet taken the city, but he was moving toward it. Overall, the bluecoats were moving in the right direction. Still, Sherman's military training told him that capturing Atlanta would be much more difficult than looking at it.

The month of July brought two changes to the Confederate army. The first involved the command structure. As of July 6, General Loring was replaced by A. P. Stewart at the head of Polk's corps. This change was simple enough, and caused no real disruption among the troops.

The second change was the most important decision of the Atlanta Campaign. President Davis had become very frustrated at Johnston's continued withdrawals. Despite holding the Federals in check in several defensive actions, the Confederates had not yet lashed out at the enemy. Davis realized that Robert E. Lee continually faced superior numbers throughout the war in Virginia, and had been able to attack his adversary and win stunning victories. Johnston had not exhibited similar aggression, and several opportunities had been missed, particularly against Schofield's small, vulnerable Army of the Ohio.

On July 18, President Davis replaced General Johnston as commander of the Confederate forces with General Hood. This decision was extremely unpopular throughout the Southern army.[85] On the other side, General Sherman was elated.[86] Both sides were astonished. There were many generals both inside and out of

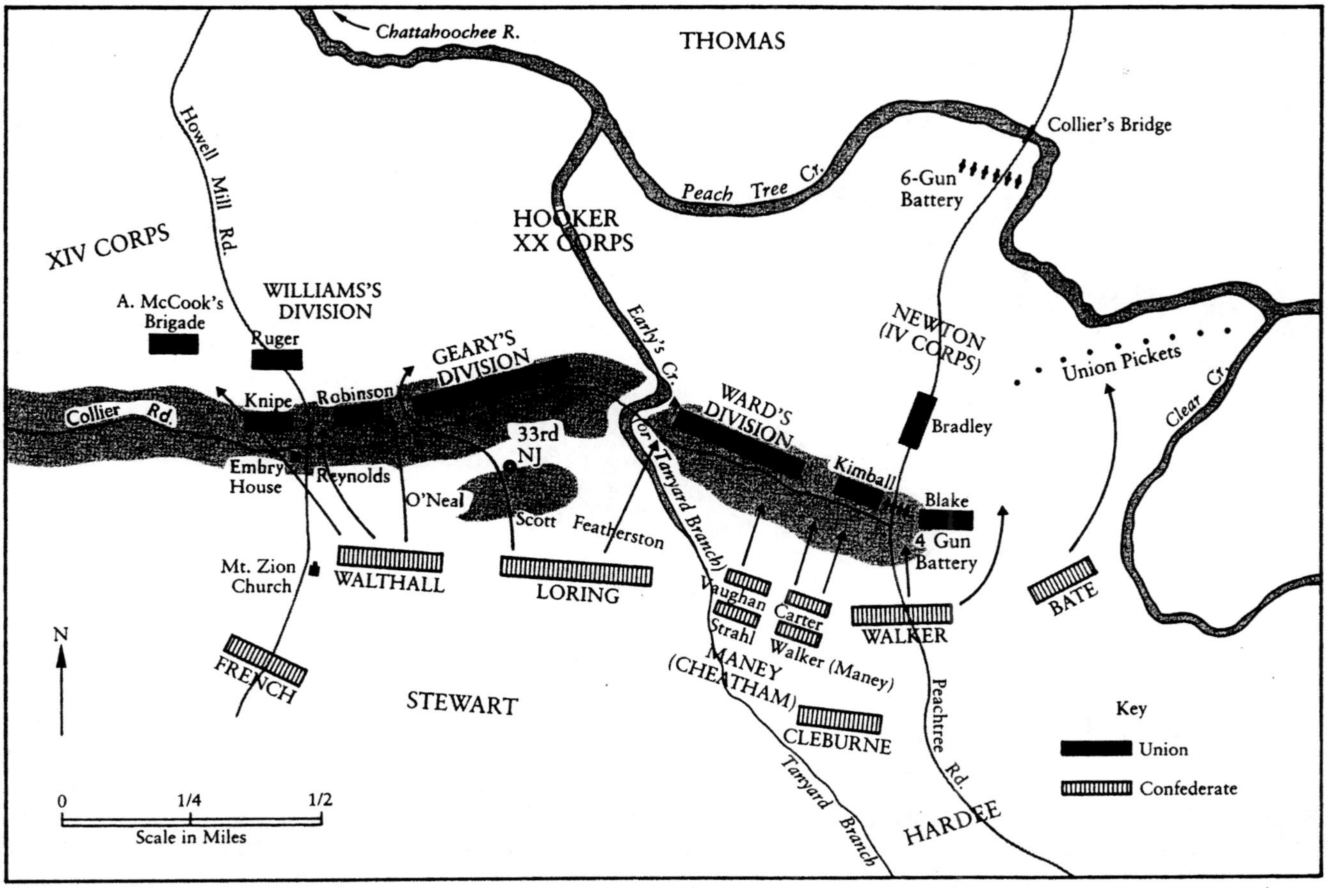

Battle of Peachtree Creek, July 20, 1864. Map by Laura Kriegstrom Poracsky.

Johnston's command who strongly disapproved of the President's action.[87]

Regardless of the clamor against the new commander, the Confederate army was about to change. Joseph E. Johnston was by nature a defensive general; John B. Hood was very aggressive, sometimes reckless. He was perhaps at his best as a subordinate under a strong hand to guide him. William T. Sherman would have a very different opponent, and one much more to his liking.

As the Union troops approached Peachtree Creek, General Hood would have an early chance to prove himself. On July 19, Hood's first full day in command, he assessed the placement of the Confederate troops. The Southerners occupied a line just south of Peachtree Creek. A. P. Stewart was on the left, Hardee held the center, and Hood's old corps, now led by General Benjamin F. Cheatham, was on the right.[88]

Once again, General Sherman had let his armies become separated. Thomas, with the Army of the Cumberland, confronted Hood. Schofield and McPherson, however, had drifted to Decatur, six miles to the east of Atlanta, and too far away to be of any assistance to Thomas.[89]

Hood's plan to save Atlanta was a simple one. Stewart and Hardee would attack Thomas just after the Northerners crossed the creek. Cheatham, combined with Wheeler's cavalry, were ordered to march on Decatur, preventing Schofield and McPherson from sending any aid to Thomas. After defeating the Army of the Cumberland, all the Confederates would then concentrate on Decatur.[90]

On July 20 Thomas brought his troops across Peachtree Creek, but they were not in a contiguous line. They were also only partially fortified. The situation looked good for the graycoats. However, General Cheatham was having a more difficult time. The Yankees were moving very slowly, but in great numbers, and Cheatham clearly did not have the strength to stop them. To remedy this problem, Hood directed Cheatham to shift one mile south. Hardee and Stewart were to move to the east, but only one half mile each. This should support the men in Decatur, and Hood was confident of victory.

However, communications began to go wrong. Cheatham moved not one mile to the south, but two.

This opened up a huge gap on his left. Hardee had a dilemma. It was not possible for him to close the gap to his right by marching half a mile. A. P. Stewart, believing that the shift to his right was unnecessary, did not follow Hardee, but he failed to notify Hood of this. Confederate coordination was coming unraveled.

General Stewart ordered all his troops to drive the Yankees back across Peachtree Creek. They were not to stop under any circumstances. If necessary, the graycoats were to drive Thomas's men from the field with the bayonet. General Hardee's corps failed to receive similar words of aggression, or if they did, the men did not heed them.[91]

Around 4:00 P.M., Hardee ordered his men forward.[92] The Southerners made some progress against the left of the Army of the Cumberland, but were turned back by Union cannon. Instead of storming the Union breastworks as Hood had desired, Hardee's attack ground to a halt. In similar fashion, Stewart's men lay down in front of the enemy fortifications.[93] The Army of the Cumberland had held its ground.

George Thomas had lost about 1,900 men killed, wounded and missing. The Confederates suffered slightly more, around 2,500 total casualties.[94] The Federals, however, were more able to take such losses. Hood blamed Hardee for the failure in front of Peachtree Creek.[95] The Union grip around Atlanta was getting tighter.

On July 21, Hood received a report from General Wheeler. The cavalryman had observed that McPherson's left flank was unprotected, or "in the air." This created an opportunity for General Hood, but the Confederates must act quickly. The new plan of attack withdrew Cheatham and Stewart closer to Atlanta, and sent Hardee's corps with Wheeler's cavalry around McPherson's left flank.[96]

The plan looked good on paper, but the Confederates would not all reach Decatur in time for an attack on the morning of July 22. A late start by several divisions rendered success impossible.

The Union Army of the Tennessee was centered on Bald Hill in Decatur. From the Federal right to left stood the IV, XXIII, XV and XVII corps, all facing west. Next to the XVII corps, but facing south, the XVI corps protected the Federal left.[97]

Facing this alignment of bluecoats was Cheatham's corps. Later that morning, Hardee's troops began to fall in on Cheatham's right. Once again, Hardee's late march would hurt the Confederate cause. Hours behind schedule, he did make a proper reconnaissance to determine just what lay in front of him. Plunging forward in a disorganized fashion, he hoped that the element of surprise would more than compensate for the lack of cohesion among his units. Unfortunately for the rebels, it would not.[98]

The disjointed efforts on the Southern side ended in dismal failure. McPherson watched his troops repulse the Confederate attacks from a knoll to the left of the XVII Corps. Suddenly, a band of graycoats appeared from the underbrush. They fired, and on July 22 the commander of the Army of the Tennessee was killed.[99] General John A. Logan assumed command, turning over the leadership of his XV Corps to General Morgan Smith.

By midafternoon the Confederates had made minimal progress. General F. P. Blair's XVII Corps had held its ground against repeated, though poorly organized attacks. Along with General Grenville Dodge's XVI Corps, Blair had beaten back every one of Hood's assaults.[100] However, around 4:00 P.M.[101] Sherman received word that Hardee was "driving" the Yankees. Confederate generals Daniel Govan and Alfred Vaughn succeeded where Pat Cleburne and George Maney had failed. The Confederates had hit Giles Smith's division simultaneously in front, flank and rear, with devastating results. They had punched a hole between the left of Blair's corps and the right of Dodge's troops, and the Union front south of Bald Hill had disintegrated.[102]

Hood reacted to the good news by ordering Cheatham forward. Originally, Cheatham was only to follow up on any success Hardee might have.[103] Now the Tennessean must attack with all the fury his men could muster.

At first the graycoats had slow going, but the day improved. The center of the XV Corps was not well protected, and two Southern brigades ripped a hole in the center of Sherman's favorite corps.[104] If Hood could only exploit this success, the entire Union left would be in serious trouble. Thomas was too far away to help. The fate of Sherman's army hung in the balance.

Two developments combined to save the men in blue from disaster. First, the Yankees rushed reinforcements to the threatened sector. Second, through some misunderstanding at the point of attack, the Confederates actually fell back instead of pouring more men into the break in the enemy lines. Speculation exists as to both the origin and the cause of the order to retreat, but there can be no doubt that there was a misunderstanding among those present. The pause in the Confederate attack allowed the XV Corps to strengthen its defenses, and the danger passed.[105]

As the summer sun began to fade away, Hardee made one last attempt at Bald Hill. The fire from Giles Smith's division stopped the Confederate assault. Govan's Arkansans attempted to take the hill from the south, but were thrown back in hand to hand fighting.[106] The fight for Bald Hill ended with the Northerners still firmly in possession of the battlefield.

July 22 had proved to be the bloodiest day of the campaign. While the Union lost approximately 3,700 men, the Confederate casualties were even greater, and can be reasonably estimated at 5,500.[107] General Hood could not afford losses like this for very long.

While Hood tried to blame the Confederate failure on Hardee once again, the fact of the matter is that he tried to do too much with too little. As soon as Hood found out that Hardee did not have all of his troops on hand, the attack should have been canceled. General Hood failed to take into account time, distance and fatigue in his plans.[108] He would have to regroup, and Sherman would have to find a better way of taking Atlanta.

General Sherman had not yet finished reshuffling the command structure of the Union army. Oliver O. Howard was promoted to lead the Army of the Tennessee, following McPherson's death. General David Stanley took over the IV Corps. Logan, for his part, was deeply disappointed, but returned to the XV Corps.

Sherman continued to try to work his way around the flanks of the Confederate army. On July 27, the Army of the Tennessee was ordered to march back around to the Union right. Thomas remained in the center, while Schofield now made up the Federal left.[109] Hopefully, this would force the graycoats to turn back and retreat.

On July 28, Howard's corps took a position centered on Ezra Curch. Opposing him, on the Confederate left, were A. P. Stewart's men. The Yankees dug in behind rails, logs or anything else they could find, and awaited the rebel charge. They didn't wait long. Around 12:30 P.M.,[110] the Southerners charged against the Union right and were handily repulsed. They charged again, only to suffer the same fate. Then the right of Stewart's corps attempted to break through the enemy lines, with similar results. The Confederate center was commanded by Stephen D. Lee. He felt that the bluecoats would break under a vigorous charge. Lee's men charged the XV Corps twice, but the Yankees held firm. As the Confederates began to bring up reinforcements, both A. P. Stewart and Loring were wounded, taking them from the field of battle. The Confederate assault at Ezra Church was over. The Federals did not have the strength to counterattack.[111] Both sides buried their dead.

The casualties at the battle of Ezra Church were devastating to the Confederates. While Howard reported a total loss of 632 men, the Southerners lost close to 3,000.[112]

Although many historians blame Hood for the disaster at Ezra Church, the fault actually lay with Stephen Lee. His disjointed attacks and disregard of Hood's instructions — which were simply to hold his position until reinforcements arrived — ruined Confederate chances of success.[113]

At the beginning of August, the rebels still held Atlanta, but Sherman was pressing hard on all sides. It would be only a matter of time before Hood would be forced to give up the city in order to save his soldiers.

In two weeks, General Hood had lost around 12,000 men, more than General Johnston had lost in three months. The morale of the Southern troops was dropping.[114]

Still, the main goal of William T. Sherman was to seize control of the railroad between Atlanta and East Point. This had not been accomplished. East Point lay on the Atlanta and West Point Railroad, and was actually southwest of the city. The Yankees must continue to push south.

Howard's corps had not been able to break through to the railroad, and cavalry raids had failed as well. Sherman turned to the Army of the Ohio. Perhaps Schofield could succeed. They now marched from the Union left, east of Atlanta, to the Union right.[115] This movement should stretch Hood's line to the breaking point.

During August 2, Schofield's men took up a position on the north fork of Utoy Creek, a small stream west of Atlanta. As Sherman had hoped, this forced the Confederate left to pull back, as they were in danger of being outflanked. After four days of shifting troops to put more pressure on the enemy, Schofield ordered the advance. The intent was to take possession of the railroad.[116]

After initial success, the bluecoats became entangled in a maze of trees which the Confederates had felled the prior night. The Southerners had an easy time of it, and the Yankees were excellent targets. Frustrated, Schofield sent two brigades on a wide sweep to the Confederate left, but darkness halted their progress. The net result to the Union was that by August 7, the rebels had fallen back.[117] However, the pursuit must continue.

The next target was further south: Jonesboro. Several weeks were spent in preparation for a large flanking movement. Ammunition was shifted, troops and wagons were moved from place to place, and the Union armies prepared themselves for the large-scale movement which was to come.

General Hardee's corps was blocking Sherman's way. The graycoats were facing west, with Patrick Cleburne on the Confederate left, Carter Stevenson in the center, and Stephen Lee on the right. They extended from just south of Jonesboro to just north of it.[118]

August 31 found the XV Corps under John Logan headed straight for the rebels. They were supported on the left by one brigade from the XVII Corps and on the right by the XVI Corps. The remainder of the XVII Corps was on the way, but had not yet arrived.[119]

At 3:00 P.M. Hardee began his attack, and Cleburne's men started forward.[120] Once again Stephen Lee failed to act in the coordinated fashion planned by his superiors.

Lee charged too soon, and the Confederates broke apart. Logan's XV Corps had an easy time with such a disorganized assault. Cleburne's unsupported attack failed miserably, and in a rare display, his men gave a poor account of themselves.

The casualty figures alone told the story. Howard's killed, wounded and missing came to only 172. Hardee's total loss at the battle of Jonesboro was at least 2,200, some 1,400 of which were under Lee's command.[121]

With the Union men still positioned in front of the graycoats, the IV and XIV corps slipped around to the Confederate right. On September 1, Jonesboro was assailed from both sides.[122] The pincer movement was a stunning success for Sherman's troops. The XIV Corps had broken through the enemy defenses at Jonesboro, and the Yankees had complete control of the area. Sherman was confident that Atlanta must soon fall into his hands.

The Ohioan was quite correct. The fall of the city was only a matter of time, perhaps helped along by the change in command. The Confederates had been at a numerical disadvantage from the start. Jefferson Davis never allowed General Forrest to operate against the Union supply lines, and Forrest was the Confederate most feared by both Sherman and Grant. There were certainly mistakes made by Johnston and Hood. However, the fact remains that within a mere seven weeks since Johnston's removal, the Confederate front in Georgia was gone.[123]

May 5–6, 1864
The Wilderness

R. E. Lee (CSA) — U. S. Grant, G. G. Meade (USA)

The Wilderness is a densely wooded area of central Virginia located just south of the Rappahannock River. Visibility is very poor there, as the canopy of larger trees blocks out the sunlight while the thick blanket of second growth saplings and vines makes it impossible for artillery to operate effectively. It is a most difficult place to fight a battle.

The Union Army of the Potomac was led by Ulysses S. Grant, with George G. Meade as second in command. The Federals were moving south. The intent was to capture Richmond, thus bringing an end to the bloody conflict which had consumed the nation. The battle of the Wilderness was the first in a series of movements in which the Union army attempted to move around the Confederate right. However, Robert E. Lee was in no mood to give up the capital of the Confederacy without a fight.

General Grant recognized the difficulty presented by the terrain. If the bluecoats could make it through the Wilderness, the surrounding country offered several positions from which the Yankees could give battle. The important thing was to keep moving.[1]

Ironically, movement was one goal which General Grant failed to accomplish. Uncertain as to the precise location of the Confederate Army of Northern Virginia, the Federals stopped in the forest.[2] The Union advance ground to a standstill in the thick woods.

Grant had some 120,000 men at his disposal.[3] The Union forces were divided into four corps. The II Corps, under Winfield S. Hancock, the V Corps, led by Gouverneur K. Warren, and the VI Corps, commanded by John Sedgwick, were in the immediate vicinity. The IX Corps, under Ambrose E. Burnside, had not yet arrived. Burnside's men were protecting the Orange & Alexandria Railroad, and though not technically part of the Army of the Potomac, they would report to General Grant.

Perhaps the combination of Burnside's absence and the lack of knowledge as to General Lee's whereabouts induced General Grant to halt his advance in the murky, overgrown forest. At any rate, it was a mistake he would live to regret.

By May 4, the Union forces were facing roughly southwest, with Hancock on the left, Warren in the center, and Sedgwick's troops on the right.[4]

Arrayed against the men in blue were two corps of Confederates. The Second Corps was under Richard S. Ewell. Marching east, the graycoats trudged along the Orange Turnpike, one of the few roads that crossed the wooded countryside. The Third Corps was commanded by A. P. Hill. Some three miles to the south, Hill's boys had taken the Orange Plank Road, running roughly parallel to Ewell's route.[5]

In addition to these men, the Army of Northern Virginia contained one more corps. The First Corps was led by James Longstreet, but General Lee had placed Longstreet near Mechanicsville, over 40 miles[6] west of the rest of the Confederates. The rebels would have roughly 65,000 men[7] in front of General Grant's advance on Richmond. But could Longstreet arrive in time to help General Lee?

The Confederates had worked hard to get in position to fight the foe. General Ewell had camped in the vicinity of Robertson's Tavern, while Hill had taken his men to Verdiersville.[8] By the next morning the graycoats would be ready for the enemy.

Longstreet, however, was another matter. His troops began leaving Mechanicsville at 4:00 P.M.[9] on May 4. The distance his men had to cover was simply too great to arrive the next morning. General Longstreet would do his best, but for now the fortunes of the Confederacy must fall upon the shoulders of Richard Ewell and A. P. Hill.

General Grant had a great numerical advantage, but General Lee was not one to let his opponent strike the first blow. He always preferred to seize the initiative. On the other hand, Longstreet had not yet reached the battlefield. Perhaps a compromise could be reached, one that would retard the Federal advance, yet let the Southerners maintain control of the action.[10]

Ewell would march his men forward on the left, with A. P. Hill on his right. In an advanced position, they could hold off the Yankees until help arrived.[11] If the Confederates could merely hold Grant where he was, the Union army would be pinned in the deep woods.[12]

On the morning of May 5, General Lee had his troops in a relatively compact formation. Ewell was on the left, Hill on the right, and, although Longstreet had not yet reached the field, Lee had every confidence that his burly lieutenant would soon appear.

On the Federal side, the men were a bit more scattered. Hancock held the Union left, but there was a gap between Hancock's right and Warren's left. The II Corps would have to march north along the Brock Road to reach Warren. On the Federal right, Sedgwick's VI Corps was moving south on the Germanna Road, but was not yet in position. Burnside would probably not be of any assistance for another day. Any fighting this morning would have to come from Warren's men.[13]

While the Army of Northern Virginia was not quite as dispersed as its Union counterpart, General Lee had a dilemma as well. As the Southerners had taken different, parallel roads to reach the front, there were three miles[14] between Ewell's right and Hill's left. If this gap were not filled, Lee might have to fight two separate, but simultaneous battles.[15]

By 10:30 A.M., the Union battle plan began to take shape. Sedgwick set his troops in motion, while Warren began to push forward against Ewell. On Warren's left, the bluecoats had sent forward cavalry under Colonel John Hammond. The horsemen were ordered to hold off A. P. Hill until Hancock's II Corps could arrive.[16]

A critical moment arose in front of A. P. Hill. The graycoats marched forward, toward the intersection of the Brock Road and the Orange Plank Road. General George Getty and his Yankees on the Germanna Road passed in front of Ewell at 11:00 A.M., heading south with the same object in mind, of seizing the intersection. If the Federals reached the intersection first, the Union position would be solidified. If Hill's rebels got there first, Hancock would be cut off from Grant. The outcome was vital to both sides. Getty had a longer march than Hill, but could Hammond delay the Confederates long enough for the Northern general to win the race?[17]

As the Yankees approached the crossroads, the remnants of Hammond's small command gave General Getty all the information he needed. Rebels just ahead! Immediately Getty ordered his men forward at double-quick time, and the bluecoats seized the junction just ahead of the Confederates.[18]

By midday on the 5th, General Grant began to deploy his troops. Facing west, Warren placed Charles Griffin's brigade astride the Orange Turnpike. To his left were the men under James Wadsworth, with Samuel Crawford's Northerners anchoring the far left. John Robinson's brigade was held in reserve, stationed behind Griffin and Wadsworth. On the Union right, Horatio Wright of Sedgwick's Corps would lead his men to Griffin's right flank. These bluecoats would soon face General Ewell's Confederates.[19]

Further south, Getty held the intersection of the Brock Road and the Plank Road, confronting A. P. Hill and his rebels. Hancock was bringing the II Corps forward, and would soon reinforce the Federal left.

Around noon,[20] Griffin and Wadsworth attempted to cautiously advance, but the dense undergrowth prevented any progress. Organization was soon lost, and visibility was nonexistent.[21]

General Meade, in his haste to bring on a battle, had yielded his advantage in numbers. The Union assault was made not with two corps, but by parts of two divisions. Any cohesive formation had long since disintegrated.[22]

Shortly before 1:00 P.M.,[23] the Union lines of blue rose from the woods and surged forward. They were greeted by an earsplitting volley of gunfire from Ewell's Confederates.[24] The battle in the Wilderness had opened!

The dense woods and steep earthworks had provided good protection for the Northerners, but as the soldiers came west into Saunders' Field, they presented tall targets for the graycoats. The Yankees dropped in rows as Ewell's troops fired into the enemy, furiously reloading only to train their muskets once again on the swarming invaders.[25]

As the afternoon wore on, thick clouds of heavy smoke covered the battlefield. Combat became more localized, as neither side had any vision. Commands on both sides became entangled, and the roar of musketry from all sides dominated the contest. Officers struggled to maintain any semblance of order. The enemy seemed everywhere, but in the early going the Confederates gained the upper hand.[26]

Suddenly, the tide turned. On the south end of Saunders' Field, Union General Joseph Bartlett led a spirited counterattack and pushed the rebels back. As his men worked their way through the thick underbrush, the

Yankees worked their way beyond any support. Soon Bartlett's troops were isolated, and the Confederates attacked the exposed right flank. This assault hurled the bluecoats back again, but many soldiers were able to reform behind the Union lines.[27]

This struggle typified the constant ebb and flow of confusion which dominated the afternoon. Groups broke apart to fight by themselves, shooting in the general direction of where the enemy was supposed to be, often firing at friends instead.

In Wadsworth's front the situation was no clearer. General John B. Gordon led his Georgians into a gap in the Union line, only to find himself surrounded. Gordon reacted quickly to adversity. He split his brigade in two, leaving three regiments facing south and one facing north. The graycoats then charged, and the surprise broke the Federal line.[28]

On the left, General Wadsworth found his men had been outflanked. Rebels had sneaked around the left side of James Rice's brigade. Junius Daniel and his North Carolinians were pouring in behind Rice's troops. The Yankees were forced to pull back in disorder, suffering heavy losses in the rout.[29]

With the collapse of the Federal attack, Crawford's division was in danger of being cut off. The Northerners pulled back, out of danger,[30] but they were no longer a threat to Ewell's right.

By 2:30 P.M., the Union offensive in Ewell's sector had ended.[31] The attack failed for several reasons. Meade had not waited long enough for Sedgwick to completely close on Warren's right. As a result, there were simply not enough men to take part in the attack. The heavy growth in the Wilderness completely negated the Union artillery advantage, and the underbrush prevented the easy movement of reinforcements from point to point.[32]

In the calm following Ewell's repulse of Warren, both sides tried to regroup and shift their forces into better positions. At 3:00 P.M., General Wright finally arrived on Warren's right flank.[33] Each army attempted to extend their lines northward, trying to outflank the other. Battle-weary units were sent to the rear and fresh troops were brought up to fill in any gaps.[34]

Thirty minutes later, the fighting resumed in earnest. The center of the action was just north of Saunders' Field.[35] General Leroy Stafford's Louisiana troops had ventured too far ahead of James Walker's Virginians on their right. A gap developed, and the Yankees poured into the hole in the Confederate lines. The bluecoats fired a murderous volley into the rebels. Stafford was wounded, and the graycoats had to fall back.[36]

Harry Hays brought his Confederate brigade up to take the place of Stafford's men. The scene repeated itself. Hays moved too far forward, Walker did not keep pace, and Hays was forced to retreat just as Stafford had before him.[37]

Still, George Meade had failed to dislodge the Confederates from their position. The second attack had failed as miserably as the first. While much of Ewell's success was due to Meade's inability to mass the Federal soldiers in a single concerted thrust, this Confederate good fortune could not last forever. Would Burnside come to rescue the Union?

Ulysses S. Grant and George G. Meade were not working well together. While Grant was in command, he tried to let Meade manage each part of the battle, and the loose arrangement was not succeeding. Grant's failure to utilize Burnside in cooperation with Wright's attack against Ewell's left flank was a serious mistake.[38]

May 5 had thus far been marked by confusion on the Union side. At 4:15 P.M.,[39] General Getty was not about to let inertia overwhelm his command on the Federal left. He threw his troops into the Confederates. Hill's men had advanced along the Orange Plank Road, and, facing east, Harry Heth's men took position along the road.[40] A collision was about to take place.

A. P. Hill commanded one other division, led by Cadmus Wilcox. However, as General Lee had become concerned about the gap between Ewell and Hill, the Confederate commander in chief had ordered Wilcox to occupy this space. As a result, Heth could not count on reinforcements. The 6,500 graycoats at his side must try to stop 17,000 Federals.[41]

Getty's regiments met a sheet of flame from General Heth, pinning the blueclad Northerners to the ground. The lead brigade were Getty's favorites, the Green Mountain boys from Vermont. The Yankees returned fire, but were soon running low on ammunition. Union casualties were frightful. The situation was truly desperate.[42]

The Federals charged, hoping to sweep the field at the point of the bayonet. Heth's front line recoiled under the shock of the onslaught, but the rebels held firm, pouring a destructive volley into Getty's troops. Federal help came from the left. Gershom Mott from Hancock's Corps had brought his brigade into line. [43]

It seemed as though the reinforcements would carry the day for the Union, but the tightly bunched Northerners presented an inviting target. Bluecoats dropped by the score as the Confederates delivered another deadly volley. The thick underbrush was impenetrable, and under heavy pressure, Mott's line collapsed.[44]

Fortunately for the Union, David Birney's brigade had been held in reserve. Birney's troops slashed their way through the jungle of vines and trees, taking Mott's place on the left of Getty. Gradually, the rebels were forced backwards, but the Yankees were unable to make any further progress. The two armies contented themselves with a static exchange of gunfire, each side determined to hold their ground.[45]

The Army of the Potomac had a decided advantage in numbers, and General Hancock was not about to waste it. He hurried forward John Gibbon's division, and the fourth Federal division moved forward against Heth's lone division of Confederates. At 5:05 P.M.[46] Gibbon formed his lines, and he attempted to turn the tide in the Union's favor. Like his compatriots, he was unable to pierce the Confederate lines. Harry Heth had held firm.

The Federal attacks on May 5 had not broken the enemy for several reasons. Ewell and Hill had performed skillfully. However, the Union assaults were made in piecemeal, unsupported fashion.[47] For the North to win in the Wilderness, the general officers would have to improve.

On the Confederate side, while Heth had been solid in his defense along the Plank Road, his men were exhausted. They would soon be overwhelmed if they were not reinforced. Longstreet was on his way, but still had not arrived. Wilcox was strung out from Heth's left all the way to Ewell's right. Without James Longstreet's men, the Confederate situation was a precarious one indeed.

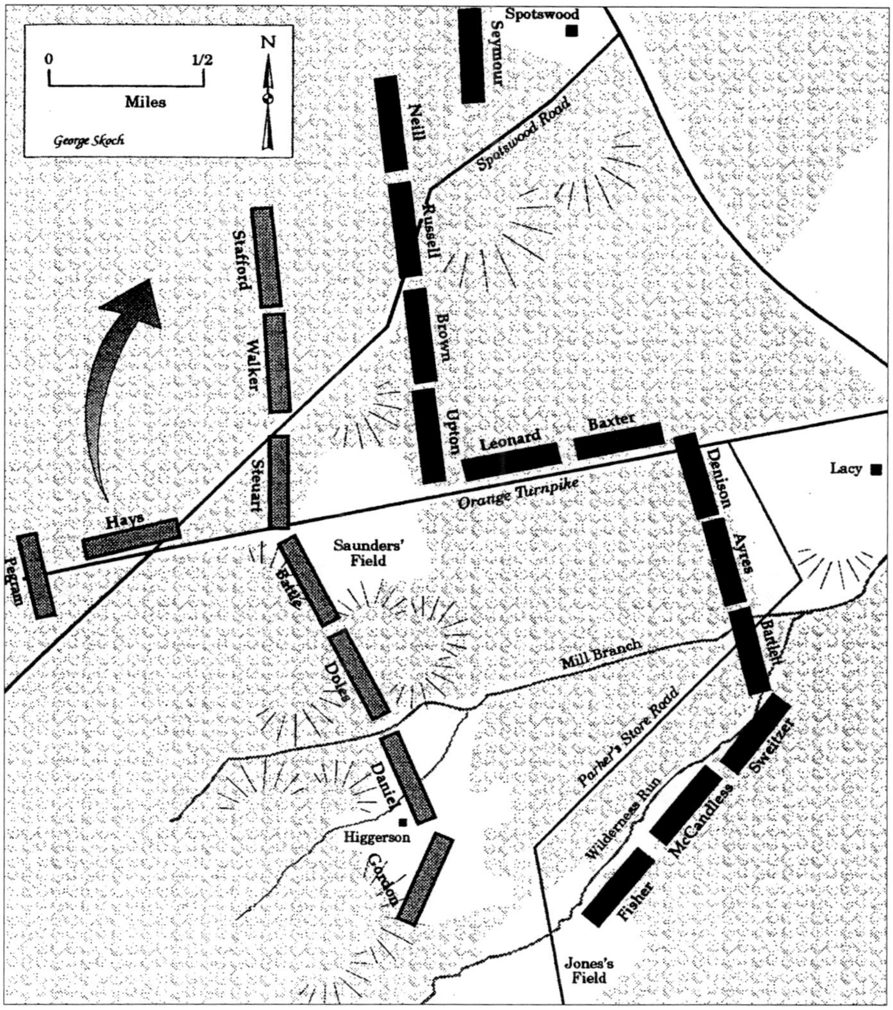

Sedgwick's assault on May 5, 1864, 3 P.M.–5 P.M. Map by George Skoch.

Late in the day, General Lee ordered Wilcox to reinforce Heth. By 5:30 P.M.,[48] the graycoats were headed into action. The Confederates now occupied the ground along the Orange Plank Road, forming their troops on either side of the dirt lane. Still facing east, the rebels extended approximately a quarter of a mile on either side of the road.[49]

As 6:00 P.M. approached, it became apparent that Wilcox did not possess the manpower necessary to relieve Heth's weary men.[50] Slowly but surely, the enemy began to assemble more bluecoats in front of A. P. Hill.

The transfer of Wilcox to aid Heth had a profound effect on the mind of Ulysses S. Grant. Grant believed that the Confederates marching in Heth's direction had been removed from Ewell's corps. The Union commander ordered Sedgwick and Warren to renew their attack on Ewell. In addition, Grant mobilized Union reserves for another attack in A. P. Hill's sector. This time the blow would come against Hill's left flank.[51]

In turn, the Federal movements provided General Lee with both hope and alarm. He correctly reasoned that Hill must guard his left flank. He also felt that with Union reinforcements moving against Hill, the enemy would not have sufficient strength against Ewell. Lee told Ewell to watch for an opening in the Union defenses. The chance for a bold counterattack just might present itself.[52]

At 7:00,[53] the worst of Lee's fears seemed to be coming true. Union troops began to work their way around Hill's left. Almost every available Confederate reserve had been already thrown into battle. The only men left were the 5th Alabama battalion, about 125 soldiers.[54] Currently assigned to guard Federal prisoners, the Alabamians would have to come forward.

Screaming wildly, the rebels charged. The trick worked, and the Federals turned away, having no stomach for smoke, battle, and an opponent who was invisible in the dense forest.

Abruptly, the fighting stopped. Both sides were

exhausted, disorganized and confused. Battle units were horribly turned around, different commands had blended together as men had become lost in the Wilderness. Darkness slowly dropped a curtain over Virginia, and the stillness of the night was broken by the agonizing cries of the wounded. There was less than 100 feet between the two sides.[55]

During the night the Federal generals worked tirelessly to coordinate their plans for the coming day. Order must be returned to the battlefield. Hancock must come up on the Union left, and Burnside's IX Corps would be available; where should his troops be placed?

The Confederates needed to adjust their plans as well. Originally, Lee had envisioned Longstreet marching forward on Hill's right, attempting to move around the Union left flank. However, reinforcements were needed, as the thin Southern line could break at any point. Longstreet would now be directed to come to Hill's support, marching right up the Orange Plank Road.[56]

General S. D. Ramseur had brought his brigade forward to reinforce Ewell. When Longstreet arrived, his rebels could replace A. P. Hill's troops. Hill's men could then shift to the north, and the gap between Hill and Ewell would be closed.[57]

The outlook on Hill's front was not as sanguine. While Ewell had an opportunity to attack Sedgwick in the morning, the situation on the Confederate right was very precarious. Heth and Wilcox had seen their commands blend together. Organization was lost, and there was not a continuous battle front. The graycoats would not be able to withstand a concerted attack.[58]

It was in this area that a point of controversy arose. Together, Heth and Wilcox made their way to A. P. Hill's quarters. Explaining their plight, the two division commanders asked Hill for instructions. Hill told them to leave their troops alone, adding that "Longstreet would soon be up," and Lee's orders were to have the men rest as they were.[59]

After a close examination of his lines, Wilcox decided to press the matter further. Around 9:00 P.M., he went to General Lee's tent.[60] He heard a report from Lee that Longstreet would soon arrive, confirming A. P. Hill's earlier statement. In the face of this welcome news, General Wilcox said nothing of his shattered lines; however, he also failed to shift his soldiers.[61]

Despite the assurances, Heth and Wilcox were still nervous about the condition of their troops. For his part, Heth visited the commander of the Third Corps twice more on the evening of May 5. On the last visit A. P. Hill's temper got the best of him. "Damn it, Heth," he erupted, "I don't want to hear any more about it; the men shall not be disturbed."[62]

The minutes seemed like hours. Very slowly, the sun crept into the sky. Morning was approaching. The graycoats looked behind them down the Orange Plank Road. Longstreet was nowhere to be seen.

May 6 dawned with a powerful Union attack against A. P. Hill. The plan was for Wadsworth to strike the left flank while Hancock overwhelmed the right, crushing Hill in a powerful pincer movement.[63]

The graycoats were unprepared for the surging tide of blue. The first contact came on the Confederate right, then rolled all along the front. The weight of the attack threw the rebels back in disorder.[64] Wadsworth's men added fury to the Federal attack, hitting the Confederate left and driving the enemy before them. Union commands became entangled, and the bluecoats paused to straighten their lines. They would try to act in concert for one final thrust.[65] If all went well, A. P. Hill would be swept from the field of battle. Winfield S. Hancock had performed magnificently in the early morning, but the fortunes of war were about to change.

Hill's Confederates were streaming to the rear along the Orange Plank Road, and the day seemed lost for the South. Suddenly, a sea of gray appeared on the road, and it was moving east with great force. Longstreet!

James Longstreet possessed many fine qualities, but his greatest was an imperturbable calm in the face of disaster.[66] For this reason, Lee always referred to him as "my war horse." There would be no disaster today if Longstreet had anything to say about it.

The troops deployed on both sides of the road, but it was John Gregg's Texans on the north side who led the way. They took heavy casualties[67] in the initial counterattack, but the powerful Union Army had been stopped in its tracks. The Federal momentum had disappeared.

North of the Orange Plank Road, Longstreet placed Charles Field's division, which included Gregg's Texans. On the south side were the troops under Joseph Kershaw, the battle-tested South Carolinian.[68]

The rebels continued to strike with devastating force. Field in particular did great damage, rendering Wadsworth's ineffective as a combat unit.[69] For its part, Kershaw's powerful thrust had taken Hancock by surprise.[70] The first Union line melted away, and the Confederates surged forward. The Yankees tried to bring up reinforcements, but the dense Wilderness hindered their efforts.[71]

While the battle raged on the Confederate right, Hill assembled the remnants of his shattered command and formed a more compact line in the space remaining between Longstreet and Ewell. This time the line held. After Longstreet's arrival, A. P. Hill's role in the battle was greatly diminished.

In the northern section of the Wilderness, there was little action. Each side probed the enemy, hoping to find a weak spot, but no opportunity arose. The troops spent

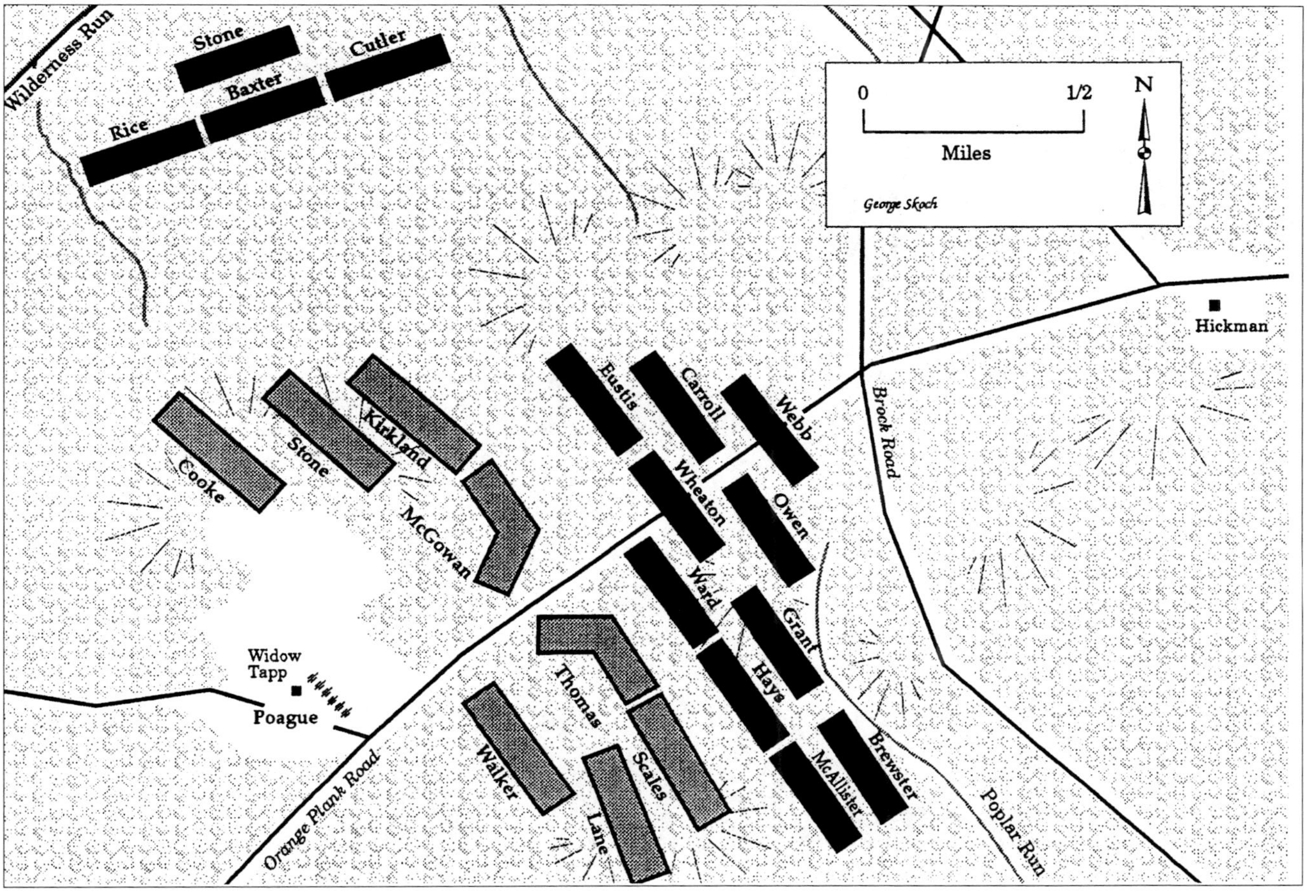

The Orange Plank Road front on May 6, 1864, at 5 A.M. Map by George Skoch.

most of the day on May 6 locked in the same stalemate they had reached the day before.[72]

General Grant realized he had the advantage in numbers. Burnside's IX Corps arrived, and was ordered to fill the space between Hancock's right and Warren's left. The problem Grant faced was how to complete the efficient movement of troops in the Virginia Wilderness. As Burnside began to deploy his Northerners, General Ramseur moved in front of the Federals. Ramseur's advance further confused Burnside, and by this point in the action A. P. Hill was moving Heth and Wilcox up to solidify the Confederate lines in the center.[73] For the rest of the morning, the IX Corps was neutralized.[74]

By 10:00 A.M.,[75] the Union advance for May 6 had stalled completely. On the right, Sedgwick and Warren were locked with Ewell, in the center Burnside had made no progress, and on the left Hancock had stretched his lines to compensate for Wadsworth's collapse.[76]

It was around this time that the Orange Plank Road sector became quiet. Longstreet and Hancock had pounded each other into exhaustion. Both sides were worn out. However, the day was not done for these two generals.

Before the outbreak of the Civil War, construction had started on a railroad link from Fredericksburg to Orange Court House. As hostilities flared, work on the railroad stopped. It was now just an unfinished roadbed, without rails or crossties.[77] It was to play a major role in the battle of the Wilderness.

The railroad cut provided a perfect opportunity for Robert E. Lee to employ one of his well known flanking maneuvers. Lee realized that any offensive operation would have to be conducted under Longstreet's direction. The path was available, but which troops should be used?

General Longstreet called his chief of staff, Colonel Moxley Sorrel, to his side. Instructions were to the point. Sorrel would lead a strike force around the Union left flank. The party would contain four brigades. From left to right, the graycoats were the troops under William Wofford, Billy Mahone and Tige Anderson. John Stone's brigade would be held in reserve.[78]

The graycoats attacked at 11:00 A.M.[79] The result was more than Longstreet could have envisioned. Sorrel led his men forward, rolling up Hancock's unprotected left flank. At the same time, Kershaw redoubled his efforts in front of the Federals. The Union left collapsed, falling back all the way to the Brock Road.[80] Resistance to the explosive

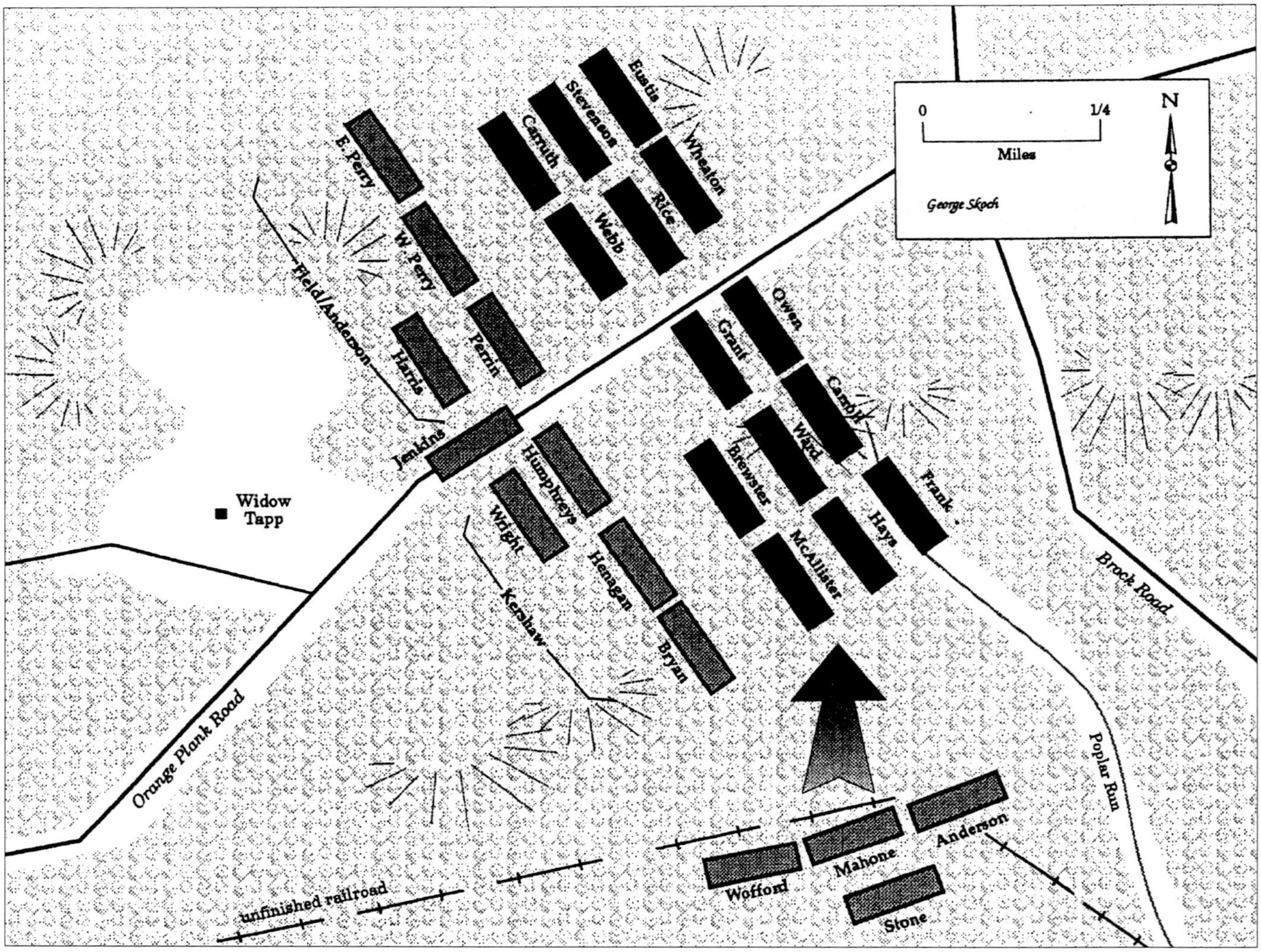

Longstreet's flank attack on May 6, 1864, at 11 A.M. Map by George Skoch.

attack was nonexistent. As Hancock conceded to Longstreet after the war, "You rolled me up like a wet blanket."[81]

To compound the difficulties for the Yankees, Longstreet then hurled General Field's division into the remnants of Wadsworth's command. North of the Orange Plank Road, the Confederates were forcing the Federals to retreat. Valiantly attempting to rally his troops, a bullet ripped through the back of the Union general's head. James Wadsworth would die two days later in a Confederate hospital.[82] The maneuver on the Confederate left was a complete success. As Hancock tried to adjust his lines to meet the attack on his flank, his men were assaulted in front. Rebels were everywhere.[83] It seemed as if nothing could stop the swarm of graycoats. However, fate was about to intervene, saving Hancock from destruction.

General Micah Jenkins commanded a seasoned brigade of South Carolinians in Field's division. Thus far, his Confederates had not played a large part in the action. However, with Hancock in disarray, Longstreet wanted Jenkins to thrust forward with his troops. With a vigorous assault, Jenkins could reclaim possession of the Brock Road intersection, slicing the enemy in two.[84]

The men from the Palmetto State understood their mission. Strutting forward, they wore brand new uniforms, made of a cloth so dark blue that they almost looked black.[85] Both Jenkins and Longstreet were confident that victory was in their grasp.

On Longstreet's right, General Mahone's Virginians were driving their way through the underbrush, forcing the Federals back. Suddenly, shots rang out. Mahone's men had mistaken the dark uniforms for those of the enemy. A shower of bullets whined through the clearing. Joe Kershaw screamed "Friends!" in an attempt to prevent a catastrophe. It was too late. A ball ripped through Jenkins' skull. He would die a few hours later. Another missile hit Longstreet in the neck. Blood spurted profusely as he tried to dismount. Lee's war horse had not been killed, but the wound was a grave one.[86]

General Field assumed command, but he was not familiar with all of the details of the flank attack, and was not sure of the position of Kershaw's Confederates. Speed was critical to the Confederate effort, but the rebels would have to stop to reform their lines. This delay saved Grant's left flank, and allowed Hancock to escape disaster.

Hancock pulled back to the Brock Road, but Robert E. Lee would not give up the initiative. Around 4:15 P.M.,[87] the Southerners attacked again. However, by this time the Federals had been able to construct strong fortifications, and the rebels were unable to pierce the Union defenses. At close range, Federal artillery was able to hold back the charging Southerners. The Federal left was at last secure.

While James Longstreet provided the Confederacy with a golden opportunity on the 6th of May, it was not the only chance General Lee had to rout the enemy. General Grant made another horrendous mistake that day, this time on the other end of the battlefield.

Confederate General John B. Gordon was one of the finest combat officers in either army.[88] On the morning of May 6, his Georgians were stationed on the far left of Ewell's command. Scouting the enemy defenses, he happened upon the opportunity of a lifetime.[89]

The far right of the Union formation was unsupported, or "in the air" in military terms. Gordon could visualize a powerful flanking movement, attacking the unsuspecting bluecoats in the right flank. He must persuade his superiors to allow him to attack.

Gordon met with both Ewell and his division commander, General Jubal Early. Early, in particular, was unimpressed. He felt Gordon must be mistaken. For his part, Gordon knew that Sedgwick's flank was unsecured. Ewell was unsure of the situation, but in the face of Early's strong objection's, the plan was overruled.[90]

A second chance for the South had evaporated. Evidence proved Gordon to be correct. Later in the day, General Lee rode up to see the Confederate left flank, and concluded that an attack might still be possible. An attempt to outflank the Federals was made, but the organization was poor, and by this time the Yankees had been able to bring up reinforcements. The Confederate effort stalled in the deep woods. A second assault was made as well, but it too was easily repulsed.[91]

The result of the battle of the Wilderness was that General Lee had foiled Grant's purpose. The Confederates had blocked the Union thrust southward, and many lives were lost in a contest that was essentially a draw, although the casualties were heavily in favor of the Confederacy.

The two days of fighting had been bloody indeed. The Union Army of the Potomac had lost 2,246 men killed, 12,037 wounded and 3,383 captured or missing, for a total of 17,666. The Army of Northern Virginia did not file completed reports, but had lost approximately 7,600 men at the Wilderness.[92]

During the night, Grant made the decision to get out of the Wilderness. The entire Army of the Potomac would continue the campaign toward Richmond. The Confederates had blocked the Union path, but the struggle had not ended. In less than two weeks, Grant would meet Lee again at the village of Spotsylvania.

May 5, 1864–April 9, 1865
BERMUDA HUNDRED

P. G. T. Beauregard (CSA) — B. F. Butler (USA)

Bermuda Hundred is a narrow projection of land located between the James and the Appomattox Rivers, about 15 miles[1] south of Richmond. The winding course of the James River created a bottleneck, with water on each side.

The Union forces were led by General Benjamin F. Butler, a political appointee from Massachusetts. On May 5, the Union Army of the James arrived at the Bermuda Hundred plantation. General Butler had 39,000 men[2] under his command. Butler was ordered to cooperate with other Union forces in a general assault on Richmond. The opposing graycoats were commanded by General P. G. T. Beauregard, who would have 30,000 Confederates at his disposal.[3]

On May 6 the Federals began moving west. A base of operations was constructed along the narrowest point of the peninsula. For the next several days minor skirmishes erupted along the trenches, as each side probed for an opening in the enemy lines.[4]

On May 12, Butler moved his troops north. His objective was Drewry's Bluff, some seven miles downriver from Richmond. By the 13th the Yankees had approached their target, and had forced the rebels back into their trenches.

The Confederates organized their defenses into three divisions, led by Robert Ransom, Robert Hoke and Alfred Colquitt.[5] General Beauregard was determined to drive the Northerners back from the outskirts of the Confederate capital.

Plans were made for a counterattack on the evening of the 15th. General Ransom was ordered to assault the Federal right flank at first light.[6] Two lines of attack were to be formed. On Ransom's right, General Hoke was to lead his men forward at the same time. He would also have two rows of Confederates. Colquitt's division would be used in a reserve role.[7]

At 4:45 A.M. on May 16, Robert Ransom moved

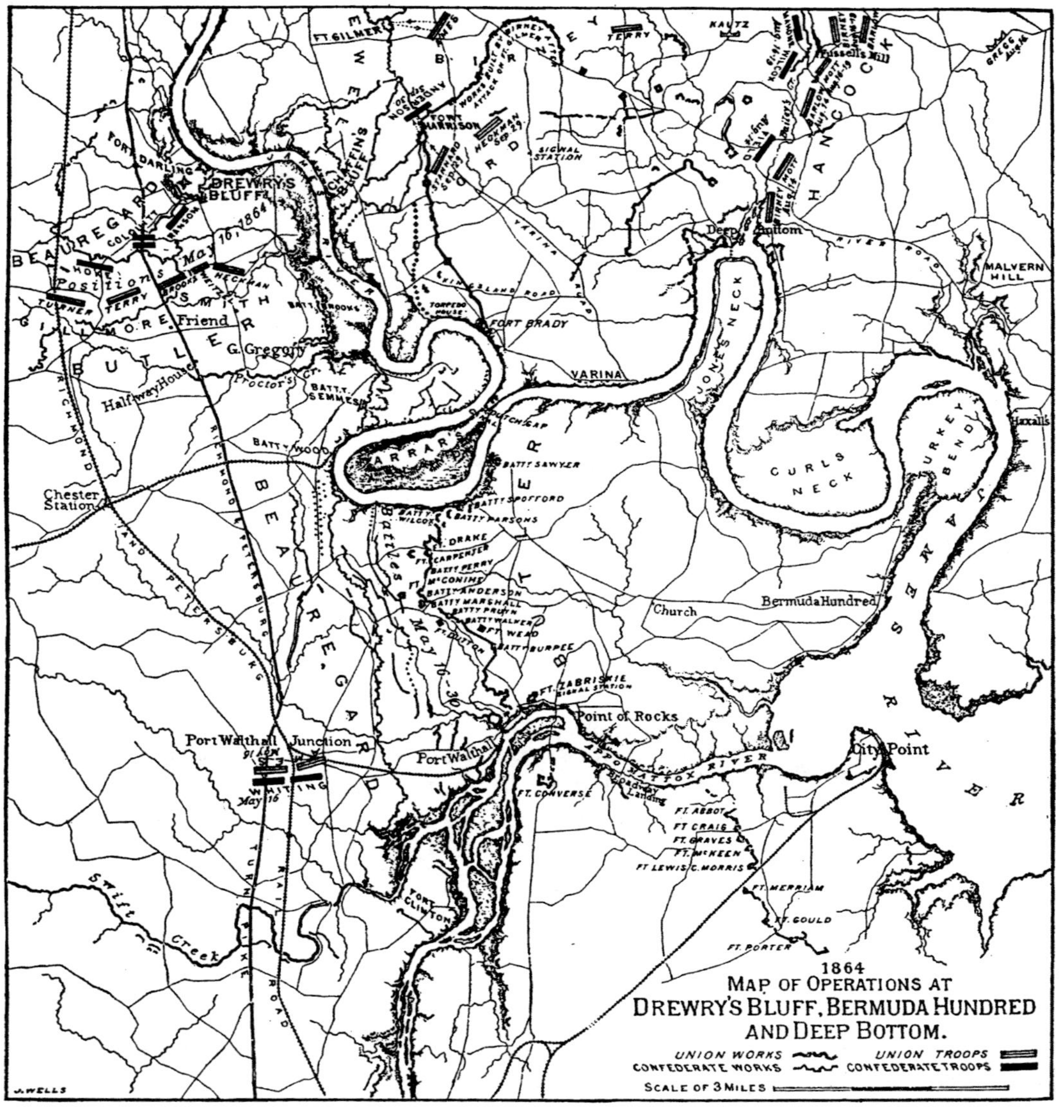

Operations at Drewry's Bluff, Bermuda Hundred and Deep Bottom, 1864.

of the James. This led the disgusted Union General Ulysses S. Grant to comment that Butler had been "bottled up."[12]

The casualties at Drewry's Bluff were heavily in favor of the Confederates. The rebels had lost 2,506 men, while the Union had lost 4,160. In addition, the Confederates had saved the southern and western approaches to Richmond, while a relatively small force under Beauregard had sealed up the entire Army of the James.[13]

In reality, Beauregard's victory was even more impressive. The Confederate forces prevented General Butler from reinforcing General Grant during the siege of Petersburg, and the rebels only left their works in front of Bermuda Hundred when Petersburg surrendered late in the war.[14]

forward through a dense fog, which covered the field.[8] At 6:30 A.M., Colquitt's troops came up to add power to the attack. However, as ammunition ran low, the action on the left died down, and the combat drifted to the right.[9]

Beauregard shifted troops from Hoke's right over to his left. Union resistance was very stubborn, and a counterattack by the Federals stopped the Southern advance. By 10:00 A.M., there was little energy left in the Confederate offensive,[10] and Butler began to withdraw back into his entrenchments.[11]

The Confederate troops had dominated the Federals, pushing the enemy back into a very narrow strip of land with the James River on both sides of them, as well as behind them. General Beauregard placed his soldiers in front of Butler's men, leaving no escape for the Union Army

May 7–19, 1864
THE SPOTSYLVANIA CAMPAIGN

R. E. Lee (CSA)	U. S. Grant (USA)

Following the battle of the Wilderness earlier in May,[1] the Union forces continued their attempt to move around the Confederate right. The ultimate goal was the capture of Richmond, but Robert E. Lee did not intend to allow the enemy to march into the capital of the Confederacy.

On May 7, General Grant's Army of the Potomac began to move.[2] The bluecoats headed southeast, in the direction of Spotsylvania. The next action would occur only 12 miles from the Wilderness.[2a]

General Lee believed that the enemy would move southeast, and it was fortunate that Lee had anticipated the intentions of his adversary. Confederate General Richard H. Anderson and the First Corps[2b] were ordered to march at once. It was imperative that the graycoats keep the enemy away from the outskirts of Richmond.

The race was close, but on May 8 General Anderson emerged victorious. The security of Spotsylvania for the Confederacy was perhaps Richard Anderson's finest hour.[3] Confederate cavalry under Fitzhugh Lee had delayed the Union infantry just long enough to allow the rebels to win the contest.[4]

Spotsylvania lies on a ridge between the Po and Ny Rivers, two of the small streams which flow into the Mattapony River. From a military standpoint, the area is well suited to defense, because the rivers are deep and difficult to cross. The banks are very steep, and are bordered by dense woods.[5]

Around 8:00 A.M.,[6]a Federal division under John C. Robinson took up a position to the north of Spotsylvania. Confederates opened fire, and General Robinson was wounded. Simon Griffin led his troops forward to the right of Robinson's men, but the Yankees were unable to hold their line, gradually falling back.[7]

In order to defend Spotsylvania, General Lee constructed a rude triangle, the top of which pointed north. Anderson, with the First Corps, held the left. Richard S. Ewell, in command of the Second Corps, occupied the center, while Jubal Early and the Third Corps manned the right of the formation, closest to the town itself. The distance between the troops at the base of the triangle was approximately three miles.[8]

As of May 9, the Federals were aligned in an arc opposite the Confederates. Ambrose E. Burnside and the IX Corps were in front of Jubal Early. To Burnside's right was the VI Corps under John Sedgwick, followed by Gouverneur K. Warren's V Corps. The far right of the Union formation was held by the II Corps under Winfield S. Hancock.[9]

May 9 was relatively uneventful. General Grant probed for a weakness in the Confederate position, but found no opening to exploit. General Lee fortified the Confederate defenses, realizing that the bluecoats intended to attack.

A constant danger to both sides in the Civil War was the presence of highly skilled sharpshooters. On this day, a Confederate sniper took aim and killed General Sedgwick. He was one of the most beloved officers in the Union army, known fondly as "Uncle John" to his men. He would be sorely missed. Command of the VI Corps went to General Horatio G. Wright.[10]

The Federal troops continued to extend their lines, hoping to move around Anderson's left flank. General Lee directed Jubal Early to move two of his divisions from the Confederate right over to the left. This would give Anderson's flank greater strength, and prevent any collapse on that side.[11]

The far left of the Southern defense was secure, but the entire formation was not. On May 10, Union Colonel Emory Upton found a weak spot.

Facing northwest, Robert Rodes' division held a vulnerable position in the Confederate center. General Ewell's graycoats had dubbed this part of the battlefield the "Mule Shoe," due to its irregular configuration. The area was only half a mile wide, but was almost one mile long. Colonel Upton formed four lines for the assault.[12]

Around 6:00 P.M., Federal cannon rained down upon the Confederates. Shortly thereafter the artillery ceased firing, and Upton's troops charged forward. The Georgians led by George Doles, along with the North Carolinians under Junius Daniel and S. D. Ramseur, felt the weight of the attack.[13]

The momentum of the charge had pierced the Confederate lines. Despite the gallantry of Upton's charge, his Yankees received no assistance. General Lee, however, had marshaled all of the Confederate troops he could find to stop the wave of blue which was pouring through General Rodes's division. Confederate artillery opened fire with deadly effect. Reinforcements slammed into the onrushing Federals. Slowly but surely, Upton was forced to withdraw.[14]

The temporary success of Upton's charge was not lost on Ulysses S. Grant. The commander of the Union forces believed that with a more concerted effort, the Confederate lines would surely break.

May 11 was spent getting the Union troops in the proper position for a massive assault. The Federals wrapped their men around Lee's formation. Warren's V Corps was on the Union right. To his left came Wright's men, with Hancock's soldiers opposite the center of the Confederate entrenchments. Burnside still held his IX Corps on the far left of the Union formation.[15] While the IX Corps clearly intended to attack on the 12th of May, it was obvious that the main Union thrust would come again on the Confederate left and center. Anderson and Ewell would have to be ready.

At 4:35 A.M.[16] on May 12, the Federal II Corps struck the Confederate center with ferocious intensity. Hancock's troops attacked the graycoats under Edward "Old Allegheny" Johnson, and the Southern lines broke.[17]

Johnson commanded the ground which would be the scene of a bitterly contested struggle. Facing northwest,

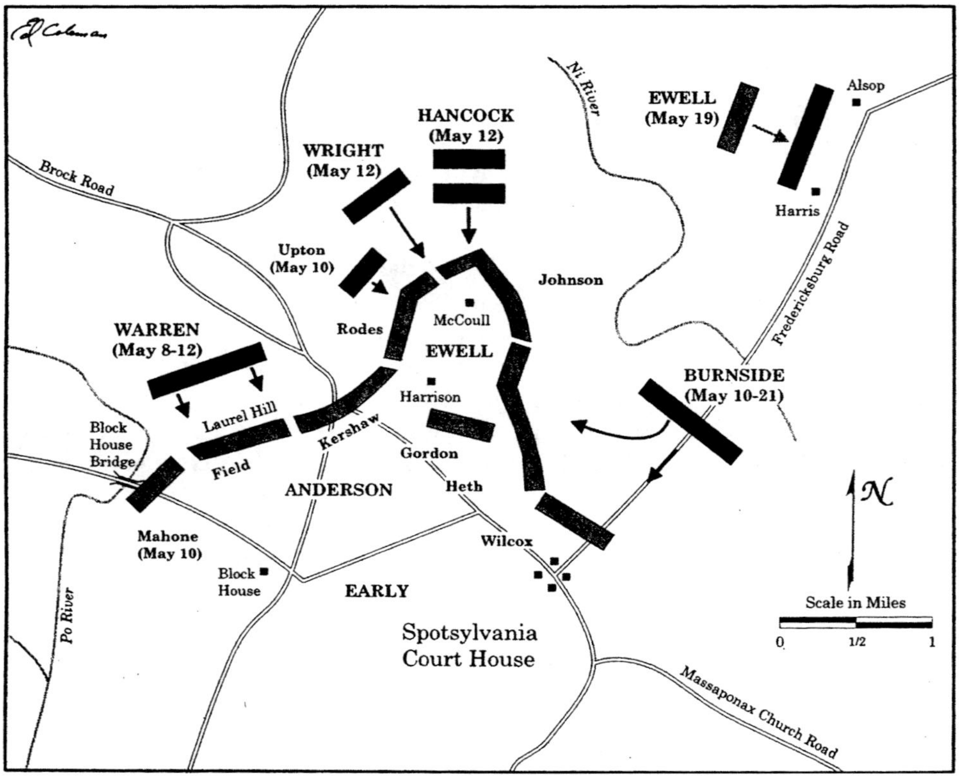

Spotsylvania Courthouse. Map by Ed P. Coleman.

this narrow strip of the "Mule Shoe" would come to be known as "Bloody Angle." Noted historian Bruce Catton called this combat "the most vicious struggle of the Civil War."[18]

As the Yankees poured over the breastworks, they captured 20 cannon, two general officers[19] and almost 4,000 men.[20] The Confederate lines had been split in two. Disaster loomed as Hancock's forces lunged forward.

Robert E. Lee refused to panic. Calmly he moved the troops under John B. Gordon into the breach. Vicious hand-to-hand fighting ensued. Flushed with success, the Yankees had lost some of their organization. Gordon's counterattack crushed the mob of bluecoats, forcing the enemy back. The two sides were so close that there was no time to load a rifle. Rocks, fists, and rifle butts became the weapons of this bitter conflict. Artillery blasted at close range, tearing huge gaps in the lines of the Union infantry.[21] By 7:00 A.M., the thrust in Hancock's sector had been checked.[22]

General Grant was not about to call off the attack. He decided to continue pounding the Confederates with a series of assaults. To Hancock's right, the two Federal corps under Wright and Warren made their way forward. Wright joined Hancock in the assault at the "Bloody Angle," and Warren struck the Confederate left, but was repulsed. Burnside attacked General Lee's right, but he too met with failure.[23]

Casualties at Spotsylvania were severe for both sides. The Union Army of the Potomac lost 2,725 men killed, 13,416 wounded, and 2,258 captured or missing, for a total of 18,399.[24] The Confederate losses were not reported, but have been estimated at approximately 10,000 total casualties.[25]

After the hotly contested action on Thursday, May 12, both sides tried to reorganize their forces. Rain came down in torrents,[26] and the survivors gained what rest they could. General Lee put together a new defensive line, running across the base of his old triangle.[27] He would await Grant's next move.

On May 17, General Grant resumed offensive operations.[28] He knew that Lee had shifted Anderson's troops to the Confederate right; this meant that Ewell now held the left flank. Grant decided to attack him on the 18th of May with Hancock's and Wright's Corps.

The bluecoats moved back to the Mule Shoe. Grant had sent some 22,000 soldiers against Ewell's 6,000 men.[29] The Union II and VI Corps began the advance at dawn, but the Confederates had felled trees as obstructions, and their position would be difficult to assault. It was not until 8:00 A.M. that Ewell's Corps observed the enemy in front of them.[30]

The Northern troops moved forward, and they were greeted by 29 Confederate artillery pieces.[31] The cannon tore huge gaps in the Union lines and Ewell's infantry was not needed as the Federals retreated in the face of the guns. By 10:00 A.M., Hancock called off the attack.[31a] Casualties in the brief action were heavily in favor of the Confederates. General Ewell had lost fewer than 30 men, while inflicting over 500 losses on the Federals.[32]

After darkness covered the field, Hancock and Wright withdrew. However, Lee was still unsure of the location of Grant's right flank. Accordingly, Ewell took his corps forward to undertake a reconnaissance.[33]

Late in the afternoon on May 19, Ewell crossed the Ny River and approached the Fredericksburg Road. Federal troops appeared on the Harris Farm,[34] located on the west side of the thoroughfare. General Ewell deployed his troops. Rodes's division took the right side; Gordon's command was on the left. The Federals belonged to General Robert O. Tyler's brigade.[35]

General S. D. Ramseur led his graycoats forward on the Confederate right. His initial success drove the Yankees back, but he realized that both of his flanks were in danger of being enveloped, and the North Carolinian was forced to retreat. After falling back some 200 yards, he reformed his lines. Tyler's Federals continued to press their advantage, but the Confederates were able to bring forward additional reinforcements.[36]

On Ramseur's left, John Pegram's Brigade[37] came up in support. In addition, cavalry under Wade Hampton rushed to the scene. Hampton had with him some artillery, and the Yankees were held until nightfall.[38]

Richard Ewell had discovered the right flank of the Union army, but not without a heavy cost. The Confederates had lost 900 men, while the bluecoats suffered 1,500 casualties.[39]

On May 19, the Army of the Potomac was still in place, but by the 21st the bluecoats were on the move again. Ulysses S. Grant was still heading toward Richmond. Robert E. Lee was still determined to stop him. The soldiers would take up new positions, and another battle would soon take place on the North Anna River.

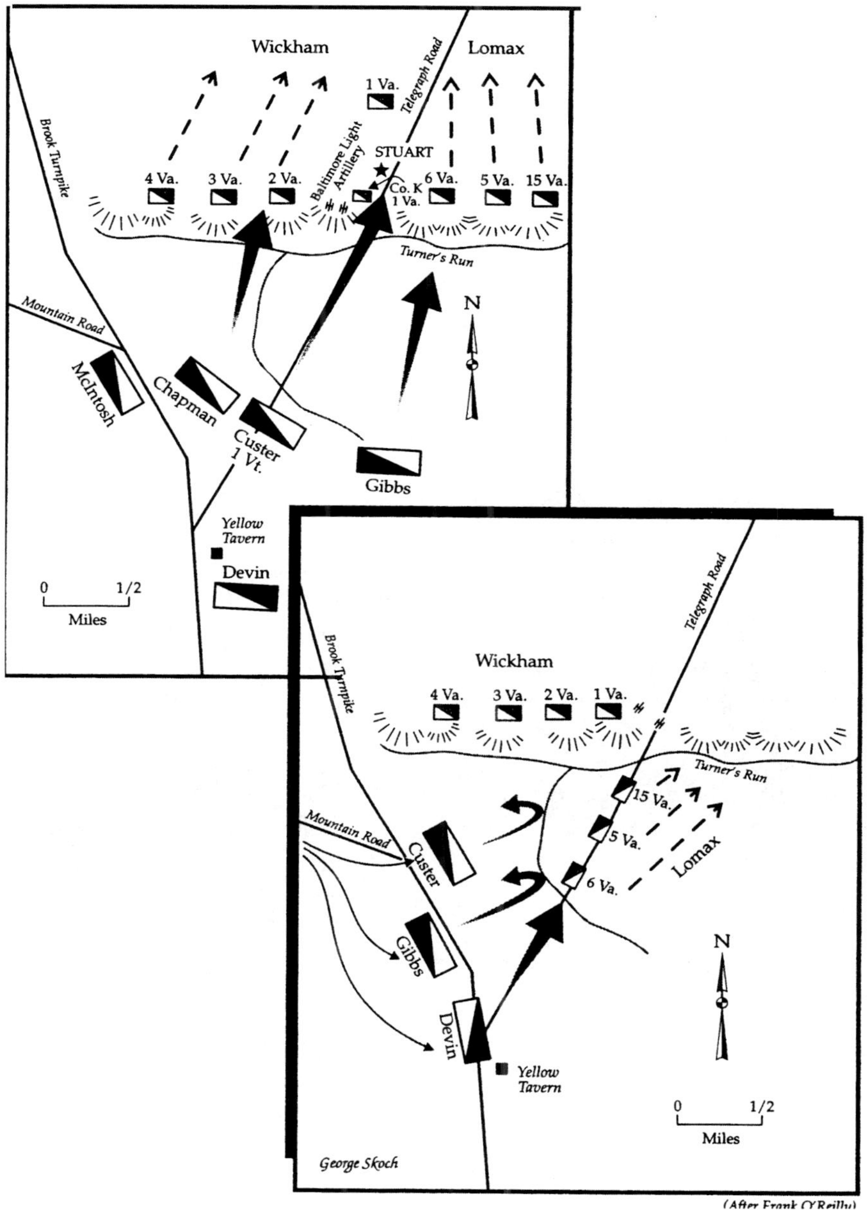

Sheridan's attack against Stuart at Yellow Tavern on May 11. Lower panel, morning action; upper panel, afternoon action. Map by George Skoch.

May 11, 1864
Yellow Tavern

J. E. B. Stuart (CSA)	P. H. Sheridan (USA)

General U. S. Grant had brought a new man to command his mounted troops: General Philip H. "Little Phil" Sheridan. Riding from Spotsylvania toward the North Anna River, the Union cavalry was moving southward in great strength, heading in the direction of Beaver Dam Station.[1]

J. E. B. Stuart led approximately 4,500 horsemen in pursuit of the Federals.[2] He knew that the enemy greatly outnumbered his band of Confederates, and it seemed like a very large force for a small raid. Sheridan might be headed to Richmond.[3]

As the rebels crossed Davenport's Bridge in the early morning of May 10, they continued south in the direction of Beaver Dam Station. They were horrified to see the sky on fire, illuminated from the destruction of warehouses. About 915,000 rations of meat and 504,000 of bread went up in flames. "Little Phil" and his men had dealt the Confederacy a punishing blow.[4] Food was very dear to General Lee's Army of Northern Virginia, and a loss of this magnitude was painful indeed.

There was nothing to do but move forward. By the end of the day, the Yankees were only 19 miles from the capital.[5] With a swift ride, Stuart reasoned, he could overtake the Federals while the garrison inside the city defended Richmond.[6]

About 8:00 A.M. on May 11, with no bluecoats in sight, the Confederate cavalry arrived at a place called Yellow Tavern.[7] It was an old abandoned stagecoach inn, about six miles north of Richmond.[8] Although small, it was important, as the Mountain Road from Louisa and the Telegraph Road from Fredericksburg joined the Brook Turnpike there, and continued on to Richmond.[9] If the Yankees were ahead of Stuart's men, they must have used one of these two roads. A quick examination of the local natives revealed that the Federals had not yet arrived.[10]

By approximately 11:00 A.M.,[11] the Federal troops were taking their positions. J. E. B. Stuart ordered General Williams Wickham to the right, with most of his men at a right angle to the Telegraph Road. On the left, Lunsford Lomax extended his line south along the road. The Confederates would have to stop Sheridan's force of seven brigades[12] with only two of their own.[13]

Presently the Union cavalry came into view. The Confederate left was the most vulnerable point of the Southern defenses. Unsupported, it was "in the air," and General Stuart rode over to encourage his men. "Steady, men, steady; give it to them!"[14] His calm voice had a reassuring effect on his troopers. The onrushing 5th Michigan cavalry rode swiftly past the general and his small band of rebels. Withdrawing his pistol from its holster, he began to fire at the Yankees. It seemed as if the Federals had disappeared when suddenly Stuart felt a shock and his body recoiled. His head dropped, and his hat fell to the ground.[15]

Crowding around their fallen leader, anxiety spread across the faces of the graycoats. He had been shot through the abdomen, and the prognosis was hopeless.[16] He was taken to Richmond in an ambulance. Jefferson Davis paid his respects to the dying man. At 7:38 P.M. on May 12, 1864, J. E. B. Stuart passed away.[17] He was not yet 32 years old.[18]

Casualties at Yellow Tavern favored the Federals. Total Confederate losses approached 300 men, while the Union lost 143 troopers, mainly in George A. Custer's Michigan brigade.[19] At first glance, it would appear that the bluecoats had won a decisive cavalry battle. However, General Sheridan's battle at Yellow Tavern had left the Union forces at Spotsylvania without their cavalry. Many Federal soldiers would fall in May due to General Grant's inability to locate his adversary, and make a proper reconnaissance.[20]

The Federals moved down the Brook Turnpike toward Richmond. However, the battle at Yellow Tavern had given the capital's defenses time to mobilize, and the Yankees turned away to the east.[21] The gallant stand by the Confederate cavalry had saved Richmond, but the price was a steep one indeed. J. E. B. Stuart's death had taken the finest eyes and ears from the Army of Northern Virgina. Robert E. Lee would have to reorganize once again.

May 15, 1864
New Market

J. C. Breckinridge (CSA)	F. Sigel (USA)

On the 8th of March, 1864,[1] President Lincoln appointed General Franz Sigel to the command of the Department of West Virginia. Of vital importance to the President was the protection of the Baltimore & Ohio Railroad. This line was critical to the United States government as it was the shortest link between Washington and Cincinnati.

Federal troops were sent to several different areas. There were numerous soldiers detailed to safeguard the railroad itself. These men were stationed at various points for a distance of approximately 300 miles[2] and were protectionist in nature. A different, attacking force of some 6,500 men[3] under General Sigel was ordered to move southwest in the Shenandoah Valley. Their target was Staunton, located in the western portion of Virginia.

Control of the valley played a prominent role in the strategy of both armies.[4] It contained some of the richest farmland in Virginia. If the Federal troops held the valley, they could cause the Confederates great hardship. On the other hand, if the graycoats maintained their grasp of the area, General Robert E. Lee would not only have easy access to a bountiful food supply, but Southern troops could interrupt Union traffic on the Baltimore & Ohio as well.

General Lee was determined to save the valley for the Confederacy. He sent General John C. Breckinridge to the Shenandoah with a force numbering just under 5,000 men.[5] The Kentuckian was aided in his search for troops by the somewhat deliberate march of General Sigel.

On May 2, Sigel's bluecoats left Winchester, at the

northern end of the valley, and headed south along the Valley Pike. By the 14th of the month they had reached Mount Jackson. They had covered 43 miles in 12 days, moving at a most leisurely pace.[6] The march was largely uneventful, though there was some minor skirmishing with 1,500[7] Confederate cavalry troops, under the command of General John D. Imboden.

The village of New Market was seven miles beyond Mount Jackson.[8] At daybreak on May 15,[9] the Federals moved out. Still facing south, the blue columns halted along the Valley Pike about one mile north of New Market,[10] confronted by the Confederates.

The battle opened with a long-range artillery duel. Breckinridge sent forward two infantry brigades, along with some dismounted cavalry. The horsemen could fight like infantry, and the Southerners pushed the Yankees back about half a mile.[11]

General Sigel took up a position to maximize the Federal strength in artillery. He found a slight rise in the terrain, and placed 17 guns[12] on the elevation, throwing showers of lead into the hard charging Confederates.

However, the Southerners were too determined for Sigel's troops. Inspired by the valiant efforts of the youthful cadets from the Virginia Military Institute, the Union line was finally broken. General Breckinridge had achieved a victory at New Market, and the Federals withdrew to Mount Jackson.

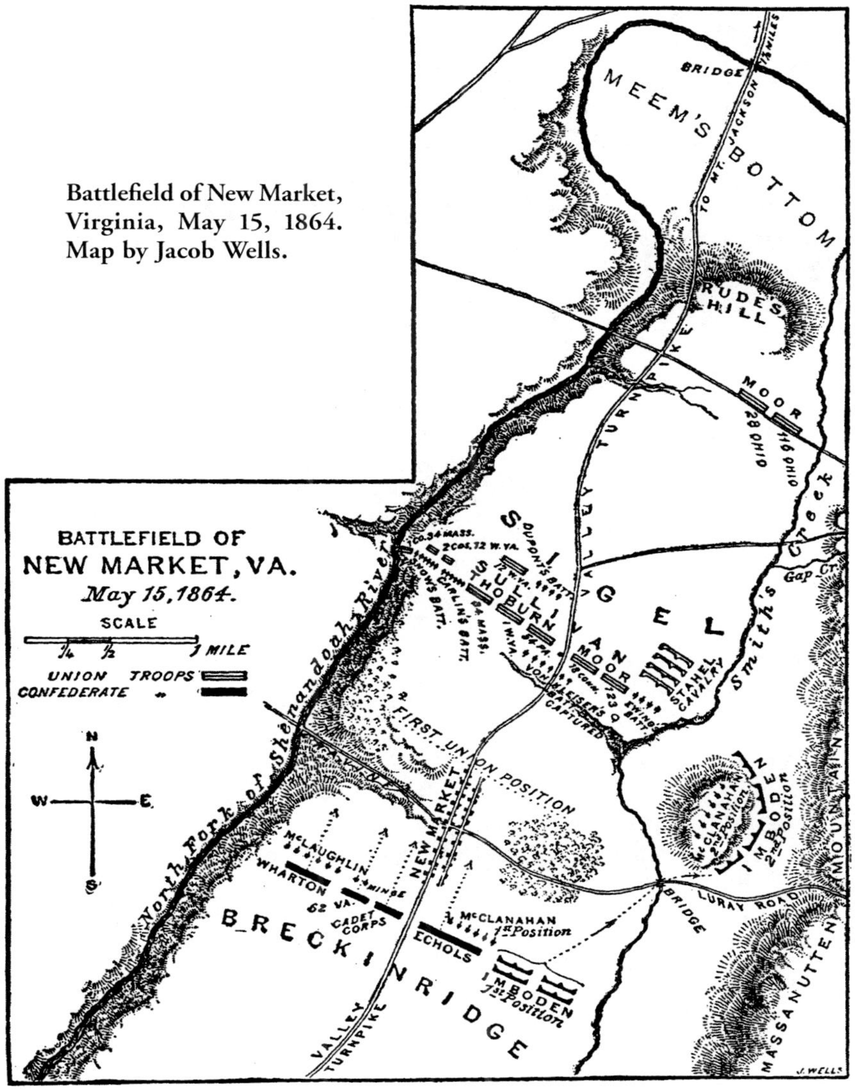

Battlefield of New Market, Virginia, May 15, 1864. Map by Jacob Wells.

Casualties on May 15 favored the Southern side. Sigel had lost 93 men killed, 552 wounded and 186 captured or missing, for a total of 831. The Confederates had 42 soldiers die in battle, 522 wounded and 13 missing, for a total of 577. The total for the Confederacy include 10 cadets killed or mortally wounded, and 47 others wounded.[13]

By Civil War standards, the action at New Market was not a major battle. Nevertheless, it did have im portant repercussions. General Sigel was relieved from command on May 19, while General Breckinridge and his troops rejoined General Lee. Although the combat this day seemed small to some, the bravery and inspiration provided by the cadets of V.M.I. would never be forgotten.

May 23–26, 1864
North Anna River

R. E. Lee (CSA) — U. S. Grant (USA)

During the month of May, the Federal army began a movement southward from the Rappahannock River in the general direction of Richmond. First at the battle of the Wilderness, then at Spotsylvania, the Confederates under Robert E. Lee turned back the Union assaults.

Strategically, the next important point in the campaign would be Hanover Junction. Some 24 miles north of Richmond and three miles south of the North Anna River[1] where the Virginia Central Railroad and the Richmond, Fredericksburg & Potomac Railroad came together. The Virginia Central brought supplies to the

Confederacy from the Shenandoah Valley, while the R. F. & P. was a major north-south artery.

General Ulysses S. Grant knew that control of Hanover Junction by his Union Army of the Potomac would severely disrupt the operations of the enemy.

Since the action at Spotsylvania on May 19, the two cumbersome bodies of troops had been in a constant race southward. Every man understood that the armies would clash again, and soon.

The Southerners, marching in a slightly more direct route, reached the North Anna first. The wooden bridges over the river were still intact, and guarded by Confederates.

The rebels crossed to the south side of the river, and General Lee decided to make his troop dispositions. The Second Corps, under the leadership of Richard S. Ewell, would be on the right. The First Corps, commanded by Richard H. Anderson, was in the center. The Third Corps, under Ambrose Powell Hill, was expected to arrive shortly.[2]

May 22 passed without the foe in sight, but the Confederate cavalry reported that the enemy was in fact approaching Hanover Junction.[3]

Robert E. Lee hoped that the enemy was coming. Very aggressive by nature, it was his nature to attack. He was hoping to prevent the Yankees from reaching Richmond. He had always been a student of Napoleon Bonaparte, and it seemed as if he remembered the Frenchman's maxim: "manoeuvre incessantly, without submitting to be driven back on the capital which it [one's army] is meant to defend or shut up in an entrenched camp in the rear."[4] Such was his thought process. If the bluecoats would show themselves, General Lee was determined to attack them.

A. P. Hill's Third Corps had made it to the river, and Lee placed Hill's veterans on the Confederate left. This alignment gave the Southerners the ability to protect Richmond and the railroads at the same time. The Confederates could block a frontal attack from the Union army, or strike the Federals if a favorable opportunity arose.[4a]

On the morning of May 23,[5] General Lee made a thorough reconnaissance of the area on the south side of the river, paying particularly close attention to the ground in front of the bridges. About noon,[6] the Federal troops came into view. For the third time in one month, Robert E. Lee had placed his men squarely in the path of the Army of the Potomac.

In the middle of the afternoon, Lee had heard sounds of Union artillery to his left, beyond the ground which General Hill's troops occupied. Yankees were visible, but they were not attempting to cross the North Anna. Lee looked through his field glasses, and determined that this was a mere demonstration. He sent instructions for A. P. Hill to leave his men where they were.[7]

General Lee's suspicions were proved correct. Further downstream, at a place called Jericho Mills, the Union V Corps had forded the water and were advancing. Fortunately, Hill had sent General Cadmus Wilcox into the area to examine the situation. When Wilcox reported his findings, Hill immediately ordered him to return to his division and attack.[8]

Cadmus Wilcox had four brigades under his command. He placed Edward Thomas on the left, Samuel McGowan in the center, and James Lane on the right. Alfred Scales stationed his men behind Thomas.[9] The graycoats were facing northeast, along the railroad tracks of the Virginia Central.

Lane and McGowan had to advance over open ground and down past a small stream before entering dense woods where the enemy was believed to be. On the left, Thomas was already in front of the forest.[10] At 6:00 P.M., Wilcox sent his troops forward.[11] The rebels succeeded in driving the enemy, but the Yankees were able to regroup without having to recross the North Anna River.[12] The Yankees retired to the safety of their artillery, and the Union guns prevented any further advance.

Overall, this was not a well-managed affair from the Southern point of view. Wilcox had lost 642 men,[13] yet had failed to drive the V Corps back across the river. A. P. Hill's performance exasperated General Lee. Not only had casualties been sustained, but the Federals had disrupted traffic on the Virginia Central Railroad as well.[14]

About 7:15 P.M.,[15] the Army of the Potomac appeared in great force on the other flank. They surged forward opposite the bridgeheads and were able to capture between 100 and 200 Confederates.[16] Robert E. Lee was now faced with a serious dilemma. The enemy had been able to cross the North Anna with relative ease on both the left and the right. On both flanks the Federals held the high ground, which was on the north side of the water.[17] The Union artillery could take command of the North Anna River. He must find a solution.

In the center, near Ox Ford, the hills rose highest on the southern side. The Confederates under General Anderson held this area, and could control the field of battle. In an attempt to maximize his advantage, General Lee pulled back Ewell's men from the right. The Confederate right would now be secured by the swampy ground in the vicinity of Hanover Junction. On the left, A. P. Hill also shifted his troops, with his left anchored on a meandering stream called Little River.[18]

The Confederates could now move reinforcements easily between Hill and Ewell. Anderson's First Corps remained the apex of the formation, with his graycoats staring straight at Ox Ford.[19] With the current arrangement of the Southern forces, General Grant would have to divide his army in order to assail the entire Confederate line. The trap was set. Would the enemy walk in to it?

General Lee had received good news in the form of additional troops. George Pickett's division, a brigade under Robert Hoke, and two brigades belonging to John Breckinridge comprised a force of some 8,500 men, and they had arrived.[20]

On May 24, fate intervened once again. General Lee was stricken with a violent intestinal illness. He was worse on the 25th, and though he was severely incapacitated, he lacked enough confidence in his subordinates to relinquish command of the Army of Northern Virginia. He must simply persevere.[21]

Grant made one attempt to unify the Union right and the left, but Anderson's troops easily repulsed the Union efforts.[22]

Both sides were busy fortifying their positions. It did not appear that Lee would receive an attack opposite Hill's men. The Federals were too numerous to be attacked, and too cautious to make an attack themselves. May 25 passed quietly with only a few demonstrations.[23]

The next day was spent with each army probing the opponent, searching for a weakness in the enemy lines. No such opportunity presented itself. When dawn broke on May 27, the Confederates looked out into the enemy trenches and found that the Army of the Potomac had evacuated their trenches.[24]

General Grant had started his bluecoats east on a march to Hanoverton, a small village on the Pamunkey River. He would continue the quest to move around the Confederate right, shifting the Federals ever closer to Richmond.

In one sense, General Lee had failed. The Confederates had been unable to bring the Army of the Potomac into a major battle. However, the action on the North Anna River was not without its benefits to the Southern cause. The Virginia Central Railroad was still open, bringing food and supplies from the Shenandoah Valley. It forced General Grant to abandon his assault on Richmond from the north, shifting his troops in an easterly direction. Third, and perhaps most significant, was the delay caused in Federal operations.[25]

In analyzing the results of the action at the North Anna River, noted historian Douglas Southall Freeman wrote: "no achievement of the entire campaign from the Rapidan to the James meant more in prolonging the struggle."[26]

The effects of Lee's maneuvers were indeed profound. Despite the advantage of a large numerical superiority, the Union Army of the Potomac discovered that this bloody conflict was far from over.

May 27–30, 1864
Totopotomy Creek (Haw's Shop)

R. E. Lee (CSA)	U. S. Grant (USA)

The Federal Army of the Potomac had spent the month of May moving south. General Ulysses S. Grant had started the month in the Wilderness, located on the Rappahannock River in central Virginia. The Union plan of attack was to continue shifting to their left, around the Confederate right flank. General Grant believed that this strategy would eventually bring the bluecoats to the gates of Richmond, and the Confederate capital must capitulate.

Progress had not been as rapid as Grant would have liked, but on May 27 the Confederates abandoned their line of defense along the North Anna River.[1]

By the 28th of May, the Federal troops had taken a new position, near Totopotomy Creek, a small tributary of the Pamunkey River. Grant's troops faced roughly southwest. Opposing the Union line of advance was Lee's Army of Northern Virginia. He was determined to prevent the capture of the capital of the Confederacy, and continued to shift his forces in order to block the Yankees' path.[2]

The rebels faced northwest,[3] and in between the two armies was a little village named Haw's Shop. The village, which lay only ten miles northeast of Mechanicsville,[4] was where the action would begin.

Still uncertain as to the whereabouts of his adversary, Robert E. Lee dispatched his cavalry in the direction of Haw's Shop. Lee wished to know if the Union cavalry in the area was supported by infantry. The 4th and 5th South Carolina Cavalry were at Lee's disposal, and the 6th South Carolina would arrive shortly. These were fine regiments of horsemen, and were a welcome addition to the Army of Northern Virginia.[5]

On May 29, the graycoats battled the 2nd Federal Cavalry Division for over seven hours.[6] One brigade of Virginians and 1,100 Carolinians held the Yankees to a draw. Most of the fighting was on foot, as the woods were so thick that it was difficult to maneuver on horseback.[7]

Union reinforcements arrived on the scene with General George A. Custer's Brigade of the 1st Division. After some difficulty the Confederates were finally able to break off the action. This reconnaissance made it certain that General Grant had a very large force under his command.[8] The fate of Richmond might soon be decided.

The Federals continued to slide to their left, while Lee changed the position of the Confederate troops to meet every contingency. Grant could maneuver around the Southern right, approaching Richmond from the east, or he could march south down the Telegraph Road and strike the capital from the north. The rebels would have to be ready for either option.[9]

Due to illness,[10] Richard Ewell had relinquished the command of the Confederate Second Corps to his trusted lieutenant, Jubal A. Early. Lee placed the head of Early's Corps at Pole Green Church. The First Corps under Richard Anderson would occupy the center, and A. P. Hill would hold the left flank with the Third Corps. The end of his column would rest near Shady Grove Church. In this manner, Lee would keep the flexibility of movement which was so vital to Confederate operations.[11] But which way would Grant move?

The remainder of the 29th was relatively quiet, but early on the morning of May 30, the bluecoats began to move. Federal troops began to disappear from A. P. Hill's front, and at the same time there were indications of Union soldiers shifting around the Confederate right flank.[12]

With the enemy on the move, General Lee felt that the best course of action would be to strike the Yankees while they were marching from Haw's Shop toward Old Cold Harbor. The assignment fell upon Jubal Early's men.[13]

General Early was eager to attack, and he failed to make a proper reconnaissance before he moved forward. Making matters worse, there was no cooperation with the First Corps. The result was a bloody repulse, and many Confederates lost their lives in this poorly executed assault.[14]

Losses for the Confederacy were not reported in the action around Totopotomy Creek. However, the Federals had 591 men killed, 2,734 wounded and 661 captured or missing, for a total of 3,986 casualties.[15]

The attack by General Early did not change the overall strategy of the Union forces. General Grant would continue to move to his left, seeking to outflank his adversary. In June, the weary participants would head toward Cold Harbor, where Grant ordered a series of attacks against Confederate lines. General Lee and his graycoats would hand the Yankees their bloodiest defeat of the entire war.

June 1–3, 1864
Cold Harbor

R. E. Lee (CSA)	U. S. Grant (USA)

Cold Harbor was the last major battle in the campaign waged by the Union forces in an attempt to capture Richmond. From the Wilderness to Spotsylvania to the action on the North Anna River, the Federal armies under General George G. Meade had continually moved to their left. Each time, the Confederates had reached the battlefield first and blocked the enemy's path.

By May 26 General Ulysses S. Grant, now personally directing the movements of the Army of the Potomac, had shifted histories once again, from the North Anna River to the south. General Lee's graycoats covered the roads between the Federals and Richmond. The only approach still available to the bluecoats led through Cold Harbor.

The next several days were spent by each army reinforcing their lines. The Confederates placed the command of A. P. Hill on their left. Next to him were the men under John C. Breckinridge. Jubal Early's troops anchored the center, with Richard H. Anderson and Robert F. Hoke to his right. On May 31, General Lee received a message from his nephew, Fitzhugh Lee, who was a general in the Confederate cavalry. It looked as if the Federal infantry was on the move again. Apparently there would be a contest to reach Cold Harbor. Robert E. Lee was optimistic, as the rebels would be led by the same man who had outrun Grant in the race for Spotsylvania: General Richard H. Anderson.[1]

Anderson's performance on June 1 was not up to the standards he had set earlier. The Confederates attacked, as Lee had wished, but the leading brigade was hampered by an inexperienced commander who was killed in the early moments of the assault.[2] Without the direction of a leader, the unseasoned troops in the 20th South Carolina gave way, and the remainder of the Southern units were forced to fall back.[3]

General Lee wished to shore up the right side, and he decided to move Breckinridge over to lengthen the Confederate right. Before the Kentuckian could shift his men, an attack developed to his left, which prevented the transfer of any troops. The Federals, however, were easily repulsed. General Breckinridge moved forward a little later, and in a separate attack managed to capture 150[4] prisoners. In a third engagement the cavalry guarding the Confederate left met a Federal advance of horsemen, and drove the Yankees back.[5]

Lee realized that the threat to the Confederate right had not disappeared and he ordered Hoke to extend his lines southward. It was strategically important that the rebels take control of Turkey Hill, but Hoke did not move his men as far as Lee would have liked. Immediately after Hoke began the movement, the Federals attacked north of the Cold Harbor Road. This connected Old Cold Harbor with New Cold Harbor. The enemy pulled back after nightfall, but Anderson and Hoke had become almost separated from the rest of Lee's Army of Northern Virginia.[6]

On June 2 General Lee awaited two developments — the arrival of Breckinridge on the right, and the resumption of the attack against the enemy.[7] Due to poor maps and a guide who was not familiar with the area, Breckinridge was late in arriving.[8] However, Lee reasoned that if Grant kept shifting troops from his right to his left in order to reach Cold Harbor, an opportunity might arise to attack the weakened Union right. General Lee gave General Early discretion to attack the enemy.[9]

Actually, Early did attack with three divisions, but after brushing aside the Federal skirmish line, the Confederates were unable to penetrate the heavy fortifications northwest of Bethesda Church.[10] Around 4:00 P.M., a heavy rain began to fall[11] and continued through the night. It made offensive operations very difficult for both sides. When morning broke, though, the weather was clear, and the rebels braced themselves for the assault they knew was sure to come.

The Army of the Potomac had placed the II Corps under Winfield S. Hancock on their left, Horatio G. Wright of the VI Corps in the center, and W. F. Smith with the XVIII Corps on the Union right.[11a]

The situation for the Confederates was truly desperate. General Lee had absolutely no reserves. If the lines were weakened at all, the Federals could punch through the Southern defenses. If Lee moved troops from the flanks to strengthen the center, the enemy could simply march around him.[12] The rebels must hold on as they were.

At 4:30 A.M. on June 3,[13] the fire of musketry crackled on the Confederate right and then spread all along the line. The bluecoats were coming! Wave after wave of Grant's men assaulted the Southern lines, and by 8:00 General Anderson had counted 14 attacks against the First Corps.[14] Still the Confederates held their ground, and the Yankees realized the futility of the repeated assaults.

By 1:00 P.M., it became obvious that General Grant had abandoned his plan of continuous assaults.[15] That evening, General Lee was able to write a short note to President Jefferson Davis: "Our loss today has been small, and our success, under the blessing of God, all that we could expect."[16]

In reality, Robert E. Lee had understated the day's results. Total casualties for the Confederacy on the 3rd of June had not been more than 1,200 to 1,500, while over 7,000 men[17] from the Army of the Potomac had fallen upon the field in the series of Grant's fruitless charges.

Total losses for the period of June 1 to June 12 also ran heavily in favor of the graycoats. The Union losses totalled 12,737,[17a] while the Confederates suffered some 4,500 casualties.[17b]

Colonel Venable, of Lee's staff, summed up the action at Cold Harbor. It was, he stated, "perhaps the easiest victory ever granted to Confederate arms by the folly of the Federal commanders."[18]

June 5, 1864
PIEDMONT

W. E. Jones (CSA)	D. Hunter (USA)

The Shenandoah Valley was an area of great importance to both sides during the Civil War. For the South, it meant an abundant supply of food, and control of the Baltimore & Ohio Railroad, which was the Union's link from Washington, D.C., to Cincinnati. For the North, while disruption of the agricultural base would bring great hardship to General Lee's Army of Northern Virginia, it was also critical to maintain operations of the railroad.

The armies had been fighting over this section of Virginia throughout the war, but the most recent action had occurred on May 15, at the battle of New Market. The events at Piedmont were set in motion by the Confederate victory there. John C. Breckinridge, the victor for the South, had rejoined General Lee. Union General Franz Sigel had been replaced in the Shenandoah Valley by David Hunter.

The Confederate defense of the Shenandoah was now entrusted to William E. "Grumble" Jones and a force of some 8,500 men.[1] General Jones was responsible for the safety of Staunton, Virginia, which was located at the southern end of the Shenandoah Valley. Staunton was important for two reasons. There was a large concentration of warehouses in the town, and it was a stop on the Virginia Central Railroad.[2] Just as the Federal government depended on the Baltimore & Ohio, the Confederacy relied on the Virginia Central.

Authorities in Washington, D.C., had no desire to see New Market repeat itself, and the Federal armies were strengthened accordingly. General George Crook was ordered to move from the Allegheny Mountains into the

Shenandoah and join General Hunter. Together, the Federals numbered almost 20,000 men.[3]

Hunter's bluecoats marched south along the Valley Turnpike until they reached Harrisonburg, where they turned east. Crook's troops would follow. "Grumble" Jones ordered two brigades of cavalry to delay Crook's advance, while he took some 5,000 rebels to block Hunter's route.[4]

On June 5, Hunter's troops came upon the advance pickets guarding Jones' graycoats near Piedmont, a small village seven miles[5] south of Port Republic. At 9:00 A.M.,[6] the Union artillery initiated the action, and one hour later the Federals attacked the Confederate left.[7]

As the rebels gradually retreated, Hunter then assaulted the Confederate right. The battle turned into a series of counterattacks, with neither side gaining much of an advantage.

Outnumbered, the graycoats finally gave way, and defeat turned into a rout. General Jones attempted to rally his men, but was hit by a bullet and killed instantly.[8]

Losses at the battle of Piedmont went in favor of the Union. The graycoats lost some 1,600 soldiers, while Hunter reported 780 casualties.[9]

The next day General Hunter's Yankees began the destruction of Staunton. George Crook's troops followed on June 8. The Shenandoah Valley was now open to Union forces, but Robert E. Lee would not passively watch the destruction of his food supply. Lee ordered General Jubal A. Early into the valley, and hostilities would begin once more.

June 10, 1864
Brice's Cross Roads

N. B. Forrest (CSA)	S. D. Sturgis (USA)

Brice's Cross Roads was an insignificant little spot in Mississippi, but here on June 10, 1864, the Union army was to receive a lesson in cavalry tactics they would not soon forget. General Nathan Bedford Forrest marched his Confederates due south from Booneville on the Wire Road, named for the old telegraph line which went to the city of New Orleans, before railroads were built. Another road running southeast crossed the Wire Road 18 miles south of Booneville and six miles west of the station of Baldwyn. It brought a much larger Union force under the command of General Samuel D. Sturgis. The intersection of these roads was Brice's Cross Roads.[1]

The Confederates were widely scattered, while the Union men were close together. To overcome this disadvantage, General Forrest had to use deception. He took advantage of the densely wooded country, which concealed the small numbers on the Southern side. Forrest then exposed just enough of his force to make the Federals believe that there were Confederate reinforcements close at hand. He preferred to wait for all of his troops before committing to battle.[2]

Nathan B. Forrest was perhaps the finest cavalry commander the Civil War produced.[2a] An unschooled officer,[3] he was simply an outstanding fighter, whose men constituted a mounted attack force. He knew that the Union cavalry would ride ahead of the infantry. The plan of attack was to defeat their horsemen before the infantry could come to the rescue, and by noon on June 10, everything was going in the Southern general's favor.[4]

By 1:00 P.M., the Union cavalry had been turned back on both flanks. As the Federal infantry began to arrive, General Benjamin H. Grierson, leading the mounted forces, asked to have his troopers relieved, stating that they were "exhausted and well-nigh out of ammunition."[5] With the first phase of his plan over, Forrest turned his attention to the infantry.

The Confederate left led the attack. The rebels managed to get around the Union right, which began to disintegrate. About 5:00 P.M., Forrest's men in the center charged forward around the Brice home, his right enveloped the Union left, and the entire Federal line started to fall back. Behind the bluecoats, a large mule train had been brought up, guarded by a brigade of negro soldiers serving in the Union Army. As the front collapsed, this became a mass of confusion. According to General Sturgis, he "now attempted to get hold of the colored brigade ... but before I could do so the troops from all directions came crowding in like an avalanche from the battlefield, and I lost all possible control over them."[6] The Confederate artillery continued to bombard the Federals running for the rear. Horses, wagons, caissons and ambulances had created a jumbled mass of men, all attempting to escape the onrushing Southerners.[7]

The final phase of the battle was the Confederate pursuit. Although the rebels were tempted by the valuable supplies which had been thrown away, they continued after the Yankees until the next morning.[8] Eventually, the exhausted troops of Forrest's command needed rest as well, and the battered bluecoats limped back to Memphis.

The victory was indeed complete, the performance by Forrest superb.[8a] The Confederate loss was 96 men killed and 396 wounded, for a total of 492. General Sturgis reported 223 Union men dead, 394 wounded and 1,623 missing, for a total of 2,240. In addition, he had lost all of his artillery, and large quantities of both firearms and equipment.[9]

Perhaps just as revealing was the perception of the Union general: "yet there is some consolation, in knowing that the army fought nobly while it did fight, and only yielded to overwhelming numbers."[10] Sturgis actually believed he was outnumbered. With only 3,500 cavalry, Forrest had routed 8,000 Union cavalry and infantry.[10a]

On a larger scale, the strategic value to the Confederacy of the result at Brice's Cross Roads was more than just men and equipment. Union reinforcements in Alabama earmarked for General Sherman in Georgia were held where they were due to Forrest's continued presence in the region.[11] His activity in Mississippi, Alabama and Tennessee would continue to haunt the thinking of William T. Sherman as the Union general marched toward Atlanta.[12]

June 15, 1864–April 3, 1865
The Petersburg Campaign

R. E. Lee (CSA)	U. S. Grant (USA)

The stage was set for the siege of Petersburg with the Union defeat at Cold Harbor.[1] During the Spring of 1864 the Union Army of the Potomac tried in vain to move through eastern Virginia. The object of their efforts was the capture of Richmond, the Confederate capital.

General Ulysses S. Grant had taken his troops into battle four times[2] since May, but had yet to emerge victorious against Robert E. Lee. Despite heavy casualties, the Union general pressed on. Grant continued to hammer at the Southern flanks. If Richmond could not be taken by direct assault, perhaps the city could be isolated and forced into submission.

Petersburg, Virginia, lies on the Appomattox River, just south of the James. In addition to being a large city, Petersburg was a railroad center: five different railroads converged there.[2a] If General Grant could take possession of the railroads, Richmond was doomed.

During the second week in June, the Confederate troops were still divided. The James River separated General Lee's Army of Northern Virginia. On the north side of the river, he had just over 20,000 men. On the south side, there were 22,600.[3] Somehow the Southerners must unify their forces.

General Grant's first attack on Petersburg came on June 15. It was to be a combined effort, with the troops from the XVIII Corps under William F. Smith, as well as the II Corps, commanded by Winfield S. Hancock.[4]

Fortunately for General Lee, cooperation on the Northern side was very poor. Both Union corps were slow in moving, and only the XVIII Corps actually attacked. The Federals captured over a mile of trenches, but accomplished little else. By June 17, the Yankees could have overwhelmed the skeleton force of Confederate defenders around Petersburg. The entire Union army was on the field, while most of General Lee's men had not yet arrived.[5] The fate of the Southern railroad center was in grave danger.

A coordinated attack had not been pressed. However, the Federals had assaulted the abandoned fortifications which surrounded the city. For all of the Union effort up to this point, General Grant had managed to lose 11,000 men in four days in order to secure a few earthworks east of the city.[6]

The next day, General Lee arrived in Petersburg. As of Sunday, June 19, the commanding general of the Confederate troops faced four problems as he evaluated the military situation.

The front of battle was 26 miles long. It stretched from White Oak Swamp on the Chickahominy River all the way past Richmond, on the James River, to Petersburg, which lay upon the Appomattox River. The entire portion of this line had to be defended. Second, it was imperative to prevent the Union forces from pinning the graycoats in Richmond. A static siege would be a disaster. Third, General Lee had to protect Richmond from a surprise attack. Finally, the railroads must remain operational. Otherwise, the Federals could starve the Confederates into submission.[7]

The Confederates had constructed an elaborate system of trenches and fortifications protecting the eastern and southern approaches to the city. Consequently, General Grant did not believe that the city could be taken by frontal assault. As a result, a long siege began. It would last over nine months. The Union soldiers began to dig a complicated set of trenches of their own. The intent was to gradually wear down the Confederates, using the Federal advantages in men, food and equipment.

On June 25, the first Union operation began. The Federals started to dig under the enemy. The long tunnel ran 511 feet into the earth, and contained additional side galleries 75 feet in length. It was designed to hold four tons of gunpowder.[8] The Union intent was to blast an opening in the Confederate defenses which would allow Federal troops to rush forward and capture Petersburg.

The work was done by the 48th Pennsylvania Volunteers, a unit comprised mainly of coal miners. The men were ideally suited to this task. Construction was slow, as the army engineers had no enthusiasm for the project, and offered very little help to the Pennsylvanians.[9]

By July 23, weeks of backbreaking labor had come to an end and the tunnel was finished. The gunpowder was to explode in one week. At 3:00 A.M., July 30, the fuse was lit, and the Yankees waited. Nothing happened. Two men crawled into the dark shaft and were able to find the problem. After relighting the fuse, the soldiers scurried back to safety before the mine exploded at 4:45 A.M.[10]

A thunderous explosion rocked the earth, leaving a giant crater in the Confederate lines. The hole was 170 feet long, 60 feet wide and 25 feet deep.[11] Men, cannon, horses and equipment were thrown skyward by the force of the blast.[12]

At last the way was open. Now the bluecoats could pour through the enemy lines and take possession of the city. Or so it seemed. Three divisions of Union troops rushed forward, followed by almost all of another division of colored troops.[13]

Despite the success of the blast itself, the situation changed in a hurry. The graycoats quickly recovered from the shock of the explosion, reformed their lines, and brought both infantry and artillery to the edge of the crater. On the right, two field pieces blasted into the Union ranks. In the center, a North Carolina battery aimed its guns directly into the crater. On the left, four 12-pound Napoleon cannon poured a deadly fire into the Union soldiers as a shower of bullets fell upon the Northerners.[14]

In the middle of the crater, the Yankees realized that they were trapped. Confusion reigned as the Federal troops jammed together. The sight of Negro soldiers in blue uniforms inflamed the Southerners. The Confederates reloaded their weapons as fast as possible, and the first Union attempt against the Petersburg trenches turned into a veritable killing field.

The slaughter in the crater was not the only action on the field. On the Confederate left, General Billy Mahone held a rise in the ground known as Cemetery Hill. Gradually the graycoats pushed the enemy back toward the Yankees still trapped in the crater. At 3:25 P.M.,[15] General Lee was able to report that the battle of the crater had ended.

The Confederates had lost approximately 1,500 men in the struggle on July 30, 278 of whom were either killed or captured when the mine exploded. The Federal troops had lost 4,008 men,[16] but Ulysses S. Grant had no intention of turning back. The bluecoats still had the advantage in numbers. Success lay in the hands of General Grant.

As the Yankees searched for an opening in the Southern armor, the Union troops shifted their attention to the north side of the James River. On the eastern side of the water Chaffin's Bluff overlooks the James. General Charles Field commanded the Southern forces in the area, located just southeast of Richmond.

Field's defenses faced south, from Chaffin's Bluff on the right, all the way to New Market Heights. At this point, the line changed direction. The Confederates extended their defenses, facing east, until the left of Field's position rested upon the Charles City Road.[17]

The line was stretched to the breaking point. On August 16, the Federals moved to within 50 yards of the thin Confederate line. A sudden rush broke the resistance, as two Confederate brigades gave way along the Darbytown Road.[18]

The Federals did not realize that they had taken advantage of the foe, and General Field counterattacked. The grayclad veterans repaired the damage, and a crisis was averted. The action was brief, but once again the Federals had been turned away.The bluecoats chose not to attack on the next day.

General Grant understood that the Confederacy lived by the railroad. The action would move from the Confederate left all the way back to Petersburg.

At 4:00 A.M. on August 18, the Federal V Corps began to advance. Led by General Gouverneur K. Warren, the Northerners were located some 3½ miles south of the Confederate right. The Yankees were opposed by only one brigade of cavalry, and Warren's men easily took possession of the Petersburg & Weldon Railroad.[19]

Both sides hurried reinforcements to the area, as the Union troops assembled around the little town of Globe Tavern. General Warren took a position just north of the village. On the afternoon of August 19, Confederate General Ambrose Powell Hill led his troops forward. At 4:30 P.M. Hill attacked.[20]

Union generals Romney B. Ayres and Samuel W. Crawford received the Confederate onslaught. Hill had brought five infantry divisions and one cavalry division, hurling them against the Yankees. The bluecoats fell back, then regrouped and counterattacked. The Federals were able to recover their lost ground, and the action subsided.[21]

The Federals had 198 men killed, 1,105 wounded and 3,152 missing, or 4,455 total casualties in the fight for the Weldon Railroad, while the graycoats lost approximately 1,600 men. However, the Union forces retained their grip on the railroad itself,[22] dealing a serious blow to the Southern cause.

By August 21, it had become apparent to General Lee that this action had been a failure. However, the rebels were about to receive some welcome news.

Confederate cavalry under General Wade Hampton had been patrolling the area on the Southern right.

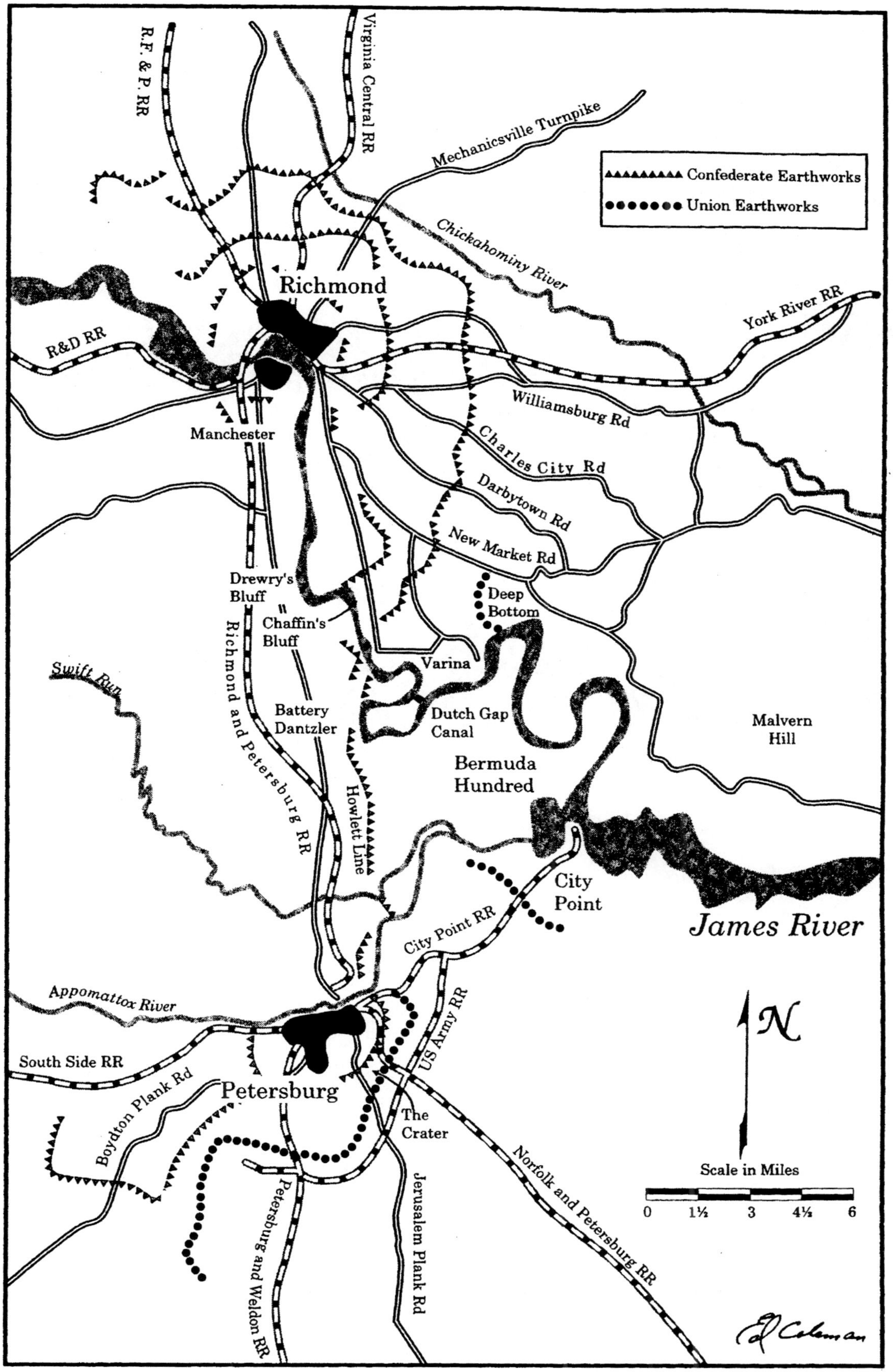

Richmond and Petersburg. Map by Ed P. Coleman.

Approximately 4½ miles south of Globe Tavern,[23] he discovered that the Federals were destroying the railroad tracks in the vicinity of Reams Station.[24]

In Hampton's opinion,[25] the Union position was not a strong one. After consultation with General Lee, a plan of attack was adopted. The Confederates would strike in force.

On August 24, A. P. Hill led 1,750 grayclad troops from their trenches in front of Petersburg. The men marched south until they came to a point about two miles west of Reams Station.[26]

Early the next morning General Hampton and the main body of cavalry rode around the left flank of the enemy. The horsemen intended to distract the Federal infantry, while General Hill moved the remainder of his forces around the enemy right flank. In front of the Confederates was the Union II Corps, under General Hancock. The bluecoats faced west, and were deployed along the tracks of the railroad.[27]

At 2:00 P.M., Hill ordered Cadmus Wilcox to assault the Federal right flank. The II Corps had felled trees for protection, and the attack was repulsed. A second attempt was also in vain. At 5:00 P.M., Confederate artillery bombarded the enemy, and the infantry charged the enemy fortifications.[28]

The fighting was desperate, hand-to-hand combat as the North Carolinians stormed the Federal position. The Federal resistance was stubborn, but gave way under the weight of the charge. General Hancock attempted to send reinforcements from his left to his right, only to have Wade Hampton's men overpower the Union left.[29] Assailed on all fronts, the bluecoats were compelled to fall back.

A. P. Hill had routed the enemy. The Federals lost 2,372 men in the debacle, including some 2,000 men lost as prisoners, while Hill suffered only 720 casualties. In addition, the Confederates captured nine artillery pieces, 3,100 small arms, and 32 horses.[30] The graycoats returned to Petersburg that night, and attacks on the railroad were temporarily suspended.

The next month was very difficult for the Confederates. In siege warfare, the Union applied constant pressure to the rebels. Each day brought new reports of casualties. Skirmishing was brief, but it seemed that there was no respite. Slowly but surely the long thin line was breaking.

General Lee was most concerned about the sector on the north side of the James River[31] which was held by fewer than 2,000 men.[32] On September 28, Lee moved Richard Anderson's troops over the river, strengthening the Confederate defenses. This part of the battlefield was under the command of General Richard S. Ewell.[33]

Grant was continuing to probe with his right toward Richmond, while he attacked with his left at Petersburg. On the morning of the 29th, the style of fighting from the trenches would change in a hurry.[34]

The Federal troops made a surprise attack and Fort Harrison was captured. This enclosure, one of the most important points of the Richmond defenses, was due east of the fortifications at Chaffin's Bluff. The loss of Fort Harrison could open the door to a direct attack on the capital itself.[35]

General Grant had made good use of the superior manpower at his disposal. Upon learning of the movement of Confederate troops across the James River, Grant had devised a plan of attack. Two separate Union forces would be involved. General E. O. C. Ord would lead the XVIII Corps across a pontoon bridge at Aiken's Landing. Once across the James River, the bluecoats would attack the southern portion of the Confederate defenses, in the vicinity of Chaffin's Farm.[36]

At the same time, 18,000 infantry and cavalry under General David B. Birney would cross a different bridge over a mile downstream, at a place called Deep Bottom. Birney's men would march north, then turn west, attacking the easternmost Confederate defenses at New Market Heights.[37]

Moving forward before daylight on September 29, General Ord's men crossed the James.[38] General Ewell had mistakenly believed that the bluecoats would assault Signal Hill, several miles south of Fort Harrison. Accordingly, much of the available Confederate strength was directed to Signal Hill, weakening the defense of Fort Harrison.

By 6:00 A.M.,[39] the fort was in Union hands, although there was a price to pay. Resistance had been stubborn, and almost 600 Yankees[40] fell at the hands of Southern artillery.

Richard S. Ewell was in serious trouble. His graycoats were outnumbered, but perhaps deception could save the capital of the Confederacy from ruin. General Ewell gathered a small force and hurried the men forward, hoping that the enemy would believe that a large number of Confederates held the area. Dense woods masked the true weakness of the Southern position, and General Ord turned most of his men south, in the direction of Chaffin's Bluff.[41]

One brigade continued north, toward Fort Johnson. The Union soldiers were met by Captain Willis J. Dance and the Powhatan Artillery. Along with troops from the Second Georgia Infantry, the rebels turned back the lone Federal brigade, driving the bluecoats back down the Varina Road.[42]

The remainder of the Union XVIII Corps had indeed headed south. They were greeted by Confederate artillery at Fort Hoke and Fort Maury. Ord was wounded, and the

Federal advance lost its power. With the loss of General Ord, the success of the Federal thrust toward Richmond would fall on the shoulders of David Birney.

While Ord was marching toward Fort Harrison,[43] General Birney and the Union X Corps struck the Confederates at New Market Heights. The graycoats under General John Gregg fought valiantly, and the X Corps was repulsed. However, fortune was smiling on the Union.

When General Ord sent his brigade northward to assault Fort Johnson, those Federals were actually between Ewell and Gregg. This development caused John Gregg to believe that the enemy had moved around his right flank.[44]

Accordingly, the order was given by General Gregg to fall back. He moved both of his brigades back to a new position, between Fort Gilmer and Fort Johnson. This would place Gregg's command on Ewell's left flank. The rebels awaited Birney's next move.[45]

Instead of massing his troops for a powerful attack against a weaker opponent, Birney sent his troops forward in a piecemeal, uncoordinated fashion. The Federals were cut to pieces by the strongly fortified Confederates. One battalion of colored troops fighting for the Union took extremely heavy casualties, as the Southerners had no sympathy for a black man in a blue uniform.[46]

With the repulse at Fort Gilmer, any remaining Union hopes of victory soon disappeared. An aggressive fighter by nature, Robert E. Lee was determined to take the offensive.

On September 29, the Confederates in this sector simply did not have enough men to mount an effective counterattack. Both Lee and Ewell understood this all too well. Nevertheless, with additional reinforcements, Lee felt it would be possible to drive the enemy away from Richmond.[47]

By the next afternoon, two divisions of General Anderson's Corps had arrived. Although General Lee had his additional troops, the delay had allowed the Federals to strengthen their position at Fort Harrison. When Lee sent his men forward, the graycoats were handily repulsed.[48]

Both sides had been disappointed in their attempts to win a decisive victory. Gradually, however, the Federal troops were gaining ground. General Grant would continue this long, slow process. By early October, the two sides had settled into a static, trench warfare, with neither side making much progress.

With the Union attempts at Richmond frustrated, Grant decided that the next move would be on his left, in the vicinity of Petersburg.

The object of Grant's plans was the Southside Railroad. If the railroad could be taken, it would be very harmful to his adversary. Winfield S. Hancock, the commander of the Union II Corps, led the advance with two of his divisions. They would assume the left wing of the attack. John G. Parke's IX Corps and Gouverneur K. Warren and the V Corps moved forward in support. Including a division of cavalry under David Gregg, Grant had assigned some 43,000 men to the assault.[49]

By noon on October 27, Hancock and Gregg had reached the Boydton Plank Road near Burgess' Mill.[50] The bluecoats were only 12 miles from Petersburg.[51]

Fortunately for the Confederacy, coordination was poor among the Union forces. Hancock waited on the Union left while Parke and Warren advanced on the right. General Parke moved forward north of a small stream known as Hatcher's Run. He was met by the Confederate division under Cadmus Wilcox, and the Yankees were thoroughly repulsed.[52]

General Warren attacked on the south side of Hatcher's Run, but was unable to work his way through the dense underbrush in the area. Wilcox was able to hold his ground.[53]

On the Union left, Hancock received a counterattack from A. P. Hill. The Confederates had also utilized the cavalry under Wade Hampton, and the Union flank was momentarily turned. However, Hancock was able to organize a charge, and order was restored in the II Corps.[54]

Confederate casualties were not reported, but the operation at Burgess' Mill had cost Grant 166 soldiers killed, 1,028 wounded and 564 missing.[55] In addition, the graycoats had held their ground, and in spite of all the Union efforts, Petersburg still belonged to General Lee.

The action along Burgess' Mill brought a temporary close to the Federal attempts to pierce the thin lines of defense around Petersburg. As the weather grew colder, there could be no doubt that General Grant had failed in his quest to conquer the railroad center south of Richmond.

On the Southern side, the winter brought additional disease, desertion and despair. The troops were pinned in their trenches. The long arms of Ulysses S. Grant stretched around the flanks of the graycoats. Sickness and hunger were working against the Confederate morale. Occasional battle casualties from static warfare further thinned the ranks. As the winter months passed, General Lee knew he was fighting a war of attrition.

There was little activity during the winter in Virginia, but in early February General Grant ordered another thrust against the Southside railroad.

The Union operations would involve one cavalry division, led by Henry E. Davies, as well as two corps of infantry. Warren's V Corps, along with the II Corps, now under the command of Andrew A. Humphreys,[56] would follow the Union cavalry.

On February 5, the bluecoats headed south. The II

Corps reached Hatcher's Run near the Vaughn Road crossing. Humphreys took a position 1,000 yards away from the enemy lines. Warren deployed his V Corps about two miles to the south of the II Corps, in the vicinity of Monks Neck.[57]

The Federal troops were opposed by Confederates under A. P. Hill and John B. Gordon. Late in the afternoon,[58] the rebels sent one division forward in a tentative counterattack, but the attempt was easily repulsed.[59]

On February 6, the Union cavalry rejoined the footsoldiers. Around 1:00 P.M., Warren probed the area south of Hatcher's Run in the direction of Gravelly Run and Dabney's Mill. In order to block the Union advance, General Gordon sent forward a division under John Pegram. Pegram's veteran soldiers hit the Federals with a fury, but the superior numbers of the bluecoats turned back the assault.[60]

General Pegram's valiant effort cost him his life. He was hit close to the heart by a musket ball, and died almost instantly.[61]

The next day the Union forces shifted their lines once again, taking a position along the Vaughn Road crossing of Hatcher's Run.

Confederate casualties were not reported, but Grant's operation saw 170 Federal soldiers killed, 1,160 wounded, and 182 missing, for a total of 1,512. This movement forced Lee to further extend the Confederate lines of defense. It was the last major shift of Federal forces to their left.[62] The next movements marked the beginning of the Appomattox campaign, which ended with General Lee's surrender on April 9.

July 9, 1864
MONOCACY

J. A. Early (CSA)	L. Wallace (USA)

During the summer of 1864 the Confederates under General Robert E. Lee were stationed around Petersburg, Virginia. The Union Army of the Potomac was holding the city under siege, using their numerical superiority to force the Southerners into submission. General Lee believed that a diversion was needed to remove the constant pressure on his beleaguered graycoats.

General Jubal A. Early and his corps were selected to lead an expedition against Washington, D.C. The purpose was to threaten the capital so that Federal troops would be transferred from Petersburg to the defense of Washington. There was another purpose to Early's mission. On the Maryland shore near the mouth of the Potomac River stood Point Lookout, home of a large Union prison camp. If the Confederates could free the 17,000 men held there, Robert E. Lee could add another corps to his infantry.[1]

General Early moved out, and on July 5 the rebels began to cross the Potomac River into Maryland.[1a] For his part, General Ulysses S. Grant reacted slowly to Early's movement.[2] Belatedly, Grant sent some dismounted cavalry troops, along with one infantry division of the Union VI Corps, to oppose the Confederates.

While negotiations were proceeding between General Grant and the Federal authorities for the protection of the capital, there was no Union force confronting the advancing graycoats. However, one Federal general was not going to sit back and watch the slow wheels of government turn.

His name was Lew Wallace. The 37-year-old general from Indiana would gain greater fame later in life as the author of *Ben Hur*, but right now the security of the nation's capital commanded his attention.

Currently the commander of the U.S. Army's Middle Department with his headquarters in Baltimore, General Wallace was very close to the corridor between Harper's Ferry and Washington. He resolved to try to prevent the Confederate invasion, or at least slow it down. Wallace believed that Monocacy Junction, located two miles east of Frederick, Maryland, offered an excellent position for defense.[3]

General Wallace had very few troops at his immediate disposal. About 3,000 men along with some inexperienced militia appeared to be all that the Federals could muster.[4] On July 6, Union luck changed for the better. The 8th Illinois cavalry arrived at Monocacy Junction, and were immediately placed under Wallace. This excellent unit[5] solved the problem of a lack of cavalry. One day later, a train arrived carrying the division of the VI Corps commanded by General James Ricketts.[6] This division, numbering some 3,350 muskets, was also placed under General Wallace.[7] Opposing this collection of Northerners, General Early had no more than 10,000 men.[7a]

By the 9th of July, the rebels had pushed forward to Frederick, Maryland. The terrain in the area is relatively flat, with roads from Baltimore and Washington converging at Frederick. The Monocacy River crossed both roads, running roughly northeast to southwest.[8]

Surveying the battlefield, General Early could see that the bluecoats had covered both river crossings, as well as a railroad bridge between the two turnpikes. An iron trestle held the tracks of the Baltimore and Ohio Railroad running from Frederick to Baltimore.[9]

The Confederate battle plan was relatively simple. One division under Robert Rodes would demonstrate on the Confederate left. The main attack, however, would come from the right.

Confederate cavalry had already crossed the river and attacked the enemy. This onslaught came against the battle-hardened veterans of the Union VI Corps. General Ricketts had ordered his infantry to hold their fire until the Southern horsemen came within close range, whereupon the cavalry was showered with bullets, driving them back. A second charge was attempted, but this too, ended in failure.[10]

General Early could see by the cavalry action just where to cross the Monocacy. The infantry division under John B. Gordon was ordered forward for a full-scale assault. Gordon's intent was to move to his right to try to get around the Union left flank. Two assaults were made by the Confederates, but both were easily repulsed.

General Gordon decided to probe the right side of Ricketts' VI Corps which was anchored on the Monocacy River. Around 4:00 P.M.,[11] a brigade of Virginians charged the Union soldiers, and drove the bluecoats back before them. Gordon's remaining brigades surged forward, increasing the Confederate pressure. The Union line crumbled under the weight of the attack, and began a hasty retreat toward the Baltimore Pike.[12]

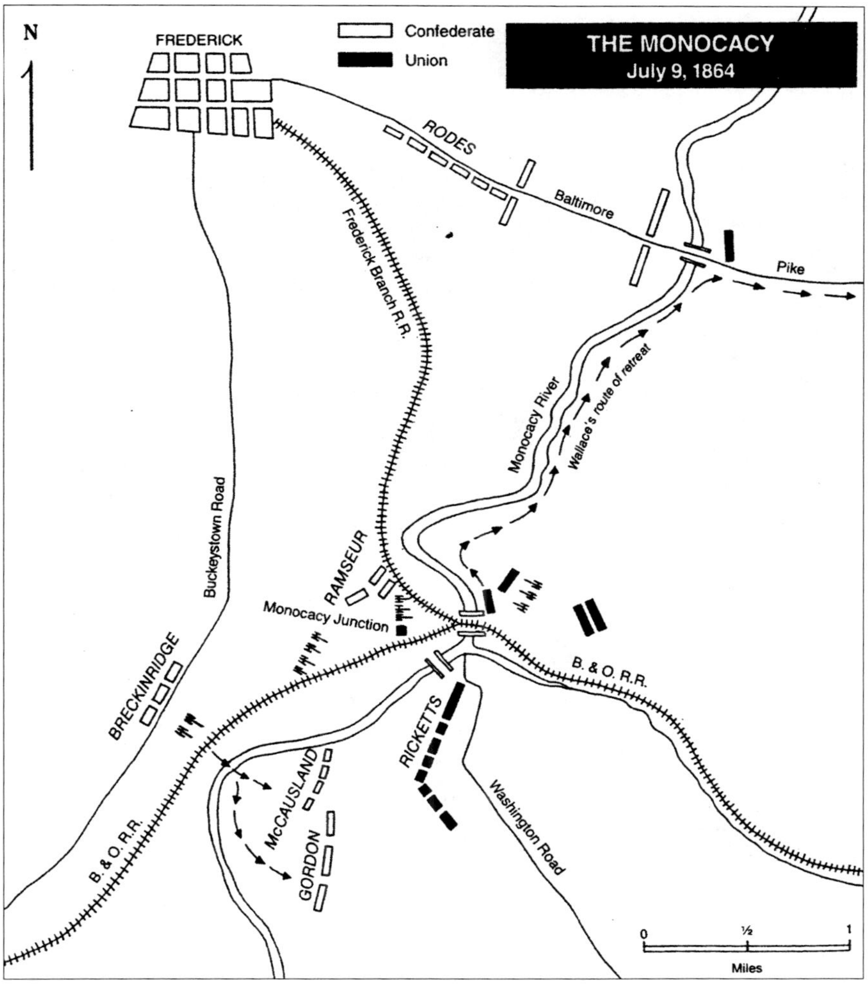

The Monocacy, July 9, 1864.

Once the VI Corps retreated, the battle was essentially over. There was some pursuit by the Confederates under General Stephen Dodson Ramseur in the center, as well as the men on the left under General Robert Rodes, but that was all.

Union losses exceeded those of the Confederacy on July 9. There were 98 bluecoats killed, 594 wounded, and 1188 captured or missing, for a total of 1,880. General Early reported his total losses as "between 600 and 700."[13]

On the surface, it would seem as if the Federals got the worst of it at the battle of Monocacy. General Wallace clearly sustained more casualties, and the Yankees were driven from the field in defeat. However, the action on July 9 ended too late in the day for the Confederates to resume their march on Washington.

By the time that Early's forces could advance again, the nation's capital had been reinforced.[14]

Lew Wallace, in the stubborn defense which he put forth that day, did his very best. The general lost a battle, but may have saved the nation.[15]

July 14–15, 1864
TUPELO (HARRISBURG)

S. D. Lee N. B. Forrest (CSA)	A. J. Smith (USA)

The events which took place in Mississippi were governed by action elsewhere in the Confederacy. During the summer of 1864, General William T. Sherman was in the

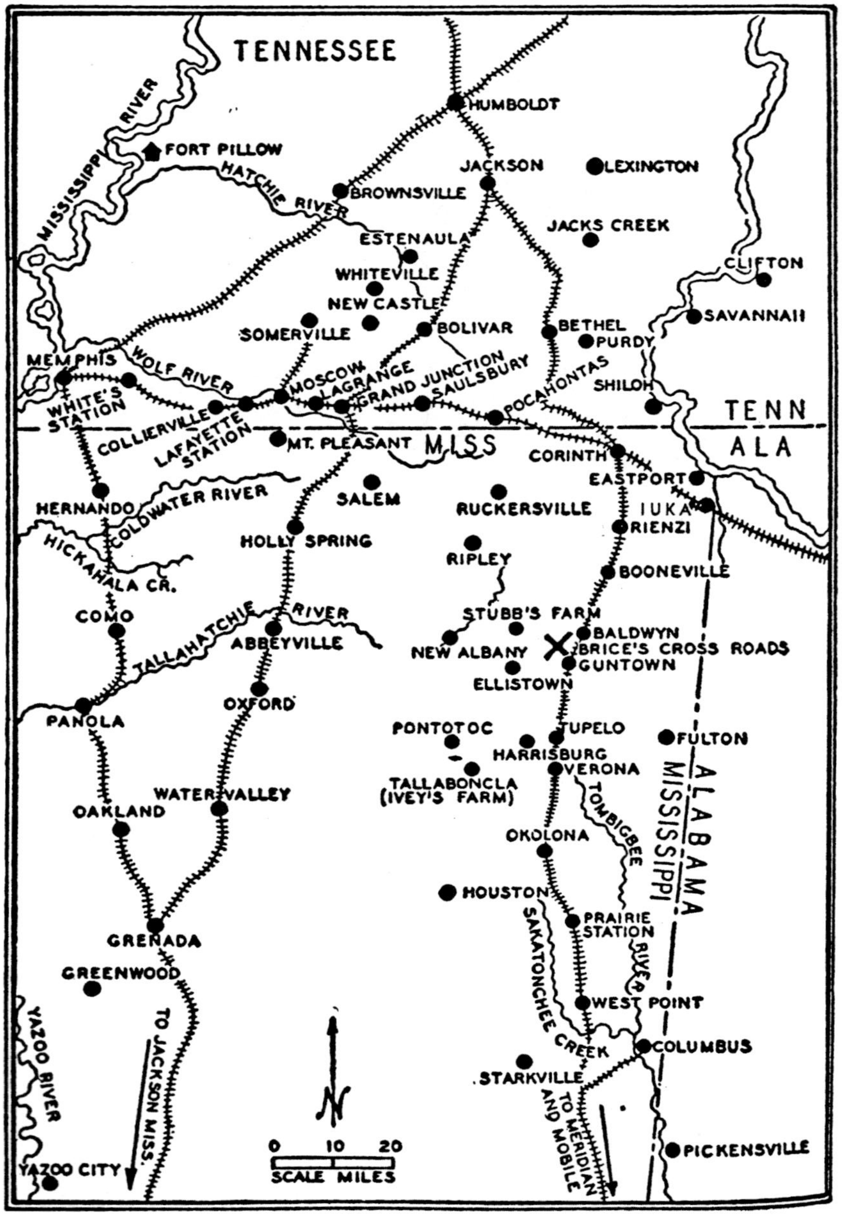

Western Tennessee and Northern Mississippi.

process of marching south through Georgia. In his attempt to reach Atlanta, the Union supply lines were growing longer and longer.

Both Sherman and Ulysses S. Grant feared the cavalry strikes of General Nathan Bedford Forrest.[1] They realized that the Union lines of communication were extremely vulnerable. The Confederate mounted attack force which had galloped across Tennessee and Mississippi, seemingly unstoppable, was currently stationed around Okolona, Mississippi.

Sherman had written "there never will be peace in Tennessee until Forrest is dead,"[2] which indicated the concern he felt over the Confederate cavalry general. In order to stop this threat, General A. J. Smith was sent forward from Memphis with about 14,000 men, including infantry, cavalry and artillery.[3]

General Smith began on July 5, 1864, with the Union cavalry under General Benjamin Grierson. By July 9, the Federal columns crossed the Tallahatchie River at New Albany, heading south toward Pontotoc, Mississippi.

Forrest had no intention of giving battle until his graycoats could be reinforced. General Stephen D. Lee was en route to Okolona from Pontotoc with some 2,000 Confederates.[3a] Upon his arrival, Lee would assume command of the Southern forces. Nevertheless, it was possible for Forrest to delay the Federal progress. He ordered General Abraham Buford to harass the enemy flanks, and General James Chalmers to put part of his division at Pontotoc, while holding the remainder between Pontotoc and Okolona.[4]

The Confederate intent was to draw the Federals toward Okolona. A. J. Smith had been quite cautious in his march southward, because his predecessors had had no luck in defeating General Forrest. Suddenly, on July 13, the Union forces shifted the direction of the advance. Smith turned to the east, and headed for Tupelo.

General Grierson and the cavalry were in Tupelo by noon on the 13th, while the Union infantry stopped that night at nearby Harrisburg. The Union force was almost two miles in length. Facing west, the Federal left was pulled back so that it faced south. The cavalry protected the flanks, while the infantry went to work building barricades with fence rails, logs and timber from the surrounding countryside.[5]

About 9:00 P.M.,[6] the Confederates made camp two miles from the Union position.[7] General Lee had ordered an attack for July 14 on the Federal position, which was a very strong one. At this point, a controversy emerges surrounding the action at Tupelo. Whether Forrest actually wanted to give battle on the next day is very debatable. Stephen D. Lee was his superior. So did Forrest agree to the attack the next day, or was he merely obeying an order he knew he could not overrule?[8]

There is considerable evidence to build a case for either side, and it has been thoroughly discussed by the adherents of both Lee and Forrest. It is not possible to reach a definite conclusion, but based on the evidence available it appears that General Forrest seems to have gone along with an order he was unable to change.[9]

The Federals had 11,000 infantry as well as 3,200 cavalry aligned in a strong position.[10] In addition, the artillery had a clear view of any attacking graycoats.[11] The Confederates had about 9,000 men, but there must be some deductions from their total to account for troops who were detailed to take care of the cavalry horses, and thus were not available to participate in a general assault.[12]

About 7:30 A.M.[13] on July 14, General Lee gave the order to move forward. He took command of the Confederate left wing, which contained Buford's and Chalmers' divisions, while Forrest led the right, made up of the division under General Philip Roddey. Given the strength of the Union position, as well as the numerical superiority enjoyed by the Northerners, Lee's attack had little chance of success. To make matters worse for the Confederates, the attack soon began to disintegrate.

The left wing under Lee began to advance well ahead of the troops under Forrest on the right. The result was a series of uncoordinated, piecemeal attacks.[14] The Yankees held their fire, then put a concentrated storm of lead into Lee's Kentuckians. With Union fortifications in front, and enemy artillery on both sides, the Kentuckians were easily repulsed.[15]

Forrest viewed the senseless casualties and held back his men. Analyzing the situation as he saw it, Forrest commented that since the enemy was "in overwhelming numbers in an impregnable position, and wishing to save my troops from the unprofitable slaughter I knew would follow any attempt to charge his works, I did not push forward General Roddey's command when it arrived, knowing it would receive the same concentrated fire which had repulsed the Kentucky brigade."[16]

As a result of Forrest's observations, the Confederate right was never seriously engaged in the action.[17] The fighting lasted about two hours, and was decided before 10:30 A.M.[18]

Casualties were high on the Confederate side on July 14. The graycoats had lost over 1,300 men — very high for a cavalry battle. The Federals, defending a strong position with infantry as well as cavalry, lost fewer than 700 soldiers at Tupelo.[19]

Neither side was particularly pleased with the outcome of the battle. The Federals were disappointed because Forrest's command had not been destroyed. The rebel was still out there somewhere, and none of the Northern high command knew where he would strike next. Still, this battle was more successful in its results than previous attempts to capture Forrest, and General Sherman's supply lines were safe for the time being. From the Confederate viewpoint, it was a fiasco. Badly planned and poorly executed, the battle should never have been fought.[20]

Curiously enough, even in defeat the Confederates had once again turned back a Union mission to get rid of Forrest. The next time the rebels would have to do much better, for the Yankees were soon to come again with a greater threat.[21]

July 24, 1864
Kernstown (Second)

J. A. Early (CSA)	G. Crook (USA)

Federal operations in western Virginia had faced little opposition during the early summer of 1864. The Union cavalry moved up and down the Shenandoah Valley with relative ease. If there was to be any peace in this section of Virginia, the Yankees must be stopped.

The area was of great importance to the Confederacy, as the rich farmland contained some of the most fertile soil in the state. On June 12,[1] Robert E. Lee detached a Confederate force to stop the Federals from laying waste to the countryside. The rebels would be led by General Jubal A. Early. Early's mission was to remove the yoke of Union domination from the counties of the valley, and threaten Washington, D.C., as well. By June 15, General Lee would be busy with the defense of Petersburg. If the enemy believed that the Federal capital was in danger, it might induce President Lincoln to remove Northern troops from General Lee's battle front.

However, three years of civil war had taken the lives of many of the best soldiers in the South. General Lee, commanding the Army of Northern Virginia, was not able to spare as many men as he might have liked. The troops under General Early would number only 10,000 infantry, along with 4,000 cavalry and artillery.[2]

The Confederates were in good spirits, despite their small numbers. After winning a victory on July 9 at the battle of Monocacy, Early's men had fought their way to the very edge of the Federal capital.. Unfortunately, Washington, D.C., was protected by a ring of forts too powerful to overcome.

During the night of July 12–13 the Southerners pulled back from the outskirts of the city, and the Federals pursued them into the Shenandoah Valley. The

Yankees were just north of Winchester, a good-sized community on the northern end of the Valley Turnpike. Early would take up a position at Strasburg, about 20 miles farther south.[2a] The Federal cavalry under General William Averell began moving forward, and General Early detached an infantry division to meet this threat.[2b]

On July 19 the graycoats under General S. D. Ramseur met the enemy at Stephenson's Depot. Averell hid his troops in the cover of dense woods, then suddenly attacked and turned the left flank of the Confederates. Ramseur's men did not fight well, and panic on the left side spread to the right. The rebels lost over 450 men and four artillery pieces[2c] in a disgraceful display.

The Union VI Corps continued to observe the Confederate movements, and by July 21 had occupied Winchester.[3] The bluecoats camped about a mile south of the town,[4] under the command of General George Crook. Still uncertain of Early's intentions, Crook sent one cavalry division forward under General Averell. Perhaps this would bring back reliable information.

On the 23rd, the Yankees came upon Confederate cavalry at Kernstown, located a short distance south of Winchester. Although there was minor skirmishing throughout the day, the two sides separated that afternoon with only minor casualties.[5]

The main Confederate position was still at Strasburg, some 20 miles south[6] of Winchester on the Valley Pike. At dawn[7] on July 24 the rebels headed north, with General John B. Gordon's division in the lead. The activity on the turnpike did not go unnoticed among the Federals, and by noon the bluecoats were well deployed on the north side of a small stream named Hogg Run.[8]

When General Early arrived, Gordon occupied the Union front while General John C. Breckinridge swung wide to the right, with the intention of attacking Crook's vulnerable left flank.[9] The Northerners put up a stubborn resistance until Breckinridge was able to force a retreat on the Federal left. The retreat became a rout, as Crook's left collapsed.[10]

Casualties for the South were not reported, but the losses on July 24 were clearly in favor of General Early. The Yankees lost 1,185 men, and retreated to Bunker Hill, 12 miles to the north.[11]

The Southern victory at Kernstown had grave consequences for the Confederacy. The United States government realized that a greater effort was needed to secure the Shenandoah Valley, and, two weeks later, General Philip H. Sheridan assumed command of the Union forces there.[12] By the end of September, this section of Virginia would be firmly in Union hands.

September 19, 1864

Winchester (Third) (Opequon Creek)

J. E. Early (CSA) — P. H. Sheridan (USA)

The summer of 1864 had indeed been a difficult one for General Jubal Early. On June 12,[1] he had met with Robert E. Lee and had received an almost impossible assignment. Union cavalry had been riding through the Shenandoah Valley with reckless abandon, and had destroyed both public and private property. The Confederate government understood the strategic value of this area to the Southern cause. In addition to providing food for Lee's Army of Northern Virginia, control of the valley offered a point of entry into Maryland and Pennsylvania. Early's Herculean task was to clear the valley of the bluecoats.

Over three years of warfare had drained the Confederacy of badly needed manpower, and General Lee did not have the troops necessary to ensure Early's success. General Early's force consisted of only 10,000 muskets, and some 4,000 cavalry and artillery.[2]

The high point in the campaign came on July 9, when "Old Jube" led his weary Confederates to victory at Monocacy. The graycoats rode close enough to look at Washington, D.C., but the Federal capital was protected by a ring of forts too strong for Early's small force to carry by assault.

Other smaller engagements dominated the summer months until September, when the action began to intensify. Both armies were encamped just north of Winchester, Virginia, located in the northern end of the Shenandoah Valley. Union General Philip H. Sheridan had devised a plan to defeat his foe, and on September 19 he would attack.

Jubal Early's infantry faced east, and were deployed between the Valley Turnpike and Opequon Creek. Stephen Dodson Ramseur's division was positioned astride the Berryville Pike. Protecting Ramseur's right flank was the cavalry of Bradley Johnson and William L. Jackson. Facing north along the turnpike, was another Confederate cavalry force under General Fitzhugh Lee, the nephew of Robert E. Lee.[2a]

The Union plan of attack was not complicated. It began with the cavalry under General James Wilson crossing Opequon Creek before dawn and moving in a westerly direction toward Winchester. General Sheridan intended for the bluecoats to strike the right flank of General Ramseur. Finally, the Yankees would hold the Valley Pike and secure it at that point.[3] This would place Wilson's cavalry between the Confederates and Winchester. Union infantry would follow the success of Wilson's men and make a direct assault on Ramseur's division.

The powerful Federal thrust surged past Ramseur's position, and the rebels began to waver. As the grayclad veterans fell back to the west, General Ramseur rallied his men and reformed his troops. Although the Northerners had the advantage of numbers, the Confederate lines held firm.[4]

The stubborn resistance of Ramseur's infantry had bought some time for the remainder of Early's men to consolidate. Around 9:00 A.M.[5] Robert E. Rodes brought his division to the field, aligning his men on Ramseur's left, with John B. Gordon's division arriving about an hour later on Rodes' left.[5a] The Confederates now had a formidable force, some four times the size it was at dawn.[6]

The performance of the Confederates was exemplary. Nevertheless, General Early did receive some aid from his enemy. General Horatio G. Wright, commander of the Union VI Corps had brought his supply train into the narrow Berryville Canyon. The animals and wagons blocked the path of two of Wright's own divisions, and prevented William H. Emory's entire XIX Corps from reaching the battlefield.

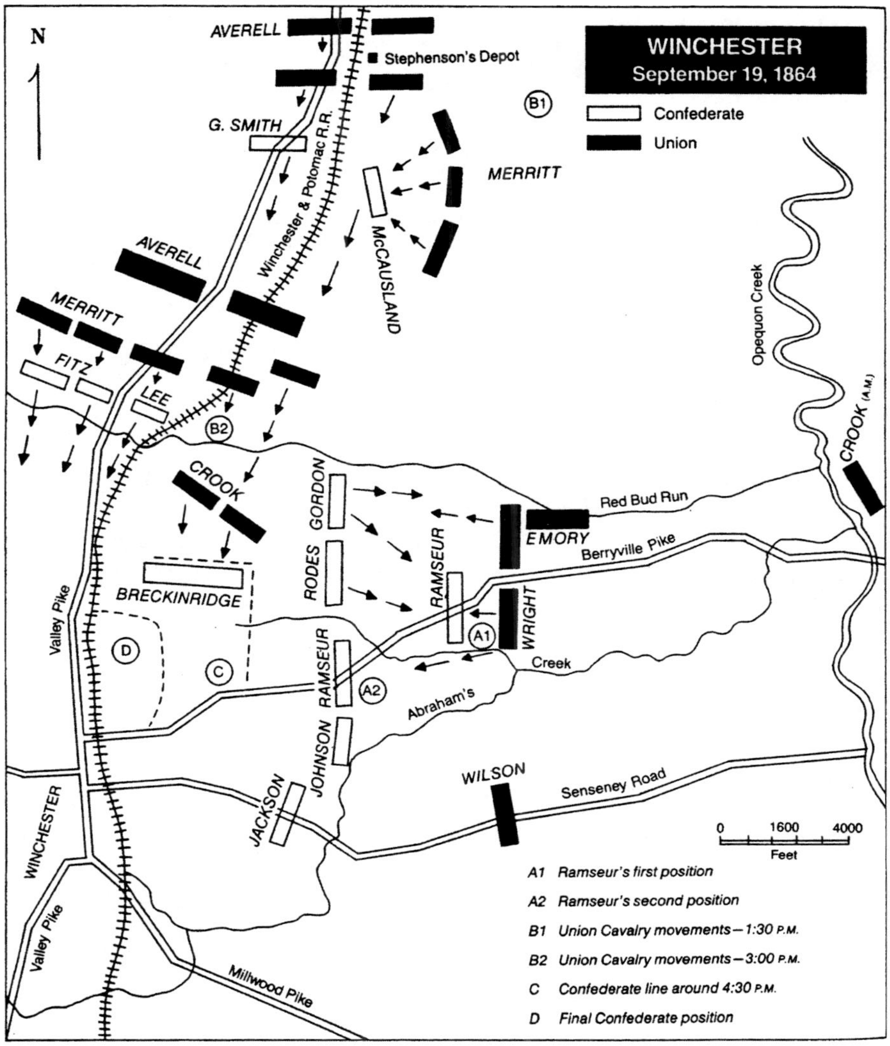

Winchester, September 19, 1864.

Disorganization on the Federal side assisted the rebels as they reached the field. General Early watched the action from behind Gordon's troops. At 11:40 A.M., blueclad infantry pressed the rebels hard, and the Southerners fell back slightly. Fortunately, they were supported by seven artillery pieces, and the guns unleashed canister at 60 yards, cutting gaping holes in the Northern ranks.[7]

Opportunity dawned for the Confederates. General Gordon had observed a gap between the VI and the XIX Corps as the Federal troops hastened back down the Berryville Pike. Conferring with General Rodes, the Confederates decided upon a swift counterattack.[8] At this moment a shell burst in midair, a and a fragment from it struck General Rodes behind the ear. He was killed instantly. General Gordon assumed command of both divisions, and urged the attack onward.[9]

The graycoats poured through the ranks of the XIX Corps, but met resistance at the hands of the VI Corps. With soldiers from each side firing volleys at point blank range, the attack lost its momentum.[10] At about 1:30 P.M.,[11] the bluecoats counterattacked. Each side was exhausted, but neither would give ground. Soon after the Union attack got under way, the fighting died down in this section of the battlefield. The action would turn elsewhere.

General Early's men had acquitted themselves well. The combat had moved back and forth, but both sides had fought valiantly, refusing to break down.

The difference in the battle would be in the numerical strength of the troops. Gordon's advance and the Union counterattack had battled to a draw, but there were reserves on both sides who had yet to be engaged. In this area, Philip "Little Phil" Sheridan had a decided advantage. The VIII Corps under George Crook numbered some 10,000 men, while the Confederate infantry under

John Breckinridge could count only 1,800 rifles. The Federal cavalry had approximately 9,000 troopers who had yet to fight, Fitz Lee had perhaps half that number.[12] If "Little Phil" could get the Union troops onto the field, the strength in numbers would soon be brought to bear.

Two Union cavalry divisions under William W. Averell and Wesley Merritt galloped forth against the small band of Fitzhugh Lee's graycoats. The Union force was overwhelming, but Fitz Lee chose to surprise the foe and he charged the onrushing troopers. In the melee that followed, Lee sustained a serious wound in the thigh. He was forced to join the remainder of the Confederates as the Southerners gave way under the weight of the Union pressure.[13]

Around 2:00 P.M., General Sheridan threw his remaining troops into the contest. Crook's VIII Corps charged forward against the Confederates facing east. With support from the VI and XIX Corps, the Federals pushed past the defenders, then turned their attack to the north.[14]

Meanwhile, the Union cavalry under Averell and Merritt had been forcing there way south along the Valley Pike. The numerical superiority of the Yankees began to turn back the rebels on all fronts. General Early tried to stop the retreat from becoming full-fledged panic. The Confederates pulled back to a position south of Winchester, and these same forces would fight another battle three days later at Fisher's Hill.

Casualties had been heavy on both sides, but the Union losses would be easier to replace. General Sheridan had lost 697 men killed, 3,983 wounded and 338 captured or missing, for a total of 5,018. The Confederates had lost a total of 3,611 in the infantry and artillery, with perhaps an additional 1,000 casualties in the cavalry.[15]

The repercussions of the third battle of Winchester were not great. The contest for possession of the valley would be decided for good three days later at Fisher's Hill. Winchester was, perhaps, of some painful significance for the Confederate side. It marked the first time in the Civil War that the Second Corps, commanded by Stonewall Jackson until his death, was driven from the field by Union troops.[16]

September 22, 1864
FISHER'S HILL

J. A. Early (CSA)	P. H. Sheridan (USA)

At the beginning of the Civil War, the Confederate cavalry was far superior to their Union counterparts, but by 1864, the bluecoats had made great strides to overtake the Southern horsemen. More than three years of constant activity had taken its toll on the rebels. Men, animals and equipment had simply worn out. The Yankees had started to gain the upper hand.

General Philip H. "Little Phil" Sheridan and his mounted troopers had wreaked havoc up and down the Shenandoah Valley. Robert E. Lee recognized the value of this food source to the Army of Northern Virginia, and he was determined to put a stop to the Union plunder.

On June 12,[1] General Lee met with General Jubal A. Early. Lee had a most important assignment for his lieutenant. Early would be dispatched to the Shenandoah to try to drive the enemy out of the valley. By this point in the conflict, however, the casualties of war had greatly reduced the manpower available to General Lee, and Early's force was not as large as it should have been.

On June 13, Early led the Second Corps out on what would be a circuitous route to reach the valley. The ultimate objective was an assault on the Federal capital. The mere threat of an invasion of Washington, D.C., would certainly bring the Northerners to their senses. Perhaps a settlement could be reached, and peace would finally come to Virginia. Because the force under General Early was so small,[2] the expedition had little chance. The Confederates numbered only 10,000 muskets, along with another 4,000 cavalry and artillery.[3] Still, General Lee felt he would have to try.

The Confederates simply did not have enough men to drive the powerful foe from Virginia. After a series of engagements, General Early would be able to look down into the city of Washington, D.C., but the ring of forts surrounding the capital was too strong too be carried by assault.

Finally, on September 19, 1864, Early's troops were defeated at the third battle of Winchester. Early realized that the Confederates would have to retreat in a southerly direction down the Valley Pike to Fisher's Hill,[4] located just west of the North Fork of the Shenandoah River.

Three days later, the graycoats took up a defensive position anchored on Fisher's Hill, but Early's troop dispositions were not compact. The Virginian placed his men in a line from Fisher's Hill, on the Southern right, all the way to Little North Mountain. This was a distance of almost four miles,[5] and much too great for the small band of Confederates to defend effectively.

A second weakness in the Confederate position was revealed when General Early placed his cavalry on the far left of the Southern lines. The horsemen under Lunsford Lomax had dismounted, so that they would be able to fight like infantry, but they were somewhat isolated in this position. Jubal Early never quite understood the cavalry, and he failed to make the best use of his troopers.[6]

To the right of the cavalry, the rebels had four divisions of infantry. These were commanded, from left to right, by Stephen Dodson Ramseur, John Pegram, John B. Gordon and Gabriel Wharton. While these four divisions had some artillery support, it must be remembered that they were no longer the size of standard Confederate infantry divisions. It would be very difficult to withstand a Federal assault. Losses at Winchester on September 19 had taken Early's force down to just under 10,000 men, while Sheridan's bluecoats numbered around 33,000.[7]

Fortunately for the rebels, General Sheridan waited until the 22nd before attacking. This gave the weary Southerners a chance to rest. The fighting commenced around 4:00 P.M.[8]

Union General George Crook moved his troops to his right and hit the Confederate left flank as hard as possible. The dismounted Confederate cavalry was the weakest point in the Southern lines, and they crumbled immediately under the weight of the Federal onslaught.

General Ramseur tried to stem the tide by shifting his men to contest the enemy's advance, but one brigade drifted too far to the left, allowing Crook's Yankees to penetrate even further behind the Confederate left and rear.[9] Hopelessly outflanked, Ramseur's men began to fall apart, and the battle turned into a rout.[10]

Early tried to stop the flight of his graycoats, but it was to no avail as they swarmed down the Valley Turnpike. Only darkness saved the Confederates, who did not stop until they had reached Woodstock, some 25 miles south along the turnpike.[11]

Confederate casualties at the battle of Fisher's Hill were only 30 men killed and 210 wounded; however there were 995 graycoats captured or missing, for a total of 1,235. In contrast, Sheridan lost 52 soldiers killed and 457 wounded, but only 19 captured or missing, for a total of 528.[12] Many of the Confederates were captured as they attempted to run down the Valley Turnpike to safety.

In retrospect, it would seem like the Shenandoah Valley operations during the summer of 1864 ended in dismal failure for Jubal Early's tattered graycoats. There had been mistakes to be sure. On the other hand, General Early had accomplished much in the face of staggering odds. The entire Union VI Corps had been drawn away from the Army of the Potomac, the powerful Federal cavalry was still in the valley, instead of going to the aid of General Grant, and Sheridan's troopers had been occupied fighting Jubal Early, instead of doing substantive damage to the Confederate supply lines.[13]

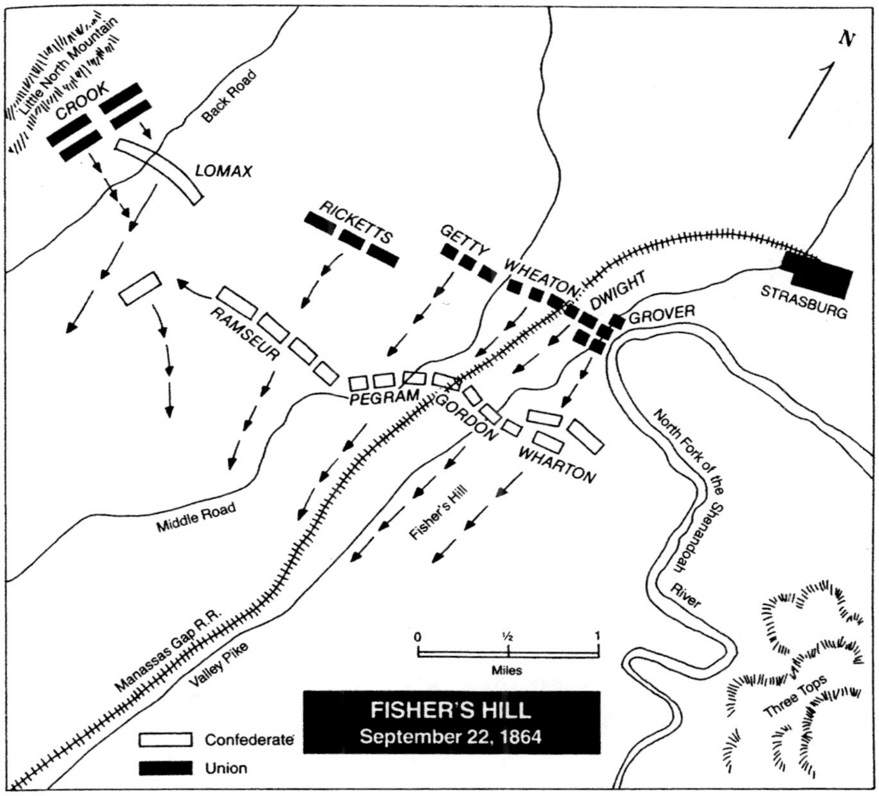

Fisher's Hill, September 22, 1864.

While the Union forces were indeed detained from more productive work, the steady succession of defeats of the undermanned Confederates would ensure that there would never again be an effective Confederate fighting force in the Shenandoah Valley.

October 19, 1864
CEDAR CREEK

J. A. Early (CSA) — P. H. Sheridan (USA)

In the early stages of the War Between the States, the Southern cavalry was far superior to that of the North.

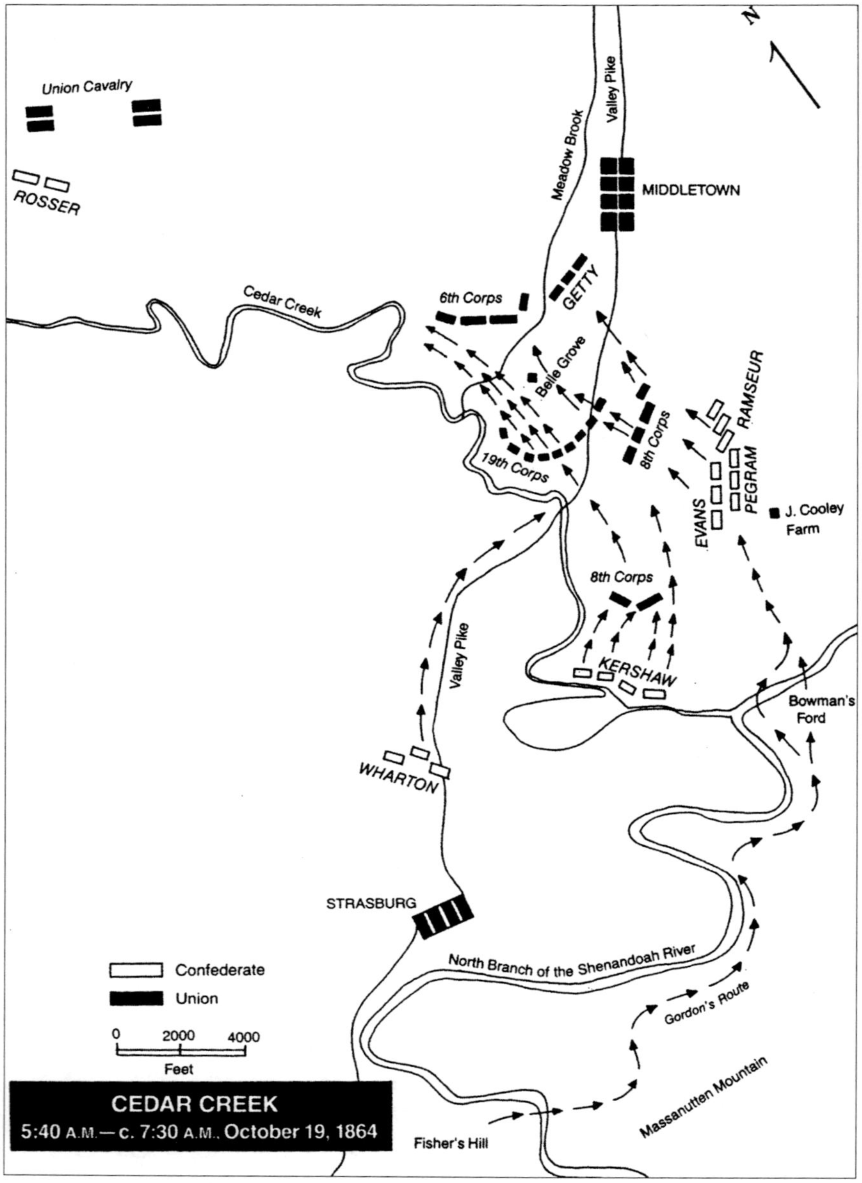

Cedar Creek, 5:40 A.M.–ca. 7:30 A.M., October 19, 1864.

This occurred as a result of several factors. Most of the soldiers of the Confederacy had grown up in a rural setting. The men were used to the outdoor way of life, and many were already excellent horsemen.[1] There was also a difference in the animals. The horses in the South were swift and athletic animals, and ideal for cavalrymen. Confederate generals such as J. E. B. "Jeb" Stuart, Nathan B. Forrest, Fitzhugh Lee and Wade Hampton dominated the early phases of warfare on horseback.

The cavalry in the North struggled. The troopers hailed from cities and towns. They were unfamiliar with these four-legged creatures which were mastered so easily by the men in gray. The horses were fine animals, but they were the strong, muscular type. The Northern men found that an animal which was perfect for pulling a plow was not always best at chasing the enemy. The Yankees would have to learn.

However, by the later stages of the Civil War, the Federal cavalry had made great progress in comparison with their Southern counterparts.[2] Experience had been a fine teacher. Horses were plentiful in the Union cavalry, but the Southern horsemen had to furnish their own mounts. If a horse was killed in battle, the Confederate trooper was responsible for its replacement, and this was not always easy.

By 1864, both man and beast in the South were wearing down.[3] Long, arduous years of warfare, little food, and the shortage of supplies such as horseshoes, saddles and bridles all combined to diminish the effectiveness of the Southern mounted forces.

Union General Philip H. "Little Phil" Sheridan had waged a very successful campaign. Moving up and down the Shenandoah Valley, his Federal horsemen had been victorious at Winchester and Fisher's Hill.[4]

On October 18 the Federal troops were encamped just north of Cedar Creek, and about three miles northeast of Strasburg. General Jubal Early had been sent by Robert E. Lee to rid the valley of the invaders and he was determined to attack. John B. Gordon would lead the assault, taking with him three divisions of the Second Corps. Led by Clement Evans, John Pegram and S. D. Ramseur, these men would make up the Confederate right. Joseph B. Kershaw was to lead his division in the center, while Gabriel Wharton would march his division up the Valley Pike, constituting the left. The intent was to converge on the unsuspecting bluecoats, drive them out of the Shenandoah Valley, and capture Phil Sheridan in the process.[5]

The Confederates moved forward in the early hours of October 19.[6] They crossed Cedar Creek and quickly overran the camps of the Union VIII and XIX Corps. However, the more formidable VI Corps still remained.[7] The Federals lost 1,300 prisoners and 18 artillery pieces in the morning's action. Jubal Early was very optimistic. No army could recover from such a blow.[8]

It was here that General Early's biggest mistake came

back to haunt him. He had sent away a large part of his cavalry,[9] led by General Lunsford Lomax, for duty along the Valley Pike. As a result, the Confederates were not able to pursue the beaten foe as vigorously as possible.[10]

There was a lull in the action until about 4:30 P.M.[11] Unknown to the Confederates was the fact that General Sheridan had been absent from the battlefield. He raced back to the scene, inspiring his troops. The Union soldiers regrouped, and delivered a vicious counterattack on the weakest point of the rebel line: the left.[12] The graycoats quickly collapsed, many veteran units retreating to Cedar Creek. General Early did his best to halt the stampede, but his efforts were useless.[13]

The Confederates had lost 2,900 men at Cedar Creek, and about 1,900 were killed or wounded.[14] In addition, Stephen Dodson Ramseur, one of the finest young generals in the South, was mortally wounded.[15] The Federals had lost 644 men killed, 3,430 wounded and 1,591 captured or missing, for a total of 5,665,[16] but these men would be easier to replace. When the day was over, the Federals remained in possession of the field. General Sheridan had routed General Early for the third time in one month, and this effectively ended Confederate operations in the Shenandoah Valley.

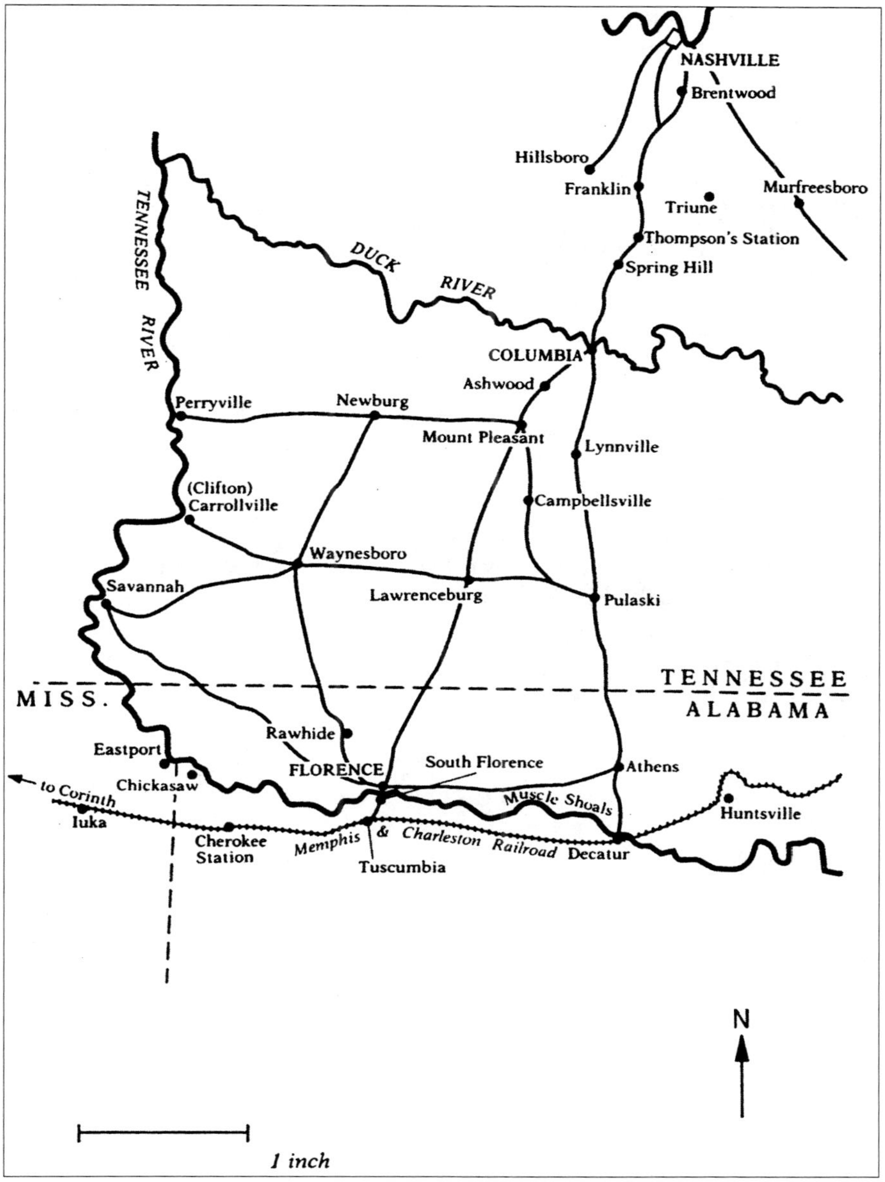

Invasion route, November 1864.

November 29, 1864
Spring Hill

J. B. Hood (CSA) — J. M. Schofield (USA)

After the fall of Atlanta in September, the Southern civilian and military population was devastated. Nothing but disaster ran through the minds of Georgians. All hope seemed lost. From a military viewpoint, there must be some way to relieve the pressure and devastation confronting the state. However, the plan which resulted was born in desperation.[1]

General John B. Hood was in command of the Confederates. It was his belief that the graycoats should march into Tennessee. This move would compel the Union forces around Atlanta to pursue him, thereby releasing the stranglehold General William T. Sherman had around Atlanta.[2]

This plan was proposed to President Jefferson Davis. General Hood would take his troops and destroy the railroads from Chattanooga to Atlanta. Sherman would then be cut off from his supply lines, and would be forced out of Georgia in order to feed his army. Both men sincerely hoped that the Yankees would simply leave the South, and follow Hood into middle Tennessee.

The weakness in this plan was that it was no longer necessary for the bluecoats to depend on Chattanooga. Once the Union forces had reached Atlanta, the Northerners could live off the land as they marched toward Savannah. Neither Hood nor Davis had the vision to grasp reality. They could only see the outcome they hoped would occur.

The offensive against Sherman's supply lines began on September 29.[3] On October 3, Confederates under General A. P. Stewart struck the Western and Atlantic Railroad. At Big Shanty, the graycoats captured the Union garrison of 175 soldiers,[4] and the next day 250 Federals surrendered at Acworth, Georgia.[5] It seemed as if the operation was a success. The next step was the large Union supply base at Allatoona.

General Samuel G. French was ordered to take his Confederates north and take control of the depot. On October 5, the rebels attacked the Federals, but were repulsed several times. French finally recalled his men about 1:30 P.M., after hearing reports that Sherman was reinforcing the position.[6] He decided that it would be wiser to rejoin General Hood. Southern casualties in the action at Allatoona were severe — French lost almost 900 men[7] from an assault force of 2,000. In contrast, the Federals lost 706 men, along with some 200 soldiers captured by the rebels. The Northerners had also used approximately 2,000 men in the defense of the post.[8]

While the fighting had been quite fierce at Allatoona, it was not a large-scale engagement. Making matters worse for the Confederates was the subsequent knowledge that the reports of Union reinforcements were nothing more than false rumors. General French had abandoned his attack for nothing.[9]

The balance of October was spent tearing up railroad tracks, burning the connections from Chattanooga to Atlanta, and generally resting Hood's weary veterans.

For his part, Sherman sent off the XXIII Corps under General John M. Schofield in a belated attempt to catch French and his rebels. General George H. Thomas, was sent north into middle Tennessee. The remainder of the bluecoats began the disagreeable task of getting the railroads back in order.[10]

The Confederates moved gradually westward, working their way through Alabama in preparation for a campaign into middle Tennessee. General Hood planned to move his infantry northward on November 5. The men would carry 20 days' rations, and the Confederate cavalry under General Nathan Bedford Forrest would join Hood's troops. The immediate destination was unclear, but the Southerners were to march in the direction of Pulaski or Columbia, and then let events unfold.[11]

Miserable weather delayed the entire operation.[12] Hood hesitated in advancing his infantry because Forrest had not yet arrived. As of November 10, Forrest had been detained by rivers swollen by rain and dirt roads which had turned into quagmires. By November 16 the cavalry had finally linked up with the infantry.[13]

The dilapidated railroads would hinder the graycoats even further. Instead of building a surplus to feed his army, the trains were barely able to furnish the daily needs of Hood's men.[14]

The lack of attention to detail was to prove disastrous in Hood's makeup as a commanding officer. There was no doubt that he was a tremendous fighter, but he did not possess all of the attributes needed to make him an excellent general.[15]

To make matters worse, the Union army vacated Atlanta on November 16, beginning what would become known as Sherman's "March to the Sea." The Confederates were now hopelessly out of position to contest such an advance.[16] Everything would be staked on the results in Tennessee.

The Federals under Schofield were stationed at Pulaski, while Thomas held Nashville. There seemed to be no sense of urgency. Schofield felt that the inclement weather would surely prevent any Confederate advance.

Unfortunately for the Federals, the situation began to change in a hurry. On November 21,[17] Federal cavalry notified General Schofield that Hood's graycoats were marching north in the vicinity of Lawrenceburg, less than 20 miles to the west. They were headed north in the direction of Columbia.[18]

John Schofield realized that he had to move fast. Orders went out immediately. Two Union divisions were to march north to Lynnville on the morning of the 22nd, a distance of some 20 miles. The two remaining divisions would take the same route on the 23rd.[19]

The Federals would concentrate their forces at Columbia as soon as possible. George Thomas realized that he did not have enough men to stop the Confederates in a pitched battle, so for the time being, he would act on the defensive. He had 12,000 men of the IV Corps, 10,000 men from Schofield's XXIII Corps, and approximately 3,000 cavalry.[20] Thomas would have to play for time and reinforce his command.

Arrayed against this Federal force were three entire corps under General Hood. The Confederates advanced along different roads leading from Florence, Alabama into Tennessee. A. P. Stewart led his men on the shortest route, heading for Lawrenceburg. Benjamin Franklin Cheatham's corps took the most westerly march, in the direction of Waynesboro. In the middle were the troops of Stephen D. Lee. They covered back roads which had seen little use.[21] General Hood intended to keep his three corps clear of each other. He could not control the weather, but he could give each corps a clear line of march.

The Confederate plan of attack was to quickly get the graycoats between Schofield's Federals at Pulaski and the troops under Thomas stationed at Nashville.[22]

By November 24, Hood had consolidated his forces. All of the Confederates were marching to Mount Pleasant, which was an intermediate stop on the way to Columbia. With his army on Schofield's western flank, the rebels were only 45 miles south of Columbia.[23]

While the rain continued for several days, the weather improved as the Confederates approached Columbia. On November 27, Hood moved his troops into position. S. D. Lee was on the left, A. P. Stewart took the center, and Frank Cheatham's Corps held the right. The cavalry under General Forrest was sent beyond the right flank to rest both men and horses. The horsemen were completely exhausted after prolonged activity.[24]

John B. Hood had finally reached Columbia. However, Schofield and his Yankees now stood between the rebels and Nashville. It was readily apparent that a battle was imminent.

The Federals were firmly entrenched in a strong defensive position. Hood knew an assault would be costly, and decided that the best way to solve the problem was to go around the enemy. Cheatham, on the Confederate right, would lead his men past the Union left flank.

Once again, the weather threw a roadblock in the path of the Confederacy. Columbia lay along the Duck River, which had swollen due to the recent rain, and the deep water blocked the path of Cheatham's graycoats. Hood would have to wait to move his troops.

On November 28, fortune smiled on the Southerners. The weather cleared, the river was falling, and during the night the Federals had unexpectedly evacuated Columbia. The Union forces had crossed the river and fortified a ridge on the north shore of the Duck River.[25] Stephen Lee led his Confederates into Columbia in the early morning.[26]

General Forrest and his troopers promptly cleared the way for the Confederate infantry. In scattering the Union horsemen, Forrest effectively removed the scouting capability of the enemy. Schofield would now be forced to guess the whereabouts of his adversary. Pontoon bridges were brought up, and the Confederates were able to safely cross the Duck River.[27]

The stage was set for the race to Nashville. Both armies were on the north side of the Duck River. The next day would answer the question: who would move the fastest?

John Schofield was in a quandary. He received periodic reports from his cavalry that Hood was marching north. These dispatches advised Schofield to retreat in the direction of Franklin. On the other hand, General Thomas believed Union reinforcements under General A. J. Smith would arrive any day. Thomas wanted his lieutenant to maintain an aggressive position. Schofield was to fall back only in an emergency.[28]

As a result, Schofield hesitated. He sent part of his command northward under General David Stanley, keeping the remainder where it was. He still had no cavalry with him, and would have to rely on a general reconnaissance of the area by his infantry. If only he knew where Hood was going.

Inexperience in combat was beginning to show. Against Thomas's instructions to keep his forces concentrated, Schofield's men were now widely scattered. Unsure of whether to hold his position or retreat back to Nashville, Schofield did neither.[29]

The activity was shifting gradually northward along the Columbia-Franklin Turnpike. Approximately halfway between the two towns lay the little village of Spring Hill. On November 29 the small town would take on great importance.

General Hood put his plan into practice on November 29. He left two divisions of infantry under Stephen D. Lee to occupy Schofield's attention, and with the remainder of his forces, some 19,621 footsoldiers,[30] set off for Spring Hill. The idea was still to get in the rear of Schofield's bluecoats. The enemy would thus be separated from their base at Nashville, and trapped between two powerful Confederate forces. Forrest was to ride forward to Spring Hill and take control of the village before Hood and Lee arrived.[31]

As Hood looked at his map, the distance to Spring Hill was only 12 miles. However, that was the straight-line distance. In reality, the troops were marching along winding country roads. The distance of the march was 17 miles. Hood's arrival in Spring Hill would be delayed.[32]

Forrest spent most of the morning on the 29th in separate cavalry actions, and had pushed the Northern horsemen back to the outskirts of Spring Hill. A courier arrived from General Hood. The gunfire was audible to the infantry as they approached the town. The grayclad veterans moved forward rapidly toward the sound of the fighting.[33]

The Federals did not march with any sense of speed. General Stanley led his troops northward in an almost leisurely fashion.[34] As they drew near the village, Stanley could hear the cavalry action up ahead, and he realized the seriousness of the situation. At approximately 12:30 P.M.,[35] the lead brigade of Union infantry charged forward, under the leadership of General Emerson Opdycke. These troops took up a position on the north side of Spring Hill, which was not under threat of Confederate attack. Forrest had been fighting on the east side of town.

Right behind Opdycke's men came John Lane's brigade. They were directed to the right, which put them directly in the path of Forrest's onrushing troopers. Lane's men charged furiously, and were able to push the Southerners back.

The last brigade in Stanley's column belonged to Luther Bradley. These bluecoats deployed south of Lane's position, but were ready to act as a reserve if the need arose. Around 2:00 P.M.,[36] Bradley sent the 64th Ohio regiment forward to act as skirmishers. Soon these Yankees were hotly engaged.

By 3:00 P.M., Forrest was still fighting the enemy. His cavalry were holding on against Union infantry, cavalry and artillery, and the rebels were running low on ammunition. The graycoats needed Hood![37]

Fortune soon was to smile on the Southerners. A Union courier with a dispatch from Thomas to Schofield was captured by the rebel cavalry. The message was a direct order to fall back to Franklin. Forrest now knew what Schofield did not: the Yankees must retreat or they would be trapped.[38]

Franklin was the Union army's next destination, but the Northerners were still south of Spring Hill. Once Hood's infantry seized the turnpike to Franklin, Schofield's entire force would be cut off. Only one question remained for Nathan Bedford Forrest: where was Hood?[39]

The next series of events were the most important moments in the battle of Spring Hill. They would determine not only the fate of that battle, but would also influence the action at Franklin and Nashville as well.

About 3:00 P.M.,[40] Hood issued several orders. Still some 2½ miles[41] south of Spring Hill, the graycoats were just crossing Rutherford Creek. General Hood had heard the fighting in the town, and acted accordingly.

Hood first issued an order to Benjamin F. "Frank" Cheatham. He was to take his troops, wade across Rutherford Creek, and join General Forrest at Spring Hill.[42]

A. P. Stewart would halt his men on the south side of Rutherford Creek. From this position he would be able to act in support of Cheatham or prevent a flanking movement by the Federals, should such an emergency arise.[43]

Hood then rode northward to the high ground on top of the Rally Hill Turnpike. From here he had a clear view to the southwest. He could see the Columbia-Franklin Turnpike filled with bluecoats streaming north toward Spring Hill. Sensing that the real Union threat would come from Columbia, not Spring Hill, Hood began changing his plans.[44]

Patrick Cleburne was the finest division commander in Hood's entire army.[45] Hood placed Cleburne's three brigades facing west, aligned in a stair-step fashion with Mark Lowrey's brigade on the right. Daniel Govan's men were in the center, and Hiram Granbury's rebels were on the left. By placing Cleburne's men in this formation, Hood was ready to move forward to the Columbia-Franklin Turnpike, then turn left and attack Schofield's men as they moved toward Spring Hill.[46]

South of Cleburne's Confederates was William Bate's division. Bate was following Cheatham's instructions, and had prepared his troops to support Cleburne. His men were aligned in a similar stair-step formation.[47]

Cheatham had ridden ahead to observe the action. He would not see Hood that day. The battle of Spring Hill would turn on this seemingly minor detail.

Frank Cheatham was working under Hood's original orders. His focus was on the enemy at Spring Hill. Hood had revised his thinking: he believed the danger was coming from Columbia.[48]

Cleburne's rebels surged forward around 4:00 P.M.[49] Lowrey's brigade encountered the Yankees under Luther Bradley. Many of these troops were new recruits without much battle experience. Hood's stair-step alignment had put the Confederates at a disadvantage, as Govan's brigade was unable to participate in the first assault. Cleburne was able to direct his Govan back into the action; however, Granbury's men continued straight ahead toward the turnpike.[50]

When the Southerners charged forward, Bradley's unseasoned Federals broke in disorder. In ten minutes, the contest was finished.[51] Both of the Southern brigades pursued the bluecoats in the direction of Spring Hill, but the rebels were halted by a blast of Federal artillery. General Stanley had had the presence of mind to place several field pieces near the Columbia-Franklin Turnpike.[51a]

Just after sundown,[52] General Cheatham began to concentrate his forces. Cleburne's men had driven the enemy back, but Cheatham ordered a halt. John Brown's division was placed on Cleburne's right, while William Bate's graycoats moved forward in support.[53] There were now some 6,800 Southerners awaiting orders from Cheatham to assault the foe, with approximately an equal number close behind.[54] The Federals in Spring Hill numbered between 4,000 and 5,000 men. Including Forrest's cavalry, Hood had some 25,000 troops in the immediate area.[54a]

Around 5:30 P.M.,[55] General Brown started to send his men forward. It appeared as if General Stanley's Yankees did not stand a chance. The Northerners at Spring Hill should be shortly overwhelmed.

The sound of Brown's gunfire was to be the signal for the entire Southern advance. However, General Brown soon discovered that the enemy front extended well beyond his right flank. To advance would invite disaster, as the Federals would envelop the Confederate right. He would stop and wait until he had consulted with Cheatham.[56]

By the time the two generals were able to confer, it was about 6:15 P.M.[57] and darkness had covered the battlefield. It was no longer possible to make an accurate estimate of the Union position or strength. Cheatham decided that he would let Hood make the final decision.[58]

Hood was still preoccupied with the activity on the turnpike. General Bate had reached the pike earlier in the day, but had pulled his men back when he received Cheatham's instructions to align himself on Cleburne's left flank. A. P. Stewart had moved his troops north of Spring Hill to strike the turnpike there, but found his corps halted before they reached the road. One of Cheatham's staff officers had directed in Hood's name that Stewart form on Brown's right. Needless to say, A. P. Stewart was astounded to see his assault suddenly stop.

From Bate on the south to Stewart on the north, the Confederates had been pulled away from Hood's intended target: the Columbia-Franklin Turnpike.

Confusion and disbelief could not have been greater. Communication had been nonexistent between the leading Southern generals.

The Union forces were in disarray. The bluecoats had been roughly handled, first by Forrest, then by Cleburne. The Confederates had a decided numerical advantage. Schofield and Stanley were still widely separated. Yet the attack never came.

General Hood believed that the Yankees would still be there in the morning. Although the graycoats were in close proximity, they had not actually taken control of the turnpike. Still, Hood was not alarmed. During the night, the entire Union army slipped right through the fingers of the Confederates, and silently marched northward on the road to Franklin. The Federal officers had realized just how dangerous the situation was. General Luther Bradley wrote the following just a few days later: "It was the most critical time I have ever seen. If only the enemy had shown his usual boldness, I think he would have beaten us disastrously."[59]

By 5:00 A.M.[60] on November 30, the bluecoats had vanished, and the action at Spring Hill was over. The lost opportunity for the Confederates was enormous. Had the Union troops been captured or destroyed as they should have been, the Federal forces at Franklin and Nashville would have been much weaker.

The responsibility for this failure must lie with John Bell Hood. He was the commanding general, yet communication with his subordinates was horrendous. Not only was Hood unaware of the enemy's position, he was ignorant of the Confederate dispositions and alignment as well.

This was a mistake the Confederacy could ill afford to make. There was nothing left to do but pursue General Schofield as the drama shifted to the fateful fields of Franklin.

November 30, 1864

Franklin

J. B. Hood (CSA)	J. M. Schofield (USA)

After their miraculous escape at Spring Hill, the Union soldiers trudged along the Columbia-Franklin Turnpike. November 30 brought a collective sigh of relief among the Federal troops, for they realized how close they had come to capture or annihilation. Located on the Harpeth River, Franklin, Tennessee was just a small village 12 miles north of Spring Hill,[1] but it was the next community of any size on the road to Nashville.

As the bluecoats arrived in Franklin, the soldiers began to construct fortifications on the south side of the town. The Confederates were coming soon, and Union General John Schofield had to make sure that his men were well prepared.

General John B. Hood believed that it was possible to move around the enemy on the road to Nashville. Unfortunately, he would not listen to his own advice that day. He sent Frank Cheatham with his corps up the Columbia-Franklin Turnpike. They were marching straight toward the center of the Union defenses. However, the Southerners also had a corps under A. P. Stewart, advancing off to the east on the Lewisburg Pike.[2] Outside the Union left flank, Stewart's men were a cause of great concern to General Schofield.

The Yankees had deployed two brigades along the road to contest Cheatham's advance. They were commanded by General George Wagner. Wagner positioned Joseph Conrad east of the pike and John Lane's brigade on the west side of the road. The Federals, about one-half mile in front of the town,[2a] intended to delay Hood's men so that the remainder of the bluecoats could reach the safety of the defenses in Franklin. Soon a second line of earthworks appeared. As the Confederates approached it became apparent that a battle was imminent.[3]

Hood's decision to send A. P. Stewart east to the Lewisburg Pike was a mistake. Stewart's men could have hidden Cheatham's troops from view prior to the main Confederate attack. As a result, both Stewart and Cheatham had their corps in plain sight of the enemy, allowing the Northerners more time to prepare for the assault that they were about to receive.[4]

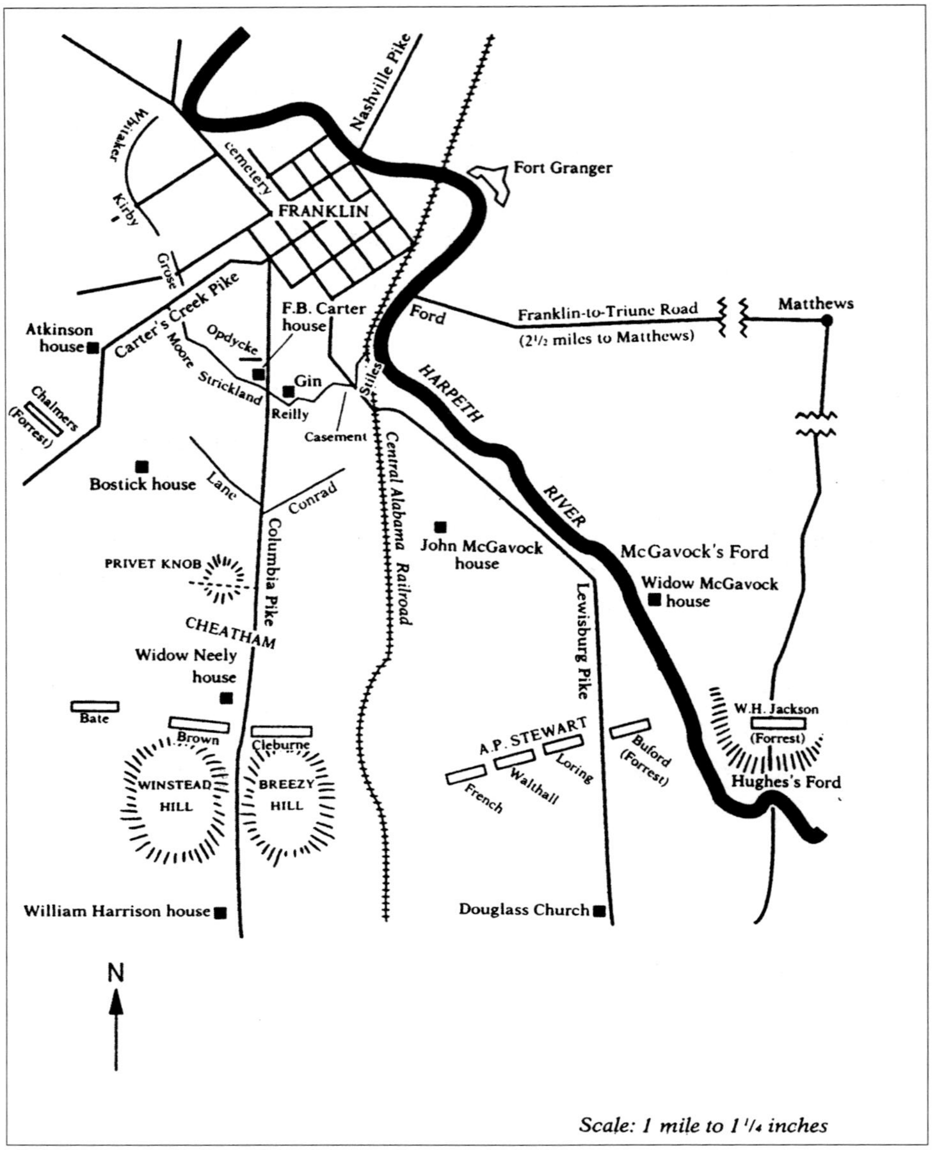

Confrontation at Franklin, November 30, 1864.

Still upset about Cheatham's failure the day before at Spring Hill, General Hood was going to make sure that Cheatham's troops fought today.[5] However, the Confederate attack at Franklin on November 30 would prove to be a horrible product of Hood's frustration.[6]

The Union troops south of each side of the Columbia Pike retreated without a fight, and around 2:00 P.M., both brigades gave up the hills in front of Cheatham's corps. The result of this move was to give General Hood a false sense of security.[6a] It reinforced his belief in the value of frontal attacks.

As John B. Hood looked out at the enemy he failed the Confederacy once again. The Federals were visible some two miles[7] in the distance. The earthworks were quite formidable. Hood summoned his generals for a conference. Unfortunately, the commanding general had already decided on his plan of attack. Despite the objections of Nathan Bedford Forrest, his chief of cavalry, Frank Cheatham, who would make the assault, and Patrick Cleburne, Hood's finest division commander, General Hood decided to charge the Union breastworks.[8]

Cheatham was ordered to use two of his three divisions, Cleburne's and John Brown's, and attack directly along the Columbia-Franklin Turnpike.[9] Cleburne was to be on the right of the road, Brown on the left. The Confederates were not to shoot their guns, but were to charge the Union breastworks and drive the foe back toward Franklin. The graycoats would first use the bayonet, then fire at the enemy as they turned and ran. Hood believed that if Franklin fell, Nashville would soon be his.[10]

Around 2:45 P.M., the Confederates began to surge forward. On Brown's left was Cheatham's third division, under the command of William Bate. To the east, along the Lewisburg Pike were the three divisions of A. P. Stewart's Corps. From left to right were Samuel French, Edward Walthall and William Loring. General Forrest was ordered to divide his cavalry, placing horsemen on each end of the line, supporting Bate and Loring.[11]

From a strategic viewpoint, Hood had his greatest concentration on the Confederate right. There were four divisions of infantry (Cleburne, French, Walthall and Loring) along with two divisions of cavalry (Abraham Buford and William Jackson) east of the Columbia Pike.[12]

By 4:00 P.M., all of the Confederates were in motion.[13] Just over 20,000 graycoats[13a] had assembled for the attack. Hood's Army of Tennessee was to encounter a novelty at the battle of Franklin. The men were used to fighting in heavily wooded terrain. For the first time they were completely exposed to the fire of the enemy and almost the entire field was visible to the men in the ranks.[14] The lack of protection would not bode well for the Southerners.

The ground along the turnpike seemed to be alive

with rebels. Both Conrad and Lane appeared headed for certain destruction, but General Wagner ordered their brigades to stand and fight. As Cleburne and Brown led their troops forward, Union fingers grew tense upon their triggers. Suddenly "Fire!" rang out along the line and the Federal earthworks erupted in flame.[15]

Graycoats fell, but gaps in the lines were quickly filled. On they came. At point blank range Cleburne's men delivered a tremendous volley. The Yankees had not been able to reload their weapons quickly enough, and the grayclad enemy surged over the makeshift defenses. Fighting was hand to hand, slashing with bayonets and clubbed muskets.[16]

Making matters worse for the Federals was the unchecked advance of A. P. Stewart along the Lewisburg Turnpike. General Conrad had been easily outflanked on his left, but the center had also given way near the Columbia Pike.[17] Combined, Lane and Conrad had fewer than 4,000 men to face approximately 8,000 Confederates.[18]

General Wagner's small force quickly turned and fled for the rear. The Confederates chased them as fast as they could, and the open field quickly became clogged with a mass of humanity struggling to gain the safety of the Union breastworks in the rear.[19] The Federals back in Franklin were unable to fire their artillery for fear of hitting their own men. All order was lost in the confusion.[20]

As the rebels reached the second Union line, a violent blast shook the ground. Federals behind the parapet had opened fire without orders. Men on both sides dropped in rows as sheets of lead cut through the air.[21]

The field was thick with bullets, shrapnel and bursting artillery shells. However, there were simply too many Confederates for the Northerners to hold back. The Yankees attempted to regroup in the rear, as the gray wave swarmed over them.[22]

John M. Schofield was now faced with a difficult problem. He had counted on the breastworks thrown up in front of Lane and Conrad to dissuade Hood from actually attacking. As Schofield peered through his field glasses, he could see that his assumption had been in error. The Union earthworks had been easily overrun, and the retreat to Nashville might be in danger.[23] The Union army was suddenly forced into fighting a battle with the Harpeth River at their backs.

The Confederates had advanced far enough so that they were actually closer to the bridges over the river than the Federals. Schofield was trapped![24]

The situation was truly desperate. Colonel Emerson Opdycke had his brigade just west of the Columbia-Franklin Turnpike. He saw Lane and Conrad disintegrate, as the Union lines streamed back in his direction. The Ohioan attempted to shift part of his force across the turnpike to meet the Confederate assault, but in the confusion, some of his men understood this to be an order to advance.[25]

The 73rd Illinois regiment surged forward, and other units along the line were carried forward in the impetus of the charge.[26] His men completely out of control, Opdycke followed his bluecoats forward. With bayonets at the ready, the Federals ran right into the advancing rebels. Vicious hand-to-hand fighting ensued. Smoke covered the battlefield and visibility was poor. With men running wildly in all directions, the combat was a disorganized brawl, with every man for himself.[27]

Opdycke's men moved forward in a very narrow area. This resulted in a condensed mass of bluecoats. When the Confederates saw how many Yankees were in their front, it appeared as if reinforcements had arrived. Temporarily, this checked the Southern advance. The vigorous countercharge of the Northern troops pushed the rebels back, and Opdycke captured 394 prisoners.[28] However, the Confederates still controlled the Columbia Pike.

Charge after charge was made, but each was repulsed. The Southern attacks had become uncoordinated; they lacked cohesion.[29] Men from Cleburne's, Brown's and Bate's divisions stormed the Federal lines, with help from some of Stewart's troops who had drifted into the area. Opdycke's brigade had been joined by the remnants of Lane and Conrad's commands. Colonel Silas Strickland added his bluecoats to the defense, and the Yankees held firm. The action was furious around the Carter House west of the road.

As the light grew dim, the killing tailed off. The slaughter on both sides had been horrific, and the contest was a stalemate. The Federals held the area west of the turnpike, while the graycoats were still in force along the road itself. The battle of Franklin would have to turn on the action in another sector.

On the Confederate right, A. P. Stewart had some 10,000 men advancing along the Lewisburg Pike. In addition, the rebels had about 1,300 dismounted cavalry of Buford's division and 4,000 infantry under Pat Cleburne.[30]

Opposing this assault force were three brigades of Union troops, commanded by General James A. Reilly. Reilly led his own brigade, and placed it on the right. In the center were Colonel Jack Casement's troops near the Cotton Gin. On the left, near the railroad cut, was Colonel Israel Stiles' brigade. Combined the Federals numbered some 5,000 men.[31]

The Federal artillery shells began to explode within the Southern ranks, but the infantry held their fire. At 75 yards, Stewart's men charged,[32] and the Yankees poured a destructive volley of lead into the rebels.

Reilly's men were well protected. They had constructed earthworks, but in front of the dirt was a four-foot-high barrier of heavily thorned osage hedges. The thickness of these hedges provided an almost impenetrable wall of protection for the bluecoats. Jim Reilly's troops were supported by the massed guns of Battery M, 4th U.S. Artillery.[33]

In less than an hour, General Loring's main charge had been defeated. Walthall met with a similar fate. The obstruction of the hedges was simply too severe. However, Cleburne's division had found an opening. His gray-clad veterans swarmed into the Union lines along the Columbia Turnpike opposite Reilly's brigade. Reilly rushed Union reinforcements to the scene, and his prompt action halted the rebel charge for the moment.[34]

Pat Cleburne's hard-hitting division did not give up so easily. The Irishman led his troops to within 40 yards[35] of the Federal works when a bullet ripped through his heart. The finest general in the Army of Tennessee lay dead on the field.[36]

The Confederate left achieved some success at first. General John Brown moved forward against Thomas Ruger's division of bluecoats. The weakest point in the Union lines was just east of some locust trees,[36a] held by the 111th Ohio regiment. The graycoats broke the Union lines, but reinforcements were quickly rushed to the scene. The superior firepower of the Federal artillery tore huge gaps in the attacking lines. The Confederates had lost so many men that they were able to hold their positions, but no longer had enough strength to attack.[36b]

A bit further west, William Bate's division advanced along the Carter's Creek Pike. Unfortunately for the rebels, Bate had decided to divide his already small division. With part of his force east of the pike and part of it on the west side, he had neither the manpower to carry the Union earthworks nor the ability to support General Brown in his attack. The men on the east side of the road made a temporary breakthrough against the Federals of the 183rd Ohio regiment, but on balance Bate's assault was a weak one.

One more Confederate corps had just arrived from Spring Hill under the command of General Stephen D. Lee. An ill-advised night attack by Edward Johnson's division yielded nothing but additional casualties.[36bb] While it would have been advisable for Hood to have had Lee's division at Franklin in the first place, it would clearly have been better to have never attempted the frontal attacks at all. A flanking maneuver to separate Schofield from Nashville would most probably have been the superior tactic, with far fewer Confederate casualties in the process.

General Hood was guilty of one more mistake on that fateful November day. General Forrest had advocated the use of his cavalry as a mobile strike force to outflank the Federals. In this manner Forrest wished to move around the Federals and head for Nashville. However, Hood had decided to split the Confederate cavalry apart, using the troopers as support for the infantry attack. As a result, both cavalry commands were weaker than they otherwise would have been, and were reduced to a minor role in the conflict.[36c]

The worst of the carnage was yet to come. The Union troops had the advantage of massed artillery firing from behind earthworks. The Confederates on the opposite side of the parapet had to face gunfire coming at them from both sides as well as from in front. Not strong enough to carry the enemy lines and too dangerous to retreat, Hood's ill-conceived frontal assault had turned into a slaughter pen. Federal reinforcements and obstructions such as the osage hedge made the Confederates' task an impossible one.

As their ammunition ran low, many Southerners chose to surrender rather than be subjected to multidirectional fire. As darkness fell upon the fields of Franklin, the fighting slackened in intensity. The cries of the wounded covered the area. Bodies thickly strewn along both sides of the parapet served as a testament to the action which had taken place.

Casualties alone do not tell the story of Franklin. The Confederates lost 1,750 men killed, 4,500 wounded and 702 captured or missing, for a total of 6,952. In contrast, the Federals had only 189 soldiers killed, 1,033 wounded and 1,104 captured or missing, for a total of 2,326.[37]

However, the damage to the Army of Tennessee went much deeper. In no other battle of the entire Civil War did either side lose so many general officers.[38] Dead upon the field were Pat Cleburne, Hiram Granbury, John Adams, S. R. Gist, and Otho Strahl. John Carter was mortally wounded. He would die on December 10. John Brown, Arthur Manigault, William Quarles, Francis Cockrell and Thomas Scott were wounded. George Gordon had been captured.[39]

The Confederacy had lost the services of 12 general officers in General Hood's poorly planned frontal assault at Franklin. Hood had accomplished nothing in his attempt to defeat Schofield, and had wrecked his army in the process.[40]

November 30, 1864
Honey Hill

G. W. Smith (CSA)	J. P. Hatch (USA)

As 1864 drew to a close, General William T. Sherman was marching through Georgia. The Ohioan was headed for Savannah, and the Federal troops in South Carolina wished to ensure that his journey was not interrupted.

On November 28, Union General John G. Foster led a contingent of some 5,500 men[1] south on an amphibious expedition. The bluecoats left Hilton Head, South Carolina and sailed down the Broad River toward Boyd's Neck, approximately 35 miles northeast of Savannah.[2]

The Union plan, upon reaching Boyd's Neck, was to march ten miles to the east and cut the railroad line near the small town of Grahamville.[3] This would prevent Confederate troops from moving south into Georgia.

On November 29, the first of the Federal transports reached their destination, and General Foster turned over command of the Union forces to General John P. Hatch. Hatch took one infantry brigade, a few sailors and eight artillery pieces toward the railroad depot at Grahamville.[4]

On the following morning the Federals reached the depot.[5] The Confederate opposition was a small, unimpressive band of troops. General Gustavus W. Smith commanded around 2,000 Georgia militia and state troops, along with a small force of cavalry and artillery.[6] These men were not bound to serve outside Georgia, but were temporarily in the area to protect the depot until other reinforcements could arrive.[7]

General Hatch advanced four regiments, supported by a second brigade of Union troops which had just arrived from Boyd's Neck. The initial attack was successful, driving the Confederates back. However, the graycoats had formed a second line of defense. About three miles south of the depot, General Smith had posted his troops along a crest of ground known as Honey Hill.[8]

Honey Hill had been constructed only two years earlier to prevent just such an attack, and it was ideal for defense. The terrain was bordered by streams, and the water on each side of the Confederate position prevented a flank attack by the Union forces.[9]

Hatch launched three separate frontal attacks, but each one was easily repulsed. The Confederate artillery fire had a deadly effect, and the bluecoats began to run low on ammunition.[10]

The Federals learned that Confederate reinforcements were on the way, and General Hatch gave the order to fall back. The action at Honey Hill ended in favor of the South, as the militia had lost only 50 men, while the Yankees had suffered 746 casualties.[11]

This minor action had no effect on the overall outcome of the war. The numerical superiority of the Union forces in the southeast was too great to overcome. General Sherman proceeded forward in Georgia, and then turned northward through the Carolinas. He would receive the surrender of the final Confederate forces east of the Mississippi River on April 26, 1865.

December 4, 1864

Waynesborough, Ga.

J. Wheeler (CSA)	H. J. Kilpatrick (USA)

As 1864 drew to a close, General William T. Sherman was marching through Georgia. Atlanta had fallen in September, and opposition to the Union infantry was almost nonexistent. However, the Confederate cavalry was still active, and the Federal horsemen needed to remain vigilant.

General Sherman and his footsoldiers were beginning the infamous "March to the Sea." He did not want any interference from the enemy cavalry, under the direction of General Joseph Wheeler.

Sherman would need the assistance of the Union troopers, currently encamped in the village of Louisville, Georgia. On December 1, the mounted bluecoats were to head northeast,[1] in the direction of Augusta.

Led by General H. Judson Kilpatrick, the Federals received orders to attack the graycoats at every opportunity. If the Union cavalry headed toward Augusta, their movement might well deceive the enemy infantry into believing that Sherman was also headed in that direction.[2]

Joe Wheeler did not intend to make life easy for his adversary. On December 3, the Confederates destroyed railroad track on the route from Millen to Augusta. The rebels darted in, accomplished their mission, and then withdrew to the safety of Waynesborough, some 30 miles south of Augusta.[3]

Confederate interference would have to be stopped. On the evening of the 3rd, Kilpatrick issued orders for the following day. The enemy at Waynesborough was to be defeated. Wheeler's troops would be assaulted early on the morning of December 4.[4]

About 7:30 A.M.,[5] the Yankees moved out. Colonel Smith D. Atkins led his brigade forward, and horsemen clashed with mounted Confederates just south of the town. The initial attack drove the Southerners back, but Atkins soon met a stronger line of the enemy, behind formidable barricades outside the town.[6]

The first assault on these lines failed to remove the foe. Colonel Atkins ordered the artillery to come up, and shelled the Confederates. Soon the enemy cannon fell silent.[7]

At this point, Atkins decided to attack from three directions. In the center, the 92nd Mounted Illinois Regiment would occupy the attention of the graycoats. On the Union left, the 9th Michigan and 10th Ohio Cavalry would charge forward. On the right, the 9th Ohio Regiment would try to envelop the left flank of the Confederates.[8]

The rebels tried to hold their ground. Resistance was stubborn, but the Confederates fell back to a second line of barricades, longer than the first. This would be too difficult to outflank.[9]

General Kilpatrick decided that a new approach was in order. He called up Colonel Eli Murray's brigade. About midday,[10] the bluecoats were hurled forward in a frontal assault. The Confederate defenses collapsed, and the rebels retreated across Brier Creek, some four miles north of Waynesborough.[11]

As the conflict at Waynesborough was a cavalry action, casualties were not high. The Confederates lost approximately 250 men, while the Federals suffered about 190 casualties. However, several bridges over Brier Creek had been burned, the Federals were in possession of the battlefield, and the Southerners were pinned in Augusta, where they would remain while General Sherman swept across Georgia.[12]

December 15–16, 1864
NASHVILLE

J. B. Hood (CSA) — G. H. Thomas (USA)

With their spirits lifted from victory at Franklin on November 30, Union General John M. Schofield and his troops began the 18-mile journey[1] to Nashville. On the morning of December 1 he led his bluecoats into the city, finally completing the junction with the Union forces already there, under the leadership of General George H. Thomas.

The Federals began constructing their defenses, in preparation for a Confederate attack. Thomas had five separate commands with which he would defend the city. Some 4,000 men had been stationed in Nashville under Thomas while Schofield had been fighting at Spring Hill and Franklin. General A. J. Smith brought about 9,000 soldiers from Missouri as reinforcements. These battle-hardened veterans were sound combat troops. The third element at Thomas's disposal were the 24,000 troops which had just arrived with Schofield. These were 14,000 men of the IV Corps, now under the command of General Thomas J. Wood, and Schofield's own XXIII Corps, which totaled approximately 10,000 men. The fourth segment under General Thomas was the 8,500 man force led by General James B. Steedman. In addition to these Federals, General James H. Wilson brought with him around 6,500 exhausted cavalrymen who had been through hard fighting during the last several days.[2] Thomas sent Wilson's cavalry across the Cumberland River to Edgefield, so that the troopers and their horses could get much needed rest.[3]

The Cumberland River winds its way around the city of Nashville so as to provide a natural barrier to an attacking army. The Federal garrison built their defensive fortifications so that the earthworks faced southwest, south and southeast. Each end was anchored on the river, with Nashville behind the Yankees.[4]

After the fiasco at Spring Hill and the destructive battle at Franklin in late November, Confederate General John B. Hood ordered his beaten army toward Nashville. On December 2, the rebels made their way up the Franklin-Nashville Turnpike and General Stephen D. Lee brought his corps into the city around 2:00 P.M. The next day, Generals A. P. Stewart and Benjamin F. "Frank" Cheatham arrived with the two remaining corps of Hood's army.[5]

The Confederate troop deployment quickly revealed the obvious problem: Hood simply did not have enough men. After the battle of Franklin, the Confederate strength was reduced to approximately 21,000 men available for battle, exclusive of cavalry.[6] To make matters worse, Hood divided his mounted arm into fragments. He kept part of his troopers around Nashville, but sent the majority of the cavalry toward Murfreesboro, Tennessee under the chief of cavalry, General Nathan B. Forrest.[6a] This would be very important in the days to come.

A four-mile gap still remained between the Confederate left and the Cumberland River, while Hood's right ended a full mile from the water.[7] Why General Hood ever thought of giving battle at Nashville with such a small force remains a mystery.

Despite his advantage, General Thomas was in no mood to attack. A defensive general by nature, Thomas had made up his mind to let his cavalry get some rest. The Yankees would wait until their commanding officer was ready to fight.[8]

The result of all of Hood's attention to Murfreesboro was that Thomas was ready to attack with an army three times as large as Schofield's force at Franklin. Arrayed against the Yankees was an army even smaller than that which Hood possessed at Franklin. The advantage was clearly with the Federals.[9] The only issue was when George H. Thomas would strike.

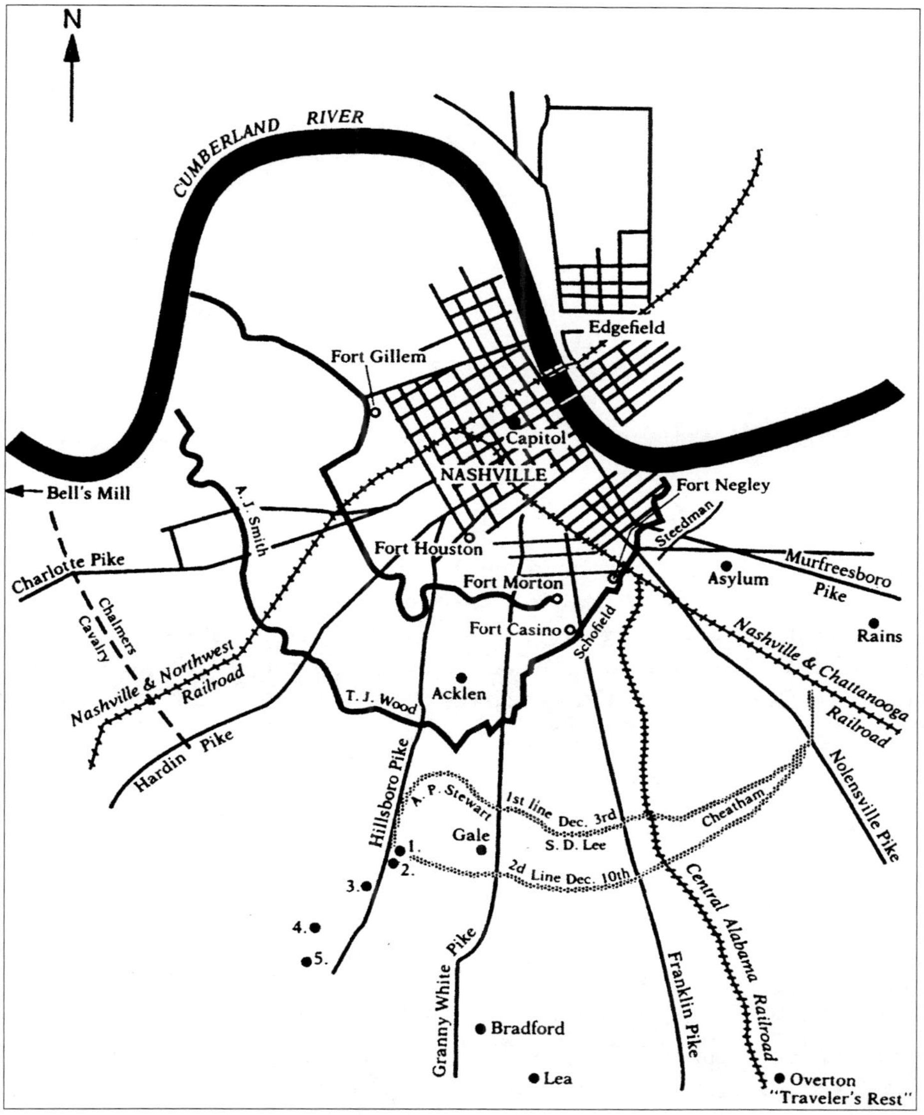

Confrontation at Nashville, December 2–15, 1864.

The weather had turned frightfully cold in December. The fields had become sheer ice. Offensive operations were out of the question, and a Federal attack planned for the 10th of the month had to be called off due to the swirling winds and heavy snow.[10] The harsh conditions persisted until the 14th when warmer temperatures quickly melted the snow, turning Nashville into "a sea of mud" according to one Michigan cavalryman.[11]

General Thomas was busy that evening as preparations were made throughout the Union army for an attack to be made early the next morning.[12]

The morning of December 15 saw heavy fog blanket the city. The bluecoats proceeded cautiously, as visibility was very poor. The Union intent was to attack the Confederate left flank. General Wilson's cavalry would lead, and take a position on the far right of the assault force. General A. J. Smith would place his comparatively fresh men on Wilson's left. The IV Corps under General Wood was to be on Smith's left. Schofield's troops were to act as a general reserve, and as such did not occupy a prominent place in Thomas's thought process.[13]

Although the main thrust would be against the Confederate left, General Thomas realized that a diversion against the enemy's right would ensure success of the Federal operations. General Steedman was ordered to take his troops along the Murfreesboro Pike and attack General Hood's right flank.

Steedman sent two brigades along the pike, commanded by Colonel Thomas Morgan and Lieutenant Colonel Charles Grosvenor. Colonel Charles Thompson would take Steedman's third brigade along the path of the Chattanooga & Nashville Railroad.[14]

Morgan's troops led the way. With Colonel Morgan in charge of overall operations, the immediate command of the advance was held by Colonel William Shafter of the 17th U.S. Colored Troops. The Yankees brushed past some rifle pits with little resistance, until they came to a deep cut for the railroad tracks. At this point the ground became a sheer drop, preventing the Federals from continuing. As the bluecoats came to a halt, they were greeted by a sudden blast of fire. The Confederates had hidden behind some logs and the surrounding underbrush, and Morgan's men were trapped.[15]

Many of Colonel Shafter's troops had never been exposed to combat before, and tremendous panic ensued. The Federals had ventured to within 30 yards of the rebel guns. They never had a chance. In less than ten minutes, Shafter lost 110 men and 7 officers.[16]

Morgan witnessed the disorder among Shafter's troops and sent Grosvenor's men into the action. They rushed the fallen logs or lunette which the graycoats had constructed. The parapet was too difficult to storm by force, but they were able to relieve some of the pressure on Shafter's men. The assault against Hood's right was a complete failure, as Grosvenor's brigade suffered 60 casualties and were thoroughly repulsed by the well-fortified Confederates.[17]

The other end of the Union line was struggling as well. The U.S. Cavalry got off to a very slow start, and the lone division of Southern horsemen still in Nashville were able to pull back before any major battle took place.

Union infantry under General Wood advanced and overran the skirmish line. When General Thomas realized what a weak attack his troops had made, it was clear that the real battle had not yet begun.[18]

General Hood felt that the Confederates held a strong defensive position, if he could only persuade George Thomas to attack. He had directed General A. P. Stewart to construct a series of five small forts or redoubts along the Hillsboro Pike. If Thomas would just make the mistake of attacking these fortifications, perhaps the battle of Franklin would repeat itself in Hood's favor.[19]

General A. J. Smith formed his Federal troops on Wood's right. Smith's men were supposed to be between Wood's infantry and the cavalry on the far right. However, they drifted too close to Wood, creating a gap on their right. General Thomas saw the problem and ordered Schofield to place his men in the open area. This would allow Wilson's horsemen to get outside the left flank of the Confederates.[20] The bluecoats had the advantage of numbers; it was up to Thomas to use them effectively.

Although Hood was clearly in a better position than he had been on November 30, the problem remained that the Southerners still did not have enough men. Redoubt No. 5 was somewhat isolated, some 600 yards[21] south of Redoubt No. 4.

Union cavalry stormed the position. The Confederates had approximately 100 men arrayed against some 1,500 Federal troopers. The graycoats at Redoubt No. 5 stood no chance against the powerful onslaught.[22] While the victory was a relatively easy one, it was short-lived. General Stewart's men in Redoubt No. 4 had turned their artillery toward the captured enclosure, and began shelling the Federal cavalry with deadly projectiles.[23] The plight of the Northern cavalry was summed up by a member of the 2nd Iowa: "to remain in our captured fort was certain death, to retreat promised little better, while to attempt the capture of this second fort seemed madness."[24]

The order was given to charge. Quickly the cavalry surged forward. Many were dismounted, fighting like infantry. They were able to capture Redoubt No. 4, but not without some help from the Confederates. Many of the Southerners were still at their posts, but one gunner had fled, taking with him the friction primers necessary to fire the artillery pieces. Resistance was brief, and the second fort was soon taken.[25]

General A. J. Smith's infantry began to move forward. The cavalry was exhausted, but the troopers were now outside the Confederate flank. The rebels were beginning to reform their lines, and the next three redoubts would certainly be more difficult. The bluecoats had the advantage in numbers. Would they be able to press the attack successfully, or could General Hood find some reinforcements?

Redoubt No. 3 appeared to be very formidable, as it was located on high ground, but the apparent advantage was misleading. General John McArthur led his enthusiastic Yankees as they charged the redoubt. The fort was elevated so much that the Confederates could not depress their artillery pieces. The rebels fired their muskets, but their aim was high. Once again, superior numbers told the story, and some of the graycoats fled the earthworks at the sight of the swarming blue horde.[26]

With firm control of the third fort, the Union grip was tightening. A. P. Stewart knew that the Confederates were in trouble. The Southerners were being rolled back. Union forces were attacking on three sides. It seemed as if only darkness would save Stewart from destruction.[27]

About 4:30 P.M.,[28] General Wood ordered Nathan Kimball's division forward to assault Redoubt No. 1. On Kimball's right, General Washington Elliott brought his division into the action. Most of the graycoats in the area had fled, and soon organized retreat turned into panic. A. P. Stewart's corps was in full flight, streaming east and south in their efforts to escape the Yankees.[29]

At first glance, it had seemed as though the five redoubts could provide a strong line of defense for Hood's men. The inherent weakness was that they were not connected by strong entrenchments. Had the forts been joined by breastworks, the Confederate position would have been a strong one indeed. As it was, the redoubts were barely more than isolated enclosures which were captured with little effort.

It seemed that there was nothing left for the Federals to do but round up the fugitives. Thomas ordered General Wood to pursue the foe at first light on December 16. The Confederates had been soundly defeated, and Thomas knew it. The enemy's logical move would be to retreat and regroup. But would the mercurial Hood change his mind again and risk everything in a desperate counterattack?[30]

As the graycoats retreated in a southerly direction, Hood contracted his lines. The Confederate right now rested firmly on Overton Hill, just east of the Franklin Pike. Stephen Lee's troops held this area. In the center was the battered corps under A. P. Stewart. On the left were the men of Frank Cheatham's Corps. The left was anchored on Shy's Hill, slightly west of the Granny White Pike.[31] Curiously, Hood still had not made use of General Forrest's horsemen.

Trees were felled, and obstructions and strong earthworks quickly appeared. General Hood wanted to be sure that his troops were protected.

Opposing the Southerners were the divisions under Steedman, Wood, Smith and Schofield, from the Union left to right. James Wilson placed his mounted troops on Schofield's right, close to the Hillsboro Pike.[32]

December 16 saw the bluecoats in the midst of inactivity. No one seemed to be giving any orders, and the lines advanced cautiously. The battle plan was to attack the Confederate left. However, Wood and Steedman would be given an opportunity to strike Hood's right if the opportunity arose.[33]

Thomas Wood realized that if Overton Hill could be carried, not only would the right flank of the enemy be turned, but Hood's line of retreat would be cut off as well. The imposing hill covered with breastworks and obstructions looked very formidable, but the reward could be well worth it. Wood had only been in command of the IV Corps a short time, as General David Stanley had been wounded at Franklin. General Wood was anxious to make a good impression.[34]

Steedman was receptive to an attack on the hill, and volunteered to cooperate. However, most of Steedman's men were colored troops who had not had much battle experience. Their task today would be a frontal assault against a strongly fortified position.[35] At 2:45 P.M.,[36] Thomas J. Wood gave the order to advance on Overton Hill.

Thompson's brigade of U.S. colored troops would lead the way with Grosvenor's brigade in close support. They were supposed to align their movements on the left of Colonel Sidney Post's men.[37] Thompson and Grosvenor were under General Steedman's command, while Post reported to General Wood.

The Union courage was unquestioned, but Stephen Lee's rebels poured a destructive fire of musketry and artillery upon the bluecoats. The Union lines became intermingled. Post's men fared no better. Wave after wave of Federal regiments attempted to scale the heights, only to be slaughtered during the ascent. The 13th U.S. Colored Troops made one last, futile attack, losing 220 officers and men on the slopes of Overton Hill.[38]

This was not the day that George Thomas had envisioned. In pointless frontal assaults against strong earthworks, the Northerners had been thoroughly repulsed, and Sidney Post had been wounded. The Union left was coming apart, due to General Wood's unchecked ambition. Would Thomas find success on the other end of his line, or would the rebels slip through his fingers and escape to fight again?

On the far right the cavalry pushed forward, Colonel Datus Coon's brigade driving the Confederate horsemen back across the Granny White Pike. General Hood's decision to send Nathan B. Forrest to Murfreesboro was coming back to haunt him. Without Forrest's troopers to block the Union advance, the rebels had lost one avenue of escape. The Franklin Pike was the only road left to the embattled Confederates.

General John McArthur commanded the 1st Division of A. J. Smith's Corps. Stationed near the Granny White Pike, his men looked south at the steep hills rising above them. The ground was rugged, but McArthur knew that if the Federals could capture Shy's Hill, Hood would not be able to hold his position.[39]

General Thomas wanted Schofield to be able to act in concert with McArthur, and around 4:00 P.M.[40] the artillery opened a furious bombardment of the entrenched Confederates. John McArthur could sense an opportunity. He sent William McMillan's brigade forward.[41] The assault was under way.

The Confederate position on Shy's Hill was a strong one. However, General Hood had created a problem without intending to do so. As Coon's cavalry passed around the Southern flank, Hood transferred troops to meet the threat. In so doing, he weakened the defenses on top of Shy's Hill. The graycoats would now have to stretch even further to protect the crest of the hill. General William Bate held the summit, but as he looked to his left he could see the Federal cavalry. At the bottom of the hill were the swarming bluecoats under John McArthur. Bate was truly in a predicament.[42]

The entrenchments on the summit were strong, but the Confederates did not fight well. Jesse Finley's Floridians broke and ran, and suddenly Bate's entire line seemed to disintegrate.[43] The panic spread to A. P. Stewart's troops, and the front line of the Confederate defense dissolved into utter chaos.[44] As the entire line broke down, Stephen Lee's men turned and ran down the Franklin Pike.

The Confederates were fortunate that the pursuit was not as vigorous as it might have been. Had the Yankees been more aggressive, even more of Hood's men would certainly have been captured.[45]

While the beaten Confederates were streaming south down the Franklin Pike, they were unaware that the Federals were racing down the Granny White Pike. If the Union troops could get behind the rebels, Hood's escape would be cut off.[46]

Confederate General James R. Chalmers had deployed his cavalry division south of the battlefield in order to protect the ambulances and wagons which had been sent along the pike prior to the fighting. General Chalmers was suddenly thrust into a most important position. In addition to the wagons, he was the last line of defense for what remained of the Confederate army.[47]

Fortunately, darkness prevailed, and after mild

skirmishing, the Confederates were saved. Heavy rains soon turned the roads to mud, which made it very difficult for an organized pursuit. The Federals would have to be content with dealing the enemy a devastating blow.

As might be expected, casualties ran heavily in favor of the Union. Thomas had lost 387 men killed, 2,558 wounded and 112 captured or missing, for a total of 3,057. Confederate losses for Nashville were not stated; however, it is possible to come up with an accurate estimate. As of December 10, Hood had between 37,000 and 39,000 men present for duty. At the close of the campaign in late December, he had 21,000.[48]

The debacle at Nashville was the crowning blow in a campaign which destroyed Hood's Army of Tennessee. As an effective fighting force it ceased to exist, although fragments of different commands were still intact. Perhaps more important was the psychological impact which the battles had on the minds of the Southern soldier. With many of their best generals killed at Franklin, and horrendous losses in battle, the Army of Tennessee would never again pose any military threat.

It is very important to note that at Nashville, just as he had at Franklin, John B. Hood made the critical and fateful decision which lost the battle for the Confederacy. His orders to send General Forrest and his cavalry off to Murfreesboro allowed the Federals to march around the Confederate left flank. In a futile attempt to protect the left flank, Hood weakened the center, and his whole line caved in.

The career of John Bell Hood is an excellent example of a man promoted beyond his capacity. As a division commander he was a ferocious fighter, as a corps commander his skill diminished somewhat, and as the leader of an entire army he shattered his troops on the rocks of Tennessee.

1865

March 2, 1865

Waynesborough, Va.

J. A. Early (CSA) | P. H. Sheridan (USA)

By the spring of 1865, the Federal cavalry had become a powerful offensive force. As the Civil War progressed, their numbers had increased. On February 27, 10,000 bluecoats headed south from their base at Winchester, Virginia, located at the northern end of the Shenandoah Valley.[1]

The target of the mounted troopers was the Virginia Central Railroad.[2] If traffic on this line could be interrupted, it would have a disastrous effect on the Confederate Army of Northern Virginia. Robert E. Lee needed the railroads to move troops, food and supplies to his weary men in the field.

The Federal horsemen were led by General Philip H. "Little Phil" Sheridan. He wanted to end General Lee's connections to the Shenandoah Valley, and bring the war to an end.

About 90 miles to the south,[3] the Confederates had camped around Staunton, Virginia. In contrast to their Northern counterparts, the war had not been kind to the Confederate horsemen. The once formidable cavalry was now in dire need of men, horses, and equipment.

On March 1, the Federal troopers arrived in Staunton.[4] One day later, the Confederates under Jubal Early marched southeast to Waynesborough. Early was determined to block the Union advance. The rebels faced west, and placed their lines on the west side of the town.[5] The graycoats had the South River at their backs, but the troops were so few that neither flank actually rested on the water.[6] The gaps on the ends of the Southern dispositions would soon prove to be disastrous to General Early's men.

Gabriel Wharton held the line for the Confederates. With 1,200 men[7] at his disposal, his formation had been stretched dangerously thin.

March 2 saw Union General George A. Custer ride toward Waynesborough, attempting to find an opening for a Federal assault.[8] One brigade of bluecoats probed the center of the Confederate line. A frontal attack seemed unlikely to succeed. Custer then sent three dismounted Union regiments around the left flank of the enemy. Armed with special repeating rifles, they soon discovered a gap about one eighth of a mile wide.[9]

General Early saw the bluecoats on his left, but before Wharton could be warned, the Yankees attacked. At about 3:00 P.M.,[10] Custer's men charged into the gap. At the same time, a mounted brigade struck the front of the Confederate line. The shattered remnants of a once proud command could not withstand the powerful Union onslaught.[11]

Wharton's men tried to fall back, but the bluecoats had cut off the escape to the river. Some of the rebels managed to make their way to safety, but many were captured.[12]

The battle had quickly turned into a rout. The bluecoats captured over 1,600 men, about 200 wagons, and 14 artillery pieces. Although it was not a large one, this victory by the Federals put an end to Confederate activity in the Shenandoah Valley.[13]

March 8–10, 1865

Kinston (Wise's Forks)

B. Bragg (CSA) | J. Schofield (USA)

On February 22, 1865, the city of Wilmington, North Carolina, fell into Union hands. This had grave repercussions for the Confederacy. General John M. Schofield commanded the Federal XXIII Corps, which had taken a position in the eastern part of the state around New Berne.[1] With the surrender of Wilmington, the bluecoats were able to turn their attention inland. If the men could march west and join the troops under William T. Sherman, perhaps the Southerners would be defeated and the long war could be brought to a close.

Schofield placed General Jacob D. Cox in charge of a contingent which numbered some 13,000 infantry, along with a small cavalry force and several artillery units.[2] The men made steady progress until early March. On March 7, Cox stopped at Southwest Creek, just below Kinston, North Carolina.[3]

Opposing the Yankees were 6,000 Confederates, principally from General Robert F. Hoke's division.[4] On March 8, the rebels were reinforced by 2,000 men under General D. H. Hill.[5] The southern troops would be under the overall direction of Braxton Bragg, a general with many administrative abilities, but one who had failed repeatedly on the field of battle.

Bragg had prepared fortifications on the west bank of the creek, hoping to prevent the XXIII Corps from joining Sherman's army in the central section of North Carolina. The Federal troops had entrenched around the village of Wise's Forks, and on March 8, the Confederates attacked.

Bragg sent General Hoke around the Union left flank, while D. H. Hill prepared to assault the enemy's right.[6] Crossing Southwest Creek, Hoke came upon a brigade under the command of Colonel Charles Upham. The bluecoats had advanced to a position one mile[7] in front of the main line of defense. Without support, Upham's men broke under the attack, losing one cannon and over 800 prisoners.[8] Unfortunately for the Confederacy, Hoke was not able to accomplish anything further.[9]

General Hill was ordered to attack Upham from the rear, but was unable to encircle the foe. His command might have been used more effectively had he united with Hoke to exploit the advantage gained at Upham's expense.[10]

On March 9, the Federals reinforced their lines, and another attack by Hoke was easily repulsed. On the next day slightly more progress was made, but both Hill and Hoke were forced back as the Federals shifted additional support to threatened areas of their lines.[11]

Casualties in the action around Kinston went heavily in favor of the Confederacy. The bluecoats had 57 men killed, 265 wounded, and 935 captured or missing, for a total loss of 1,257 soldiers. The Southerners lost only 11 men killed, 107 wounded, and 16 captured or missing, for a total of 134 casualties.[12]

Braxton Bragg had been unable to stop the westward movement of his enemy. Better tactics would certainly have helped, as once again Bragg saw an apparent Confederate victory turn into defeat. Overall, the action around Kinston, North Carolina had little impact on the outcome of the war. Schofield and the XXIII Corps marched into Goldsboro a week later and secured a base of supply for General Sherman.[13]

March 10, 1865
Monroe's Crossroads

W. Hampton (CSA)	J. Kilpatrick (USA)

General William T. Sherman began the month of March with the desire to sweep across the Carolinas in one powerful thrust, using his numerical superiority to bring the hostilities to a close. Located on the northern border of South Carolina, the Union Army was made up of four infantry corps, plus a division of cavalry under the command of General Judson Kilpatrick.[1] These forces marched in a northeasterly direction, toward the town of Goldsboro, North Carolina.

In addition to these troops, the Union XXIII Corps under General John M. Schofield had taken a position to the east of Goldsboro. If the Federal forces could unite with one another, their combined strength would be overwhelming.

Although the Federal forces had encountered little opposition as they moved northward through the Carolinas, the bluecoats were not as concentrated as they might have been.

The Union troops were separated into two "wings." The northern, or left wing consisted of the XIV and XX Corps, and was led by General Henry W. Slocum, a 57-year-old West Point graduate who was a battle-hardened veteran. The right, or southern wing was commanded by General Oliver O. Howard, a courageous fighter who had lost his right arm in 1862 at the battle of Seven Pines. He had both the XV and XIV Corps at his disposal.[2]

The Union cavalry guarded the army's left flank, and continued onward toward the small North Carolina hamlet of Monroe's Crossroads. It was here that General Kilpatrick's men would clash with the Confederate horsemen under Wade Hampton.

On March 8, Kilpatrick led his men east along the Morganton Road. The general learned that Confederate infantry had already passed by, heading in the direction of Fayetteville, North Carolina. To the Federals' surprise, the southern Cavalry had not yet arrived. The graycoats were north, and slightly west of the Union position.[3] Hampton's command was approaching on the Yadkin Road. Through a great stroke of luck, General Kilpatrick now found himself between the divided Confederate forces. If he could only defeat the cavalry, he would be able to prevent a junction of enemy troops.[4]

While the opportunity looked good to the Yankees, there was a flaw in the calculations. As of March 1, General Kilpatrick had 4,317 mounted soldiers, compared to about 4,000 Southerners under Hampton. However, the Federals had divided their forces, leaving each one vulnerable to attack. In his zeal to annihilate the Confederate cavalry, Kilpatrick was in reality setting a trap for himself.[5]

Twelve miles away lay Morgan's Crossroads.[6] The small village was formed by the intersection of two main roads. The Morganton Road ran east to Fayetteville, while Blue's Road meandered in a roughly north-south direction.[7] It seemed like an insignificant little spot for the cavalry action which was to come.

On March 9, the Confederates thundered down the Yadkin Road. Matthew Butler's division was in the lead, followed by three divisions under Joseph Wheeler. In a very brief encounter, the Southerners clashed with the Union 5th Kentucky cavalry regiment, capturing 16 prisoners.[8] Although General Kilpatrick was able to escape, the action was only beginning.

Evening found two Union brigades in close proximity on the west side of Blue's Road. Colonel George Spencer's men pitched their tents to the south, while Colonel William Way placed his command further to the north, close to the Morganton Road. General Smith Atkins and his bluecoats were some five miles to the west. A Union scout company under Captain Theo Northrop camped on the east side of Blue's Road.[9] All told, the Yankees had some 1,500 troopers at Morgan's Crossroads, against Hampton's force of some 4,000 graycoats.[10] The scattered deployment of Kilpatrick's cavalry would not bode well for the coming day.

Shortly before midnight,[11] Hampton, Butler and Wheeler reached Kilpatrick's camp. The Federals were asleep, clearly not expecting the onslaught which was to come.

The Confederates prepared for the action. Wheeler would attack with his three divisions from the west. William Allen would anchor his left flank upon the Morganton Road, and to his right were the troopers under William Humes. George Dibrell's division would be held between the two as a mounted reserve.[12]

North of the Morganton Road, Matthew Butler gave instructions to his men. Facing south, they would assault the bluecoats under Colonel Way.[13]

In the early morning fog of March 10,[14] the graycoats charged forward. Initially, the Yankees broke and ran, but were quickly able to reform. The Northerners found cover behind some trees and put up a stubborn resistance.[15]

The rebels had charged forward all at once, instead of obeying General Butler's orders to remain in a regimental alignment. As a result, the men had become somewhat confused. Making matters worse, the Confederates had paused to plunder the Union wagons which had been parked along Blue's Road.[16] Supplies were always in great demand in the Confederacy, and this may have been a temptation too great to pass up.

As the action neared the Monroe house, located just south of the crossroads, battle formations on each side became quite compact. Fighting was furious, and at close quarters.[17] The left half of Wheeler's command had made good progress, as Allen's men surged forward, but Humes and his graycoats were stymied by a swamp in their front. The soggy ground allowed the Federals more time to regroup.[18] The capture of Kilpatrick's cavalry would not be as easy as it looked.

The Union scouts under Captain Northrop quickly moved to support Colonel Way. Suddenly, there was a new enemy force attacking the Confederate left flank. It seemed as if the Federals were receiving reinforcements.[19] By 7:30 A.M.,[20] the Confederates had seen the strength of their charge disappear, and the battle was essentially over.

Casualty figures at Monroe's Crossroads were very sketchy for both sides. General Kilpatrick reported a total loss of 19 men killed, 68 wounded and 103 missing, for a total of 190. However, Colonel Spencer listed almost identical losses in his brigade alone.[21] The Confederates claimed to have inflicted some 500 losses in the action.[22]

On the Confederate side, Wheeler lost 12 men killed, 60 wounded and 10 missing, but there were no returns for General Butler's division. Kilpatrick stated that Union forces had killed about 80 rebels and taken 30 prisoners.[23]

From a tactical standpoint, the battle was poorly conducted by both sides. General Kilpatrick's Federals were asleep and unprepared for a sudden attack. The Confederates failed to exploit their advantage, and did not account for the difficulties presented by a swamp. Moreover, they stopped to plunder Union supply wagons, instead of pressing the advantage gained by surprise.[24]

Amazingly, both sides claimed victory. Kilpatrick reported that he had retaken his camp and equipment, while the Confederates pointed out that they had taken hundreds of prisoners, and had opened the road to Fayetteville.[25] Objectively, it would seem that neither side was entitled to very much credit.

March 16, 1865
AVERASBOROUGH

W. J. Hardee (CSA) — W. T. Sherman (USA)

As the Spring unfolded in 1865, the Federal troops had almost completed their journey through the South. Different commands of the United States Army began to move closer together. The union of large bodies of soldiers would make the defense of the Confederacy all the more difficult. This was the background for the events which were about to take place in North Carolina.

The Federals were under the command of General William T. Sherman, and had camped in the vicinity of Fayetteville, North Carolina. Sherman divided his forces into two wings. The left wing, led by General Henry W. Slocum, would march north, in the direction of Raleigh. The right wing, comprised of General O. O. Howard's men, would advance to the northeast, toward Goldsboro.[1]

On March 15, General William J. Hardee had approximately 6,000 Confederates at his disposal. The graycoats were entrenched facing south, with the Black River to the left and a swamp on the right.[2] Hardee had placed his men in three lines. Lafayette McLaws and his division would form the back line of defense. Some 600 yards further forward,[3] William Taliaferro placed his troops. General Taliaferro advanced one brigade under Colonel Alfred Rhett south an additional 200 yards.[4] Rhett's command would receive the initial Federal assault in this sector.

Federal cavalry skirmished with Rhett's troops during a rainy[5] afternoon, and the colonel from South Carolina was taken captive.

The next day the Union XX Corps clashed with Hardee's troops. Including the cavalry, General Slocum led 20,000 men into battle. The action began with a Federal attack on the Confederate left, but the bluecoats were swiftly beaten back. Two divisions[6] of Federals held the Confederates' attention in the center. About 10:30 A.M.,[7] Sherman ordered one brigade to attack the enemy right flank. This assignment fell to Colonel Henry Case. His instructions were to turn Colonel Rhett's[8] position. The rebels put up a stubborn defense, but the Yankees had too many men.[9] Still, the Confederates had forced General Sherman to deploy all of his cavalry and some 12,000 infantry in a fight which lasted some five hours.[10] Rhett's brigade, now led by Colonel William Butler, had performed admirably under difficult conditions. Nevertheless, Hardee was forced to retreat to a second position along the Smithfield Road.[11]

The Confederates tried to form a second line of defense, but it too crumbled under the weight of the Union assault. The rebels buckled, but were soon reinforced by cavalry under Joseph Wheeler. This brought their strength up to roughly 8,000 men against Sherman's 20,000, and the graycoats were finally able to entrench, extending their right flank all the way to the Cape Fear River.[12] Heavy rains and General Hardee's strong fortifications prevented any further Union advance.

Darkness ended the action for the day, but not before Hardee had lost about 700 men. For his part, Slocum's Northerners had suffered only 554 casualties.[13]

The rebels slipped away during the night, as Hardee attempted to unite his command with other forces in the area. The fighting just south of Averasborough had delayed the Union left wing, and it widened the gap between Slocum and Howard. The Confederates would hope to capitalize on this advantage only three days later at the battle of Bentonville.[14]

March 19–21, 1865
BENTONVILLE

J. E. Johnston (CSA)	W. T. Sherman (USA)

By March 1865, the Federal columns were marching through North Carolina with relative ease. After General William T. Sherman had captured Atlanta in the fall of 1864, his movements to the coast of Georgia and through South Carolina had met with little opposition.

It was the Confederate belief that the Federals would try to move through North Carolina to Virginia and effect a junction with General Ulysses S. Grant. Grant's troops already outnumbered the Army of Northern Virginia, and the graycoats feared a combination of the two giant Union forces would deal a devastating blow to Robert E. Lee's exhausted veterans.[1]

General Joseph E. Johnston was given the task of stopping Sherman's Federals. He was assigned command of the department on February 23, and Johnston needed to consolidate the widely scattered Confederate soldiers.[2]

Sherman was moving east from Fayetteville, North Carolina in the direction of Goldsboro.[3] The Confederates had brought their men together at Smithfield,[4] determined to do whatever possible to check Sherman's progress.

The Confederate cavalry was encamped at Bentonville, a small village which lay between Fayetteville and Goldsboro. Johnston ordered the horsemen to meet the enemy on March 18 and detain the bluecoats until the infantry arrived.

Sherman had divided his large force. The Yankees moved forward with General Henry W. Slocum on the left, while the right was commanded by General Oliver O. Howard.[5]

The Confederates braced themselves for the coming attack. Johnston placed Braxton Bragg's troops on the Goldsboro Road, blocking the Union advance. He was to be supported on his right by Joseph Hardee's Corps.[6] On the far right of the alignment were the men under A. P. Stewart. Bragg's command faced almost due west, while Stewart's men faced in a southerly direction.[7] Unfortunately, Hardee had not yet arrived, so a gap developed between Bragg's right and Stewart's left.[8] This opening was quickly closed by the placement of two batteries[9] of artillery which belonged to the Confederate cavalry.

On March 19, the Union XIV Corps attacked Bragg's men but were easily repulsed.[10] The graycoats counterattacked, and were able to drive the Federals backward. The XIV Corps would find reinforcements later in the form of the XX Corps, but these troops had not yet reached the action.

Although the Union attack had not broken the Confederate lines, the bluecoats had been able to alter the course of the battle. General Johnston had shifted the division under Lafayette McLaws from the center of the battlefield to the Confederate left flank. This movement severely weakened the striking power of the center.[11]

Despite the reinforcements, Braxton Bragg waited over an hour to attack. The delay would give the Federals valuable time to regroup.[12]

The action had ground to a stalemate on the Confederate left, but on the right the battle was just beginning. North of the Goldsboro Road, two Union brigades under General William Carlin faced A. P. Stewart's troops. W. W. Loring held the left, with D. H. Hill in the center and William Bate on the right.[13] William Taliaferro was leading his graycoats up in support, and would take a position on the far right of the line.[14] Carlin would soon discover that the enemy extended past both of his flanks.[15]

The Federals were unable to withstand the pressure. Carlin's men crumbled, and the Southerners surged forward. The Yankees fell back along the Goldsboro Road and were finally reinforced by Nathaniel Jackson's division of the Union XX Corps.[16] Thus far, the Confederates had done relatively well, though they had failed to capitalize on several opportunities. However, the tide of the battle was about to turn.

Finally, Braxton Bragg decided to move forward on the Confederate left. General Robert Hoke and his rebels attacked the Federal lines several times, but were unable to pierce the stubborn defenses. By 4:00 P.M.[17] the exhausted graycoats were vulnerable to a counterattack. Suddenly, the 14th Michigan and 60th Illinois regiments bounded over their fortifications and routed the stunned Southerners, capturing more than 100 prisoners.[18] South of the Goldsboro Road on the Federal right, the XIV Corps had finally regained control.

The reinforcements from the XX Corps began to stabilize the Union left flank, but the Confederates seemed to have lost none of their aggression. General Taliaferro sent two brigades forward, marching almost due south. Without warning, gunfire erupted from an unexpected quarter. There were Yankees on their right flank!

The 13th New Jersey and the 82nd Illinois poured a murderous fire into the column of gray.[19] The Confederates under Taliaferro were surprised, then shattered. As darkness covered the field, General Johnston ordered a withdrawal.[20] Each side had had their opportunities, but the first day at Bentonville had been a draw.[21]

Casualties for the action on March 19 favored the Northern side. Total losses for the Confederates were approximately 2,000 men of some 16,000 on the field of battle.[22] Union losses were roughly 1,100 of some 20,000 men present at Bentonville.[23]

On the next day the Confederates received some ominous news. Union troops were moving toward the left flank of the Southern line. The enemy belonged to the Federal XV Corps, commanded by General John A. "Black Jack" Logan, and were marching west along the Goldsboro Road.[24] This section of the Confederate defenses, currently manned by General Hoke's division, was ordered to change position so that the troops faced south and east. Reinforcements were sent to Hoke's assistance to strengthen his position.[25]

However, the problem had not vanished. By 4:00 P.M.,[26] William Tecumseh Sherman had united his two wings. The Confederates now faced an enemy almost three times their size.[27] With the 16th Illinois Regiment on the left and the 14th Michigan on the right, the Federals moved forward. North of the Goldsboro Road, General Hoke deployed Kirkland's Brigade on the left, with the North Carolina Reserves to his right.[28] The Confederates faced south, determined to resist the growing numbers of their foe. Despite repeated attacks by the Yankees, they failed to break the Southern lines. Hoke's grayclad veterans had held firm, and finally darkness enveloped the battlefield.

The battle of Bentonville was noteworthy in that neither side particularly wanted to take the offensive.[29] Johnston hoped that if Sherman would attack entrenched Confederates, perhaps the Federal advantage in numbers could be negated. Sherman had no desire to seize the town of Bentonville; his only objective was to continue his eastward march toward Goldsboro.[30]

March 21 would bring a more vigorous attack from General Sherman. The Yankees under "Fighting Joe" Mower were able to break through the cavalry pickets on the Confederate left. If the Federals got behind Johnston's army to the Mill Creek Bridge, the Southerners route of escape might be cut off. Around 1:30 P.M.,[31] General Mower could sense the victory that was within his grasp. One more step and his troops would be in the town of Bentonville.

Suddenly, the Union general received some very disturbing news. His right brigade, led by John Fuller, was headed northwest, and straight for Bentonville. However, the left brigade, under the command of John Tillson, had veered to the southwest, creating a gap between the two forces.[32]

In an uncharacteristic move, "Fighting Joe" held his troops back, shifting most of his men to the left in an attempt to unite his brigades. All alone, the 64th Illinois regiment moved on ahead, unsupported by the remainder of the union army. The Midwesterners forced General Johnston to evacuate Confederate headquarters, and they continued forward, hoping to cut off the Confederate route of escape.[33]

All available men were rushed to the scene to try to stop the swarming tide of onrushing bluecoats. Confederate cavalry led by Wade Hampton hit the 64th Illinois in the right flank, while infantry under Robert Henderson[34] burst into the Union left. The attack was so sudden that the Union troops recoiled at the charge.[35] To

Henderson's right, two cavalry units[36] and approximately 600 infantry from Brown's Division[37] charged forward into Tillson's bluecoats.

While the Confederates were able to see momentary success, at this point General Johnston simply did not have enough men to mount a serious assault on the Union forces. Nonetheless, this gallant charge on March 21 drove the Federals back, and effectively ended the battle of Bentonville.

The rebels lost 239 men killed, 1,694 wounded and 673 captured or missing, for a total of 2,606 for the three days of fighting. Union casualties were 191 men killed, 1,168 wounded and 287 captured or missing, for a total of 1,646.[38]

Obviously, the Confederates could ill afford to trade casualties with the powerful United States government. The Southern losses were gone for good. There were no more troops to take the place of their fallen soldiers. As soon as a Union man went down, another man quickly appeared in his stead. The action in the Carolinas would not continue much longer, for on April 26, General Johnston surrendered, and the Civil War in the east was over.

March 25–April 9, 1865
THE APPOMATTOX CAMPAIGN

R. E. Lee (CSA)	U. S. Grant (USA)

The surrender at Appomattox Court House of the Army of Northern Virginia was really just the last event in a race which the Confederates were not able to win. Closing in on all sides of his adversary, Grant simply had too many men for Lee's troops to escape.

In an attempt to break the Union stranglehold around the city of Petersburg, Virginia the Confederates launched an attack on Fort Stedman. Operations at Fort Stedman can best serve to illustrate the value of both sound military reconnaissance and accurate information. It was in part a desperate measure, with perhaps little chance of success. Nevertheless, it seemed worth a calculated risk, and it was for no lack of effort that it failed.

In the spring of 1865, the Confederates under Robert E. Lee were still besieged around Petersburg. Federal soldiers were believed to occupy several forts, or redoubts, constructed primarily of earth and logs.

The focal point of the Southerners' attention was Fort Stedman, a redoubt in the center of the Union line.[1] It was situated on high ground known as Hare's Hill, approximately three-quarters of a mile southeast of the Appomattox River.[1a] As the Confederates assessed the situation, there were two Union artillery batteries to the left of the fort and two batteries to the right. Further along on the Confederate right was another enclosure, Fort Haskell.[2]

The battle plan for the assault on Fort Stedman was a simple one. Confederate General John B. Gordon would lead three divisions from the Second Corps, with additional troops from the First and Third Corps. The Confederates were expected to capture the Federal garrison inside the fort.

The Union infantry was commanded by General Orlando B. Willcox, and the footsoldiers were supported by a regiment of heavy artillery.[3]

Initially, the attack was a success. At 4:00 A.M.[4] on March 25, the graycoats stormed past the Union pickets and took possession of the redoubt and three supporting batteries. The difficulty arose when it was discovered that the three satellite forts believed to be in the vicinity of Fort Stedman were simply old Confederate works long since abandoned.[5]

The Southerners ventured out after the other redoubts, but finding no worthy prize for the taking, pulled back to Fort Stedman. Gordon's attack had collapsed. The Federals regrouped, and delivered a vicious counterattack. General Willcox and General John F. Hartranft led their divisions against the rebels, unleashing both muskets and artillery on the occupants of Fort Stedman.[6]

By 8:00 A.M.,[7] General Lee realized that the attack had been a failure. The Confederates in Gordon's sector were withdrawn.

Approximately 5,000 Confederates became casualties, while the Northern side lost about 1,500 men.[8] The conflict at Fort Stedman signified the last attempt by General Lee at an offensive. The remainder of the Civil War saw the Army of Northern Virginia fighting desperate actions against an enemy closing in on all sides.

In the wake of the failure at Fort Stedman, the graycoats continued to retreat in a westerly direction. The purpose now was to feed the starving army. The Confederate commissary had ordered food and forage to be sent to Danville and Lynchburg. Lee's object was to get there first, before General Grant could destroy the supplies.[8a]

General Lee believed that the Federals would move across Hatcher's Run, a meandering stream which ran roughly parallel to the Appomattox River, then as it approached Petersburg, completely changed direction to run north and south.[9] Between Hatcher's Run and the river was the Southside Railroad, which was vital to the communications and supplies of the Army of Northern

Virginia. General Grant wished to capture the railroad, which would place the Confederates in a very precarious situation.

The best route for Grant's purpose took the bluecoats to Lee's right. The Federals would then turn north, blocking the path of the retreating Confederates and intercepting the railroad as well.

As Lee's men moved west, the commanding general issued orders to secure the flanks against attack from the enemy.[10] On the morning of March 31, General Lee inspected the enemy lines. To his surprise he discovered that the Union left flank was unsupported, or "in the air."[11] Here was a great opportunity, and Lee issued orders for the advance.

The graycoats attacked with great gallantry. There were but four brigades to attack an entire Federal corps. Two of these were under General Bushrod Johnson. Sam McGowan and Eppa Hunton led the other two brigades. The assault succeeded at first, and the exposed left flank of the enemy was rolled up. However, the bluecoats promptly dispatched reinforcements to the scene, and the Confederates were forced to withdraw. General Lee realized that the Union lines could be extended around the Southern flanks; the opponent simply had too many men to contest.[12]

Ulysses S. Grant had given orders to General Philip H. "Little Phil" Sheridan, his chief of cavalry, to pursue the graycoats as vigorously as possible. General Lee had instructed his nephew, Fitzhugh Lee, a Confederate cavalry general, as well as the infantry under General George E. Pickett, to attack Sheridan if he drew near the Confederate lines. The rebels would strike Sheridan's men at a place called Five Forks.[13]

This small community lay due west of Petersburg. At the village, the road from Dinwiddie Court House approached from the southeast. The intersection of the Dinwiddie Road and the White Oak Road formed the hamlet of Five Forks.

Saturday, April 1 was to bring a disaster so unexpected that General Lee could never have seen it coming. He elected to return to the works so thinly held by the men under Bushrod Johnson, and he left the defense of Five Forks to the troops under his nephew, Fitzhugh Lee, combined with General Pickett's men.

This was the time of year when the shad were running in the Virginia rivers. It was a tempting delicacy to hungry men. Around noon on April 1,[14] cavalry General Thomas L. Rosser had some of the fish baked, and invited Fitzhugh Lee and George Pickett for a delicious feast. Unfortunately, the two men yielded to their appetites and abandoned their commands.[15]

The Confederates had discovered the presence of the Union V Corps in the vicinity, and began to deploy their troops. They numbered about 6,000 infantry.[16] Against this ragged band of Confederates General Sheridan had approximately 30,000 Federal soldiers.[17] The Southern cavalry was not concentrated, leaving the flanks vulnerable to Union advances.

The power of the Union V Corps simply overwhelmed the graycoats, and with General Pickett absent, the Union infantry easily rolled up his four brigades, driving them from east to west.[18] Sheridan's intent was to force Pickett's command to the west, thereby separating it from General Lee and the remainder of the Southern troops which were closer to Petersburg.[19]

The estimates of prisoners taken vary widely, but the result of the battle of Five Forks was that General Pickett's command no longer existed as an effective fighting force.[19a]

Early in the morning of April 2, General Grant began to pound away at the city of Petersburg itself. As the Confederate strength was severely diminished, the rebels were forced out of their entrenchments around the city and into earthworks closer to Petersburg. The Confederates under General Gordon and General A. P. Hill no longer possessed the manpower to withstand such a furious bombardment.

Ambrose Powell Hill was a furious combat fighter, who never lacked for personal courage. He realized that the grasp of the Union fingers was growing somewhat tighter. He had remarked only four days earlier that he did not want to survive the loss of the Confederate capital.[20]

In the dim light of the morning, General Lee observed some skirmishers moving quietly toward the Confederate camps. Without waiting for orders, General Hill had mounted his horse and was off to reconnoiter the enemy. General Lee would never see him alive again. In performing his duty, A. P. Hill would be shot from his horse only seven days before the surrender of the Army of Northern Virginia. In his death around the lines of Petersburg, A. P. Hill had gotten his wish.[21]

At approximately 10:00 A.M.,[22] General Lee dictated a message to Richmond, providing for the evacuation of the capital. Lee made it apparent that Petersburg could not hold out much longer.

Outside the inner fortifications at Petersburg were two walled enclosures, Fort Whitworth[22a] and Fort Gregg. Fort Whitworth contained a mere three artillery pieces, while Fort Gregg had only two. General Lee assembled every available man, but was able to place only 214 Confederates in Fort Gregg. Moving against the graycoats were several thousand Yankees.[23]

The fighting was furious, and lasted much longer than one would have expected. The bluecoats dominated the vicious fighting, and finally took possession of the fort. When the action was over, there were 55 dead Confederates, and 129 wounded soldiers, and only 30 men left uninjured. This had cost the Union 714 casualties — a tremendous price to pay.[24]

As darkness covered the battlefield, General Lee shifted his lines. Only 15,000 survivors[25] of the Army of Northern Virginia left Petersburg with Robert E. Lee. The army was but a shell of the fighting force he had seen cover the fields of Virginia in glory with its triumphs of the past four years.

On April 3 the Confederates continued their flight. General James Longstreet's troops led the way, with the 5,000 men of General Gordon's corps acting as the rear guard.[26] The destination was Amelia Court House, just under ten miles away.[27] General Lee had made arrangements for food to be delivered to the small town. Gordon waited for two other commands to join him before moving out. William Mahone brought his troops from the Bermuda Hundred area, while Richard S. Ewell's men were scheduled to arrive from Richmond. All told, the graycoats might be able to count 30,000 muskets, while the enemy constantly nipped at their heels, 100,000 strong. [27a]

The Confederates were not a compact marching force. Each command was marching in a westerly direction, but on separate roads, and were strung out as they headed on their journey. Various Confederate forces entered Amelia Court House on April 4. Through some misunderstanding, the graycoats found that no food had been delivered. The newly appointed chief of the commissary, Isaac M. St. John, had stockpiled food at Richmond, Danville, Lynchburg and Greensboro, but only artillery ammunition had been sent to Amelia.[28]

General Lee heard from General Ewell that he was en route to Amelia Court House. Following the same general line of march as Lee's troops, Ewell had still not reached the main body of Confederates. Due to the food shortage, a new destination would have to be determined. Burkeville, a small village about 20 miles southwest of Amelia, was the immediate objective. At that point, the Southside Railroad arrived from Lynchburg.[29] Perhaps it would be possible to ship food to Burkeville.

The next day, April 5, brought the arrival of General Ewell's men. As the Southerners headed for Burkeville Longstreet again took the lead, followed by men formerly under A. P. Hill's command. Next came George Pickett's remnants, followed by Ewell. Gordon remained as the rear guard.[30]

The Federals had been pursuing Lee's hungry band of men, and the bluecoats had taken the Burkeville route. This blocked any escape further south. Once again, General Lee would have to change his line of march. Seeking a point to the west, Lee's mind now centered on Farmville. On the way to Farmville, the next day would witness yet another disaster for the Army of Northern Virginia. It would take place along the muddy shores of Sayler's Creek.

By 10:00 A.M. on April 6, Robert E. Lee had ridden on ahead of the rebels, to a place called Rice's Station. The men were so famished that even the heartiest soldiers began to fall from the ranks.[31]

At this juncture, the long, unconnected nature of the Confederate columns would prove to be their undoing. General James Longstreet was still in the lead, and reasonably close to General Lee. However, during the middle of the day,[32] the Federals struck hard. Union cavalry under General George A. Custer attacked between Mahone, who was in the rear of Longstreet's columns, and Pickett, who was in the lead of the next command under Ewell and Richard Anderson. This separated the two Confederate forces. At the same time, the Union II Corps of infantry assaulted Gordon's rearguard. Gordon and Ewell had a long, cumbersome wagon train in between them, and this second Union attack prevented their forces from connecting as well.[33]

The problem worsened when General Anderson failed to notify General Mahone that he had stopped his march. As Mahone continued on, the gap between them widened. For his part, General Ewell diverted his wagon train in an attempt to safeguard his supplies, but did not inform General Gordon. Unable to see Ewell's column in front of him, Gordon followed the wagon train.[34]

The Confederates had been split into three separate entities: Longstreet and Mahone in front, Ewell and Anderson in the middle, with Gordon bringing up the rear. As the day wore on, the space in between these isolated forces became even wider.

Completely cut off from any assistance, General Ewell was attacked in front, flank and rear. Despite ferocious hand-to-hand fighting, Ewell's Corps was forced to surrender. Ewell had lost some 2,800 men; Anderson approximately 1,500.[35] Gordon hardly fared any better, losing 1,700 men by capture.[36] With battle casualties included, General Lee had lost at least 7,000 men, perhaps as many as 8,000 at Sayler's Creek.[37]

The results of Sayler's Creek were devastating to an Army already in a shambles. The Confederates had simply run out of men, food and forage. All routes of escape were cut off. General Lee gradually moved his weary men toward the village of Appomattox Court House. On April 9, Robert E. Lee would surrender the Army of Northern Virginia, and the conflict in Virginia would be over.

March 31–April 2, 1865

Selma

N. B. Forrest (CSA) — J. H. Wilson (USA)

By the early spring of 1865, the fortunes of the Confederacy had reached their very depths. The Army of Tennessee had been shattered at the battle of Franklin. John B. Hood had resigned the command of the troops, and had been replaced by Richard Taylor.

The cavalry, under General Nathan B. Forrest, had retreated to Corinth, Mississippi.[1] The Confederate horsemen would now head southeast, to Selma, Alabama. Selma was important both for its close proximity to the iron and coal region in Alabama, as well as for its railroad link with the state of Mississippi.[2]

On March 30, the graycoats had reached the small town of Scottsville, Alabama, about 25 miles[3] southeast of Tuscaloosa. Forrest and his troopers were now only five miles[4] from the bridge over the Cahaba River at Centreville. This bridge would become an important factor in the campaign.

The Federal cavalry was located at Elyton,[5] known today as Birmingham. Led by General James H. Wilson, the Northerners crossed the Cahaba and made their way toward Montevallo, in the coal district of Alabama.

General Forrest had sent an advance force of cavalry and infantry to Montevallo under Philip Roddey. Although it was only a small party, the Union troops believed it was Forrest himself. The clash at Six Mile Creek, just below Montevallo, would begin the ongoing battle which would culminate in Selma, 50 miles to the south.[6]

Forrest approached from the west when he heard the fighting. He hit the Federals from behind, slicing the enemy cavalry in two. One segment was driven northward, while the other galloped to the south, with General Forrest close behind.[7] By 10:00 P.M., the action had drifted 16 miles south of Montevallo.[8]

Despite the success on the 31st, Nathan Bedford Forrest wanted to consolidate all his cavalry. He sent messages to William H. Jackson at Tuscaloosa and James Chalmers at Plantersville. The intent was to attack Wilson's Yankees in front, flank, and rear.[9]

Unfortunately for the Confederates, the courier carrying the messages was captured. General Wilson now understood the plans of his adversary, and from that point forward Wilson was in control of events.[10] The first order of business was to burn the bridge at Centreville. Suddenly, the Union rear was secure.[11]

On April 1, Forrest took up a position at Ebenezer Church, located six miles[12] north of Plantersville. The Confederates numbered no more than 1,500 men. The bluecoats sent forward two divisions, led by Eli Long and Emory Upton, a force five times the size of the graycoats. In addition, the Federals possessed repeating rifles, giving them a decided advantage in firepower.[13]

The fighting was desperate, hand-to-hand combat. The Confederates were thrown back, and Forrest was slashed across the arm by a Union saber. There was no recourse but to fall back and camp at Plantersville. The battle was now only 19 miles north of Selma.[14]

On the next day the Federal cavalry left Plantersville at daylight. By 2:00 P.M., the bluecoats had reached the outskirts of Selma. The Confederates could muster barely 3,000 men to defend over three miles of fortifications.[15]

Just before dark,[16] Wilson attacked. Nearly 9,000 men[17] swarmed down upon the city. With only one third of the Federal force — and many of these confederates were older men or young boys — Forrest's men never had a chance. The center of the Southern line caved in, retreating back into Selma.[18]

By the evening of April 2, Selma was firmly in Union control. There had been some 2,700 prisoners captured, as well as 102 cannon and large quantities of military supplies.[19]

General Forrest was able to escape, but the damage to the heart of the Confederacy was irreparable. James Wilson had plunged deep into the South, and would soon ride into Georgia. His momentum would not stop until after the South had surrendered, with the capture of a fugitive Jefferson Davis.

April 9, 1865

Lee's Surrender

R. E. Lee (CSA) — U. S. Grant (USA)

The Confederate soldiers had finally come to the end of the line. The indomitable spirit which had characterized the Army of Northern Virginia was still willing to fight. However, men were few, food was scarce, and the rebels were virtually surrounded. There was no feeling so odious as the thought of surrender, but Robert E. Lee did not wish to sacrifice the lives of the men who had served him so bravely in a cause that would not succeed.

After much communication with both his own officers and Union General Ulysses S. Grant, General Lee decided that on April 9, 1865, the Civil War would come to a close.

The surrender at Appomatox, based on the lithograph "The Dawn of Peace." Drawing by Walton Taber. (2) General Robert E. Lee; (1) Colonel Charles Marshall of General Lee's staff; (8) Lieutenant-General Ulysses S. Grant; (15) Major-General Philip H. Sheridan; (7) General Edward O. C. Ord; (14) Brevet Major-General Rufus Ingalls; (10) Brigadier-General John A. Rawlins, Chief-of-Staff; other members of General Grant's staff: (4) Major-General Seth Williams; (12) Brevet Major-General John G. Barnard; (9) Colonel Horace Porter; (3) Colonel Orville E. Babcock; (5) Colonel Ely S. Parker; (6) Colonel Theodore S. Bowers; (11) Colonel Frederick T. Dent; (13) Colonel Adam Badeau.

The surrender of the Army of Northern Virginia represented the end of the most powerful fighting force in the Confederate States of America. The ceremony took place in the home of Wilmer McLean, a Virginian who had lived in Manassas Junction in 1861. After the first battle of Manassas, McLean decided to take his family far away from the military conflict. Ironically, he chose to move to the village of Appomattox Court House, a distance of almost 200 miles.[1] For Wilmer McLean, the war had come full circle. From the first large-scale battle which had scarred his property in 1861, to the conclusion of hostilities in his parlor four years later, Wilmer McLean lived in the center of the Civil War.

At approximately 12:30 P.M.,[1a] General Lee rode forward toward the enemy lines. He was impeccably dressed, and his horse, Traveller, was marvelously caparisoned. Accompanied by Colonel Charles Marshall, the two Confederates followed a Union party into the little town of Appomattox Court House.

Wilmer McLean conducted the men to his own house. Locust and elm trees dotted the lawn, and there was a wide verandah across the front of the two-story home.[1b] A hall ran through the center of the house from front to back on the ground floor. There was a large room on each side of the hall. Lee and Marshall entered the room on the left. At 1:30 P.M., General Grant entered the room.[2]

General Grant took a seat at a marble-topped table in the center of the room; General Lee sat next to a small oval table near the front window, facing his adversary for the last time. Colonel Marshall stood behind Lee, and several Federal officers assembled behind Grant.[3]

The appearance of the two famous generals was a striking contrast. Ulysses S. Grant was about five feet eight inches in height, almost 43 years of age and slightly stooped. He wore no spurs, and his boots were spattered with mud. Robert E. Lee was 16 years older than Grant, but fully six feet tall. His carriage was still erect, despite his years. The new uniform was Confederate gray, and his long sword had a hilt studded with jewels. On the table lay a pair of long gauntlets and a gray felt hat.[4]

The two men exchanged a few words, and then began to talk in earnest. General Grant began to write out the terms for surrender. When he had finished, he handed the document to General Lee. It was two pages long. The terms were generous. Confederate infantry officers would be allowed to retain their side-arms, private horses and baggage.[5]

General Grant was unaware that in the Confederate Army the cavalrymen and artillerists owned their own horses. This was not the practice in the United States Army. General Lee inquired as to whether these men would also be able to keep their mounts. Admitting that he was unaware of the situation in the Confederate Army, General Grant made allowances for these men as well.[6]

The two leaders then addressed the exchange of prisoners, and the possibility of food for the famished Confederates. General Grant issued 25,000 rations[7] from Union supplies to relieve the hunger in the Army of Northern Virginia.

Just before 4:00 P.M., General Lee shook hands with General Grant, and with Colonel Marshall left the room.[8] Raising his hat to the Union officers, Lee rode back to the Confederate lines with a heavy heart.

The next few days were spent with each side attending to the details of a formal surrender. Confederates stacked their arms, although many would have preferred to escape and fight elsewhere. At this point Lee issued what has become well known as his General Order No. 9. It was a farewell to his men.

> After four years of arduous service, marked by unsurpassed courage and fortitude, the Army of Northern Virginia has been compelled to yield to overwhelming numbers and resources.
>
> I need not tell the brave survivors of so many hard fought battles, who have remained steadfast to the last, that I have consented to the result from no distrust of them.
>
> But feeling that valor and devotion could accomplish nothing that would compensate for the loss that must have attended the continuance of the contest, I determined to avoid the useless sacrifice of those whose past services have endeared them to their countrymen.
>
> By the terms of the agreement officers and men can return to their homes and remain until exchanged. You will take with you the satisfaction that proceeds from the consciousness of duty faithfully performed, and I earnestly pray that a Merciful God will extend to you His blessings and protection.
>
> With an increasing admiration of your constancy and devotion to your country, and a grateful remembrance of your kind and generous considerations for myself, I bid you all an affectionate farewell.[9]

For Robert E. Lee, a new life was just beginning. The next five years would see him become the president of Washington College, known today as Washington and Lee University, in Lexington, Virginia. It would be his task to guide the Southern people in a long, arduous journey as they struggled to rebuild a broken land.

April 26, 1865
Johnston's Surrender

J. E. Johnston (CSA)	W. T. Sherman (USA)

It is generally assumed that the surrender of Robert E. Lee and the Army of Northern Virginia on April 9 brought an end to the Civil War. This is not the case, although the fighting in Virginia was over. The largest, most powerful and most famous Confederate body of troops had indeed capitulated; however, Joseph E. Johnston still led Southern forces in North Carolina.

General Johnston commanded an outnumbered army of Confederates, perhaps 30,000 men.[1] This was less than half the strength of his adversary, General William T. Sherman. The Federal numbers were further increased on March 24, when General John M. Schofield's forces united with Sherman's Yankees. The Federals could now put approximately 80,000 troops in the field.[2]

Johnston continued to follow Sherman as the bluecoats marched through North Carolina. He had hoped to combine his forces with the men under Robert E. Lee in Virginia, but on April 10 Johnston learned of the surrender of the Army of Northern Virginia.

Realizing the hopelessness of the situation, the popular general began to explore the opportunities for the surrender of his troops as well. General Sherman was receptive, and the two men met for the first time on April 17 near Durham Station.[3]

Terms of the agreement between the two men included points of civil policy, and officials in Washington, D.C., rejected the accord.

On April 26, Sherman and Johnston worked out a more narrow agreement, confined solely to military matters. Union General Ulysses S. Grant wired his approval of the terms, and on May 3 Johnston's army laid down their arms, closing hostilities east of the Mississippi River.[4]

Epilogue

What conclusions can we draw from four years of turmoil? What were the most significant events which determined the outcome of the Civil War? Obviously, a book could be written and then debated on that subject alone. However, there are three events from each side which had a tremendous impact on the outcome of the conflict. They are presented not as the most famous, nor the most documented, but as the most influential.

From the Confederate point of view, the single most important moment would have to be the death of Stonewall Jackson at the battle of Chancellorsville. His troops under Lee represented the most potent striking force in the Civil War, and their leader was no longer present. It was not merely the loss of one man; it changed the organization of the entire Army of Northern Virginia. Promotions were made throughout the army as a result of his death which elevated men beyond their capacity. This would continue to be a factor for the duration of the war.

This is most visibly seen with the promotion of Richard S. Ewell, an excellent subordinate under Jackson, to the head of the Second Corps. Clearly, he was not fit for this post. Ewell's hesitation at Gettysburg cost the Confederates dearly. While one can only speculate, it is extremely unlikely that Jackson would have made a similar mistake. As it was, the Southerners won the field on the first two days. Had Stonewall Jackson been present, the battle would likely have ended at that point. This led Robert E. Lee to believe that Gettysburg was lost at Chancellorsville.[1] Ewell would hesitate again at the battle of the Wilderness. The Union right flank was unprotected or "in the air." Prompt action was required to deal a crushing blow to the enemy. General Lee received vacillation.

A second, yet extremely important event was the unfortunate election of Jefferson Davis as President of the Confederacy. Without doubt, his character and credentials were impeccable. His military judgment was not. His loyalty to some of his appointments proved to be very costly. Davis stood by Braxton Bragg as the commander of the Army of Tennessee, Lucious B. Northrop as Commissary General, and Samuel Ruth as Railroad Superintendent, who actually turned out to be a Union spy, long after these men should have been replaced. His replacement of Joseph E. Johnston with John B. Hood during the Atlanta Campaign had disastrous consequences. The failure to utilize the cavalry under Nathan B. Forrest early in the Atlanta Campaign was a terrible mistake. Both Sherman and Grant were constantly worried that Forrest would be unleashed upon the vulnerable Union supply lines. Certainly as poor as any decision he ever made was the choice to defend every inch of the Confederacy at the same time.[2] This policy of diffusion shuffled troops throughout the South, with the result that the defense of each sector was compromised. Politics weakened his selections for the members of his cabinet. In an attempt to placate everyone, Davis chose one cabinet member from each state. This may have been politically adroit, but it did not bring the best men to the government of the Confederacy. Finally, in perhaps his most interesting decision, Jefferson Davis kept Robert E. Lee in Richmond as an administrative advisor to the president. Were it not for a stray bullet which wounded General Joseph E. Johnston at the battle of Seven Pines, the most famous soldier to come out of the Civil War would never have left his desk.

Third, would obviously be that stray bullet. While this would not usually be given mention as an influential event in the Civil War, the wounding of General Joseph E. Johnston was simply critical.[2a] Without Robert E. Lee in command of the Army of Northern Virginia, how long would the war have lasted? General Lee was not without his faults, but he was unquestionably the outstanding figure of the war.

From the Union perspective, the most important development in the Civil War was the selection of Ulysses S. Grant to lead the Army of the Potomac.[3] This came after a succession of failures. Grant's outstanding characteristic was his pugnacious nature. He realized that the United States government had resources which the Confederacy simply could not match. He was a very determined leader who would not stop until he had accomplished his objective. This resulted in extraordinary casualties, but when the day was done, Grant's persistent pounding had succeeded.

Absolutely vital to the Union war effort was the campaign waged on Atlanta by General William T. Sherman. Militarily, the South was not able to win the war, but Abraham Lincoln's Republican Party was in serious trouble in the summer of 1864. The South had a very real chance for peace on the political front. General Grant was making no progress against Lee in Virginia, and the casualties were staggering. If Sherman were to be defeated in Georgia, or simply be stalemated with heavy losses in a fashion similar to Grant's, the clamors for peace would be deafening. The invasion of the South was not a war which many Northerners wanted or cared for. As the war was originally fought on economic principles, Lincoln's later attempts to portray it as a struggle over slavery carried little weight in either the Union military or civilian population. Not only was victory at Atlanta important, it had to be accomplished before the 1864 elections.

The third factor, and extremely important, was accomplished on the political front. It had to do with the secession, or lack thereof, of Maryland, Kentucky and Missouri. The retention of these states in the Union was of paramount importance to President Lincoln.[4] Without these three border states, the Union would have been severely weakened. Had these states seceded, not only would the Confederacy have received additional manpower, but the South would also have had easier entry into northern states. States vulnerable to attack might well have chosen to retain additional troops at home for protection rather than send them to fight in Virginia or Tennessee. The capital of the United States of America would have been completely surrounded by the Confederacy. The potential repercussions of this seemingly nonmilitary event are almost endless.

There were many other influential factors throughout the war. On the Southern side, Longstreet's wounding at the Wilderness by his own men, along with Ewell's failure to attack the Federal right at the same battle, was another lost opportunity to cripple Grant's Army of the Potomac. The Federals might point to General Buell's rescue of Grant at Shiloh. Without a Union victory there, Grant's career might not have taken off as it did. The lost orders by the Confederates prior to Sharpsburg alerted the Federals to Lee's plans. A duplicate set of Lee's plan of attack were carelessly wrapped around three cigars and found by Union troops. Without that oversight, another important battle may have turned out differently. This particular oversight may be claimed as significant by either side.

At this point, the reader may ask: but what about Gettysburg? It is the most famous battle of the war, and more books have been written about it than any other battle. The Confederates lost the battle, yet the war went on another 21 months. The Union Army of the Potomac blocked Lee's thrust into Pennsylvania, nothing more. The Federals lost over 23,000 men at Gettysburg; the Confederates over 20,000. In addition, it contained the most famous charge in American military history. It was certainly important, but there were many other events with far greater influence upon the actual outcome of the conflict.

NOTES

1861

April 12–14, 1861, Fort Sumter

1. Chester, James: *Battles and Leaders* Vol. I p. 51

2. Strode, Hudson: *Jefferson Davis* Vol. II p. 31

3. Strode: p. 31

4. Strode: p. 34

5. Strode: p. 40; Chester: p. 65; Lee, Stephen D.: *Battles and Leaders* Vol. I p. 75

6. Strode: p. 40; Chester: p. 65

7. Strode: p. 40; Chester: p. 65; Catton, Bruce: *The American Heritage Picture History of the Civil War* p. 66; Lee: p. 75

8. Strode: p. 40

9. Strode: p. 40

10. Strode: p. 42

11. Strode: p. 42; Lee: p. 75

12. Chester: p. 66; Strode: p. 42; Catton: p. 66

12a. Chester: p. 71; Lee: p. 79

12b. Strode: p. 46

13. *Historical Times Illustrated Encyclopedia of the Civil War*: p. 280; Strode: p. 46 gives the time as "shortly before one o'clock"; Lee: p. 78 writes that the flag was shot down at "about 12:30"

14. Strode: p. 46

15. Strode: p. 46

16. Catton: p. 66

17. Catton: p. 66; Strode: p. 47

18. Catton: p. 66

19. *Historical Times Illustrated Encyclopedia of the Civil War*: p. 280, Strode: p. 47, Lee: p. 81

June 10, 1861, Big Bethel

1. Freeman, D.S.: *Lee's Lieutenants*, Vol. I, p. 18; *Historical Times Illustrated Encyclopedia of the Civil War*: p. 59

2. Freeman: pp. 16–17

3. Freeman: p. 17

4. Freeman: p. 17

4a. Freeman: *R. E. Lee* p. 528

5. Freeman: *Lee's Lieutenants* pp. 17–18

6. Freeman: p. 18

7. *Historical Times Illustrated Encyclopedia of the Civil War*: p. 59; Freeman: *R. E. Lee* Vol. I p. 528. The encyclopedia lists the Confederate forces engaged at 1,200; Freeman lists 1,400.

8. Freeman: p. 19, 22

9. Freeman: *R. E. Lee* Vol. I p. 528

July 11, 1861, Rich Mountain

1. West Virginia did not become a state until June 20, 1863

1a. Strode, Hudson: *Jefferson Davis* Vol. II p. 61; Cox, Jacob D.: *Battles and Leaders* Vol. I p. 126

2. *Historical Times Illustrated Encyclopedia of the Civil War*: p. 633; Cox: p. 130 sums up the Union force as "about 20,000" men

3. Freeman, Douglas S.: *Lee's Lieutenants* Vol. I p. 26 states that the Confederates were "about 4,000" men; *Historical Times Illustrated Encyclopedia of the Civil War*: p. 633; Cox: p. 129

4. *Historical Times Illustrated Encyclopedia of the Civil War*: p. 633; Cox: p. 129 states that Garnett was able to recruit only 23 new men

5. Freeman: p. 26

6. Freeman: p. 32; Cox: p. 132

7. *Historical Times Illustrated Encyclopedia of the Civil War*: p. 633; Cox: p. 129 gives the figure as "about 1,300" men

8. *Historical Times Illustrated Encyclopedia of the Civil War*: p. 633

8a. Cox: p. 132

9. Freeman: p. 33

10. Freeman: p. 34

11. Freeman: p. 34

12. Freeman: p. 34

13. Freeman: p. 35

14. Warner, Ezra J.: *Generals in Gray* p. 100; Freeman: p. 37

15. *Historical Times Illustrated Encyclopedia of the Civil War*: p. 185; Freeman: p. 36 points out that the total Confederate casualties were approximately 700 men

July 21, 1861, First Manassas (Bull Run)

1. Freeman, Douglas S.: *Lee's Lieutenants* Vol. I p. 41

2. Alexander, E. Porter: *Fighting for the Confederacy* pp. 41–42

3. Alexander: pp. 41–42

4. Freeman: p. 43

5. Freeman: p. 44

6. Eckenrode, H.J. & Conrad, Bryan: *James Longstreet* p. 14; Pfanz, Donald C.: *Richard S. Ewell* p. 130

7. Eckenrode & Conrad: p. 14

8. Tucker, Glenn: *High Tide at Gettysburg*: p. 5; Eeckenrode & Conrad: p. 233; Freeman: p. xliv

9. Eckenrode & Conrad: p. 17

10. Eckenrode & Conrad: p. 17

11. Eckenrode & Conrad: p. 19; Robertson, James I.: *Stonewall Jackson* p. 259; Vandiver, Frank E.: *Mighty Stonewall* p. 158

12. Robertson: p. 259

13. Robertson: p. 259, Vandiver: p. 160 The Union attack force of 13,000 men represented the Second and Third Divisions commanded by Generals David Hunter and Samuel Heintzelman

14. Freeman: p. 53 Freeman notes that

General Evans reported the start of the firing at 5:15

15. Freeman: p. 53
16. Freeman: p. 54
17. Freeman: p. 55
18. Freeman: pp. 55–56; Robertson: p. 261; Vandiver: p. 160
19. Freeman: p. 56; Vandiver: p. 160
20. Freeman: p. 57; Vandiver: p. 159 also gives the time as 9:00 A.M.
21. Freeman: p. 61; Govan & Livingwood: p. 55; Vandiver: p. 159 gives the time of Johnston's departure as closer to 11:30 A.M.
22. Freeman: p. 63
23. Freeman: p. 64
24. Freeman: p. 64, Vandiver: pp. 160–161
25. Freeman: p. 66
26. Freeman: p. 69
26a. Robertson: p. 264; Vandiver: p. 161
26b. Robertson: p. 264. For a detailed analysis and discussion of Stonewall Jackson's nickname, refer to footnote 37, Vandiver: p. 161
27. Freeman: p. 70; Vandiver: p. 161
28. Freeman: p. 71
29. Freeman: p. 71
30. Freeman: p. 72; Vandiver: p. 164
31. Freeman: p. 72
32. Freeman: p. 73
33. Freeman: pp. 73–75; Pfanz: p. 138
34. Freeman: p. 78
35. *Battles and Leaders* Vol. I: pp. 194–195
36. Freeman: p. 76; Pfanz: p. 139
37. Beauregard, P.G.T.: *Battles and Leaders* Vol. I pp. 219–221

September 10, 1861, Carnifix Ferry

1. The state of West Virginia was admitted to the Union as the 35th state on June 20, 1863
2. Strode, Hudson: *Jefferson Davis* Vol. II p. 61; Freeman, Douglas S.: *R. E. Lee* Vol. I pp. 502–503
3. *Historical Times Illustrated Encyclopedia of the Civil War*: p. 113
3a. *Historical Times Illustrated Encyclopedia of the Civil War*: p. 114
4. *Historical Times Illustrated Encyclopedia of the Civil War*: p. 113
5. *Historical Times Illustrated Encyclopedia of the Civil War*: p. 113; Cox, Jacob D.: *Battles and Leaders* Vol. I p. 145
6. Cox: p. 145
7. Cox: p. 145
8. *Historical Times Illustrated Encyclopedia of the Civil War*: p. 113
9. Cox: p. 146
10. *Historical Times Illustrated Encyclopedia of the Civil War*: p. 114

September 11–13, 1861, Cheat Mountain

1. *Historical Times Illustrated Encyclopedia of the Civil War*: p. 135
2. *Historical Times Illustrated Encyclopedia of the Civil War*: p. 135; Freeman, Douglas S.: *R. E. Lee* Vol. I p. 561 notes that approximately half of these men were sick and unfit for combat
3. Freeman: p. 550
4. Freeman: pp. 561–562
5. Freeman: p. 560
6. *Historical Times Illustrated Encyclopedia of the Civil War*: p. 135; Freeman: p. 563
7. Dowdey, Clifford: *Lee* p. 172
8. Dowdey: p. 171; Davis, Burke: *Gray Fox* p. 42
9. *Historical Times Illustrated Encyclopedia of the Civil War*: p. 135; Freeman: p. 565
10. *Historical Times Illustrated Encyclopedia of the Civil War*: p. 135; Davis: p. 49; Freeman: pp. 570–571
11. Freeman: p. 567
12. Freeman: pp. 574–575
13. Freeman: pp. 575–576
14. Freeman: p. 577

October 21, 1861, Ball's Bluff (Leesburg)

1. Dowdey, Clifford: *The Seven Days*: p. 28; Sears, Stephen W.: *Controversies & Commanders* p. 34
2. Dowdey: p. 28; *Historical Times Illustrated Encyclopedia of the Civil War*: p. 36; Irwin, Richard B.: *Battles and Leaders* Vol. II p. 124; Sears: p. 33
3. Dowdey: p. 28; Irwin: p. 124; Sears: pp. 34–35
4. *Historical Times Illustrated Encyclopedia of the Civil War*: p. 37; *Battles and Leaders* Vol. II p. 126; Sears: p. 33 states that casualties for both sides were less than 1,100 men, with 85 percent of the casualties on the Federal side
5. Dowdey: pp. 28–29; *Historical Times Illustrated Encyclopedia of the Civil War*: p. 37
6. *Battles and Leaders* Vol. II p. 126
7. Dowdey: p. 30
8. Dowdey: p. 30

1862

January 1–February 23, 1862, The Romney Campaign

1. Robertson, James I., Jr.: *Stonewall Jackson* p. 302
2. Robertson: p. 302
3. Robertson: p. 302
4. Robertson: p. 302
5. Robertson: p. 302; Tanner, Robert G.: *Stonewall in the Valley* pp. 68–69
6. Robertson: p. 304; Vandiver, Frank E.: *Mighty Stonewall* pp. 186–187
7. Robertson: p. 304
8. Robertson: p. 305
9. Robertson: p. 305; Vandiver: p. 187
10. Robertson: p. 305
11. Robertson: p. 306
12. Robertson: p. 306
13. Robertson: p. 306 states that the temperature did not rise above 18 degrees
14. Robertson: p. 307
15. Robertson: p. 307
16. Robertson: p. 307
17. Robertson: p. 307
18. Robertson: p. 307
19. Robertson: p. 308
20. Robertson: p. 308
21. Robertson: p. 308; Tanner: p. 73; Vandiver: p. 188
22. Robertson: p. 309 states that six inches of snow blanketed the ground on January 6, 1862
23. Robertson: p. 309
24. Robertson: p. 309; Tanner: p. 75
25. Robertson: pp. 309–310
26. Robertson: pp. 310–311; Tanner: pp. 75–76
27. Robertson: p. 311; Tanner: p. 76
28. Robertson: p. 311
29. Robertson: p. 312
30. Robertson: pp. 312–313
31. Tanner: p. 78
32. Tanner: p. 79
33. Robertson: p. 313
34. Robertson: p. 315
35. Tanner: pp. 80–83; Robertson: p. 315
36. Robertson: pp. 315–316
37. Robertson: p. 317; Tanner: p. 82; Vandiver: p. 192
38. Robertson: p. 317; Vandiver: p. 192
39. Robertson: pp. 319–321; Vandiver: pp. 192–195
40. Robertson: pp. 321–322
41. Robertson: p. 322
42. Robertson: p. 322

January 19, 1862, Mill Springs (Logan's Crossroads)

1. Daniel, Larry J.: *Shiloh* p. 20 states that the actual battlefield is only eight miles west of Somerset; Sword, Wiley: *Shiloh: Bloody April* p. 60 states that Logan's Crossroads was ten miles from the Confederate camp

1a. Kelly, R. M.: *Battles and Leaders* Vol. I p. 387

1b. *Battles and Leaders*: Vol. I p. 392

2. Kelly: p. 387

3. *Battles and Leaders*: p. 392; *Historical Times Illustrated Encyclopedia of the Civil War*: p. 495

4. Kelly: p. 387

5. Kelly: pp. 387–388; *Historical Times Encyclopedia*: p. 495 states that contact was made about daylight

6. Kelly: p. 388

7. Kelly: p. 389

8. Kelly: pp. 389–390; *Historical Times Encyclopedia*: p. 495

9. *Battles and Leaders*: p. 392; *Historical Times Encyclopedia*: p. 495 lists total Confederate losses at 533, but places the total Union loss at 261

10. Kelly: p. 391

February 6, 1862, Fort Henry

1. *Historical Times Illustrated Encyclopedia of the Civil War*: p. 274; Sword, Wiley: *Shiloh*: Bloody April p. 52

2. Henry, Robert S.: *Forrest "First With the Most"* p. 40; *Historical Times Encyclopedia*: p. 274

3. *Historical Times Encyclopedia*: p. 274

4. *Historical Times Encyclopedia*: p. 756

5. Henry: p. 49

6. *Historical Times Encyclopedia*: p. 756

7. Henry: p. 50

8. *Historical Times Encyclopedia*: p. 756

9. Sword: p. 53

10. Henry: p. 50

11. Henry: p. 50

12. *Historical Times Encyclopedia*: p. 274

February 13–16, 1862, Fort Donelson

1. *Historical Times Illustrated Encyclopedia of the Civil War*: p. 272

2. Henry, Robert S.: *Forrest "First With the Most"* p.40

3. *Historical Times Encyclopedia*: p. 272

4. Henry: pp. 53–54

5. *Historical Times Encyclopedia*: p. 272; Strode, Hudson: *Jefferson Davis* Vol. II p. 197; Sword, Wiley: *Shiloh: Bloody April* p. 56

6. *Historical Times Encyclopedia*: p. 272

7. Henry: p. 54 states that the attack began at 5:30 A.M.

8. Henry: pp. 53–54. He gives the temperature as "20 degrees below freezing"

9. Sword: p. 56; Henry: pp. 55–56. This order was very controversial. Generals Buckner and Forrest were strongly against the order to withdraw

10. *Historical Times Encyclopedia*: pp. 272–273

11. *Battles and Leaders*: Vol. I p. 572; Strode: *Jefferson Davis* Vol. II p. 198 gives the figure at "some 12,000"; Mitchell, Joseph B.: *Decisive Battles of the Civil War* p. 48 states "approximately 11,500"

12. *Battles and Leaders*: Vol. I p. 429

March 23–June 9, 1862, The Valley Campaign

1. Sears, Stephen W.: *Chancellorsville* p. 33; Freeman, Douglas S.: *Lee's Lieutenants* Vol. II pp. 477–478; Strode, Hudson: *Jefferson Davis* Vol. II p. 403; Dowdey, Clifford: *Lee* p. 297; Tucker, Glenn: *High Tide at Gettysburg* p. 18

2. Tanner, Robert G.: *Stonewall in the Valley* p. 101; Vandiver, Frank E.: *Mighty Stonewall* p. 198

3. Tanner: p. 115; Pfanz, Donald C.: *Richard S. Ewell* p. 169

4. Tanner: p. 115; Robertson, James I., Jr.: p. 390

5. Tanner: p. 119

6. Tanner: p. 119

7. Ecelbarger, Gary L.: *We Are in for It* pp. 74–75; Tanner: p. 119; Robertson, James I., Jr.: *Stonewall Jackson* p. 339

8. Ecelbarger: p. 74; Robertson: p. 332 states than Jackson's army consisted of "no more than 3,600 soldiers"; Freeman, Douglas S.: *Lee's Lieutenants* Vol. I p. 312 gives the Confederate strength at March 22 at "a few more than 3,000 infantry and 290 cavalry"

8a. Robertson: p. 331. Johnston had begun retreating from the Manassas line on March 7, 1862

9. Ecelbarger: p. 80

10. Ecelbarger: p. 74; Robertson: p. 339; Freeman: *Lee's Lieutenants* Vol. I p. 312; Vandiver: p. 204

11. Robertson: p. 339

12. Ecelbarger: p. 75; Freeman: p. 312

13. Robertson: p. 339

14. Robertson: p. 340

15. Robertson: p. 340; Ecelbarger: p. 104

16. Ecelbarger: p. 100; Freeman: *Lee's Lieutenants* Vol. I p. 313

17. Tanner: p. 123

18. Freeman: p. 314; Robertson: p. 344; Vandiver: p. 207

18a. Ecelbarger: pp. 175–178

18b. Eclebarger: p. 196

18c. Freeman: p. 314; Vandiver: p. 207

19. Freeman: pp. 315–316; Robertson: p. 346; Vandiver: p. 207

20. *Battles and Leaders*: Vol. II p. 307; Robertson: p. 346; Tanner: p. 136

21. Sears: p. 32; Tanner: pp. 139–141; Robertson: p. 347; Dowdey, Clifford: *The Seven Days*: p. 48; Ecelbarger: pp. 225–226

22. Robertson: p. 347

23. Robertson: pp. 350–351; Freeman: p. 326; Vandiver: p. 212

24. Robertson: p. 353; Freeman: p. 330

25. Robertson: p. 357

26. Robertson: p. 357

27. Robertson: p. 363; Freeman: p. 352; Pfanz: p. 160 lists Ewell's force as approximately 8,000 infantry, 500 cavalry and 14 guns

28. Robertson: p. 363

29. Robertson: p. 364; Freeman: p. 341

30. Robertson: p. 366

31. Robertson: p. 366; Vandiver: p. 229

32. Robertson: p. 366

33. Robertson: pp. 367–369

34. Robertson: p. 372; *Historical Times Encyclopedia*: p. 460; Vandiver: p. 229

35. Robertson: p. 374

36. Tanner: pp. 190–191

37. Tanner: p. 192; Robertson: p. 375

38. Tanner: p. 193; Robertson: p. 376

39. *Historical Times Illustrated Encyclopedia of the Civil War*: p. 741

40. Robertson: p. 376. Estimates vary on casualties; Freeman: p. 354 gives the Federal losses as 296, and the Confederate casualties as 498; *Battles and Leaders* Vol. II pp. 299–301 lists Federal losses as 256, and Confederate losses at 499; Vandiver: p. 230 also gives Federal losses as 256, with Confederate casualties of 498

41. Robertson: p. 383

42. Robertson: p. 385; Freeman: p. 363

43. Robertson: p. 387; Pfanz: pp. 180–181

44. Robertson: p. 387

45. Robertson: p. 391

46. Robertson: p. 392; Freeman: p. 374

47. Robertson: p. 392; Freeman: p. 374

48. Freeman: p. 377; Robertson: p. 393; Vandiver: p. 240

49. Freeman: p. 378 For a more complete description of the reaction of the townspeople, see pp. 378–379

50. Freeman: p. 378; Robertson: p. 395

51. Freeman: p. 379; Vandiver: p. 243

52. Freeman: p. 381

53. Freeman: p. 381; Robertson: p. 398; Tanner: p. 263

54. Freeman: pp. 381–382; Robertson: p. 398 lists the Federal force as simply "over 1,000"; Vandiver: p. 247

55. Freeman: p. 382; Robertson: p. 398 gives the Confederate loss as "under 100"; Vandiver: p. 247 F12

56. Robertson: p. 398

57. Tanner: pp. 296–297; Robertson: p. 412; Vandiver: p. 257

58. Tanner: p. 265

59. Robertson: p. 400

60. Robertson: p. 405

61. Robertson: p. 405

62. Tanner: p. 284; Robertson: p. 407

63. Tanner: p. 285

64. Tanner: p. 283 This was originally Colonel John Campbell's brigade, but after he was wounded in the initial action, Colonel John Patton of the 21st Virginia assumed command

65. Tanner: p. 286; Freeman: p. 402

66. Tanner: p. 330; Pfanz: p. 197 includes the 7,000 Federals at Harper's Ferry, and states that "nearly 60,000" men were ready to close in on Jackson

67. Robertson: p. 419

68. Robertson: p. 420

69. Robertson: pp. 421–422; Pfanz: p. 201

70. Robertson: p. 423; Freeman: p. 423; Pfanz: p. 202

71. Robertson: p. 424; Freeman: p. 423

72. Robertson: p. 425; Pfanz: pp. 203–204

73. Robertson: p. 425

74. Robertson: p. 428

75. Robertson: p. 429; Pfanz: p. 205; Vandiver: p. 273

76. Robertson: p. 430; Freeman: p. 435

77. Freeman: p. 439; Robertson: p. 432; Vandiver: p. 275 gives the time as "sometime around 9:00 A.M."

78. Freeman: p. 439; Robertson: p. 432

79. Robertson: pp. 432–433

80. Robertson: p. 433

81. Robertson: p. 435; Freeman: p. 445; Pfanz: p. 209

82. Robertson: p. 435; Pfanz: p. 209

83. Robertson: p. 435

84. Robertson: pp. 435–436; Freeman: p. 445; Pfanz: p. 211

85. Robertson: p. 436; Freeman: pp. 447–448 gives the Confederate casualties as 288, and places the Federal losses at 684; Pfanz: p. 214 lists Confederate losses at 288 men, and states that Frémont reported 684 casualties; however, Ewell's own belief was that Union losses were much higher; Vandiver: p. 277 also gives the Confederate loss as 288 men

86. Robertson: p. 437

87. Robertson: p. 437; Vandiver: p. 274

88. Robertson: p. 438

89. Robertson: p. 438

90. Robertson: p. 441; Vandiver: p. 280

91. Robertson: p. 442; Pfanz: p. 216; Vandiver: p. 280

92. Robertson: p. 443; Vandiver: p. 281 quotes Jackson as saying "those batteries"

93. Robertson: p. 443

94. Robertson: p. 444

95. Robertson: p. 444; Vandiver: p. 282

96. Robertson: p. 445; Vandiver: p. 282 gives Tyler's losses at 1,018, and places Jackson's casualties at "over 800" men

97. Robertson: p. 445

98. Robertson: p. 446; Vandiver: p. 283

April 6–7, 1862, Shiloh (Pittsburg Landing)

1. Sword, Wiley: *Shiloh: Bloody April* p. 15; Daniel, Larry J.: *Shiloh* p. 105

2. *Battles and Leaders* Vol. I p. 539 gives the Confederate return for April 3, 1862, as 34,727 infantry, with 1,973 cavalry and 2,073 cavalry, or a total of 38,773. This does not include the 47th Tennessee regiment, which is counted as "probably 550" men; Daniel: p. 322 gives the aggregate a bit higher, at 44,699, less the strength of the 47th Tennessee (counted as 731 men) which did not reach the battlefield until April 7

3. Sword: p. 99

4. Sword: pp. 99–104; Daniel: pp. 120–123

5. Daniel: p. 128; Sword: p. 106; *Historical Times Encyclopedia of the Civil War*: p. 684

6. Catton, Bruce: *The American Heritage Picture History of the Civil War*: p. 123 gives the Union strength under Grant as 37,000; *Battles and Leaders*: p. 538 lists Union totals as of April 6, 1862, as 37,331

7. Catton: p. 123; *Battles and Leaders*: p. 538

7a. Sword: p. 97

8. Daniel: p. 102

9. Daniel: p. 102

10. Daniel: p. 102

11. Daniel: p. 120; Mitchell, Joseph B.: *Decisive Battles of the Civil War*: pp. 56–57

12. Mitchell: pp. 56–57; Catton: pp. 126–127; Grant, Ulysses S.: *Battles and Leaders* Vol. I p. 470

13. Mitchell: pp. 56–57

14. Daniel: p. 144; *Historical Times Encyclopedia*: p. 684

15. Daniel: p. 146

16. Daniel: p. 146

17. Daniel: p. 152

18. Daniel: p. 152

19. Daniel: p. 152

20. Sword: p. 175; Daniel: p. 165

21. Daniel: pp. 158–159

22. Daniel: pp. 158–159

23. Daniel: p. 159 notes that the 6th Mississippi regiment lost 70.5 percent of its men

24. Daniel: p. 162

25. Daniel: p. 165. The regiments were the 2nd Tennessee, 24th Tennessee, 15th Arkansas, and 5th Tennessee

26. Daniel: p. 162

27. Daniel: pp. 163–165

28. Daniel: p. 172

29. Daniel: p. 176

30. Daniel: pp. 176–177

31. Daniel: pp. 178–179

32. Daniel: pp. 179–181

33. Daniel: p. 185

34. Daniel: p. 185

35. Daniel: pp. 185–187

36. Daniel: p. 188

37. Daniel: p. 191

38. Daniel: p. 199

39. Daniel: pp. 199–200

40. Daniel: p. 200

41. Daniel: pp. 200–201

42. Daniel: p. 202

43. Daniel: p. 206; Sword: p. 243; Mitchell: p. 57

44. Daniel: p. 214

45. Daniel: p. 214

46. Daniel: p. 234

47. Daniel: p. 234

48. Daniel: p. 236

49. Catton: p. 129; Daniel: p. 236; Grant: p. 474

50. Buell, Don Carlos: *Battles and Leaders* Vol. I p. 523; Catton: p. 129; Daniel: p. 237

51. Johnston, W. P.: *Battles and Leaders* Vol. I p. 565; Daniel: pp. 226–227. For a thorough discussion of General Johnston's wounding, and the possibility that he may have been killed by Confederate gunfire, see Sword: Appendix A

52. Daniel: p. 261 states that Wallace began to arrive around 5:00 P.M.

53. Sword: p. 365; Catton: p. 130; Strode, Hudson: *Jefferson Davis* Vol. II p. 233

54. Sword: p. 382

54a. Grant: p. 477

55. Daniel: pp. 281–282
56. Daniel: p. 283
57. Daniel: pp. 284–286
58. Daniel: p. 285
59. Daniel: p. 287
60. Daniel: p. 289
61. Daniel: p. 291
62. Daniel: p. 291 gives the time as 5:00 P.M.
63. Sword: pp. 460–461; Daniel: p. 322
64. Sword: p. 438
65. Daniel: p. 305

April 7, 1862, Island No. 10

1. *Historical Times Illustrated Encyclopedia of the Civil War*: p. 386
2. *Historical Times Encyclopedia*: p. 386
3. *Historical Times Encyclopedia*: p. 386
4. Walke, Henry: *Battles and Leaders of the Civil War* Vol. I p. 440
5. *Historical Times Encyclopedia*: p. 386
6. *Historical Times Encyclopedia*: p. 386; Walke: p. 445
7. Walke: p. 445 states that Mackall replaced McCown "ten days before the surrender"
8. *Historical Times Encyclopedia*: p. 386
9. Walke: p. 445 gives the date of the surrender as April 7, with additional Confederate prisoners being taken on the 8th; *Historical Times Encyclopedia*: p. 386 gives the surrender date as April 8

April 10–11, 1862, Fort Pulaski

1. Gillmore, Q. A.: *Battles and Leaders of the Civil War*, Vol. II p. 1
2. Gillmore: p. 1
3. Gillmore: p. 2
4. Gillmore: p. 4
5. Gillmore: p. 6
6. Gillmore: p. 8
7. Gillmore: pp. 8–9
8. Gillmore: p. 9
9. Gillmore: p. 10
10. Gillmore: p. 12

April 5–May 3, 1862, Yorktown

1. Sears, Stephen: *To the Gates of Richmond* p. 24
2. Sears: p. 24
3. Sears: p. 30
4. Sears: p. 36
5. Sears: p. 37; *Historical Times Illustrated Encyclopedia of the Civil War*: p. 847; Catton, Bruce: *The American Heritage Picture History of the Civil War* p. 142
6. Sears: p. 38
7. Sears: p. 39; Catton: p. 141
8. Sears: p. 45

8a. *Historical Times Encyclopedia*: p. 847

9. Sears: p. 51; Freeman, Douglas S.: *Lee's Lieutenants* Vol. I pp. 161–162

9a. Sears: pp. 46–48; Freeman: pp. 149–150

10. Sears: pp. 55–56
11. Sears: pp. 58–59
12. Sears: p. 59; Freeman: p. 154
13. Sears: p. 60; Freeman: p. 156 puts the Confederate troop total at 56,500
14. Dowdey, Clifford: *Lee Takes Command* p. 58; Freeman: p. 155
15. Sears: pp. 61–62
16. Sears: p. 66

May 5, 1862, Williamsburg

1. Sears, Stephen: *To the Gates of Richmond* p. 68
2. Sears: p. 68; Freeman, Douglas S.: *Lee's Lieutenants* Vol. I p. 174
3. Sears: p. 69
4. Sears: p. 70
5. Sears: p. 71
6. *Historical Times Illustrated Encyclopedia of the Civil War*: p. 409; Sears: p. 71
7. Sears: p. 71
8. Sears: p. 73
9. Sears: p. 73
10. Sears: p. 74 These were the 70th, 72nd, 73rd and 74th New York regiments
11. Sears: p. 75
12. Sears: pp. 75–77
13. Sears: p. 74
14. Sears: p. 78
15. Sears: p. 78
16. Sears: p. 79
17. Sears: p. 79
18. Sears: p. 79 From left to right the Confederate alignment was 24th Virginia, 38th Virginia, 23rd North Carolina and 5th North Carolina; Freeman: p. 182
19. Sears: p. 79; Freeman: p. 183
20. Sears: p. 81
21. Sears: p. 82
22. Sears: p. 82
23. Sears: p. 82

May 7, 1862, Eltham's Landing

1. Sears, Stephen W.: *To the Gates of Richmond* p. 84
2. Sears: p. 85
3. Sears: p. 85
4. Sears: p. 85
5. Sears: p. 86
6. Sears: p. 86
7. Sears: p. 86
8. Sears: p. 86; *Historical Times Illustrated Encyclopedia of the Civil War*: p. 242

May 15, 1862, Drewry's Bluff (First)

1. Sears, Stephen W.: *To the Gates of Richmond*: p. 24. Included is a full description of all of the camp equipment, animals and wagons in General McClellan's operation

1a. Yorktown was evacuated by the Confederates May 3, 1862. The battle of Williamsburg was fought on May 5, 1862

2. Freeman, Douglas S.: *Lee's Lieutenants* Vol. I p. 155; Dowdey, Clifford: *Lee Takes Command* p. 58; Sears: p. 60
3. Robertson, James I., Jr.: *Stonewall Jackson* p. 218
4. *Historical Times Illustrated Encyclopedia of the Civil War*: p. 227
5. *Historical Times Encyclopedia*: p. 227
6. Sears: p. 93
7. Sears: p. 93
8. Sears: p. 93

8a. Freeman: p. 210; *Historical Times Encyclopedia*: p. 227

9. Sears: p. 94

May 27, 1862, Hanover Court House

1. *Battles and Leaders*: Vol. II p. 219
2. Sears, Stephen W.: *To the Gates of Richmond* p. 115
3. Sears: pp. 113–114
4. Sears: p. 114
5. Sears: p. 114
6. Sears: p. 114
7. Sears: p. 114; Freeman, Douglas S.: *Lee's Lieutenants* Vol. I p. 219
8. Sears: p. 114 would indicate a Union force of some 12,000 men opposing Branch. *Battles and Leaders*: p. 219 states that Porter's Corps contained 17,546 men.
9. Sears: p. 114
10. Sears: p. 114
11. Sears: p. 115
12. Sears: p. 114; Porter, F. J.: *Battles and Leaders* Vol. II p. 320
13. Sears: p. 114
14. Sears: p. 114; Porter: p. 321
15. Sears: p. 116
16. Sears: p. 116

17. Sears: pp. 116–117; Porter: pp. 322–323
18. Sears: p. 117; Porter: pp. 322–323
19. Sears: p. 117

May 31–June 1, 1862, Seven Pines (Fair Oaks)

1. *Battles and Leaders* Vol. II: p. 219
2. *Battles and Leaders*: p. 219
3. Sears, Stephen W.: *To the Gates of Richmond* pp. 100–102
4. Freeman, Douglas S.: *Lee's Lieutenants* Vol. I p. 220
5. Sears: p. 118
6. Freeman: p. 225
7. Freeman: p. 225
8. Freeman: p. 225 states that the Nine Mile Road and the Williamsburg Road were never more than 2.25 miles apart from Richmond to Seven Pines; Sears: p. 118
9. Sears: p. 118; Freeman: p. 225
10. *Battles and Leaders*: p. 219; Sears: pp. 119–120 states that the Union force totalled "just under 33,000" men
11. Freeman: p. 226; Sears: p. 119, 132
12. Freeman: p. 233
13. Freeman: p. 234
14. Freeman: p. 236
15. Sears: p. 139; Freeman: p. 238
16. Dowdey, Clifford: *Lee Takes Command* pp. 120–121
17. Freeman: p. 238 states that Whiting lost 1,283 men; Johnston, Joseph E.: *Battles and Leaders* Vol. II p. 214 asserts that "no advantage was gained on either side"
18. Freeman: p. 240; Johnston: p. 215
19. Freeman: p. 240
20. Freeman: p. 240
21. Freeman: p. 241
22. Freeman: p. 241
23. Freeman: pp. 241–242
24. Freeman: p. 242; Johnston: p. 24
25. Freeman: p. 242
26. Freeman: p. 242
27. Sears: p. 138
28. Sears: p. 138; Eckenrode & Conrad: *James Longstreet* p. 48
29. Sears: p. 140
30. Freeman: p. 243; Eckenrode & Conrad: p. 50
31. Govan, Gilbert & Livingwood, James: *Joseph E. Johnston* p. 152; Sears: p. 130
32. Dowdey, Clifford: *The Seven Days* p. 114; Eckenrode, H. J. & Conrad, Bryan: p. 46
33. Eckenrode & Conrad: p. 47
33a. Eckenrode & Conrad: p. 50
34. Sears: pp. 146–147; Freeman: p. 244

June 6, 1862, Memphis

1. Fort Henry fell to the Union on February 6, 1862. Fort Donelson was captured on February 16. Federal troops were victorious at Shiloh on April 6–7, and at Island No. 10 on April 7
2. Freeman, Douglas S.: *R. E. Lee* Vol. IV p. 166; Strode, Hudson: *Jefferson Davis* Vol. II pp. 208–209; Robertson, James I., Jr.: *Stonewall Jackson* p. 371; Dowdey, Clifford: *Lee Takes Command* p. 11; Eckenrode, H. J. & Conrad, Bryan: *James Longstreet* p. 155
3. *Historical Times Encyclopedia of the Civil War*: p. 486
4. *Historical Times Encyclopedia*: p. 486
5. *Historical Times Encyclopedia*: p. 486
6. *Historical Times Encyclopedia*: p. 486
7. *Historical Times Encyclopedia*: p. 486

June 16, 1862, Secessionville

1. *Historical Times Encyclopedia of the Civil War*: p. 664
2. *Historical Times Encyclopedia*: p. 664
3. *Historical Times Encyclopedia*: p. 664
4. *Historical Times Encyclopedia*: p. 664
5. *Historical Times Encyclopedia*: p. 664
6. *Historical Times Encyclopedia*: p. 664
7. *Historical Times Encyclopedia*: p. 664
8. *Historical Times Encyclopedia*: p. 664
9. *Historical Times Encyclopedia*: p. 664

June 25–July 1, 1862, The Seven Days

1. Sears, Steven: *To the Gates of Richmond* pp. 156–157; *R. E. Lee* Vol. II p. 230
2. Strode, Hudson: *Jefferson Davis* Vol. II p. 247; Sears: p. 92; Freeman: *R. E. Lee* Vol. II p. 48
3. Freeman, D. S.: *R. E. Lee* Vol. II pp. 116–117 (O.R.)
4. Freeman: *R. E. Lee* Vol. II pp. 116–117 (O.R.)
5. Freeman: *R. E. Lee* Vol. II pp. 232–238; Fergurson, E. B.: *Chancellorsville 1863* p. 81; Davis, Burke: *Gray Fox* p. 88
6. Freeman: *R. E. Lee* Vol. II pp. 232–238
7. Freeman: *R. E. Lee* Vol. II p. 110; Vandiver, Frank E.: *Mighty Stonewall* p. 296
8. Sears: p. 189 F6 (O.R.)
9. Freeman: *R. E. Lee* Vol. II p. 135; Sears: p. 198, 208; Robertson, James I., Jr.: *Stonewall Jackson* p. 473
10. Freeman: *R. E. Lee* Vol. II p. 135; Sears: p. 208; Robertson: p. 473 gives the Union losses as "barely a fourth" of the Confederate losses of "close to 1500"
11. Sears: pp. 208–209; Freeman: *Lee's Lieutenants* Vol. I pp. 515–516
12. Sears: pp. 208–209; Freeman: *Lee's Lieutenants* Vol. I pp. 515–516
13. Robertson: p. 473
14. Sears: p. 214
15. Sears: p. 213
16. Sears: p. 214; Hassler, W. W.: *A. P. Hill* p. 56 lists Porter's numbers as "30,000"
17. Sears: p. 219; Vandiver: p. 304
18. Sears: p. 223; Freeman: *R. E. Lee* Vol. II p. 142
19. Sears: p. 224; Freeman: *R. E. Lee* Vol. II p. 146 also states the time as 2:30 P.M.; Porter, F. J.: *Battles and Leaders* Vol. II p. 337 gives the time as "soon after 2 P.M." Hassler: *A. P. Hill* p. 55 gives the time as 2:30
20. Sears: p. 226; Dowdey, Clifford: *The Seven Days* p. 192
21. Sears: pp. 228–229; Freeman: *R. E. Lee* Vol. II p. 149; Dowdey: *The Seven Days* p. 215 states the time as "around three o'clock"
22. Sears: pp. 229–230; Freeman: *R. E. Lee* Vol. II p. 149–150; Pfanz, Donald C.: *Richard S. Ewell* p. 225
23. Sears: p. 233; Freeman; *R. E. Lee*, Vol. I p. 153
24. Sears: p. 236
25. Sears: p. 236; Vandiver: p. 307 states that only three hours of daylight remained
26. Sears: pp. 237–239
27. Sears: p. 240
28. Sears: pp. 241–242; Freeman: *R. E. Lee* Vol. II p. 155
29. Sears: pp. 244–246; Porter, F. J.: *Battles and Leaders* Vol. II p. 340 The artillery loss for the U.S.A. was 19 guns captured in the assault, plus three additional cannon lost during the evacuation, for a total of 22
30. Sears: p. 248
31. Sears: p. 249; Freeman: *R. E. Lee* Vol. II p. 157 while acknowledging the inaccuracy of Confederate records, states that Confederate losses "could not have fallen below 8,000" and lists Federal casualties as 894 killed, 3107 wounded, and 2836 missing, for an identical total of 6,837
32. Sears: p. 250; E. Porter Alexander: *Fighting for the Confederacy*: p. 100–103; Dowdey, Clifford: *Lee Takes Command*: p. 242

33. Sears p. 255

34. Sears: p. 255; Freeman: *Lee's Lieutenants* Vol. I p. 538 (O.R.), 540

35. Sears: pp. 255–256

36. Sears: p. 258

37. Sears: pp. 260–261

38. Sears: p. 261; Eckenrode, H. J. & Conrad, Bryan: *James Longstreet* p. 74 It should be noted that a fifth road, the Nine Mile Road, runs north of, and roughly parallel to, the Williamsburg Road, but is not mentioned as it was not used by the Confederates in this particular attack

39. Sears: p. 261

40. Sears: p. 267; Freeman: *R. E. Lee* Vol. II p. 174. Jackson was never to explain what his "important duty" had been

41. Sears: p. 269

42. Freeman: *Lee's Lieutenants* Vol. I pp. 559–560

43. Sears: p. 271

44. Sears: pp. 272–274. Adding the morning's fighting at Allen's Farm, the Federals lost a total of 1,038, the Confederates 473.

45. Sears: p. 274; Robertson, James I., Jr.: *Stonewall Jackson*, p. 489

46. Sears: p. 277; Freeman: *R. E. Lee* Vol. II pp. 177–178

47. Freeman: *R. E. Lee* Vol. II p. 178

48. Sears: pp. 278–279

49. Sears: p. 279

50. Sears: p. 279; Davis: p. 94 gives rounded figures of 44,000 and 25,000, respectively

51. Sears: p. 279

52. Sears: p. 279

53. Sears: p. 280

54. Sears: pp. 279–280; Dowdey: *Lee*, p. 263; Dowdey: *The Seven Days*, p. 304; Freeman, *R. E. Lee*, Vol. II p. 199; Alexander: *Fighting for the Confederacy*, pp. 97, 110

55. Sears: p. 281

56. Sears: p. 281

57. Sears: p. 287; Freeman: *Lee's Lieutenants* Vol. I pp. 577–579; Vandiver: p. 316

58. Sears: pp. 287–289 For a full discussion of Jackson's exhaustion, see Freeman, D. S.: *Lee's Lieutenants* Vol. I pp. 655–669; Alexander: *Fighting for the Confederacy* p. 98; Robertson, J. I., Jr.: *Stonewall Jackson* pp. 466–467, 474; Dowdey, Clifford: *The Seven Days* p. 314; Strode, Hudson: *Jefferson Davis* Vol. II p. 273

59. Dowdey: p. 314

60. Sears: p. 288

61. Sears: p. 282

62. Sears: p. 293

63. Sears: pp. 297, 300–301 and Appendix III

64. Sears: pp. 299–300

65. Sears: pp. 300–304

66. Hassler: p. 62

67. Davis: p. 96

68. Sears: p. 306; Freeman: *R. E. Lee* Vol. II p. 191

69. Sears: p. 307

70. Freeman: *R. E. Lee* Vol. II pp. 192–196

71. Sears: p. 307; Freeman: *R. E. Lee* Vol. II p. 202. This was Robert E. Lee's response in a conversation with Confederate General Jubal A. Early

72. Sears: p. 310

73. Sears: p. 310

74. Sears: pp. 310–311; Robertson: p. 500

75. Sears: p. 312

76. Sears: p. 314; Robertson: p. 502

77. Sears: p. 313

78. Sears: p. 315

79. Sears: p. 316

80. Sears: pp. 316–317

81. Sears: p. 317

82. Sears: p. 317

83. Sears: p. 317

84. Sears: pp. 317–318

85. Sears: pp. 318–320

86. Sears: p. 326

87. Sears: p. 330

88. Sears: p. 335

89. Eckenrode & Conrad: p. 81; Freeman: *R. E. Lee* pp. 200–212, 218; Dowdey: *The Seven Days* pp. 316–317

90. Sears: p. 335; Catton, Bruce: *The American Heritage Picture History of the Civil War*: p. 165 gives the Confederate casualties at Malvern Hill as 5,500

91. Freeman: *R. E. Lee* Vol. II pp. 230–231; Sears: pp. 343–345 places the casualties slightly higher. On the Confederate side: 3,494 killed, 15,758 wounded, 952 missing, for a total of 20,204. For the Army of the Potomac: 1,734 killed, 8,066 wounded, 6,055 missing, for a total of 15,855

92. Refer to footnote 56

August 9, 1862, Cedar Mountain

1. Robertson, James I., Jr.: *Stonewall Jackson* p. 513

2. Robertson: p. 514

3. *Battles and Leaders* Vol. II p. 496

4. Freeman, Douglas S.: *Lee's Lieutenants* Vol. II p. 1. This was Rufus King's Division and Abner Doubleday's Brigade

5. Robertson: p. 513

6. Robertson: p. 519; Vandiver, Frank E.: *Mighty Stonewall* pp. 335–336

7. Freeman: p. 19; Robertson: pp. 522–523

8. Robertson: p. 522

9. Robertson: p. 523

10. Robertson: p. 523; Vandiver: pp. 337–338; Pfanz, Donald C.: *Richard S. Ewell* p. 240

11. Robertson: p. 526; Freeman: p. 24

12. Robertson: p. 527

13. Freeman: pp. 25–26

14. Robertson: p. 527

15. Robertson: p. 528; Vandiver: p. 339

16. Robertson: p. 528

17. Robertson: pp. 530–531; Freeman: p. 37; Osborne, Charles C.: *Jubal* p. 97

18. Robertson: p. 533; Osborne: p. 98

19. Robertson: pp. 533–534; Pfanz: p. 242

20. Robertson: p. 535; Freeman: p. 43. The medical director lists casualties of 229 killed and 1,047 wounded, or a total of 1,276. Jackson's own report lists 223 killed, 1,060 wounded, and 31 missing, for a total of 1314; Vandiver: p. 344 also lists Confederate losses as 1,276, with Federal casualties at 2,381

21. Freeman: p. 45

22. Osborne: p. 99; Freeman: p. 46; Vandiver: p. 344

August 14–October 8, 1862, The Kentucky Campaign

1. Kelly, R. M.: *Battles and Leaders* Vol. I p. 373

2. Strode, Hudson: *Jefferson Davis* Vol. II p. 150; Catton, Bruce: *The American Heritage Picture History of the Civil War* p. 242 refers to Kentucky as "the key border state"

3. The year had seen Union victories at Fort Henry on February 6, Fort Donelson on February 16, Shiloh on April 6–7, and Island No. 10 and New Madrid on April 7

4. Wheeler, Joseph: *Battles and Leaders* Vol. III p. 6; Catton: p. 242

4a. *Historical Times Illustrated Encyclopedia of the Civil War*: p. 414

5. *Historical Times Encyclopedia*: p. 629

6. *Historical Times Encyclopedia*: p. 629; Buck, Irving: *Cleburne and His Command* p. 105

7. Buck: p. 104

8. Wheeler: p. 4; Buck: p. 105

9. Buck: p. 105

10. Buck: p. 105

11. Buck: p. 105

12. Buck: p. 105; Wheeler: p. 4 says that it was "early on the 30th"

13. Buck: p. 105; Wheeler: p. 4 states that the Federal troops were "about a mile north" of Kingston

14. Buck: pp. 105–106

15. Wheeler: p. 4; Buck: p. 106

16. Buck: p. 106; Wheeler: p. 5

17. Wheeler: p. 5

18. Buck: p. 107

19. Buck: p. 107; Wheeler: p. 5

20. Buck: p. 107

21. Wheeler: p. 5; Buck states the Confederate loss was "about 400," while giving Federal casualties as 1,050 killed and wounded, with 4,303 captured, also a total of 5,353

22. Buck: p. 108

23. Wheeler: p. 7

23a. *Historical Times Encyclopedia*: p. 414

24. Wheeler: p. 8

24a. *Historical Times Encyclopedia*: p. 414

25. *Historical Times Encyclopedia*: p. 517

26. *Historical Times Encyclopedia*: p. 517

27. *Historical Times Encyclopedia*: p. 517

28. *Historical Times Encyclopedia*: p. 517

29. *Historical Times Encyclopedia*: p. 517; Wheeler: pp. 9–10

30. Wheeler: p. 10; *Historical Times Encyclopedia*: p. 517 does not list casualties, but does state that the garrison numbered 4,076 men

31. Wheeler: p. 14

32. Wheeler: pp. 15–16

33. *Historical Times Encyclopedia*: p. 576

33a. Gilbert, Charles C.: *Battles and Leaders of the Civil War* Vol. III p. 59

34. Buck: p. 112; Wheeler: p. 16 states that Cheatham moved forward "between one and two o'clock"

35. Wheeler: p. 16; Buck: p. 112

36. Buck: p. 112

37. Wheeler: p. 17

38. Wheeler: p. 17

39. *Battles and Leaders*: p. 30

40. Catton: p. 245; Wheeler: p. 17; Buck: p. 114

41. Catton: p. 245

August 28, 1862, Groveton

1. Robertson, James I., Jr.: *Stonewall Jackson* p. 546

2. Robertson: p. 546

3. Robertson: p. 546

4. Robertson: p. 547

5. Robertson: p. 549 gives the starting time as 3:00 A.M.; Freeman, Douglas S.: *Lee's Lieutenants* Vol. II p. 84 gives the start as at the "half-dawn"; Hennessy, John J.: *Return to Bull Run* p. 96 also gives the time of Jackson's departure as 3:00 A.M.

6. Robertson: p. 548; Hennessy: p. 111 lists Jackson's strength as 24,000 soldiers

7. Robertson: p. 549; *Historical Times Illustrated Encyclopedia of the Civil War*: p. 329

8. Robertson: p. 550; Pfanz, Donald C.: *Richard S. Ewell* p. 249 states that Ewell's division had covered 25 miles

9. Robertson: p. 551

10. Robertson: p. 551; Vandiver: p. 356

11. Robertson: p. 552; Vandiver: pp. 356–357; Pfanz: p. 250

12. Robertson: p. 552; Taliaferro, William B.: *Battles and Leaders* Vol. II p. 504 states that the march was in fact "over fifty-six miles"

13. Robertson: p. 552

14. Robertson: p. 554; Freeman: p. 93 gives Trimble's strength as "less than 800 muskets"; Vandiver: p. 358 states that Trimble took 500 men plus Stuart's cavalry; Hennessy: p. 115 lists Trimble's force at 500 men

15. Robertson: p. 554

16. Robertson: p. 554; Hennessy: p. 115 states that Trimble captured "several hundred" prisoners and eight cannon. However, he lists Confederate casualties at only two killed and two wounded.

17. Robertson: p. 554; Freeman: p. 96

18. Robertson: p. 554; Freeman: pp. 97–98

19. Freeman: p. 98

20. Freeman: pp. 98–99; Robertson: p. 556; Vandiver: p. 359

21. Robertson: p. 558; Hennessy: p. 138

22. Robertson: p. 560

23. Robertson: p. 560; Pfanz: p. 254

24. Robertson: p. 560 gives the time as "around 3 o'clock"; Vandiver: p. 370 states that it was between 2:00 and 4:00 P.M.; Hennessy: p. 151 places the time as "before evening"

25. Robertson: p. 560; Hennessy: p. 167

26. Robertson: p. 562; Hennessy: pp. 187–188 note that the Federals lost approximately 1,025 men at Groveton, while the Confederates suffered some 1,250 casualties

27. Robertson: p. 562; Freeman: pp. 109–110; Pfanz: pp. 257–258; for a detailed description of losses on both sides, see Hennessy: pp. 187–188. Hennessy confirms the losses in the Stonewall Brigade at 40 percent of its strength, or 340 men of some 800 present

August 29–30, 1862, Second Manassas (Bull Run)

1. The Seven Days was fought from June 25 to July 1, 1862

2. Pope, John: *Battles and Leaders* Vol. II pp. 449–451. The Union troops were called the Army of Virginia, not to be confused with the Confederate Army of Northern Virginia

3. Freeman, Douglas S.: *R. E. Lee* Vol. II p. 289; Mitchell, Joseph B.: *Decisive Battles of the Civil War* p. 89 states that the Confederate force was "about 54,000" men; *Battles and Leaders*: Vol. II p. 500 also estimates the Confederate strength at 54,000 men

4. *Battles and Leaders*: Vol. II p. 500; Mitchell: p. 89; Robertson, James I., Jr.: *Stonewall Jackson* p. 540

5. Robertson: p. 540

6. Robertson: p. 540

7. Robertson: p. 541; Hennessy, John J.: *Return to Bull Run* pp. 50–51

8. Robertson: p. 541; Hennessy: pp. 50–51

9. Freeman: p. 290; Hennessy: p. 66

10. Robertson: p. 546

11. Taliaferro, William B.: *Battles and Leaders* Vol. II pp. 501–503; Freeman: pp. 300–301; Eckenrode, H. J. & Conrad, Bryan: *James Longstreet* pp. 97–98; Robertson: p. 548 lists Jackson's strength at 23,500 men; Hennessy: p. 111 puts Jackson's command somewhat larger, at 24,000 troops

12. Eckenrode & Conrad: pp. 97–98; Freeman: pp. 300–302

13. Robertson: p. 549 states that Jackson got under way "around 3:00 A.M."; Taliaferro: p. 501 says that the march began "on the morning of" August 25; Hennessy: p. 96 gives the time of Jackson's departure as "at 3:00 A.M."

14. Eckenrode & Conrad: pp. 98–99

15. Eckenrode & Conrad: pp. 98–99; Catton, Bruce: *The American Heritage Picture History of the Civil War* p. 217; Hennessy: pp. 117–118 explains that had Pope attempted to join forces with McClellan at Fredericksburg, he would have left Washington uncovered

16. Dowdey, Clifford: *Lee* p. 189; Catton: p. 217; Freeman: pp. 313–315

17. Freeman: p. 317

17a. General Taliaferro had been wounded three times at the battle of Groveton. General Starke assumed command of Jackson's old division

18. Richard Ewell received a severe leg wound at the battle of Groveton; Robertson: p. 564; Hennessy: p. 182. General

Lawton assumed command of Ewell's division

19. Freeman: p. 321; *Battles and Leaders*: p. 473; Robertson: p. 564

20. Freeman: p. 322; *Historical Times Illustrated Encyclopedia of the Civil War*: p. 93; *Battles and Leaders*: p. 473

21. *Battles and Leaders*: p. 497 It should be noted that a sixth corps, under General Nathaniel P. Banks, was part of Pope's command, but these troops, with the exception of some of the cavalry, did not participate in the battle of Second Manassas

22. Robertson: p. 568; Eckenrode & Conrad: p. 104

23. Pope: p. 474; Eckenrode & Conrad: p. 104; Hennessy: p. 211; Hennessy: p. 223 states that Reno's troops began to arrive on the field around 11:30 A.M.

24. Robertson: p. 565; Vandiver, Frank E.: *Mighty Stonewall* p. 366

25. Robertson: pp. 565–566; Vandiver: p. 367

26. Robertson: p. 566; Vandiver: p. 367

27. Robertson: p. 566

28. Robertson: p. 567; Hennessy: p. 230

29. Robertson: p. 567

30. Hassler, W. W.: *A. P. Hill* p. 90; Robertson: p. 568

31. Robertson: p. 568; Hassler: p. 92; Osborne, Charles C.: *Jubal* pp. 110–111 states that the attacks against Hill lasted from around noon until 6:00 P.M.; Freeman: pp. 325–326 gives the time of the attacks as from around 3:00 P.M. to 6:00 P.M.; Hennessy: pp. 283–284

32. Robertson: p. 568

33. *Battles and Leaders*: p. 473

34. Freeman: pp. 328–329

35. Freeman: p. 329; Robertson: p. 570

36. Freeman: p. 330

37. Catton: p. 220; Robertson: p. 571

38. Robertson: p. 571

39. Robertson: p. 571; Eckenrode & Conrad: pp. 106–107

40. Robertson: p. 571 gives the times as "almost 3 P.M."; Freeman: p. 331 explains that the estimate of the time ranged between 1:00 P.M. and 4:00 P.M., but the most probable time was "about 3 o'clock"

41. Robertson: p. 572

42. Robertson: p. 573; Hennessy: pp. 282–284

43. *Battles and Leaders*: p. 482; *Historical Times Encyclopedia*: p. 94; Eckenrode & Conrad: pp. 107–108; Catton: p. 220

44. Robertson: p. 574; Dowdey: 294; Vandiver: p. 370

45. Robertson: p. 574; Sears, Stephen W.: *Controversies & Commanders* p. 64

46. Catton: p. 220

47. Catton: p. 220; Dowdey: p. 294; Vandiver: pp. 370–371

48. Robertson: p. 575; Hennessy: p. 459 points out that had Jackson attacked sooner, the Confederate victory might well have been even more decisive

49. *Battles and Leaders*: pp. 495–500. These estimates may well be too low for both sides, as some commands did not complete casualty reports

September 1, 1862, Chantilly (Ox Hill)

1. Freeman, Douglas S.: *Lee's Lieutenants* Vol. II p. 129; Robertson, James I., Jr.: *Stonewall Jackson* p. 578

2. Robertson: p. 578; Freeman: p. 128; Hennessy, John J.: *Return to Bull Run* p. 443

3. Freeman: p. 130

4. Robertson: p. 579; Freeman: p. 130; Osborne, Charles C.: *Jubal* p. 113

5. Robertson: p. 579; Freeman: p. 130; Osborne: p. 113

6. Robertson: p. 579; Hennessy: p. 448

7. Robertson: p. 579

8. Robertson: pp. 579–580; Hennessy: p. 449

9. Robertson: p. 580; Hennessy: p. 449 places the time of Stevens' advance slightly later, at 5:00 P.M.

10. Freeman: p. 131

11. Freeman: p. 132; Osborne: p. 113; Hennessy: p. 449

12. Robertson: pp. 580–581; Freeman: p. 133; Hennessy: pp. 449–450 notes that General Stevens was leading his old regiment, the 79th New York

13. Robertson: p. 581

14. Freeman: p. 134 cites the report from A. P. Hill of 306 casualties, and the report from Ewell of 200; Robertson: p. 581 says that "each side lost about 500 men"; *Historical Times Encyclopedia*: p. 130 lists Jackson's losses at "about 500 men," while the bluecoats lost "probably 1,000 casualties"; Osborne: p. 114 also states that Union losses were "twice those of the Confederates"; Hennessy: p. 450 gives the Confederate losses as "something on the order of" 500 men

15. Robertson: p. 581

September 13–15, 1862, Harpers Ferry

1. Vandiver, Frank E.: *Mighty Stonewall* p. 373; Freeman, Douglas S.: *R. E. Lee* Vol. II pp. 350–351; Robertson, James I., Jr.: *Stonewall Jackson* pp. 581–582

2. Vandiver: p. 373; Freeman: pp. 350–351; Robertson: pp. 581–582

3. *Historical Times Encyclopedia of the Civil War*: p. 19

4. Vandiver: p. 379; Freeman, Douglas S.: *Lee's Lieutenants* Vol. II p. 159

5. Robertson: p. 591

6. General James Longstreet would occupy Hagerstown, while the troops under General D. H. Hill would guard the passes through South Mountain

7. Robertson: p. 591

8. Robertson: pp. 591–592

9. Robertson: pp. 591–592; Freeman: p. 160

10. Robertson: p. 592

11. Robertson: p. 592; Freeman: pp. 161–162

12. Robertson: p. 593; Vandiver: p. 381; Dowdey, Clifford: *Lee* p. 303

13. Robertson: p. 593; Dowdey: pp. 303–304

13a. Robertson: p. 595 states that the first elements of Jackson's command entered Martinsburg "by midmorning"; Freeman: p. 165

14. Robertson: p. 597

15. Robertson: p. 597; Freeman: p. 165

16. Robertson: p. 598

17. Robertson: p. 598

18. Robertson: pp. 598–599 asserts that McLaws had four brigades of his own plus six brigades belonging to General R. H. Anderson's division; Freeman: pp. 186–187

19. Robertson: p. 599

20. Robertson: p. 599; Freeman: p. 187

21. Robertson: p. 599; Freeman: p. 187 states that the last Federal soldier was gone from Maryland Heights "by 4:30 P.M."

22. Robertson: p. 600

23. Robertson: p. 604

24. Robertson: p. 604

25. Robertson: pp. 604–605; Freeman: p. 198

26. Robertson: p. 606

27. *Battles and Leaders* Vol. II p. 618; Robertson: p. 606; Dowdey: p. 307; Vandiver: p. 388 and Freeman: p. 199 place the figure of captives at about 11,000 men. The higher figure is used in the text as it comes from the Official Records

28. Robertson: p. 606

September 14, 1862, South Mountain

1. Freeman, Douglas S.: *Lee's Lieutenants* Vol. II p. 159; Vandiver, Frank E.: *Mighty Stonewall* p. 379

2. Freeman: pp. 159–160; Dowdey, Clifford: *Lee* p. 302

3. Freeman: p. 160; Vandiver: p. 380

4. Freeman: p. 161; Vandiver: p. 380

5. Freeman: pp. 161–162; Vandiver: p. 381

6. Freeman: p. 168

7. Freeman: p. 169

8. Freeman: p. 170

9. Freeman: p. 170

10. Freeman: p. 171

11. Freeman: p. 171; Hill, Daniel H.: *Battles and Leaders* Vol. II p. 560; Freeman, Douglas S.: *R. E. Lee* Vol. II p. 367

12. Freeman: *Lee's Lieutenants* p. 173

13. Freeman: *Lee's Lieutenants* pp. 173–174. For a discussion on the possibility that McClellan did not actually possess the Confederate battle plans, see Freeman, Douglas S.: *R. E. Lee* Vol. II p. 369. With all respect to the historical acumen of Douglas S. Freeman, the change in behavior of General McClellan would seem to indicate that he did in fact become aware of the Confederate plans. The sudden aggression exhibited by the Union commander was most out of character. For a discussion of the fact that the Union was in fact in possession of the lost orders, see *Battles and Leaders* Vol. II p. 603, and Davis, Burke: *Gray Fox*: p. 138

14. Freeman: *Lee's Lieutenants* p. 174. Hill had brigades under Colquitt, Garland, G. B. Anderson, Ripley and Rodes at his disposal, though Garland was not yet on the crest of South Mountain

15. *Battles and Leaders*: p. 598

16. *Battles and Leaders*: p. 569

16a. Freeman: *R. E. Lee* pp. 370–371

16b. Freeman: *R. E. Lee* p. 371

16c. Freeman: *R. E. Lee* p. 372

17. Dowdey: p. 306; *R. E. Lee* p. 372

18. Freeman: *R. E. Lee* p. 372; *Historical Times Illustrated Encyclopedia of the Civil War*: p. 20

September 14, 1862, Crampton's Gap

1. Freeman, Douglas S.: *Lee's Lieutenants* Vol. II p. 169

1a. Franklin, William B.: *Battles and Leaders* Vol. II p. 592

2. *Battles and Leaders*: Vol. II p. 553; Franklin: p. 592 states that the distance from Crampton's Gap to Maryland Heights was only five miles

3. Robertson, James I., Jr.: *Stonewall Jackson* pp. 591–592; Franklin: p. 595

4. *Historical Times Illustrated Encyclopedia of the Civil War*: p. 189

5. *Historical Times Encyclopedia*: pp. 189–190

6. Freeman: p. 190

7. *Historical Times Encyclopedia*: p. 189; Franklin: p. 594

8. Freeman: pp. 190–191; *Historical Times Encyclopedia*: p. 190

9. Freeman: p. 191

10. Freeman: p. 192

11. *Historical Times Encyclopedia*: p. 190; Franklin: p. 596

12. *Battles and Leaders*: Vol. II p. 618; Robertson: p. 606; Dowdey, Clifford: *Lee* p. 307 and Freeman: p. 199 place the figure of captured soldiers at Harpers Ferry at approximately 11,000. The higher figure is used in the text as it comes from the official records

September 17, 1862, Sharpsburg (Antietam)

1. Freeman, Douglas S.: *R. E. Lee* Vol. II p. 387; Mitchell, Joseph B.: *Decisive Battles of the Civil War* p. 98; Robertson, James I., Jr.: *Stonewall Jackson* p. 581 states that it was the "bloodiest single day in American history"

2. Robertson: p. 607 states that Sharpsburg "contained no more that 1500 residents"

3. Robertson: p. 607; Walker, John G.: *Battles and Leaders of the Civil War*: Vol. II p. 675. A. P. Hill collected prisoners at Harpers Ferry, but it must be remembered that as of September 14, the divisions of Richard Anderson and Lafayette McLaws had also not reached General Lee

4. Strode, Hudson: *Jefferson Davis* Vol. II p. 305; Alexander, E. Porter: *Fighting for the Confederacy* p. 146; Mitchell: p. 94; Franklin, William B.: *Battles and Leaders* Vol. II p. 629 refers to notes on pages 565 and 603 for the strength of each side. The troops at Lee's disposal increased as different commands reached the field

5. Catton, Bruce: *The American Heritage Picture History of the Civil War*: p. 235; Robertson: p. 609

6. Catton: p. 235; Robertson: p. 609

7. Catton: p. 235; Robertson: p. 609

8. Freeman: p. 387; Robertson: p. 612 states that Hooker attacked "at daylight"; Osborne, Charles C.: *Jubal* p. 121 says that the battle opened "as soon as there was light enough to see"

9. Freeman: pp. 388–389; Osborne: p. 125

9a. Robertson: p. 613

10. Robertson: p. 613

11. Robertson: p. 614; Freeman: p. 390 states that the Federals "were driven back almost to the point where the battle had opened"

12. Robertson: p. 614

13. Freeman: p. 389. These were one brigade under Colonel G. T. Anderson and two under General J. G. Walker

14. Mitchell: p. 95

15. Mitchell: p. 96; Cox, Jacob D.: *Battles and Leaders* p. 639

16. Mitchell: p. 96; Cox: p. 645 states that it was "between 9 and 10 o'clock"

17. Mitchell: p. 96

18. Freeman: p. 391; Mitchell: p. 97; Catton: p. 235

19. Catton: p. 235; Mitchell: p. 97

20. Catton: p. 237

21. Freeman: p. 391

22. Freeman: p. 393

23. Mitchell: p. 95

24. Cox: p. 646

25. Catton: p. 237

26. Catton: p. 237; Mitchell: p. 97; Freeman: p. 393

27. Cox: p. 651; Freeman: p. 397; Mitchell: p. 97

28. Catton: p. 239

29. Catton: p. 239

30. Mitchell: p. 97; Catton: p. 239; Hassler, W. W.: *A. P. Hill* p. 105

31. Mitchell: pp. 97–98

32. Franklin, William B.: p. 629; Freeman: p. 398; Mitchell: p. 98

33. Catton: p. 241; Freeman: p. 402

34. Freeman: pp. 400–401

35. Catton: p. 241; Freeman: p. 402

36. Catton: p. 241

37. *Battles and Leaders* Vol. II pp. 598–603. The Confederate totals are carefully reconstructed estimates. Mitchell: p. 98 states that the Confederates lost "about 10,000" men, while the Union lost "over 12,000" troops; Catton: p. 241 says that the two sides combined lost "about 23,500" men; Freeman: p. 402 cites E. P. Alexander's computation of the Confederate losses at around 10,700, with Federal casualties at 12,410

38. Robertson: p. 612; Freeman: p. 281; Cox: p. 643

39. Catton: p. 241

40. Vandiver, Frank E.: *Mighty Stonewall* p. 379; Freeman, Douglas S.: *Lee's Lieutenants* Vol. II p. 159

September 19, 1862, Iuka

1. Sword, Wiley: *Shiloh: Bloody April* p. 66

1a. *Historical Times Illustrated Encyclopedia of the Civil War*: p. 387

2. *Historical Times Encyclopedia*: p. 387

3. *Historical Times Encyclopedia*: p. 386; Snead, Thomas L.: *Battles and Leaders* Vol. II p. 731

4. *Historical Times Encyclopedia*: p. 387; Snead: p. 731

5. *Historical Times Encyclopedia*: p. 387; *Battles and Leaders*: p. 736

6. *Historical Times Encyclopedia*: p. 387; *Battles and Leaders*: p. 736

7. *Historical Times Encyclopedia*: p. 387

8. Snead: p. 732

9. Snead: p. 732; *Historical Times Encyclopedia*: p. 387

10. *Historical Times Encyclopedia*: p. 387

11. Snead: p. 732

12. Snead: p. 732

13. *Historical Times Encyclopedia*: p. 441; Snead: p. 733

14. Snead: p. 734; *Battles and Leaders*: p. 736. In the returns compiled from the *Official Records* the Confederate losses are listed as 85 killed and 410 wounded

September 19–20, 1862, Shepherdstown (Boteler's Ford)

1. Mitchell, M. B.: *Battles and Leaders of the Civil War* Vol. II p. 686

2. Vandiver, Frank E.: *Mighty Stonewall* p. 401; *Historical Times Illustrated Encyclopedia of the Civil War*: p. 679; Robertson, James I., Jr.: *Stonewall Jackson*: p. 621

3. Vandiver: p. 402 states that the time was "sometime after midnight"

4. Vandiver: p. 402; Robertson: p. 621

5. Vandiver: p. 402; Hassler, W. W.: *A. P. Hill* p. 108; Dowdey, Clifford: *Death of a Nation* p. 80; Freeman, Douglas S.: *Lee's Lieutenants* Vol. II p. 244

6. Hassler: p. 108

7. Hassler: p. 108

8. Hassler: p. 108; Robertson: p. 622

9. Hassler: p. 108; Vandiver: p. 402

10. Vandiver: p. 402

11. Hassler: p. 108; Vandiver: p. 402

12. Hassler: pp. 108–109; Vandiver: p. 402

13. Freeman, Douglas S.: *R. E. Lee* Vol. II p. 407; Vandiver: p. 402; Robertson: p. 622

14. Vandiver: p. 402; Hassler: p. 109; Robertson: p. 622

October 3–4, 1862, Corinth

1. Daniel, Larry J.: *Shiloh* p. 315 states that Jefferson Davis considered Corinth of paramount importance

1a. *Historical Times Illustrated Encyclopedia of the Civil War*: p. 166 states that Chewalla is ten miles to the north; Rosecrans, William S.: *Battles and Leaders of the Civil War*: p. 743 gives the direction as ten miles to the northwest of Corinth

2. *Battles and Leaders of the Civil War*, Vol. II: p. 760; *Historical Times Encyclopedia*: p. 166

3. Rosecrans: p. 744; *Historical Times Encyclopedia*: p. 166

4. *Historical Times Encyclopedia*: p. 166

5. Rosecrans: p. 744

6. Rosecrans: pp. 744–745

7. *Historical Times Encyclopedia*: p. 166

8. Rosecrans: p. 744

9. Rosecrans: p. 745; *Historical Times Encyclopedia*: p. 166

10. Rosecrans: p. 746

11. *Historical Times Encyclopedia*: p. 166 give the temperature as 90 degrees

12. Rosecrans: p. 746

13. Rosecrans: p. 748

14. *Historical Times Encyclopedia*: p. 166

15. *Historical Times Encyclopedia*: p. 166; Rosecrans: pp. 748–749 states that the attack began at "half-past four"

16. *Historical Times Encyclopedia*: p. 167

17. *Historical Times Encyclopedia*: p. 167

18. *Historical Times Encyclopedia*: p. 167

19. *Battles and Leaders*: p. 760. The Confederate figures include the action on October 5 during the retreat

October 16 1862–July 4, 1863, The Vicksburg Campaign

1. Hill, D. H.: *Battles and Leaders* Vol. III p. 639; Moore, J. N.: *The Confederate Commissary General* pp. 69–71

2. Bearss, Edwin: *The Vicksburg Campaign* Vol. I p. 428

2a. Grant, Ulysses S.: *Battles and Leaders* Vol. III p. 501

3. Bearss: Vol. I p. 22; *Historical Times Illustrated Encyclopedia of the Civil War*: p. 781; Martin, David: *The Vicksburg Campaign*: p. 73

4. Bearss: Vol. I p. 43

5. Warner, Ezra J.: *Generals in Gray* p. 162; Govan, Gilbert & Livingwood, James: *Joseph E. Johnston* p. 164

6. Grant: p. 493

7. *Historical Times Encyclopedia*: pp. 365–366

8. Martin: p. 74; Govan & Livingwood: pp. 172–173

9. Martin: p. 74; *Historical Times Encyclopedia*: p. 366; Bearss: Vol. I p. 292

10. *Historical Times Encyclopedia*: p. 366; Bearss: Vol. I p. 296

11. *Historical Times Encyclopedia*: p. 366

12. *Historical Times Encyclopedia*: p. 366; Martin: p. 76

13. *Historical Times Encyclopedia*: p. 366 states that "$1.5 million and several buildings" were destroyed, including a new, 2,000-bed hospital; Martin: p. 76 states that the damage was closer to $2 million; for a more complete description of the materiel captured at Holly Springs, see Bearss: Vol. I pp. 311–315

14. *Historical Times Encyclopedia*: p. 366

14a. Johnston, Joseph E.: *Battles and Leaders* Vol. III p. 475

15. Martin: p. 77

16. Martin: p. 77

17. *Historical Times Encyclopedia*: p. 138

18. Martin: pp. 77–78; Bearss: pp. 171–172

19. Bearss: Vol. I p. 176 gives the time as 8:00 A.M.

20. Bearss: Vol. I p. 176

21. *Historical Times Encyclopedia*: p. 138

22. Martin: p. 78

23. Martin: p. 78

24. Catton, Bruce: *The American Heritage Picture History of the Civil War* p. 310; Martin: pp. 78–79

25. Martin: p. 79

25a. The Desoto Canal, Lake Providence expedition, Yazoo Pass project and Steele's Bayou expedition were abandoned as miserable failures; Catton: p. 309; Mitchell, Joseph B.: *Decisive Battles of the Civil War* pp. 134–137

26. Catton: p. 310; Mitchell: pp. 134–137

27. Bearss: Vol. II p. 297

28. Bearss: Vol. II p. 305

29. Bearss: Vol. II p. 307

30. Bearss: Vol. II p. 309

31. Bearss: Vol. II p. 309

32. Bearss: Vol. II pp. 311–315

33. Bearss: Vol. II p. 317

34. Martin: p. 100; Bearss: Vol. II pp. 351–352

35. Bearss: Vol. II p. 318

36. Bearss: Vol. II p. 318; Catton: p. 310

37. Bearss: Vol. II p. 319

38. Bearss: Vol. II p. 357

39. Bearss: Vol. II p. 384

40. Bearss: Vol. II pp. 357–360

41. Bearss: Vol. II pp. 361–363

42. Bearss: Vol. II p. 363

43. Bearss: Vol. II p. 363

44. Bearss: Vol. II p. 364

45. Bearss: Vol. II p. 379

46. Bearss: Vol. II pp. 405–407

47. Bearss: Vol. II pp. 405–407; *Battles and Leaders*: Vol. III p. 549

48. Catton: p. 310

49. *Battles and Leaders*: Vol. III p. 550 places the Confederate total in the campaign at close to 28,000 men; Bearss: Vol. II pp. 563–564 places Pemberton's force at a somewhat lower figure, 22,971 men, as of May 14, 1863
50. Martin: p. 108
51. Bearss: Vol. II p. 486
52. Bearss: Vol. II p. 486
52a. Bearss: Vol. II p. 502
53. Bearss: Vol. II p. 502. These were the 1st Tennessee Infantry battalion and the 41st Tennessee regiment
54. Bearss: Vol. II p. 491
55. Bearss: Vol. II p. 491 gives the distance as two miles southwest of Raymond; Martin: p. 108 states that the distance is two miles south of Raymond; Grant: p. 503 states that the action occurred "about two miles out of Raymond"
56. Bearss: Vol. II p. 494
57. Bearss: Vol. II pp. 494–495
58. Bearss: Vol. II p. 497
59. Bearss: Vol. II pp. 515–517. Bearss: p. 511 notes that casualty reports for the Confederates totalled 515, while McPherson reported Union losses to General Grant as 66 men killed, 339 wounded and 37 missing, for a total of 442. *Battles and Leaders*: Vol. III also lists Union losses as 442 men. However, Union burial details claim 103 dead Confederates, plus an additional 720 captured, bringing the Confederate totals to 823 total casualties. Martin: p. 108 lists Confederate losses as 505, with Federal casualties at 432. As Bearss: pp. 515–517 has used the most detail in breaking down the battle reports, his figures are used
60. Bearss: Vol. II p. 514
61. Grant: *Battles and Leaders* pp. 518–519; Strode, Hudson: *Jefferson Davis* Vol. II p. 414
62. Bearss: Vol. II p. 536
63. Bearss: Vol. II p. 537
64. Bearss: Vol. II pp. 537–539
65. Bearss: Vol. II pp. 538–542
66. Bearss: Vol. II p. 538
67. Bearss: Vol. II p. 542
68. Martin: p. 108
69. Strode: pp. 401–402; Grant: *Battles and Leaders* Vol. III p. 518
70. Bearss: Vol. II pp. 557–558; Martin: p. 108; *Battles and Leaders*: Vol. III p. 549
71. Bearss: Vol. II p. 559
72. Bearss: Vol. II p. 580
73. Martin: p. 110
74. Bearss: Vol. II p. 591
75. Martin: p. 110; Bearss: Vol. II pp. 563–564 places Pemberton's strength at 22,971 men
76. Bearss: Vol. II p. 588
77. Bearss: Vol. II p. 590
78. Bearss: Vol. II p. 596
79. Bearss: Vol. II pp. 596–598; Grant: p. 510
80. Bearss: Vol. II p. 599
81. Bearss: Vol. II pp. 600–603
82. Bearss: Vol. II p. 605
83. Bearss: Vol. II p. 609
84. Bearss: Vol. II p. 609 Cockrell commanded Bowen's 1st Brigade, while Green led the 2nd Brigade
85. Bearss: Vol. II p. 611
86. Bearss: Vol. II p. 611
87. Bearss: Vol. II p. 617
88. Bearss: Vol. II pp. 622–623
89. Bearss: Vol. II pp. 642–651; Martin: p. 111 gives the figures as 400 men killed, 1,000 wounded, and 2,400 missing, for a total of 3,800, which does not include figures for Loring's division. Loring's troops did not suffer many battle casualties, but their heavy straggling resulted in many soldiers falling into Union hands. Bearss: p. 642 estimates Loring's loss at approximately 3,000 prisoners. Martin: p. 111 places the number much higher, at 5,000 men. According to Bearss: p. 642, the Federal reports, and *Battles and Leaders*: Vol. III p. 549, 410 men were killed, 1,844 wounded and 187 missing, for a total of 2,441.
90. Bearss: Vol. II p. 664
91. Bearss: Vol. II p. 675
92. Bearss: Vol. II p. 675
93. Martin: p. 119
94. Bearss: Vol. III pp. 773–780 states that the Union losses on May 19 were 157 men killed, 777 wounded, and eight missing, for a total of 942. Confederate casualties, while not separately reported, were very light. On May 22, Grant lost 502 men killed, 2,550 wounded and 147 missing, for a total of 3,199. Again, Confederate battle reports were not complete for the second assault on Vicksburg, but the casualties, while heavier than in the first assault, were only a small fraction of the Union losses.
95. *Battles and Leaders*: Vol. III p. 550. This includes some noncombatants, such as cooks, musicians, and medical personnel.

December 13, 1862, Fredericksburg

1. Osborne, Charles C.: *Jubal* p. 131; Freeman, Douglas S.: *R. E. Lee* Vol. II p. 441; Fergurson, Ernest B.: *Chancellorsville* p. 12; Vandiver, Frank E.: *Mighty Stonewall* p. 422 gives the Confederate strength as 78,500 men
2. Osborne: p. 131; Freeman: p. 441; Vandiver: p. 420; Fergurson: p. 12 places the Union force slightly lower, at 122,000 men
3. Eckenrode, H. J. & Conrad, Bryan: *James Longstreet* p. 141; Dowdey, Clifford: *Lee* pp. 326–327; Longstreet, James: *Battles and Leaders* Vol. III pp. 71–72; Robertson, James I., Jr.: *Stonewall Jackson* p. 662
4. *Battles and Leaders*: p. 72; Robertson: pp. 641–642
5. Robertson: p. 662
6. Robertson: p. 651; Hassler, W. W.: *A. P. Hill* p. 119
7. Robertson: p. 651
8. Robertson: p. 651
9. Freeman: p. 453
10. Robertson: p. 652
11. Hassler: p. 118; Freeman, Douglas S.: *Lee's Lieutenants* Vol. II p. 342 gives the distance of the gap as 500 to 600 yards wide
12. Freeman: *Lee's Lieutenants* p. 394; Robertson: p. 661
13. Hassler: p. 119
13a. Robertson: p. 655; Hassler: p. 119; Freeman: *R. E. Lee* p. 455
14. Robertson: p. 656
15. Robertson: p. 657
16. Robertson: p. 656; Vandiver: p. 428
17. Trout, Robert J.: They Followed the Plume p. 208
18. Robertson: p. 656; Vandiver: p. 428
19. Hassler: p. 120; Robertson: p. 657
20. Robertson: p. 656; Vandiver: p. 429
21. Freeman: *R. E. Lee*: pp. 351–352; Robertson: p. 656
22. Robertson: p. 657
23. Robertson: p. 657
24. Robertson: p. 658; Vandiver: p. 431
25. Robertson: p. 658
26. Robertson: p. 658
27. Robertson: p. 658
28. Robertson: p. 658
29. Longstreet, James: *Battles and Leaders* Vol. III p. 78
30. Freeman: *R. E. Lee*: p. 460
31. Longstreet: p. 81; Freeman: *Lee's Lieutenants* p. 364
32. *Battles and Leaders* Vol. III pp. 144–146; Sears, Stephen W.: *Chancellorsville* p. 3; Freeman: *R. E. Lee* Vol. II p. 471 gives the Union losses as 12,653, but places the Confederate loss slightly lower, at 5,309

December 31, 1862, Parker's Crossroads (Red Mound)

1. Henry, Robert S.: *Forrest "First with the Most"* p. 102; Catton, Bruce: *The*

American Heritage Picture History of the Civil War p. 358

2. Henry: p. 114

3. Bearss, Edwin: *The Vicksburg Campaign* Vol. I p. 258; *Historical Times Illustrated Encyclopedia of the Civil War*: p. 557

4. Henry: p. 115

5. *Historical Times Encyclopedia*: p. 557; Henry: p. 118

6. Henry: p. 118; *Historical Times Encyclopedia*: p. 557 gives the time of the Confederate attack as "between 12 and 1 P.M."

7. Henry: p. 118

8. Henry: p. 118 states that Fuller's attack was "between fifteen and thirty minutes" after the cease fire

9. Henry: p. 119

10. *Historical Times Encyclopedia*: p. 557; Bearss: p. 268 states that Forrest's estimates were slightly higher, at 25 men killed, 75 wounded and 250 soldiers captured. Federal casualties were 27 men killed, 140 wounded and 70 missing

11. Henry: p. 120

December 31, 1862–January 3, 1863, Stones River (Murfreesboro)

1. Sword, Wiley: *Embrace an Angry Wind* p. 316

2. Sword: p. 279. The distance varies according to the position of the armies. Sword lists the distance as 28 miles; Mitchell, Joseph B.: *Decisive Battles of the Civil War* gives the distance as 32 miles, while Cozzens, Peter: *No Better Place to Die* p. 55 indicates that the actual distance may vary according to which route one takes

3. Cozzens: p. 30

4. Cozzens: p. 30

5. Cozzens: p. 30

6. *Historical Times Illustrated Encyclopedia of the Civil War*: p. 722; Kniffin, G. C.: *Battles and Leaders* Vol. III p. 613

7. *Historical Times Encyclopedia*: p. 722; Kniffin: p. 613

7a. *Historical Times Encyclopedia*: p. 722; Mitchell: p. 112

8. *Historical Times Encyclopedia*; p. 722 It should be noted that these represent "effective forces." According to Kniffin, G. C.: *Battles and Leaders* Vol. III p. 613 the December 15 return for the Union Army shows a total of 51,822 infantry and artillery, plus 4,849 cavalry for a total of 56,671. Bragg's return for December 10 listed 39,304 infantry, 10,070 cavalry and 1,758 artillery, for a total of 51,132. From these totals one must subtract men detailed for noncombat duty, such as transportation, hospital, musical band and the like, to get what is termed "effectives." Bragg placed his "effectives at 37,712, Rosecrans listed an effective force of 43,400. Buck, Irving: *Cleburne and His Command* p. 122 lists Union strength at 43,400, and Confederate totals at 37,712.

9. Mitchell: p. 112

10. Kniffin: p. 617

11. Cozzens: p. 76

12. Cozzens: p. 76; Kniffin: p. 618; Mitchell: p. 112

13. Cozzens: p. 83

14. Cozzens: p. 83; Kniffin: p. 618 states that the battle began "at daybreak"

15. Cozzens: p. 83

16. Cozzens: p. 83

17. Buck, Irving A.: *Cleburne and His Command* p. 119; Cozzens: p. 83

18. Cozzens: p. 86; Kniffin: p. 619

19. Cozzens: p. 87; Kniffin: p. 619

20. Cozzens: p. 88

21. Cozzens: p. 89

22. Cozzens: p. 91

23. Cozzens: p. 92

24. Cozzens: pp. 92–94

25. Cozzens: p. 95

26. Cozzens: pp. 96–97

27. Cozzens: p. 110

28. Catton, Bruce: *The American Heritage Picture History of the Civil War* pp. 284–287; Cozzens: pp. 132–134; *Historical Times Encyclopedia*: p. 723; Mitchell: p. 113

29. Cozzens: p. 134

30. Cozzens: pp. 150–151

31. Cozzens: p. 157

32. Cozzens: p. 157

33. Mitchell: p. 115; Buck: p. 124; Cozzens: p. 159

34. Cozzens: p. 165

35. Cozzens: p. 179

36. Catton: p. 287; Cozzens: p. 179

37. *Historical Times Encyclopedia*: p. 723; Cozzens: p. 183

38. Cozzens: p. 191

39. Cozzens: pp. 192–193; Catton: p. 287

40. *Battles and Leaders* Vol. III pp. 610–612; Mitchell: p. 116 states that the Confederates lost "about 10,000" and the Federals "about 13,000"

41. Catton: p. 289

42. Sword: p. 293

1863

March 17, 1863, Kelly's Ford

1. Thomason, John: *Jeb Stuart* p. 353; *Historical Times Illustrated Encyclopedia of the Civil War*: p. 411; Freeman, Douglas S.: *Lee's Lieutenants* Vol. II p. 457

2. Thomason: p. 353

3. Thomason: p. 354

4. Freeman: pp. 458–459

5. Freeman: p. 459

5a. Thomason: p. 355; Freeman: p. 459

6. Freeman: p. 459

7. Freeman: pp. 460–462

8. Freeman: p. 462

9. Freeman: pp. 462–463

10. Freeman: pp. 462–463; Thomason: p. 357

11. Freeman: p. 463

12. Freeman: p. 465

13. Freeman: p. 465

14. *Historical Times Illustrated Encyclopedia of the Civil War*: p. 568

15. Freeman: p. 464; Thomason lists the Union loss as 80 men, and Confederate casualties at 133

April 27–May 6, 1863, Chancellorsville

1. Sears, Stephen: *Chancellorsville* pp. 65–67

2. Bigelow, John A: *The Campaign of Chancellorsville* pp. 491–492

3. Hassler, William W.: *A. P. Hill* p. 127

4. Bigelow: p. 54. These were the divisions of General John B. Hood (6,965 men) and General George E. Pickett (6,169 men)

5. Sears: p. 168

6. Freeman, Douglas S.: *R. E. Lee* Vol. III p. 6

6a. Furgurson, Ernest B.: *Chancellorsville 1863*: p. 105

7. Sears: p. 193

8. Furgurson: p. 88; Bigelow: pp. 134–136; Osborne, Charles C.: *Jubal* p. 160 states the troop totals as "about 60,000 vs. about 133,000." For the command structure of each army at Chancellorsville see Sears: Appendix I. Vandiver, Frank E.: *Mighty Stonewall* p. 456 lists the Confederate strength at 62,500, while Hooker had some 130,000 troops at his disposal

9. Furgurson: p. 67

10. Furgurson: p. 67

11. Furgurson: p. 67

12. Furgurson: p. 336; Bigelow: pp. 269–270; Sears: p. 266; Thomason, John: *Jeb Stuart* p. 371; Vandiver: 488

13. *Historical Times Illustrated History of the Civil War*; Vandiver: p. 488

14. Furgurson: pp. 94–97

15. Furgurson: p. 97

16. Furgurson: p. 100
17. Bigelow: p. 251
18. Furgurson: pp. 111–112
19. Furgurson: p. 115; Bigelow pp. 232–233
20. Furgurson: p. 115. Estimates vary slightly on General Early's infantry. Freeman: *R. E. Lee* Vol. II p. 517 places Early's force at 10,400; Bigelow lists it as 11,600; Osborne: p. 145 calculates it as 10,500
21. Bigelow: p. 244
22. Bigelow: p. 248
23. Freeman: *R. E. Lee* Vol. III p. 3; Bigelow: p. 263
24. Furgurson: p. 123; Sears: p. 202 lists the number as 72,000
25. Bigelow: p. 482
26. Sears: p. 207
27. Bigelow: pp. 254–255; Sears: p. 181
28. Furgurson: p. 130
29. Bigelow: p. 255
30. Furgurson: p. 45
31. Sears: pp. 231–232
32. Freeman: *Lee's Lieutenants* Vol. II pp. 546–547; Furgurson: p. 142; Freeman: *R. E. Lee* Vol. II p. 523, 525; Robertson, James I., Jr.: *Stonewall Jackson* p. 714; Vandiver: p. 468
33. Furgurson: p. 152; Sears: p. 246
34. Sears: p. 240
35. Howard, Oliver O.: *Battles and Leaders* Vol. III p. 194; Bigelow: p. 275; Sears: pp. 244–245
36. Furgurson: p. 151
37. Furgurson: p. 154
38. Furgurson: p. 154; Sears: p. 268; Bigelow: p. 286; Howard: *Battles and Leaders* Vol. III p. 220
39. Furgurson: p. 259; Vandiver: p. 472
40. Furgurson: p. 157
41. Furgurson: p. 157
42. Furgurson: p. 158
43. Furgurson: p. 158
44. Furgurson: p. 158
45. Furgurson: p. 166. Estimates of the distance between each Confederate line vary. Furgurson: p. 166 puts it at 100 yards; Bigelow: pp. 291–292 has it at 150 yards; Sears: p. 261 places the distance at 200 yards
46. Bigelow: pp. 291–291; Furgurson: p. 168. While Nicholl's brigade was part of Colston's second line, Bigelow and Furgurson disagree on its position. Furgurson places Nicholls on the left of the second line, and Bigelow states that Nicholls dropped back to Heth's left, in the third line
47. Furgurson: pp. 167–169
47a. Sears: p. 269; Bigelow: p. 286 lists Howard's troop strength as 10,500
47b. Sears: pp. 237–238
47c. Sears: p. 133
48. Sears: p. 237
49. Sears: p. 237
50. Sears: p. 238 These were the 54th New York and the 153rd Pennsylvania, some 700 men
51. Sears: p. 238
52. Furgurson: p. 171; Robertson: p. 722 also places the time at 5:15 P.M.; Sears: p. 272 states the time as 5:30 P.M.; Vandiver: p. 473 gives the time as 5:15
53. Furgurson: p. 171; Robertson: p. 722; Sears: p. 272
54. Sears: p. 272
55. Sears: p. 272
56. Sears: p. 272 These were the 41st and 45th New York under General von Gilsa
57. Sears: p. 272
58. Sears: p. 277
59. Furgurson: pp. 189–190; Bigelow: p. 298; Freeman: *Lee's Lieutenants* Vol. II p. 559; Sears: pp. 279–280
60. Sears: p. 278
61. Sears: p. 287
62. Sears: p. 293
63. Sears: p. 294
64. Freeman: *Lee's Lieutenants* Vol. II p. 600; Sears: p. 296; Furgurson: p. 214
65. Sears: p. 297; Robertson: p. 733
66. Bigelow: p. 459
67. Furgurson: p. 329; Robertson: p. 753; Vandiver: p. 494
68. Sears: p. 298
69. Sears: p. 298. Jackson and A. P. Hill were both incapacitated. Rodes was a brigadier general, so Stuart was the most senior officer on the field
70. Sears: p. 312
71. Sears: p. 312
72. Sears: p. 313; Bigelow: pp. 344–345
73. Sears: pp. 314–315
74. Sears: p. 314
75. Sears: p. 328
76. Sears: p. 328
77. Sears: p. 336
77a. Furgurson: p. 227. For an analysis of the artillery duel at Hazel Grove and Fairview see Bigelow: p. 348
78. Sears: pp. 336–337
79. Sears: p. 338; Bigelow: p. 403. For an in depth analysis of the injury and its after effects, see Bigelow: pp. 362–363
80. Furgurson: p. 248
81. Furgurson: p. 249
82. Furgurson: p. 258
83. Sears: pp. 349–350
84. Furgurson: p. 261
85. Furgurson: pp. 262–263
85a. Sears: p. 357
86. Furgurson: p. 267
87. Furgurson: p. 267
88. Furgurson: p. 253
89. Furgurson: p. 268
90. Furgurson: p. 274
91. Furgurson: pp. 276–277
92. Furgurson: p. 277
93. Furgurson: pp. 278–279
94. Furgurson: p. 280
95. Sears: p. 385
96. Furgurson: p. 280
97. Furgurson: p. 284
98. Furgurson: p. 290
99. Furgurson: p. 293; Dowdey, Clifford: *Death of a Nation* p. 175; Freeman: *R. E. Lee* Vol. II p. 551
100. Furgurson: p. 297; Sears: p. 411 gives the time as 5:30 P.M.
101. Furgurson: p. 299
102. Furgurson: p. 317
103. *Battles and Leaders*: Vol. III pp. 233–238; Furgurson: pp. 364–365; Sears: pp. 475–492 lists Federal casualties as 1,694 killed, 9,672 wounded and 5,938 missing, for a total of 17,304. Freeman: *R. E. Lee* p. 5 gives the total Union loss as 16,845 men
104. *Battles and Leaders*: Vol. III pp. 233–238; Freeman: *R. E. Lee* Vol. III p. 5 lists Lee's losses as 1,683 killed, 9,277 wounded, and 2,196 captured or missing, for a total of 13,156
105. Strode, Hudson: *Jefferson Davis* Vol. II p. 452; Dowdey: *Lee* p. 394; Freeman: *R. E. Lee* Vol. III p. 153
106. Freeman: *R. E. Lee* Vol. III p. 153
107. Bigelow: p. 337; Castel, Albert: *Decision in the West*: p. 95

June 9, 1863, Brandy Station

1. *Historical Times Illustrated Encyclopedia of the Civil War*: p. 76
2. *Historical Times Encyclopedia*: p. 76
3. *Historical Times Encyclopedia*: p. 76
4. *Historical Times Encyclopedia*: p. 76
5. *Historical Times Encyclopedia*: p. 76
6. *Historical Times Encyclopedia*: p. 76
7. *Historical Times Encyclopedia*: p. 76
8. *Historical Times Encyclopedia*: p. 76
9. *Historical Times Encyclopedia*: p. 76
10. Freeman, Douglas S.: *Lee's Lieutenants* Vol. III p. 13; *Historical Times Encyclopedia*: p. 76; Thomason, John: *Jeb Stuart* p. 408; *Battles and Leaders*: Vol. III p. 263 and Freeman: *R. E. Lee* Vol. III p. 32 both list the Confederate casualties at 485 and the Union losses at approximately 930
11. Tucker, Glenn: *High Tide at Gettysburg*: p. 67
12. Freeman: *Lee's Lieutenants* Vol. II p. xxiv; Thomason: p. 137. For a scathing article on General Stuart's performance at

Brandy Station in the *Richmond Examiner*, see *Lee's Lieutenants* Vol. III p. 19

13. Dowdey, Clifford: *Lee* p. 394; Freeman: *Lee's Lieutenants* Vol. III p. 170, 175

June 14–15, 1863, Winchester (Second)

1 *Historical Times Encyclopedia of the Civil War*: p. 834; Pfanz, Donald C.: *Richard S. Ewell* p. 281 gives the distance from Berryville to Winchester as ten miles

2. Pfanz: p. 281 states that there were "between 6,000 and 8,000" Federal troops stationed at Winchester; Freeman, Douglas S.: *Lee's Lieutenants* Vol. III p. 20 places "an estimated 6,000 to 8,000" force at Winchester, plus an additional 1,800 man garrison at Berryville

3. Osborne, Charles C.: *Jubal* p. 168; Freeman: p. 20; Pfanz: p. 282 states that Jenkins had 1,600 men

4. Pfanz: pp. 282–283

4a. Fort Milroy was also know as Flag Fort

5. Pfanz: pp. 284–285

6. Pfanz: pp. 284–285

7. Pfanz: p. 286; Osborne: p. 170 places the time of the bombardment closer to 5:30 P.M.; Freeman: p. 22 gives the time as "6:00 P.M. or a little later"

8. Pfanz: p. 286; Osborne: p. 172

9. Pfanz: pp. 286–287; Freeman: p. 24

10. Pfanz: pp. 286–287; Freeman: pp. 23–24

11. Pfanz: pp. 285–287

12. Pfanz: p. 287; Freeman: pp. 25–26

13. Pfanz: p. 287; Freeman: p. 26 states that Federal prisoners numbered "more than 2,300"

14. Pfanz: p. 287

15. Pfanz: pp. 287–288

16. Pfanz: p. 288; Mitchell, Joseph B.: *Decisive Battles of the Civil War* p. 145; Freeman: p. 27 and Osborne: p. 173 also state that 23 guns were taken, at a cost of 269 Confederate casualties, but assert that Union prisoners amounted to only 3,358 men. The difference in the two numbers may be due to prisoners being counted at two different points in time

17. Pfanz: pp. 287–289 explains that Milroy and about 200 men escaped to Harper's Ferry

June 17, 1863, Aldie

1. Dowdey, Clifford: *Death of a Nation*, preface

2. *Historical Times Encyclopedia of the Civil War*: p. 5

3. Thomason, John: *Jeb Stuart* p. 414

4. Thomason: p. 414

5. Thomason: p. 414

6. Thomason: p. 414

7. Thomason: p. 414

8. Thomason: p. 414

July 1–3, 1863, Gettysburg

1. General Hooker was a native of Massachusetts

2. Eckenrode, H. J. & Conrad, Bryan: *James Longstreet* p. 176; Mitchell, Joseph B.: *Decisive Battles of the Civil War* p. 159 lists the totals as between 70,000 and 75,000 men; *Battles and Leaders of the Civil War*: Vol. III p. 440; Pfanz, Donald C.: *Richard S. Ewell* p. 291 states that General Lee had "approximately 75,000" men

3. Freeman, Douglas S.: *R. E. Lee* Vol. III pp. 37–39

4. Freeman: *R. E. Lee* pp. 37–39

5. Freeman: *R. E. Lee* pp. 37–39

6. Freeman: *R. E. Lee* p. 40

7. Tucker, Glenn: *High Tide at Gettysburg* p. 33; Thomason, John: *Jeb Stuart* p. 423; Freeman: *R. E. Lee* pp. 40–41

8. Freeman, Douglas S.: *Lee's Lieutenants* Vol. III p. 170; Tucker: p. 386; Dowdey, Clifford: *Death of a Nation* p. 38

9. Mitchell: pp. 146–147

10. Thomason: pp. 429–430; Dowdey: pp. 71–72; Mitchell: p. 147

11. Mitchell: p. 147 General Meade replaced General Hooker on June 28, 1863

12. Freeman: *R. E. Lee* p. 57; Hassler, W. W.: *A. P. Hill* p. 150; Pfanz: p. 301

13. Catton, Bruce: *The American Heritage Picture History of the Civil War* p. 326

14. Pfanz: p. 302 gives the population as 2,400 residents in 1863; Tucker: p. 99 states that Gettysburg was "a town of about 3,000 people"

15. Osborne, Charles C.: *Jubal* p. 189; Alexander, E. Porter: *Fighting for the Confederacy*: p. 233; Freeman: *Lee's Lieutenants* p. 81

16. Freeman: *Lee's Lieutenants* p. 78

17. Freeman: *Lee's Lieutenants* pp. 79–80 explains that while the proper name for the road was the Chambersburg Turnpike, it was also called the Cashtown Road

18. Freeman: *Lee's Lieutenants* pp. 79–80

19. Freeman: *Lee's Lieutenants* p. 80; Hassler: p. 154

20. Freeman: *Lee's Lieutenants* p. 80

20a. Tucker: p. 120 explains that immediate command of the Union I Corps fell to Abner Doubleday; it would later be assumed by John Newton

21. Hassler: p. 154; Freeman: *Lee's Lieutenants* p. 81

22. Hassler: p. 155 gives the times as 2:30 P.M.; Freeman: *Lee's Lieutenants* p. 82 states that it was "between 2:30 and 3:00 o'clock"

23. Freeman: *Lee's Lieutenants* p. 83

24. Freeman: *Lee's Lieutenants* p. 83

25. Freeman: *Lee's Lieutenants* pp. 83–87; Davis: p. 223

26. Freeman: *Lee's Lieutenants* pp. 86–88

27. Freeman: *Lee's Lieutenants* p. 89

28. Catton: p. 332

29. Davis, Burke: Grey Fox p. 223, and Hassler: p. 156 both state that Heth lost 2,700 men; Pfanz: p. 310 lists Rodes' losses as 2,500 men and Early's casualties as "under 500"

30. Freeman: *Lee's Lieutenants* p. 90

31. Freeman: *Lee's Lieutenants* p. 90

32. Freeman: *Lee's Lieutenants* pp. 90–92; Dowdey: p. 139 gives the time as "somewhere between three thirty and four o'clock"

33. Freeman: *Lee's Lieutenants* p. 93; Dowdey: pp. 139–142; Tucker: pp. 176–177

34. Mitchell: p. 153; Thomason: p. 438; Freeman: *R. E. Lee* p. 91; Dowdey: p. 144; Tucker: p. 196

35. It will be remembered that General Newton assumed command of the I Corps when General Reynolds was killed on July 1

36. Hunt, Henry J.: *Battles and Leaders* Vol. III p. 308; Mitchell: p. 154; Sears, Stephen W.: *Controversies & Commanders* p. 213 places the distance at about three quarters of a mile

37. Strode, Hudson: *Jefferson Davis* Vol. II p. 452; Thomason: p. 439; Hunt: p. 307

38. Mitchell: p. 155; *Historical Times Encyclopedia of the Civil War*: p. 306; Hunt: p. 308

39. Hunt: p. 308

40. Catton: p. 335

41. Catton: p. 335; Tucker: p. 300

42. Freeman: *Lee's Lieutenants* p. 118

43. Longstreet, James: *Battles and Leaders* Vol. III p. 339

44. Freeman: *Lee's Lieutenants* p. 118; Longstreet: pp. 339–341; Mitchell: pp. 153–155

45. Catton: pp. 336–337; *Historical Times Encyclopedia*: p. 306; Mitchell: p. 155

46. Mitchell: p. 154; Tucker: p. 236; Hunt: p. 306

47. Castel, Albert: *Decision in the West*

p. 58; Freeman: *R. E. Lee* p. 94; Tucker: p. 236

48. Freeman: *Lee's Lieutenants* p. 128; Freeman: *R. E. Lee* pp. 150–152; Tucker: p. 287; Mitchell: p. 154

49. Hunt: p. 307; Dowdey pp. 205–207; Hood, John B.: *Advance and Retreat* pp. 57–59

50. Mitchell: p. 155; Catton: pp. 336–337; Sears: p. 213 states that casualties in the III Corps exceeded 30 percent

51. *Historical Times Encyclopedia*: p. 688; Catton: p. 338

52. Tucker: p. 269

53. Tucker: p. 259

54. Tucker: p. 259

55. Tucker: pp. 257–259

56. Tucker: pp. 266–267

57. Tucker: p. 267

58. Tucker: p. 283

59. Tucker: p. 283 explains that Colonel David Lang had temporarily assumed command of the brigade normally led by Edward A. Perry, who was ill with typhoid fever

60. Tucker: p. 288

61. Tucker: p. 288

62. Catton: p. 340

63. Catton: pp. 340–341

64. Catton: pp. 340–341

65. Dowdey: p. 258; Freeman: *R. E. Lee* p. 108

66. Catton: p. 342; Tucker: p. 344; Alexander, E. Porter: *Battles and Leaders* Vol. III p. 367; Mitchell: p. 157

67. Tucker: p. 347

68. Tucker: pp. 342–343

69. Archer's command had been decimated on July 1. The troops in this charge were led by Colonel Birkett D. Fry, who aligned his men on Garnett's left

70. Pettigrew exercised command of all four brigades. His own brigade was led by Colonel James K. Marshall

71. Colonel Mayo led John Brockenborough's brigade

72. Catton: p. 342; Mitchell: p. 157

73. *Battles and Leaders*: p. 370; Dowdey: p. 202; Freeman: *Lee's Lieutenants* p. 179; Freeman: *R. E. Lee* p. 152

74. Freeman: *R. E. Lee* p. 130. Exact language varies, but Lee accepted complete blame for the Confederate defeat

74a. Dowdey: p. 338

75. *Battles and Leaders* Vol. III p. 384 and 440. Casualty reports vary slightly; however, it is well documented that the Confederates lost slightly more than 20,000 troops and the Federals lost just over 23,000 men

76. Freeman: *R. E. Lee* p. 154

77. Freeman: *R. E. Lee* p. 154

78. Dowdey, Clifford: *Lee* p. 394; Strode: p. 452; Freeman: *R. E. Lee* p. 153

July 14, 1863, Falling Waters

1. Freeman, Douglas S.: *Lee's Lieutenants* Vol. III p. 165; Imboden, John D.: *Battles and Leaders* Vol. III p. 423

2. Imboden: p. 423; *Historical Times Illustrated Encyclopedia of the Civil War*: p. 253

3. Pfanz, Donald C.: *Richard S. Ewell* p. 328

4. Imboden: p. 426

5. Freeman: p. 166; Imboden: pp. 427–428

6. Freeman: p. 166; Pfanz: p. 328 states that Falling Waters is four miles from Williamsport

7. Freeman: pp. 166–167; Pfanz: p. 328

8. Freeman: p. 167; *Historical Times Encyclopedia*: p. 253

9. *Historical Times Encyclopedia*: p. 253

10. Freeman: p. 167; *Historical Times Encyclopedia*: p. 253 lists the Southern losses at 719 men

September 19–20, 1863, Chickamauga

1. Cozzens, Peter: *This Terrible Sound* p. 71; Buck, Irving: *Cleburne and His Command* p. 138 states that at this point Crittenden was 15 miles from Thomas

2. Cozzens: pp. 72–74

3. Cozzens: p. 75; Tucker, Glenn: *Chickamauga* p. 71; Eckenrode, H. J. & Conrad, Bryan: *James Longstreet* p. 221

4. Tucker: p. 71

5. Cozzens: p. 81

6. Tucker: p. 71

7. Cozzens: p. 83

8. Cozzens: p. 85

9. Cozzens: p. 89

10. These were the infantry divisions of John B. Hood and Lafayette McLaws, along with artillery under E. Porter Alexander

11. Opdycke, Emerson: *Battles and Leaders* Vol. III p. 670

12. Tucker: p. 126

13. Tucker: p. 127

14. Tucker: p. 127; Cozzens: p. 123

15. Tucker: p. 127; Cozzens: p. 123

16. Cozzens: p. 127

17. Cozzens: p. 127

18. Cozzens: p. 129

19. Cozzens: p. 133; Tucker: p. 133

20. Cozzens: pp. 137–138

21. Cozzens: pp. 141–143

22. Cozzens: p. 144

23. Cozzens: p. 146; Tucker: pp. 133–134

24. Cozzens: pp. 149–150

25. Cozzens: p. 169

26. Cozzens: p. 171

27. Cozzens: pp. 184–185

28. Cozzens: p. 186

29. Cozzens: p. 186

30. Cozzens: p. 192

31. Cozzens: p. 239

32. Cozzens: pp. 239–241

33. Cozzens: p. 233

34. Cozzens: p. 233

35. Cozzens: pp. 243–244

36. Cozzens: pp. 247–248

37. Cozzens: p. 248

38. Cozzens: pp. 248–249

38a. Cozzens: pp. 256–257

39. Cozzens: p. 198

40. Cozzens: p. 208

41. Cozzens: p. 214

42. Cozzens: p. 214

43. Cozzens: p. 214

44. Cozzens: pp. 221–222

45. Cozzens: pp. 226–229

46. Cozzens: p. 267; Tucker: p. 182 indicates that the time of the assault was between 5:00 P.M. and 6:00 P.M.

47. Cozzens: p. 274

48. *Battles and Leaders* Vol. III p. 670; Cozzens pp. 537–542. It should be noted that technically General Johnson was under McCook's command and General Palmer was under Crittenden's command, but on September 20 Thomas controlled all six Union divisions.

49. *Battles and Leaders*: p. 670

50. Cozzens: p. 315. A. P. Stewart, Bushrod Johnson and William Preston belonged to Buckner's corps, but for this assault, Longstreet commanded the entire left wing. Eckenrode & Conrad: p. 230

51. Tucker: p. 261; Cozzens: p. 368; Sword, Wiley: *Mountains Touched with Fire*: p. 13

52. Cozzens: p. 368

53. Cozzens: p. 369; Eckenrode & Conrad: p. 232 state that Longstreet advanced "about noon"; Sword: p. 13 gives the time as 11:10 A.M.

54. Cozzens: p. 330

55. Cozzens: p. 330

56. Cozzens: p. 391

57. Cozzens: p. 428

58. Cozzens: p. 424

59. Cozzens: p. 477

60. *Battles and Leaders*: pp. 672–676; Alexander, E. Porter: *Fighting for the Confederacy*: p. 296

61. *Battles and Leaders*: pp. 672–676; Alexander: p. 296 places Confederate losses at 16,171, while Tucker estimates Confederate casualties at 20,950. Most estimates fall in the 16,000 to 18,000 range

62. Tucker: pp. 377–379

63. Cozzens: pp. 535–536; *Battles and Leaders*: p. 662

October 5–10, 1863, Blue Springs

1. On November 4, 1863, General James Longstreet would leave Chattanooga with two divisions, and place Knoxville under siege
2. *Historical Times Encyclopedia of the Civil War*: pp. 68–69
3. *Historical Times Encyclopedia*: p. 69
4. *Historical Times Encyclopedia*: p. 69
5. *Historical Times Encyclopedia*: p. 69
6. *Historical Times Encyclopedia*: p. 69
7. *Historical Times Encyclopedia*: p. 69
8. *Historical Times Encyclopedia*: p. 69
9. *Historical Times Encyclopedia*: p. 69
10. *Historical Times Encyclopedia*: p. 69
11. *Historical Times Encyclopedia*: p. 69
12. *Historical Times Encyclopedia*: p. 69
13. *Historical Times Encyclopedia*: p. 69
14. *Historical Times Encyclopedia*: p. 69
15. *Historical Times Encyclopedia*: p. 69

October 14, 1863, Bristoe Station

1. Freeman, Douglas S.: *R. E. Lee* Vol. III p. 170
2. Freeman: *R. E. Lee* p. 170 lists the Union forces as 80,700 effectives, and Lee at "under 50,000."
3. Freeman: *R. E. Lee* p. 170
4. Freeman: *R. E. Lee* p. 174
5. Freeman: *R. E. Lee* pp. 176–177
5a. Freeman, Douglas S.: *Lee's Lieutenants* Vol. III p. 241
6. Freeman: *R. E. Lee* p. 180
7. Freeman: *R. E. Lee* p. 181
7a. Freeman: *R. E. Lee* p. 181
8. Freeman: *Lee's Lieutenants* p. 241
8a. Hassler, W. W.: *A. P. Hill* p. 176; Freeman: *Lee's Lieutenants* p. 241
9. Freeman: *R. E. Lee* p. 181; Hassler: pp. 176–177
10. Freeman: *R. E. Lee* p. 182
11. *Historical Times Illustrated Encyclopedia of the Civil War*: p. 80
12. Freeman: *R. E. Lee* p. 183
13. Freeman: *R. E. Lee* p. 183
14. Freeman: *R. E. Lee* p. 183 lists total losses in Cooke's brigade at 700, and Kirkland's at 602
15. Freeman: *R. E. Lee* p. 183; *Battles and Leaders* Vol. IV p. 84 lists Confederate losses as 136 killed, 797 wounded and 445 captured or missing, for a total of 1,378; Osborne, Charles C.: *Jubal* p. 204 lists Confederate losses at 1,378
15a. Historical Times: p. 81; *Battles and Leaders* Vol. IV p. 84 lists Union losses as 50 killed, 335 wounded and 161 captured or missing, for a total of 546
16. Freeman: *R. E. Lee* p. 183; Hassler: p. 180

November 14–December 14, 1863, The Knoxville Campaign

1. *Historical Times Encyclopedia of the Civil War*: p. 420. The divisions were infantry troops under Generals Lafayette McLaws and Micah Jenkins, along with two artillery battalions, commanded by Colonel E. Porter Alexander and Major Austin Leyden.
2. *Historical Times Encyclopedia*: p. 420
3. *Historical Times Encyclopedia*: p. 420; Eckenrode, H. J. & Conrad, Bryan: *James Longstreet* p. 253 state that Longstreet had "something more than 15,000 men"
4. Eckenrode & Conrad: p. 252; *Historical Times Encyclopedia*: p. 420
5. Eckenrode & Conrad: pp. 252–253; Sword, Wiley: *Mountains Touched with Fire* p. 29
6. *Historical Times Encyclopedia*: pp. 108–109
7. *Historical Times Encyclopedia*: p. 109
8. *Historical Times Encyclopedia*: p. 109
9. Poe, Orlando M.: *Battles and Leaders* Vol. III p. 733
10. Poe: p. 733
11. *Historical Times Encyclopedia*: p. 109; Poe: p. 733
12. *Historical Times Encyclopedia*: p. 109; Poe: p. 734 lists Union losses at 300, Jenkins' command at 174, and estimates that with the inclusion of McLaws' losses, total casualties were approximately equal
13. Eckenrode & Conrad: p. 257
14. Poe: p. 743; Eckenrode & Conrad: pp. 263–264 state that the attack took place at first light
15. Eckenrode & Conrad: p. 264; Poe: p. 743 mentions specifically the 13th and 17th Mississippi and the 16th Georgia regiments
16. *Historical Times Encyclopedia*: p. 51
17. *Battles and Leaders*: p. 752

November 7, 1863, Rappahannock Station

1. *Historical Times Encyclopedia of the Civil War*: p. 615
2. Pfanz, Donald C.: *Richard S. Ewell* p. 343
3. Freeman, Douglas S.: *Lee's Lieutenants* Vol. III p. 264; Pfanz: p. 343
4. *Historical Times Encyclopedia*: p. 615, Pfanz: p. 344
5. Freeman: p. 264
6. Freeman: p. 266; Osborne, Charles C.: *Jubal* p. 208
7. Freeman: pp. 266–267. These were the brigades under Harry Hays and Robert Hoke. Hays was absent while serving on court-martial duty, and his brigade was temporarily commanded by Colonel Davidson Penn. Hays arrived around 4:00 P.M. Hoke was also absent, being on detached duty. His brigade was led by Colonel Archibald Godwin. Freeman states that "not more than 600 escaped" while *Historical Times Encyclopedia*: p. 615 says that the Confederates had "a loss of some 1500 men"; Osborne: p. 208 states that "only about 450 escaped"
8. Osborne: p. 209; Freeman: p. 267; Pfanz: p. 244 states that Early lost "approximately 1,700 men" and that the Rodes and Early combined losses "topped 2,000"
9. Pfanz: p. 344
10. Freeman: p. 269

November 23–25, 1863, Chattanooga

1. The battle of Chickamauga was fought September 19–20, 1863.
2. Hill, Daniel H.: *Battles and Leaders* Vol. III p. 662; Buck, Irving: *Cleburne and His Command* pp. 151–152, 154; Tucker, Glenn: *Chickamauga: Bloody Battle in the West* pp. 377, 379; Cozzens, Peter: *This Terrible Sound* p. 518
3. Cozzens: p. 518
4. Grant, Ulysses S.: *Battles and Leaders* Vol. III p. 711; Strode, Hudson: *Jefferson Davis* Vol. II p. 482
4a. *Historical Times Illustrated Encyclopedia of the Civil War*: p. 134; Cozzens, Peter: *The Shipwreck of Their Hopes*: pp. 390–391; Sword, Wiley: *Mountains Touched with Fire* pp. 77–78
5. *Civil War Times Illustrated*: August 1971 p. 30; Sword: p. 179 states that Orchard Knob rises about 100 feet above Chattanooga Valley. Sword: p. 86 by comparison, states that Lookout Mountain is 2,146 feet above sea level
6. *CWTI*: p. 30
7. *CWTI*: p. 30
8. Cozzens: *The Shipwreck of Their Hopes* p. 130; Sword: p. 181 places the time at 1:50 P.M.

9. Cozzens: *The Shipwreck of Their Hopes* p. 130
10. Cozzens: *The Shipwreck of Their Hopes* p. 132
11. Cozzens: *The Shipwreck of Their Hopes* p. 132; Sword: p. 183 states that it was 2:20 P.M.
12. Cozzens: *The Shipwreck of Their Hopes* p. 133; Sword: p. 183
13. Cozzens: *The Shipwreck of Their Hopes* pp. 140–141
14. Cozzens: *The Shipwreck of Their Hopes* pp. 141–142; Sword: p. 188 infers that this deployment was Hardee's decision; however, it seems likely that Bragg must have approved the order, as he was also stationed on Missionary Ridge, and was the overall commander of the Confederate forces
14a. Sword: p. 86 states that the mountain was 2,146 feet above sea level
15. Cozzens: *The Shipwreck of Their Hopes* p. 144
16. Cozzens: *The Shipwreck of Their Hopes* p. 168; *CWTI*: August 1971 p. 31; Sword: p. 207
17. Cozzens: *The Shipwreck of Their Hopes* p. 168; Sword: p. 207
18. Cozzens: *The Shipwreck of Their Hopes* p. 171
19. Cozzens: *The Shipwreck of Their Hopes* p. 171
20. Cozzens: *The Shipwreck of Their Hopes* p. 173
21. Cozzens: *The Shipwreck of Their Hopes* p. 174
22. Cozzens: *The Shipwreck of Their Hopes* p. 175
23. Cozzens: *The Shipwreck of Their Hopes* p. 187; Sword: p. 218
24. Cozzens: *The Shipwreck of Their Hopes* pp. 187–188
25. Cozzens: *The Shipwreck of Their Hopes* pp. 188–191
26. Cozzens: *The Shipwreck of Their Hopes* p. 193
27. Cozzens: *The Shipwreck of Their Hopes* p. 197; Sword: p. 241 verifies that a lunar eclipse occurred during the night of November 24–25; Sword: p. 227 also states that the Confederates had evacuated Lookout Mountain by 3:00 A.M., November 25
28. Cozzens: *The Shipwreck of Their Hopes* p. 201; Sword: p. 223
29. Cozzens: *The Shipwreck of Their Hopes* p. 204
30. Cozzens: *The Shipwreck of Their Hopes* pp. 204–205; Sword: p. 241
31. Cozzens: *The Shipwreck of Their Hopes* p. 205. Sherman's attack should have started at approximately 6:30 A.M.; it got under way around 8:00 A.M.
32. Cozzens: *The Shipwreck of Their Hopes* pp. 205–210
33. Cozzens: *The Shipwreck of Their Hopes* pp. 213–216
34. Cozzens: *The Shipwreck of Their Hopes* pp. 218
35. Cozzens: *The Shipwreck of Their Hopes* pp. 218
36. Tucker: p. 182; Cozzens: *No Better Place to Die* p. 34; Sword: p. 24
37. Cozzens: *The Shipwreck of Their Hopes* p. 227
38. Cozzens: *The Shipwreck of Their Hopes* p. 232
39. Cozzens: *The Shipwreck of Their Hopes* p. 232
40. Cozzens: *The Shipwreck of Their Hopes* pp. 232–233
41. Cozzens: *The Shipwreck of Their Hopes* pp. 236–239; Sword: pp. 256–257
42. Cozzens: *The Shipwreck of Their Hopes* p. 239
43. Cozzens: *The Shipwreck of Their Hopes* p. 240
44. Cozzens: *The Shipwreck of Their Hopes* pp. 241–243
45. Cozzens: *The Shipwreck of Their Hopes* p. 244
46. Cozzens: *The Shipwreck of Their Hopes* pp. 244–245
47. Cozzens: *The Shipwreck of Their Hopes* p. 245; *CWTI*: August 1971 p. 36; Grant: *Battles and Leaders* Vol. III p. 708
48. Cozzens: *The Shipwreck of Their Hopes* p. 249; Sword: p. 321
49. Cozzens: *The Shipwreck of Their Hopes* pp. 250–251; Sword: p. 188 notes that Bragg had occupied Chattanooga for 62 days without constructing any fortifications
50. Cozzens: *The Shipwreck of Their Hopes* p. 251
51. Cozzens: *The Shipwreck of Their Hopes* pp. 251–252; Sword: p. 287
52. Cozzens: *The Shipwreck of Their Hopes* p. 253; Sword: p. 320
53. Cozzens: *The Shipwreck of Their Hopes* pp. 253–254
54. Cozzens: *The Shipwreck of Their Hopes* p. 255
55. Cozzens: *The Shipwreck of Their Hopes* pp. 263–264
56. Cozzens: *The Shipwreck of Their Hopes* p. 265; Grant: *Battles and Leaders* Vol. III p. 707
57. Cozzens: *The Shipwreck of Their Hopes* pp. 268–269
58. Cozzens: *The Shipwreck of Their Hopes* pp. 272–273
59. Cozzens: *The Shipwreck of Their Hopes* p. 281
60. Cozzens: *The Shipwreck of Their Hopes* pp. 282–283
61. Cozzens: *The Shipwreck of Their Hopes* p. 286
62. Cozzens: *The Shipwreck of Their Hopes* p. 287; Sword: p. 299
63. Cozzens: *The Shipwreck of Their Hopes* p. 289
64. Cozzens: *The Shipwreck of Their Hopes* p. 290
65. Cozzens: *The Shipwreck of Their Hopes* p. 291
66. Cozzens: *The Shipwreck of Their Hopes* pp. 293–294
67. Cozzens: *The Shipwreck of Their Hopes* p. 295
68. Cozzens: *The Shipwreck of Their Hopes* p. 345
69. Cozzens: *The Shipwreck of Their Hopes* pp. 345–346
70. Cozzens: *The Shipwreck of Their Hopes* p. 391; *CWTI*: August 1971 p. 45 lists the casualties as follows: the Confederates lost 361 killed, 2,160 wounded and 4,146 captured, for a total of 6,667. The Federals lost 752 killed, 4,713 wounded and 350 captured or missing, for a total of 5,815. The slightly higher Union total includes casualties in subsequent fighting on November 26 and 27. *Battles and Leaders* Vol. III p. 729 also includes these two days for the Union casualties, listing a total of 5,815 casualties too. *Battles and Leaders* Vol. III p. 730 gives a total of 6,687 for the southern side

November 27, 1863, Ringgold Gap

1. Sword, Wiley: *Mountains Touched with Fire* p. 357
2. Sword: p. 24; Henry, Robert S.: *Forrest "First with the Most"* p. 390; Castel, Albert: *Decision in the West* p. 36; Tucker, Glenn: *Chickamauga* p. 182
3. Buck, Irving: *Cleburne and His Command*: p. 179 states that the gap is "about half a mile in length"; Cozzens, Peter: *The Shipwreck of Their Hopes* p. 370 describes the passage as "about a thousand feet wide and four thousand feet long"
3a. Sword: p. 335
4. Sword: p. 327; Cozzens: p. 378; Buck: p. 179
5. Cozzens: p. 368; Sword: p. 335
6. Sword: p. 335
7. Cozzens: p. 371; Buck: pp. 179–180
8. Cozzens: p. 372
9. Cozzens: p. 373
10. Cozzens: p. 373
11. Cozzens: p. 374 gives the time as "a few minutes after 8:00 A.M."

12. Cozzens: p. 375; Sword: p. 338; Buck: pp. 181–182
13. Cozzens: p. 375; Sword: p. 336 states that the 13th Illinois first came under fire at 150 yards
14. Cozzens: pp. 375–377; Sword: pp. 336–337
15. Cozzens: p. 377; Sword: pp. 338–339; Buck: p. 182
16. Cozzens: pp. 380–381; Sword: pp. 339–340
17. Cozzens: pp. 381–382
18. Cozzens: p. 382
19. Cozzens: p. 382
20. Cozzens: p. 383; Sword: p. 341
21. Cozzens: p. 383
22. Cozzens: p. 383
23. Cozzens: p. 384; Buck: p. 183 gives the time as "between 12 and 1 o'clock"
24. Cozzens: p. 384
25. Sword: p. 343; Buck: p. 184
26. Sword: p. 343 calls this action "one of Pat Cleburne's finest hours"

1864

April 12, 1864, Fort Pillow

1. Catton, Bruce: *The American Heritage Picture History of the Civil War* p. 358; Castel, Albert: *Decision in the West* p. 53; Henry, Robert S.: *Forrest "First with the Most"* p. 16
2. Henry: p. 249; *Historical Times Illustrated Encyclopedia of the Civil War*: p. 277
2a. Henry: p. 249
3. Henry: p. 249
4. Henry: p. 249; *Historical Times Encyclopedia*: p. 257
5. Henry: p. 251; *Historical Times Encyclopedia*: p. 257
6. Henry: p. 253
7. Henry: p. 254
8. Henry: p. 254
9. Henry: p. 254
10. Henry: p. 255
11. Henry: p. 255
12. Henry: p. 256
13. Henry: p. 256
14. Henry: p. 257
15. Henry: p. 259
16. Henry: p. 261
17. *Historical Times Encyclopedia*: p. 257

May 1–September 2, 1864, The Atlanta Campaign

1. *Historical Times Illustrated Encyclopedia of the Civil War*: p. 28; Castel, Albert: *Decision in the West* p. 112; *Civil War Times Illustrated: The Campaign for Atlanta* p. 34; Sherman, William T.: *Battles and Leaders* Vol. IV p. 252
2. *Historical Times Encyclopedia*: p. 28; Castel: p. 112; Howard, Oliver O.: *Battles and Leaders* Vol. IV p. 294 states that the entire Union force was 100,000 men
3. Castel: p. 112; *CWTI* p. 34
4. *Historical Times Encyclopedia*: p. 28
5. Castel: pp. 111–112 There were many noncombatants in a Civil War army. These were men such as cooks, musicians, and teamsters who did not carry a gun. The Union army had 110,000 men "present for duty" and 98,000 "effectives," while the Confederate army had just over 60,000 men "present for duty" and approximately 43,000 "effectives"
6. Govan, Gilbert and Livingwood, James: *Joseph E. Johnston* p. 241
7. Castel: p. 149
8. Castel: pp. 149–150
9. Castel: pp. 150–151; *CWTI* p. 37
10. Castel: p. 150
11. Castel: p. 151
12. Castel: p. 152
13. Castel: p. 155
14. Castel: p. 159
15. Castel: p. 161
16. Castel: p. 161
17. Castel: p. 162
18. Castel: p. 162
19. Castel: p. 163
20. Castel: p. 164
21. Castel: p. 164
22. Castel: p. 164
23. Castel: pp. 165–166
24. Castel: p. 166
25. Castel: p. 166
26. Castel: p. 166
27. Castel: pp. 166–167
28. Castel: p. 167
29. Castel: p. 171
30. Castel: p. 173
31. Castel: p. 173
32. Castel: p. 173
33. Castel: p. 173
34. Castel: p. 173
35. Castel: p. 175
36. Castel: p. 179; Howard: p. 302
37. Castel: p. 180
38. Castel: p. 188
39. Castel: p. 192
40. Castel: pp. 192–193
41. Castel: p. 193
42. Castel: p. 194
43. Castel: p. 195
44. Castel: p. 198 gives the number as "between 70,000 and 74,000 troops"
45. Castel: pp. 198–200
46. Castel: p. 200
47. Castel: p. 202
48. Castel: pp. 204–205
49. Castel: p. 213
50. Henry, Robert S.: *Forrest "First with the Most"* p. 308; Castel: p. 329; Johnston, J. E.: *Battles and Leaders* Vol. IV p. 276; Govan & Livingwood: p. 286
51. Henry: p. 308; Castel: p. 329
52. Freeman, Douglas S.: *R. E. Lee* Vol. III 462
53. Castel: p. 209
54. Castel: p. 209
55. Castel: p. 218
56. Castel: p. 221
57. Castel: p. 225
58. Castel: p. 226
59. Castel: p. 226
60. Castel: p. 226
61. Castel: p. 237
62. Castel: p. 238
63. Castel: p. 239
63a. Castel: p. 242
64. Castel: pp. 243–245
65. Castel: p. 246
66. Castel: p. 246
67. Castel: p. 246
68. Castel: pp. 261–262 gives Confederate losses as about 9,000 of some 70,000, while Union losses were approximately 12,000 of 100,000.
69. Castel: p. 262 states that "two divisions of the XVII Corps, another of the XV Corps and miscellaneous units from Kentucky and Tennessee" would soon join Sherman
70. Castel: p. 269
71. Castel: p. 269
72. Castel: p. 269
73. Castel: p. 270
74. Castel: p. 270; *CWTI* p. 39; Johnston, J. E.: *Battles and Leaders* Vol. IV p. 270
75. Castel: p. 287
76. Castel: p. 292
77. Castel: p. 294
78. Castel: p. 295
79. Castel: p. 306
80. Castel: p. 308
81. Castel: pp. 313–314
82. Castel: pp. 316–317
82a. Castel: pp. 319–320
83. Castel: pp. 317–318
84. Castel: p. 319
85. Castel: pp. 363–365; Govan and Livingwood: p. 314, 321; Freeman: *R. E. Lee* III pp. 461–462
86. Buck, Irving: *Cleburne and His Command* p. 229; Sherman: p. 253 states that "at this moment the Confederate Government rendered us most valuable service"
87. Castel: pp. 352–353; Govan: p. 314
88. Castel: p. 366; Hood, John B.: *Battles and Leaders* Vol. IV p. 336

89. Castel: pp. 366–367
90. Castel: p. 367
91. Castel: p. 375
92. Castel: p. 375
93. Castel: p. 377
94. Castel: p. 381
95. Hood, John B.: *Advance and Retreat* p. 171
96. Castel: pp. 385–386
97. Castel: p. 390
98. Castel: p. 394
99. Castel: p. 398
100. Castel: p. 403
101. Castel: p. 404
102. Castel: pp. 404–405
103. Castel: p. 405
104. Castel: p. 406
105. Castel: p. 407
106. Castel: p. 408
107. Castel: pp. 411–412
108. Castel: p. 413
109. Castel: p. 424
110. Castel: p. 428
111. Castel: pp. 428–433
112. Castel: p. 434
113. Castel: p. 435
114. Castel: p. 450
115. Castel: p. 455
116. Castel: p. 459
117. Castel: p. 460
118. Castel: p. 501
119. Castel: p. 501
120. Castel: p. 502
121. Castel: p. 503
122. Castel: pp. 512–514
123. Dowdey, Clifford: *Lee* p. 502

May 5–6, 1864, The Wilderness

1. Rhea, Gordon C.: *The Battle of the Wilderness* p. 52
2. Rhea: pp. 92–93
3. Rhea: p. 34 states that Grant had 120,000 men; Freeman, Douglas S.: *Lee's Lieutenants* Vol. III p. 345 lists the Union strength at 116,000 troops; *Battles and Leaders* Vol. IV: p. 182 gives the Union troop totals as 118,000 men of all arms
4. *Battles and Leaders*: p. 155; Pfanz, Donald C.: *Richard S. Ewell* p. 365
5. Pfanz: p. 361; Catton, Bruce: *The American Heritage Picture History of the Civil War* p. 448; Freeman: *Lee's Lieutenants* p. 346
6. Hassler, W. W.: *A. P. Hill* p. 186; Freeman, Douglas S.: *R. E. Lee* Vol. III p. 428; Alexander, E. Porter: *Fighting for the Confederacy*: pp. 348–350 states that Longstreet's camps were in Mechanicsville; Eckenrode, H. J. & Conrad, Bryan: *James Longstreet* p. 198 state that part of his command was in Mechanicsville, part in Gordonsville
7. Freeman: *Lee's Lieutenants* p. 345 gives the Confederate strength at approximately 64,000 men; Rhea lists the Confederate army as 65,000 troops; *Battles and Leaders*: p. 184 states that the Southern forces were "not less than 61,000" men
8. Rhea: pp. 84–85; Hassler: p. 187; Pfanz: p. 362
9. Rhea: p. 85; Freeman: *Lee's Lieutenants* p. 346
10. Rhea: p. 87
11. Rhea: p. 87
12. Rhea: p. 90; Eckenrode & Conrad: p. 300
13. Rhea: p. 109; Law, E. M.: *Battles and Leaders* Vol. IV p. 121; Grant, U. S.: *Battles and Leaders* p. 145
14. Rhea: p. 129
15. Rhea: pp. 128–129; Freeman: *R. E. Lee* Vol. III p. 278
16. Rhea: p. 133
17. Rhea: p. 134
18. Rhea: pp. 134–135
19. Rhea: p. 137; Eckenrode & Conrad: p. 305
20. Rhea: p. 141
21. Rhea: p. 142
22. Rhea: p. 143
23. Rhea: p. 142; Pfanz: p. 364 states that Warren attacked "at 1:00 P.M."
24. Rhea: pp. 143–144
25. Rhea: p. 145
26. Rhea: pp. 151–152
27. Rhea: pp. 154–156
28. Rhea: pp. 160–161
29. Rhea: pp. 164–165
30. Rhea: p. 167; Freeman: *Lee's Lieutenants* p. 351
31. Rhea: p. 172; Freeman: *Lee's Lieutenants* p. 351
32. Rhea: p. 173; Freeman: *Lee's Lieutenants* p. 351
33. Rhea: p. 176
34. Rhea: p. 179
35. Rhea: p. 180 states that the hottest fighting took place "a quarter mile or so" above Saunders' Field
36. Rhea: pp. 180–181
37. Rhea: p. 182
38. Rhea: p. 186
39. Rhea: p. 191; Webb, A. S.: *Battles and Leaders* Vol. IV p. 157 states that the time was 4:30 P.M.
40. Rhea: pp. 191–192; Webb: p. 157
41. Rhea: p. 194. These were the divisions of Getty, Mott and Birney
42. Rhea: pp. 195–197
43. Rhea: pp. 197–198
44. Rhea: p. 199
45. Rhea: pp. 199–200; Webb: p. 158
46. Rhea: p. 206
47. Rhea: p. 222
48. Rhea: p. 225
49. Rhea: p. 225
50. Rhea: p. 228
51. Rhea: p. 231
52. Rhea: p. 232
53. Rhea: p. 237
54. Freeman: *R. E. Lee* p. 280; Hassler: p. 191 and Dowdey, Clifford: *Lee* p. 432 list the strength at about 125 men; Rhea: p. 237 gives the strength as closer to 150 soldiers
55. Rhea: p. 238; Hassler: p. 192; *Battles and Leaders*: p. 123; Freeman: *Lee's Lieutenants* p. 353
56. Rhea: p. 272
57. Rhea: p. 275
58. Rhea: p. 276; Freeman: *R. E. Lee* p. 281
59. Rhea: pp. 276–277; Dowdey: p. 433
60. Rhea: p. 277
61. Rhea: p. 278; *Battles and Leaders*: p. 123
62. Rhea: p. 279; Dowdey: p. 434; Hassler: p. 193
63. Rhea: p. 283; Catton: p. 448 and Freeman: *R. E. Lee* p. 285 state that the attack occurred at 5:00 A.M.; Grant: p. 145 also confirms the time as 5:00 A.M.
64. Rhea: pp. 285–287; Hassler: pp. 194–195
65. Rhea: p. 292
66. Rhea: p. 298; Eckenrode & Conrad: p. 310
67. Rhea: p. 302; Freeman: *R. E. Lee* p. 290
68. Rhea: pp. 302–304; Freeman: *Lee's Lieutenants* pp. 356–357
69. Rhea: p. 308
70. Rhea: p. 309; Eckenrode & Conrad: p. 311
71. Rhea: pp. 310–311
72. Rhea: pp. 323–324
73. Rhea: pp. 328–329
74. Rhea: p. 331
75. Rhea: p. 341
76. Rhea: p. 340
77. Rhea: p. 351; Freeman: *Lee's Lieutenants* p. 360
78. Rhea: pp. 356–357
79. Eckenrode & Conrad: p. 313; Freeman: *R. E. Lee* p. 293 also places the attack at about 11:00 A.M.
80. *Historical Times Encyclopedia*: p. 827
81. Rhea: p. 362
82. Rhea: p. 365; *Historical Times Encyclopedia*: p. 795
83. Rhea: p. 366
84. Rhea: p. 368
85. Rhea: p. 369
86. *Historical Times Encyclopedia*: pp.

394–395; Rhea: pp. 369–371; Dowdey: p. 440; Freeman: *R. E. Lee* p. 294

87. Rhea: p. 392; Freeman: *R. E. Lee* p. 295

88. Rhea: p. 404; Dowdey, Clifford: *Death of a Nation*: p. 123; Freeman: *Lee's Lieutenants* p. 448

89. Rhea: p. 404

90. Rhea: pp. 408–409; Freeman: *Lee's Lieutenants* pp. 369–370

91. Rhea: pp. 424–425; Freeman: *Lee's Lieutenants* pp. 370–371; Davis, Burke: *Grey Fox*: pp. 293–294; Pfanz: pp. 373–374 asserts that Lee never met with Ewell on May 6, and did not see him until May 7

92. *Battles and Leaders*: pp. 182–184; Osborne, Charles C.: *Jubal* p. 238 states that Grant lost "about 17,000 men" while Lee lost 7,500 troops

May 5, 1864–April 9, 1865, Bermuda Hundred

1. *Historical Times Illustrated Encyclopedia of the Civil War*: p. 57

2. *Historical Times Encyclopedia*: p. 57; *Battles and Leaders* Vol. IV: p. 182 states that the Union effective force was approximately 36,000 men

3. *Battles and Leaders*: p. 184

4. *Historical Times Encyclopedia*: p. 58

5. Beauregard, P. G. T.: *Battles and Leaders* Vol. IV p. 200

6. Beauregard: p. 200 says that the attack would begin "at daybreak"

7. Beauregard: pp. 200–201

8. Beauregard: p. 201; Encylopedia: p. 228

9. Beauregard: p. 202

10. *Historical Times Encyclopedia*: p. 228

11. Beauregard: p. 203

12. Dowdey, Clifford: *Lee* p. 457; Beauregard: p. 204

13. *Historical Times Encyclopedia*: p. 58

14. Petersburg capitulated April 2, 1865. General Lee formally surrendered the Army of Northern Virginia on April 9, 1865

May 7–19, 1864, The Spotsylvania Campaign

1. The battle of the Wilderness was fought May 5–6, 1864

2. Webb, Alexander S.: *Battles and Leaders* Vol. IV p. 163; Catton, Bruce: *The American Heritage Picture History of the Civil War* p. 455; Osborne, Charles C.: *Jubal* p. 239; Pfanz, Donald C.: *Richard S. Ewell* p. 375

2a. Osborne: p. 239 states that Spotsylvania Court House was "about twelve miles" from the battlefield of the Wilderness; Dowdey, Clifford: *Lee* p. 446

2b. General Anderson had assumed command of the First Corps when General Longstreet was wounded at the battle of the Wilderness

3. Freeman, Douglas S.: *R. E. Lee* Vol. III p. 306; Dowdey: p. 449; Rhea, Gordon C.: *The Battles for Spotsylvania Court House and the Road to Yellow Tavern May 7–12, 1864* p. 60

4. Osborne: p. 239; Webb: p. 164; Catton: p. 455; Alexander, E. Porter: *Fighting for the Confederacy*: p. 366; Rhea: p. 47

5. Freeman: p. 309

6. Webb: p. 165

7. Webb: p. 165

8. Freeman: pp. 309–310; Osborne: p. 239; Dowdey: p. 450

9. Webb: p. 167

10. Alexander: p. 371; Catton: p. 455; Webb: p. 165 calls Sedgwick "our most esteemed general"; Rhea: pp. 94–95

11. Freeman: p. 311; Dowdey: p. 449

12. Alexander: p. 372; Webb: p. 168; Freeman: pp. 312–313; Catton: p. 455

13. Alexander: p. 373; Pfanz: p. 379 gives the time as "just before 6:00 P.M."; Rhea: pp. 169–170

14. Alexander: p. 373; Webb: p. 168; Catton: p. 455; Rhea: p. 174 notes that Upton's charge was over by 7:30 P.M.

15. Alexander: p. 375; Webb: p. 169; Rhea: p. 215

16. Webb: p. 169; Alexander: p. 376; Pfanz: p. 384; Rhea: p. 430

17. Pfanz: p. 384; Catton: p. 456 gives the time of the attack as 4:30 A.M.

18. Catton: p. 456; Pfanz: p. 387; Rhea: pp. 291–292

19. These were Edward Johnson and George H. Steuart. For details of both captures, refer to Rhea: p. 238

20. Alexander: p. 376 says that "nearly 4,000" men were captured; Galloway, G. Norton: *Battles and Leaders* Vol. IV p. 170 gives a figure of "over 3,000" men; Freeman: p. 317 states that "most of the division" was captured; Osborne: p. 239 gives the figure as "more than 4,000 men"

21. Catton: p. 458; Galloway: p. 170; Pfanz: p. 387

22. Alexander: p. 377; Rhea: p. 266

23. Alexander: pp. 377–378; Rhea: pp. 252–255

24. *Battles and Leaders*: Vol. IV pp. 179–182; Alexander: p. 379 uses various estimates to compute troop totals

25. Dowdey: p. 455; *Battles and Leaders*: Vol. IV pp. 182–184 gives reported casualties as 4,001, but it must be remembered that actual losses were much higher than that. As the Confederates were fighting from a defensive position behind fortifications, it may be assumed that the losses on the Southern side were lower than 18,399

26. Freeman: p. 334; Pfanz: p. 387

27. Catton: p. 456; Rhea: p. 290

28. Pfanz: p. 391; Freeman, Douglas S.: *Lee's Lieutenants* Vol. III p. 437

29. Pfanz: p. 391; Freeman: *Lee's Lieutenants* p. 439

30. Freeman: *Lee's Lieutenants* p. 437

31. Pfanz: p. 391; Freeman: *Lee's Lieutenants* p. 437

31a. Freeman: *Lee's Lieutenants* p. 439

32. Pfanz: p. 391

33. Pfanz: p. 392

34. Pfanz: p. 392; Freeman: *Lee's Lieutenants* p. 440 puts the time of day at approximately 3:30 P.M.

35. Pfanz: p. 392; Freeman: *Lee's Lieutenants* p. 441

36. Freeman: *Lee's Lieutenants* p. 440

37. Freeman: *Lee's Lieutenants* p. 440 notes that Pegram was wounded, and the brigade was temporarily commanded by Colonel John S. Hoffman

38. Freeman: *Lee's Lieutenants* pp. 440–441

39. Pfanz: p. 393; Freeman: *Lee's Lieutenants* p. 441

May 11, 1864, Yellow Tavern

1. Freeman: Douglas S.: *Lee's Lieutenants* Vol. III p. 413

2. Freeman: p. 414; Dowdey, Clifford: *Lee* p. 456 puts the number at around 4,000; Rhea, Gordon C.: *The Battles for Spotsylvania Court House and the Road to Yellow Tavern May 7–12, 1864* p. 194 note 11 places the Confederate force at approximately 3,000 men, and Sheridan's strength between 9,000 and 11,000 men

3. Freeman: p. 414

4. Freeman: p. 414

5. Freeman: p. 417

6. Freeman: p. 419

7. Freeman: p. 419

8. *Historical Times Illustrated Encyclopedia of the Civil War*: p. 847; *Battles and Leaders* Vol. IV p. 117; Rhea: p. 200

9. Freeman: p. 419; Rhea: p. 201

10. Freeman: p. 419

11. Freeman: p. 420; *Historical Times*

Encyclopedia: p. 847 states that Federal horsemen arrived "before noon"

12. *Historical Times Encyclopedia*: p. 847
13. Rhea: p. 202
14. Freeman: p. 424; *Battles and Leaders* Vol. IV p. 194
15. Freeman: p. 424; Rhea: pp. 208–209 note 57 explains that historian Robert E. L. Krick has documented over twenty different accounts of General Stuart's death
16. Freeman: p. 426. For a complete description and a surgeon's analysis of the mortal wounding of J. E. B. Stuart refer to Appendix III; Rhea: p. 209
17. Freeman: p. 431
18. Thomason, John: *Jeb Stuart* p. 501; Warner, Ezra J.: *Generals in Gray* p. 296. Stuart was born February 6, 1833
19. Rhea: pp. 211–212
20. Rhea: p. 212
21. *Historical Times Encyclopedia*: p. 847; Dowdey: *Lee* p. 456

May 15, 1864, New Market

1. Sigel, Franz: *Battles and Leaders* Vol. IV p. 487
2. Sigel: p. 487
3. *Historical Times Illustrated Encyclopedia of the Civil War*: p. 527; Sigel: p. 488 states that he had 5,500 infantry, 28 artillery pieces and 1,000 cavalry; Osborne, Charles C.: *Jubal* p. 246
4. *Historical Times Encyclopedia*: p. 527; Osborne: p. 246
5. *Historical Times Encyclopedia*: p. 527; Sigel: p. 488 estimated the Confederate infantry to be 5,000 men; Osborne: p. 247
6. *Historical Times Encyclopedia*: p. 528; Sigel: p. 488 states that he arrived at Mount Jackson on the 14th
7. *Historical Times Encyclopedia*: p. 528; Sigel: p. 488 had estimated Imboden's force to be 2,000 men
8. Sigel: p. 488; *Historical Times Encyclopedia*: p. 528
9. *Historical Times Encyclopedia*: p. 528
10. *Historical Times Encyclopedia*: p. 528; Sigel: p. 489 gives the distance as three quarters of a mile north of New Market
11. *Historical Times Encyclopedia*: p. 528
12. *Historical Times Encyclopedia*: p. 528
13. *Battles and Leaders* Vol. IV p. 491

May 23–26, 1864, North Anna River

1. *Historical Times Illustrated Encyclopedia of the Civil War*: p. 535; Davis, Burke: *Gray Fox* p. 310 gives the distance from Richmond as 23 miles
2. Freeman, Douglas S.: *R. E. Lee* Vol. III pp. 350–351
3. Freeman: p. 351
4. Freeman: p. 351
4a. Hassler, W. W.: *A. P. Hill* p. 205
5. Freeman: p. 351
6. Freeman: p. 352
7. Freeman: p. 353
8. Freeman: p. 353; Hassler: p. 206
9. Freeman: pp. 353–354; Hassler: p. 206
10. Freeman: pp. 354–355
11. Hassler: p. 206
12. Freeman: p. 355
13. Hassler: p. 207; Freeman: p. 357
14. Hassler: p. 207
15. Freeman: p. 355
16. Freeman: p. 355
17. Freeman: pp. 355–356
18. Freeman: p. 356; Davis: p. 314
19. Freeman: p. 356
20. Freeman: p. 356; Hassler: p. 207 lists the reinforcements as "over 8,000 fresh troops"
21. Freeman: pp. 356–358; Hassler: p. 208
22. Freeman: p. 358; Hassler: p. 208
23. Freeman: p. 359
24. Freeman: p. 360; Pfanz, Donald C.: *Richard S. Ewell* p. 396
25. Freeman: p. 361
26. Freeman: p. 361

May 27–30, 1864, Totopotomy Creek (Haw's Shop)

1. Alexander, E. Porter: *Fighting for the Confederacy* p. 395; Pfanz, Donald C.: *Richard S. Ewell* p. 396
2. Alexander: p. 396
3. Alexander: p. 396
4. Freeman, Douglas S.: *R. E. Lee* Vol. III p. 362
5. Freeman: p. 364
6. Freeman, Douglas S.: *Lee's Lieutenants* Vol. III p. 499
7. Freeman: *Lee's Lieutenants* p. 499
8. Freeman: *Lee's Lieutenants* p. 500
9. Freeman: *R. E. Lee* p. 364
10. Freeman: *Lee's Lieutenants* p. 498; Pfanz: pp. 396–397; Alexander: p. 397. Freeman states that Ewell fell ill from an "acute intestinal malady," while Pfanz states that on May 26 he fell ill with diarrhea
11. Freeman: *R. E. Lee* pp. 364–365
12. Freeman: *R. E. Lee* p. 369
13. Freeman: *R. E. Lee* p. 369
14. Freeman: *Lee's Lieutenants* p. 502; Alexander: p. 397
15. *Battles and Leaders* Vol. IV p. 182 Figures include casualties sustained at the North Anna River

June 1–3, 1864, Cold Harbor

1. Freeman, Douglas S.: *R. E. Lee* vol. III pp. 375–376
2. Freeman: p. 377. This was Colonel Lawrence M. Keitt, who had been named to lead Joseph B. Kershaw's brigade. Kershaw's promotion to major general had created a vacancy at the brigade level
3. Freeman: pp. 377–378
4. Freeman: p. 378
5. Freeman: p. 378
6. Freeman: pp. 379–380
7. Freeman: p. 381
8. Freeman: p. 382
9. Freeman: p. 382
10. Freeman: p. 384
11. Freeman: p. 385; Hassler, W. W.: *A. P. Hill* p. 209
11a. McMahon, Martin T.: *Battles and Leaders* Vol. IV p. 215
12. Freeman: p. 389; Alexander, E. Porter: *Fighting for the Confederacy*: p. 400
13. Freeman: p. 386; Alexander: p. 401; *Historical Times Illustrated Encyclopedia of the Civil War*: p. 150
14. Freeman: p. 389
15. Freeman: p. 390
16. Freeman: p. 391
17. Freeman: p. 391; *Historical Times Encyclopedia*: p. 150 states that "fewer than 1,500" Confederates fell, while "nearly 7,000" Federals did; Alexander gives the figure of "about 1,700" as the Confederate total, though his numbers seem a little high for both Union and Confederate casualties
17a. *Battles and Leaders*: p. 187; Alexander cites the Union army's chief surgeon as a source for the following tabulation of Union casualties: 1,920 killed, 10,345 wounded, and 1,864 missing, for a total of 14,129
17b. Alexander: p. 414
18. Freeman: p. 391

June 5, 1864, Piedmont

1. *Historical Times Illustrated Encyclopedia of the Civil War*: p. 584
2. *Historical Times Encyclopedia*: p. 584
3. *Historical Times Encyclopedia*: p. 584
4. *Historical Times Encyclopedia*: p. 584
5. *Historical Times Encyclopedia*: p. 584

6. *Historical Times Encyclopedia*: p. 584
7. *Historical Times Encyclopedia*: p. 584
8. Warner, Ezra J.: *Generals in Gray* p. 167; *Historical Times Encyclopedia*: p. 584
9. *Historical Times Encyclopedia*: p. 584; Imboden, John D.: *Battles and Leaders* Vol. IV p. 486 states that the Confederate loss was "not less than 1,500"

June 10, 1864, Brice's Crossroads

1. Henry, Robert S.: *Forrest "First with the Most"* p. 287. The Cross Roads is named for the two-story dwelling of William Brice
2. Henry: p. 288
2a. Castel, Albert: *Decision in the West* p. 53; Martin, David: *The Vicksburg Campaign* p. 81; Henry: pp. 16, 307; Catton, Bruce: *The American Heritage Picture History of the Civil War* p. 358
3. Henry: p. 14. Forrest had received no formal military training
4. Henry: p. 290
5. Henry: p. 291
6. Henry: pp. 293–394
7. Henry: p. 294
8. Henry: pp. 295–296
8a. Castel: p. 274 evaluates this battle as follows: "the most spectacular victory of Forrest's career, it enhances his already awesome reputation for genius and invincibility"; Martin: p. 82 says "the battle, which is considered Forrest's masterpiece, cost him 500 casualties while he inflicted over 2,200"; Mitchell, Joseph B.: *Decisive Battles of the Civil War* p. 187 calls this "one of the most outstanding examples of brilliant tactics in American military history"
9. Henry: p. 300; Castel: p. 274 lists Union casualties as "well over 2,000; Forrest's under 500"
10. Henry: p. 300
10a. Castel: p. 274
11. Henry: p. 303
12. Warner, Ezra: Generals in Gray p. 92; Henry p. 307

June 15, 1864–April 3, 1865, The Petersburg Campaign

1. The Battle of Cold Harbor was fought June 1–3, 1864
2. The Battle of the Wilderness occurred May 5–6, followed by a campaign to Spotsylvania May 7–19. The troops moved to the North Anna River May 23–26, and ended at Cold Harbor June 1–3.
2a. Pfanz, Donald C.: *Richard S. Ewell* p. 407. The Southside, Petersburg & Weldon, Norfolk & Petersburg, City Point, and Richmond & Petersburg railroads all came together at Petersburg
3. Freeman, Douglas S.: *R. E. Lee* Vol. III p. 413; *Battles and Leaders*, Vol. IV pp. 590–594 lists total Union strength as of June 30 as 107,419 men. Total Confederate strength as of June 30 was 54,751 troops
4. Mitchell, Joseph B.: *Decisive Battles of the Civil War* pp. 209–212
5. Mitchell: p. 212
6. *Historical Times Encyclopedia of the Civil War*: p. 578
7. Freeman: p. 448
8. Mitchell: pp. 212–213; Powell, William H.: *Battles and Leaders* Vol. IV pp. 545–546. For a detailed description of the mine, see pp. 548–549
9. Mitchell: p. 212
10. Mitchell: p. 213; Davis, Burke: *Gray Fox* p. 341
11. Mitchell: p. 213; Powell: p. 551 gives the dimensions as 170 feet long, 60 feet wide, and "about 30 feet deep"; Pfanz: p. 410 also states that the crater was 170 feet long
12. Powell: p. 551
13. Mitchell: p. 213; Powell: p. 550. These were the white divisions of James Ledlie, Orlando Willcox and Robert Potter
14. Freeman: pp. 470–473
15. Freeman: p. 477
16. Freeman: p. 477; Davis: p. 343 states that "fewer than 300 Confederates" died in the explosion
17. Freeman: p. 483
18. Freeman: pp. 483–484
19. Freeman: p. 485; *Historical Times Encyclopedia*: p. 812
20. *Historical Times Encyclopedia*: p. 813
21. *Historical Times Encyclopedia*: p. 813
22. *Historical Times Encyclopedia*: p. 813; Freeman: p. 485 states that Hill captured 2,700 prisoners
23. Freeman: p. 488
24. Freeman: p. 488; Hassler, W. W.: *A. P. Hill* pp. 225–226
25. Freeman: p. 488; Hassler: p. 226
26. Hassler: p. 226
27. Hassler: p. 226
28. Hassler: pp. 226–227; Willcox, Orlando B.: *Battles and Leaders* Vol. IV p. 573
29. Hassler: p. 227
30. *Historical Times Encyclopedia*: p. 618 states that "nearly 2,000" men were captured; Hassler: p. 227 list the total prisoners as 2,150 soldiers
31. Freeman: p. 500
32. Freeman: p. 500
33. Freeman: p. 500; Dowdey; Clifford: *Lee* p. 505
34. Freeman: p. 500; Pfanz: p. 411
35. Freeman: p. 500; Pfanz: p. 414; Dowdey: p. 505
36. *Historical Times Encyclopedia*: p. 123; General W. F. Smith had been replaced on July 19 as the commander of the XVIII Corps
37. *Historical Times Encyclopedia*: p. 123
38. Pfanz: pp. 413–414 states that Union troops crossed the river in force at 4:00 A.M.
39. Pfanz: p. 414
40. Pfanz: p. 414
41. Pfanz: p. 416
42. Pfanz: p. 416
43. Pfanz: p. 416
44. Pfanz: p. 416
45. Pfanz: pp. 415–416
46. Pfanz: pp. 416–417
47. Pfanz: p. 417; Freeman: p. 501
48. Freeman: pp. 502–503; Pfanz: p. 417
49. *Historical Times Encyclopedia*: p. 95
50. *Historical Times Encyclopedia*: p. 95
51. *Historical Times Encyclopedia*: p. 95
52. *Historical Times Encyclopedia*: p. 95
53. *Historical Times Encyclopedia*: p. 95
54. *Historical Times Encyclopedia*: p. 95; Freeman: p. 514
55. *Historical Times Encyclopedia*: p. 95
56. General Hancock had been forced back to Washington, D.C., due to ill health
57. *Historical Times Encyclopedia*: p. 350
58. *Historical Times Encyclopedia*: p. 350 states that the time of the attack was "about 5:00 P.M."
59. *Historical Times Encyclopedia*: p. 350
60. *Historical Times Encyclopedia*: p. 350
61. Warner, Ezra J.: *Generals in Gray* p. 232
62. *Historical Times Encyclopedia*: p. 350

July 8, 1864, Monocacy

1. Osborne, Charles C.: *Jubal* p. 267
1a. *Historical Times Illustrated Encyclopedia of the Civil War*: p. 504; Early, Jubal A.: *Battles and Leaders* Vol. IV p. 495
2. Osborne: *Jubal* pp. 268–269; *Historical Times Encyclopedia*: p. 504

3. Osborne: p. 269

4. Osborne: p. 270; *Battles and Leaders*: p. 499 lists the effective strength under Wallace at 2,700 men

5. Osborne: p. 270

6. Osborne: p. 270; *Battles and Leaders*: p. 495. U. S. Grant, writing in his Personal Memoirs, stated that Ricketts arrived on July 8

7. Osborne: p. 270; *Battles and Leaders*: p. 499 places the effective troop strength under Wallace at 2,700 men, while Rickets division was listed at 3,350, for a total of 6,050 Federals

7a. *Battles and Leaders*: p. 499

8. Osborne: p. 271

9. Osborne: p. 271

10. Osborne: p. 273

11. Osborne: p. 274; *Historical Times Encyclopedia*: p. 504

12. Osborne: p. 274

13. *Battles and Leaders*: p. 499; *Historical Times Encyclopedia*: p. 504 does not list Southern casualties, but gives the Northern losses as an aggregate figure of 1,880.

14. Osborne: p. 275; *Historical Times Encyclopedia*: p. 504

15. Osborne: p. 275; *Historical Times Encyclopedia*: p. 504

July 14–15, 1864, Tupelo (Harrisburg)

1. Castel, Albert: *Decision in the West* p. 213; Henry, Robert S.: *Forrest "First with the Most"* p. 16

2. Henry: p. 307; Catton, Bruce: *The American Heritage Picture History of the Civil War* p. 358

3. Henry: p. 313

3a. *Historical Times Illustrated Encyclopedia of the Civil War*: p. 765

4. Henry: p. 314

5. Henry: pp. 315–316

6. Henry: p. 316

7. Henry: p. 316

8. Henry: pp. 316–318

9. Henry: p. 318. The reader is invited to explore Henry: Chapter XX for a full examination of conflicting evidence on this point

10. Henry: p. 318

11. Henry: pp. 318–319

12. Henry: p. 319

13. Henry: p. 320; *Historical Times Encyclopedia*: p. 765

14. Henry: pp. 320–321; *Historical Times Encyclopedia*: p. 765

15. Henry: p. 321

16. Henry: p. 321

17. Henry: p. 321

18. Henry: p. 322

19. Henry: p. 322; *Historical Times Encyclopedia*: p. 765

20. Henry: p. 326

21. Henry: p. 327

July 24, 1864, Kernstown (Second)

1. Osborne, Charles C.: *Jubal* p. 245

2. Osborne: p. 263; Freeman, Douglas S.: *Lee's Lieutenants* Vol. III p. 558

2a. *Historical Times Encyclopedia of the Civil War*: p. 415

2b. Osborne: p. 300

2c. Osborne: p. 301; Freeman: p. 570 lists the Confederate casualties as 73 men killed, 130 wounded, and 267 captured, for a total of 470

3. *Historical Times Encyclopedia*: p. 415

4. *Historical Times Encyclopedia*: p. 415

5. *Historical Times Encyclopedia*: p. 415

6. *Historical Times Encyclopedia*: p. 415

7. *Historical Times Encyclopedia*: p. 415

8. *Historical Times Encyclopedia*: p. 415

9. *Historical Times Encyclopedia*: p. 415; Osborne: p. 301

10. *Historical Times Encyclopedia*: p. 415

11. *Historical Times Encyclopedia*: p. 416; Osborne: p. 301 states that Crook left "nearly 1,200" casualties on the field; Freeman: p. 571 gives the Union loss as 1,185, of which 479 were prisoners

12. *Historical Times Encyclopedia*: p: 415

September 19, 1864, Winchester (Third) (Opequon Creek)

1. Osborne, Charles C.: *Jubal* p. 245

2. Osborne: p. 263; Freeman, Douglas S.: *Lee's Lieutenants* Vol. III p. 558

2a. Osborne: p. 334

3. Osborne: pp. 332–334

4. Osborne: p. 333

5. Osborne: p. 335

5a. Freeman: p. 578 states that Gordon arrived on the battlefield at 10:00 A.M.

6. Osborne: p. 335

7. Osborne: p. 336

8. Osborne: p. 337; *Historical Times Encyclopedia of the Civil War*: p. 835

9. Osborne: p. 337; Freeman: p. 578 states that although General Rodes heart beat feebly for a few minutes, he knew nothing

10. Osborne: p. 337

11. Osborne: p. 337

12. Osborne: pp. 337–338

13. Osborne: pp. 338–339

14. Osborne: p. 339

15. *Battles and Leaders* Vol. IV p. 532; *Historical Times Encyclopedia*: p. 835 states that Sheridan lost "slightly more than 5,000 men" while Early's army had been "reduced by more than 3,500 casualties"; Freeman: p. 581 gives Confederate losses as 3,611 plus "probably 1,000 of his cavalry"

16. Osborne: p. 340

September 22, 1864, Fisher's Hill

1. Osborne, Charles C.: *Jubal* p. 245

2. Osborne: p. 263; Freeman, Douglas S.: *Lee's Lieutenants* Vol. III p. 558

3. Osborne: p. 263; Freeman: 558

4. Freeman: pp. 583–584

5. Freeman: p. 584

6. Osborne: p. 351; Freeman: p. 327

7. Osborne: p. 341

8. Osborne: p. 342; Freeman: p. 584 gives the time as "late on the afternoon of September 22"

9. Osborne: pp. 342–343

10. Osborne: pp. 343–344

11. Osborne: p. 344

12. *Battles and Leaders*: Vol. IV p. 524; Osborne: p. 344; Freeman: p. 584 commenting on the large amount of Southern captured or missing troops, states that "almost 1,000 were prisoners or stragglers who did not return to the ranks"

13. Freeman: p. 585

October 19, 1864, Cedar Creek

1. *Battles and Leaders* Vol. III: p. 258; Thomason, John C.: *Jeb Stuart* p. 75; Catton, Bruce: *The American Heritage Picture History of the Civil War* p. 357

2. Thomason: p. 76

3. Freeman, Douglas S.: *Lee's Lieutenants* Vol. II p. 412; Thomason: p. 76; Osborne, Charles C.: *Jubal* p. 339

4. Winchester and Fisher's Hill were fought September 19 and 22, 1864, respectively

5. Freeman: Vol. III pp. 597–598

6. Freeman: p. 600; Early, Jubal A.: *Battles and Leaders* Vol. IV p. 526

7. Freeman: pp. 603–604

8. Freeman: p. 604; Osborne, Charles C.: *Jubal* p.365

9. Freeman: p. 609 Early had detached 1,700 of his 3,900 cavalrymen

10. Freeman: p. 598
11. Freeman: p. 607
12. Freeman: p. 607; Osborne: pp. 371–372
13. Freeman: p. 607
14. *Historical Times Illustrated Encyclopedia of the Civil War*: p. 121; Early, Jubal A.: *Battles and Leaders* p. 529
15. Freeman: p. 610
16. Freeman: p. 610; *Historical Times Encyclopedia*: p. 121; Early, Jubal A.: *Battles and Leaders* p. 529

November 29, 1864, Spring Hill

1. Sword, Wiley: *Embrace an Angry Wind* p. 2
2. Sword: p. 46
3. Sword: p. 54
4. Sword: p. 54
5. Sword: p. 54
6. Sword: p. 54; Buck, Irving: *Cleburne and His Command* pp. 261–262
7. Sword: p. 54
8. *Historical Times Illustrated Encyclopedia of the Civil War*: p. 7
9. Sword: p. 56
10. Sword: p. 59
11. Sword: p. 66
12. Sword: p. 68
13. Sword: p. 68 gives the arrival of Forrest as "November 14th through the 16th"; Buck: p. 263 states that Forrest arrived on the 14th
14. Sword: p. 68
15. Sword: p. 70
16. Sword: p. 72
17. Sword: p. 83
18. Sword: p. 83
19. Sword: p. 83
20. Sword: p. 83; Buck: p. 283
21. Sword: p. 89; Hood, John B.: *Advance and Retreat* p. 281
22. Sword: p. 89; Hood: p. 281
23. Sword: pp. 91–92
24. Sword: pp. 94–95
25. Sword: p. 96
26. Sword: p. 96 states that Lee arrived "at first light"
27. Sword: p. 98
28. Sword: p. 108
29. Sword: p. 109
30. Sword: p. 114
31. Sword: p. 114
32. Sword: pp. 114–115
33. Sword: p. 120
34. Sword: p. 120
35. Sword: p. 121
36. Sword: p. 121
37. Sword: p. 122
38. Sword: p. 122
39. Sword: p. 123
40. Sword: p. 124
41. Sword: p. 124
42. Sword: p. 124
43. Sword: p. 124
44. Sword: pp. 124–126
45. Sword: p. 126
46. Sword: p. 126
47. Sword: p. 126
48. Sword: p. 127
49. Sword: p. 126
50. Sword: pp. 126–128
51. Sword: p. 129

51a. Sword: p. 129

52. Sword: p. 131 does not give a specific time of day
53. Sword: p. 131
54. Sword: p. 131

54a. Buck: pp. 265–266 lists Hood's infantry total at 16,000; Sword: p. 139 states that with the arrival of one division from Stephen D. Lee's corps, the Confederates had some 19,000 infantry against a Union force of approximately 6,000 men.

55. Sword: p. 131
56. Sword: pp. 133–134
57. Sword: p. 135
58. Sword: p. 135
59. Sword: p. 152; Buck: pp. 57–58; Henry, Robert S.: *Forrest "First with the Most"* p. 395
60. Buck: p. 273; Sword: p. 152

November 30, 1864, Franklin

1. Sword, Wiley: *Embrace an Angry Wind* p. 158; *Historical Times Encyclopedia of the Civil War*: p. 284
2. Sword: p. 181

2a. *Historical Times Encyclopedia*: p. 284

3. Sword: pp. 175–177
4. Sword: pp. 177–178
5. Sword: pp. 177–178
6. Castel, Albert: *Decision in the West* p. 556

6a. Sword: p. 178

7. Sword: p. 178
8. Sword: pp. 178–179; *Historical Times Encyclopedia*: p. 284
9. Sword: p. 179
10. Sword: pp. 179–180
11. Sword: pp. 180–182; *Historical Times Illustrated Encyclopedia*: pp. 284–285; Buck, Irving: Cleburne and his Command: p. 182 gives the time of the advance as approximately 3:30; Hood, John B.: *Battles and Leaders* Vol. IV p. 433 places the time at roughly 3:00 P.M.
12. Sword: pp. 181–182
13. Sword: p. 183

13a. Sword: p. 180

14. Sword: p. 183; Buck: p. 281
15. Sword: pp. 189–191
16. Sword: p. 191
17. Sword: p. 191
18. Sword: p. 191
19. Sword: p. 192
20. Sword: pp. 193–194
21. Sword: p. 194
22. Sword: p. 195
23. Sword: pp. 197–198
24. Sword: p. 199
25. Sword: p. 199
26. Sword: p. 201
27. Sword: p. 202
28. Sword: p. 206
29. Sword: p. 208
30. Sword: p. 214
31. Sword: p. 214; Stone, Henry: *Battles and Leaders* Vol. IV p. 450
32. Sword: p. 216
33. Sword: p. 216
34. Sword: pp. 222–223
35. Sword: p. 223
36. Sword: pp. 223–224

36a. Sword: p. 237

36b. Sword: p. 237

36[b]b. Sword: p. 247 lists total casualties in Johnson's division as 587 men

36c. Sword: p. 241

37. Alexander, E. Porter: *Fighting for the Confederacy* p. 499; *Battles and Leaders* Vol. IV: pp. 473–474
38. Buck, Irving: *Cleburne and His Command* p. 284
39. Buck: p. 284; Sword: p. 270 adds the name of Zachariah Deas to this list, who was "lightly wounded" in Edward Johnson's night attack
40. Castel: p. 557; Buck: p. 284 calls this battle: "a needless and horrible butchery"

November 30, 1864, Honey Hill

1. *Historical Times Illustrated Encyclopedia of the Civil War*: p. 368
2. *Historical Times Encyclopedia*: p. 368
3. *Historical Times Encyclopedia*: p. 368
4. *Historical Times Encyclopedia*: p. 368
5. *Historical Times Encyclopedia*: p. 368 states that the Federal troops arrived "after 9:00 A.M."
6. *Historical Times Encyclopedia*: p. 368
7. *Historical Times Encyclopedia*: p. 368
8. *Historical Times Encyclopedia*: p. 368
9. *Historical Times Encyclopedia*: p. 368
10. *Historical Times Encyclopedia*: p. 368
11. *Historical Times Encyclopedia*: p. 368

December 4, 1864, Waynesborough, Ga.

1. *Historical Times Encyclopedia of the Civil War*: p. 810
2. *Historical Times Encyclopedia*: p. 810
3. *Historical Times Encyclopedia*: p. 810
4. *Historical Times Encyclopedia*: p. 810
5. *Historical Times Encyclopedia*: p. 810
6. *Historical Times Encyclopedia*: p. 810
7. *Historical Times Encyclopedia*: p. 810
8. *Historical Times Encyclopedia*: p. 810
9. *Historical Times Encyclopedia*: p. 810
10. *Historical Times Encyclopedia*: p. 810
11. *Historical Times Encyclopedia*: p. 810
12. *Historical Times Encyclopedia*: p. 810

December 15–16, 1864, Nashville

1. Sword, Wiley: *Embrace an Angry Wind* p. 272
2. Sword: p. 277
3. Sword: p. 277
4. Sword: p. 275
5. Sword: p. 278
6. Sword: p. 279
6a. Sword: p. 282
7. Sword: p. 279
8. Sword: pp. 290–292
9. Sword: pp. 292–293
10. Sword: p. 308
11. Sword: p. 317
12. Sword: pp. 317–318
13. Sword: p. 320
14. Sword: pp. 322–324
15. Sword: p. 324
16. Sword: p. 325
17. Sword: p. 325
18. Sword: p. 329
19. Sword: p. 330
20. Sword: p. 332
21. Sword: p. 334
22. Sword: pp. 335–336
23. Sword: p. 336
24. Sword: p. 336
25. Sword: p. 337
26. Sword: pp. 337–338
27. Sword: p. 337
28. Sword: p. 341
29. Sword: p. 342
30. Sword: p. 347
31. Sword: pp. 348–349
32. Sword: p. 349
33. Sword: p. 355
34. Sword: p. 355
35. Sword: p. 356
36. Sword: p. 356
37. Sword: p. 359
38. Sword: pp. 361–363
39. Sword: pp. 365–366
40. Sword: p. 367
41. Sword: p. 367
42. Sword: p. 372
43. Sword: p. 373. Finley's Florida Brigade was under the command of Colonel Robert Bullock
44. Sword: pp. 375–376
45. Sword: p. 386
46. Sword: p. 388
47. Sword: p. 388
48. *Battles and Leaders* Vol. IV: pp. 473–474

1865

March 2, 1865, Waynesborough, Va.

1. Osborne, Charles C.: *Jubal* p. 386; *Historical Times Encyclopedia of the Civil War*: p. 810
2. *Historical Times Encyclopedia*: p. 810
3. *Historical Times Encyclopedia*: p. 810
4. *Historical Times Encyclopedia*: p. 810
5. Osborne: p. 388
6. Osborne: p. 387
7. Osborne: p. 387; Freeman, Douglas S.: *Lee's Lieutenants* Vol. III p. 635 states that Early had "little more than 100 infantry." About 100 additional cavalrymen formed under Thomas Rosser
8. *Historical Times Encyclopedia*: p. 810
9. Osborne: p. 387
10. Osborne: p. 387–388; *Historical Times Encyclopedia*: p. 811 gives the time as "shortly after 3:30"
11. Osborne: p. 388; Freeman: p. 635
12. Freeman: p. 635
13. *Historical Times Encyclopedia*: p. 811

March 8–10, 1865, Kinston (Wise's Forks)

1. Bradley, Mark L.: *The Battle of Bentonville* p. 73
2. *Historical Times Illustrated Encyclopedia of the Civil War*: pp. 418–419
3. *Historical Times Encyclopedia*: p. 419
4. Bradley: p. 75. Bradley also states that the North Carolina Junior Reserves Brigade was included in this force, and the total was approximately 6,000 men. *Historical Times Encyclopedia*: p. 419 gives the Confederate total under Hoke as "6,500 effectives"
5. Bradley: p. 75; *Historical Times Encyclopedia*: p. 419
6. *Historical Times Encyclopedia*: p. 419
7. *Historical Times Encyclopedia*: p. 419
8. Bradley: p. 75
9. *Historical Times Encyclopedia*: p. 419
10. *Historical Times Encyclopedia*: p. 419
11. *Historical Times Encyclopedia*: p. 419
12. *Battles and Leaders*: pp. 698–700
13. *Historical Times Encyclopedia*: p. 419

March 10, 1865, Monroe's Crossroads

1. Bradley, Mark L.: *The Battle of Bentonville* p. 70
2. Bradley: p. 70
3. Bradley: p. 86
4. Bradley: p. 86
5. Bradley: pp. 86–88 note 14 states that estimates of Confederate strength are derived from Hampton's earliest returns, dated March 27, 1865
6. Bradley: p. 88. According to Bradley, p. 90, Morgan's Crossroads also lies 17 miles west of Fayetteville
7. Bradley: p. 95
8. Bradley: pp. 88–89
9. Bradley: pp. 90–91
10. Bradley: p. 102 explains that Kilpatrick had about 800 men from Spencer's brigade, 600 under Colonel Way, 50 men in one artillery section, and 50 scouts led by Captain Northrop
11. Bradley: p. 92
12. Bradley: p. 95
13. Bradley: p. 95
14. Bradley: p. 94
15. Bradley: p. 96
16. Bradley: p. 97
17. Bradley: p. 97
18. Bradley: p. 98
19. Bradley: p. 100
20. Bradley: p. 100
21. Bradley: p. 100; *Historical Times Illustrated Encyclopedia of the Civil War*: p. 506
22. *Historical Times Encyclopedia*: p. 506
23. Bradley: p. 102; *Historical Times Encyclopedia*: p. 506
24. Bradley: pp. 102–103
25. Bradley: p. 104

March 16, 1865, Averasborough

1. *Historical Times Encyclopedia of the Civil War*: p. 31; Slocum, Henry W.: *Battles and Leaders* Vol. IV p. 692

2. *Historical Times Encyclopedia*: p. 31; Bradley, Mark L.: *The Battle of Bentonville* p. 115 states that as of March 15, 1865, General Hardee had "only 6,455 effectives"
3. Bradley: p. 116
4. Bradley: p. 116
5. Bradley: p. 116
6. Bradley: p. 124. These were the divisions of General Nathaniel J. Jackson and General William T. Ward, both of Slocum's XX Corps
7. Bradley: p. 125
8. Bradley: p. 121 notes that Rhett's brigade was now under the command of Colonel William Butler, Rhett having been captured the previous day
9. Bradley: p. 123 lists the strength of Butler's command as 1,051 men.
10. Bradley: p. 123
11. *Historical Times Encyclopedia*: p. 31; Slocum: p. 691
12. Bradley: p. 128
13. *Battles and Leaders* Vol. IV pp. 698–700; Bradley: p. 132 places Confederate losses at approximately 500 men, and Union losses at 682
14. *Historical Times Encyclopedia*: p. 31

March 19–21, 1865, Bentonville

1. Hampton, Wade: *Battles and Leaders* Vol. IV p. 700
2. Hampton: p. 701
3. Hampton: p. 701; *Historical Times Illustrated Encyclopedia of the Civil War*: p. 56
4. Hampton: p. 701
5. *Historical Times Encyclopedia*: p. 56
6. Bradley, Mark L.: *The Battle of Bentonville* pp. 302–303 note 14 explains that General Hardee's command sent one division to the Confederate left (McLaws) and one to the Confederate right (Taliaferro). Hardee himself was placed in overall command of the right wing. This left Bragg on the left, Stewart in the center, and Hardee on the right
7. Bradley: p. 162
8. Hampton: p. 703; Govan, Gilbert, and Livingwood, James: *Joseph E. Johnston "A Different Valor"* p. 355; Bradley: p. 166
9. Hampton: p. 703. These were South Carolina Batteries under Captain William E. Earle and Captain Edwin L. Halsey. These units belonged to the Confederate Horse Artillery
10. Bradley: p. 179
11. Bradley: pp. 179–180
12. Bradley: p. 232
13. Bradley: p. 185
14. Bradley: p. 192
15. Bradley: p. 211
16. Bradley: p. 227
17. Bradley: p. 251
18. Bradley: p. 254
19. Bradley: pp. 280–283
20. Bradley: p. 294
21. Bradley: p. 309
22. Bradley: p. 309 note 31 explains that Livermore's estimate of 2,118 total casualties is too high, with General Johnston's return of 1,915 a bit on the low side.
23. Bradley: p. 309 note 31. Federal data is more precise, though there is some variance, with Sherman's estimate of 1,186 slightly higher than Slocum's final tally of 1,144. Slocum's figure is for all three days at Bentonville, and Union losses on March 20 and 21 were slight. Livermore estimates Slocum's total casualties for March 19 at 1,103
24. Bradley: p. 327
25. Bradley: p. 330
26. Bradley: p. 341
27. *Battles and Leaders* Vol. IV: p. 698. The Union returns for March 1 show an effective fighting force of 57,696 men. Confederate returns for March 17 list 9,513 effectives. However, General Johnston's returns for March 23 gives his effective strength as 15,027 men. Based on Bradley: p. 347, it may be assumed that Johnston's returns do not include some 4,000 cavalry under Wade Hampton. Bradley: p. 347 states that "the addition of Wade Hampton's 4,000 troopers gave Johnston roughly 20,000 men of all arms with which to oppose Sherman's army of 55,000." Govan and Livingwood: p. 357 state that Sherman had approximately 56,000 men
28. Bradley: p. 332
29. Bradley: p. 348
30. Bradley: p. 352
31. Bradley: p. 380
32. Bradley: p. 380, see notes 11 and 36
33. Bradley: p. 380
34. Bradley: p. 381 notes that Cumming's Brigade was led at this point by Colonel Robert J. Henderson
35. Hampton: p. 705; Bradley: p. 384
36. These were the 4th Tennessee and 8th Texas. See Bradley p. 387
37. Bradley: p. 386. Bradley points out in note 53 that it is possible Lowrey's Brigade was also present, which would have given Brown some 800 men
38. *Battles and Leaders*: pp. 698–700; Bradley: p. 404 also gives the Confederate losses as 2,606, but gives the casualties on the Federal side as 194 killed, 1,112 wounded and 221 missing, for a total of 1,527. Bradley believes that these estimates for both sides are "probably low"

March 25–April 9, 1865, The Appomattox Campaign

1. Hartranft, John F.: *Battles and Leaders* Vol. IV p. 584

1a. Freeman, Douglas S.: *R. E. Lee* Vol. IV p. 14

2. Hartranft: p. 584
3. *Historical Times Encyclopedia of the Civil War*: p. 279
4. *Historical Times Encyclopedia*: p. 279; Dowdey, Clifford: *Lee* p. 530; Freeman: p. 17
5. Dowdey: p. 531; Davis, Burke: *Gray Fox* p. 366
6. *Historical Times Encyclopedia*: p. 279; Freeman: p. 18
7. Dowdey: p. 531; Davis: p. 365
8. Davis: p. 366; Freeman: p. 19 states that the "Union estimate of gross Confederate casualties of 4,800 to 5,000 was not greatly exaggerated"

8a. Dowdey: p. 533

9. Freeman: p. 22
10. Freeman: pp. 31–32; Dowdey: pp. 533–534 lists cavalry of 5,400 with infantry of 6,400, for a total of 11,800
11. Freeman: p. 33; Dowdey: p. 534; Sears, Stephen W.: *Controversies & Commanders* p. 269
12. Dowdey: p. 535; Sears: p. 270 notes that the Federals lost over 1,800 men on March 31, while Confederate losses were "something less than half that number"
13. Dowdey: p. 534
14. Dowdey: p. 536
15. Dowdey: p. 536; Freeman: p. 39
16. Freeman: p. 39; Davis: p. 368
17. Dowdey: p. 536; Sears: p. 263 states that the cavalry portion of the Union army began the Appomattox campaign with approximately 9,000 troopers
18. Dowdey: p. 537
19. Dowdey: p. 537

19a. Sears: p. 281 lists Pickett's losses at "more than 500 dead and wounded and some 2,500 captured"

20. Dowdey: p. 540
21. Dowdey: p. 541. For a more complete description of A. P. Hill's death, see Freeman, Douglas S.: *Lee's Lieutenants* Vol. III pp. 678–679
22. Dowdey: p. 542

22a. Freeman: *Lee's Lieutenants* p. 45 also called Fort (Battery) Baldwin

23. Dowdey: p. 543
24. Dowdey: p. 544; *Historical Times Encyclopedia*: p. 274 gives the Federal losses as 714, but states that 57 Confederates died. This would add up to 216 men. Freeman: *Lee's Lieutenants* p. 51–53 places the

total occupants of Fort Gregg at 400–600, and states that while there were 55 Confederates killed, there were some 300 captured

25. Dowdey: p. 545; Freeman: *Lee's Lieutenants* p. 58 puts the number closer to 12,500

26. Dowdey: p. 546

27. Dowdey: p. 546

27a. Freeman: *Lee's Lieutenants* p. 689

28. Dowdey: p. 548; Freeman: *R. E. Lee* p. 66

29. Dowdey: p. 550

30. Dowdey: p. 551; Freeman: *Lee's Lieutenants* pp. 692–693

31. Dowdey: p. 555

32. Dowdey: p. 556 gives the time as "sometime after one o'clock"

33. Dowdey: p. 556

34. Dowdey: p. 557

35. Freeman: *R. E. Lee* p. 91

36. Freeman: *R. E. Lee* p. 93; Pfanz, Donald C.: *Richard S. Ewell* p. 439 also states that Ewell lost some 2,800 men to capture, along with 150 men killed or wounded. General Wright reported losses of 442 total casualties, while Sheridan's losses in the Union cavalry have been estimated at 1,000 troopers

37. Freeman: *R. E. Lee* p. 93; *Historical Times Encyclopedia*: p. 660

March 31–April 2, 1865, Selma

1. Henry, Robert S.: *Forrest "First with the Most"* p. 418

2. Henry: p. 422

3. Henry: p. 429

4. Henry: p. 429

5. Henry: p. 429

6. Henry: p. 429

7. Henry: p. 430

8. Henry: p. 430

9. Henry: p. 430

10. Henry: p. 430

11. Henry: p. 430

12. Henry: p. 430

13. Henry: pp. 430–431

14. Henry: p. 431

15. Henry: pp. 431–432

16. Henry: p. 432 states that the attack came "after 5:00 and not long before dark"

17. Henry: p. 432

18. Henry: p. 432

19. *Historical Times Encyclopedia of the Civil War*: p. 666

April 9, 1865, Lee's Surrender

1. Alexander, E. Porter: *Fighting for the Confederacy* p. 544

1a. Freeman, Douglas S.: *Lee's Lieutenants* Vol. III p. 739

1b. Dowdey, Clifford: *Lee* p. 577

2. Porter, Horace: *Battles and Leaders* Vol. IV p. 735; *Historical Times Illustrated Encyclopedia of the Civil War*: p. 735

3. Porter: pp. 735–736

4. Porter: p. 737; Dowdey: p. 578

5. Porter: p. 737; Dowdey: pp. 579–580; Freeman, Douglas S.: *R. E. Lee* Vol. IV p. 138

6. Porter: p. 740; Dowdey: pp. 579–580

7. Porter: p. 742; Dowdey: p. 580

8. Porter: p. 742; *Historical Times Encyclopedia*: p. 735 gives the time as 3:45 P.M.

9. Dowdey: p. 583

April 26, 1865, Johnston's Surrender

1. *Historical Times Illustrated Encyclopedia of the Civil War*: p. 736; Govan, Gilbert & Livingwood, James: *Joseph E. Johnston* p. 359 state that Johnston had "less than 29,000" men

2. Govan & Livingwood: p. 358; *Historical Times Encyclopedia*: p. 736

3. *Historical Times Encyclopedia*: p. 736; Govan & Livingwood: p. 363

4. *Historical Times Encyclopedia*: p. 736

Epilogue

1. Dowdey, Clifford: *Lee* p. 394; Strode, Hudson: *Jefferson Davis* Vol. II p. 452; Freeman, Douglas S.: *R. E. Lee* Vol. III p. 161

2. Robertson, James I., Jr.: *Stonewall Jackson* p. 371; Eckenrode, H. J. and Conrad, Bryan: *James Longstreet* p. 155; Dowdey, Clifford: *Death of a Nation* p. 16; Strode: Vol. II pp. 208–209; *Battles and Leaders*: Vol. I p. 221; Freeman: *R. E. Lee* Vol. IV pp. 166–167

2a. Catton, Bruce: *The American Heritage Picture History of the Civil War* p. 149 states that the wounding of General Johnston "affected profoundly the story of the Confederate States of America"

3. Daniel, Larry J.: *Shiloh* p. 308 terms this "one of the crucial decisions" of the entire war

4. Strode, Hudson: *Jefferson Davis* Vol. II p. 150

Bibliography

Alexander, E. Porter. *Fighting for the Confederacy.* Chapel Hill: University of North Carolina Press, 1989.

Battles and Leaders of the Civil War. 4 Vols. 1884–1887. Reprint, Secaucus, N.J.: Castle Books, n.d.

Bearss, Edwin C. *The Vicksburg Campaign.* 3 Vols. Dayton: Morningside, 1985–1986.

Bigelow, John A. *The Campaign of Chancellorsville.* 1910 Reprint, Dayton: Morningside, n.d.

Bradley, Mark L. *The Battle of Bentonville.* Mason City, IA: Savas, 1996.

Buck, Irving A. *Cleburne and His Command.* Wilmington, NC: Broadfoot Publishing, 1995.

Castel, Albert. *Decision in the West.* Lawrence: University of Kansas Press, 1992.

Catton, Bruce. *The American Heritage Picture History of the Civil War.* 1960. Reprint: New York, Bonanza Books.

_____. *Grant Moves South, 1861–1863.* 1960. Reprint, Secaucus, N.J.: Castle Books, 2000.

Civil War Times Illustrated. August 1971 Issue. Harrisburg, PA: Civil War Times Illustrated, 1971.

Connelly, Thomas L. *Autumn of Glory.* Baton Rouge: Louisiana State University Press, 1971.

Cozzens, Peter. *No Better Place to Die.* Urbana, IL: University of Illinois Press, 1990.

_____. *Shipwreck of Their Hopes.* Urbana, IL: University of Illinois Press, 1994.

_____. *This Terrible Sound.* Urbana, IL: University of Illinois Press, 1992.

Daniel, Larry J. *Shiloh.* New York: Simon & Schuster, 1997.

Davis, Burke. *Gray Fox.* New York: Rinehart, 1956.

Dowdey, Clifford. *Death of a Nation.* New York: Alfred A. Knopf, 1958.

_____. *Lee.* Boston: Little, Brown, 1965.

_____. *Lee Takes Command.* 1964. Reprint, New York: Barnes and Noble, 1992.

_____. *The Seven Days.* 1964. Reprint, Wilmington, NC: Broadfoot, 1988.

Ecelbarger, Gary. *We Are in for It.* Shippensburg, PA: White Mane, 1997.

Eckenrode, H.J. & Conrad, Bryan. *James Longstreet.* 1936. Reprint, Chapel Hill: University of North Carolina Press, 1986.

Freeman, Douglas S. *Lee's Lieutenants.* 3 Vols. New York: Scribner's, 1942–1944.

_____. *R.E. Lee.* 4 Vols. New York: Scribner's, 1934–1936.

Furgurson, Ernest B. *Chancellorsville 1863.* New York: Alfred A. Knopf, 1992.

Govan, Gilbert & Livingwood, James. *Joseph E. Johnston: "A Different Valor."* 1956. Reprint, New York: Smithmark, 1995.

Hassler, W.W. *A.P. Hill.* 1957. Reprint, Chapel Hill: University of North Carolina Press, 1962.

Hennessy, John J. *Return to Bull Run.* New York: Simon & Schuster, 1993.

Henry, Robert S. *Forrest "First with the Most."* 1987. Reprint, Wilmington, NC: Broadfoot, 1991.

Historical Times Illustrated History of the Civil War. Patricia Faust, editor. New York: Harper & Row, 1986.

Hood, John B. *Advance and Retreat.* 1880. Reprint, Edison, NJ: Blue & Gray Press, 1985.

Martin, David. *The Vicksburg Campaign.* Conshohocken, PA: Combined Books, 1990.

Mitchell, Joseph B. *Decisive Battles of the Civil War.* New York: G.P. Putnam's Sons, 1955.

Moore, Jerrold N. *The Confederate Commissary General.* Shippensburg, PA: White Mane, 1996.

Osborne, Charles C. *Jubal.* Chapel Hill: Algonquin, 1992.

Pfanz, Donald C. *Richard S. Ewell.* Chapel Hill: University of North Carolina Press, 1998.

Rhea, Gordon C. *The Battle of the Wilderness May 5–6, 1864.* Baton Rouge: Louisiana State University Press, 1994.

_____. *The Battles for Spotsylvania and the Road to Yellow Tavern May 7–12, 1864.* Baton Rouge: Louisiana State University Press, 1997.

Robertson, James I., Jr. *Stonewall Jackson.* New York: Macmillan, 1997.

Sears, Stephen W. *Chancellorsville.* Boston: Houghton Mifflin, 1996.

____. *Controversies & Commanders.* Boston: Houghton Mifflin, 1999.

____. *To the Gates of Richmond.* New York: Ticknor & Fields, 1992.

Strode, Hudson. *Jefferson Davis.* 4 Vols. New York: Harcourt, Brace, 1955–1966.

Sword, Wiley. *Embrace an Angry Wind.* Columbus, OH: The General's Books, 1994.

____. *Mountains Touched with Fire.* New York: St. Martin's, 1995.

____. *Shiloh: Bloody April.* New York: William Morrow, 1974.

Tanner, Robert G. *Stonewall in the Valley.* 1976. Reprint, Mechanicsburg, PA: Stackpole, 1996.

Thomason, John. *Jeb Stuart.* Lincoln: University of Nebraska Press, 1994.

Tucker, Glenn: *Chickamauga: Bloody Battle in the West.* 1961. Reprint, New York: Smithmark, 1994.

_____. *High Tide at Gettysburg.* 1958. Reprint, New York: Smithmark, 1995.

Vandiver, Frank: *Mighty Stonewall.* 1957. 1988. College Station: Texas A & M University Press, 1992.

Warner, Ezra. *Generals in Gray.* Baton Rouge: Louisiana State University Press, 1989.

Index